FREE AT LAST?

P9-DDY-782

ALSO BY FRED POWLEDGE

You'll Survive
The New Adoption Maze
Fat of the Land
A Forgiving Wind
Water
So You're Adopted
Journeys Through the South
The Backpacker's Budget Food Book
Born on the Circus
Mud Show
Model City
To Change a Child
Black Power / White Resistance

FREE AT LAST?

THE CIVIL RIGHTS MOVEMENT AND THE PEOPLE WHO MADE IT

FRED POWLEDGE

HarperPerennial

A Division of HarperCollins*Publishers*

For Tabitha

A hardcover edition of this book was published in 1991 by Little, Brown and Company. It is here reprinted by arrangement with Little, Brown and Company.

FREE AT LAST? Copyright © 1991 by Fred Powledge. All rights reserved. Printed in the United States of America. No part of this book may be used or reproduced in any manner whatsoever without written permission except in the case of brief quotations embodied in critical articles and reviews. For information address HarperCollins Publishers, Inc., 10 East 53rd Street, New York, NY 10022.

HarperCollins books may be purchased for educational, business, or sales promotional use. For information, please call or write: Special Markets Department, HarperCollins Publishers, Inc., 10 East 53rd Street, New York, NY 10022. Telephone: (212) 207-7528; Fax: (212) 207-7222.

First HarperPerennial edition published 1992.

LIBRARY OF CONGRESS CATALOG CARD NUMBER 91-55515

ISBN 0-06-097463-X

92 93 94 95 96 MB 10 9 8 7 6 5 4 3 2 1

Let me give you a word of the philosophy of reform. The whole history of the progress of human liberty shows that all concessions yet made to her august claims, have been born of earnest struggle. The conflict has been exciting, agitating, all-absorbing, and for the time being, putting all other tumults to silence. It must do this or it does nothing. If there is no struggle there is no progress. Those who profess to favor freedom and yet depreciate agitation, are men who want crops without plowing up the ground, they want rain without thunder and lightning. They want the ocean without the awful roar of its many waters.

This struggle may be a moral one, or it may be a physical one, and it may be both moral and physical, but it must be a struggle. Power concedes nothing without a demand. It never did and it never will.

FREDERICK DOUGLASS,
speaking in Canandaigua, New York,
August 3, 1857

85013

CONTENTS

■ ────────────────

PART EIGHT: VICTORY

PREFACE

The civil rights movement did not start on May 17, 1954, when the United States Supreme Court struck down racially segregated education. The Movement did not begin on December 1, 1955, when Rosa Parks was arrested for refusing to leave a "white" seat on a bus in Montgomery, Alabama, or four days later, when Montgomery blacks began a successful bus boycott. Nor did it start (though many would argue otherwise) on February 1, 1960, when four Negro college students sat down at a whites-only dime store lunch counter in Greensboro, North Carolina. The civil rights movement was not something spontaneous, but the inevitable outcome of centuries of mistreatment of black people by white people and their governments.

The civil rights movement did not grow out of the dream of any one man, or woman, or even a small group of people, or a formal organization, and it was not guided by any number of sage strategists from the North. The people who made up the Movement were almost as diverse as America itself. Their numbers included lifelong believers in the American system. They were leftists who had cut their eyeteeth on radicalism as preached from the soapboxes of New York's Union Square. They were South Carolina undertakers who would have voted Republican if they had been allowed to vote. They were teenagers who were tired, even before they started, of waiting for segregation to end itself, and who, like all young people, rejected the patience of their elders. They were very old people, and they were very young people, and they were all ages in between.

They were members of the black establishment: the Baptist ministers who served black people in churches that were as strictly segregated as the schools and lunch counters. They were the executives of the old-line black organizations, the National Association for the Advancement of Colored People and the National Urban League, that had been fighting segregation for as long as anyone could remember. And they were people whose scorn for that black establishment was nearly as great as their dislike for the white-run system.

They were blacks who lived in the urban centers of Atlanta and Birmingham, in both stylish brick homes and neglected public housing. And they were people who lived in deepest isolation in parts of rural Mississippi and Alabama where the plantation era had never ended.

The people who made the Movement were far from being all the black people in America, and far from being all the black people in the South. An enumeration would have been impossible, but surely the work of the Movement was carried out by a tiny percentage of all those who could have taken part. And yet this small group was able to generate a wave that washed over the entire nation, that spawned similar movements in a dozen fields.

The civil rights movement in America was not the effort of a single race of people. It was a movement by and for black people, and it was a campaign that was directed against a system that had been thought up, maintained, and enforced by white people. But many white people helped the Movement. Some gave their lives for it. So it is impossible to talk about the civil rights movement without talking, too, about its white participants. And, of course, it was white people of another sort who made the civil rights movement necessary.

In America now, in the nineties, the civil rights movement is not the same movement that commanded so much attention in the sixties. This is not to say that the earlier movement ended. Its membership has changed, and its rhetoric has been altered. Some of its original goals have been met. But many other goals remain elusive, and efforts to cope with some of the early problems of racism have uncovered others just as serious, if not more so. The Southwide campaign that some of its first proponents thought would last at most a few years now promises to go on indefinitely and nationally, even internationally. This is because America's and the world's resistance to the elimination of discrimination seems to be without end, and because many of the nation's opinion leaders and policymakers seem preoccupied with other matters, indulging in the illusion that in the field of race relations there is no more to be done.

Americans must understand what happened in the days of the Movement, for without a comprehension of what occurred in the past, we cannot hope to finish the job of subduing racial discrimination — and until we do that, we will continue to waste the minds and talents of a large part of the population.

And our understanding of the Movement is in serious jeopardy. The events of decades ago — the marches and mass meetings and murders, the triumphs and setbacks and speeches — all seemed at the time so clear and precise and memorable that they could never fade from understanding or suffer the terrible fate of misinterpretation.

But we have started now to forget how it happened. It has been thirty-seven years since the *Brown* decision; thirty-six since the Montgomery bus boycott; thirty-one since the Greensboro sit-ins. A generation has grown up knowing of the Movement's active days only at second hand. That generation, furthermore, has no experience with an America where politicians are at least circumspect about their corruption, where a political assassination is a remarkable event, where television gathers its news by 16-millimeter film cameras set on heavy wooden tripods. This generation has trouble believing some of the things that happened in the fifties and sixties. There are teenagers who will argue that "COLORED" and "WHITE" signs over drinking fountains were an aberration; that they existed only in a handful of the worst Deep South communities. It is unbelievable, they say, that black people could have let such an indignity happen on a regionwide scale. Maybe they are right, and it *is* unbelievable. But it happened.

America has developed a compulsion about condensing events, even the most complicated issues, to tiny chunks of "news" that fit into one sentence on the television screen or one paragraph in the newspaper. Serious information has little chance these days in the mass media. An "in-depth" examination of a social problem as likely as not means a television "docudrama" that distorts some truths and ignores others, twists the fundamental character of actual people, abuses time and geography to fit into the script, and substitutes "production values" for honesty. Because Americans now get more of their information from what they see on a screen than what they read from paper, and because what reaches the screen has such profound influence on what people think, historical truth is in deep trouble.

And so, like precious documents that were carelessly engraved onto cheap paper, the truth of what happened in those years is fading and is in danger of being lost.

Pseudo-truths replace it. In the minds of untold numbers of Americans, for example, the Reverend Dr. Martin Luther King, Jr., *was* the civil rights movement. Thought it up, led it, produced its victories, became its sole martyr. Schoolchildren — including black schoolchildren — are taught this.

America has a near-pathological need to codify everything of importance in terms of personalities (even better, in terms of a single personality), and King's charisma and sincerity make him the prime candidate for *the* person who was *the* Movement. It is much easier and quicker to say (as countless teachers, politicians, and miscellaneous other public figures do when encountered on television during the annual celebration of Black History Month) that "Martin Luther King led the civil rights movement and freed the black people" than it is to explain what really happened — which is that Martin Luther King and an awful lot of other people, many of them far less charismatic than he, created a movement and freed themselves.

Jesse Jackson is widely perceived as a hero of the Movement, a perception he rarely has denied, although he spent most of the Movement years in Chicago. Jackson's major claim to Movement fame rises from the fact that he was with Martin Luther King in April, 1968, when the leader was assassinated in Memphis, and that some of King's blood stained Jackson's shirt, which Jackson wore back to Chicago. Jackson did little work in the Southern movement and was on hand for few of its significant events. What he has built on the foundation created by the Movement — a popular political effort that seems truly interracial — is impressive. But to refer to Jesse Jackson as a civil rights leader from the Movement of the sixties is simply wrong, and it does great injustice to the leaders and followers who *were* there.

The degree to which Americans have been kept in ignorance about any but a handful of the Movement's chief personalities is illustrated by a story (almost certainly apocryphal, since it has been reported by several sources, always as something that happened to a friend of a friend) about a teacher who, during Black History Month, assigned reading on various figures, including the black nationalist Malcolm X. One young student returned from his research and asked for more. He had become interested, he said, in the things that were said back then by "Malcolm the Tenth." The teacher didn't know whether to be depressed that his student hadn't known enough about Malcolm X to get his name right or overjoyed that the child understood Roman numerals.

History is in danger of being bent out of shape, too, in the current-day recollections of those whites who were in positions of power in the South in the fifties and sixties, who roused the rabble at every opportunity in favor of white supremacy, and who now proclaim that they didn't really mean it — that they were saying what the electorate (the white electorate, since there was hardly any other kind) wanted to hear, and that the only reason they did *that* was to keep the rednecks from getting violent. George Wallace has announced he was wrong and begged blacks' forgiveness. Herman Talmadge recalls with great fondness his black childhood playmates. Strom Thurmond takes to the Senate floor in an appeal for fairness for a black political nominee.

It may be true, and in many cases it was obvious back then, that the great majority of the segs (as they were known in the

South to reporters and civil rights activists) did not have their whole hearts in their racism. But that should not obscure the fact that at the time, some of them were inciting violence and all were inciting hatred against black people. They were actively pursuing policies that denied Negroes their constitutional and human rights. They spread the message throughout their jurisdictions (to those same violence-prone whites they now say they were trying to calm down) that violence against black people was no big deal, nor was defiance of federal authority. Their actions and inactions are responsible for countless incidents of violence, years of indignity, and no one knows how many murders and premature deaths.

The revising historians of the Movement, in their relentless drive for simplification at the expense of truth, are coming closer and closer to establishing the federal government as Martin Luther King's great collaborator, as the other saviour of the black people. A movie released in 1989, *Mississippi Burning*, which many Americans no doubt mistook for a factual account of the investigation into the 1964 murder of three civil rights activists, portrays the Federal Bureau of Investigation as a major force in the prosecution of those who deprived voter registration workers of their rights. Few claims could be as obscene as this one. The FBI (which in those years meant, more than anything else, its all-powerful director, J. Edgar Hoover) was one of the Movement's more unrelenting enemies. Its agents collaborated with local policemen who were widely known as friends of, and in some cases members of, the Ku Klux Klan. The FBI had on its payroll members of white terrorist organizations, and it had formally declared war on Negro organizations promoting integration. The FBI was un-American in the sixties. Despite frequent announcements by successive directors that "we don't do that anymore," revelations of its continuing disrespect for the law and its negative attitude toward members of minority groups, even among its own agents, keep popping up.

Other agencies of the federal government were less blatant in their dealings with the Movement, but they all managed to compile what a proper recollection of those years can only conclude to be a dismal record. At a time when national leadership was so badly needed, one president (Eisenhower) was waffling and talking about how difficult it was to change people's emotions; another

(Kennedy) was appointing journeymen racists to be judges in the South.

To claim that the FBI was the Movement's friend and that George Wallace was actually a cuddly fellow is to strain the limits of even a short-memoried public. But other, more subtle changes to the historical record have gained ground as the actual events (and those who remember them at first hand) grow dimmer.

According to one notion, the Movement, after its initiation by Southerners, was actually just a bit of detail on a broader, grander canvas. This deeper agenda concerned not merely the achievement of a peaceful meal at a previously all-white lunch counter, but the economic and social reform of the entire nation. And it was masterminded and directed by activists from the North, seasoned veterans of the organized labor movement who with great effort restrained themselves from overt condescension toward their worthy but less advanced Southern cousins.

This version of things, only slightly exaggerated here, can be heard now (indeed, it was heard even then, though in more respectful tones) from people who are, by and large, more Northern than Southern in their viewpoint; who are more inclined toward socialism of the Norman Thomas variety than the more fundamentalist, literal-interpretation view of democracy shared by many Southern blacks and some Southern whites; and who lack that essential ingredient that propelled and sustained the Southern movement and its people, a strong religious belief. There is no question that the larger agenda existed and that those who promoted it were sincere and hardworking. But the movement in the South was self-generated, self-fueled, self-motivated, and freestanding. It did not need the help of anyone else, well-meaning or not. To assume otherwise is to flirt with the position of the racist Southern politicians who kept insisting, in the face of much evidence to the contrary, that "our nigras" were happy with segregation and that some sinister force from outside had obviously been required to "stir them up."

The Movement was not as simple as the revisionists paint it — not as planned, not as centrally directed. The Movement consisted largely of playing it by ear, of trying something and seeing what worked and what didn't work, of testing the limits of democracy, the resources of resistance, and the reliability of those

who said they wanted to help, and then trying again. And again.
The Movement was exciting, not predictable. It existed in thoughts
and dreams, not in strategies and memoranda. Those who are its
veterans say now that it was the most exciting time of their lives,
and they wouldn't have missed it for the world.

Many of those veterans are outraged, too, at the way the history they lived through and made is being revised. In recent years,
groups of those who were active in the Movement have gathered
to analyze what happened, what didn't, and what should happen
now. The veterans, like everyone else, aren't getting any younger,
and there is a clear need on the part of many of them to tie up
loose ends (as there is among veterans of the Vietnam War, another
era of American life that never had a real ending date). One such
meeting was held by former members of the Student Nonviolent
Coordinating Committee in April, 1988, at Trinity College in Hartford, Connecticut. The organizer, Jack Chatfield of the Trinity history department, had been a SNCC field secretary in southwest
Georgia in the sixties. Another, more a reunion than a formal examination, was held later that same summer in New Orleans by
former members of the Congress of Racial Equality. The organizers
went to some pains to disguise the name and purpose of their gathering, since CORE was taken over in post-Movement years by a
faction that the old-timers strongly dislike.

At both meetings there was the camaraderie that must characterize reunions of military units that have survived memorable
campaigns. Participants recalled events that were a quarter-century
old but that remained, in the minds of the recollectors, as sharp
and humorous and painful as if they had happened earlier that day.
There was much celebration of the fact that the participants had
survived, and there were bowed heads and soulful songs for those
who had not. There was good food and, after the meetings were
over, lengthy sessions around open bottles.

There was also, at both meetings, an anger that history was
being rewritten. Much of the resentment was centered around the
popular characterization of Martin Luther King, Jr., as the creator,
leader, and embodiment of the Movement. Participants at the
SNCC and CORE meetings spoke of their admiration for Dr. King,

but they also expressed their determination that the rest of the Movement be remembered, as well. Martha Norman, a SNCC worker in Mississippi and Alabama and former wife of another SNCC activist in the sixties, spoke at the Hartford conference about this. "I have three children," she said, "and I have read interpretations that have made me cry, to think that my boys would be left with such ridiculous explanations of what it was that their mother and their father were doing in those days — and why it was that their parents decided to put their lives on the line in the early sixties."

Those who put their lives on the line have a right to be alarmed. For what was happening back then was far more exciting than a docudrama or a news simulation. The heroism of a Martin Luther King was inspiring, but equally important were the heroic acts of thousands of other people who joined the Movement for a day, a year, five years, a lifetime.

This book makes no claim on absolute truth, but it can do better than a docudrama. Nor can I promise a neat, crisp lack of bias; everybody who lived through those years was terribly partisan — had to be and should have been.

The reader deserves, at the least, some warning on where the author's biases lie. I am a white male, born in rural North Carolina in 1935, raised in Raleigh, brought up in an environment that was totally segregated but not as brutally so as it was in some states farther to the south. My parents, like those of far more Southern whites than is generally acknowledged, did not question the segregated system, but they would not tolerate racism. Racism, they would have said if anyone had asked them, was vulgar and common. They thought of themselves as gentle and friendly toward black people, and they acted that way, but always within the framework of the segregated society in which we lived. The slack-jawed Southern-white pronunciation of "nigra" might be allowed, with a frown, but "nigger" was not. That was something the trashy whites said. More often, the term was "colored." But my parents and the other people around me did not challenge the system. Hardly any white people did that, and in those days very few black people did, either, at least within the earshot of whites. Southern whites seemed to accept the system as unchanging and unchangeable.

For reasons that I never have been able to understand but never thought of as remarkable, I grew up with an intense dislike for segregation. Perhaps it was the well-known adolescent rebellion against my environment; more likely I was merely taking the lessons my parents, teachers, and preachers taught (the Golden Rule, compassion for the downtrodden, all the basic stuff of organized religion of the Southern Methodist variety) and applying them to what I saw around me. At any rate, I had no trouble smelling out the hypocrisy of the white society in such matters.

When the Greensboro sit-ins started in 1960, I was a young newsman for the Associated Press in New Haven, Connecticut, with a wife and infant daughter. Desperate to go south and help cover what clearly was going to be the biggest story of my time, I signed on as television columnist for the *Atlanta Journal.* When I confessed that our family income had never allowed us the luxury of a television set, the city editor of the *Journal* did two things that would forever change my life: He gave us an old television that had been in his garage, and he hired another television columnist. What he wanted anyway, he said, was a reporter to help cover the civil rights revolution that was sweeping the region. It was my great fortune that my city editor was Pat Watters, who went on to write some of the most perceptive articles and books on the era. Most important at the time, however, was the fierceness with which Watters went to bat for his reporters and for what we in the newsroom all felt, at least for a year or so, was our absolute license to cover this story thoroughly. Later I was to be blessed with two other editors, at the *New York Times,* who were equally dedicated to getting the story: Harrison Salisbury and Claude Sitton.

I was and am, then, biased in favor of the Movement. More than that, I was and remain completely taken by it. I still believe it is the most important social event in American history since Independence.

The reader also deserves a few guidelines on technology and technique.

With very few exceptions, the material spoken by people in this book in interviews comes from tape-recorded conversations conducted in person by the author. A couple of the interviews were obtained by telephone, and in rare instances quotations were taken down by hand. Material that comes from published and broadcast sources is cited in the endnotes.

For the purposes of this book, "civil rights movement" designates the era that roughly started with the May 17, 1954, Supreme Court school desegregation decision and that began to peter out in the mid- and late sixties, and that had completely lost its original flavor by the time of the April, 1968, murder of Martin Luther King. Having said that, I must immediately point out that much that is the Movement started before 1954 and much went on after 1968, and that it is probably a waste of time trying to set beginning and ending dates.

When the Movement started, whenever that was, it was considered correct (by black people as well as others) to refer to persons of color in the United States as "Negroes." The term "black," which in earlier years could be interpreted as a slur, did not come into widespread use until later in the sixties. I have tried to use the terms interchangeably in this book, emphasizing "Negro" early on and "black" later. The use of one term over another does not necessarily imply anything important. The term "African-American," which enjoyed a modest burst of popularity earlier, was not widely promoted by some black leaders and thinkers until the late 1980s, and it isn't used here unless it is a direct quotation. I respect the desire of any group, particularly those who are oppressed, to choose the name by which they prefer to be known. I also respect the need of oppressed groups to choose new names from time to time, to mark the way stations along their march out of oppression. The test ought to be whether the term catches on with the masses of people.

Terms such as "racist," "white supremacist," and "segregationist" are tougher to deal with, largely because many of those who would not have been disturbed by such labels in the fifties and sixties would now, in their sunset years and with the benefit of a mellowing sort of hindsight, prefer that posterity remember them as being a bit more decent. As far as this book is concerned, that is their problem. Often, when the segs of the sixties used the time-tested technique of red-baiting to attack the Movement, they threw out the old line about how "if it walks like a duck and quacks like a duck, it must be a duck." That seems like a good technique to use here. If a politician acted like a segregationist, racist, white supremacist, or demagogue in the sixties, when he was at his peak of power and influence, then that is what he was. I have tried, however, to note any conversions that were proclaimed later in life, since I have always believed in the ability of humans, and especially Southerners, to transcend themselves.

I am grateful to each of those veterans of the Movement years who took the time to talk with me and share their recollections. Their names appear throughout the book; they are the ones who, in the words of the book's subtitle, made the Movement.

I am also grateful to Essie Borden, who transcribed most of the tapes and did so not only at amazing speed but correctly; to F. Joseph Spieler, my literary agent, and Jennifer Josephy, my editor. The computer software programs XyWrite, by XyQuest, Inc., and MaxThink, by Neil Larson, never failed me, though most others did. Steven Edward Vagle, of Advocates at Law in Washington, gets my special thanks, as do Alice Ma and Peggy Leith Anderson of Little, Brown and Company, Val Coleman, Charles Pou, Bill Minor, Samantha Biro, Lucy Montgomery, David Crosland, Charles McDew, Leslie B. McLemore, Tom Hayden, Walter Naegle, Dorothy Dawson Burlage, Anthony Scotto, Jack Chatfield, and the staff members of the library of the United States Commission on Civil Rights. Leslie Dunbar was, as always, a magnificent source of knowledge and inspiration. Among my old friends who went the extra mile, in some cases to the point of providing room and board, are Alice and Calvin Trillin, Claire Cooper, Truman Moore, Naomi Morrison, Kerry and Dick Snyder, and Camille and Chuck Morgan. These are the ones who learned early on never to ask how far along I was with the book.

A number of libraries were especially helpful. They include, in addition to the fine facility at the Civil Rights Commission, the Vanderbilt University Law Library, where Mary Colosia was a godsend; the Mississippi Department of Archives and History; the

Alabama Department of Archives and History; the Saint Mary's College Library in Maryland; the people who thought up and operate interlibrary loan; Beth M. Howse of the Fisk University Library; the Dougherty County (Georgia) Public Library (which certainly has changed since 1962, when I saw black people turned away from its doors); and the library of the United States Naval Academy.

Most of all, I am grateful to Tabitha M. Powledge. As always, she stretched her interpretation of "for better or for worse" to include her spouse's writing. This book simply could not have been done without her.

PART ONE

A WAY OF LIFE

ONE

■

THE COST OF OPPRESSION

■

L. C. Dorsey was born on December 17, 1938, in Washington County, Mississippi, on the Walker Plantation. It was a cotton plantation, and Dorsey learned to chop cotton about the same time she learned to walk.

Dorsey's family moved from plantation to plantation, white employer to white employer, always within the cotton country of Mississippi's Delta, that flat plain of rich soil that runs along the Mississippi River in a strip some twenty miles wide and two hundred miles long, from Vicksburg to Memphis, Tennessee.

L.C. (she disliked her given name from childhood, and has always insisted on using the initials) did not leave Mississippi until she was nineteen, and even then she did not go far. The family moved to Memphis, just across the state line. The geographic distance was slight, but other differences were enormous. Mississippi had been another society, another world, a place where people yearned to cross the borders of neighboring states just so their poverty could be a little less painful. Dorsey said not long ago: "We were very isolated. You had no way of really knowing what was happening in other states as far as behavior and equality were concerned. We had heard from people who came back and forth across the river from Arkansas that it was easier to make a living there.

"Now, that doesn't mean an awful lot. It means that when we were earning two cents a pound to pick cotton here in Mississippi, in Arkansas people were earning three or three and a half cents a pound. So we aren't talking about large-scale differences.

"Memphis was the Mecca. If you could make it to Memphis, you could have a job and you could go home and there was running water and you could take a bath. Or you could go out and nobody'd beat you on the head. So Memphis was a Mecca, and people left north Mississippi in large numbers and went to Memphis, looking for economic opportunity more than anything else."

Often the emigrants did not stop at Memphis, but pushed farther north, to St. Louis or Chicago. (In the East, a similar migration route took Negroes from Florida and Georgia and the Carolinas up into Washington, D.C., Baltimore, Philadelphia, Newark, and New York City.) The Dorsey family remained in Memphis. "The difference in living was *so* great between Mississippi and Memphis," recalled Dorsey. "That's where the majority of my folks are. They never got farther than Memphis, because it represented to them the best of both worlds — rural enough so they could have all the things they enjoyed about rural Mississippi, and urban enough where their labor was competitive for wages, where they could make money and buy homes and buy cars and live decently." The family would return to Mississippi only "when somebody was sick or dead or when they had gotten a new car or new baby or something like that."

Memphis was another step, too, on the ladder up from a life largely controlled by terror. Negroes in Mississippi in the time when L. C. Dorsey was growing up, and for many of the years that followed, were accustomed to hearing about, and sometimes witnessing, violent and brutal examples of the whites' efforts to keep them down, economically and every other way. A lynching was among one of Dorsey's earliest childhood memories.

"I don't think I even knew the term was 'lynching,' because the words that I remember earliest were 'the mob crew.' That was the name they gave the people who came and got folks. And I'm not even sure that the mob crew was the same folks as the Ku Klux Klan as we know them now, or whether they were simply a group of local white people whose mission it was to keep uppity niggers in their place. . . .

"But, yes, I remember when Odell Gray disappeared. And all the whispering that went on around it. He had been in the military, as best as I can remember all of this, and had come back to town, and then he disappeared. The whisper around was that he had been put in the bayou. I found out much later that there was a lot of animosity toward black servicemen." White men who had not served in the military in World War II, she said, resented the Negroes who did. But there was another, murkier reason: "There was this concern that all these black men in the service had been over there sleeping with white women. And there's evidence to document that that was the cause of some of the bloodiest lynchings back in Georgia and other places."

As for social and political equality, that was a distant dream. For many of the plantation families such as Dorsey's, the concept of "freedom" meant little more than an absence of slavery. Segregation was just the way of life. Things *would* get better — God would make sure of that, the preachers kept saying — but they would get better later on, not right now.

L. C. Dorsey's family was a strong and supportive one, and it never relaxed its efforts to make sure she got an education. On one plantation where they lived, the owner's agents, or employment bosses, didn't want the children of the workers to go to school. They were more useful as cotton choppers. So no school bus came to the farm. Dorsey's father walked her a mile or so every morning to a gravel road where the bus did pass, to make sure she got an education.

Her mother came from Alabama, from a family that owned land. In a time when blacks had to pay for their education if they wanted one, this woman learned to read and write and achieve the equivalent of a junior high school education. Dorsey's father, who influenced her life even more, was, she now realizes, "quite a radical person in a nonradical way. On weekends, Dad would walk into whatever town we lived close to and would buy the *Pittsburgh*

Courier and the *Chicago Defender,"* black-owned and -edited newspapers that had national circulation, "and my mother would spend the weekend reading those papers out loud to us. So we had some black consciousness from my earliest remembrance.

"Dad had a traveling trunk with a tray. In it he had all of the important stories clipped from the newspaper. Joe Louis was one of his favorites. He had stories about all of the black boxers. My parents made sure we had a radio even if we didn't have food, and all of the folks on the plantation were invited in to hear the big fights. And he bought bigger and bigger radios. I remember at one point we had a radio two feet long with a five-cell battery so that everybody in the house could hear the fight.

"They loved baseball, and at the risk of the boss man's wrath, they would stay home during the World Series and root for their folks. They loved Jackie Robinson and Roy Campanella. I mean, they *loved* those folks. They loved the white players, but the blacks were their heroes. And we used to talk about equal rights around the house. So I think, if I was predisposed to the Movement when it came, that maybe I was born that way. Some of us are born that way."

The family into which L. C. Dorsey had been born had a lot to do with her feelings about equality, but her own experiences were equally important. "I really think I had been made that way by something that happened when I was thirteen," said Dorsey. "Even the disappearance of Odell Gray didn't do the trick, because I was only eight or so when that happened, but what happened when I was thirteen did."

What happened in the summer of 1951, when L. C. Dorsey was in the eighth grade, was based on what she had learned from her parents about equality. "My father's definition of equal rights was very simple," she said. "He didn't really care about voting. That was not his priority, and I think he represented the thinking of a lot of people. To him, the basic thing was justice and economics — and when you look at them, they're the same principles.

"He wanted equal pay for equal work. He wanted, if he and a white man were out logging together, or picking cotton together, or plowing mules together, for both of them, if they did equal work, to receive equal pay. And the other thing that he wanted was if he and a white man got into a fight, he wanted the best one of them to win. And that would be the end of it — not that when he went to bed at night, a mob crew would come, dragging him out of his house or killing him and his family in the house. He wanted, when you went to court, that the justice was fair. If he had not bothered the man and the man attacked him, then the man should be punished, not him.

"And those were the only things he wanted. He didn't want to go to their churches. He didn't want to go live in their neighborhoods. In fact, we were always so upset with him because he didn't want to live in the neighborhoods with *black* folks, either. Whenever we'd move on a plantation, he always got the house that was farthest away from everybody. And I think he had a lot to do with influencing me about things. Of course, to a child, at the time, this was just talk.

"But when I was thirteen, I had been going to school and I had been listening to him, and I figured out that he'd had a lot of exploitation and abuse from white folks. He worked on one plantation for twenty-one years, making crops. Making lots of cotton. And he had never cleared any money. He'd never come out of a crop year with even a break-even. It was always the plantation owner saying, 'Well, Will, you didn't quite get out this year. You still owe me.' And I figured out when I was thirteen that what was wrong with people, the reason they always got exploited this way, was because nobody kept records. And that *this* crop year, we were going to keep records.

"We were going to set down all of our expenses and we would keep track of the cotton futures, which they broadcast on the radio every day, and which they printed in the [Memphis] *Press Scimitar*. And all we had to do was just figure that out and we would know how much we owed and how much we had earned, and we'd subtract what we owed from what we'd earned and we would have some figures. And when we walked up to the white people with this information, they would be fair. But if we didn't bother enough to keep up with our own bookkeeping, we couldn't blame the people for taking everything.

"Well, I'll never forget: It was a little blue composition book. The trade name was Blue Horse. I don't even know if they still make them. But if you wanted to *keep* anything, you got the composition book, because it was stitched. It wasn't glued together; it was stitched together. And then there was a thing on the back that glued the stitching together. So it was well put together. It would last forever.

"So we got a blue composition book, and I started setting down the figures: Expenses in one half of the book, and later on, when the cotton was in, the price they got for it. Part of the expenses were the 'furnishings.' " A regular fixture of plantation and sharecropper economics, this was an advance for living expenses. "We got six months of furnish'. Fifty dollars a month for a family of four. So you start putting in all of that. If somebody had to go up to the doctor's, you didn't get a bill, but you assumed it was going to be a lot, so you estimated it.

"And the crop expenses. In theory, the way the process was supposed to work is that one half of the cost of producing the crop was your expense and the other half was the landowner's expense. We knew that didn't work, so you always put down the total cost of the crop." L.C. had to estimate other expenses, such as the cost of fuel for running the tractor.

When the cotton was grown and picked and carried to the gin, there were other adjustments that had to be entered into the Blue Horse. A standard bale of cotton was five hundred pounds; the proceeds from any overage went to the landowner. There were many variables — the fluffiness of the cotton, its moisture content — that made bale-weight a tricky maneuver. If a bale came in at *less* than five hundred pounds, the tenant lost money, too. That was an important part of the Mississippi system.

The summer of 1951, Dorsey recalls, was a good year for cotton, with lint (cotton that had been ginned, and was now without its seeds) hitting forty cents a pound and never going below thirty-five cents. One fall morning it was time for the accounting. Dorsey's father was going to see the white folks for his yearly settlement, and L.C. was going off to school.

"My father was dressing to go up to the people's house, and I got out the book. Now, he knew I was doing this all the time, and he'd been cooperating with me all the year. And I told him, 'Now, when you walk in there today, you tell Mr. Carl' — that was the white man's name — 'you tell Mr. Carl that this is your record, and that you're going to sit with him and compare records and stuff.' And the last thing I remember before leaving the house was seeing him take the composition book and put it in his pocket. We'd gone over how much we anticipated the expenses were.

"I thought I was so smart: I'd added 'plantation expenses,' which is what they always told black folks when they'd question or challenge why they weren't getting any money. 'Well, you know, we got "plantation expenses." ' It was a joke in the black community. 'Plantation expenses' was a catchall. It was like, 'I done took everything I can from you, and if you still want to know what I'm taking, I'm taking "plantation expenses." ' If you applied it to a modern business practice, it was overhead. It was the cost of managing. It was the cost of thinking. It was the cost of oppression.

"We put in a huge amount for that, 'cause it was always what white people used as their out. And after we got through with all of that, based on what cotton was going for, and multiplied it by all the pounds, we came up with a huge amount of money. We subtracted all of these inflated expenses that I'd attribute to the boss man, and we *still* would've gotten two thousand some dollars back for our part. That's being extremely generous and paying for everything and anticipating huge 'plantation expenses' and everything else."

L.C. saw her father off and left for school.

"When I came home, I think my folks had cleared four hundred dollars. Or two hundred dollars. But it was less than five hundred dollars. I was devastated. And from that point on, I couldn't be reconciled that there was any fairness at all in that system. That set the foundation of a woman becoming ready for the Movement.

"It was like the making of a terrorist. I had played by the rules as I understood the rules, and I had applied my learning in one-room classrooms to solve the problem. I really *had* been blaming black folks for this exploitation. I had just assumed that because we hadn't taken initiative to deal with the white people as business people, that that's why we were being exploited, and that all we had to do to *correct* that was just to be businesslike, and they would be businesslike with us. And — to prove how naive I was — that somehow being businesslike would mean fair. I mean, I had equated all of that to mean *fair*."

L.C. asked her father what had happened. "And he said nothing had happened. What I didn't ask him, because I didn't know to ask him, and I still don't know, was whether he even pulled out the figures. As an adult, I'm sure he never even brought these figures up. Or if he brought them up, it was like looking at them without really making a big to-do about them. Because he understood that the system wasn't fair. And I expect that he was being a good and gentle father and not really wanting to expose me, at that age, to the ugliness of the system."

L. C. Dorsey paused in her telling of the story. It was now the late 1980s, and she was a grown woman with children of her own. She had been to Mecca but returned to Mississippi. Now she lived in Canton, not all that far from the Delta.

"Oh," she said, "I really grieve sometimes at how much pain I must've caused my folks, with all my questions, with all my challenges to them about, 'Why don't you do this, and why don't you do that?' And I know my father must have worried someday that 'This education I'm making sure that this girl gets is going to get her killed.' Because we lived on plantations."

America in the 1950s before the *Brown v. Board of Education* decision was a thoroughly segregated place, and in the South the separation was almost complete. In the Mississippi of L. C. Dorsey it was total; it was segregation at its most Gothic and grotesque. Racial segregation throughout the South was truly the *way of life* that white Southerners so frequently said it was. Lynching and brutal repression were practiced by only a small number of the most violent and vindictive whites, but the philosophy behind the terror was accepted by almost everybody white, from governor to sheriff to schoolchild.

Racial separation was rarely contested in public even by black Southerners, who knew from painful experience that to do so was to invite consequences far more terrible than just segregation.

The whites seemed hardly to notice segregation and its components and effects, even though it was such an integral part of *their* lives, too. If they did notice it, it was in the way they noticed water flowing from a tap or hot weather in the summertime — it was unremarkable, to be taken for granted. It was the "plantation expenses" of Southern living, a part of the overhead. It was the *way of life*, for quiet shopkeepers and high school math teachers, for Methodist ministers and big-city bankers. There were almost no inducements to challenge it or even suggestions that it be challenged. Even those who thought of themselves as humanitarians, and who would feel truly insulted at being labeled "racist," practiced segregation as a *way of life*. A few whites in every sizeable community were known for their outspoken opposition to segregation, but they were regarded as eccentrics, consigned to the same category as the recluse who lived down the road or the village idiot who hung around the courthouse square. No one who was taken seriously spoke out against segregation. Those whites who spoke out really seriously were regarded as troublemakers, as enemies of the society, and as agents of some foreign conspiracy.

The great majority of white Southerners showed, by their actions and inactions, that they considered black people to be something less than human. Negroes were useful, to be sure, for economic purposes, but only in the sense that mules and tractors were useful.

The national media seemed to assume that if any Negroes were reading or listening, their feelings were unimportant. Black people were not counted or sought out among the audience. A popular radio program such as "Amos and Andy" could ridicule the way black people talked, thought, and lived, and no complaints would be expected. No performers seemed to have considered the possibility that they were belittling or insulting fellow members of the human race when they put on blackface and whitened their teeth for minstrel sketches.

Just as whites had used the labors of blacks in the plantation fields a century before (and, in the Deepest South, in present times, as well), blacks were used in other areas of American life, but they were always kept segregated. A Negro might become a great athlete and bring fame and financial reward to a predominantly white sporting team, but he was always subject to the indignities of segregation, and he never was allowed to actually manage or reap the fortunes of the team. It was not until 1947, when Jackie Robinson joined the Brooklyn Dodgers, that the color barrier was dropped in major league baseball — and *that* was in the presumably enlightened North. When a Negro athlete achieved greatness on his own, as did Joe Louis, the prizefighter so admired by L. C. Dorsey's family, a frantic search was begun for a "great white hope" to dethrone him. White Southerners danced and rolled their eyes back in ecstasy to the songs created by black musicians, but those artists could not perform in desegregated facilities in the South. When musician Nat "King" Cole sang in a Birmingham, Alabama, theater in 1956, he was attacked by a gang of whites. Louis Armstrong could bring his band (an integrated one, in fact) to a prestigious and "liberal" Southern university for a concert, but the audience, except for the janitors who watched from the wings, would be all white. It was as if Negroes existed only for the whites' profit and amusement, as they had in the days of slavery.[1]

Negroes were certainly not considered eligible for full citizenship, though some of the more thoughtful whites did admit to a feeling that some day in the vaguely defined future (always with the comforting caveat, "not in my time"), Negroes would have improved themselves to the point where they had earned the right to equality.

The idea of Negroes as less than complete Americans had received the sanction of the nation's highest court back in 1857. A slave named Dred Scott, who lived with his master in the free territory of Wisconsin, demanded his freedom on the grounds of his residence. But the Supreme Court, in the case of *Dred Scott v. Sanford*, ruled that Congress had no power to prohibit slavery in the territories. Chief Justice Roger B. Taney's decision declared, furthermore, that Negroes were not citizens.[2]

Few white Southerners (or other Americans, for that matter) seemed to raise the obvious question of how Negroes could "improve" themselves to the point where they could attain full citizenship and equality as long as they were denied the raw materials of self-improvement. The black educator Booker T. Washington, in his famed speech at the Atlanta Exposition of 1895 (which more militant Negroes ridiculed as his "Atlanta Compromise"), told the region's white leaders that black people should forgo equality and integration in favor of education and economic assistance. The speech's most memorable line was, "In all things that are purely social we can be as separate as the fingers, yet one as the hand in all things essential to mutual progress."[3] It played to rave reviews by Southern white movers and shakers who would have welcomed anything that sounded like a delay in ending segregation. But how could black Americans get the education they needed if it was taught in rundown schools with poorly paid teachers, using textbooks that were the secondhand refuse of white students? Or when plantation masters actively discouraged their black workers from sending their children (always counted among the work force) to school at all? And how could a race of people "improve" itself when most of the components of its life were, by design, inferior, from water supply to transportation to — especially — employment opportunities?

The citizenship issue raised by the *Dred Scott* decision was finally settled after the Civil War. In 1866, Congress passed a civil rights act that extended citizenship to "all persons born in the U.S. and not subject to any foreign powers, excluding Indians not taxed." Members of "every race and color" were guaranteed the right to enter into contracts, go to court, and buy and sell property. President Andrew Johnson, a former slaveholder born in North Carolina who succeeded the murdered Abraham Lincoln as president and who ended up being impeached by the House of Representatives, vetoed the legislation, but Congress overrode the veto. In the same year discussions began that led to the adoption of the Fourteenth Amendment, which was ratified in 1868. The amendment declares among other things that no state shall "deny to any person within its jurisdiction the equal protection of the laws."

Without question, Negroes now had citizenship, but how much citizenship they had was quite a different matter. In 1896 the Supreme Court heard a case brought by a black man from New Orleans, Homer Plessy, who had been arrested for riding in a railroad car reserved for whites.

The majority of the court, in the landmark case *Plessy v. Ferguson*, ruled that it was legal for states to provide "separate but equal" facilities for Negroes. Separate but equal accommodations, found the court, were a "reasonable" use of a state's power. The

Fourteenth Amendment, said the court, was not intended "to enforce social as distinguished from political . . . equality, or a comingling of the two races upon terms unsatisfactory to each other."

As memorable as the majority decision was, it was Justice John Marshall Harlan's dissent that has rung most unforgettably through the succeeding century: "The judgment this day rendered will, in time, prove to be quite as pernicious as the decision made by this tribunal in the *Dred Scott* case. The thin disguise of equal accommodations . . . will not mislead anyone nor atone for the wrong this day done."[4]

Because segregation and inequality in the schools had come under legal attack, most notably and consistently from the National Association for the Advancement of Colored People and an offshoot that later became completely independent, the NAACP Legal Defense and Educational Fund, Inc. (known as the Inc. Fund), Southern states tried to maintain the fiction of "equal" schools for blacks. Perhaps because they sensed that the rules were about to change, Southerners in the early 1950s built new schools to replace the shacks to which Negroes previously had been sent. But improving the physical structure wasn't enough. The whites still provided unequal educations within those new buildings, and blacks who pursued their studies to the high school level were likely to be steered firmly into "vocational" tracks such as bricklaying and carpentry, at schools almost invariably named after Booker T. Washington, while their white contemporaries across town were learning about the humanities and sciences and business administration. It was a relatively rare occasion when a Negro youth was able to escape from the white-designed and -imposed system to the campus of one of the black colleges or universities of the South, where his or her real intellectual potential could finally be nurtured.

Beginning in 1938 and into the 1950s, a number of lawsuits pointed toward a different "way of life," at least for students at the graduate degree level. But even those were decided within the framework of *Plessy v. Ferguson*. In one, a black student named Lloyd Gaines was denied admission to the all-white University of Missouri law school but was offered tuition money to attend any out-of-state school that would accept him. (Such practice was widespread among Southern state universities that didn't want to desegregate. Another scheme was to operate separate state graduate schools for Negroes, which, of course, the states claimed were equal to the white institutions. In the real world, however, the reputations of these schools — among whites as well as blacks — were those of proud but second-rate institutions.) Gaines sued, with the assistance of the NAACP, and in 1938 the Supreme Court ruled that the Constitution's equal protection clause meant Missouri must either provide a separate but equal law school for Gaines or admit him to the white school. The decision was reaffirmed in 1948 in a case involving the University of Oklahoma law school, *Sipuel v. Board of Regents.*[5]

Inroads on the system continued to be made by Negro plaintiffs and their lawyers, a hardy band of dedicated graduates from Washington, D.C.'s Howard University law school. But the white resistance continued. After the *Sipuel* decision, the University of Oklahoma started admitting blacks to its graduate and professional schools, but once they got there they faced rigid, cruel segregation. G. W. McLaurin, a graduate student in education, found himself segregated in the cafeteria; he was assigned his own table in the library; and he was even kept in a separate classroom that was adjacent to the one in which professors lectured to white students.

The Supreme Court put an end to such practices on June 5, 1950, when it handed down two school segregation cases. One of them involved McLaurin in Oklahoma; the court found the Negro's chances for intellectual interchanges with his fellow students were severely diminished by the school's actions, and ordered them ended.[6] And in another case that would be remembered as one of the landmarks in the law of education equality, separate but equal got a damaging blow.

The court said, in essence, that it was very difficult for separate to be equal. The suit, *Sweatt v. Painter,* had been brought by Heman M. Sweatt, a black man who had applied for admission to the University of Texas law school. He was rejected because of his race, and Texas, seeking to avoid the consequences of the Missouri and Oklahoma cases, created a separate, black law school.

Sweatt attacked the move on the grounds that it still constituted segregation, that the black school was inferior, and that he
still was denied equal protection of the law. The Supreme Court
ruled in his favor. In its decision, the court noted that there were
intangible characteristics of segregation that must be considered:
"The University of Texas possesses to a far greater degree [than the
black school] those qualities which are incapable of objective mea-
surement but which make for greatness in a law school," wrote
the court.[7] Still, the court did not strike down *Plessy*.

While these rulings were important in setting the stage for
the massive change that would be proclaimed in 1954 with *Brown
v. Board of Education*, education in the southern United States, as
well as in most other regions, remained segregated and unequal.
Those white state officials who could agree grudgingly to desegregate graduate schools, where presumably responsible adults were
concerned, were unwilling to deal with the less predictable emotions involved in opening up elementary and high schools.

Similarly, in the field of transportation, progress at administrative
levels as well as in the courtroom had been made for some time,
but the average Negro in the South was unlikely to benefit from
the decisions.

A Negro congressman from Illinois, Arthur Mitchell, purchased a first-class train ticket from Chicago to Hot Springs, Arkansas. When the train passed into segregated territory in
Arkansas, Mitchell was ordered to move into a second-class car
because the train did not carry a "Negro" first-class car. Mitchell,
who was no stranger to discrimination (he had been born in 1883
in Alabama), complained to the Interstate Commerce Commission, the agency designated by the Interstate Commerce Act to
carry out Congress's constitutional mandate "to regulate commerce with foreign nations, and among the several States, and with
the Indian tribes." The commission ruled against him, and Mitchell took his case to court. The Supreme Court ruled in 1941 that
it was all a matter of "equality of treatment" rather than a "question of segregation," and that the issue lay within the purview of
the Interstate Commerce Act, which prohibited "undue or unrea-
sonable prejudice or disadvantage." In finding for Mitchell, the

court wrote: "The denial of appellant of equality of accommodations because of his race would be an invasion of a fundamental individual right which is guaranteed against state action by the Fourteenth Amendment."[8]

Five years later, the Supreme Court broadened the notion of equality in transportation. The court sided with a Negro woman who was traveling by bus from Virginia to Baltimore, Maryland. Virginia criminal law required all bus companies to keep white and Negro passengers separate. When the woman was ordered to move to the back of the bus, she refused. She was arrested, tried, and convicted. The Supreme Court reversed the conviction. And on June 5, 1950, the same day it handed down the *McLaurin* and *Sweatt* education cases, the court ruled that segregated seating was illegal in railroad dining cars. In that decision, the court called attention to the elaborate paraphernalia of signs, warnings, and dual facilities that had grown up around transportation segregation: "The curtains, partitions and signs emphasize the artificiality of a difference in treatment which serves only to call attention to a racial classification of passengers holding identical tickets and using the same public dining facility."[9]

But for the typical Negro and white stepping on a municipal bus or entering a Greyhound or Trailways terminal in the South in the early fifties, segregation was all too clearly pointed out. The signs directing passengers to sit or stand behind a certain line, or to enter a certain waiting room, were mere extensions of a system that tried to keep the races separate in everything that could be thought of as public accommodations. Water fountains, theaters, lunch counters, restaurants, department store dressing rooms — all were either operated under the system of separation or were operated for whites only. Not only was this the situation at the time; it was assumed by practically all the whites (and quite likely a good number of the Negroes, too) that this was the way it would always be. Even a lawsuit that was settled in the nation's highest court, and settled in favor of the blacks, did not figure into the scheme of things. Such a decision, they thought, was distant; it was inapplicable; it took place in a different land entirely.

Discrimination in places of public accommodation was outlawed in 1875 by Congress in a civil rights act that guaranteed equal rights in transportation, theaters, juries, and places of lodging. But eight years later, the Supreme Court ruled that the Constitution did not allow Congress to tell private persons they could not deny equal access to privately operated places of public accommodation. In reaction to this decision, a number of non-Southern *states* enacted laws guaranteeing equal access in publicly owned and operated accommodations, and in 1947 a Committee on Civil Rights appointed to advise President Harry S Truman recommended the widespread enactment of such laws at the state level. In 1953, Oregon passed such a law that applied to privately owned and operated enterprises, and a number of other states north of Mason and Dixon's Line followed suit.[10]

An extraterrestrial visitor to the American scene in the early fifties would have been hard put to come up with rational explanations for any of the forms of discrimination and segregation that were so manifest in society. But there seemed even less reason behind the prohibitions against equality in public accommodations. The same whites who nailed into place the "WHITES ONLY" and "COLORED THIS WAY" signs were the ones who would discourse interminably about their deep fondness for Negroes. They could talk at length about "growing up with nigras," about eating the food prepared by black people, even being fed at a black woman's breast (though this last was probably in the same category as the claim some men made to have worked their way through college by hustling at billiards, a recollection based more in fantasy than in reality).

Surely the reason for all the "WHITES ONLY" signs was not simple fear of being close to black people. A more likely explanation was that the whites needed ways to deprive Negroes of their dignity and humanity as part of the general effort to keep blacks down. People whose dignity had been usurped were easier to terrorize, and that meant they were more easily manipulated economically. And a lot of what went on in the South in the name of racial segregation, as L. C. Dorsey learned, was based on economics.

To say, publicly, and sometimes in harsh block letters, that Negroes are not sufficiently human to eat in the same room with white people, or to ride on the same end of the bus — indeed, that the gentlest, most aged black woman is expected to give up her seat to the most robust white man, and, if the seats in the "black" section are all filled, to *stand* while seats go begging in the "white" section — that was to aim major weaponry at a people's dignity. To twist the knife further, the supremacists took a name that was acceptable to most blacks at the time, "Negro," and corrupted it into something vile — or, on those occasions when they used the correct term, they refused to capitalize it. (Even the opinions of federal judges frequently spelled the word "negro.") It was, in one sense, a masterstroke for the segregationists, this business of destroying the dignity of a subjected people in order to keep them even more firmly subjected and economically manipulable. But it had a dangerous side, too, as do all attempts to repress people. Sometimes the victim rebels, quickly and forcefully.

Government — the means, according to the myth of the American system, by which grievances could peacefully and reasonably be redressed — was an integral part of the racist system. The White House was only beginning in the forties and fifties to appear dedicated, at least rhetorically, to favoring an end to discrimination.

President Truman issued an executive order in late 1946 creating his Committee on Civil Rights, with a charge to determine how "current law-enforcement measures and the authority and means possessed by Federal, State, and local governments may be strengthened and improved to safeguard the civil rights of the people." When the committee met with Truman in January, 1947, he said: "I want our Bill of Rights implemented in fact. . . . We are making progress, but we are not making progress fast enough."[11] One of the committee's first actions was to criticize the high degree of segregation in the District of Columbia, the government's own hometown. Under pressure from government, local organizations, irate citizens, and court attacks, segregation in the District gradually declined. Washington's places of public accommodation desegregated (after court pressure) in 1953, much earlier than other Southern cities.

Other indicators of the federal government's commitment were less encouraging. Black people remained virtual strangers to the federal system of justice — there were no black faces on the bench, among the ranks of prosecutors and courtroom officers, even on juries. The practice was duplicated in state, county, and local jurisdictions, with the added insult that members of the justice system were often outspoken racists. Throughout the South (and elsewhere, for that matter), the police had one policy for white people and another for Negroes. A police reporter checking the desk sergeants and deputies on his Saturday night rounds in a small Southern city in the early fifties was told, "Nothing happening — just a couple of nigger stabbings." The horror was that the officers were not joking. They *meant* that stabbings of and by Negroes were not important. And when it came time to parcel out space and select headline sizes, the reporter's newspaper agreed.

Blacks had little political power in America. They had virtually none in the South, except in a few cities where they could, one, register and vote without taking their lives in their hands and, two, form loose and useful coalitions with those voters known as "decent whites." The result of these coalitions (Atlanta provided one important example) was to insure the election and reelection of politicians who were the least of several evils or, sometimes, even progressive and enlightened public servants.

The lack of voting power was central to the predicament of black Americans in the days before the civil rights movement began in earnest. It could be and was argued that if blacks had the right to register and vote freely, many of the other obstacles to their progress would be reduced, if not wholly eliminated.

Henry Lee Moon, who later was to become the press information officer for the National Association for the Advancement of Colored People, published a comprehensive book in 1948 titled *Balance of Power: The Negro Vote*. In his preface, dated early in 1948, Moon wrote: "Intent upon attaining full equality of citizenship in his native land, the Negro American today sees in the ballot his most effective instrument in the long and hazardous struggle toward this goal. From such equality, he realizes, flow all the good things of life in a democratic society — the freedoms and enjoyments long denied him."[12]

The Negro American, wrote Moon, had come to such conclusion by a long route that involved earlier, short-lived political action during Reconstruction; land ownership, which proved difficult indeed; education, à la Booker T. Washington, which helped, but left the educated Negro just as disfranchised as the uneducated Negro; and, finally, the ballot again. The ballot, he wrote, was no longer considered "a magic key," but it was "recognized as the indispensable weapon in a persistent fight for full citizenship, equal economic opportunity, unrestricted enjoyment of civil rights, freedom of residence, access to equal and unsegregated educational, health, and recreational facilities. In short, a tool to be used in the ultimate demolition of the whole outmoded structure of Jim Crow."[13]

———————————— ■

When Charles Jones was growing up in South Carolina, he knew he was a Negro. Society made sure of that.

Jones was born in Chester in the summer of 1937. The place was a textile mill town that had been settled in the 1750s. His father was a Presbyterian minister, and his mother taught in the segregated school system — a situation that insured a family status of what Jones now says was "middle class, for black folk. Of course, we were 'colored people' at that point."

There was, he said, "very strong awareness" of segregation, of its meaning, and of its ubiquity. "Back in Chester, you were always aware that you were black."

Charles Jones was a child playing near his home when the Incident occurred. People almost always refer to them as "Incidents," and from their recollections of these events it is clear that they are experiences that profoundly affect the participants' lives. The rejection of her painstaking plan to end her family's economic exploitation was an Incident that shaped L. C. Dorsey's life. It is likely that every black person in America above the age of thirty, and more Southern whites than would admit it, can recall some moment from his or her childhood in which the difference between the races was suddenly, clearly, vividly, chillingly made apparent. These events, these introductions to the system, almost always served to demonstrate the awful injustice of a process that considered and treated persons of color as inferior to those with lighter skins. The cruelty of these incidents was magnified by the fact that the blacks were almost invariably innocent children.

A Negro schoolteacher had gone into one of Chester's drugstores to get a prescription filled. The pharmacist counted out the pills and handed the prescription to the woman.

"Thank you," she said.

"Thank you *what?*" said the pharmacist.

"Thank you," she said, again.

"Thank you, *sir,*" corrected the pharmacist.

"The teacher said, 'I beg your pardon,' " recalled Jones. "And he slapped her right hard, and told her that anytime she came in there to refer to him as 'sir,' because he was white."

Always, in those days before the Movement started, the message was there: You are colored and we are white, and we are your superiors. The command was issued a dozen times a day and in a dozen different ways. Conform to our society. Keep your mouth shut (except to address us as "sir" and "ma'am") and keep your eyes averted, hooded with feigned ignorance. When we meet on a sidewalk, even the high, wide ones of dusty Deep South county seats, step off it and down into the gutter until we have passed. Take what we prescribe for you and thank us *sir* and never complain. You are the equivalent of a child, and we are doing you a favor by taking care of you. In return, we expect you to perform for us at wages we, not you, consider reasonable.

You certainly cannot take care of yourself. You are lazy beyond comprehension, you have no control over your sexual urges, and your odor is offensive to us. If we paid you more for your work, you would just feel "nigger rich" and throw it away on whiskey, a car, or a woman. Your brain is inferior to ours, is actually lighter in weight, and you cannot be expected to perform the more sophisticated tasks, such as thrift and planning ahead. You should be pleased that we give you as much attention as we do, and we become quite displeased when you do not acknowledge our beneficence. Do not even show disappointment. Make your face an unmovable mask. If you do have any fleeting thoughts of resentment toward us, you must never let us guess that they exist.

If you do all these things, conform in all these ways and never complain, then you may expect to live a relatively safe life. We will treat you as if you were invisible. We say "relatively" safe because we cannot promise complete safety; random physical and economic violence by whites against Negroes has always been an important part of our system. And if you deliberately refuse to do these things — if you step out of line, if you forget "your place" or even act as if you have forgotten — you can get in a lot of trouble. You can have your face slapped, or you can be lynched. Or we can starve you economically.

And Charles Jones and L. C. Dorsey heard all this, and they understood it, though they hated it. And somehow, they maintained their belief that the system, once challenged properly, would respond properly and fairly, as they had been taught in school that it would. They were Americans, after all, and they believed in the American way of life.

■ ———————————————————

TWO

RACE, CREED, COLOR, OR NATIONAL ORIGIN

If there had been no discrimination in employment, the condition of the American Negro would have been remarkably different. As it was, the nation maintained two distinct systems, one for whites and a handful of Negroes who somehow managed to overcome the manifold obstacles, and another for the rest of the blacks. This scheme was crystal clear in its operation in the South, somewhat less so in the rest of the nation. The two systems were not "separate" as the South's schools were — whites and blacks could work under the same roof and sometimes even eat their lunch at the same table — but they certainly were not "equal."

Equal employment would have hastened the end of the economic subjugation that was such an important part of the Southern system. And it would have cost Southern whites, both individual and corporate, a great deal of money. Grown men, called "yard boys" to insure that their self-esteem did not get out of hand, were paid a few dollars a week to perform the laborious work of maintaining the white families' gardens, lawns, and houses; inside the house, their wives were paid another few dollars, plus carfare to get them to and from their side of town via segregated buses, for rearing the whites' children, cooking their meals, scrubbing their floors, and washing their clothes. Even the most ardent white humanitarians were unwilling to bypass a bargain like this, despite the obvious similarities between this system and the one that had prevailed during the days of slavery.

Such an unbalanced economic system did not escape challenge, however, and some of the challenges sounded a lot like those that would follow in the sixties. When America went on a war footing in the early forties and defense plants employed thousands of workers, A. Philip Randolph, who in 1925 had founded the Brotherhood of Sleeping Car Porters, saw an opportunity to force the issue of equality in employment. He threatened a massive march on Washington if the White House failed to act to change the situation. Randolph conducted mass meetings around the nation promoting the march. One acquaintance recalled Randolph's saying, "This is the age of mass pressure, masses on the march." President Franklin Delano Roosevelt felt the pressure and came up with an executive order banning discrimination in defense and government work and establishing the Fair Employment Practices Commission. (CORE's James Farmer quotes Walter White of the NAACP as saying he doubted Randolph could have led five hundred people to Washington — because of poor organizing techniques — but that fortunately for Randolph, President Roosevelt didn't know that.)[1]

World War II gave black military men a taste of the world outside the plantation-mentality domain of the South, and it taught them the ultimate lesson in employment equality — for in wartime, practically anyone could suddenly die, with alarming parity. The war produced an enormous migration of whites and blacks from the South to the industrial centers of the Northeast and Midwest, leaving the South with an increasingly unpredictable labor pool that made it more difficult for whites to operate their mini-plantations with the same contempt for blacks' human needs.

------------------------------------- ■

Executive orders were one way — and, as it turned out, a rare one — by which the White House could act on behalf of civil rights, even if the other branches of government were not as sympathetic. Joseph L.

Rauh, Jr., wrote a bit of history in the forties by drafting such an order.

Rauh was born in Cleveland in 1911 to well-to-do German immi-grants. Like many, if not most, Northern whites of the pre-Movement days, he thought little about racial matters, though this was not because of any insensitivity on his part, he says now. He just didn't notice. It wasn't until around 1929, when he was at Harvard, that his eyes opened and he received what he called "an introduction to racial problems."

Rauh was a member of the Harvard basketball team. "There was one Jew, me, and one black, William Baskerville," Rauh recalled. The team had a game in New York City. "We traveled to New York, and the team went to a hotel. The Vanderbilt Hotel in New York on Thirty-fourth Street wouldn't have Bill Baskerville.

"So Bill started out the door. I said, 'Where are you going?' He says, 'I'm not staying here.' I said, 'Why?' That's how little I knew about it: I said, 'Why?' which was a rather dumb thing to have said to a black person in such circumstances. That shows you how little one's life may connect with that problem. . . .

"Anyway, there was a little rebellion and we all went out of the hotel. And I don't know where. They got us in somewhere, and we played the next day, and of course we got beat, because we weren't any good anyway. Some people have always claimed we got beat be-cause of the incident. We got beat because we had a lousy team."

In 1935 Rauh went to Washington to work in government. He held jobs with the executive branch, and for three years he was law clerk for Supreme Court Justices Benjamin Cardozo and Felix Frankfurter. By 1941, when World War II was starting, he was employed as assistant general counsel for the Lend-Lease Administration, which supervised the selling, giving, lending, and leasing of munitions and other materiel to nations whose defense was considered vital to that of the United States.

The administration became heavily involved with President Roose-velt's Office of Emergency Management, which Rauh described as "a holding company for all the defense agencies." With the increase of Hitler's activities in Europe, America suddenly had become a huge em-ployment agency for the builders of ships, bombs, guns, airplanes, tanks, uniforms, and jeeps. Part of Rauh's work involved drafting legal lan-guage for proposed legislation to prohibit discrimination in such em-ployment.

"Anyway," said Rauh, "I came in one morning in June and the secretary said, 'Mr. Coy [Wayne Coy, the head of the Office of Emergency Management] is looking for you.' I called over there. His secretary said, 'You get over here. Mr. Coy wants you very badly.' So I ran the six blocks and, out of breath, I went in. It's early June of '41. And he said, 'Can you write an executive order?'

"And I said, 'Well, any jackass can write an executive order. What do you want in it?' He said, 'There's a fellow named Randolph in New York who is going to march on Washington if we don't have an executive order for employment of Negroes.' " A. Philip Randolph was calling for a march of a hundred thousand blacks on Washington to force the government to open employment for Negroes, particularly in war-related industries.

"And I said, 'Well, that's not very hard to write.' So he said, 'All right. They're waiting for you downstairs at the Budget Bureau. They're going to give you what you need — secretaries and so forth. I need it in the morning.' "

Rauh did not flinch, since he still thought writing the order for President Roosevelt's signature would be a fairly simple task. "Anyway," he said, "as I'm walking out the door, Wayne hollers at me: 'Hey, Joe, put in something about the Poles. The president said, when he told me to get this order out, he says, 'We've got to satisfy Randolph on the Negroes, but I've had a couple of complaints from Buffalo that they're not hiring Poles.'

"Roosevelt had a couple of congressmen screaming about how they weren't hiring Poles in Buffalo," said Rauh. "So that's my instructions. I've got to do something to stop Randolph, and we've got to hire Poles, by tomorrow morning. But it wasn't hard. . . . I worked out the wording. It said there'd be no discrimination because of race, creed, color, or national origin. And nowadays there's a big dispute among historians: Where did I get 'race, creed, color, or national origin'? Several people said they'd never seen the word 'national origin' before that. Well, it's there in the order, and I wrote it, but I can't remember. I have no idea where the goddamn phrase comes from.

"So at any rate, we wrote the order. I finally had a draft, and at nine o'clock the next morning I gave it to Coy."

From Rauh's office the proposed executive order went to Fiorello

La Guardia and Eleanor Roosevelt, the president's wife, who then were at the Office of Civilian Defense. They read the draft and then called up A. Philip Randolph and read it to him.

It was now early June. Randolph's March on Washington was set for July 1. There was no question, says Rauh, that the Negro leader was serious about the demonstration. Rauh's boss called him later in the day and told him the bad news: "Mr. Randolph says your executive order isn't strong enough."

"And here I had put every goddamn thing in it I could think of. I says, 'All right, Wayne. I'll work on it all evening. We'll have a draft for you in the morning.' And we did. I didn't change very much. I *tried* to strengthen it, but I didn't change much. Randolph says, 'It isn't strong enough' again. The second time. It goes up the ladder and comes back. So when Wayne calls me again, I said, 'Look, there is no *way* I can make it stronger on anything than we have now, but I've got an idea. I'll turn it upside down. Change paragraphs, you know: Change the order and everything else.'

"And I suggested that Mrs. Roosevelt and La Guardia read it to him and say, 'Now, if this isn't strong enough, we insist on *your* input in how to make it stronger.' So they read it to him, and he says, 'It's just right.'

"He thought it was great. Called off the march. . . . It was a great experience for me." President Roosevelt issued Executive Order 8802 on June 25, 1941, forbidding employment discrimination in all defense and government industries.

■ ─────────────────────────

President Truman declared on July 26, 1948, that the military itself would henceforth be an equal opportunity employer, with no more "separate but equal" facilities and training.[2] It took years, however, and in some branches decades, for the executive order to be fully implemented. The problem remained longest in the units furthest from direct control by Washington — the Reserves and National Guards. These were often little more than playthings and personal militias for the governors (especially Southern, although Connecticut had a contingent that dressed up in colonial uniforms, fired muskets, and beat drums), which proved most effective in such tasks as directing traffic during hurricane evacuations.

On the same day he ordered the military desegregated, President Truman issued an executive order proclaiming a policy of "fair employment throughout the Federal establishment, without discrimination because of race, color, religion or national origin."[3] And when Korea provided the United States with a new war in the fifties, the federal government began insisting that its contractors hold to policies of nondiscrimination in employment. The executive orders and promises did some good, to be sure; but any candid assessment of the situation in the early fifties had to conclude that in America, Negroes were the victims of deep, pervasive employment discrimination.

Discrimination was equally widespread in housing. In the North the question was handled by simply stuffing blacks and other people of color into specific neighborhoods. White society made sure they stayed there by refusing to rent or sell or even show them housing in "white" sections. In the South, for once, the system was a bit more subtle. Blacks often lived on the same streets as whites, particularly in the older cities along the Atlantic and Gulf coasts. But the quality of the housing was decidedly different, and if a Negro had tried to move into an all-white neighborhood, he or she would have faced the same brick-wall opposition that was the rule in the North.

A favorite way to keep neighborhoods just as they were was the restrictive covenant. This was a contract, signed by homeowners or new purchasers, promising not to sell to members of a specific racial or religious group. A seller who violated the covenant could be sued by others in the neighborhood, and the new owner could even be prevented from occupying the house. The Supreme Court ruled in 1948 that such contracts could not be enforced, on the grounds that they denied prospective purchasers the equal protection of the laws. Nobody ordered anybody to remove the covenants from deeds, however, and they may be found today in legal papers accompanying the sales of houses. A purchaser may be horrified at discovering such wording on closing day, only to be told by a lawyer that it doesn't matter; it's not enforceable. But the covenants remain as reminders not only of the way things once were in law, but also of the way things all too often now are in reality.

Organized religion was also a segregated institution. This might have actually been a plus for black Americans, since it would be their own rock-solid religious faith, rather than religion generally, that would sustain many of them through the tough Movement years that were soon to come, just as it had fortified them through 350 years of slavery and persecution. Black religion, which in the South came almost exclusively in Baptist and Methodist flavors, was far more joyous, emotional, and political than the white variety, and in the Movement it was much more attuned to dealing with real-world problems, such as how to transport several thousand people a day during a bus boycott, or how to get a hundred children out of jail by nightfall, or how to get two hundred potential demonstrators together to give them the details of a planned protest and the spirit and courage to undertake it.

At the beginning of the Movement years, however, the religion of the black South also contributed to retarding Negroes' appetite for challenging and changing the status quo. Black ministers who rightly saw little advantage in promising immediate change to their congregations were wont to preach instead that better times would come, but the timing would be by and by. When everybody died and gathered up in heaven, *that* was when there would be equality. And the yard boys and housemaids who had suffered for so many years would finally achieve the glory they so profoundly deserved. (There was also the understanding that simultaneously their white tormenters might well be roasting in hell, although black religion has always been reluctant to speak out publicly about revenge.)

Furthermore, the question should be asked, What blacks would *want* to join forces with a religion that counted active, unrepentant white supremacy among its major tenets? There were important exceptions, of course, as in all the institutions. But taken as a whole, organized white Protestant and Roman Catholic religion in the South was anti-Negro. The white Baptists and Methodists did allow for one or more of the Wise Men in their Christmas manger scenes to be persons of color, but that was just about their only concession, and even then the explanation often was that this dusky-skinned magus was a Persian, or Moroccan, but certainly not a Negro of the American sort. The same ministers and congregants who spoke warmly of sending this Sunday's collection to missionaries saving the ignorant savages of Africa could rattle on endlessly and earnestly about God's having made bluebirds and blackbirds (and making sure they didn't interbreed), along with the biblical passage about the goats going on one side and the sheep on the other. One never had to guess who was represented by which animal.

The major media were as white and segregated as any other of society's institutions. The local press, particularly, nurtured and amplified the national assumption that segregation was the way America worked. The Southern white newspapers that harbored dissenters to this rule among their editorial and column writers could be counted on the fingers of one hand.

Newspapers had no black reporters, editors, or executives, with a couple of exceptions: There was often a Negro manager who supervised circulation in the black community, and there was the occasional moonlighting high school teacher who was hired on a piecework basis to assemble a few news items of interest to blacks each week. The items ran, often on a Saturday (a traditionally slow day), under a headline such as "News of Our Colored Community." The reporter generally dropped the material off and didn't occupy a desk or use a typewriter in the newsroom. The *Atlanta Journal*, one newspaper that did that, continued the practice well into the sixties.

A news story about a white person referred to the subject as "a man" or "a woman" or "a Lee County resident," but a story about a Negro always made the distinction clinically clear: A "Negro male," a "Mississippi Negro." For many newspapers, the spelling was negro, not Negro. And when stories about black people appeared, they almost always had to do with the harsher chapters of life — the shootings and stabbings and breaking and enterings. The *normal* condition, according to the press and most of the rest of white society, was one of whiteness. Blackness was the exception. Many newspapers and other news organizations follow that rule even today. Radio was a weak instrument of communication, and television was even weaker. When radio did speak out on community issues it spoke, as often as not, from the far right side of its mouth. The mainstream broadcast media were as white as their print cousins.

There was a vigorous black press, represented by a handful of national newspapers such as the Baltimore *Afro-American* and the *Pittsburgh Courier*, but there was also a feisty collection of local weeklies, such as the *Atlanta Daily World* and the *Birmingham World*, that the white community never even knew existed. Between these, and a handful of magazines edited in Chicago by Johnson Publications (*Jet* and *Ebony* were prominent among them), Negroes in even some of the most isolated portions of the South were able to sustain their knowledge that not everything was white. They read of black heroes and accomplishments, they saw black beauty, and far too often they learned of black lynchings.

Social exchanges between adult whites and blacks fell into two categories: nonexistent and clandestine. The word "adult" is used here because age made a difference. Many a nonurban white Southerner above the age of fifty can recite pleasant memories of "growing up with blacks" of the same age; playing with them day after day, building tree houses together, tormenting frogs together, picking blackberries together, until a certain age was reached — one that roughly corresponded to the onset of puberty — after which the massive door of race clanged forever and completely shut.

Or maybe not so forever and completely. Dark-of-the-night liaisons were still possible (and in some strata of society expected), as long as it was a white male who was in charge. Throughout the South, "social" went through the tortured translation of race to become "sexual." Many was the white supremacist who could deliver a stem-winder of a speech on the terrors of the "mongrelization" of the races that would follow instantly if "mixing" were allowed to occur in the schools or anywhere else — and who could then repair, oblivious to his hypocrisy, to the unpaved streets of the local "Harlem" or "Browntown" or "niggertown" to wallow and snort in the musky passions of a black mistress. Or, more likely, a light-skinned one, a woman of the very pigmentation that the segregationist, once back on his side of the tracks, would revile as a "high yellow." These debauches were never discussed openly by the white public, or possibly even dreamed of by some of its more high-minded members. But those whites whose careers kept them in touch with humanity's more fundamental urges — the cops on the night shift, the funeral home attendants, the bordello operators, the hotel desk clerks — they knew. So did the Negro community, to be sure.

Having participated as frequently as possible in the "mongrelization" process himself, the segregationist would then condemn in strongest terms its light-skinned products. Perhaps these children reminded him of how easy and even pleasant it was to integrate. The same white supremacist might condone a hastily assembled lynch mob to go after any "black buck" who attempted the same entanglement with a white woman, of course.

Perhaps the most important characteristic of American race relations in the early 1950s was the degree to which terror reigned in the black community and in the black mind. Black Southerners lived in a police state, a place where violence — officially sanctioned violence — could be visited upon them in a moment, and for no reason at all. (White Southerners lived there, too, but most of them did not know or acknowledge it.) And the oppressors could do anything they wanted and get away with it. Members of a lynch mob could be reasonably certain of never being arrested. But if a lynching became a famous case, and attracted the eye of those Northern, Jewish-owned newspapers, and the sheriff did have to arrest a few of his friends, they could be certain that no prosecutor would try very hard to convict them. And if by some fluke a prosecutor *did* try, then no jury would ever bring in a guilty verdict.

For white supremacists whose tastes did not run to physical violence, there was always the tool of economic intimidation against Negroes who stepped out of line. That produced almost as much terror as did violence.

And as a kind of halfway house between economic intimidation and lynching, the system offered jail. Jail was operated by the white segregationist establishment, and it could be used to frighten a Negro into submission, not only by shaming him but also by taking him out of circulation, removing him from his community. Or it could be the place where violence could be practiced on him with nobody watching. Jail was an instrument of economic terror, too; Southern jurisdictions routinely ordered prisoners to build roads, lay pipelines, clear land, and do all sorts of strenuous labor for no pay. In some places, notably Mississippi, prisoners were rented out to private corporations and plantation owners.

▪

White society, even that part that was horrified at lynch-type violence, was always prepared for what it called the "uppity" Negro: the black who, through ignorance or inadvertence or youthful impetuosity or — God forbid — sheer disgust with the system, stepped across the line that white society had drawn. Blacks were expected to learn early where this line lay and never to forget it.

But there were Negroes everywhere in the South (and in the North, too, as the whites were later to learn) who considered the line not a rule but a challenge. For some reason — a quirk in their personality, acceptance of what they had learned in school about America the land of equality — these people not only stepped across the line but stamped on it in contempt, and did so at every opportunity. Any white person with good sense would have known that threats and repression would not work with these Negroes; but often the confrontations did not involve whites with a great deal of sense.

Many of those who helped create the history of the fifties and sixties have two dates for the beginning of the civil rights movement: a public one, such as a recognition of the *Brown* decision or the Montgomery boycott or the Greensboro sit-ins, and a personal one. For Floyd McKissick, who became a civil rights lawyer and a chair of the Congress of Racial Equality, this personal Movement started very early on, and it involved repeated trips across the separating line. Floyd McKissick considered himself the equal of whites, and he frequently proved it.

"I think when one defines when the Movement started," said McKissick not long ago, "one has to think in terms of when one consciously became aware that he was regarded differently from other people. I think for each of us — when we found out that we were black, and then when we later discovered the effects or sentiment or attitudes that grew out of that — it then becomes a secondary phase of saying what one will do about it, or what action one will take.

"I was born in Asheville, North Carolina, on March 9, 1922, and I became conscious of being of another hue when I was four or five years old. It might have been earlier, but that's when I became conscious that I was black. 'Black' is what I say." McKissick explained that his father, who was "an outspoken preacher," and his mother were members of the African Methodist Episcopal Zion Church, and the word "black" was closely associated with the thought of Africa, although at the time the term was shunned by some Negroes. The word, he said, "carried the true meaning of 'African.' It had a connection with the old country." His parents, said McKissick, "tried to protect me from the effects of being black, but they never tried to keep me from being aware of it."

It was inevitable that McKissick would experience an Incident, but in his case there were several. He had "two or three bad experiences" when he was a child, and because of them, he feels, he became a fighter. "I've been fighting, I've been in civil rights, ever since high school," he said.

One of the Incidents happened, as it did for many blacks, on public transportation. In Asheville, the streetcars converged on Pack Square, at the center of town, where passengers transferred to other cars taking them into other neighborhoods. "I got on the car. I was with my Aunt Mattie and somebody else. A little white boy went up to see the conductor operate the streetcar, and I wanted to go up there, too. I said I wanted to sit up there so I could see him operating the car. All the kids, when they got on the streetcar, wanted to see him operate the thing, and I didn't know any difference then. I was four years old.

"And my Aunt Mattie said, 'No, come on back here.' And I had turned around and gone back up to the front of the car — just sashaying up there; you know, just like kids do. And the man turned around and said, 'Get your ass back to the back of the car there.' I was just a kid, you know; I didn't know anything. I think he said, 'Get your black ass back there before somebody *throw* it back there, boy.' And my aunt ran up to the front of the car and grabbed me and told him, 'That's no way to talk to a child.' And he made some comment about a nigger not being a child. He said, '*This* is a child,' and he pointed to the white boy. . . . There was a white fellow there who got up and said something to the conductor, and Aunt Mattie went on back to the back of the streetcar.

"It had a hell of an effect on me, because when I went back home my Aunt Mattie cried and cried and cried for days. It never left her. And she repeated it to Mother and Daddy, and neighbors came over and everybody came over to the house, and it was a major matter. They found out who was the conductor and they were talking about him and they had a prayer meeting on what they were going to do about him, and they stopped Aunt Mattie's husband from going back to the street-car.'' The family was worried that Floyd's uncle might thrash the conductor.

''This was my first time of realizing, as a child, the impact of what I had caused, and I had mixed emotions of being guilty for having brought on all of Aunt Mattie's crying. My thinking at that time was as a child, so I knew that I had done something wrong to have hurt my Aunt Mattie, who was real sweet to me and my uncle, and my momma and my daddy and all the rest of them. And the trouble that it was causing, the telephone calls that were being made about it, and this man had said this ugly thing and he looked at me in an angry way and I was mad at that man, never realizing the fullness and impact of that statement that he had made.

''They always told me from then on to 'Get on the car and go all the way back to the back.' But they jumped on the conductor, too. They called him and they called the NAACP about this man and the remark.

''That was my first experience. That was not my last, but that was my first experience.''

Another Incident occurred not long afterward, said McKissick, ''that really put the icing on the cake.'' In his preteenager days, Floyd worked at a white-owned barbershop in a commercial neighborhood not far from his home. He fired the furnace, cleaned up, and shined the shoes of customers inside the small shop and on the sidewalk outside.

One day a neighborhood bully, the ''darling little blue-eyed blond boy of the neighborhood,'' jumped Floyd. ''He grabbed me,'' recalled McKissick, ''and I grabbed him and I whipped him a fare-thee-well. He tried to hit me with rocks, a piece of wood, a bottle of shoe polish, and every time he missed, and I slipped up under him and I finally got him down. . . . And I swung around and hit him on the side of his face and in his eye. I got him a *good* blow then. Then I got off of him and hit him another blow. And by that time, everybody and his brother was running out there across the street, wanting to kill me. And Terperville, the barber, came out there and said, 'Floyd, come in here right quick.'

He grabbed me and told me, 'Get the hell on out of here. Go through the bakery.' There was a bakery in the same building with the barbershop. And he said, 'You get on home.'

"The cops were coming in the door. Somebody had called the policemen. They hunted for me for days." Floyd successfully eluded the police and went to the nearby home of some friends. They and the white barber alerted Floyd's parents to the manhunt that was under way. "My parents told me to stay put. So I didn't go home that night. The cops were going to come to my house. That was the way they did in those days. That was the way they did if you beat a white boy up."

Eventually things calmed down and Floyd went home. The barber told the authorities that the white boy had started the fight, and that helped matters some. McKissick does not think the fight was a racial incident, but that the system in which it occurred caused it to be racial. "It was a two-boy-of-any-color fight, as far as I was concerned," he said, "but everybody else made it racial."

Floyd McKissick spent his younger years pursuing a rich variety of interests in Asheville, which at that time was a small city at a gateway to the fairly primitive mountains of western North Carolina. There was a community market on Lexington Avenue where people could buy and sell produce, hunting equipment, wild foods, squirrels, rabbits, and raccoons. Floyd used to collect glass bottles and sell them at the market. With the proceeds he would purchase ice and fish and sell them door to door. There was another fight with a white boy, one promoted by a group of whites, "but that was basically a fair fight. They let me win it, so things were progressing.

"At that time, in the mountains, you had to fight. Fighting was a part of life. You had to know how to box. You had to know how to wrestle. And when somebody challenged you, you might as well accept the challenge, because if you didn't, in the black community *or* in the white community, you were a coward. We were young then, don't forget. If somebody challenged me, I'd rather get beat than to say that I was a coward.

"Coming up, I was taught nonviolence by my grandfather. He would not let me fight until I came home beaten up one time, and then he and my momma had a discussion, and they sent me back out so I could fight that boy who had been beating me up for about three days in a row because I wasn't supposed to fight. A lot of times when we went on Lexington Avenue we knew that somebody was going to fight that day."

If McKissick's life was a rambunctious one, it also was marked by sign after sign that the youth wanted desperately to participate in the greater society he saw around him in Asheville. And there was sign after sign that the white society would not let him participate.

He hauled the ice and fish and bottles in wagons. Boys with enough money bought red Radio Flyers, but Floyd made most of his wagons. "I could make a good wagon," he said. "We made a wagon for the Soap Box Derby, and they wouldn't let us get in the Soap Box Derby. So when the derby started, we jumped in with our wagon and outran the whole derby. But they wouldn't let us in it. They wouldn't let black boys in it. We beat them to death. There wasn't any wagon in that race that could compete with our wagon. *No* wagon!"

By the time he was eleven or twelve, McKissick was pretty sure he would follow his father and become a minister. But another Incident occurred that changed his plans somewhat (although he did eventually receive a minister's license).

During the Christmas holidays one year, Floyd and other members of his segregated Boy Scout troop had been stationed along a city intersection, at one of Asheville's few flat stretches of pavement, to direct traffic during a roller skating competition. Floyd was proud of his assignment and his smart scout uniform and of his Union Hardware Number 5 skates, which he felt were the fastest and strongest roller skates available.

The city's director of recreation for Negroes and the scoutmaster roped off the roadway. It was the scouts' job to direct traffic around the event and to make sure the younger participants didn't duck under the ropes and expose themselves to danger.

"We were bigger than the other kids," remembered McKissick, "and we were in uniform so we could be identified. And then a white cop came up and told me, 'Get back under that goddamn rope, boy.' The cop was a motorcycle policeman.

"I said, 'I'm out here directing this thing, and if you don't believe it ask the scoutmaster.' Douglas Clark was the scoutmaster. He was an old navy man — roamed the seven seas and could tie any kind of knot in the world. He had taught us everything in the world. We loved that old man.

"The officer told us to 'Get the hell out of the street.' I was trying to line up the kids and I felt sure he was not talking to me at first. Then I told him that I was out here working for the scoutmaster and it was the scout's duty to obey. We'd just gone through all of the scout laws, you know: honor, obedient, cheerful, everything you go through. And he told me, 'Boy, didn't I say get the hell out of that street?' He was on the motorcycle and he had great big reflector gloves — these gloves that had a big band on them and little red shiny reflectors. And he took off his gloves and he slapped me upside the head. And the little glass reflectors hit me. I remember the glove coming into my mouth.

"Other people were hollering, 'What did he do?' I said, 'I ain't done nothing but trying to do my job.'

"He said, 'Take off them damn skates; we going to take you to jail.' He took me. I was trying to take off my skates. He had knocked me down and my skate had jammed, and he had twisted the thing so it'd take a pair of pliers to straighten out the part of the lock so that you could pull the strap out. But you couldn't take that one off. So I was trying to take off the other and he grabbed at me. And I swung at him with the skate and he slapped me down with the big glove."

Floyd was hauled away to the police station. But word of the unusual confrontation — a Negro had actually fought back at a white policeman — had spread and his father and minister were already at the station. There was "a long conversation and then they took me home." McKissick had to appear in court a week or so later. He had no lawyer — there were no black attorneys in Asheville at the time — but a black minister and another prominent Negro, "the people who got out the vote in Asheville," spoke to the judge. Floyd's father told the court that "he had punished me enough, that he had whipped me."

Had he?

"No. He had admonished me that I should never do anything against a police officer. He and everybody in the group had told me that swinging the skate was wrong. I had so many little knots and bruises from the fight already that no one even mentioned beating me."

There was an effort at punishment when Floyd returned to high school. The school's principal, who was a friend of the family, ordered

Floyd not to associate with other students for a week. In this bonus of extra time, Floyd read some of the literature on the NAACP and black history that one of his favorite teachers had thrust on him. "I started reading everything about the NAACP that I could find," said McKissick — "about the lawyers, *black* lawyers. And that was when I decided I was going to become a lawyer. There was no doubt then."

There was also no doubt in Floyd McKissick's mind that an alternative — employing violence against the system that had been brutal toward him — would be the wrong one. "That wasn't the way that you were going to get anything done," he said. "That was not the practical solution, and I don't think anybody really wanted violence. If anybody suffered by violence it would've been us. We could become *emotionally* violent, but that was not any practical solution. I think that was well understood. You couldn't win, in the first place, and violence would not help anybody, in the second place. So violence just doesn't bring peace and happiness to anybody."

■ ───────────────────────────

THREE

■

THE SOUTH'S UNIQUE LIABILITY

■

In a small public park in the seat of St. Mary's County, Maryland, not all that far below Mason and Dixon's Line, there is a memorial to local soldiers and sailors "who made the Supreme Sacrifice" in World War I. The names of those who died are engraved on the front and back of the monument. One list of names starts beneath the word "WHITE." Another runs below the word "COLORED." In both lists, some of the family names are the same. These are names that are not all that common. Through the centuries, the whites of St. Mary's County have bestowed their names on black people, and some have bestowed their genes as well. They fought and died in the same war. But in death a thankful society felt it must segregate them.

Southern life in the early fifties and much life elsewhere in America was segregated, as the cliche puts it, from the cradle to the grave. It was literally true: White babies and black babies were not allowed to be born in the same hospitals, and when Americans died they were buried in separate cemeteries. Even burial plots were the subject of restrictive covenants.

Throughout the years, however, there were forces at work to change those conditions.

It would be easy to attribute the birth of the Movement to a single event or a single person, and many people try to do just that. They see its very origin in the decision by a brave, lone black woman with tired feet to refuse a bus driver's order to give up her seat, and they see its execution as the words and deeds of a single charismatic and courageous black man. But only in television docudramas are things so simple. The challenge to segregation was the yield of a number of sources — a challenge that said, above all, that blacks would no longer allow themselves to be victims of the terror.

One factor was the decreasing isolation of the South. That was brought on partly by the end of World War II. Soldiers and sailors, black and white, were returning home with memories of a world outside the South. Agriculture was no longer holding people to the land. The South was developing urban centers that were more vulnerable to black pressures for reform than a South that was overwhelmingly agrarian.

This is not to say that the downtown white business community of a typical Southern city was overly enlightened. The correct term was "practical minded." This group, also known as the "downtown elite" and the "power structure," embraced segregation wholeheartedly as a necessary cost of doing business. If community sentiments had been the opposite, the group just as enthusiastically would have promoted integration. Under the system that did prevail, providing separate water fountains, dressing rooms, toilets, and eating places was on a par with securing annual business licenses and health department inspections. This accommodation to the system was not restricted to country boys who covered their red necks with white collars and ties when they moved to the city to operate businesses; it was amazing how quickly the graduates of Harvard and Yale, people who undeniably understood the moral score, were able to make the adaptation.

For Southern business, segregation meant a way to keep the peace. As long as people were segregated and nobody kicked up too great a fuss, that itself was a definition of "peacefulness," and that meant a healthy business climate. There was the additional fact that Negroes didn't have all that much discretionary income anyway.

There were, however, occasional signs of rebellion, indications that some people *were* ready to kick up a fuss. Floyd McKissick was not unique. Every community had many Floyd McKissicks. It may have happened as a result of a lynching that was designed to show a returned soldier that he was still a nigger. Or maybe the Negroes had read in the *Afro-American* about some of the early efforts to integrate lunch counters by sitting at them until the owners either brought food or closed down. Or maybe part of it was white guilt over being the repressor, a guilt that translated itself into fear (because all repressors surely must wonder if the day will come when the tables are turned, when they are caught without their weapons and their victims are in control). Kind, gentle colored housemaids pushed their white infant charges to a shady spot and sat and talked in low voices, rocking the baby carriages slowly, and when a white person approached they would stop talking. *What are they plotting? Why are they scowling at me?* It was like seeing a dangerous animal in the zoo; a tiger who suddenly stops pacing and looks you in the eye. *What if the cage door somehow opens?*

On more than one occasion, a black man or woman would plunk down in the first available seat on the bus and, chin thrust forward and mouth set in a straight line of defiance, silently dare the driver to make an objection. And the smart driver would know better than to make one. Sometimes the miscreant was dismissed as "just a crazy nigger," deemed not to be fooled with on grounds of unpredictability. And it was always possible that the white, guessing at the depth of the black's rage and perhaps even sympathizing with it a bit, just decided not to raise the issue.

Occasionally it would be a white who would thumb his or her nose at the way of life and march to the back of the bus, causing the other white passengers to shake their heads in disbelief and the blacks to squirm and wonder if this crazy ofay was about to bring a load of trouble down on them.

A number of institutions that operated within or for the black community were part of the growing rebellion. The National Association for the Advancement of Colored People, which was founded in 1909 as the amalgam of a militant black group and a number of white social workers who wanted to help Negroes, had been active in Southern big city and dusty hamlet almost from the beginning. In 1950 the NAACP, reflecting the postwar impatience that characterized much of the black population, changed its antisegregation legal strategy from one that accepted separate but equal to one that demanded an end to segregation.

The National Urban League, founded in 1911, was, as its name implied, more urban in its operations, and its presence in the South was not nearly so great as the NAACP's. In many communities across the region, local black ministerial alliances effectively gathered and directed black energies, anger, and outrage. In every Southern city of any size, too, there were other sources of relatively independent Negro wealth and influence that were, in some but not all cases, starting to bring pressure on segregation. These included the operators of black funeral homes, newspapers, insurance companies, sometimes banks, and personal service establishments such as barbershops.

And the black church. As noted above, black Southern religion had the capability of helping the Movement (and, as things turned out, it helped mightily) and also of retarding it. In any event, as civil rights activist Lawrence Guyot was later to put it in an interview reflecting on the Movement years, "There couldn't have been a civil rights movement without the black church. . . . That was the only institution controlled, run, financed, and dictated by black folks. The only question [for a Movement worker] was getting in on them; getting into the church and moving it."

One form of rebellion had been carried on for a long time by the black legal profession. The relative handful of Negro NAACP lawyers, the Howard University gang, had been contesting racial discrimination in court for decades. Among them was a loose network of local black lawyers, in some cases as few as one per Deep South state. These attorneys were eager to help out on the big cases that brought in high-caliber courtroom types such as Thurgood Marshall, the Inc. Fund's counsel, and Charles Houston, the head of Howard's law school and a legendary NAACP lawyer, but they also took local cases that before might have been handled by no lawyer at all. In doing so, they made themselves highly visible to the white supremacist contingent and were always in some danger.

An active segregationist might not know the names of local Negro morticians or life insurance executives, but he certainly would remember the uppity black man who strode into *his* courtroom wearing a suit and tie, exuding self-confidence and citing the law in two- and three-dollar phrases. Even the less extreme whites had trouble with this; in Atlanta, the well-known Austin T. Walden, who for a time was the only black lawyer in town, and who had been fighting for civil rights all his life, was always called Colonel Walden by court employees who could not bring themselves to refer to him as Mister. In Birmingham, Arthur Shores, who had been an NAACP lawyer since the 1940s, was well known to the racists. His house was dynamited twice in the sixties.

------------------------------------   ■

One means by which an independent-minded Negro could survive in the segregated South was by taking up one of the professions. As supremacist as some Southern whites were, they never denied that Negroes had a right to produce their own lawyers, doctors, morticians, ministers, barbers, hairdressers, dentists, and teachers (to be sure, most whites simply would not have taken on the tasks of healing, embalming, taking communion with, or trimming the hair of Negroes). The practice of law was one particularly attractive means of remaining both independent and at least moderately financially secure, and it usually brought with it a degree of respect within the community. It was practically guaranteed that a black lawyer would also be a "civil rights lawyer," with ample opportunities to be as uppity as he or she desired. Floyd McKissick was licensed as a minister, but he made his living practicing law in North Carolina. Arthur Shores pretty much had the field to himself in Birmingham.

When Shores finished at the University of Kansas and was admitted to the Alabama bar in 1937, there were three other black lawyers in Birmingham. Within two years, however, two of the lawyers died, and the third was elevated to grand master of Alabama's black Masons, an honor that kept him quite busy. "Then for ten years I was the only black lawyer," said Shores, who reached the age of eighty-five in 1990. For much of the time he served as the NAACP's legal representative in

Alabama. But he also devoted his energies to the nuts-and-bolts work of defending black people who had gotten into trouble with the law in ways unrelated to the Movement.

"I went over all this state alone," said Shores. "Whenever I put my briefcase on the desk, I had a .45 army automatic, which I had a license to carry. And I never had an unpleasant situation in many of the rural sections that I had to go to. The worst situation that I had was here in Birmingham, on occasion when the NAACP had retained me to prosecute a white police officer for police brutality.

"The NAACP indicated that they had hired white lawyers before, and they hadn't had any success, so they might as well hire me to do it. But to the surprise of everybody, this officer was found guilty. They suspended him for thirty days and put him on probation for a year. This was back in the forties.

"The courthouse was packed with black and white. This was a white city police officer, being prosecuted in the county. And after the case was over, I was being congratulated on the sixth floor of the courthouse. And a black man came up and said, 'Shores, I'd like to speak to you.' I thought he wanted to congratulate me. And the moment I stepped out from the crowd, he swung at me.

"But I ducked and he missed me. My friends beat him down in the corridor of the courthouse; closed both of his eyes. White officers came up and arrested two of the blacks — the rest of them ran and they couldn't catch them — and they included me. Arrested me. Put us in the city jail. I was there for about thirty minutes, and then I was bonded out.

"Well, on the very next day they tried us in city court. Naturally, I was found not guilty. The two who protected me were fined five dollars and court costs. And the one who had attacked me, they fined him ten dollars.

"A week later, he came to my office and said he was what we call a police informer, a police pimp, who worked for the cops. He said he had been paid to start an altercation during the recess of the case so that would break it up. They would come in and arrest us all, and that would break it up. He said he didn't have the nerve to do that, so he just did the next best thing."

The fact that the informer waited until the trial's completion, said Shores, "was worth a fortune to me. There were blacks who didn't realize I was practicing law in Birmingham who would come by my office and say, 'I don't have any legal business now, but if I ever need a lawyer, I know where to come.' And from that day to this, I haven't had to look for any cases."

In the years that followed, Shores's legal business profited not only by word-of-mouth boosting in the black community, but also by the heavy-handedness of Birmingham's racist white political leadership. Police pimps were just one weapon in racist Birmingham's arsenal.

■ ─────────────────────────────────

The South was also, albeit with painful slowness, developing a body of white people who were at the very least concerned about the negative effects of racial segregation. Some of them saw it as bad for business. Some saw it as harmful for the notion of the "new South" that, according to the region's spokesmen, was always just around the corner. Some saw it as a moral travesty. Very often Southern whites with these feelings could gather under the banner of "moderates" and, if nothing else, make it impossible to honestly issue a blanket denunciation of the region.

Some of the more deeply concerned whites took things a step further. At the beginning of 1944, a number of white and black Southerners formally chartered an organization that had been in the discussion stage for several years. The Southern Regional Council, which had and still has its headquarters in Atlanta, was an effort, according to one account of its origins, "to try to do something about problems arising from culture and history that crippled this southern land and people they loved."[1] The council started life less enthusiastic (or at least its white members were) about integration and more interested in the idea that if the South's economic problems could be solved, the others, including race, would fall into line. But by the early fifties, much earlier than other Southern organizations containing influential whites, the SRC was publicly tackling the real problems. It provided a place where the "decent whites" could work and express their opinions, where black intellectuals could break out of segregation's isolation, and where journalists and others could go for reliable information on the region. Indeed, according to Harold Fleming, SRC's director from 1947 to 1961, until late in the fifties the U.S. Justice Department didn't have accurate information on black voter registration in the South and had to get it from SRC before it could try to prove that there was discrimination on the registration books. "We were the first to try to compile any data," said Fleming, "and we had the only figures as late as 1959."

------------------------------ ■

It was not just the returning black soldiers who came back to the South with new ideas. World War II exposed white Southerners to the world, too.

Harold Fleming is a white Southerner, born in Atlanta in 1922 in Georgia Baptist Hospital, although he says now that such credentials never seemed to help him with contemporaries who disagreed with his integrationist ideas. "They'd say, 'You ought to know better, being a native-born Georgia white.' " He grew up in Atlanta during the Depression and then moved to the old family home in Elbert County, in south Georgia. It was, he says, "a very conventional upbringing."

Things got unconventional, however, when Fleming went into the U.S. Army, which made him an officer and placed him in command of a company of black "service" troops. In those days, black military men performed service functions — the dirty work — to support their white counterparts. The military, and particularly the army, was strictly segregated.

The army experience was a profound one. "It meant different things to different people," said Fleming, "but for me it — 'radicalized' would be too strong a word. It wasn't that I came to love Negroes; it was that I came to despise the system that did this. I mean, the nearest thing you could be in the army to being black was to be a company officer with black troops, because you lived and operated under the same circumstances they did, and they got crapped all over.

"I ended up commanding a company — a company was two hundred and eight men — on Okinawa. We were part of that massing of troops for the invasion of Japan. . . . The brass were overtly prejudiced. They were just overtly racist. And oddly enough, in some fashion . this rubbed off on the white officers of those units. You were sort of a second-class officer or second-class white because of your assignment. Now what this did was, it turned some people who grew up in the

Harriet Beecher Stowe culture into raving racists themselves. Because you had a lot of unattractive men in those units, and they had every technique of avoiding and evading. Passive resistance was an art. Well, I did a little better than some of them because I knew it was bullshit so I said, 'Look, don't give me that Stepin Fetchit act, please. You know. Come on.' "

After the war ended Fleming entered college, at Harvard. He was by then, he sees now, "a kind of a do-nothing snob about race relations. I felt that I was literate, I had read a lot of things that my contemporaries had not read; I was sort of a corn pone intellectual. And the cruder founts of racism were beneath me. But I wasn't about to do anything about it.

"That's what I meant when I said 'radicalized' isn't the right term. It wasn't that I was radicalized, but the army experience activated me, so that I was prepared to feel strongly about it."

Harold Fleming planned to return to Georgia after the war and college. The state was offering a glimmer of hope to people like him that it could react to postwar change in a progressive way and avoid turning into a hotbed of racism. Ellis Arnall, a somewhat forward-looking politician, had been governor. But Eugene Talmadge, a demagogue of the first order, who won the decisive Democratic primary to succeed Arnall, died before taking office and was replaced (through a series of those cynical manipulations that have characterized much Southern political history) by his son, Herman, who was almost as accomplished at milking the race issue as his father.

Arnall's term, said Fleming, "was a spirit of hope that went gurgling down the drain when Gene Talmadge was elected and further gurgled when Herman Talmadge took over with storm-trooper tactics." It might be a good time, he thought, to get out of Georgia. "My reaction was not, 'Let me get down there and get in the battle' but, 'Good God, I don't want to live in that kind of a thing.' It just made sense to go to New York. New York was a paradise then." He would look for a job in publishing.

Fleming was in Georgia that summer of 1947, and he made it a point to see Ralph McGill before he left for the North. McGill's column appeared every day on the front page of the *Atlanta Constitution,* and it contained the most liberal comments that most Georgians had ever read. "He was saying some things that I had never heard before," said

Fleming. "As vacillating as he was in those days and as incompletely reconstructed as he may have been, he was still a phenomenon that I had never seen in the South. So I decided, 'Well, I've got to go talk to this man.'

"Characteristically, McGill says, 'Aw, I think you've got the right idea; go on to New York. We're in for a long, dark night down here.' And I was saying that I didn't know that people held the kind of ideas that he was talking about, and things like that. And finally, probably in order to get rid of me, he said, 'There's an outfit that you really ought to know about before you go. It's called the Southern Regional Council. A struggling outfit, but good people. . . .' "

Fleming investigated the council, which then was headquartered in the Wesley Memorial Church building, on the end of downtown Atlanta's Auburn Avenue. The street, known as Sweet Auburn by black Atlantans, was a center of Negro commerce and culture.

Fleming talked with George Mitchell, the council's director. After a few pleasantries, Fleming recalled, Mitchell said: " 'You in any hurry to get on up there to New York?'

"I said I wasn't working against any deadline.

"Then he said, 'Well, my director of information has just left and there are some unfinished things here. . . . Would you be willing to hang around for a month to six weeks and finish these things up for me? I haven't got any money, but I'll scrape up something.'

"Well," said Fleming, "he honest to God *didn't* have any money, as I discovered to my sorrow for quite a while after that. But I stayed on to finish those odd jobs, and fourteen years later I left Atlanta."

During the fourteen years, Fleming managed to change the Southern Regional Council from an organization dominated by polite white Southerners who hoped the region's economic progress would have a trickle-down effect on its race relations to one unabashedly in favor of, and working for, integration.

The council had been wrestling since its founding with its feelings on segregation. As Fleming explained it, SRC at the outset "equivocated in its public statements and position-taking, and equivocated on segregation. . . . It had a lot of people in it who would not have been in it in the beginning if they had been required to face the world naked and say, 'Jim Crow must go.' "

The Southern historian Howard Odum had a lot to do with SRC's tendency to bog down in equivocation and paternalism. Odum's position, Fleming said, was that the interracial organization that the council was becoming should "transcend race" rather than concentrate on it. Odum and others who shared his view wanted a Southern force "that worked through, and advocated, and pointed the way to economic development, modernization, sound urbanization — all those good things. It would involve people of both races and would speak to the needs of people of both races, but would not be viewed as a racial organization. It would be *above race.* He genuinely thought that in the first place, you could do that, and, secondly, that it was the way to lead the South into a racially enlightened society."

Such thinking is similar to modern-day arguments that America should encourage economic growth in South Africa, not boycott it. "It's the philosophy that all good things flow from a healthy, growing, economically sound, developing society, and that all your social problems get taken care of without direct confrontation simply by the process of healthy social and economic growth.

"Well, I thought it was impossible then, and I think it's impossible now. . . . Where I think Odum was wrong or mistaken is that that approach underestimates the depth and force of the segregated tradition of the South — to suppose that you could transcend it and really spend very little of your time thinking about it, and that you could move on into some 'postsegregationist society.' You avoid the confrontation, or at least not tear *our*selves apart, or get ourselves torn apart, by being a combative force here, a confrontational force.

"It was not possible in the South to do that. The country club couldn't do it. The Chamber of Commerce couldn't do it, much less an organization like the SRC that had no intrinsic power. There was no way it could not become focussed on race, and advocacy."

Eventually, others at SRC came to similar conclusions, and at the group's annual meeting in 1950, the members instructed their executive committee to return in a year's time with a recommended statement of purpose. Fleming wrote it. The resulting document, titled "Toward the South of the Future," was adopted in December, 1951.

The policy statement placed SRC on record as seeking "working solutions" to the South's problems "rather than spectacular pronouncements." It still favored finding solutions to the region's problems "that transcend the question of race," the old approach. "But, for the present," the statement added, "the unique liability under which the South labors arises out of an unreasoning racial disharmony." It would be the council's goal "to create here the atmosphere in which artificial distinctions and discriminations based upon race will no longer persist. Only when that goal has been attained will the energies of enlightened men be fully released for the great task of realizing all our potential resources, natural and human."[2]

By 1990s standards, it was not exactly an inflammatory statement of purpose. But in 1951, before even the *Brown* decision, it was radical enough to attract the attention of the racist establishment. Fleming recalls that Herman Talmadge went on a statewide radio hookup and blasted the SRC as a "haven for communist fronters."

Fleming said that as he worked on the document in 1951, he had to overcome the "strategic" thinking that characterized so many of the Southern liberals of the forties and fifties. It was, he said, a brand of thinking "that gives you a lot of latitude for rationalizing almost anything. Like the preachers used to say: 'Gosh, I'd love to speak up on this, but if I do they'll fire me and then they'll hire somebody worse. And so, okay, we don't do anything, right?'

"My feeling was that the Southern Regional Council barely escaped waiting too long to take a flat-footed public position on segregation."

■ ─────────────────────

Most white Southerners in those years felt no need whatever to revise their positions on the way of life they shared with the region's black people. It was a commonplace expression among the whites that "our Negroes [or nigras] are happy." When unhappiness did manifest itself, it was necessary to assign blame for it to that infinitely handy, all-purpose villain, the Outside Agitator — whose role was played, almost always, by the NAACP. (Southern politicians skilled at what they thought of as political debate would often deliberately mix up the initials, saying "enn-double-a-pee-cee" to show their contempt for an organization that was so totally unimportant as to not have a name they could remember. Their other words and deeds showed that they felt otherwise, however. They routinely spoke of the nation's oldest black organization as a danger far worse than godless international communism, drought, and the boll weevil all combined.)

To a certain extent, it had been in the blacks' interest to allow and even encourage this fantasy of childlike happiness among the whites with whom they shared their region. It bought peace, and that was a welcome commodity, though the rebellion continued beneath the placid surface. James Farmer, a founder of the Congress of Racial Equality and its national director from 1961 to early 1966, said in a recent interview that he thinks many whites believed that "their colored" really were happy.

"You know how the human mind can work on those things," said Farmer. "You can convince yourself. You say a thing over and over again, and you believe it to be true. And I think that they had convinced themselves that it was true. They *believed* that 'their colored people were happy.' And there was so much evidence to join in that convincing process: Many of them smiled when they saw a white face. That was part of the delusion. There was a fine art in the black community — the fine art of fooling the white man. And blacks learn it early.

"And those blacks who learned it well survive and make a lot of money. Not sur*vived* and made money but sur*vive* and make money. It's still happening." Farmer said these people no longer have to employ a public shuffling gait and head-scratching routine in order to appear harmless to whites; rather, they "just say the right thing. Say the thing that the white community wants to hear." He declined to supply names, but added that some of these people were "political," some were "media personalities" who had learned how to sound militant but still tell whites what pleased them.

It should be clear that the Movement, when it happened, was anything but an eccentricity, an outburst, a surprise — at least to anyone who had been paying attention, and most white people hadn't. The civil rights movement was the logical outgrowth of everything that had happened before, and a lot had happened. The Movement started not long after 1619, when a Jamestown, Virginia, settler noted in his journal that "there came in a Dutch man-of-warre that sold us 20 negars."[3] It probably *really* started even before that. The first thing that prisoners of war may be expected to do is to start plotting their escape.

America was headed toward a change in its way of conducting relations between the races. But the nature of the change, in the early fifties, was not so apparent. Who or what would be the catalyst? What would kick it off?

For many people, it would be the May 17, 1954, decision by the Supreme Court in *Brown v. Board of Education* declaring that separate but equal, in education at least, was no longer the law of the land. Even for those who had known that the old system was bound to change, and to change soon, the *Brown* decision meant that a totally new universe of possibilities was opening up.

PART TWO

A MOVEMENT IS BORN

FOUR

THE REVOLUTION GOT OUT OF HAND

The Supreme Court's *Brown* decision was one of three critical events in the years 1954 to 1960 that gave the Movement a forward motion that could not be halted or reversed. Each of the three — *Brown*; the Montgomery, Alabama, bus boycott that started in December, 1955; and the sit-ins that occurred in Greensboro, North Carolina, in February, 1960 — contributed to the inevitability and invincibility of the Movement. Somewhere in those years, the modern Movement started.

Observers of the era are not of one mind about precisely when the Movement began. Indeed, the only thing that seems certain is that it didn't start at any precise time. Perhaps the strongest case can be made for the Greensboro sit-ins. The Montgomery boycott — as important as it was in demonstrating that Negroes previously pronounced "happy" and "satisfied" and "docile" could get together and defeat an opponent who not only owned the deck of cards but also wrote the rules — was, for all its importance, a local event. The Greensboro sit-ins, although they came far closer to being a spontaneous display of disgust with the system of segregation, started something that swept the region, the nation, and even the world.

Whenever the Movement started, it is important to understand that it was not just an impromptu occurrence. In *Brown*, Greensboro, and, most notably, Montgomery, there had been a good deal of planning by a good many people who had yearned for a good long time to attack and defeat racial segregation.

It is important to remember this, too, about the Movement: It was not a series of discrete events, most easily remembered by the names of the major battlefields, as in a world war. It was not a collection of film clips that can be squeezed neatly into an hour of television during Black History Month. Rather it was (like the rest of real history) a flow, a continuum, an ongoing mishmash of events, places, and people — of violence, legislation, legal decisions (not all of them favoring the Movement, by any means), murders, shootings, beatings, arrests, marches, mass meetings; of songs, speeches, ultimata, threats, promises both kept and broken, crosses both carried and burned, votes both cast and denied, terror both inflicted and vanquished.

For many survivors of those years, the *Brown* decision was the beginning of all that.

-- ▪

Leslie W. Dunbar was born in Lewisburg, West Virginia, just to the east of the coalfields. Somewhere along the way he developed that characteristic, which manifests itself strongly every now and then in people from the Appalachian highlands, of unflinching liberalism bordering on radicalism. Perhaps it is the personal knowledge of so many people so close to poverty, the close familiarity with a system in which a few people exploit the rest and the land to boot. At any rate, Dunbar became one of those white Southerners who believed in integration and put his actions behind his words.

He taught political science at Emory and Mount Holyoke, and joined Harold Fleming's Southern Regional Council in Atlanta in 1958. When Fleming left the job in March, 1961, Dunbar became executive director. He ran the council until October, 1965, when he moved to New York City to become executive secretary and director of the Field

Foundation, which supported projects and organizations interested in Southern issues. Since 1980, Dunbar has served as a teacher and consultant for various organizations and has been a frequent author of tracts and books, always dealing with the fundamental issues of poverty, racism, war, and peace.

For Dunbar, the thing that is called the civil rights movement began with *Brown v. Board of Education.*

"You can give other dates, and you can give earlier dates," said Dunbar. "If you like to think 'Movement' means when something transformed itself into a campaign of lots of people, you might put the date off until the Montgomery bus boycott.

"But I think *Brown v. Board of Education* has a very special historical claim. I guess you could say the same thing, in a way, about 1865, with the Thirteenth Amendment [which abolished slavery and involuntary servitude]. But that got ignored. Up until *Brown v. Board of Education,* in 1954, segregation had been legal. Up to *Brown v. Board of Education,* the constitutional rights of black people *not* to be legally discriminated against were, to say the least, unclear. After that, they were not. From 1954 on, it was as though the Constitution had been clarified. So I think that's the date."

■ ────────────────────────────

In *Brown* (the full title of which was *Oliver Brown et al. v. Board of Education of Topeka, Shawnee County, Kansas, et al.*), the court rendered a decision in cases coming not only from Kansas but also Clarendon County, South Carolina; Prince Edward County, Virginia; and New Castle County, Delaware. Three of the four were Negroes' appeals from lower court decisions favoring segregation, while the fourth involved a state, Delaware, that was appealing a decision ordering desegregation. The NAACP originally brought a case in the District of Columbia as well. NAACP lawyers representing black schoolchildren in those states had attacked the separate but equal doctrine enshrined in *Plessy v. Ferguson* as an unconstitutional means of excluding the children from "white" schools.

Chief Justice Earl Warren delivered the court's unanimous decision. In a statement that stands as one of the court's, and the nation's, landmarks, Warren wrote: "We conclude that in the field of public education the doctrine of 'separate but equal' has no place. Separate educational facilities are inherently unequal. Therefore, we hold that the plaintiffs and others similarly situated for whom the actions have been brought are, by reason of the segregation complained of, deprived of the equal protection of the laws guaranteed by the Fourteenth Amendment."

"Separate but equal" and *Plessy* were dead. Or perhaps not quite. The basic issue of constitutionality had been settled, but the court still needed time to consider how to implement the decision. All the parties involved, along with the attorney general of the United States, were invited to present further arguments on how best to carry out the ruling. The court set the following October 1 as the date for submission of briefs.[1]

The ruling had profound consequences that are being felt even a third of a century later. One of its most positive effects was to put the federal government squarely on the side of desegregation, at least in name. Before, this had really happened only in relation to the armed forces, and even there incompletely and with many an official wink in the direction of discrimination. Other government programs, where they existed at all, were aimed more at preventing discrimination. But now the highest court in the land had spoken of affirmative effort; had said that (as both blacks and whites who had given more than a moment's thought to it certainly knew) there could be no equality in separation.

The decision also told Negroes that the legal approach produced success — that there was some justice to be gained by working within the system. The decision said that equity didn't have to wait for the sweet by-and-by, after everybody was dead and in heaven; that it could be realized perhaps not later today or tomorrow, because of the inherent slowness of the legal system, but certainly by next year. And it said that this was so in the area of American life that Negroes respected above all others: education. It was the field in which Booker T. Washington had advised them to excel, and the field that the white people said held the key to the end of discrimination. When Negroes pull themselves up to our level, the whites had so often said, *then* we can exist equally in society.

▪

Harvey Gantt was born in Charleston County, South Carolina, in 1943. A year or so later he and his parents moved to Charleston, the city, into a public housing project near the naval base. As World War II progressed, Gantt's father built a house for the family.

"You have to understand," said Gantt later, "that as a kid growing up in Charleston, I was pretty happy, pretty much enjoying what I had been used to: close family relationships; small, blue-collar, salt-of-the-earth neighborhood; people just working hard every day. No matter that I didn't understand that many of them worked in domestic jobs and menial-type labor, and very few of them had college degrees.

"Around the corner there was a doctor and lawyer, and those were the people we were supposed to emulate. We never questioned walking past white schools to get to black schools, or sitting at the back of the bus, or that our parents were always saying, 'You've got to be quiet. . . . White folks expect you to be quiet.'

"And you always wondered why white kids always seemed to be unruly and nobody cared, but you had to sit prim and proper. The point is: I was a happy child in existence right in the midst of rigid segregation, which is probably the story of millions of black kids who grew up in the forties and fifties. Except when 1954 hit. For a kid like me, that May seventeenth was a very significant day. I don't forget it."

Initially, the Supreme Court decision was confusing for this eleven-year-old black child.

"I didn't understand it at first. All I remember was the *Charleston Evening Post*'s bold headlines: "Supreme Court: Segregation Is Unconstitutional." And then we started talking. My father had been an NAACP member for years, and I really started to question him about all this stuff. What's this all about?"

▪

The reaffirmation of the legal approach, as opposed to what many felt were self-defeating alternatives such as violence and mass emigration to a newly established black nation, or even milder ones such as street demonstrations, found easy acceptance in the hearts of Negro Americans. For Negro Americans had, and still have, a solid record of being good Americans. As much as any other group in the country, and more than most, they have always tried to play by the rules. When the rules made the system unfair to them, they sought redress of their grievances through the channels that society certified as the proper ones. They did this even when their lawyers could not enter the whites' law schools and when they knew their jury boxes would not contain a black face and when the seating in the very courtrooms was segregated. And through the Movement years, blacks' faithfulness to the American system and dream has remained touchingly strong, despite fierce attacks on that dream by that system.

As evidence of this, consider communism and the American Negroes. Few areas of American life offered a riper opportunity for proselytizing by other ideologies than the black experience. Few Americans, save perhaps the original ones, were treated more undemocratically by democracy. And yet the number of Negroes who abandoned democracy for communism was miniscule.

Finally, for many people, particularly the younger blacks but also quite a few Southern whites who had been looking for a way out of the segregation labyrinth, *Brown* was the beginning of a beginning that had been long awaited. It told the young Negroes — when they were in their formative years, when they were at that age that assumes immortality and an unquestioned ability to change the world — that segregation was all but over, that what had seemed eternal to their parents could be ended now. For many of those who in a few years would become the foot soldiers and lieutenants of the activist army, it was a starting point. It said "Something can be done, finally."

When the *Brown* decision came down, on May 17, 1954, some white Southerners were surprised. Those who had kept themselves even minimally current on public affairs had known for several years, of course, that the school cases were in the courts and that change was all but certain. The four cases that made up *Brown* had reached the Supreme Court back in 1952, and they had been making their ways through the lower courts before that.

Many people had *not* kept themselves up to date on public affairs, however. Some had believed their political leaders' declarations that "it'll never happen here"; some were fooled all of the time by this rhetoric, and almost all of them were fooled some of the time. And some actually believed that "their" Negroes didn't really want integration and would decline it if it were offered.

The segregationists in elective office knew that a big decision was on its way, and most of them surely had more than an inkling of what it would be. In November, 1953, Governor Herman Talmadge proposed a constitutional amendment allowing the Georgia legislature to convert public schools into private facilities and to provide tuition grants for the children who attended them. The obvious motivation for such a drastic move would be a court-ordered desegregation of public schools. The Georgia legislature agreed, and the state's voters (few of whom were black) approved the amendment a year later by a close margin.[2] Other states took similar actions later on.

While some of the supremacists had been preparing for change, so had some of the moderates and integrationists in the white community. Before the *Brown* decision, the Ford Foundation had established a Fund for the Advancement of Education, whose task was to conduct research on the South's reactions to the expected desegregation order. Harry Ashmore, then the executive editor of the *Arkansas Gazette,* was chosen to head the project, the end result of which would be a series of books. (The key publication in the series, *The Negro and the Schools,* was published on the same day that the court handed down its decision.)

■

When Harry Ashmore took his leave from the *Arkansas Gazette* to collect information on the forthcoming Supreme Court decision, he knew that much depended on the region's reaction. Ashmore knew, and so did the study's sponsors, that a decision from the nation's highest court pretty much had to do one of two things: "It was either going to demand that the Southern school system be equalized, which would have bankrupted every state because the differences were so great," said Ashmore, "or they would order them integrated, which would cause an even greater social dislocation. But one of the two things was going to happen."

Ashmore and his colleagues found a glacial unwillingness to consider the subject publicly. "Nobody in the South," he said, "was willing to even discuss the possibility. You couldn't bring the subject up among politicians. They just ran like hell." So the fund went to Southern universities, both private and public, and stated its case, in hopes of getting help in collecting regionwide data: "Look, this court's going to rule twelve months from now. There isn't any accurate information about what kind of changes will be required." The point was made, said Ashmore, that "there are going to be changes either way, but the figures on the disparities of the school system had been cooked and the damn state departments of education had been lying so long that none of these normal statistics are any good. . . .

"And also there were the great differences between the states and among the states and within the states. There were places where desegregation wouldn't make much difference, and there were places where it would be probably impossible for quite a long time. These distinctions had never been drawn. And every university turned them down, public or private. They said, 'No, this thing's too hot to handle. We just can't touch it.' But the same thing was true of every politician you talked to in those days. They wouldn't even discuss the goddamn thing."

The project eventually got rolling when the Fund for the Advancement of Education abandoned its efforts to involve entire schools and sent Ashmore, as its head researcher, to recruit academics on an individual basis. The newspaper editor continued his discussions, in the meantime, with politicians and, particularly, business leaders. "I wanted to know what the hell they were going to do. I was trying to see what their reaction was going to be, which I was convinced was what ultimately it would be: that they would finally decide they couldn't put up with the damn violence, that it was bad for business. But they, like the politicians, were absolutely unwilling to say anything publicly."

Some of the business leaders knew the score — knew what was likely to happen, knew that it was right to happen, knew that to resist it was wrong and futile. "But they didn't want to believe it. There was an awful lot of rationalization. People who didn't want to believe this would simply dismiss it.

"Somewhere in the middle of this, I ran into an old Arkansas politician, a member of the legislature, a little old redneck fellow. He said, 'What the hell are you up to these days?' I said, 'Well, I'm writing this book.' He said, 'What's it going to be called?' I said, 'Well, it's a book about what's going to happen to the schools. It's called *The Negro and the Schools.*' And he said, 'Son, sounds to me like you got yourself in the position of the man running for son of a bitch without opposition.'"

———————————

As he grew into adolescence in Chester, South Carolina, Charles Jones became increasingly aware of the more strident forms of white resistance. The Ku Klux Klan was active in South Carolina, and Jones and every other Negro were, as he put it, "constantly aware of the differences of being black."

He entered high school in Chester, but in 1952 his family moved to Charlotte, North Carolina, about fifty miles away. Charlotte was much larger than Chester, and it had more progressive ideas — or perhaps it was just that Charlotte's political and social climates did not encourage the more repressive ones. "Charlotte was a bit more enlightened, but not much," recalled Jones.

At first, Jones did not spend much time in Charlotte. Through the connections his father had as a Presbyterian minister, he transferred for his last two years of high school to Harbison Junior College, a church-related school near Columbia, South Carolina, that had a high school department. Students at Harbison, which was a black school, attended classes half a day and worked half a day.

Jones was about to graduate, in the spring of 1954, when he heard about the Supreme Court's decision in the case of *Brown v. Board of Education.* His heart soared. He did not pay all that much attention to the slight delay that the court had allowed. Segregation, the court had said, was ended.

"I remember walking on the campus" after hearing the decision, recalled Jones. "All kinds of feelings that I wasn't even aware were inside; I was all excited about what that might mean. Schools were going to be opening up, I thought. Society was going to be opened up. Finally we were going to develop some kind of rational society, I thought."

He thought it would happen quickly. After all, the Supreme Court of the United States had spoken. "This shows my naivete: I thought it ought to be by that noon, or next year. Within the year. Just a matter of working out the details. I remember very clearly when I heard it. It was a bright day, and I was all excited."

■ ————————————————————————

The *Brown* decision produced great positive change, but one outcome of the ruling was decidedly negative and long-lasting: that the federal government, no matter how hopeful the words of its highest court might be, was clearly not committed to taking either quick or strong affirmative action to see that blacks' constitutional rights were enforced and that discrimination was ended.

The court itself hinted strongly at this in the May 17 decision, when it declined to set enforcement guidelines immediately, announcing instead that it would ask the interested parties for help in writing them. Because the school cases were class actions, "because of the wide applicability of this decision, and because of the great variety of local conditions," wrote the court, "the formulation of decrees in these cases presents problems of considerable complexity."[3]

Actual desegregation, said the court, would start at some later date. Justice for some ten million American citizens was instantaneously delayed, and thus further denied, on the grounds (unstated, but crystal clear) that to start the change immediately would be to place too great a burden on those who had been the deniers.[4] The history of American race relations, and especially of school desegregation, is chock full of assumptions that integration, though desirable, will somehow place a hardship on white people and that any change in the status quo must take the whites' comfort into consideration. It is an unspoken way of saying that blacks, whose own hardships are rarely mentioned, are inferior. In the case of *Brown*, it meant that uncounted thousands of Negro children had to continue receiving their education under conditions that everyone, including the Supreme Court of the United States, knew were unequal and unfair.

When the litigants in *Brown* gathered in the fall of 1954 to tackle the "problems of considerable complexity" cited by the court, the NAACP argued for desegregation by September, 1955. On May 31, 1955, the court released its guidelines, and they were a disappointment for the NAACP and others who wanted firm action. Local school boards were instructed to draw up desegregation plans "with all deliberate speed."⁵

Whatever "all deliberate speed" may have meant to the members of the court, to the segregationist school boards and Southern politicians it meant a comfortable period of delay that was the equivalent of going back to business as usual. Just drawing up a plan could consume a good part of a black child's educational years, and "all deliberate speed" could mean just about anything — and often did. As it turned out, the NAACP's disappointment was well founded. Fourteen years after the decision, a survey showed that close to 80 percent of America's Negro children were still attending all-black schools.⁶

When the Little Rock school desegregation crisis occurred in 1957, it clearly was one of the legacies of this hesitation. The Eisenhower administration, in its initial handling of the situation, which was characterized by white violence, demonstrated that unless the federal government were strictly forced to do so by a challenge to its sovereignty, it would not intervene forcefully on behalf of black people. It would intervene, however, if its own authority were challenged. Government was reactive, not innovative, even when matters of the Constitution were clearly involved. Constitutional issues, including those believed to have been settled by the Supreme Court, were negotiable, with the parties who had violated the Constitution having negotiating rights equal to everybody else's.

The inescapable message of such behavior was: This is a white nation and a white government. Black people are outsiders, petitioners. Anything that happens — any proposed changes, all decisions by the judiciary, the executive, and the legislature — is and will be judged in terms of that event's relationship to the white community.

This was a pattern that would manifest itself again and again through the administrations that followed, including the Kennedy years. It was a major failure for America.

As we shall see in the sections devoted to the segregationists' reactions, the years after *Brown* were marked by the construction of a massive barricade of delay and resistance, aided and abetted by the almost deliberate sluggishness of the federal government, as well as the quite deliberate defiance of the Southern state governments. Resistance groups formed in the South, some connected with state and local politics, some independent. The first Citizens Council, part of a collection of groups sometimes referred to as the White Citizens Councils, was organized on July 11, 1954, in Indianola, in the Mississippi Delta. Others were formed quickly afterward throughout the South. The councils were sometimes referred to by their critics as "uptown Ku Klux Klans," or racist organizations for business and professional people who weren't up to wearing hoods and robes. The Klan itself, actually a number of local and state terrorist organizations that had split off from one another with the frequency of fundamentalist religious offshoots (with which they shared several characteristics), thrived during the period.[7]

Racists in Congress, such as Senators James Eastland and John Stennis and Representative John Bell Williams of Mississippi and Senator Strom Thurmond of South Carolina, worked the halls of the Capitol in the cause of white supremacy. Eastland and Williams introduced legislation to invalidate the *Brown* decision, but failed to get it out of committee. The racists kept up the attack, however, using the Southern-biased seniority system and the power of the filibuster.[8]

Lynching, which had been on the decline, returned to the South. There were three such incidents in 1955, all in Mississippi. The Reverend George W. Lee was lynched after he led a voter registration drive at Belzoni; Lamar Smith was murdered at Brookhaven; and Emmett Till, a fourteen-year-old from Chicago who was visiting in Leflore County, was killed and sexually mutilated after he was accused of whistling at a white woman. The enormity of the Till lynching touched the public, both black and white. For many blacks who read about the crime in the Negro press and saw pictures of Till's open-casket funeral in Chicago, it is one of the milestones they mention now when they recall their growing involvement in the civil rights movement.[9]

Negroes worked harder than ever in the years after *Brown* to break down the walls that had been built since 1619. At a meeting after the 1954 decision, the NAACP pondered ways to continue its battle. There was debate over whether to concentrate on education lawsuits, in which NAACP lawyers could go initially after the presumably more pliant border states* and then work down through the Deep South, or whether to attack segregation in other areas of Southern life. NAACP branches, meantime, filed a number of petitions in local jurisdictions requesting desegregation, as well as lawsuits demanding it.

The Defense Department announced that as of August 31, 1954, all-Negro units no longer existed in the armed forces. Also in that year, Benjamin O. Davis, Jr., became the first Negro general in the air force.[10]

Some Southern jurisdictions extended desegregation into the area of publicly supported facilities generally. Atlanta opened its public recreation facilities to all races in 1954, as did several cities in the border states.[11]

The NAACP announced a Fight for Freedom campaign, with its goal the total elimination of discrimination by January, 1963 — the one hundredth anniversary of Lincoln's Emancipation Proclamation. The goal was not met.[12]

School desegregation began showing a pattern, one that could have been predicted by anyone familiar with the Southern scene: The farther south the community, the more resistance to desegregation. When the school year opened in the fall of 1954, there was at least partial public school desegregation in eight Deep South and bordering states — Arizona, Arkansas, Delaware, Kansas, Maryland, Missouri, New Mexico, and West Virginia. Some fairly quick and quiet desegregation had occurred, but little of it was in the South. As of the beginning of the 1956–57 school year, 797 school districts had desegregated, with 319,184 Negro students attending desegregated schools. However, some 2.4 million Negro children in the South continued to receive their education in a segregated setting. There were no desegregated public school dis-

---

*The term "border states" as used in these pages is more flexible than the original Civil War definition. It refers to those states that, during the Movement years, were South but not Deep South, either geographically or temperamentally. The definition is a somewhat sliding one, depending on year and issue. Thus, North Carolina is generally a "border state," but Virginia, to its north, sometimes acted quite Deep South.

tricts in Alabama, Florida, Georgia, Louisiana, Mississippi, North Carolina, South Carolina, and Virginia.[13]

Desegregation in education was a major topic of interest for Southerners both black and white and anyone else concerned about race relations in America. But something happened on December 5, 1955, that dramatically broadened the growing movement against discrimination. The Montgomery bus boycott began.

———————————————————— ■

Constance Baker Motley was a Northern Negro who went south more than once to help. She was an NAACP lawyer, and a woman to boot, and very smart and articulate, and that combination was almost too much for some of the segregationists she opposed in the Southern courtrooms.

Motley was born in 1921 in New Haven, Connecticut, to West Indian parents who had, she recalls, "great middle-class values." Her father and mother were natives of Nevis, in the Lesser Antilles, a place whose black citizens have a longer history of freedom than their American counterparts. Her father even looked down on black Americans. "In Nevis, *everybody* was free," she said. "There was no racial segregation in Nevis as such. So they didn't grow up cowering with fear of the white man's putting them in jail because they walked on this or that side of the street. They didn't know anything about that." So when Motley's parents came to America, in 1907, "naturally they were shocked by segregation and by what they felt was the black American's inability to fight for himself and take hold of his life. . . .

"All that is to say that I came from a middle-class kind of background. Not that we had any money. But we had these middle-class values, and we had what the social workers call a stable home — a home with a father, in other words. And there was order in the house." The family lived in an integrated neighborhood in New Haven, and Constance attended integrated schools. She didn't really have firsthand experience with racism until she entered Fisk University in Nashville and found, when the train got to Cincinnati, that Negroes had to move into the Jim Crow car, the car for blacks.

Constance Baker Motley got to Fisk, and later to New York University and Columbia law school, through the generosity of a white New

Havener. Clarence W. Blakeslee was a contractor who used a portion of his wealth to help Negroes. Among other things, he had built a community center in a black neighborhood. The center's board was controlled by white people from Yale. A meeting was convened to explore ways to attract more Negroes to participate. Constance, a recent high school graduate, went to the meeting. She stood up and said the reason blacks stayed away was that there weren't any of them on the board.

A black lawyer with connections to Blakeslee scolded Constance for this impertinence, but the next day she got a call from the contractor, asking her to come see him. She went to his office.

"And he said to me, 'You know, I looked up your high school record, and I see you graduated with honors. Why aren't you in college?' I said, 'I don't have the money to go to college.'

"So he said, 'Well, I'd be willing to pay for college as long as you want to go. What would you like to be?' And I said, 'I'd like to study law.' He said, 'Well, I don't know anything about women going into law, but I'm paying my grandson's way to Harvard law school, so if you want to go to law school it's all right with me.' "

Motley went to Fisk for a year and a half, then transferred to NYU and finished up with a law degree at Columbia. All the while her benefactor kept in touch, asking if she didn't need money for clothes or other expenses. Once he told her, "I think you ought to take a course in public speaking. If you're going to be a lawyer you've got to know how to speak in public." When she graduated from Columbia, Blakeslee came to her graduation.

In October, 1945, half a year before she finished law school, Motley went to work for the NAACP Legal Defense and Educational Fund, Inc. It was an exciting time, she remembers, but not many people realized "we were at the threshold of one of the biggest legal developments in this century."

When the development did occur, on May 17, 1954, Motley and other Inc. Fund lawyers hoped that Negroes would participate more willingly in desegregation lawsuits and that blacks would insist that officials integrate schools immediately. But the next step was not that easy for the masses of Southern Negroes to take. The terror was too deep.

"Right after the *Brown* decision," recalled Motley, "the NAACP convention was in Dallas. And we were talking about, 'What are we going to do now? We've got this *Brown* decision; how are we going to proceed?' And so forth and so forth. And we thought, 'Well, we'll proceed in the border states and work down.' And Oliver Hill from Richmond, Virginia, who was one of the lawyers in the Virginia case [that had gone before the Supreme Court], said, 'I think what we ought to do is to bring suits to desegregate the buses. Because that's something which black people meet every day, and it just riles them to think that they have to pay money and get on the bus and then stand while some white person sits.'

"And someone said, 'Look, Oliver, we're here to implement *Brown;* we can't be bothered with that at this time. We have called the meeting for that purpose.' And we said, 'Oliver, he's off the wall. Right?'

"He wasn't. That's exactly what happened: The black parents were reluctant to desegregate schools because the whole black community's economic lifeline is tied to those schools. The black teachers had regular salaries, so they didn't want to destroy that. They were interested in other things which would *not* destroy the economic lifeline — like riding the bus, and drinking at the fountain, and eating at the five and ten when they went to town. And that was something we had not perceived.

"We felt that we had a purpose, a mission, and that was to desegregate the schools. Here the Supreme Court had done this great thing for us, and it was up to us, obviously, to get it implemented. Right? And not go off on something else and abandon it. We couldn't conceive of abandoning *Brown.* We thought we had to devote what resources we did have, and the staff, to trying to implement *Brown.* So we couldn't be off doing something else. And that's why the revolution got out of hand, so to speak, as far as we were concerned. We couldn't control everybody, and there we were. But Southern blacks like Oliver Hill had perceived what it was that really got black people upset."

■ ────────────────────────

FIVE

■

OLD BLACK WOMEN WALKING
IN THE SUN

■

The Montgomery bus boycott will be remembered for several contributions to the Movement, most notably as the campaign that
gave Martin Luther King, Jr., his start. When King came to Montgomery he was a little-known, young Baptist pastor. When he left
a few years later, he was clearly headed for the position of national,
perhaps world leader and spokesman for an end to segregation. But
the boycott also provided the important lesson that black people
could work together toward a goal that was difficult to attain and
that involved considerable inconvenience to themselves.

The Montgomery boycott was not the first of its kind. This
should not be surprising, considering that bus companies throughout the South had demanded for years that the customers who
provided most of their income should subsidize an insulting regulation aimed only at them, and that those companies threatened
customers who resisted with arrest and imprisonment. There had
been a ten-day boycott in Baton Rouge, Louisiana, in June, 1953.
It was led by the Reverend T. J. Jemison, and it resulted in slightly
more relaxed segregation.[1] But the Baton Rouge campaign did not
capture the nation's attention in the way that Montgomery's did.

The boycott grew out of the arrest, on December 1, 1955, of Rosa Parks, a Negro woman who ignored an order by a municipal bus driver to relinquish her seat to a white man. At the time of her arrest, there were about 50,000 Negroes in Montgomery, which had a total population of about 110,000. About three-quarters of the riders of Montgomery buses were Negroes.[2]

The tradition (and city law) in Montgomery and in many other Southern communities was that the first ten rows of seats in municipal buses were reserved for whites. If there were more Negroes than whites riding the bus, Negroes still could not occupy the "white seats," but would have to stand in the rear — even if the seats reserved for whites were empty. If whites filled their section, Negroes would have to move from theirs to make room. In some places, and often at the whim of the driver, a Negro would have to enter the front door, pay the fare, step back out on the pavement, and reenter the bus through the back door. (Segregation was many things to many people in the South, but certainly one of its universal characteristics was that it was insanely complicated.)

On December 1, Rosa Parks and other blacks occupied seats in the first row behind the white section. The white seats filled up, and a white man remained standing. The driver ordered the Negroes in row eleven to move — all of them, since the rule also forbade whites and Negroes to sit in the same row. All the Negroes but Parks moved. When she refused, the driver called the police and Parks was arrested.[3]

Rosa Parks was not, as some versions of civil rights history would have it, just a simple black woman whose feet were tired from working all day for the white folks. Parks, who was an assistant tailor at a Montgomery department store, had been the secretary of the local NAACP chapter since 1943, and in the late forties she became the first secretary for the Alabama State Conference of NAACP Branches. Also in the forties, she organized an NAACP Youth Council chapter in Montgomery, and she had been ejected from a bus for refusing an order to move by the same driver whom she defied in 1955. In the fifties, members of the youth council had engaged in some direct action by attempting unsuccessfully to borrow books from the "white" library.[4] Parks was an active member of St. Paul AME Church, and in the summer prior to her arrest she had attended an interracial meeting at Highlander Folk School, in Tennessee. Highlander, run by Myles and Zilphia Horton, was a well-known center for education in the fields of labor organizing and antidiscrimination work. It served as a friendly place where like-minded people from throughout the South could meet, regardless of their skin color, and where those who had showed themselves to be potential leaders could learn of others' experiences and, perhaps most important, discover that they were not alone. Because of all this, Highlander was a frequent and convenient target for white supremacists, who seized on the school's labor-union orientation as a reason to red-bait it unmercifully.

After Rosa Parks was arrested on that December day, word spread quickly through the black community. Leaders, especially E. D. Nixon, a former NAACP chapter president and a Pullman porter who was a member of A. Philip Randolph's union, saw the Parks arrest as the perfect way to press the issue they had been planning — an attack on segregation in Montgomery. The Women's Political Council became involved, largely through the efforts of Jo Ann Gibson Robinson, its president. Robinson, who was an English professor at Alabama State College, a Negro institution, and her group had earlier asked the city for a revision of its bus seating policy. Negroes, they suggested, could sit from the back of the bus toward the front until all the seats were taken. Such a rule was in effect in some other Southern cities, but the whites who ran Montgomery had been unresponsive, and the Women's Political Council had been discussing the possibility of direct economic action.[5]

After the Parks arrest, plans for a boycott moved into high gear. Much of the effort was coordinated through the Women's Political Council, local churches, and other organizations. Someone asked E. D. Nixon why he did not choose the NAACP as the command post for the campaign, and he replied that the NAACP president at the time had said he would have to clear everything through the New York headquarters, and that there was no time for such bureaucratic deliberation.[6]

An umbrella organization was formed and named the Montgomery Improvement Association (MIA). Though Nixon was the logical choice for commander in chief of the operation, he urged that a minister be chosen. Churches provided a built-in organizational structure, along with large captive audiences, and preachers were skilled at dealing with big groups. Martin Luther King, Jr., who had come to Montgomery less than two years before, was chosen on December 5 to head the boycott campaign. For one thing, King was relatively new in town and thus more immune than most of his clerical colleagues to jealousies and infighting.

King was pastor of Dexter Avenue Baptist Church, a handsome building that rises from one of Montgomery's major streets a few blocks from the state capitol. Ralph Abernathy, pastor of the First Baptist Church, became the MIA official in charge of negotiating with the city.[7] Thus Abernathy started an association with Martin Luther King that was to last until King's death.*

When the boycott began, on December 5, 1955, the Negroes immediately sought discussions with the city. In its early negotiations, the MIA did not ask for an end to bus segregation at all, but rather for a policy, similar to the one presented by the Women's Political Council, whereby customers would seat themselves on a first-come, first-seated basis. Whites would fill seats from the front toward the rear, and Negroes would seat themselves from the rear forward. Because the request, if granted, would result in continued segregation, the local NAACP chapter refused to support the proposal at its outset. (This was one of the relatively infrequent instances when the NAACP rejected a civil rights initiative on the grounds that it wasn't militant enough; later on, the shoe would often be on the other foot.) MIA also asked for more courteous treatment of Negroes and for the hiring of black drivers for bus routes that served black customers. The city refused to negotiate, however, and the boycott stayed in place.

As photographs started appearing around the nation of proud Negroes walking and taking car pools to work rather than give in to racism, money flowed in from outside Alabama. Much came

---

*Throughout the time King was alive, people in the Movement and the media referred to Abernathy as "the Reverend Ralph Abernathy"; most didn't even know his middle name. After King's assassination, when Abernathy took over King's reins at the Southern Christian Leadership Conference, associates and the press immediately started referring to him as "Ralph David Abernathy" — as if the person who succeeded Martin Luther King must have a name with similar cadence to it. Abernathy died in April, 1990.

from Negro churches and organizations, notably the NAACP, in the North. There were contributions from some labor organizations; the United Auto Workers in Detroit sent thirty-five thousand dollars.[8]

Northern activists, who had fought discrimination almost as long as their Southern counterparts, saw in the Montgomery uprising an exciting new chance to advance the cause, a breakthrough of the sort of militancy they had long hoped for in the South. Bayard Rustin, who at that time was the executive secretary of the War Resisters League, raised money from labor and peace groups and went to Montgomery to deliver it, to help out, and to offer advice to King.

Tall, handsome, articulate, and well educated, Rustin had been a lifelong laborer in the antisegregation crusade. In 1947 he helped organize a freedom ride to test the previous year's Supreme Court decision, in a case named *Morgan v. Virginia*, that segregated seating on interstate buses was unconstitutional.[9] Rustin went on the ride and was arrested eighteen times in the South. As a result of one of the arrests, he did time on a North Carolina chain gang.

Rustin became executive secretary of the War Resisters League in 1952. By the mid-sixties he had been arrested more than twenty times for his civil rights activities. One other arrest, in 1953 in Pasadena, California, on a morals charge that involved two other men, was to cause Rustin to remain in the background in parts of the country, such as Montgomery or anywhere else in the South, where his homosexuality would certainly be used to tar the whole movement. (And not just in the South. In the sixties the Federal Bureau of Investigation, in one of its several efforts to smear the Movement and its influential members, circulated among Northern newspaper reporters and others copies of the Pasadena arrest record.)[10]

Much of the income that flowed into Montgomery during the boycott was used to buy vehicles to transport boycotters to and from work. At first, black-owned taxicab companies had done much of the hauling, at prices equal to the fares charged by the bus company, but the city forced the taxis to charge their normal forty-five-cent minimum. Martin Luther King and others in the MIA consulted with Rev. T. J. Jemison about the logistical details of the

1953 boycott in Baton Rouge. Cars and station wagons were dispatched from central points, which often were Negro churches. The churches opened early on chilly winter mornings to accommodate the crowds.[11]

Martin Luther King blossomed during the boycott. Any of those who had attended his services at Dexter church knew he was a fine speaker, but the boycott demonstrated to a larger audience the twenty-six-year-old preacher's talents as an orator. Aldon D. Morris, a sociologist who studied the organizational structure of the early Movement, writes that "King clearly understood the social power of oratory and used it as a tool for agitating, organizing, fundraising, and articulating the desires of the black masses." Morris also points out that King was far more educated than most preachers. It had been the tradition in the South (and is still, to some extent) for black preachers to choose their vocation as a result of receiving a "call" from a supernatural force, rather than through a combination of emotional and intellectual desire and religious education. Some of the "called" preachers lacked the ability to read and write and had never seen the inside of a seminary, and so it was not surprising that they urged their congregations to be skeptical of ministers with an abundance of book learning. One characteristic that set King apart from many others was the fact that he came from the deepest tradition of religious background (his father was a prominent minister in Atlanta) *and* he was well educated, having studied at Morehouse College and at Boston University. Says Morris: "One of King's talents was to use metaphors that communicated to the 'cultured' and educated as well as the uneducated and downtrodden. He coherently wove together the profound utterances of ditchdiggers, great philosophers, college professors, and floor-scrubbing domestics with ease."[12]

King's religious commitment was not driven solely by intellectual energy; he also was to speak of having heard the voice of Jesus during the beginnings of the Montgomery boycott. King's assumption of leadership had been somewhat involuntary, and so, when he received a death threat, he understandably wondered whether he shouldn't adopt a more placid life. Then he heard an "inner voice" that he identified as that of Jesus, telling him to persevere.[13]

It was not too difficult, then, to understand why many people could conclude that King was a prophet, an almost divinely selected leader for the newly forming movement. Also, growing up in a large and successful church with a strong pastor-father had taught King many political lessons about how to raise funds, subdue tensions, cope with jealousies, seek consensus, and negotiate.

Alan Gartner, a founder and officer of the Congress of Racial Equality, notes that charisma and oratorical skill were not the only reasons King was selected to lead the boycott. King was chosen in Montgomery, said Gartner in an interview, "because he was a young newcomer who wasn't involved in the conflicts within the black leadership community." Also, if King failed, he could be more easily discarded than someone who was more deeply entrenched in the black community structure.

There was a certain amount of bureaucracy evident in the Montgomery operation. This would be the case in all Movement activities where a firmly settled local leadership received the assistance of a charismatic leader from elsewhere. Even in Montgomery, where Martin Luther King wasn't exactly an outsider and where his charisma was just beginning to be discovered, things went too slowly for some longtime Movement warriors.

---- ■

Fred Shuttlesworth, who took part in the Montgomery campaign, was perhaps the Movement's most outspokenly courageous participant. The Baptist minister from Birmingham would not hesitate to tell a segregationist what he thought of segregation, and it did not matter to Shuttlesworth if the man was carrying a pistol, a court order, or a bomb. One segregationist did carry the last, and tried to blow up Shuttlesworth and his house in 1966. Through it all, Fred Shuttlesworth was known as a man who had no fear.

Asked about this not long ago, in his parsonage (which is now at a large church in Cincinnati), Shuttlesworth replied simply and factually, as though modesty were not part of the equation. "I think I've always had forthrightness and directness. It's just been part of my disposition. I guess in times where it's needed, innate things that are in people come out.

"I had the drive to get things done — an obsession, really, about overcoming segregation — and fear just didn't bother me. Especially after the bombing, when I knew that God could take care of me above and beyond anything you could imagine or dream. Get a house blown down around your head, flames going out from under your bed, wall between your head and the dynamite gets shattered, and you don't get a scratch — that must mean that somebody or something is real, and somebody or something is for you . . . and that you have a job to do. I think that reinforced it, to the point where nothing could have driven me out of Birmingham, actually."

Shuttlesworth's impatience extended to his fellow activists, as well. When the Montgomery boycott began, he frequently made the hundred-mile trip down from Birmingham to help out. He preached and spoke at mass meetings, and he participated in the Montgomery Improvement Association's strategy sessions. Shuttlesworth had been the membership chairman for the NAACP in Birmingham, and he was in the process of organizing an umbrella group there that would be called the Alabama Christian Movement for Human Rights, so he was interested in encouraging and stimulating activism in the state capital. He found in Montgomery a tad more sluggishness and bureaucracy than he had been accustomed to back home.

"The Montgomery Improvement Association did all right," he said, "but they could find *more* to argue about. And they would eat chicken, and they would eat chicken.

"I remember losing my license on one of the trips down. I lost my driver's license coming through Thorsby, Alabama. Our phones were tapped, you know, and they knew I was going. They took my license for speeding. I had to get to a ten o'clock meeting. King and Abernathy *lived* in Montgomery, and they didn't get there till twelve o'clock. I walked in, and King was ordering chicken. I told him, I said, 'You all are gonna eat yourselves to death.' It was very frustrating to me.

"And they were doing a lot of talking. They had so much to *talk* about. Strategy. Points about points which weren't points about anything. I told them, I said, 'We don't do this in Birmingham. We don't spend our breath arguing among ourselves. We hit the road in Birmingham.' "

■ ────────────────────────────

King quickly proved to be a spellbinder. On the night of his selection to head the boycott, just four days after Rosa Parks's arrest, the minister told a mass meeting that its participants were "the disinherited of this land, we who are tired of going through the long night of captivity. And now we are reaching out for this daybreak of freedom and justice and equality. And the only weapon that we have in our hands this evening is the weapon of protest."[14]

The organizational success of the Montgomery boycotters caught the eye of those all over America who had labored for equality. James Farmer, who had been toiling in the field of nonviolent civil rights protest for a dozen years, long before his Congress of Racial Equality had become a significant force, saw Montgomery and King's emergence as its leader, with national acclaim, as the event for which he had long waited. But in his joy there was also sadness that he was not the one leading the parade.

In his autobiography, *Lay Bare the Heart*, Farmer wrote of his bittersweet feelings upon hearing of Montgomery:

> The great day has come at last. The nonviolent movement in America is airborne. Why am I not more exuberant? Is it because it is not I who leads it? Is there a green-eyed monster peering through my eyes? I had labored a decade and a half in the vineyards of nonviolence. Now, out of nowhere, someone comes and harvests the grapes and drinks the wine. I am only human. What I have hated most in people is pettiness. Am I now consumed by that which I hate? I must kill the green beast inside if I am to battle the dragons outside. . . . But can I? Am I enough of a person to see the spotlight on another while I do my dance in the low lights and shadows?[15]

───────────────────────────────── ■

James Farmer was asked not long ago what he would have done if there had been no civil rights movement.

"I would have had to start one," he replied, instantly. "I started

CORE. CORE may never have gotten off the ground, though. Because it *didn't* get off the ground before King. Remember?"

Was Farmer being too hard on himself? Was it Martin Luther King who got the Movement going, or was it a conglomeration of people and events, some of which King was part of, some of which Farmer himself was a part of?

"Of course, that's true," Farmer said. "But they did congeal around the man, King."

Isn't it reasonable to expect that, given the direction society was traveling in the fifties and sixties, the emerging Movement would have formed itself around *someone* — if not King, then Farmer or someone else?

"Oh, I don't think so. No, I don't think so. It had to be the Montgomery bus boycott which had the charisma to capture the imagination of people. Other things happened that didn't capture the imagination of the nation. But King did. King *did* have a combination of qualities: He was a Southern Baptist preacher, speaking with a Southern accent — that was important — who could *preach*. He could make 'em shout. And that, too, was important.

"Same time, he could address a Harvard audience and do it intelligently. Quite a rare combination. There are many black Baptist preachers who can make them shout. But how many of them can speak to Harvard at the same time? How many of them at that date — 1955, '56 — knew of Gandhi and Gandhi's work and could speak of nonviolence?"

Farmer himself did, for one.

"Yes, yes, yes, yes. But I was not a Baptist preacher. It had to be Baptist; couldn't be Methodist. And it had to be in a Southern setting. It could not be a Northerner; it had to be a Southerner. No, King was just perfect."

Recent accounts of King's life, and observations made at the time, suggest that Martin Luther King did not actively pursue the job of Movement leader. It always seemed that he was being thrust into the leadership by forces that were beyond his control.

"A reluctant knight?" Farmer laughed. "Well, yes, there was a bit of that." He laughed some more. "But not as much as you think, no. He *enjoyed* it, too."

■ ────────────────────────

The Montgomery bus boycott was about as successful an undertaking as could have been imagined by those who opposed segregation. It was far more successful than could have been imagined by those supremacists who had been saying for decades that Negroes were too shiftless, uneducated, disorganized, and unmotivated to gather around a complex project and stick with it. And it wasn't just white segregationists who made these arguments. Some self-critical blacks deplored the lack of previous success at organization, though they were more likely to attribute the cause to jealousies and infighting, particularly within the church, or to generations of repression, rather than some mysterious biological shortcoming. The boycott was ample proof that Negroes could get together on something and stick to it.

Furthermore, they sustained themselves in a campaign that was especially difficult to sustain. The method chosen in Montgomery — the boycott — was one of the toughest to initiate and adhere to because of its built-in inconvenience. It's easy to boycott the gasoline refined by a notorious polluter or the beer brewed by an ultraconservative zealot, for there are plenty of alternatives available at little or no penalty. There was, however, no alternative bus company in Montgomery. The blacks maintained the boycott through the cold winter months and the moist heat of a south Alabama summer. The depth of their sincerity and determination should have been apparent to the white segregationists, but the supremacists apparently missed the obvious, just as they would keep missing it throughout the Movement years. Indeed, one of the blacks' major allies in the fifties and sixties was their opponents' inability or unwillingness to discern and act upon the obvious.

In the preface to her memoir of the boycott, Jo Ann Gibson Robinson refers to the false stereotype of Negro disorganization. She says the main reason she compiled her book is "so that the world will know that black people of America are not, as stereotypes have depicted them for generations, a 'happy-go-lucky,' self-satisfied, complacent, lazy, good-for-nothing race that has nothing good or worthwhile to offer society.... The second reason ... is ... to show that black Americans can endure hardship and suffering for the cause of justice."[16]

The Montgomery example was not lost on young Negroes who had been raised on segregation, who were appalled at what the system had done to their elders, and who had no intention of allowing things to stay that way. James Forman, who had been born in Chicago but raised on his grandparents' farm in northern Mississippi, spent his formative years back in Chicago, where he demonstrated his distaste for segregation in numerous confrontations with white individuals and authorities. When Forman entered the military in the late forties, he encountered more racism there; by the time he was discharged, he was convinced he had been, as he wrote later, "supposedly protecting a system of government which I had grown to hate."[17] It was not long before Forman started thinking about the creation of a movement that could change all this. He set down his theories about such a movement in fictional (and as yet unpublished) form. Later, Forman would become the executive director of the Student Nonviolent Coordinating Committee, one of the major forces in the Movement.

Until the Montgomery boycott, wrote Forman in a memoir of the Movement years, black Americans constantly railed at themselves for their reputed inability to stick together on an issue. "We can never act as a unit," Forman quoted Negroes as saying; "we can't unify to protest against this man. We're like a bunch of crabs — the minute one of us crawls through the top, the rest of us drag him back down." Forman blamed the "colonizing force" for the attitude, along with the ingrained belief in the by-and-by principle — that God would balance the books later on. Montgomery, says Forman, changed all this.

The Montgomery boycott, he wrote, "had a particularly important effect on young blacks and helped to generate the student movement of 1960." And it "woke me to the real — not merely theoretical — possibility of building a nonviolent mass movement of Southern black people to fight segregation."[18]

Another significant product of the boycott was the demonstration, to Negroes in the South and to Americans generally, that the "legal approach," as personified by the NAACP, was not the only method. Massive action, or direct action, as it was coming to be called, could be used, too, and could often bring faster and more far-reaching results than the courtroom technique. Direct action also provided a way for the individual Negro — the single proud, patriotic citizen — to make his or her contribution to the protest. The individual Negro could actively march in a demonstration or join a bus boycott, but in most cases could participate in a lawsuit only passively.

There was, furthermore, something deliciously inviting about the here-and-now nature of direct action that did not characterize the legal approach at all. Granted, the courtroom route, when finally followed to its ultimate conclusion in the Supreme Court, might result in a decision far more wide-ranging in terms of geography and political jurisdictions than a local boycott. (*Brown* showed, however, that court decisions did not necessarily insure speedy change.) Montgomery proved that there was nothing wrong, and a lot right, with using both approaches at once.

As the boycott continued into early 1956, the segregationists again demonstrated their near-infallible facility for inadvertently lending aid and comfort to their enemy. Whenever the Movement needed a boost, it seemed, the white South — and, later, the white North — served it up with an act of violence or misjudgment or crudeness or legal shenanigans that was guaranteed to undercut the segregationists' case at home and provoke outrage and increased financial contributions for the activists from abroad.

In the case of Montgomery, it was the combination of violence and flimsy legal footwork that was to distinguish official Alabama's response to the Movement throughout the fifties and sixties. In late January, 1956, Montgomery policemen started harassing drivers in the Montgomery Improvement Association's car pool. On January 30, Martin Luther King's house was bombed. In late February, a grand jury returned indictments for some ninety MIA supporters and leaders, including King. They were charged with conspiring to conduct an illegal boycott.

The NAACP came to the boycotters' legal defense and took the case to federal court. When it was obvious to practically everyone that the courts would strike down segregated bus transportation, the Montgomery bus company, which was losing money, announced that it was ending its segregation policy. The city

responded with a threat to arrest any bus driver who allowed interracial seating. (This was to become another characteristic that
made segregation in Alabama a little different from segregation
elsewhere. While other Southern states might rely on peer pressure
or economic intimidation to force their white citizens to maintain
segregation policies, Alabama frequently used the threat of arrest
to achieve the same goal — even in private or semiprivate places
such as churches and department store changing rooms. It was as
if official Alabama didn't trust its white citizens to be as racist as
it wanted them to be.)

On June 5, 1956, a three-judge federal court in Montgomery
ruled two to one that bus segregation was unconstitutional. By so
doing, Judges Richard T. Rives and Frank M. Johnson, both Alabamans (Rives came from an old Montgomery County family), insured themselves a rich supply of threats and hate mail. The city
appealed the decision. On November 13, 1956, the Supreme Court
of the United States upheld the lower ruling. Almost a month later,
federal marshals served Montgomery officials with copies of the
ruling, and segregated seating was abolished. The next day, December 21, 1956, MIA ended its boycott and Negroes returned to the
municipal buses.

NAACP members and officials, some of whom were still ruf-
fled by the fact that the boycott had pretty much proceeded without their direction, were quick to point out that they eventually
saved the demonstrators' bacon. Thurgood Marshall, the special
counsel for the NAACP and director of its Inc. Fund, was said to
have commented that if the demonstrators had just stayed home
and saved all that walking and waited for him to get the court's
ruling, they could have spared themselves a lot of trouble. And
John Morsell, the second in command at the NAACP's national
headquarters, was quoted as saying that someday some bright reporter would discover that it wasn't the boycott that desegregated
Montgomery's buses, but an NAACP lawsuit.[19] Although there
were elements of truth in both these statements, they didn't do
much to alleviate the feeling, which would grow over the years,
that the NAACP was used to being top dog and now was having a
hard time adjusting to being anything else.

In the minds of some observers and participants, Montgomery marked the beginning of a decline in influence for the NAACP. The NAACP's officials and loyalists knew this and seemed to be hurt and surprised by it. The organization's leadership had never before been questioned by opponents of segregation. Although its influence never disappeared or even came close to vanishing, the NAACP's prestige and dominance lessened when the challenge to segregation moved into the direct action stage. The spotlight that formerly had shone only on the NAACP now had widened to include a number of organizations and individuals.

There were several reasons why the NAACP's influence never disappeared. For one thing, there would always be a market for the time-tested, albeit time-consuming, legal approach. Similarly, there would always be a need for a forum in which blacks of all occupations and social strata, but predominantly middle-class, could meet. Like all of its sisters and brethren in the evolving civil rights movement — from the conservative, white-collar-and-tie Urban League to the overalls-clad Student Nonviolent Coordinating Committee, from the black-and-white-together Congress of Racial Equality to the militants of the Black Panther Party — the NAACP filled a niche that was absolutely necessary. And the NAACP was as rock-solid and stable as any nongovernmental organization in America. It had been there before the others, and there was every reason to believe it would be there long after the rest had gone.

After bus segregation ended in Montgomery, the segregationists turned back to violence. Martin Luther King's home was shot up. Sniper fire was directed at buses. On January 10, 1957, bombs went off at four Negro churches and at the homes of two pro-integration ministers, one Negro and one white. The city reacted to this by briefly stopping bus service.[20] Eventually, though, the violence diminished, and today the city of Montgomery has a long street named Rosa L. Parks Boulevard. The boulevard connects neighborhoods of pleasant, shady homes where black people live with the downtown business section. The municipal bus that traverses the boulevard bears the destination sign "ROSA PARKS."

■

Charles Jones graduated from junior college in South Carolina just after the Supreme Court handed down its *Brown* decision. The following fall, he entered Johnson C. Smith University, a black school in Charlotte, North Carolina. It was that fall, he said later, "that I began to be aware that we were in for a long, hard battle." There were signs all around that "the organized legal opposition was formulating itself. And it became very clear very quickly that that was another dream, another promise, that was yet to be realized. And that was when I began to understand, particularly through the violence, the killing, that the South or the country was not about to give up, and that the cost of changing was going to be very high, including human life."

Jones's earlier ideas about the ease with which *Brown*'s promise would be kept had to be revised, but he was not disillusioned. "I still believed the Declaration of Independence: 'We hold these truths to be self-evident. That *all* men are created equal.'

"You see, my father was a Presbyterian minister. My mother was an English teacher. So between Jesus of Nazareth, Hegel, Homer, and some of the great philosophical thinkers, I believed that this country was based on sound, solid Christian principles, and all you had to do was believe, and somehow the church was going to do it. Because that's right. This country was based on the church, on Christianity. I believed that. At school, I was in the hotbed of intellectual pursuits, so in a sense you could play around with all of the great concepts. And delude yourself. However, thank God, I had a couple of professors. . . ."

One of Charles Jones's mentors was named Winston Coleman. He taught philosophy and logic. The other, A. O. Steele, taught religious education. Jones at the time was strongly considering following his father into a religious career.

Jones remembers that Dr. Steele used a text that he had written, titled *The Bible and the Human Quest,* that challenged the assumption that the Bible was a perfect rendition of history. The message, said Jones, was that "one must be very skeptical and critical in reading the Bible. And particularly in taking it literally, because the consequences of that, particularly for black people, in an economic and social environment that used Christianity to further justify enslavement, segregation, et cetera, simply delayed the process for confrontation with the issues."

Equally challenging to the student's assumptions was the teaching of Dr. Coleman, a man Jones found to have "the most rigorous and disciplined mind I have ever encountered." Jones studied logic and deductive reasoning with Dr. Coleman, and learned that "two and two is four, *if* you assume the value of two, or zero. But not necessarily."

Both teachers compelled Jones and his fellow students to exercise their brains as never before. "I remember," said Jones, "that it was agonizing because it was much easier to accept the so-called truths that had been interpreted by the larger society, primarily through European perceptions: Man is basically good, and given enough time, he will basically do right. So colored people, be patient, and good white folk are going to take care of you. I remember the contradictions increased as my knowledge of history and my knowledge of human nature increased. And my freedom increased to accept or not accept what the Bible or what theology of the Western church had said as fact."

Although his father had been shaped by that very same Western church, Jones found his teaching valuable, too. "My father was more intuitive than intellectual. . . . Daddy saw life from his relationship to the earth, the natural laws of the universe, and whatever contradictions he found between that and the intellect, he tended to resolve based on what the natural laws were.

"He was black, there was no question, but he was able to transcend the trap of ethnicity, or of blackness, or any particular ethnic . . . which probably was a part of my freedom, thank God.

"And my mother: English teacher, English history, European history. Intellect. And there was a balance, an interesting balance as I look back now, between Mom and my father: I don't mean to suggest in any sense that my father wasn't smart. He was much smarter than most of the intellectuals I knew. *Much* smarter, because on basic survival issues, his instincts were always right. And on basic business issues, basic decisions, he was inevitably accurate in terms of what people were going to ultimately do, how they were going to behave, and therefore how to govern yourself and position yourself to protect yourself and to survive. Much more so than the sort of paralysis of analysis in an intellectual, which turns out sometimes to be garbage, because generally it was based on the assumption that man is basically good.

"I couldn't square man being basically good with what was happening to black folk in the South. It just didn't make any sense. . . . And *under the banner of Christianity!* Not only under the banner of Christianity, but with the absolute blessings of the church, that segregation continued, discrimination continued. Although the ministers in the white church or most of the members would not go along on Klan activities, they certainly blessed them from the pulpit. So trying to square the contradictions of the concepts of Christianity and the practices of the major society, I had great difficulty, and those instructors helped my own intellectual pilgrimage through the pitfalls of by and by in the sky, when life is over, we'll get some kind of relief. At this point, I'm in my late teens. I'm middle-class."

And then, as Charles Jones wrestled with not only the meaning of life, a common experience for college students, but also the meaning of black life in America, the Montgomery bus boycott started.

"And coming out of that media of negative stuff was Dr. King, Rosa Parks. . . . I'll never forget the pictures of old black women walking in the sun.

"And though the context was always interpreted through the perceptions of the white press, my intuition saw and cut through all of that. When you see an old black woman in her seventies walking with her shoes in her hand, you know that there is something very profound about that.

"And then, when Dr. King began to talk with all of the European finesse, when he was able to cut through the analytical context that he was forced into in answering questions — I mean, the questions assumed a certain answer: 'Aren't you upsetting white folk and is that, in fact, not going to make them uneasy?' His answers were not, 'Well, yes, we got to be careful.' His answers were, 'The system is immoral. The system is contradictory. The system does not behave as the great Western thought in Christianity professes. So the *system* is wrong, not the concepts.'

"Ah! That was not only a fresh ray of light, but just food for the intellect and the soul. All of a sudden, someone who understood the philosophy and the history was interpreting it totally differently. Was not attempting to justify the behavior of the major society through some sort of intellectual gymnastic bullshit."

Jones excitedly got and devoured the book *War Without Violence,* written by Krishnalal Shidharani in the late thirties. Shidharani, a follower of Mohandas K. Gandhi, chronicled his leader's efforts in the independence movement in India. He described the concept of *satyagraha*, the power of truth, or — as it was widely referred to in Movement years — "soul force," as a weapon more formidable than anything the oppressors could wield. *Satyagraha* was a vital component of nonviolence, and it had been promoted for many years by the Fellowship of Reconciliation, a pacifist group that was born in England in 1914 and in the United States the following year. FOR staffers went to Montgomery when the boycott started there in 1955, preaching their doctrine to all listeners. Martin Luther King, Jr., was one of the most attentive.

"It was a very interesting concept," said Jones. "It was more in tune with my nature. I don't tend to be a violent person — in addition to which it seemed the white folk had all the guns."

Jones smiled. "About this time, the conflicts I was having with the Bible as a source of infallible history and truth were being supplanted by Dr. Steele and Dr. Coleman with some very solid, analytical tools. So all of a sudden, with Montgomery, I felt free from other people's perceptions and contexts and premises. And my God, the *power* that that meant was that you, on the one hand, could resist the behavior and attitudes and practices of the system with a positive alternative, which, from everything I could see, had caught the system off guard.

"The system had no defenses for black folks walking with their bodies into the system, talking about its contradictions, but prepared to put their bodies there rather than guns or bullets or violence."

■ ─────────────────────────────

SIX

■ ─────────────

PILGRIMS

■ ─────────────

The remainder of the fifties after Montgomery was a time of organization and experimentation for the growing Movement, with periods of isolated direct action. For the segregationists, it also was a time of strength-gathering, much of it thanks to a federal government seemingly reluctant to provide leadership, as if it had not yet decided whether segregation was right or wrong.

Those who were political leaders, or who hoped to be, appeared uncertain of what the white majority wanted or how far it would allow desegregation to go, and they based their public positions on this uncertainty rather than on a fundamental assumption that segregation was wrong and must be changed. It was as if they felt (as did the Supreme Court with *Brown*'s implementation) that the issue was negotiable. In the 1956 presidential election, both major parties and their candidates were vague and hesitating in their celebration of civil rights. Dwight Eisenhower, seeking reelection on the Republican ticket, and Adlai Stevenson, the Democratic candidate, both promised they would not use force to carry out a court's desegregation order — a gold-plated tip-off to anyone who wanted to defy such an order. Stevenson, a former Illinois governor with a reputation as an intellectual liberal, would say only that the 1954 *Brown* decision had produced "consequences of vast importance."[1]

Congress passed a civil rights act in 1957. It upgraded the Justice Department's civil rights section to division status, which gave it more power within the bureaucracy, and designated an assistant attorney general to run it. The new law strengthened the right of all people, regardless of race, color, or previous condition of servitude, to vote and sit on juries. It authorized the federal government to bring civil suits in cases where persons were denied the right to vote; previously, only private parties could sue. And it established the U.S. Commission on Civil Rights, with the power to investigate charges of voting abuses, among other things.

Originally, the 1957 legislation gave the attorney general the power to go into federal courts to seek injunctive relief on behalf of those whose constitutional rights had been abridged. But white supremacists in the Senate fought that provision and it was taken out of the bill. When the legislation was snagged in the Southerner-dominated Senate Judiciary Committee, Republicans sought to bypass the committee and go straight to the Senate calendar with it. The technique worked, but not without opposition from many Democrats, including John F. Kennedy and Lyndon B. Johnson. Johnson, who was the majority leader, did play an important part in eventually convincing his fellow Southerners that they could hardly oppose legislation guaranteeing the right to vote.[2]

The National Association for the Advancement of Colored People, which long before had recognized the vote as a key to solving many of the Negroes' problems, announced after passage of the Civil Rights Act a campaign to register three million blacks in four hundred cities and counties by the 1960 election. The goal was not met.[3]

In January, 1957, the Movement gained a major new organization, one that was to instantaneously achieve the power and prestige that groups such as the NAACP and National Urban League had labored long to attain. At a meeting in Atlanta, the Southern Christian Leadership Conference was founded.

SCLC was an outgrowth of the Montgomery Improvement Association and the boycott. It was not really a new organization, formed from scratch, but rather a merging of the talents of a number of Movement leaders in Southern cities, all of them black and almost all of them Baptist preachers. Martin Luther King, Jr., was its leader. The day-to-day running of the organization was largely handled by the associate director, Ella Baker. She was a Southerner who had worked in several important positions for the NAACP in New York City before returning to the South.[4]

When SCLC held its organizational meeting in Atlanta on January 10–11, 1957, it was called the Negro Leaders Conference on Transportation and Nonviolent Integration. (This soon was changed to Southern Leaders Conference, then to Southern Christian Leadership Conference.)[5] An important feature of the gathering was the presentation of several working papers, prepared by Bayard Rustin, that discussed segregation and ways to fight it. Rustin and Stanley Levison, a white attorney from New York City who had expressed interest in the Montgomery campaign and who had raised funds for the Southern cause, took part in much of the conference planning.

Rustin's working papers argued that direct action was now the blacks' most powerful weapon. (That term, "direct action," was gaining currency now; it was an effective shorthand symbol for everything from boycotts to street demonstrations, and pretty nearly everything else except lawsuits.) Rustin advocated nonviolence as an effective tactic, and pointed out that Negro economic power, as demonstrated in Montgomery, was considerable. He wrote that blacks could profit by dividing the white community according to its interests, which for some whites would be economic, for others political. And he stressed the importance of the church, "the most stable social institution in Negro culture," as an effective and proper base for the forthcoming campaign against racism.[6]

The black ministers who attended the organizing session hardly needed to be reminded of that last point; already, in city after city around the South, the Negro church was assuming the role of social action center, often to the consternation of local NAACP officials. By the time of SCLC's establishment, one researcher found, the organization could be thought of as "the decentralized political arm of the black church."[7]

SCLC was, in effect, the clearinghouse for a number of local, church-based movements. Ministers in cities such as New Orleans, Tallahassee, Atlanta, Nashville, Birmingham, and Baton Rouge, as well as Montgomery, had established communications with one another during the bus boycott, and in some cases well before it. King's new organization was the logical way to keep in touch and to combine resources and strengths. Through the Movement's later years, leaders from one city would visit other jurisdictions that were in the direct action spotlight to serve as guest speakers at mass meetings and to absorb information on strategy and techniques — and to absorb along the way, too, some of the brilliance that radiated from Martin Luther King. These visitations were nothing new for the ministers; since time immemorial Southern clergymen, black and white, had been invited to one another's churches to take part in or conduct periodic revival sessions. The visitor, it was believed, would bring some excitement to the project; "revival" meant a resurrection of the congregation's interest in the doctrines of the church, and a fresh voice from elsewhere was a welcome relief from the same old face in the pulpit. As this technique was used in the Movement, such visitations served to impress the local participants with their own importance and the significance of their cause. Many was the mass meeting that opened with the announcement that "Reverend So-and-so has traveled all the way from Such-and-such-a-place to be with us here tonight and to lend his voice to our cause."

The establishment of SCLC also provided King with a base from which he could ride circuit for civil rights causes around the South, with frequent fund-raising expeditions into the North.

King's first national SCLC forum was a Prayer Pilgrimage for Freedom, which was held May 17, 1957, the anniversary of *Brown*, and which was an attempt, unproductive as it turned out, to goad President Eisenhower into speaking out on desegregation matters. On February 12, 1958, SCLC kicked off its Crusade for Citizenship program, which was designed to encourage Southern Negroes to register and vote. The campaign was not spectacularly successful, but then few observers could have predicted that the resistance to black voting in much of the South would be as fierce as it was. And in November, 1959, Martin Luther King left his church in

Montgomery to devote all of his time to SCLC, at its headquarters in Atlanta. In a prepared statement to his congregation, King said: "The time has come for a broad, bold advance of the Southern campaign for equality. . . . Not only will it include a stepped-up campaign of voter registration, but a full-scale approach will be made upon discrimination and segregation in all forms. . . . We must employ new methods of struggle involving the masses of our people."[8]

———————————————— ■

Fred Shuttlesworth, the Birmingham minister, was one of the founders of SCLC. He recalls that the organization really centered around five or six men, all of them ministers. At first, he said, when SCLC revolved about the Montgomery boycott, the ministers were less than totally militant, no matter what the segregationists might have thought.

"You must remember that this was really around bus desegregation. Just asking for it, not fighting. We weren't talking about fighting. All of us had the idea that all you had to do was just shame the conscience of the country, to grip the soul, redeem the soul. So we started off like that, not by attacking segregation. It was a call to 'redeem the soul of America.' I remember Martin expostulating those words."

But before long, Shuttlesworth discovered, along with others, the truth of the matter: that white America didn't necessarily want its soul redeemed. And he started expostulating some other words.

"I said that a rattlesnake don't commit suicide, and ball teams don't strike themselves out," said Shuttlesworth. "You got to *put* them out."

■ ————————————————

From the very beginning, SCLC was black led and run. This may have surprised or dismayed some whites who had been committed for decades to ending segregation, who thought of themselves as equal partners with blacks in the struggle, and who considered any sort of separatism to be repugnant. But others understood the blacks' need to make their own decisions and form their own strategies, free of the white paternalism of the past, be it deliberate or inadvertent, which had automatically assumed that whites would be among those who made the decisions.

■

Will D. Campbell has been called "a pioneer trouble shooter in areas of racial tension."[9] He has also been called a white Southern Baptist preacher who chews tobacco, curses fluently, plays a guitar, hangs out with country musicians, and drinks whiskey, some of which is made the old-fashioned way, which is to say out in the woods of Tennessee. But the word that describes Will Campbell best, probably, is one that he has used to describe himself: pilgrim. Campbell, along with several other white people, Northerners and Southerners, automatically attached themselves to the civil rights movement when it started. It was, for them, a perfectly unremarkable thing to do. It was their movement, too, after all. The cause had always been their cause, too.

Campbell was born in southern Mississippi. He aimed early at a life in the Baptist church, and studied first at a small church school in Louisiana, then Wake Forest, then Tulane, and finally Yale Divinity School. His first pulpit was in a northern Louisiana town. From there he became director of religious life at the University of Mississippi. As Campbell, referring to himself in the third person, put it in one of the books he has written: "It was 1954 and the Supreme Court had recently ruled that public school segregation was unconstitutional. He could be an invaluable ally to the university which, he was sure, would draw on his enlightenment and liberalism as it moved to full equality. Somehow that was not the case. So by middle 1956, he was seeking fuller fields of service."[10]

Campbell joined the National Council of Churches as a specialist in race relations, and he became the director of the Committee of Southern Churchmen. What he did, mostly, was travel from one civil rights crisis to another, and attend as many meetings in between, being a witness — bearing witness, in the religious sense. Always in the background, Campbell tried to reconcile black and white, and he paid particular attention to the less-well-off whites of the South. (That last mission once earned Campbell the uncomfortable appellation of "minister to the Klan.") Campbell went to Little Rock during the school desegregation crisis in 1957, and when no one else stepped forward to escort the terrified black students into Central High School, he literally extended his hand. He describes himself in his memoir, in a tone half sarcastic and half self-deprecatory, as "a missioner to the Confederacy, bridge between white and black, challenging the recalcitrant, exposing the Gothic politics of the degenerate southland; prophet with a Bible in one hand and a well-worn copy of W. J. Cash in the other."[11] Now he lives on a small farm outside Nashville with his wife, Brenda, and writes in a small cabin heated by hickory logs and splattered with evidence of his imperfect marksmanship as a tobacco chewer.

When did the Movement start? Well, he drawled one day in his cabin, for Southern blacks it probably started as soon as the first slave ship arrived in America. For Southern whites, it was a different matter. "Harmonious race relations" existed in their minds as long as they "had their foot on black people's necks and the blacks weren't struggling to get up." Therefore, for them, the Movement began when the blacks started struggling.

"So I guess in that sense the crisis began, or the Movement began, in '55 with the Montgomery bus boycott. Because in 1954, not many people took the *Brown* decision seriously, at least where I was living. I was living in north Louisiana.

"I was in my first, last, and only parish, up in Bienville Parish, Taylor, Louisiana, a little sawmill village, and we would go to the Lions Club, and the mill owners and people would say to the school principal, 'Well, how many little darkies are you going to have this fall, Professor?' And he'd say, 'Oh, I'm expecting about twice what I had last year,' and everybody would laugh, you know, because twice nothing is nothing.

"And I'd preach on it about every other Sunday — not about the decision, but about race — and they thought it was kind of cute, you know: Our little preacher, he's the cutest thing, he's talking about our children going to school with little darkies. He's so cute."

It was talk like that, and suggestions that the lumber mill could stand a little union organizing, that hastened Campbell's departure from Taylor. At first it wasn't so much that his congregation got angry at what he said, recalls Campbell, as it was that they thought he was crazy. As time passed, however, and he continued to preach his sermons, the population was "beginning to not think that was so cute any more."

"But I think they really didn't envision the possibility," said Campbell. "The thought of black children going to school with their children was so outrageous that they just didn't see it as an eventuality. It was like somebody saying, 'Hey, you gonna die.' Well, you know, you are someday, so they said, 'Well, someday this might happen, but not in our time, so don't worry about it.'

"But the Montgomery bus boycott, that was a different thing. I would say that the Movement as white people experienced it began with Rosa Parks and ended on the balcony of the Lorraine Motel." It was at the Lorraine, in Memphis, that Martin Luther King, Jr., was murdered on April 4, 1968.

Will Campbell developed a habit of turning up, sometimes with a guitar case slung across his back, at the scenes of many of the Movement's important events in the years following Montgomery. He was working for the National Council of Churches as sort of a circuit-riding pilgrim when SCLC was formally organized in Atlanta in January, 1957. The council, he said, "was seemingly sympathetic to the Movement that was emerging," so he went to the meeting. Campbell remembers that he was one of the very few whites who showed up in Atlanta, or maybe the only one.

Martin Luther King, Jr., had been scheduled to attend the meeting, of course, which was being held at Atlanta's Ebenezer Baptist Church, whose pastor was the Reverend Martin Luther King, Sr., known to practically everyone as Daddy King. But a series of bombings in Montgomery damaged the homes of Movement activists and sympathizers. Ralph Abernathy's church and parsonage were among those hit, and he and King hurried to Alabama instead.

"When I got to the meeting, at Daddy King's church, there was somebody presiding at the door, and there was this kind of hush in the conversation. They explained to me, well, they didn't know who I was or anything.

"I knew King by then — not well, but I'd been with him on a number of occasions. And it was, 'We appreciate your coming and your interest, and we are not practicing segregation, which is what we are fighting, but this is a consultation, a family affair, and we hope you understand.' And I did, you know, and I was getting ready to leave. And Bayard Rustin came out and saw what was happening and just took over. Rustin said, 'Oh, no, no; before this thing is over we are going to need whites, we are going to need browns, we are going to need all the help we can get, and the National Council of Churches is an ally and you come on in and participate any way you choose to.'

"I chose to be silent. And I learned a great lesson at that meeting. It was probably there that I first knew for sure in my head as well as in my heart that this was a black movement; that it was black led, and that all I could ever do was to stay out of the news. A statement was read and adopted at the meeting, and afterward, I got up and said, 'I will see to it that every [congressional] representative has a copy of this document placed on his desk.' And there was this kind of tentative scattering of applause, and then somebody spoke. I think it was C. K. Steele, from Tallahassee. He said, 'Well, we appreciate what our brother is offering. But I move, Mr. Chairman, that it be the responsibility of the council secretary to see that that is done.'

"It was not hostile. But I knew what he was saying, and everybody else did: that 'If it hadn't been for the "beneficence" of good white people, we wouldn't be sitting where we are today.' " Campbell roared with laughter and spat at the open door of his wood stove. "So then I knew that this was *their* ball game.

"So during all this time I was *on hand.* That's the only claim I make. I don't know whether I was just lazy or timid or uncertain or what, but I did spot very early that this was a black movement, and would be led by blacks, and if I wanted a role in it, it was only going to be in the second or third echelon. And that I would be, at best, support troops. Now, a lot of white people didn't really understand that."

■ ────────────────────────

Some of what King called "new methods of struggle," or at least new variations on old ones, were already being used in various places around the South, but the nation's attention in the mid-fifties, when it focussed on race relations at all, was most usually riveted on education matters. A pattern seemed to be developing in education, and it was a predictable one. One stratum of Southern and border state communities found desegregation relatively easy to accomplish and did so, without much fanfare. True, much of what was done was the minimal acceptable amount. The term "token desegregation" entered the vocabulary of race relations, where it remains today. North Carolina, a border state that traded heavily on its "progressive" reputation, particularly when it was trying to snatch industry away from the North, provided a typical example of tokenism: By 1959, only thirty-four Negroes in that state attended public schools with whites.[12] Other Southern communities, most of them in the Deep South but several in Virginia, dug in their heels against desegregation and stayed dug in for as long as possible.

Violence became part of the education equation with the case of Autherine Lucy. A black student, Lucy was admitted to the University of Alabama under a federal court order in February, 1956. Her fellow students who were white rioted over this intrusion, and the university, rather than punish the perpetrators of the violence, removed *her*. Lucy applied for reinstatement but was permanently expelled for making "outrageous" allegations in her lawsuit. Eventually she gave up. The racists won, and the university wasn't desegregated for another seven years.

One important factor in the Alabama fiasco was the lack of moral or other leadership. That it did not come from state government or the university administration may have been deplorable, but it surely wasn't surprising. But neither was it offered by the nation's chief executive. President Eisenhower said, at the time of the rioting:

> While there has been an outbreak that all of us deplore, when there is a defiance of law, still the chancellor and the trustees, the local authorities, the student body and all of the rest of them have not yet had an opportunity, I should think, to settle this thing as it ought to be settled. I would certainly hope that we could avoid any interference with anybody as long as that state, from its governor on down, will do its best to straighten it out.[13]

▪

When Autherine Lucy won the first federal case ordering her admission as a student to the University of Alabama, Constance Baker Motley and other lawyers in the NAACP Legal Defense and Educational Fund, Inc., thought there was a good chance the transition would be peaceful. Not necessarily friendly, but at least peaceful.

"There was only one student that they had to be worried with," Motley said she reasoned. "And they could say, 'Well, she'll feel so harassed that she'll leave'; or 'She'll flunk out or something.' It wouldn't be any big deal. There wasn't that much for them to be concerned about. They viewed Autherine Lucy as just somebody picked by the NAACP to desegregate the school, and she was a girl, and blah, blah, blah. They didn't see it up to that point as something that was going to strike at the whole system.

"But the Montgomery boycott changed the whole atmosphere. Once the bus boycott started, once the average black got involved, the guy on the street, they knew it was the end. Because they understood that when the average black was out there, ready to demonstrate and to sit in the front of the bus, that was the end."

■ ───────────────────

Alabama's handling of the Lucy case was almost polite compared to the treatment Clennon King got in Mississippi. King, a Negro who taught at the black Alcorn A&M College in southwestern Mississippi, applied for admission to the University of Mississippi in Oxford in the summer of 1958. He wanted to do graduate work in history. King, a somewhat eccentric man who had spoken out in favor of segregation (someone who knows him well referred to him as "a genius but not practical"), showed up on the campus and was met by Governor James P. Coleman and a number of policemen. The state officials hustled King off to a mental institution on the floorboards of a highway patrol car, but after lawyers intervened on King's behalf, the staff there said he was sane. A year later, a Negro named Clyde Kennard tried to enter Mississippi Southern College at Hattiesburg and was thrown off the campus. Soon afterward, the authorities tried and convicted him of stealing five bags of chicken feed, and he was sent to Parchman Penitentiary. During his time in prison, Kennard became a victim of cancer. He was released shortly before his death.[14]

The Little Rock school crisis further illustrated official unwillingness to confront segregation with anything approaching courage. The city's school board had prepared a desegregation plan, in compliance with the *Brown* decisions. At the last minute, on September 2, 1957, the night before nine Negroes were to walk through the doors of Central High School, Arkansas governor Orval Faubus announced he was sending the National Guard to the school "to preserve order." When the Negro students appeared, they were greeted by a howling racist mob and a National Guard contingent that refused to let them enter. Eventually, President Eisenhower sent in federal troops and federalized the guard, but not before the supremacists had been allowed to strengthen their positions.

Eisenhower occupied a notable niche in Movement history. At a time when federal leadership was called for, he vacillated and spoke of his inability to change people's hearts and minds. One result was that the segregationists gained time and energy; another was that the disfranchised, repressed Negroes of the American South were offered a reason to distrust their national government and to continue regarding it as a white operation. It was not to be the only such lesson.

In the 1952 election, in which Eisenhower first came to office as a hero of World War II, former college president, and ex-commander of the North Atlantic Treaty Organization, only 21 percent of the Negroes who voted had cast their ballots for him. One reference work attributes this to blacks' memories of Ike's earlier testimony against President Truman's effort to end segregation in the military. But in the year after his election, the Eisenhower administration ordered an end to segregation in schools on military installations and in other areas of the military, as well as Veterans Administration hospitals.[15]

In 1954, however, Eisenhower declined to ask Congress to pass civil rights legislation, and he failed to support a rights amendment to the Taft-Hartley Labor-Management Relations Act. His partisans in the House kept a bill outlawing segregation in interstate travel from coming to the floor for a vote. In 1955, Eisenhower spoke against legislation that would have required the desegregation of National Guard units. In the 1956 election, about 40 percent of the blacks who voted went for Eisenhower over Stevenson; the increase was attributed to the fact that Ike had appointed Earl Warren, the author of the *Brown* decision, to the Supreme Court. But Negro voting was a relative thing; in the South, only 25 percent of voting-age Negroes, or about 1.2 million people, were registered to vote.[16]

Eisenhower proposed a civil rights act in 1956, but originally he did not want a provision, favored by Attorney General Herbert

Brownell, that would allow the Justice Department to intervene on behalf of Negroes who were denied the right to vote. Ike reversed his position only after the campaign got under way.

Eisenhower's lethargy reflected the attitude of much of the American public — or at least the white portion of it. The fifties were known, by those who were not preoccupied by thoughts of bus segregation, lunch counter discrimination, and public school integration, as bland and noncontroversial. The decade produced political witch hunts for communists and their "sympathizers," and surely caused many Americans with ideas to suppress them. It produced, too, an entire category of young people who would become known as the "silent generation." As it turned out, only the whites (and not all of them) were silent. Their black contemporaries were boisterous enough to change the course of world history.

The education issues were important, but equally so were the direct action campaigns that sprang up in cities and towns in the South and elsewhere. In 1958, the NAACP Youth Council of Oklahoma City protested segregation at lunch counters by sitting down at the counters and refusing to move. Before long, more than three dozen of the eating places had decided to desegregate. Sit-down demonstrations were also held at the Dockum Drug Store chain in Wichita, Kansas. In other places, notably college towns, black and white college students registered their displeasure with segregation by holding sit-ins at restaurants and other public accommodations.[17] Alan Gartner, the white man who was to become an executive of CORE, recalls that in the fall of 1956, in his freshman year at progressive Antioch College, in Yellow Springs, Ohio, he joined a sit-in at a local movie house. The theater desegregated without incident, and the students moved on to demonstrate at a barbershop whose barbers refused to cut Negroes' hair.[18]

After Montgomery, Negroes in several cities instituted their own defiance of segregated municipal buses. A boycott was begun in 1956 in Tallahassee, and blacks in Birmingham were arrested in that year for refusing to seat themselves by the rules.[19] Municipally owned recreational facilities such as golf courses and parks were desegregated in a number of Southern cities. Again, the pattern was that some places, after hemming and hawing and erecting a few roadblocks, went ahead and desegregated, while others became even firmer in their resistance. The former group included communities such as Atlanta and Charlotte — cities that were seeking attractive business and that cared about their images abroad — while the latter was made up of towns such as Birmingham, Baton Rouge, and virtually anyplace in Mississippi. People began to speak of "hard-core" areas; generally, these included parts of the South where the proportion of Negroes to whites was high and places where restrictions on Negro voting were strongest. These two characteristics often went hand in hand. A number of other cities teetered somewhere in the middle — communities such as Savannah and Mobile and Nashville — but they tended toward a little quiet, token desegregation rather than a "segregation forever" stance.

A. Philip Randolph, the perennial trekker against discrimination, led a Youth March for Integrated Schools in Washington, D.C., on October 25, 1958. The students sent a delegation to speak with President Eisenhower, but he refused to meet with them. In the spring of 1959, a second march was held.[20]

In the non-hard-core areas, where resistance to black participation in the political process was not so severe, the difference began to show. Negroes were elected to city councils and other local offices in Nashville and Oak Ridge, Tennessee, several North Carolina towns, and Virginia. The black vote was felt even in hard-core Hinds County (Jackson), Mississippi, where two vocal segregationists were defeated in an election.[21]

In the spring of 1959, Negroes formed the Fayette County Civic and Welfare League in western Tennessee, which had a long history of repressing the black vote and of acting like Mississippi on racial matters generally. The whites responded by trying to drive the blacks off the land. One particularly effective technique they used was to deny the Negroes annual crop loans, which are the lifeblood of most small farmers. In Monroe, North Carolina, NAACP official Robert Williams spoke of meeting violence with violence. Roy Wilkins, who had become executive secretary of the national NAACP in 1955 and would hold the post through the Movement years, promptly suspended Williams from his post.[22]

Antisegregationists continued their efforts to eliminate discrimination across the board, in transportation, housing, and employment, but the successes came slowly during the late fifties. Organized labor spoke eloquently of its affinity for the cause, but its actions spoke louder. Many Northern unions were as white as many Southern schools, and would remain so even after the schools had desegregated. And when A. Philip Randolph criticized the leadership of the American Federation of Labor and Congress of Industrial Organizations at its 1959 national convention for not doing enough, the executive committee censured him. AFL-CIO president George Meany said Randolph was to blame for Negroes' antipathy toward organized labor.[23]

By the end of the fifties, direct action was decidedly on the Movement's agenda, although few were calling it that. What was later to be categorized under that somewhat bureaucratic-sounding term was already evident in the South: sit-down demonstrations, picket lines, boycotts. More activities were in the planning stages. Martin Luther King and his colleagues in and around the Southern Christian Leadership Conference, along with activists in general, quickly learned that direct action, by focussing the attention of the nation and the world on the evils of segregation, could bring enormous pressure to bear on those who were trying to perpetuate discrimination, as well as on those who had sought to hide behind the banner of "moderation" and do nothing. And if, as often turned out to be the case, the whites' reaction to direct action was violence, that helped build public opinion for the activists, too.

Direct action brought money and volunteers into the Movement. It produced quick results, though not always pleasant ones. And, most important, it was the best way for black people to overcome the terror that centuries of segregation and repression had inflicted on them.

So it should not have been surprising when, on February 1, 1960, in Greensboro, North Carolina, a handful of black college students took the era of direct action into high gear with their sit-in demonstration. Sit-ins were not totally new. Negroes had used the technique before, as had the labor movement. James Farmer and his friends had held sit-ins in segregated facilities in Chicago back in the forties. Floyd McKissick says *his* began in 1953. But nothing that had gone before had the impact of the Greensboro demonstration.

Unlike the others, Greensboro spawned a regionwide, even a nationwide, campaign. And it removed the newly born civil rights movement from the exclusive control of adults. Just as Montgomery had shown that people other than NAACP types could effectively fight segregation, Greensboro showed that there was a definite place in the Movement for young people.

It could be argued, and sometimes was, that there was nothing new under this particular sun: that direct action of this sort had been employed since slave days, and that young people had previously been represented in the Movement through their activities in NAACP youth councils. But something different had happened with Greensboro-by-way-of-Montgomery-by-way-of-*Brown*. The rules of engagement, as military commanders say, had changed. The calendar had changed, too: All of a sudden there was a hollow sound to the exhortation that justice would come in the by-and-by. The schedule had been rewritten, compressed. What the demonstrators were saying, and meaning with all the impatience and assumed immortality of youth, was "Freedom *now!*" with the emphasis on the second word. And suddenly no other option seemed worth even considering.

The impetus behind the movement for freedom that had been going on for so long had changed. The agenda now was being written by the young people, who joyfully abandoned their junior status, where they had been dispatched to watch and learn from their elders. In some cities they practically replaced the older black leadership, or certainly banished it to the far background. In other cities a real competition between older and younger started brewing. This was especially true in Atlanta.

People's lives were suddenly changed by all this. Those who had been fighting segregation for decades were reinvigorated (and in some cases peeved that the younger warriors were getting all the attention). The energy flowed to those who, because of their youth, had never engaged in the formal struggle before. Young, smart black men who had planned to become ministers or teachers started considering a period of activism first. Young, smart black women who ordinarily would have gone into teaching were drawn to the same calling. It was a sort of dues-paying ritual. Most thought it would be a temporary assignment, if they thought at all about the time involved. It was simply the thing they had to do. Surely the struggle would be over before long, and they could return to their more normal lives.

It would take longer than any of them dreamed. The "law of the land," and the decisions of the federal courts, and the boycotts and picket lines and sit-in demonstrations, ran headlong into the curtain of resistance that the segregationists were erecting. "Now," as in "Freedom *now*," would come only after a long, difficult, and dangerous struggle.

────────────────── ■

One obvious reason that the Movement began for different people at differing times was the simple matter of age. Some of those who were to play important roles in destroying segregation were just children when the *Brown* decision came down. For others, like A. Philip Randolph and Joseph Rauh and the NAACP's Roy Wilkins and Thurgood Marshall, the struggle started decades before. To them, milestones such as *Brown* and the Montgomery boycott were welcome and sometimes surprisingly so, but always understandable in the context of an evolutionary transition that had been developing for a long, long time. For these people, the Movement was part of the Long Haul.

"We were all left-wingers," said Wyatt Tee Walker, who fell somewhere in between these two age groups. During the sixties, the Reverend Mr. Walker was the chief logistician and strategist for the Southern Christian Leadership Conference and Martin Luther King's chief of staff. Now he is the pastor of the prestigious Canaan Baptist Church in New York City's Harlem.

"The question nobody wants to say, or has not said, or doesn't *know* to say, is that the people around Dr. King, and Dr. King himself — we were all left-wingers. I belonged to the YCL here in New York when I was a kid. The Young Communist League. And I'm proud of my left wing. I wasn't in it for politics. I was trying to get next to white girls, you know. But some of the things I heard helped to radicalize me. Then I worked downtown in the garment district. Eighteenth Street and Fourth Avenue. I used to go to Union Square Park to eat my lunch. And I heard the Trotskyites and those folks over there.

"And that's what radicalized me. It just further radicalized me, because my father was a race man. You know, in retrospect, I see the pieces that have created the persona that I have. I grew up in a black preacher's house. In south Jersey. With a picture on the wall which was not Booker T. Washington. It was Frederick Douglass, the abolitionist. And I can remember things my father said. He told us why he left the South. He was sitting in a train station in North Carolina. There was a white waiting room. There wasn't any colored waiting room. It was cold.

"And a constable came in, and he told my father that he had to get out of there. And my father told him he wasn't going to leave; he was waiting for the train. And the constable raised his billy stick to hit him, and my daddy said he had his finger on the trigger of a Smith and Wesson nickel-plated .32 caliber. He said if that billy stick had started down, he was a dead constable. My daddy did not like white folks.

"The chip didn't fall far from the block. At nine years old, I was sitting in at a white-only theater in Merchantville, New Jersey, with my two older sisters. Nine years old. That was 1938. So the YCL and Union Square Park just further radicalized me. My senior paper at Merchantville High School in 1946 — you would never dream what it was about: the five-year plan of the Soviet Union. In a town with two thousand people, that's where my mind was."

To younger participants in the Movement such as Charles Jones of Charlotte, everything that was happening seemed fresh and new and revolutionary, not evolutionary. They hardly thought, at first, about a Long Haul. Of course segregation was wrong, and the federal government had finally said it was wrong, and that was that. It would be over, and over soon.

So the younger activists made slight corrections to their courses. Charles Jones, whose earlier inclination had been toward the church, found himself edging more toward the law as a way to make his contribution.

Others remained convinced that the church was the way. In Petersburg, Virginia, Charles Sherrod was studying at Virginia Union University, on his way to becoming a Baptist preacher. When Sherrod was born, in 1939, his mother was fourteen years old and his father was not present in the home. Sherrod was the eldest of six children. The family received welfare funds, and Charles shined shoes to help out.

On a farm in Pike County, Alabama, in the 1950s, John Lewis thought that becoming a preacher would be the best way for him to do his part toward ending discrimination. Lewis was born in 1940, the third of ten children in a sharecropper family. When he was a small child, his parents bought a hundred-acre farm for three hundred dollars.

The farm was in the Black Belt, the broad crescent of fertile soil that sweeps from eastern Virginia through coastal North Carolina, South Carolina, the center of Georgia, Alabama, Mississippi, and into parts of Louisiana and Arkansas. The term is sometimes mistakenly used to mean a heavy concentration of black people, but it originally referred to the richness and color of the soil. It was because of that soil, however, that plantations grew along the Black Belt. Slavery provided the large work forces for the plantations, and that resulted in a large population of black people.

Among his other jobs on the farm, John Lewis was in charge of the chickens. For practice, because he was so certain of his calling, he preached the chickens' funerals when they died.

Lewis despised segregation from the beginning. In 1970 he told author John Egerton:

> I had come to resent segregation and discrimination at an early age. We had the poor schools, the run-down school buses, the unpaved roads; and I saw that those were penalties imposed on us because of race. So race was closely tied to my decision to be a minister. I thought religion could be something meaningful, and I wanted to use the emotional energy of the black church to end segregation and gain freedom for black people.[24]

In 1956, one year before he graduated from high school, John Lewis became an ordained Baptist minister. He paid close attention to the Montgomery boycott. When he finished high school and headed off to Nashville to enter American Baptist Theological Seminary, he knew the pulpit was the logical place from which he should conduct his attack on segregation.

――――――――――

The shady, well-groomed campuses of the Atlanta University Center, a collection of black universities and colleges, formed a focus for Negro middle-class and intellectual life in Atlanta and much of the South. What Julian Bond really wanted was to run a coffeehouse there and write poetry. Bond was born in 1940. His father, the well-known black educator Horace Mann Bond, was the president of a state college in Georgia, but there were no hospitals nearby that would accept Negroes. So when Julian's mother went into labor, the Bonds traveled to Meharry Medical College in Nashville for the birth. In the late fifties the family moved to Atlanta, where Julian's father became dean of the school of education at Atlanta University. Julian, his sister, Jane, and brother, James, who also were to become active in the Movement, lived in the intellectually stimulating atmosphere of one of the South's finest centers of education.

And not just intellectually stimulating. Julian Bond was and is a handsome man. In the early sixties he made some money modeling in an advertisement for a soft drink that ran in publications aimed at Negroes, and he joked about how he should be ashamed of it. The Bond family lived on the campus near the home of Whitney Young, then dean of the school of social work at Atlanta University and later to become the head of the National Urban League.

Young and Atlanta scholar and activist Carl Holman had produced a pamphlet titled *A Second Look at Atlanta*. Using census and other data, the booklet attacked the prevailing notion (prevailing in the white business community, and largely through that business community's own self-promotion efforts) that Atlanta was a center of racial tolerance. In actuality it had many of the problems of other Southern cities.

The booklet nagged at Bond and made him want to get more involved in the Movement that he saw growing on the campus in the late fifties, but the temptations to go the other way were strong. Bond's sharp mind and attractive features, his ease with the upper-class community, his fluency with words, the lightness of his skin — they all pulled him away from the struggle. They made it possible to think of pursuing the academic life, becoming a teacher, perhaps opening a coffeehouse on the edge of the campus, and writing poetry for a living.

But he could not do it. Julian Bond knew that he would have felt ashamed if he hadn't joined up. "And now," he said with a laugh, "people would be asking, 'What were *you* doing then?' And I could say, 'I was getting my Ph.D.' "

■ ──────────────────────────

PART THREE

---- ■

RESISTANCE: THE SEPARATE
BUT NOT EQUAL

■ ----

SEVEN

THE POWER OF THE BALLOT BOX

The reaction of the majority of the white South to attacks on segregation was massive. It was horrified and indignant, and it expressed hurt surprise, though the *Brown* decision and allied events had hardly been unanticipated. "Massive" was the correct term, for the response came from politicians and opinion leaders throughout the entire white South, from Black Belt to border state, and it came in huge doses, flooding the legislatures and courtrooms and the campaign trails and the front pages of newspapers.

"Massive resistance" was, in fact, the name the white Virginians attached to one of their rhetorical schemes for replying to the Supreme Court's actions. The Virginians, in their aristocratic way, had always thought of themselves as the intellectuals, the Jesuits, of segregation (or, as they would have put it, of state sovereignty). Now, in the wake of *Brown*, their white leaders seemed to believe they could use flowery words and speechifying about the past — about the true aims of John C. Calhoun and James Madison, for example — to rescind the decision, or at least to whip up public sentiment for its reversal. The rest of the Southern states went along with the rhetoric, but the time soon came when they, and the Virginians, too, would back up their flowery words of gentlemanly rhetoric with laws, resolutions, repression, threats, intimidation, state-condoned violence, and in some cases even state-engineered violence.

There had been resistance all along, but *Brown* elevated it to a higher level, giving it a different and stronger urgency.

Southern whites in the fifties, and to a great extent even now, cannot abide being told what they must do. Harry Ashmore, the former editor of the *Arkansas Gazette*, referred to this in an interview as "the 'ain't no son of a bitch gonna tell me what to do' syndrome." The characteristic, thinks Ashmore, is stronger in the South than elsewhere in the nation, and it grows out of the region's experiences during the Civil War and the Reconstruction that followed. The South is full of white men (women are hardly ever afflicted by this preoccupation) who speak of the glories of The War and the crushing indignities of Reconstruction as if they had happened last month. This is particularly the case in small county seats in Mississippi, where the lone granite Confederate soldiers stand eternal guard over the courthouse squares. But the phenomenon may be observed anywhere in the present-day South, save perhaps for the biggest cities.

Even to a white Southerner who is not particularly inclined toward racism, the idea of an entity (a "foreign power," in the minds and words of some Southerners) telling him what he must do is cause for tooth-gnashing anger. With *Brown*, it was a case not only of being told what to do, but of being told to do something that most white Southerners had been taught was beyond abhorrent — it was unthinkable.

Never mind that resisting the Supreme Court's demand put these Southerners in the position of being hypocrites (for, if their love for and relations with Negroes had been half as delightful as they had always said, they would have ardently embraced integration decades before). The Southern white male mind (white females were rarely heard in public on this matter, either) had long experience with such convoluted thinking. White Southerners have a celebrated bent for self-delusion and displacement, and it was with almost imperceptible ease that they translated the Supreme Court's rather patient and overdue, and certainly reasonable and moderate, order from what it was — a recognition that segregation was evil and could never produce the equality that separate but equal had promised — into a calamity that better suited the fantasies of the white South.

Brown thus became, more than anything else, the usurpation of states' rights by a small group of twisted minds in Washington. It was communist inspired. It was *socialist* inspired. There was probably more than a smattering of Jewish conspiracy involved, too. The Florida senate, in a 1956 special session, passed a resolution lambasting the court for, among other things, using the advice of social scientists in arriving at its decision. (In *Brown* the court had written, "Whatever may have been the extent of psychological knowledge at the time of *Plessy v. Ferguson*, this [new] finding is amply supported by modern authority," and then, in its famous Footnote 11, cited the work of several researchers, among them social psychologist Kenneth B. Clark, who had helped the NAACP in its preparation for the cases.)[1] The Florida legislators declared that the court

> has cited as authority for the assumed and asserted facts the unsworn writings of men, one of whom was the hireling of an active participant in the litigation. Others were affiliated with organizations declared by the attorney general of the United States to be subversive, and one of whom, in the same writing which the court cited as authority for its decision stated that the Constitution of the United States is "impractical and unsuited to modern conditions."[2]

Several of the critics were particularly outraged because the court had used the writings of a Swedish (translation: "foreign," "socialist," and, no doubt, "communist") economist in arriving at its conclusion. When Gunnar Myrdal's *An American Dilemma* was published in two volumes in 1944, as *Brown* historian Richard Kluger has written, Myrdal accomplished "what no white American had ever done — to document, analyze, and excoriate the nation's continuing mistreatment and evident hatred of the Negro."[3]

The railing against the court went on and on, employing in some places roadside billboards to call for the impeachment of

Chief Justice Earl Warren. The outraged segregationists always managed to overlook the explanation more likely than social-scientist-crypto-communist conspiracy, which was that the white South knew, and knew with the conviction of the profoundly guilty, that school desegregation was but the beginning of an attack on a system that rested solidly on the economic and political exploitation of an entire race of people, people who were sorted into their category solely by the color of their skin.

■

James P. Coleman occupied two top positions in the Mississippi state government during the early Movement years. He was the state's attorney general from 1950 until January of 1956, when he was sworn in as governor. He held that position until 1960, when he was succeeded by Paul Johnson, who campaigned as a more strident segregationist. Later Coleman served as a judge on the U.S. Fifth Circuit Court of Appeals. Now he is back in his hometown of Ackerman, in central Mississippi, practicing law.

He said recently that it was obvious to him long before the *Brown* decision which way the segregation issue was heading. He had watched the higher education cases move toward the Supreme Court and be decided in the Negro plaintiffs' favor. "So the shape of things to come was very apparent. When the school desegregation cases kicked off, I, as attorney general of Mississippi, went to Washington, and I listened to all of the arguments in the Supreme Court, including the implementation arguments. So we were well aware of what was going on.

"We also knew what I think the Supreme Court itself recognized when it deferred the implementation of its decision: that since the law had been exactly the opposite, at least since the 1890s, to turn it around would be very much like trying to stop the Panama Limited express train in a very short distance. From the very beginning my concern was to try to keep Mississippi from being burnt up in the conflagration. Or at least severely singed."

There were in Mississippi, he said, "a lot of red-hot segregationists . . . who thought that we just ought to go to war with the United States — which, of course, I knew better about. I knew you couldn't defy the United States government." But the courts, with their longtime

endorsement of the doctrine of separate but equal, had given segregationists hope that their position would prevail. In a celebrated case in
the late twenties, the Supreme Court had even upheld Mississippi's
school segregation law against a Chinese student.

A further complication arose, said Coleman, when Chief Justice
Warren, in the *Brown* decision, "cited no legal authority whatever for
his position. He really infuriated a lot of people by relying on the writings
of a fellow named Gunnar Myrdal from Sweden, who had come over
here and stayed some time — I don't know how long — and had gone
back and proceeded to judge the whole thing. Mississippi never did —
and the South never has — taken very well to being judged by foreigners
or others outside the United States.

"I think we demonstrated with the Civil War that we don't always
listen to judgments from *within* the United States. But the main thing
was, the law had been turned completely around from what everybody
thought it would be.

"Now, let me say here that I was well aware of the fact that with
separate but equal — the way things were, the South had lived up to
the separate but not to the equal. And that was the beginning of our
real problems, because when these suits were first filed, they were filed
as suits for equal treatment. And then finally Thurgood Marshall decided,
'Well, what the heck, they'd been delayed, and they'd been delayed,
and delayed. . . . I'll just amend my suit, and I'll go for the whole deal.'
And did, and succeeded."

■ ─────────────────────────────

Although for many white Southerners who were not in official
positions the Movement did not start until *Brown*, they had been
fighting against a "movement" or anything that looked like a
movement, or anything that might conceivably turn into a movement, for decades. Negroes' attempts to register and vote had always been seen as terrible threats to the status quo (as well they
were), and these threats ran parallel with the whites' fear that Negroes might somehow improve their economic positions and no
longer be dependent upon the "beneficence" and "paternalism"
and "good will" of their white masters. So the white resistance had
been going on for a long time, even during the period when it was
a reaction to a stimulus that was more imagined than actual.

Walter White explained it all in 1929, but the whites had not paid attention. For one thing, White was black, at least by the standards of American society, since he had "Negro blood."* (He also had blond hair, blue eyes, and light-colored skin and was able to travel in the white South and listen with grim amusement to whites grumble about the Negro problem.)⁴ For another, White was the executive director of the National Association for the Advancement of Colored People.

White wrote a book in the twenties about violence against Negroes. It was titled *Rope & Faggot: A Biography of Judge Lynch*, and it was a chilling account of the methods some Southern whites used to keep blacks in their place. White collected his information from official sources but also from consultations in the field, and in his preface he thanks the "many lynchers with whom I have talked and who have expressed themselves freely, unaware of my racial identity."

Lynching means putting someone to death, often by hanging, by mob action and without legal sanction. A widely accepted explanation for its name has it that a Virginian named Charles Lynch, of what is now Lynchburg, became upset with the lack of law and

---

*The lawbooks of the states (not all of them Southern, by any means) were replete with rules about who is black and who isn't. Most of them were dependent on an impossible assessment of the "color" of blood. Arkansas defined as Negro "any person who has in his or her veins any Negro blood whatsoever," while Tennessee's pertained to those "having any blood of the African race in their veins." Virginia decided that "every person in whom there is ascertainable any Negro blood shall be deemed and taken to be a colored person"; whether the ascertaining was to be conducted intravenously or by eyeballing was not specified. Virginia, always cautious in these matters, provided a definition of white folks, as well: The term "white persons," said the state's code, shall apply "only to such persons as has [*sic*] no trace whatever of any blood other than Caucasian; but persons who have one-sixteenth or less of the American Indian and have no other non-Caucasic blood shall be deemed to be white persons." Mississippi, as usual, carried things a bit further than most by expanding its definition to include those who had "one-eighth or more Mongolian blood."

Several jurisdictions defined a Negro as having one-eighth or more of his or her "blood" black. This would include anyone who had one great-grandparent who was a full-blooded member of the Negro (or "African") race. Under these guidelines, then, it is likely that Negroes are not a minority in the United States after all.

The laws were aimed primarily at preventing interracial marriage, but Florida's also provided that children born to parents of different races could not inherit property. *Race Relations Law Reporter* (1958), "Legal Definition of Race" survey, 571.

order in the western part of his state in the years before the Revolutionary War. The nearest trial court was two hundred miles away. Lynch and friends formed an extralegal court, with Lynch as chief magistrate. The rights of the accused were said to have been protected in this court, but out of it the current term "lynch" has come to mean capital punishment without a trial or other constitutional safeguards and, as White pointed out, capital punishment meted out in communities "where the excuse cannot be offered that there are no courts of law."[5] While lynching has been largely associated in the public's mind with black victims, it also has been used extensively against whites who get out of line.

White found, and other researchers have agreed, that lynch-type violence against Negroes was rooted in economics. Slavery was in decline until the cotton gin was invented, bringing an increased demand for cheap labor to work the crop. Lynching was a convenient way to discourage slave revolts and abolitionist talk and to keep Negroes on the plantation; but whites could not lynch indiscriminately, since the Negro was worth more alive than dead or mutilated. This precaution was abandoned, however, after the Emancipation Proclamation reduced the cash value of Negroes to zero; violence and the threat of violence became the main tool for enslaving Negroes in fact, if not in law. Lynching became popular again during World War II, when the flow of cheap immigrant labor slowed in the South and blacks started their great migrations to the cities of the North and Midwest. White Southerners panicked at this potential economic loss and returned to what White had called "the old standby" of violence.

Among the conditions that White found closely associated with lynching were "the influence of evangelical religions, the use [by] unscrupulous politicians of mythical fear of 'Negro domination,' the important role of sex, and the strenuous efforts to keep the Negro ignorant and intimidated that he may the more easily be exploited." The author was especially critical of Southern white religion, noting, "It is exceedingly doubtful if lynching could possibly exist under any other religion than Christianity. Not only through tacit approval and acquiescence has the Christian Church indirectly given its approval to lynch-law and other forms of race prejudice, but the evangelical Christian denominations have done much towards creation of the particular fanaticism which finds an outlet in lynching."[6]

As for sex (since the reasons given for lynching often had to do with purported sexual approaches by Negro males to white females), White observed, "Lynching has always been the means for protection, not of white women, but of profits." And he found that the low intellectual levels of the white Southern community provided plenty of fuel for violence. "Lynchings seldom occur where there is enlightenment," he wrote. "The holding fast to outworn and faulty ideas, the retention of ignorance with all its vicious by-products, provide the fertile soil from which springs the rule of the mob, whether it be one to burn a Negro or flog a white woman or to wage a campaign for compulsory reading of the Bible or to enact an anti-evolution law."[7]

This ignorance also fertilized campaigns by Southerners to convince themselves and each other that Negroes were biologically and anatomically, as well as legally, inferior. Throughout American history, and well into the Movement years, there have been efforts by scientists and others to show that Negroes have smaller brains than whites, or some sort of genetic abnormalities that made them different and that, therefore, justified their subjugation. White recounted one attempt by a University of Virginia researcher in 1906 to demonstrate that "white" brains were heavier than "Negro" brains. Another researcher checked the data and found that his colleague's test brains had been clearly labeled as to head of origin, and thus personal bias could have crept into the study. As things turned out, it had crept quite a bit; reweighing showed that the white brains had been overweighted and the black ones shortweighted. Intelligence quotient tests in one "large Southern city" revealed that black children were superior to the whites. "It is hardly necessary to add," wrote White, "that the results were promptly suppressed!" Others have noted that if brain size were all that crucial, women would be dumber than men, since their heads are smaller on the average. And examinations given soldiers in World War I indicated that the "average" Northern Negro was smarter than the "average" Southern white male.[8]

As almost always in the white South's dealings with segregation, some effort was made to justify actions by using legal (or at least legal-sounding) explanations. In 1893 the Georgia legislature enacted a law providing prison terms for anyone found guilty of "mobbing or lynching any citizen . . . without due process of law," raising the intriguing question of how lynching could be carried out *with* due process. Walter White found a variety of reasons given in official documents for cases of lynching. They included attempting to vote in a presidential election; "insanity"; "associating with white women"; jilting a girlfriend; "introducing smallpox"; talking back to a white man; testifying against a white man; "frightening children"; "jumping labor contract"; and "a Fourth of July celebration."[9]

What Walter White had been examining was a phenomenon that has long fascinated thoughtful Southerners of all colors, as well as others who have studied the region. It is the peculiar, complex, and frequently contradictory nature of the South and of white Southerners. Researchers have tried to capture and explain the essence of what one of the best-known of them, W. J. Cash, referred to as "the mind of the South," but few have succeeded. It seems that part of the region's nature is its mystery. Frequently, students of the subject fall back on the forces of nature, which are so manifestly present in the South, in attempts to describe their subject. James McBride Dabbs, a Southerner who has written often of the region, referred in one of his books to the elusive Southern character this way: "Non-Southerners visiting in the South sense the character, Southerners visiting beyond the South recall it. It is as distinctive as the balmy air blowing inland across the sea-islands of South Carolina." Even the stultifying homogenization brought by modern-day television, interstate highways, and assembly-line hamburger joints has failed to take completely from the South that balmy feeling — part reality, part history, part geography, big part fantasy — that makes the South the South.[10]

One element of the fantasy, a trap that snares most who talk about it, blacks included, is that "South" and "Southerner" are almost always used to refer to the *white* South and the *white* Southerner. And yet the black South and the black Southerner are essential ingredients in the term "the South." Without them, people might speak of the South as only a geographic region, much as weather forecasters refer to the Upper Great Lakes or the Lower Ohio Valley.

Another element of the Southern character, and one that has been mentioned here before, is the half fact, half fantasy of some kind of closeness between black and white, even in their strictly enforced separation. Dabbs, more cynical about this than most observers, refers to it as the whites' claim of a "degree of personal relationship"; of their pretending that Negroes were happy in their segregation. "They had to be happy," he writes, "because we who created the myth were happy, and we didn't like unhappy people around us."[11]

Southern whites are fond of talking about how solicitous they are (or were in pre-Movement days) of the welfare of "their" Negroes, particularly those who work for them. It is an attitude not far from that expressed by an adult for a child, or perhaps for an idiot relative. Dabbs destroys this one, as well. A white employer, he writes, may express personal interest in a Negro employee's personal situation,

> but he does not feel bound to extend that interest into the world in which the employee lives, nor to seek such changes in that world as to give the Negro employee the same general chance that his white employee has. His friendliness is limited to the alleviation of evident distress; it is not extended to any modification of that world which, largely, creates the distress. . . . It is, if you please, an over-personal relationship. Its goodness is not built into the total structure of society.[12]

One aspect of the contradictory nature of the South is far less mysterious or rooted in emotions, and this hasn't been subjected to much inspection. In and before the Movement days, it was possible — likely, even — for white officialdom to function simultaneously on a number of seemingly conflicting levels in its dealings with Negroes and hardly ever notice the inconsistency. On one side of a half-dozen square blocks in Atlanta, for example, there existed a state capitol, its gold-plated dome an ironic comment on the poverty of the state's educational and cultural resources. At the time of the early civil rights movement, the building beneath the dome was filled with legislators and, almost always, a governor, who could be described only as iron-collar reactionary. Some had gotten to the uncontrollable-hatred stage. These were the people who, in the early sixties, could easily have passed the 1893 act forbidding lynching without "due process of law." They had great difficulty pronouncing the word "Negro" as it ought to be pronounced, tending toward "nigra" and "nigger." A little downhill from the capitol was the high-rise Atlanta City Hall, which during most of the period was populated by officials who knew that segregation was not only bad for the city's business but morally wrong, and who for the most part acted at least politely, and sometimes solicitously, toward Negroes. The pronunciation here was more on the order of "KNEE-grow." And at the bottom of the hill was the Fulton County Courthouse, containing officials and judges who ran the gamut from reasonable to moderate to white supremacist, and whose pronunciation of the so very important word was all over the lot.

The differences could be seen even in the physical plants. The Georgia capitol, and many others in the South, resembled a cold and musty mausoleum, a dark and brooding place of the past where ancient colored men in white jackets were "porters" and fetched ice water for the white politicians (some of whom mixed it with their Wild Turkey and Jack Daniel's on the very floor of the Senate). The city hall building was not a modern one, but it had been updated so that it at least acknowledged the existence of the twentieth century, with telephone cables fed through old walls, self-service elevators replacing the porter-driven ones, and more than one Negro employee who was not at the menial level. The courthouse was almost as neutral as a piece of putty-colored modern office equipment, making no promises or statements about its attitude toward civilization. It was possible to cross from one century into another just by walking from one governmental building into the next. The only constants were taxes — each jurisdiction levied them — and the Southern accents of the people, almost all of them white, who populated each of the buildings.

What made the differences, of course, was the vote. As the Movement began, Negroes in much of rural Georgia, which through legislative machinations maintained an inordinate hold on the state's general assembly, were effectively prevented from exercising their right to vote. In Atlanta, blacks were not prevented from registering; a coalition of well-informed Negro voters and "decent whites" kept die-hard segregationists out of office and sometimes installed competent mayors and council members. In Fulton County, whites outside Atlanta balanced the Negro vote and provided a government that was sometimes equitable in its treatment of blacks, sometimes brutal.

Another aspect of the white Southern character that confuses outside observers is that, although one of its facets is a certain dead-setness in its ways, those who possess it are often capable of majestic changes of mind, and even of heart, once they have seen the light. Many white Southerners are emotional, moody types, almost begging for an excuse to make dramatic conversions and bear boisterous witness. The success of fundamentalist religion in the South is evidence of this. A Southern white's pendulum does not often swing, but when it does, it can fairly clang against the other side.

Howard Odum, the North Carolina social historian, in mid-century did as much as any other white Southerner to understand the nature of the South and to suggest ways to end segregation. But in 1910, his pendulum was somewhere else. Back when he was a student, he demonstrated a mindless, unscientific prejudice that was typical of many Southerners. In his doctoral dissertation, published by Columbia University, Odum wrote that the Negro "has little home consciousness or love of home . . . no pride of ancestry . . . few ideals and perhaps no lasting adherence to an aspiration toward real worth. . . . He is shiftless, untidy, indolent . . . ." Negro women were "inefficient and indisposed to be faithful."[13] Odum was to undergo quite a conversion in the succeeding years, and one that was to benefit the entire South mightily.

Of course there are those, perhaps of a more psychological bent, who argue that the white Southerner has acted as outlandishly as he has on racial matters because he wanted someone to make him change his ways.

Another component of the region's nature was the fact that in the places where the black population was greatest, white repression of blacks was strongest. Central South Carolina, south

Georgia, lower Alabama, Mississippi, a big part of Louisiana — these were the places where racist sentiment was highest, and they were also the places with the most blacks. Reasons for this were obvious. If Negroes in these places overcame their fears, they could very easily take control of the traditional units of economic and political power — the county commission, tax assessor's office, sheriff's department; in fact, the whole courthouse gang could turn from white to black overnight. Blacks could get control of the state legislature. They could start controlling juicy public works budgets, such as highway paving contracts, and assorted other plums that the whites had been enjoying exclusively for decades. And there was the old creeping fear that if the blacks got control, they might treat their white neighbors as badly as the whites had treated *them.*

Some whites, to be sure, honestly felt that the blacks around them were immoral, smelled sweaty, and were intellectually inferior — though it was a perception created, perhaps, by the way white society had treated the blacks in terms of sanitary facilities, employment prospects, and educational opportunities. But an unmeasured amount of this sort of prejudice grew from the whites' knowledge, if only subconscious, that if they took their foot off the Negro's neck long enough for him to scramble to his feet, they wouldn't have anybody to look down on anymore. Southern whites of the supremacist class have always needed "niggers" to give themselves status; if true Negroes have not been handy they have substituted the poorest of the whites, whom they call "white trash."

Whatever motivated the "Southern character," it and what one author called the white South's "emotional fixation upon the Negro" were never represented more unremittingly than in the area of Southern politics.[14] Politics in the South took in practically everything, while at the same time its practitioners railed against the national government for its efforts to meddle in people's lives. Southern politics oversaw education. It tried to regulate sex. It sometimes slopped over into (but more often got slopped into by) religion. It controlled the varying qualities of justice that were available to Southerners, depending on their skin color. And most of all, it was the command post from which Negroes were held powerless and, when the machinery was running smoothly, in a constant state of low-level terror. Politics was the be-all and end-all of economic controls on black people.

Although politically centered resistance took some dramatic turns after the *Brown* decision, the machinery had been firmly in place for many years. And it had been durable; even the Civil War had produced hardly a dent. Its principal mission had been to keep Negroes from voting.

After the Civil War, the federal government's Reconstruction program took power from the Southern governments and gave it to the controllers of the five military districts established for that purpose. These districts registered more than 700,000 Negroes within one year, 1867. The total slightly exceeded the number of registered white Southerners. Negroes took part in all Southern governments, though they controlled none. The lieutenant governors in South Carolina, Mississippi, and Louisiana were Negro. Fourteen Negroes went to Congress from the South, and Mississippi sent two Negroes to the Senate. A study of the era notes that the new officeholders were "seldom vindictive in their use of their newly gained political power and were generally conservative on all issues except civil and political rights."[15]

The whites *were* vindictive, however. A congressional inquiry showed that in the weeks before the 1868 presidential election in Louisiana, in which Negroes were attracted to the Republican party, more than two thousand persons were killed or wounded in forays against those who were not supporting the supremacist Democratic party. A federal study reported that "half the state was overrun by violence; midnight raids, secret murders, and open riot kept the people in constant terror" until the beneficiaries of Reconstruction, the Republicans, surrendered their claims to the election.[16] Then the regular Democrats "won."

------------------------------------ ■

"I think it's historically correct," said James P. Coleman, "that the South, and Mississippi in particular, didn't have any real bias or malice or hatred about the Civil War, because they knew they had fought their hearts out and had done everything they could do, and they got beat. What really did it was Reconstruction. . . . You know, action always begets its reaction. And of course we had that period in Mississippi where we had men like James K. Vardaman and Theodore G. Bilbo, who ran against the black race, although the blacks couldn't vote. And they got elected to office by denouncing the rest of the country. . . ."

When he was governor, Coleman said, he once told his legislature, "Because of the Civil War, Mississippi will always be a hundred years behind where it otherwise would have been if it hadn't happened.

"But," he added now, "you can't get around the fact that it did happen."

■ ─────────────────────────────────

Other methods used throughout the South to keep Negroes away from the polls included simple warnings that they would die if they voted, the removal of names from ballots, and election officials' harassing Negroes with unnecessary questions. In a Georgia precinct the police blocked the door to a polling place and let only Democrats in, a surefire way to minimize Republican turnout. In Mississippi, the newspapers reported that boxes containing the ballots of anti-Democratic voters had been eaten by mules and horses.[17]

By 1877, blacks' newfound political power had been diluted almost to nothing. National politics issued the final insult with the Great Compromise of that year. In the compromise, Southern Democrats helped out national Republicans by supporting GOP candidate Rutherford B. Hayes for president in a contested election. The quid pro quo was that Washington would remove federal forces from the South, permit Southern whites to run their own election machinery, and treat Southern white political demands more kindly than in the past. Henry Lee Moon, the scholar of black voting, referred to this as "a compromise between northern and Southern white folk, with democracy and the Negro as the sacrificial victims."[18]

By the 1940s and 1950s, the machinery of political repression was firmly in place and humming. White officials had a well-stocked armory of weapons to use against the black who dared to try to register or vote. Mules no longer "ate" ballot boxes, but county registrars frequently had attacks of disappearing when Negroes came to the courthouse to register. Or they simply refused to register Negroes. States denied the vote to those who had been convicted of crimes such as petty larceny, and that removed a number of potential Negro voters. On election day, polls were set up in places far removed from black communities, or their location was changed with no notice to Negroes.

Political parties today frequently go over registration records to purge them of the names of voters who belong to the opposing party and who have died or moved, the object being to remove the temptation that someone will "vote" those who are absent. In the South, the technique was used to purge black voters, usually for no real reason. The poll tax — a fee charged for the privilege of voting — was levied on whites as well as blacks, but blacks were less able to afford it, not to mention less likely to think of it as an investment that might result in any sort of meaningful return. (It was not until 1964 that the Twenty-fourth Amendment to the Constitution was ratified, outlawing the poll tax in federal elections. The Supreme Court banned it in state elections two years later.)

The states, which under federal law had great latitude in deciding who got to vote, set up discriminatory qualification tests. A typical test would require potential voters to adequately read and interpret, to the white registrar's satisfaction, a section of the state constitution. White voters were not given the same test, which in most cases would have been impossible for anyone to pass. In Georgia, someone hoping to qualify on the basis of literacy had to be able to read intelligibly and write legibly any article of the United States or Georgia constitution. If he or she was weak in reading or writing, qualification was possible on the basis of "good character and . . . understanding of the duties and obligations of citizenship under a republican form of government." To meet that criterion, the prospective voter faced a personal appearance before the board of registrars to answer thirty questions, including "How may a county site be changed?" and "What legislative acts of the General Assembly of Georgia are void?"

Literacy tests were widely used, but since their equitable administration would have disenfranchised vast portions of the white population as well as Negroes, some states enacted "grand-father clauses" that waived the tests for anyone who was a direct descendant of a person who was entitled to vote prior to a certain date. Whatever the date, it was sure to be one on which no Negroes could vote. This scheme was quickly declared unconstitutional by the federal courts.

Economic pressure was a major technique used to keep blacks from voting. A Negro farmer who tried to register could have his credit cut off and find it impossible to buy fuel for his tractor; a black schoolteacher could lose her job. And blacks who were not directly affected by such actions could see from them that perhaps it was best not to go down to the courthouse. The choice of can-didates was usually between bad racist and worse racist, anyway. Only in a few urban centers such as Atlanta were blacks talking about running their own candidates or were moderate or progres-sive whites trying to solicit the Negro vote.

The most formidable obstacle against voting, though, was none of these. It was the white primary.

This was the ruling by the Democratic party (the only one that counted in the South after Reconstruction had been effectively repealed) that only white people could vote in its primaries. The basic assumption was that political parties were private organiza-tions and could make whatever rules they liked. By 1930, the party in eleven Southern states was using the white primary. The strat-egy was so effective that violence became less necessary for keep-ing blacks away from the political process.

The antivoting devices worked well. By 1900, according to one government document, "the Negro vote in the South virtually had disappeared." In Louisiana in 1896, for example, 130,334 Ne-groes were registered. In 1900, there were 5,320. By 1904, there were 1,342.[19]

The Supreme Court, in its 1944 ruling in *Smith v. Allwright*, found the white primary to be unconstitutional. Some Southern states fell back on literacy tests to keep blacks from voting. But in South Carolina, a further twist was added. A federal judge (a proper Charlestonian, and certainly not a socialist dupe or bleeding-heart liberal) had announced in a white primary case, "It is time for South Carolina to rejoin the Union. It is time to fall in step with the other states and to adopt the American way of conducting elections." But the Democrats ignored his advice. They changed their rules to require that party membership (and therefore the right to vote in Democratic primaries) be limited to those who were twenty-one years of age and "a white Democrat."

Negroes who couldn't join the party could participate in the party primary, though, *if* they were qualified voters and if they would raise their right hands and declare: "I . . . solemnly swear that . . . I believe in and will support the social, religious, and educational separation of the races. I further solemnly swear that I believe in the principles of states' rights, and that I am opposed to and will work against any [fair employment] law and other federal law relating to employment within the states."[20]

The time, expense, and ingenuity devoted to denying Negroes their right to vote demonstrated clearly the high regard in which those who ran the Southern system held white-only politics. Blacks' sitting next to whites on city buses and interstate trains was one thing, but the power of the ballot box was serious — so serious that there was little challenge to the system even from Washington. Ever since the Fifteenth Amendment was ratified in 1870, Negroes in America had been promised by their Constitution that their right to vote "shall not be denied or abridged by the United States or by any State on account of race, color, or previous condition of servitude." But virtually every effort that was made to secure that right, until the Movement years, was the result not of federal action but privately brought lawsuits. Even after the Civil Rights Act of 1957 was passed, giving the attorney general the authority to bring cases on behalf of Negroes whose voting rights had been denied, Washington was a passive partner. In voting, as in everything else, Negroes discovered that they would have to do the hard work themselves.

There was hope, though, that another component of the 1957 act would work enthusiastically in desegregation's behalf. The fledgling U.S. Commission on Civil Rights exercised its new powers by going to Alabama in December, 1958, to investigate allegations of voting rights abuses in six Black Belt counties. At the time, there were no Negroes registered to vote in Lowndes or Wilcox counties,

4 in Bullock, 125 in Dallas, and 1,110 in Macon. There were no figures on the sixth county, Barbour. Blacks outnumbered whites in all the counties.

Voting registrars refused to testify or hand over subpoenaed records at the commission's December hearing. And circuit judge George Wallace, who a few months before had been defeated by Attorney General John Patterson for the governorship, also announced that he was defying the federal authority. Patterson, meantime, who in his state position was serving as a counsel for the registrars, declared that the state would "take advantage of every means we have available" to protect the registrars "from this invasion by the . . . legislative and executive branches of the government." The Civil Rights Commission asked the Justice Department to compel the state to comply.[21]

It was evident by then that Wallace, who had been beaten because white voters perceived him as softer on desegregation than Patterson, had decided to retool himself as a racist. (Such rapid political makeovers are commonplace nowadays, but they were less brazen back then.) Patterson's term as attorney general had been marked by frequent attacks on opponents of segregation, and his campaign had been assisted, said two Alabama newspapers, by the Ku Klux Klan.[22] Wallace had made a similar allegation. Now Wallace wanted to become the white supremacists' darling.

When Wallace refused to appear at the Civil Rights Commission hearing, he quickly called two grand juries into action and handed the disputed voting records over to them. The reasoning was that now the records were out of Wallace's hands, and he could not be forced to produce them.

When Justice Department lawyers went into federal court and asked that Wallace be held in contempt, the move delighted Wallace, since it strengthened his segregationist credentials. A court-ordered trip to jail would bring in no end of votes from antiblack, anti-Washington Alabamans. Wallace even tried to enter a plea of guilty. But one Alabaman saw through the charade. District judge Frank M. Johnson, Jr., refused to satisfy the man who had taken to calling himself "the fightin' little judge." On January 26, 1959, Judge Johnson acquitted Wallace of the contempt charge and pointed out that Wallace had been playacting all the time.

Wallace, wrote Johnson, "through devious methods, assisted [the commission's] agents in obtaining the records" by actually giving some of them to officials and telling the commission where the others might be found. "Even though it was accomplished by means of subterfuge," wrote Judge Johnson, "George C. Wallace did comply with the order of this court. As to why the devious means were used, this court will not now judicially determine. . . . If these devious means were for political purposes, then this court refuses to allow its authority and dignity to be bent or swayed by such politically generated whirlwinds."[23]

EIGHT

∎

THE DESIRE TO SURVIVE
POLITICALLY

∎

White resistance was by and large a state-run operation. Some communities — Birmingham, Alabama, and Plaquemines Parish, Louisiana, were the most notorious — operated their own campaigns of applied racism, but generally the headquarters of Segregation Central were found under the domes of the South's capitol buildings, in the governors' offices and the legislative chambers.

The level of courage shown by these politicians was not extraordinarily high. In state after state there was evidence that, even before the *Brown* decision was delivered, plenty of political figures in high offices saw the inevitability of segregation's end and didn't seem all that disturbed by it. The prevailing atmosphere in many places seemed one of moderation, or at least one of seeking moderation. Some politicians even made public statements of acceptance when the 1954 decision came down. But one by one, like weather vanes in a passing thunderstorm, they changed their positions frequently.

The attorney general of Virginia, J. Lindsay Almond, Jr., who had argued before the court on behalf of segregation in one of the *Brown* cases, provided a case study in vacillation. After the May

17 decision, Almond sounded like a good loser: "The highest court in the land has spoken and I trust that Virginia will approach the question realistically and endeavor to work out some rational adjustment." The *Richmond News Leader*, the state's politically connected newspaper, proposed a plan of gradual implementation of the Supreme Court's order.

Only a few years later, all this had turned 180 degrees. The *News Leader* practically foamed at the mouth on matters of desegregation, and Lindsay Almond, who in the meantime had sought and won the governorship, in his January, 1958, inaugural speech was asking the legislature to "stand firm with unfailing unity of purpose and high resolve against every assault upon the sovereignty of this commonwealth. . . . Against these massive attacks, we must marshal a massive resistance."[1] One year later, Almond was fulminating before the legislature about the "daggers of political expediency" that armed those federal officials engaged in "the unholy alliance of a conspiracy to destroy the Constitution," and about "the ruthless hand of federal power under the driving urge of a minority pressure group" that was trying to open the schools to children of all races.[2]

What had happened? Had politicians who had been middle-of-the-road on race questions suddenly turned into white supremacists? Had the Negroes — the people whom the white folks had always loved and taken such good care of, et cetera, et cetera — suddenly turned into monsters who, if allowed to attend schools with white children, would poison their morals and their minds?

Of course not. What did happen is that delay occurred, and along with it, resistance blossomed. The Supreme Court created some of the delay by not providing a plan for implementation in its initial decision, but the Southern states themselves furnished the remainder by dragging their feet as if they thought desegregation would go away. In the vacuum of leadership that followed, politicians who were more unscrupulous than most seized the integration issue as their own. They used it to terrorize the moderates into self-induced suspended animation. They used it to make the more gullible and ignorant segments of the white population believe that not only would desegregation go away, it would be totally vanquished. Since Reconstruction, Southern white politics had run on the fuel of racism, to one degree or another. Now, after *Brown*, it ran almost exclusively on it. From this time until late in the sixties, no decision was made in Southern political life that did not take race into consideration.

Samuel DuBois Cook, now the president of Dillard University in New Orleans, was teaching at Atlanta University in 1964 when he wrote about the ingredients of Southern politics. It was, he said, the product of

> a stream of historical forces and sequences: plantation agrarianism, slavery, one-party politics, cultural isola-
> tion, a profound sense of self-consciousness and national alienation, a penchant for conformity and intolerance, the scars of the Civil War and Reconstruction, a nativist mentality, and excessive poverty and illiteracy. But the chief animation of the broad framework of Southern pol-
> itics has been the Negro as an object of action, manipu-
> lation, exploitation, and control. Although, in the main, voteless, the Negro has been, strangely, the prime mover in the politics of Dixie. . . . Somehow, the Negro unwit-
> tingly has exercised a tyranny over the mind of the white South, which has found continuous expression in the politics of the region.[3]

The arrival of a fresh issue of racism was a godsend for poli-
ticians who were devoid of ideas of their own, and for old-timers who seemed to be losing their touch and needed political transfu-
sions. The Virginians' apparent change of heart resulted largely from the decision by the aging head of the state's premier political machine, Harry F. Byrd, to abandon moderation or compliance in favor of a position that claimed to be opposing federal usurpation of states' rights but that amounted to a campaign of white supremacy. The same sort of thing happened in Alabama and Mississippi and Georgia; it was just that the politicians in those states were less genteel in their racism.

Although many white Southerners (and, presumably, all black Southerners) were opposed to the developing resistance, there were few active channels through which moderate or prointegra-
tionist whites could make themselves heard. Only a handful of

representatives of organized religion spoke out. University presidents and school board superintendents were largely silent. With exceptions that could be counted on the fingers of one hand, the white bar was struck dumb. Much of the press found other things to talk about. And all the while, the segregationist politicians were exploiting the vacuum.

---------------------------------- ■

"The biggest problem," said Judge Frank Johnson, "was white folks' not doing anything."

The judge was now, in 1989, seventy-one years old, as solid as the rock he was in the Movement years. Johnson ruled consistently during that time and later against racism and (as George Wallace learned in his voter registration charade) attempts to simulate racism. Johnson was acquainted with Wallace back when both were at the University of Alabama law school. Wallace ran as the independent candidate, against the fraternities' nominee, for the presidency of the student body. Johnson voted for him. Now Johnson continues to sit as a federal judge in Montgomery.

"That was the biggest problem," said Judge Johnson again. "The large majority of white people were not active in opposing the rights of blacks. Their inactivity allowed those that were willing to be active in opposing to be more effective. So if you condemn them — and I don't necessarily condemn all of them — you have to condemn them for standing aside and watching something wrong be done. . . .

"Organized religion not only failed to act, but they acted in a negative way in the Montgomery area. I'm talking about *some* of them. They put members of the board of deacons outside to keep blacks from coming into the [white] First Baptist Church. And not only the First Baptist Church, but the big organized religions in Montgomery. So they not only failed to act, they acted adversely.

"The bar did nothing. I condemn the bar for that and have publicly. They were under a duty to support the court and the court's rulings when they were following the law. There are exceptions to all of these, you know. But you had some very, very poor leadership. It was not just failure to act, but people who occupied leadership roles, from the governor on down, who acted in very, very negative ways. And that made it . . . that made it harder."

■ ─────────────────────

The movement for desegregation was growing in many areas, as the Montgomery bus boycott proved, but the segregationist's first priority was education.

Government's reaction to most crises to which it has no immediate answer is to appoint commissions to study the situation, and in the South after *Brown* it was no different. Virginia's Commission on Public Education, known as the Gray Commission, was turned loose on the problem in summer, 1954, and came back with a final report in November, 1955. North Carolina's Advisory Commission on Education turned in its report in the spring of 1956. Both commissions recommended the passage of a number of laws, all of them designed to circumvent desegregation.

Politicians in Virginia, in the meantime, had been reading the extensive editorial campaign being waged by the *News Leader*'s young editor, James Jackson Kilpatrick, Jr., an Oklahoman who, since moving to Virginia, had become more Southern white than most Southern whites. (This is the same Kilpatrick who survives today as a conservative newspaper columnist.) Kilpatrick and his newspaper had excavated an old and dubious doctrine called "interposition" and wrote extensively about it as if it were a viable strategy for insuring segregation. The doctrine grew largely out of the writings of John C. Calhoun, who referred to it as "the fundamental principle of our system." It held that a state had the right to "interpose" its "sovereignty" between the federal government and the people when it felt the federal government wasn't doing the right thing. A study of interposition, done at the time by the prestigious *Race Relations Law Reporter*, which was published during the Movement years by the Vanderbilt University school of law, explained that "interposition" (the study put quotation marks around the term) "assumes a legitimate authority in a state to suspend within its borders, for a time at least, the binding effect of an exercise of federal power — in this instance, the action of the Supreme Court of the United States . . . until such time as there has been submitted to the states, and ratified, a constitutional amendment giving the power against which the state has interposed its sovereignty."[4]

The state derives this power, according to the doctrine, from the fact that the federal government is but a creature of the states, created by the states' compact, and thus the states have the right to question that institution's actions and authority.

The Virginia legislature received its interposition bill in January, 1956. It declared that "this commonwealth is under no obligation to accept supinely an unlawful decree of the Supreme Court . . . based upon an authority which is not found in the Constitution . . . nor any amendment thereto. Rather this commonwealth is in honor bound to act to ward off the attempted exercise of power that does not exist lest other excesses be encouraged."[5] By the end of 1956, interposition resolutions had been passed in Virginia, South Carolina, Georgia, Alabama, and Mississippi.

Scholars at the time regarded the resolutions as mostly the strutting talk of political peafowl. Federal judge John Minor Wisdom of Louisiana, writing in a case a few years later in which Mississippi segregationists had raised the interposition argument, commented that the supremacy clause, found in Article VI of the U.S. Constitution, "makes hash of the so-called Doctrine of Interposition. All informed persons know that this political poppycock has never been recognized in a court of law."[6] All but the most ignorant politicians were aware of this all along, but there is no telling how many white Southerners believed the rhetoric and newspaper campaigns and thought that their statehouse leaders really would be able to "interpose themselves" between the "Southern way of life" and the incursions of the diabolical Supreme Court.

Another rhetorical flourish was unleashed on the floor of Congress in March, 1956, when the Declaration of Constitutional Principles was introduced. Better known as the Southern Manifesto, the declaration was signed by nineteen Southern senators and eighty-one of the region's representatives. It accused the Supreme Court of substituting "naked power for established law"; it defended segregation as based on "elemental humanity and common sense"; and it claimed the *Brown* decision was "destroying the amicable relations between the white and Negro races that have been created through ninety years of patient effort by the good people of both races," planting "hatred and suspicion where there has been heretofore friendship and understanding." It warned that "outside agitators are threatening immediate and revolutionary changes in our public school system." If that last happened, said the manifesto, the destruction of the public school system would certainly follow.

In the end, though, the manifesto retreated from an open declaration of war on the United States government. "We pledge ourselves to use all lawful means to bring about a reversal of this decision," said the signatories, who included such prominent politicians as Senators Richard B. Russell, J. William Fulbright, and Sam Ervin, and Representatives Wright Patman, Brooks Hays, Carl Vinson, and L. Mendel Rivers.[7]

In all the tons of rhetoric that issued from the white politicians in the weeks and months after the Supreme Court decision, those Southerners who viewed politics with a certain cynical detachment asked themselves, How much of this is sincere opposition to the federal government's intruding on the states' legitimate rights, how much is just political posturing, and how much is certifiable, authentic racism? And how much is just economics — an involuntary, instant reaction against anything that might disturb the cozy arrangement by which the South's whites had been enslaving their black neighbors, in one form or another, since 1619?

It was, of course, some of all of that. No doubt some of the learned or partially learned Southern politico-lawyers, such as North Carolina's Senator Sam Ervin, were genuinely distressed by what they perceived as unwarranted trespass by the federal government on the rights that the Constitution reserved for the states. (These politicians were invariably referred to, in the pompous hyperbole of Southern politics, as "great constitutional lawyers" and "celebrated constitutional scholars." Ervin only enhanced this excess by referring to himself as just a "simple country lawyer.") These men saw a dangerous trend that, if not halted, would lead to central control like that in communist countries. But there was racism and economic exploitation, too; for if there were none, why had the Southern states not eliminated segregation and begun a program of economic equality long before *on their own*, without the need for federal "usurpation"?

The truth of the matter is that racism and states' rights were, in the fifties and sixties, concepts that could not be weighed separately. Judge Johnson, who heard both concepts discussed almost continuously in his Montgomery courtroom, said later that "most people who talked about states' rights were equating the term with racial discrimination. So that's what states' rights meant in Alabama at that time, and I'm sure it was the same in Mississippi and Georgia. . . . And that's what states' rights, to some extent, still means."

And a great deal of it was political posturing, the words and actions of men desperate either to win elections rigged to prevent Negroes from participating or to keep from being thrown out of office by those more vocally rabid than themselves. Political power anywhere is a reward that tempts some men and women beyond all imagination, and in the South it was ever more so. The Southern states for the most part lacked the big-city political machinery that, lubricated with bribe money and rakeoffs, kept metropolises such as Boston and New York and Philadelphia humming, and most of them lacked the extra level of economic-political power that came from having an active collaboration between organized crime and some of the more essential unions.

But more rurally oriented Southern states did pretty well with what they had. Scandals were uncovered with great consistency in Southern public works programs, particularly highway departments. Alabama was notorious for this.[8] Because Southern religious fundamentalists opposed alcohol, the states imposed strict regulations on liquor, wine, and beer, and this provided ample opportunity for corruption. (And in places where alcohol was outlawed completely, robust relationships between politicians and bootleggers and moonshiners flourished. Mississippi led the field here.) Southern politicians, who could be counted on to portray themselves, particularly while campaigning, as not only friends of the "little man" but actually little men themselves, were generally quite willing to betray their "little" constituents in favor of sweet and personally lucrative deals with big business.

The dread of losing power was tempered by the politicians' knowledge that they could go a long way toward assuring political longevity by the simple, inexpensive, and (for most of them) ethically painless expedient of sounding as racist as they thought their white constituents wanted them to be, always being careful to sound more so than their competitors.

This was the easy part. Southern politicians have always been wonderful talkers, with a gift for political oratory that rivals the blarney of Irish-American officeholders. Since most of them believed in segregation anyway, and since demagoguery occupied a favored place in the history of Southern government, it was relatively easy to take the next step into out-and-out racism. The trick was to "out-nigger" your opponent, as the saying went — speak more harshly, promise more segregation, and, while you were at it, promise it in perpetuity. "Segregation forever" was the shout of a score of Southern politicians who knew full well that integration was inevitable.

Early in 1955, in a lawyer's office in Birmingham, a small group of Southern politicians gathered out of the public's view to discuss just that last problem: how to square the "never" of popular rhetoric with the "inevitable" of common sense.

Those attending, according to two of those present, included John Patterson, the attorney general of Alabama (and, in three years, to be its governor); an assistant attorney general on Patterson's staff who specialized in constitutional matters; Joe Johnston, a Birmingham lawyer who advised the state on constitutional matters and the host for the meeting; Charles Bloch, of Macon, Georgia, a "great constitutional lawyer" who had been a member of the state board of regents and head of the Georgia Bar Association; and Griffin Bell, a lawyer from Americus, Georgia, who later would become a federal judge and then attorney general of the United States under President Jimmy Carter. Both Bell and Bloch had skin-tight connections with Georgia politics. Mississippi politicians had been invited as well, but only Georgia and Alabama were represented at this initial meeting. (In a year or so, such strategy meetings with Southwide representation would become commonplace.)

The men met for half a day, John Patterson recalled later, and discussed what was likely to happen as a result of the *Brown* decision and what the states could do about it. Already looming very large on the horizon, at least in the mind of anyone who seriously thought about it (and Patterson was one of those), was the obvious fact that the principles enunciated by the court in *Brown* would inevitably be applied to other areas of segregation, such as public transportation, higher education, housing, employment, and justice in general. In short, to the entire way of life.

The consensus, said Patterson in an interview much later, was that "we could never legally win." The best the white leadership could do, the conferees concluded, was to fight a delaying battle.

And that is what they, and the Southern states in general, did. For years, the Southern white leadership threw roadblock after roadblock in desegregation's way, often totally confusing and bamboozling the federal government, which naively assumed that elected officials were honorable people who would keep their word and obey their oaths of office. Layer upon layer of administrative delays kept school boards from obeying the Supreme Court's order to develop implementation plans. Then, once these plans were finally submitted, aeons of courtroom palaver removed any possibility that a black six-year-old would even be in the school system by the time the classrooms were desegregated. By using rhetoric, skillfully manipulating their constituents, trying to out-nigger their white supremacist legislatures and challengers, and turning their great constitutional lawyers loose on the courtrooms, Southern white politicians — who knew that segregation was over — managed to keep that fact a secret from those who elected them.

-- ■

John Patterson did not start out political life as a racist, but rather as a crime fighter. In 1954, the summer of the *Brown* decision, his father won the Democratic party's nomination for Alabama attorney general. Albert L. Patterson's platform was to clean up Phenix City, a wide-open town across the Chattahoochee River from Columbus, Georgia, the home of Fort Benning. Just before the general election in the fall of 1954, Patterson was assassinated. The son, who was also his father's law partner, became the fill-in candidate. He won, and immediately scoured Phenix City clean.

John Patterson also started building a constituency for a run at the governorship. Between the time of Phenix City and 1958, when he defeated George Wallace for governor, Patterson became an implacable white supremacist. By the time he was elected, he was telling Negro schools they could not send their bands to march in his inaugural parade.[9]

Now Patterson is a judge in the Alabama Court of Criminal Appeals. He sounds mellower than he did in the Movement years — a condition that affects virtually all white politicians surviving from those times. He also seems of better temperament than he did back then, when the *New York Times* commented in a profile that "he is said to be humorless and rather rough in speech, although he has a lawyer's education."[10] Patterson spoke in a 1988 interview of the meeting he convened a few months after *Brown*, when he was Alabama's attorney general.

"In the first year that I was attorney general," he said, "there was a lot of interest in Alabama among certain people about what was in store for us in the integration of public facilities battle. And so we had a meeting." The meeting was the one Patterson held in Birmingham with the other "constitutional lawyers."

"It was very hush-hush. We didn't want anybody to know it. We didn't want any publicity. We wanted a cold-blooded — we wanted to lay it out on the table and discuss it like lawyers like to discuss things sometimes, to see where the hell we were, and to see if we could come to any conclusions about what we should do. We discussed this thing for about half a day. And we went into it.

"And if my recollection is right, when we left there that day, the consensus was amongst us that we could never legally win. And that the only thing that we could do was to fight a delaying battle in an effort to gain time so that people could adjust gradually to the changes without violence. It was understood amongst all of us that any efforts that we ever made to delay would be legal and aboveboard. There would be nothing undercover. It would be a legal and aboveboard delay. And this became our policy as attorneys general."

Patterson said he was relatively new to the field of race relations. "I was doing more work, really, in the law enforcement field and I was dabbling in the racial thing," he recalled. But he said he nevertheless felt that the delay he was engineering reflected the desires of the majority.

"The consensus of the white community in Alabama at that time — which, of course, is sixty percent of the people of Alabama — and my own belief at that time was that it was better at that time to operate a segregated education system in order to get the best possible education for both races, *at that time*. Now, I never believed in the segregated system because I thought that one race was inferior to another race. I never believed that and never have. But I thought that as a practical matter this was the best way to run the school system at *that particular time*, and to run it without violence and difficulty and to get the best possible education for the people. That was my belief, and that was the consensus, I think."

What Patterson and others created was a package of legislation, similar to that of other Southern states, that changed school laws to make it more difficult for the NAACP or other plaintiffs to win court victories quickly. "An effort was made to get legislation passed to decentralize control of the school systems to force the NAACP and others to have to file a multitude of suits," he said, "rather than taking us on in one suit and integrating all the schools at one time.

"Our whole program of delay was to decentralize, avoid confrontation, avoid going to court, avoid litigating with the government, because we knew we were going to lose. This was our whole idea.

"And it worked for me for eight years. It worked when I was attorney general, and it worked for me when I was governor, as far as delaying the ultimate day. Now, looking back, as to whether that was advisable or not from a long-range point of view was debatable."

Looking back, in fact, Patterson now thinks desegregation has been beneficial. "The thing has been a good thing," he said. But in the fifties, politicians were pulled between the rhetoric of their constituents (he didn't say so, but it was rhetoric the constituents got from the politicians themselves) and their own knowledge of what the outcome would be.

"I was confronted with groups like the White Citizens Council out here, and the Ku Klux Klan crowd — that's a vocal bunch, but they're very small. . . . The White Citizens Council and your average white voter were opposed to integrating the schools. And the average white Alabaman would say, you know, 'I'm not going to put up with this. I'm not goin' to do it. We're not going to integrate that school. I'd go down there and burn that thing down before I'll let it be integrated. I don't intend to send my child to an integrated school.'

"Of course, I always figured that when the day came that he'd have to go down there and stand up, that he wouldn't be there. But anyway, when the day came and when Judge Johnson integrated the schools of Alabama — when the day came that that fellow had to make a choice whether to send his kid down there to that integrated school or pull him out and dig up the money and send him to a private school, he'd just send him on down to that public school and cuss the federal judge." Patterson laughed.

As a result, said the former governor, not only are the schools of Alabama integrated now with relative peace, but so are other areas of the state's life. "Not only has the attitude changed in the schools, but it's changed everywhere else." He gestured in the direction of Montgomery's downtown business district, which adjoins the state office buildings. "The Elite Cafe, you know, has sort of been the political headquarters in this town all my life." He spoke of a Montgomery landmark that is the city's premier noontime gathering place for politicians and state workers. (There is an Elite in Jackson, Mississippi, too, and the habitués of both refer to them not as "Ay-LEET" but "EEE-lite." Both restaurants are operated by Greek-Americans who feed state government workers lunches that somehow combine continental and Southern rural tastes at reasonable prices.) Patterson said his father once introduced him at the Elite to "a young freshman legislator who walked in there looking like he was about fifteen years old, named George Wallace.

"Twenty years ago you wouldn't have gone in there with a black fellow for nothing. And today, you know, you go in there and blacks are in there, and they're there with whites. I have black friends that I take to lunch at the Elite. It's really a tremendous thing."

Patterson said he attended a symposium on the occasion of the twenty-fifth anniversary of the Montgomery bus boycott — it was held in the state's Archives and History Building, where black fellows could not have gone for nothing, either — and more than one participant said, "Why in the world couldn't we do this twenty-five years ago? Why couldn't we sit down twenty-five years ago around the table and work these things out?"

"And that's a great question mark. I have to agree that there must be something wrong with people who can't do that. Why *couldn't* we do that? Why couldn't we have seen the handwriting on the wall?

"Of course, it was a political thing. You know — I wanted to run again. You always want to run again. You always have that feeling.

"I wanted to run again. And I figured that if I wasn't well grounded on this question, and if I couldn't do what I could to maintain the system, that they'd turn me out for sure. Of course, I got turned out anyway! I ran for reelection and Lurleen [Wallace, George's wife] beat me. They'd superseded the issue and they beat me. So I got defeated anyhow." Patterson laughed again, not so loudly this time.

The conversation turned to Judge Frank Johnson, whose office was in the Federal Building a few hundred yards away. Central Montgomery is a compact place, with the state capitol, the courthouse — both state and federal — Martin Luther King's former church, and the Elite Cafe all pretty much within each other's shadows.

"I like Judge Johnson," said Patterson. "He and I are friends. And always have been. Even back when we were litigating a lot, and I was in his court a lot, we were always friends, and we always handled our business there for the state in a legal manner. And I think he appreciated that.

"Johnson is a stickler for the law. Johnson has always attempted, I think, to follow what he thought the Constitution of the United States required. And to follow the decisions of the United States Supreme Court. Of course, being a lawyer, I know — I don't necessarily fault him for what he did. I don't think he had any choice."

Patterson was asked if he was also saying that *he* had had no choice.

"Well," he replied, "I think under the circumstances, that's correct. Under the circumstances at the time, and the way I perceived it — I mean, I didn't particularly want to be a martyr for anybody's cause. I wanted to survive politically, and I wanted to run again. And in order to do so, I had to do what I thought the majority of the voters of Alabama expected me to do."

And did that extend to providing the white voters with a sort of theater, a playacting that told them there would always be segregation even when he knew it was all over?

"No question about it."

And for many of the black people, it was deadly serious theater?

"That's correct."

And a lot of the poorer whites never knew it was theater, did they?

"No. They thought that we were standing up for them, to the bitter end."

And when they were in the presence of someone who was "a great constitutional lawyer" they thought, "This guy's going to go out and whip those folks. He's going to win."

"That's right."

And massive resistance and interposition and all that had a lot more meaning to them than perhaps they did to you?

"Yes. The desire to survive politically, whether you do what is necessary to stay popular politically, or whether you do what the statesman ought to do and do what you think is right in the matter — it's a conflicting situation sometimes. It's a weakness of the system."

Arthur Shores, the black Birmingham lawyer who persevered through bombings and other acts of attempted intimidation, was frequently in the fifties and sixties the victim or intended victim of racists who put into action the words of some of their leaders. When a Patterson or a Wallace said "Never" and "Segregation forever," these people assembled sticks of dynamite, and a lot of them thought of Arthur Shores first. But Arthur Shores survived, just as John Patterson did, and today the walls of his law office are covered with certificates, citations, and proclamations, some of them signed by those who proclaimed "Never" in the old days and all of them attesting to Arthur Shores's sagacity and brilliance as a lawyer, an Alabaman, and a great human being. One of the certificates, the first one you see when you walk through the office door, is signed by John Patterson. Shores was asked how he felt now about people like Wallace and Patterson.

"Wallace wasn't basically a segregationist," he replied.

He was just a politician?

"Sure. Blacks had no political clout, and in order for a politician, a white politician, to be elected, he had to give the impression that he wanted to keep blacks in the status that they were.

"I knew Wallace. And when he became governor, two of his most important cabinet members were black. He appointed a black circuit judge here. He appointed a black woman a circuit judge down in the Black Belt counties. And, well, he did a lot of things."

So you don't dislike him?

"No, I don't. I don't. Now, for John Patterson — I never had much association with John at all. We've been together on occasion, though.

"The thing about it was, all of it was politics. Just politics. As long as blacks didn't have any clout — and they kept them where they *didn't* have any — then individuals who were not really segregationist at heart, in order for them to get what they wanted from the majority, they had to give the appearance that they were strict segregationists. The way they could maintain their position was to *appear*."

■ ————————————————————

NINE

─────────────── ■

FAITH IS NOT ENOUGH

■ ───────────────

A well-used staple of the rhetoric of delay was the white politicians' threat — it often sounded more like a promise — of violence if desegregation were allowed to occur.

The picture that the white political leaders liked to draw of themselves, and that they still draw today when they recall the Movement years, is one in which they heroically counselled against desegregating the public schools (or anything else) not because they believed desegregation was morally wrong but because continued segregation kept the white natives peaceful. Let there be some "race mixing," they liked to say, and violence would surely follow. The whites, they said, wouldn't stand for desegregation; they would take matters into their own hands. The politicians couldn't guarantee that they would be able to control the tempers of the "little people" should the law of the land be implemented. John Patterson put it in terms of fighting "a delaying battle . . . so that people could adjust gradually to the changes without violence." James P. Coleman of Mississippi now says that he saw the inevitability of desegregation way back, and sought in his public statements and actions as governor only to keep his state "from being burnt up in the conflagration." He also says that many of the statements he made back in the fifties about supporting "Mississippi institutions until they were otherwise declared unconstitutional" were designed "to keep the lid on, or at least keep the kettle from blowing out through the roof."

Harry Ashmore of Arkansas, who heard a good deal of this talk when assembling his data on the South's potential reaction to the *Brown v. Board of Education* decision, referred to it as the "blood in the streets" rationale. Politicians all over the South said the people "will never stand for this," and in many cases the media bought this argument, which provided the politicians with a way to avoid taking any sort of meaningful leadership role. "Blood in the streets" was particularly likely to flow if "outside agitators" (whose initials invariably spelled NAACP) were allowed to continue working up the local Negro population, which was well known to be docile and quite happy with the system in its segregated form.

The politicians were fond of combining the blood-in-the-streets warning with the integration-will-close-our-schools promise. In reality, there was precious little evidence that anything approaching the majority of the white Southern population (and no evidence that the black population) wanted to go that far. Indeed, when some public schools actually were closed, the white community showed clearly by its public outcries that it wanted them opened again.

But the close-the-schools threat was another valuable weapon in the arsenal of demagoguery, as were appeals to the white South's perceived fears that integrating grammar schools, which was widely called "mixing," would immediately lead to widespread interracial fornication, usually referred to by politicians as "amalgamation" and by hard-core supremacists as "mongrelization." This argument was based on the notion that has long run through the secret and not-so-secret depths of the Southern white male psyche that Negro males, despite their inferior intellect, hygiene, and so forth, were nevertheless irresistible sexually to white women — or, in this case, that fifth-grade white girls would fall immediately under the spell of their black male classmates and would be carrying mulatto babies by senior prom time.

John Patterson threw the demagogue's complete armory into one speech on January 20, 1959, the day he took the oath as governor of Alabama. By this time, Patterson was an experienced and articulate racial politician. He had defeated state judge George Wallace by the largest majority in Alabama's history thus far, and he had done so by being the consummate segregationist office seeker. Patterson had courted and gladly accepted the backing of the Ku Klux Klan, while Wallace had, of all things, the endorsement of the National Association for the Advancement of Colored People — perhaps the most soulful kiss of death a white Alabama politician of those years could have received. Wallace learned well from that campaign, and when he returned a term later to win the governorship, he was the racist's racist.[1]

Patterson's inaugural combined all the proven elements of supremacist oratory, from blood-in-the-streets to school-closing to federal-government-as-ogre to they're-going-to-marry-your-sister to outside-agitator to our-colored-are-happy, crowning it all with we-must-protect-our-way-of-life. He told the people of Alabama, both white and black, that their children should have access to equal school facilities,

> . . . but they must be segregated. I will oppose with every ounce of energy I possess and will use every power at my command to prevent any mixing of the white and Negro races in the classrooms of this state. I dedicate every capacity to prevent segregation in the schools. . . . The people of this state will not tolerate nor support integrated schools, and any attempt by the federal government or anyone else to integrate the schools of this state by force would cause turmoil, chaos and violence, and would result in the destruction of our public school system.
>
> There can be no compromise in this fight. There is no such thing as a "little integration." The determined and ruthless purpose of the race agitators and such organizations as the NAACP is to bring about as fast as possible an amalgamation of our society. They seek to destroy our culture, our heritage, and our traditions. If

we compromise or surrender our rights in this fight, they
will be gone forever, never to be regained or restored.

Patterson asked the legislature to give him the power to close
public schools that might be ordered desegregated by the federal
courts, and to enact a law cutting off funds to any school that
might be integrated.

> I am well aware that as governor of Alabama I am
> the governor of all the people of Alabama, white and Ne-
> groes alike. The overwhelming majority of the Negro cit-
> izens of this state are opposed to integration of the
> races. . . . The trouble between the races is being caused
> by a handful of race agitators who are not natives of this
> state, but who have been sent here to stir up racial trou-
> ble and strife.

Alabama's new governor threatened Negroes with the loss of
even segregated schools if they failed to repel those who were
trying to interest them in integration. "If you do not do so, and
these agitators continue at their present pace," he declared, "in a
short time you will have no public school system at all. Our public
schools, once destroyed and closed down, may not be reopened in
your lifetime or mine. Our children will suffer the consequences."2

Now, many years after the cries of "agitators" and "amalgamation"
and "never" (and, most important, many years after black Southerners won for themselves the right to vote), the politicians acknowledge what many have always suspected — that they were
engaged in playacting. Southern journalists and other observers
said at the time that they suspected much of what issued from the
statehouses of the South was a particularly grisly form of show
business, designed to soothe and retain the votes of the white electorate. The politicians' statements were simply expedient things
to say, positions as easily adopted and later cast aside as stands on
agricultural price supports or the need to eradicate the scourge of
fire ants.

Harold Fleming, the director of the Southern Regional Council in those years, said that different politicians felt varying degrees

of certainty about what they told the electorate. The "vindictive-ness with which [Herman] Talmadge pursued the people who didn't agree with him" in Georgia, he said, "sort of makes you feel that he had his back in it more than most. I mean, he had people full-time on his payroll who were doing nothing but harassing and spying on the so-called race mixers." Talmadge's father, Eugene, said Fleming, seemed to be relatively free of true antiblack senti-ment. Other politicians seemed deeply and incurably white su-premacist; they appeared incapable of determining where the rhetoric left off and true racism began.

Senator Strom Thurmond of South Carolina was one of these. When Southern members of Congress composed their Southern Manifesto in 1956, Thurmond was its most ardent supporter. Harry Ashmore, on leave from the *Arkansas Gazette* to work on the pres-idential campaign of Democrat Adlai Stevenson, consulted Thur-mond's Senate colleague, Olin Johnson, in hopes that Johnson would persuade Thurmond (then a Democrat) to downplay the manifesto at least until after the party primaries, since it could only harm the Democratic candidate in much of the nation. "It's no use trying to talk to Strom," Ashmore quoted Johnson as telling him. "He *believes* that shit."[3]

"It's not just the politicians," said Harold Fleming, who con-fessed to feeling "a little scornful" of all sorts of white professional, legal, educational, and financial leaders who once sounded like dedicated segregationists but who now have changed their tunes. "Whenever I go back home to Atlanta, and I see and hear these recognizable figures, talking very piously about race and giving each other awards for their good works, I can't help but think, Where have all the segregationists gone? There *used* to be a lot of them down there. I can't find anybody who acknowledges ever hav-ing been one."

Much of the resistance may have been theater, but it was a theater of reality. Rhetoric designed to create delay produced schools that really closed and children, both white and black, who really spent part of their formative years in ignorance. As resis-tance spread into other areas, and as violent racists interpreted the rhetoric as license to resist integration by any means, real people lost their lives. An uncounted but very real number of Southerners, white as well as black, were denied the opportunity to develop to their best potential because of the pronouncements that flowed so effortlessly from governor's mansion and legislative floor. And the damage was made all the worse by the fact that white institutions such as the bar, organized religion, finance, education both higher and lower, and the press did not exert the pressures that could have fostered more moderation on the part of the politicians.

――――――――――――――――   ■

Judge Frank Johnson was well acquainted with the politicians' argument that they were engaging in delaying tactics because they wanted to minimize white-led violence. But he did not buy it at the time, and he does not buy it now.

"That's rationalization," he said. "I never had the lawyers for people who opposed desegregation in a public facility come before me and say, 'Judge, give us a year to work this out. Give us two years to work it out.' A lawyer argued this before me in a sports desegregation case in my courtroom, on the second floor of this building, where I tried all these cases. He said, 'There'll be blood running in the field if you put whites playing against blacks.'

"That's not a delay argument. That's the argument that we got in all of these cases. . . . It wouldn't have bothered me if they'd have come up and said, 'We need some time. This changes a way of life in our state, and we can work it out, and we will take affirmative steps to work it out in a manner in which there'll be no likelihood of violence and we'll eliminate, by doing it, a lot of the resentment that has grown and may continue to grow toward the federal judiciary and the federal government itself.' But that's not the public position that they took. So for them to say it now — to say that 'we realized it,' and then to look back and know that that's not the position that they took, doesn't give me a reaction that's very favorable. . . .

"That's what John Patterson was saying. When you analyze and evaluate what he told you, it was that 'I was willing to take a position that I knew was wrong in order to preserve and perpetuate my political career.' And that's just not a very good position to take."

It was, however, a position that was taken widely throughout the South.

"No question about it. It was. That made it harder. Made it harder on people, not only just federal judges. Made it harder on people who were living under an atmosphere like that."

∎ ─────────────────────────

In the first four years following the school desegregation decision, Southern legislatures passed 196 laws designed to overcome or circumvent the ruling.[4] The specially appointed state commissions returned with their studies and the legislatures adopted their recommendations, which fell generally into the categories of pupil placement laws, school closings, and devices for using public funds to shift support from public schools to newly created private ones — which would, of course, be free to continue the tradition of segregation.

The pupil placement laws usually required that local boards of education control the assignment of pupils to public schools, using several criteria, none of which mentioned race specifically. These included schoolroom capacity, availability of transportation facilities, geographical location of the school, pupil's residence, and (from a Tennessee law) "the psychological effect of the attendance of such pupil at a particular school." There was ample leeway in such laws to guarantee perpetual segregation. Furthermore, the laws could be used to keep Negro challengers in court almost forever as they satisfied the legal doctrine of exhausting their remedies at the administrative level before seeking relief in federal court.[5]

The resistance legislation usually also contained school closing laws. These allowed the governor or others to act to close public schools if a certain trigger were squeezed — such as the receipt of an integration order from a federal court. The Georgia law, passed February 3, 1959, provides an example. Section 1 reads:

> Whenever the Governor shall determine, from such facts as he may find to exist, of the sufficiency of which he shall be the sole judge, that the continued operation of any public school . . . is likely to result in or cause violence or public disorder in the community in which such school is situated, or that it is necessary to preserve

the good order, peace and dignity of the State, or any subdivision thereof, that any such school be closed, he shall make public proclamation of such findings, and such school shall thereupon be closed.[6]

Tuition plans, too, were part of the package. States promised tuition grants to pupils who either didn't want to attend integrated public schools or who attended private schools because their public schools had been abolished. And the states enacted a plethora of other laws intended to thwart desegregation. The Nashville board of education filed a "desegregation" plan with federal court in 1957 that would have provided for *three* sets of schools. One would be for Negroes, one for whites, and the third "for those students whose parents prefer that their children attend schools available to both Negro and White children." An annual "parents preference census" would be conducted to sort everybody out. The court quashed that idea quickly. A Georgia law provided that "contributions" to private schools could be deducted from state income tax — a form of bribery for whites who might waver in their dedication to segregation.[7]

The chief weapon contained in all the legislation was delay. Put off a final decision, went the reasoning, put off the day when those little black children walk up to the front of the formerly all-white school, and political tranquillity will persist, at least in the white community. And political longevity will persist for the politicians, as well.

The delaying strategy worked well for the segregationists. They knew that once a challenge to their laws or actions reached the federal courts, they would be overruled. But that moment was far off in the future — even farther when the lower federal judges were segregationists, too, as many of them were. The case of *Borders et al. v. Rippy et al.* demonstrated this clearly.

Hilda Ruth Borders, a black child, sought to force Edwin Rippy, president of the board of trustees of the Dallas, Texas, Independent School District, to admit her to public school on a nonsegregated basis. When the case reached the U.S. Court of Appeals for the Fifth Circuit, three years after the *Brown* decision, Judge Richard T. Rives, in his decision, summarized the events so far.

More than a year after the *Brown* decision, wrote Rives, the Dallas board asked its superintendent of schools to conduct an "intensive study" of schools, students, teachers, administrators, parents, athletic programs, curricula, "relative intelligence quotient scores," and "social life of the children within the school." The board, said the judge, declared that "it will be impractical to attempt integration until these studies have been completed," and that therefore there should be no desegregation in the fall of 1955.

A year after *that*, in June, 1956, the board issued another delaying statement. "The board recognizes its responsibility to implement the decree of the Supreme Court," it said, "but it reaffirms its studied opinion that it would be derelict in this regard if it ordered an alteration in the status of its schools until its understanding of the problems involved is as comprehensive as possible and its plans for such changes are completed." The board could not "in good conscience" accept the responsibility of carrying out the Supreme Court order, it said, "until it has had sufficient time within which to formulate plans which must be to the best interests of this school district, its children, and the community. Therefore . . . the board . . . instructs the Superintendent of Schools to continue a segregated school system for the school year 1956–1957."

When Hilda Ruth Borders took her suit into federal district court, the local judge (who apparently had not got the word about the death of *Plessy v. Ferguson*) ruled that white and black schools in Dallas were substantially equal. He found that the Supreme Court's 1955 *Brown* implementation ruling required that school boards and lower courts engage in planning on how they should fulfill the order, noted that no planning had yet taken place in the present case, and dismissed the suit on *those* grounds! The Fifth Circuit Court of Appeals quickly reversed this bizarre ruling and sent it back to the district level.

The indefatigable district judge then ruled that it would be a "civil wrong" to admit Negroes to white schools that were already crowded. He dismissed the case again so that the school board might have "ample time . . . to work out this problem." The plaintiffs returned to the court of appeals, which overruled the district judge again and sent the case back to him with directions to order the school board to desegregate "with all deliberate speed."

Judge Rives, in his court of appeals decision, pointed out what any competent federal district judge (let alone any local school administrator) should have known: "So long as they are excluded from any public school of their choice solely because of their race or color the plaintiffs are being denied their constitutional rights." Rives said the appeals court was not impugning the school board's motives. "Faith by itself, however, without works, is not enough," he wrote. Quoting from the Supreme Court, he added, "There must be 'compliance at the earliest practicable date.' "[8]

Between May, 1954, and May, 1957, there were no court decisions on public school desegregation in Georgia, Alabama, and Mississippi. And delaying tactics were widely used in the Southern states in higher education, as well. Georgia tried to require applicants to its colleges and university to produce vouchers of good character from alumni, and Louisiana required them from county school officials — thus practically insuring that no Negroes could get them. The courts eventually knocked these obstacles down, but again, there was much delay and many potential students were denied.

The politicians' pronouncements about never giving in to federal tyranny and so forth were widely reported by the press, one of whose basic rules is that whatever a prominent person says is news, even if it is demonstrably false or calculated or irresponsible. But the Southern governors and their lieutenants were not the only ones engaging in rhetoric. A torrent of oratory, ranging from eloquent to obscene, flowed from the leaders of private segregationist organizations, ministers of the gospel, and diverse citizens who appointed themselves spokesmen for the Cause. Another deluge of pseudoscientific "findings," similar to (and in some cases based on) the rash of brain-weight "studies" that had appeared in the forties, entered the marketplace of Southern racism as well. Rarely did members of the moderate white community publicly and actively challenge these assertions. They seemed more inclined to just wait and let the white supremacist rhetoric run its course —

which it did, eventually, but while it was running a great deal of harm was done.

The tone of much of this privately produced oratory is familiar. It criticized the Negro as subhuman, blasted the federal government for its usurpation of rights that lawfully belonged to the states, and warned that if a mighty resistance were not mounted, Southerners might soon become the color of café au lait. Private citizens often took their cues from the politicians' speeches. When John Patterson was governor of Alabama, a Montgomery resident wrote him to express his admiration for "your valiant efforts to circumvent integration." The writer was wise enough to see that the object of his praise was trying to find a way around integration, rather than to defeat it. He enclosed a copy of a letter he had written to the *Saturday Evening Post,* which began by discussing "labor domination and Centralized Socialism" and quickly moved to "mongrelization, which inevitably must be the result of FORCED INTEGRATION."[9]

Austin Earle Burges of Texas provided a handy guide to racism in his little book *What Price Integration,* published in 1956. Burges, a Louisianian who moved to Texas in 1907, at the age of sixteen, was a newspaperman, biology teacher, interviewer with the state employment commission, and, after *Brown,* the first secretary of the Associated Citizens Councils of Texas, a Citizens Council group. He was, he wrote, a lifelong friend of black people: "Yes, I like Negroes. I also like children; but that does not keep me from recognizing that they are children and have the traits that are characteristic of children."

That was just a warm-up to Burges's explanation of why Negroes should not be allowed to attend schools with whites. Burges wrote that he had learned, largely through his experience in interviewing them for jobs, that Negroes were "notoriously lax in their sex morals"; "proverbially careless about property rights"; lacking in honor and integrity; "proverbially indolent"; given to "careless, slovenly speech"; more afflicted with disease than whites; mentally inferior to whites; "generally . . . unable to deal with abstractions"; consumed by a love for gambling; and marked by contentiousness. Furthermore, wrote Burges, "Negroes, as a group, are definitely deficient in a sense of time and spacial relations. I have often noticed their haziness about time when I was interviewing them."[10] Burges apparently did not consider that any Negro being interviewed by him might consider it prudent to be hazy about everything.

While such diatribes seem absurd now and did then to many people, Southerners as well as others, they provided reassurance and food for thought for many white Southerners who didn't want integration and who were searching for some sort of "expert" support for their feelings. These Southerners were also assured by statements issued by people with impressive-sounding initials after their names. Southerners have always treated academic honorifics with a superabundance of respect; some of the most fanatical segregationists referred to Martin Luther King, Jr., as "Dr. King," almost without thinking about it.

W. Critz George was one academic who enjoyed a lengthy popularity among that subspecies of racists who specialized in proving that Negroes were biologically and mentally inferior to whites. George was emeritus professor of histology and embryology and former head of the University of North Carolina's anatomy department. In the mid-fifties, when he was an active researcher in the UNC medical school, he organized the Patriots of North Carolina, Inc., a group similar to the Citizens Councils.

George had a habit of popping up in print to say that Negroes were biologically inferior, claiming such purported scientific evidence as the "facts" that one of the brain's tissues was thinner in the average Negro than in the average white and that Negroes have lighter brains than whites. While the Negro "should be treated with courtesy, consideration and generosity," wrote George in one of his tracts, he should never be allowed to enter the white social sphere. George, who was happy to share his theory with practically anyone who would listen, sold it for three thousand dollars in report form to the state of Alabama under the Patterson administration. He threw in the extra "scientific" observation that "integration is not Christian." When asked by a reporter to explain this, George replied, "Integration is evil. Doing evil is not Christian."

Other members of the scientific community were quick to disassociate themselves from the likes of George's work. The

American Association of Physical Anthropologists passed a resolution deploring "the misuse of science to advocate racism," and the chair of Emory University's psychology department said, "No moderately reputable psychologist could come up with these conclusions."[11]

The pronouncements, both official and nongovernmental, would not have had the force they did if the federal government had taken a more positive role in seeking compliance with the school decision and in preparing the South for the desegregation that was obviously on the way in other areas, such as transportation, housing, employment, and justice.

But the national government provided opportunities that were too tempting for the segregationists to ignore: Washington expected Southern racists to behave like gentlemen, negotiate honestly, and keep their word; it expected school boards and governors to act in good faith in establishing their own deadlines to meet goals that many of them vowed publicly they would never seek.

This characteristic of the federal government to allow itself to be gulled by the Southern segregationists got a thorough workout with the Little Rock school crisis of the fall of 1957. In a sense, Little Rock was a test of Washington's feelings about violence. The segregationists had already gotten some mileage out of wild promises of "blood in the streets" if desegregation were allowed to occur; now they found that the government had an amazingly high tolerance for the real stuff.

It was not until the mobs had pretty much taken over the streets outside Central High School and succeeded in keeping the nine Negro children out of the classrooms, as well as successfully challenging the federal court order for desegregation, that President Eisenhower finally acted by sending the Airborne in. Governor Orval Faubus and the segregationists seemed never to let up, however. After desegregation had actually occurred, the Little Rock school board asked a federal judge to suspend the desegregation plan for two and a half years, and the judge agreed. After he was overruled by the Supreme Court, Faubus closed the high schools to prevent what he called "violence and disorder." The schools remained closed during the 1958–59 academic year.

Early in 1959, a reporter from the *Chicago Daily News* told President Eisenhower at a news conference that "many persons feel you could exert a strong moral backing for desegregation if you said that you personally favored it," and asked why, if the president did favor it, he had not said so. Eisenhower's reply was: "I do not believe it is the function or indeed it is desirable for a president to express his approval or disapproval of any Supreme Court decision. His job is, for which he takes an oath, is to execute the laws."[12]

A president can (or can not) exert moral suasion, but a Justice Department can enforce laws and bring lawsuits. However, the Justice Department in this period, and later, seemed not much more eager to get involved than Eisenhower. The department had a civil rights section starting in 1939, and since passage of the 1957 Civil Rights Act it had a civil rights division, with the power to bring lawsuits in voting rights cases on behalf of aggrieved citizens. But the department was reluctant to use its powers. It viewed its mission as one that should be performed under what is called a "policy of strict self-limitation." The policy reflected the thinking that prosecutions in civil rights cases involved somewhat delicate relationships between federal and state authorities. "Furthermore," said a 1958 study of the Justice Department policy, "the defendant may often be a state or local official of some prominence in the community, whereas the complainant is not necessarily a respected member of the [presumably white] community."[13] The department required all U.S. attorneys to consult with headquarters before initiating lawsuits or even investigations, with the result that few prosecutions were brought. Most of the progress that was made, during these years and later, came through the efforts of private citizens and civil rights organizations that took tremendous risks and incurred enormous expenses, with little help from the national government.

Federal judges were the willing instruments of delay in a number of places, as in the case of Hilda Ruth Borders of Dallas. In Prince Edward County, Virginia, one of the most hard-core areas of resistance, a judge ruled against setting a finite date for implementation and added: "Action which might cause mixing the schools at this time, resulting in closing them, would be highly and permanently injurious to children of both races. . . . At this time the children of both races are being afforded opportunities for an education under an adequate system that has been formulated over the years."[14] Such patent disregard for the law of the land on the part of one of the nation's judges stood no chance of surviving beyond the appeals level, but it delayed desegregation. It gave local white supremacists hope that massive resistance really would work, and it gave politicians more reason to engage in the theater of Never. And black and white children and their parents who could have benefited from truly equal education were denied the experience.

Some (though by no means all, or even a majority) of the federal judges, many of them Southern whites themselves, consistently refused to play the delaying game and saw easily through the machinations of posturing legislatures and governors, scheming school boards, and grandiloquent great constitutional lawyers. Indeed, it is perhaps *because* they were white Southerners themselves, and familiar with the way Southern politics and politicians operated, that some of the federal judges did such consistently good jobs. One Alabama civil rights leader commented, "The federal judiciary was a sign of hope." Frank Johnson, a native of Winston County, Alabama, he said, was a fine example of this: "Frank Johnson was one who ruled against the mores of his own surroundings and survived. Judge Hobart Groomes of Birmingham, also. It took a lot of guts to take some of the stands that he did, and [to make] the rulings that he issued." Richard Rives of Alabama was another outstanding example. And there were others. When school officials in Charlottesville, Virginia, did nothing to implement *Brown*, a federal judge there commented that two years had passed, summarized all the inaction, pointed out that the school officials had shown no evidence that they were willing to comply ever, and ordered the schools desegregated right away.[15]

One of the tasks the judges were often called upon to perform was taking the blame for desegregation. Many a politician who knew that delay was at an end found himself deserted by courage and welcomed the opportunity to turn the matter over to a federal judge, whom he knew would deflect the condemnation of the segregationists and provide a convenient target for the politician's own denunciations.

■

"If there's any one big mistake of my administration," said former governor John Patterson, "it was not making some effort to bring the black community into the Alabama political process. This thing was so polarized when I was elected governor that there were no moderates left. There was no middle ground. You were either on one side or the other. The black community had been practically excluded from the political process in Alabama.

"I was in a position at that time, being the spokesman for the segregation forces and having the background that I had at that time — I could, in my judgment, have made some positive moves in the direction of bringing the right to vote to the black citizens of Alabama and making them a part of the political process.

"I could have done it, and I believe that if there is any one big mistake, it was a mistake in not doing that."

Patterson was asked what specific actions he could have taken. Appoint the usual commission?

"No, no. You'd have had to have moved toward registering people. You could have appointed boards of registrars who were willing to register qualified blacks. You could have made some inroads. And *particularly* you could have made some inroads in those counties where there was less friction.

"You know, all this is hindsight, of course. It didn't do me any good to not do it. I was defeated." He laughed. "As George Wallace said, his *wife* beat me. It didn't do me any good.

"But, you know, there is no question — I have always believed, from the very beginning, that the black citizen has a right to participate in the political process. It's like everybody else. I've always believed that. I've never disbelieved that. It had reached the point, though, that by the time I was elected governor that they did not participate anywhere. . . . Unfortunately, it was such a political situation here at that time, and the thing had become so polarized politically, that there was no middle ground. There was no ground for compromising without grave risk to your political career. And really, that's what kept people here from possibly doing something themselves.

"We are very fortunate that we had a system whereby the federal judge could ultimately be the valve that made it possible to bring about change that could not be done politically.''

The federal judge was the valve, but wasn't he also often made the goat?

''Yes. The valve *and* the goat.''

''They failed to take affirmative action,'' said Judge Johnson, his face as stern as any courtroom judge's, ''in the cases where the law was clear, and they punted their problems to the federal court.''

It is human nature for people to do so, he added. ''Particularly with politicians. Patterson wasn't the only one that did it. George Wallace did it. A lot of state judges did it. And I don't condemn them for that. I have *criticized* them for it. But if you think that your status and your tenure are important enough — these are strong words, but I think they're applicable — to compromise your integrity, then that's the route you go.''

Judge Johnson was asked if he could imagine a situation in which he would go that route.

''Well,'' he said, ''I can't imagine a situation where I could function as a politician.''

■ ———————————————

TEN

NOTHING PERSONAL, YOU UNDERSTAND

With inaction, court-approved delay, and obfuscation even on the Washington level, a lack of constructive leadership in the state-house, and widespread reticence on the part of most of those who considered themselves moderate whites, desegregation took a real drubbing during the later part of the fifties. The civil rights movement was broadening and strengthening itself, but so too was the resistance. The segregationists were devising ways other than pupil placement and school closing laws to frustrate their enemies. Economic and physical intimidation expanded, especially in the Deep South, while politicians and professional segregationists found new ways to say "Never."

Resistance became a self-generating thing. The politicians encouraged the hard-core racists, and the hard-core racists influenced the political climate, silenced many of the moderates, and made the politicians feel they had better do nothing that could be characterized as "soft on segregation" by those who wanted their jobs. What had started out as Virginia-style oratory about John C. Calhoun and "interposition" turned quickly into state-sponsored repression.

*   *   *

As the Movement matured through the sixties, the National Association for the Advancement of Colored People would become known as one of the more conservative organizations working for integration and equal rights. Groups such as the Congress of Racial Equality and the Student Nonviolent Coordinating Committee embodied the militant younger wing of the Movement, and they and officials of the Southern Christian Leadership Conference were wont to criticize the NAACP, at least privately, as too mired in bureaucracy. But to the white supremacists of the late fifties, the NAACP was the enemy incarnate. It was the organization that dragged state attorneys general and other "great constitutional lawyers" into court in their Palm Beach suits and Panama hats and courtly drawls and humiliated them before the eyes of their constituents. It was the NAACP that was directly responsible for marching those well-scrubbed little black children up the steps into the white schools. (Actually, it was the NAACP and its affiliated, but separate, organization, the NAACP Legal Defense and Educational Fund, Inc. — the Inc. Fund — but the segregationists rarely bothered with such distinctions.)

And so it was the NAACP that the resistance sought to eradicate, to drive from the region, to restrain from its continued meddling with the "Southern way of life." This was an ambition roughly comparable to convincing all Negroes they should go back to Africa.

The NAACP *was* a formidable opponent in those years, and not only because of its ability to send first-rate lawyers into courtrooms with well-researched lawsuits against segregation. The NAACP was everywhere in the South, if not in actual meeting rooms and offices then in the minds of black people. Even on Mississippi plantations there were Negroes who were known — to other Negroes, at least — as the people to see on NAACP matters. L. C. Dorsey remembered a couple from a neighboring plantation who would drive from place to place at night, recruiting for the organization. "To avoid detection," she said, "they did this without turning their truck lights on."

An opinion written by two federal court judges in the fifties included an objective status report on the organization. The

NAACP operated in forty-four states through approximately one thousand community branches. Dues started at $2 a year and went up to $500, the latter for a life membership. Other funds came from special campaigns and contributions. In 1956 the organization received almost $600,000 in income.

Delegates from the branches met at the annual convention to set policy and programs, which were executed by the board of directors and the staff that it supervised. Activities at the state level were overseen by state conferences. These state groups maintained legal staffs, made up of lawyers living in various communities in the state. When an appropriate legal case arose, the state conference authorized lawyers, usually members of the legal staff, to bring suit. These lawyers were compensated for their expenses and given per diems. The fees were never large — certainly not in comparison to the sums spent by state governments to fight desegregation.

The Inc. Fund, which operated from offices in New York City, had a small staff. It kept lawyers on annual retainers in Richmond, Dallas, Los Angeles, and Washington, and also used local lawyers for research. Some one hundred lawyers around the country were on call for Inc. Fund work, as were social scientists who volunteered their help. The Inc. Fund was a nonprofit organization that, unlike the NAACP, did not seek to influence legislation. It obtained its money from contributions and luncheon and dinner benefits.[1] Its reputation as an expert in research and litigation was superior to that of the NAACP, and over the years resentment built at the parent organization because of this.

White Alabama had tried as early as 1955 to eliminate the NAACP's ability to function. The legislature passed a law, over the veto of Governor James Folsom, placing excessively high licensing fees on organizations that were soliciting membership in Black Belt Wilcox County. For those who couldn't figure out what that meant, the bill's sponsor explained that otherwise, "it would be very easy for the NAACP to slip into Wilcox County and teach the Negroes undesirable ideas."[2]

In 1956 Georgia's rabidly segregationist attorney general, Eugene Cook, asked the legislature to restrict organizations that promoted litigation. Cook alleged that some NAACP officers "have communist or subversive records," and added that "it has been demonstrated beyond any doubt that the NAACP is the enemy of the South, that it is the most potent enemy of our segregated system of public schools, and that its leadership represents the most effective sponsors of insidious and unconstitutional civil rights measures."[3] Within a year, legislation had been passed in Georgia, Alabama, and Louisiana seeking to obtain information about NAACP finances and membership, and soon Mississippi, South Carolina, Virginia, Florida, Arkansas, and Texas joined the list. The politicians were especially interested in getting the names of white supporters of the organization.

The Arkansas attorney general released a six-point plan of attack against the NAACP in 1959. Most such offensives avoided mentioning the enemy by name, lest some sort of liability be incurred, but this one was unusually straightforward. The attack was based, said the attorney general, on the simple principle of "No NAACP, no NAACP-inspired lawsuits, no federal integration orders, no more Little Rocks." Among the six steps, he said, should be the formation of "economic safety committees" in local communities to ferret out "troublemakers" and take "necessary steps to effect economic reprisals against such people."[4]

The anti-NAACP actions, like school integration circumventions, were soon dissolved by the federal courts, but again, time passed and the segregationists gained the luxury of delay. In Alabama, the state sued the NAACP for refusing to comply with laws requiring it to register as a foreign (that is, non–state chartered) corporation. Then the state went after the organization's papers and membership lists. A state court sided with the attorney general, John Patterson, in all of this, and when the NAACP refused to produce the documents, it was found in contempt and hit with a hefty fine.

When the case went to the Supreme Court, the high court returned an unusual verdict: "The immunity from state scrutiny of membership lists which the Association claims on behalf of its members is here so related to the right of the members to pursue their lawful private interest privately and to associate freely with others in so doing as to come within the protection of the

Fourteenth Amendment." It was, observers noted, a novel extension of judicial thinking. The respected *Race Relations Law Reporter* said it was "a new constitutional right — or at least a new official concept of constitutional law — called 'freedom of association.' "[5] This pro–civil rights theory, generated by the actions of the very white supremacists who opposed it, took a while being absorbed into white Alabama judicial consciousness; the state supreme court continued holding the NAACP in contempt, despite the U.S. Supreme Court's ruling, until eventually it gave up.

■

John Patterson was the architect of harassment of the NAACP in Alabama, and, in fact, the landmark Supreme Court decision bears his name — as the loser.

"It became quite apparent to me," he said in 1988, "from what was happening in Virginia, that the prime mover in this thing was the NAACP and that the NAACP Legal Defense and Educational Fund was putting up the money and recruiting the plaintiffs. I don't think that this was my idea originally; I think I could have gotten that idea from somebody else. But anyway, I finally concluded that there was a possibility of putting them out of business in Alabama because they had failed to comply with the corporate domestication statutes, being a foreign corporation doing business in Alabama."

Was this, he was asked, also another delaying tactic?

"Right. Oh, yes."

So if the NAACP had been a lobbying group for an association of railroads —

"We wouldn't have paid any attention to them. This was part of the delaying tactics."

As far as he knew, said the former governor, the NAACP was really an honorable, legal organization. "I knew the leaders. I knew their lawyers, and I knew they were honorable people. There was no question about it."

His opposing lawyers were Robert Carter, general counsel of the NAACP (now a federal judge in New York City), Fred Gray from Tuskegee, and "a fellow from Birmingham, Arthur Shores."

Patterson was reminded that Shores now has a framed certificate in his office, signed by Patterson and attesting to Shores's high quality. Shores was, said Patterson, "a fine fellow. Very fine fellow."

But you were trying to put his organization out of business?

Patterson laughed. "Nothing personal, you understand," he said. "This was a bitter battle, a bitter political thing."

Patterson's attack on the NAACP, he explained with a grin, was founded partly on a New York State case in which a chapter of the Ku Klux Klan was successfully prosecuted for doing business without properly registering as a foreign corporation. The New York law, passed in 1923, was aimed solely at the Klan. It ordered the registration and production of membership lists of any association of twenty or more members which "required an oath as a prerequisite or condition of membership, other than a labor union or a benevolent order." When some college fraternities registered under the law, the New York legislature amended it to narrow its application even more closely to exclude everything but the Klan.[6]

"That was absolutely on all fours with what we wanted to do then to the NAACP," said Patterson. "We used that case as the basis for our suit to oust the NAACP from Alabama. The whole idea of that thing was to dry up those legal funds and to make it more difficult for them to prosecute those cases.

"And it worked. We had a very favorable circuit judge here who granted the injunctions. But there was no question; they had not complied with the corporate laws." Those laws, he said, required a foreign corporation wishing to do business in Alabama to register with the secretary of state, designate a local person as a representative to receive legal papers, and arrange with the state revenue department for payment of taxes and fees.

"And they did not do that. New York ousted the Ku Klux Klan on the same basis, and so we ousted the NAACP. They refused to give up their records, and we wanted their records to show what they were doing in Alabama, and of course we wanted to look at their membership." Patterson laughed.

Why?

"Well, we felt like there were people that were members of that thing that didn't want us to know that they were members. There was a lot of white folks that were members of that thing." He laughed again. "So we wanted to see who the members were."

The NAACP at first tried to work out a compromise and then refused, and an Alabama circuit judge held the organization in contempt and levied a $100,000 fine.[7] Then the U.S. Supreme Court found, as Patterson phrased it, "that the black people of Alabama didn't have the power themselves to exercise their constitutional rights, and the NAACP was the vehicle by which they exercised their constitutional rights, and therefore, the NAACP, Incorporated, was entitled to essentially the same protection that they would be entitled to as individuals.

"Which was really a new law. It was a landmark decision. . . . A very interesting case. . . . You find a lot in that case. I've cited that case as an authority since I've been on the appellate court here." The former governor of Alabama laughed again.

■ ————————————————

NAACP and other civil rights lawyers were attacked in other ways, as well. NAACP attorneys who worked on the Autherine Lucy school desegregation case at the University of Alabama were threatened with a $6 million libel suit. Constance Baker Motley recalled later that she and the Inc. Fund's chief lawyer, Thurgood Marshall, "didn't dare go back. As Thurgood always said, he only had five million dollars to give them, and they wanted six! Anyway, the point was that if we had gone there, we'd go before an Alabama jury, in Alabama. They would certainly rule with the plaintiffs, and there we would have a judgment against us that would have been enforceable against us in New York. There was no question about it. So we couldn't go to Alabama." Then came the state's suit and contempt action against the NAACP, and Motley and others were effectively prevented from working in Alabama for almost a decade, until 1963.

Several states passed laws defining and outlawing wicked-sounding practices such as champerty (encouraging litigation); maintenance ("officious intermeddling in a suit that no way belongs to one"); barratry ("exciting groundless judicial proceedings" with malicious intent to annoy); and running and capping (soliciting business, or at least soliciting it in ways that nonintegrationist lawyers didn't employ). In addition, state bar associations bore down on what they chose to call "unprofessional conduct." Mississippi passed a law requiring out-of-state lawyers to be "cleared" by the Mississippi Bar Association, and the Louisiana Bar Association reprimanded a lawyer in 1955 who sought to enroll black children in a white school.[8]

The segregationists demonstrated a fear, one that they were to reveal throughout the Movement years, that their fellow white Southerners might fall victim to integrationist brainwashing and commit acts of treason against their region unless they were deterred by laws and threats of punishment. In some places (more of them the farther South one went), any hint that a white person was "getting out of line" and treating Negroes with too much parity could mean ostracism, intimidation, time in jail, or worse. It was important to keep whites and blacks from meeting, talking, or playing together. Louisiana passed a law in 1956 providing for the removal of any schoolteacher who was charged with, among other things, belonging to a group that advocated "bringing about integration of the races" in any school in the state. The state also prohibited "all interracial dancing, social functions, athletic training, games, sports or contests and other such activities." Religious gatherings were exempted, however.[9]

Mississippi quickly became the South's leader in attempts to suppress criticism of white supremacy. (This situation was shortly to lead one of the state's few outspoken white academics, University of Mississippi history professor James W. Silver, to courageously deliver a paper, and later write a book, *Mississippi: The Closed Society*, which provided chapter and verse on the state's self-imposed moratorium on free expression.)[10]

The general assembly in 1956 enacted legislation making it "unlawful for any person or persons within the territorial limits of the State of Mississippi or the jurisdiction thereof to incite a riot, or breach of the peace, or public disturbance, or disorderly assembly, by soliciting, or advocating, or urging, or encouraging disobedience to any law of the State of Mississippi, and *nonconformance with the established traditions, customs, and usages of the State of Mississippi*" (emphasis added). The maximum penalty for violating this clearly unconstitutional law was a thousand-dollar fine and six months' imprisonment.

Most of the Southern states tried, in one form or another and with varying degrees of intensity, to exert control over their citizens' minds on matters of race relations. Among the first targets of segregationist politicians were the educators in public schools and colleges who, if not intimidated into silence, might infect their innocent students with the sorts of libertine and un-Southern ideas teachers were long suspected of harboring. In a society as rigidly racist as Mississippi's, controls over thought and speech became every bit as important as sanctions on actions. The government of Birmingham, Alabama, behaved in much the same fashion, enforcing laws that prohibited whites from even voluntarily engaging in integrated activities. In addition to laws, several communities used the grand jury method to intimidate those who might speak out. Grand jury "investigations" were used in several counties to harass citizens, both black and white, who spoke out against the prevailing order. This technique was used in south Georgia in 1957 against Koinonia Farms, an interracial cooperative that had been shot up by night riders. The grand jury not only rejected the farm's claims that it was the object of violence; it blamed the victims for their own predicament and threw in several paragraphs of red-baiting for good measure.[11]

-- ■

When Harold Fleming went to work for the Southern Regional Council, he recalled later, "it was a world I never knew existed. It was like starting over. I kept very few friends from my prewar days, and I was on a different track."

He was now in a desegregated world — not integrated, for integration was far away in those days, even in organizations that promoted racial equality. A meeting could be integrated, an office party could be integrated, but one step outside onto the sidewalks of Atlanta brought back the grating reality of segregation. His world was filled with talk of race relations, for that was what the council was all about. And his world was filled with black people whom most white Atlantans never knew existed — college presidents, physicians, millionaire insurance executives, highly intelligent and sophisticated people — all of them united with their white counterparts in the effort to do something about segregation and something about the South.

Some of Fleming's friends and associates from the old days wanted to know "what happened" to him, a drawling Southern white, to make him embrace the cause. This is a question that often is asked of white Southerners of an integrationist bent, a little less now than before but still with some frequency. The assumption is that white Southerners are born with the supremacist gene in their blood, and they must have undergone some wrenching experience in order to shed it.

"It's not like that, of course," said Fleming. "It's evolution, isn't it?"

Part of the evolution was the new people, the new friends. "Isolation" was not the correct word to describe the way Fleming felt in those days, he said, because even then, "maybe in a way *especially* in those days, there was a little band of folks, most of whom knew each other. There was a chapter of the American Veterans Committee, for example: The unifying principle was veterans, usually young veterans, just back from the war, white and black, who thought there was or ought to be a new day on this race stuff. And I exchanged my old friends for a new set of friends and co-workers and collaborators." He hesitated. "The right word is 'pariah.' You were very much a pariah in a whole lot of respects and you kind of felt like the Underground Man.

"I suppose it's sort of the way a spy feels in another country: As you walk down the streets you realize that if all these white people knew what you really stood for and what you were doing, they'd at best spit in your face and at worst knock the hell out of you."

Some Southern whites who have been in positions similar to Fleming's have reported feelings of something approximating guilt — feelings of sadness that they were betraying their fellow white Southerners, despite their absolute certainty that their actions were correct. Fleming never felt this way. "I felt something, though," he said. "I guess what I felt was *painful.* It was painful in lots of ways. Because I'm not like some people I've known in the liberal movement, South and elsewhere, who really relish the battle and are really motivated by a desire to dissent.

"They're not the dissenter-in-spite-of-himself but the dissenter-first-and-we'll-find-the-issue-later. I never was that kind of person. I'm a kind of a good old boy at heart. I like the idea of community, I like peaceable relations, I like to feel a part of whatever society I'm living in. I identify with people very easily and a lot. So I really wasn't a very good crusader, in the sense that I wasn't out to punish or vilify the white

South, bad as it was, because I understood how people could behave that way and hold those beliefs. I'd grown up in the society and it was just chance that I got exposed to some things that changed me.

"I didn't feel particularly morally superior because of that. But I did feel pained that I was cut off from the mainstream. And also there was a certain amount of shit that went with it."

Fleming and his wife and their young children moved into their first house, a Veterans Administration–financed home in a subdivision. "And it wasn't long before word of my nefarious connections spread through this little development." A neighbor, who had been a high school friend, told him that the "Fleming issue" had come up at a meeting of the subdivision's civic association. It was a question of "What were they going to do with this communistic race mixer who had even been known to have blacks in his house? And the rumor went that we gave interracial dances in the house."

Two of Fleming's Negro friends from Atlanta University had been to the house, and they tended to wear dark suits, white shirts, and bow ties. "So the rumor was that there were niggers in tuxes coming to a dance at our house. Of course — I was not a dancer, but if we had had dancing, they'd been welcome to come.

"And there was talk — all these people were veterans — about getting out the trusty old M-1 and so on, and 'We're not going to have this.' My friend, bless his heart, made some kind of appeal for sanity in the meeting, and so someone said, 'Well, I knew there was something wrong with him; he and his wife aren't even members of the civic association.' My friend said, 'Did anybody ever ask them?'

"And it turns out that the woman who was charged with signing up everybody on our block finally spoke up timidly and said, 'I know I should have done it, but I was afraid to go to their door.'

"Well, some of the people who had kids wouldn't let them play with my kids, and all that. But I was never in a situation where there weren't x-number of decent people who just wouldn't play that game, and that was true there in Atlanta, too. And we were enriched in a sense by all the friends, colleagues, and interesting people that the others didn't have because they didn't have anything to do with the black community. There was a kind of camaraderie because, you know, it was our brave new world."

Will Campbell, the circuit-riding pilgrim, worked a while on the University of Mississippi campus as a student chaplain. His ideas, his mouth, and his actions kept him in fairly consistent trouble at Ole Miss. Once Campbell was caught in the act of playing Ping-Pong with a black person. "The dean said, 'You know, Will, I don't object, for God's sake. I'm from Columbus, Ohio; *I've* played Ping-Pong with a black man — in my basement. But don't do it in public because, you know, you're just asking for trouble, and you've got to protect the institution.' "

As word spread of Campbell's deviations from what the law called the "established traditions, customs, and usages of the State of Mississippi," reprisals began against him. His secretary told him that a law student came to Campbell's office every evening to collect carbons from the wastebasket. Campbell learned that the student took the carbons to his home and held them up against a lamp to see what the minister was writing. And at a social function hosted by Campbell, he discovered human excrement floating in the bowl containing the beverage. It had been decorated with powdered sugar — or perhaps it was talcum powder; there was no close examination. Campbell lamented the mind that thought it clever to produce an actual "turd in a punchbowl."

When the Little Rock crisis occurred, Campbell — then an employee of the National Council of Churches and with Ole Miss behind him — immediately went there. On the morning schools were scheduled to open, the students and their parents and lawyers met to plan their strategy, and Campbell was with them. Then word came that Governor Faubus had stationed National Guard troops around Central High School. "And when the children started out," said Campbell later, "it was just too much for me to sit there drinking coffee and let them go. Part of it was just sheer curiosity with me. Hell, I thought, something historic is taking place here and I want to see it. So I walked beside the kids."

Reporters and persons who introduce after-dinner speakers welcome pithy, one-sentence biographies of those with whom they deal, and Will Campbell became known as "the white man who walked to school through the mobs with the black kids at Little Rock." Campbell cringed at this at the time, and does today, because he realized early on that he could be most effective by staying out of the public eye.

"My greatest contribution in Little Rock," he says, "was letting some of the ministers, primarily, and some others, who were trying to get the schools reopened and so on — letting them use my National Council of Churches telephone credit card. That was something I could do. I'm sure that the people in New York at the treasurer's office wondered, 'How in the world does this man talk that much on the telephone?' And, 'How could he be in that many places? How could he be in Searcy, Arkansas, calling Little Rock, and then five minutes later he was calling Forrest City from Little Rock?' But anyway, I was *there,* and I did whatever I could. Then when the direct action started, there were things that I could do that black people couldn't do, certain people I could talk to who they could not comfortably talk to. I had an access by the accident of birth, this incurable skin disease." Campbell displayed a pale arm sprinkled with freckles, the unmistakable mark of a white Southerner.

■ ─────────────────────────────

ELEVEN

A SUBTLE, GRADUAL TIGHTENING DOWN

The unwillingness of the politicians to provide leadership and the torrent of rabid rhetoric encouraged a good deal of private and semi-public racist activity. In the twenties, the Ku Klux Klan had grown considerably as a center of often violent activity for those lower-income and lower-class Southern whites (and Northern, too) who hated Negroes, Jews, and in some cases Catholics; who claimed an allegiance to fundamentalist Christianity while ritually burning crosses and murdering people; and who preferred to conduct their business while wearing hoods and robes. But after its initial burst of popularity the Klan lost influence, and postwar Southern politicians started regarding a Klan endorsement as a genuine liability.

This all changed after the *Brown* decision. Klan influence waxed again; the organization underwent a resurgence in Alabama, Mississippi, Georgia, Florida, Arkansas, and, to a lesser extent, North and South Carolina. The Klan was always afflicted, however, by a tendency toward intramural quarreling, followed by splits in the style of warring religious factions, and challenges from one grand dragon to another. As the Movement flourished later in the sixties, the Klan declined greatly in importance.

Other organizations took up the slack, however. Segregationist groups such as W. C. George's Patriots in North Carolina and the Defenders of State Sovereignty and Individual Liberties in Virginia provided a somewhat more genteel brand of racism, while hard-core racist groups such as the National States Rights Party, a pro-Nazi organization founded in 1957 in Knoxville and headquartered in Birmingham, provided an outlet for racists who liked to sport Sam Browne belts and flip Nazi salutes.[1]

The haven of choice for upscale segregationists was the Citizens Council, which was sometimes referred to as the White Citizens Council.

The councils were born in the summer of 1954 in Mississippi in direct response to the Supreme Court's desegregation ruling. From the beginning they represented an attempt to provide a less outrageous alternative than the Klan for whites who wanted to band together to fight integration. The idea caught on quickly. Within eight months, there were 167 local councils operating in Mississippi, and the council went into the business of producing weekly fifteen-minute films promoting its cause. The films, which were shown on sympathetic television stations around the region and nation, were usually devoted to discussions of the evils of integration and to allegations of communist infiltration in the civil rights movement, with occasional excursions into Negroes' purported biological inferiority. The Mississippi state government supported the films with taxpayers' money.[2]

A major difference between the Citizens Councils and segregationist organizations such as the Klan, according to some observers, was that the councils considered violence just one of many tools to use against the threat of integration, while the Klan and like groups thought of violence as the only weapon. Indeed, the councils considered propaganda a tool of far greater value. At an October, 1956, meeting of the Citizens Councils of America, members adopted a four-point "blueprint for victory." The points were support for interposition; a national propaganda effort, a "sharp counterattack" on the National Association for the Advancement of Colored People and other prointegration groups; and greater organization of white Southerners behind the ideals of white supremacy.[3]

Although the councils were unable to achieve their goal of a Southwide supremacist organization and although they had lost much of their steam by the mid-sixties, they served well in the early days as spokesmen for the segregationist, though not necessarily violent, ambitions of "respectable" local people — bankers, lawyers, public officials, businessmen, well-to-do farmers. They were vehicles for putting the fear of God not just into Negroes, but also into politicians and other influential whites who might be tempted to soften up on integration. Samuel DuBois Cook, in his assessment of Southern political movements in the era, wrote:

> White Citizens Councils, employing the powerful weapons of economic reprisal, political pressure, psychological and emotional terror, and social ostracism, sought to frighten and to silence not only Negroes but moderate and liberal whites as well and to keep them from participating in desegregation activities, and, indeed, from any sympathy with, or discussion of, the issue. Negro allies or potential and suspected sympathizers were as much the object of abuse, retaliation, and intimidation as Negroes themselves.[4]

Cook added that the councils acted as political pressure groups, advocating specific legislation, inviting candidates to appear before them to seek their endorsements, and keeping tabs on administrators. At election time, council members challenged Negroes who dared try to vote.

─────────────────────────── ■

William J. Simmons was a food broker who lived in Jackson, Mississippi, when the Citizens Councils started their rapid growth. He helped organize the Jackson Citizens Council in 1955 and stayed on long after the councils began their decline in the mid-sixties. He now is the administrator of the national group and publisher of its bimonthly journal, *The Citizen.* When he speaks of "the movement," he is talking not about the civil rights movement but the one that formed in resistance to it.

Simmons became involved in the councils, he said, because "I was interested in the movement and becoming attached to some kind of organization that I thought was responsible and with a respected leadership that could command some popular support." While the council promoted a philosophy of conservative opposition to liberalism, Simmons did not like the frequent descriptions of his organization as an "uptown Ku Klux Klan."

"The Citizens Councils, I think, made a considerable contribution to general stability, social stability, and racial peace during those years," he said, "particularly after the massive integration of the public schools. . . .

"The general feeling, and I think I'm correct on this, was that activities such as those of the Ku Klux Klan were extremely harmful to the movement, because they brought it to discredit and made it easy to introduce high emotional reactions among the general public and the opposition. And brought the federal government in directly. . . . I mean, it would lead one to suspect that it was not done for a legitimate purpose, the effects were so harmful." Simmons said he and others were "highly suspicious" of one man who affiliated himself with the Citizens Council movement, John Kasper of Clinton, Tennessee. Kasper's organization, which he called the Seaboard White Citizens Council, fought fiercely against the peaceful desegregation of Clinton's public schools in September, 1956, and he eventually was convicted by a white jury of violating a federal district judge's injunction against interfering with the desegregation order.[5]

"A correspondent of mine sent me some clippings from New York," said Simmons, "that indicated that Kasper had an association with some people who were . . . engaged in some kind of violent, anti-Semitic activity to bring disrepute on people." These people, he said, "were used by a Jewish organization to make it easier to raise money to combat anti-Semitism, as agents provocateurs." The organization, said Simmons, was the Anti-Defamation League of B'nai B'rith.

"And so I was really concerned about this, because I could see a parallel. If some stalking-horse were created that would bring disrepute on the Citizens Council, it was a matter of great concern."

Anyone could easily tell, said Simmons, that the sort of violence that was advocated and practiced by the Klan and similar groups was harmful to the conservative cause. "It is obvious," he said. "Any act of violence has raised money for the civil rights movement. It's caused oceans of tears and all kinds of sympathy. Nothing could have been worse from our point of view. Nothing."

What the councils tried to do, he said, was to serve "not so much as an organized group, but to be an information agency; to provide an information service. Then people could act on their own initiative based on whatever information they had." Thus the councils spread the word of Negroes' attempts to desegregate all-white churches. Later the councils put their energies into supporting private schools as alternatives to desegregated public schools.

And the councils tried to explain their position, and what they took to be the position of the white South generally, to the rest of the country. Simmons recalled that in 1964, during the height of rioting by blacks in New York City and other Northern communities, he was riding a train through Harlem to a meeting in Rye, New York. The train passed through 125th Street Station, which rests on elevated girders astride the eastern end of Harlem's busiest street.

"Each coach on the train had an armed guard on it. The trains were pelted from time to time with bricks and other debris from the buildings. We got out to Rye. While I was there, I went to a club that gave me some insight into Yankee tolerance. No blacks, no Jews, no Catholics, and no Southerners allowed. And I met a gentleman there named Mr. Moncrief — whose name is almost as if it came out of a storybook, it fit him so well — who was on Wall Street. And I was introduced to him, and he said, 'You're from Mississippi?'

"I said, 'Yes.'

" 'You actually live there? At that place with all those racial troubles? Oh, you poor fellow.'

"There was a total lack of intellectual curiosity. They simply dismissed our point of view as due to bad character or prejudice or some other thing that's just not worth consideration, without thinking that you can live in a situation and be a firsthand observer and maybe know a little bit about it — have a feeling for it that's not just a malevolent attitude."

What was missing in the Movement days, said Simmons, was a continued allegiance by the white South to massive resistance. "I thought that the best chance, and in retrospect I still think it was the best chance, was massive resistance. If they had provided the political leadership — and the South at that time still had enough political power in Washington to make it work — I think it would have been a totally different story."

If the politicians had stuck with massive resistance, would Mississippi still be segregated today?

"Well, it might be."

But some of the politicians are saying now that it was all theater — that they knew segregation was all over.

"I'm prepared to believe that a hundred percent, because that's exactly what I thought they were doing." Simmons laughed. "But I'm amazed that they'd say it."

But you were not engaging in theater yourself?

"No. No, sir."

You were quite serious about it.

"You bet."

■ ————————————————————————

The Mississippi State Sovereignty Commission was an attempt to perform Citizens Council–type work through a governmental agency. Although copied by some other states, the Mississippi commission was the most active one. It was established by the state legislature in 1956, during the administration of Governor James P. Coleman, in reaction to the *Brown* decision and what its director called "the federal usurpation of states' rights." As was often the case, no mention of segregation or integration was made in the founding legislation, which did, however, attempt to extend the commission's powers beyond the state's borders. The law said the commission's duty would be "to do and perform any and all acts and things deemed necessary and proper to protect the sovereignty of the State of Mississippi, and her sister states, from encroachment thereon by the Federal Government or any branch, department or agency thereof; and to resist the usurpation of the rights and powers reserved to this state and our sister states by the Federal Government."

To carry out its mission, the commission was given wide-ranging powers to subpoena and examine "any persons" and to demand access to "any books, records, papers or documents." If a witness refused to testify or produce documents on the grounds of self-incrimination (a right clearly guaranteed Americans by the Fifth Amendment to the national Constitution), the commission was authorized to "consider such refusal as a part of the evidence and shall inform the public of the refusal of such witness to so testify, and the facts and circumstances under which such refusal was made." The commission was empowered to employ any help it needed to carry out its mission. And the legislation alerted all state, county, and municipal employees, as well as those of the University of Mississippi "and other institutions of higher learning," that they must "co-operate with the commission."[6]

Governor Coleman, who in more recent years has sought to downplay his enthusiastic attitude toward the commission (which, by law, he headed), at the time was quoted as saying that the organization would retain private investigators to serve as the "eyes and ears" of segregation and to keep records on potential trouble-makers. But another and more important role for the commission was to serve as a propaganda device. Coleman, who was smart enough to know the true score in the game of South v. Nation, also knew that Mississippi, which was at the bottom of most national indices of education, income, and employment, needed relief from continued negative publicity, which increased tension levels at home and produced pressures from elsewhere in the nation. Segregation could be promoted, thought Coleman, by a policy of "friendly persuasion."[7] So, in addition to compiling dossiers on "agitators" and others who favored an end to racism and to engaging in several extralegal activities, the Sovereignty Commission sent emissaries to the North to address groups on how splendidly the state's Negroes and whites got along together and to point out, from time to time, that there was a great deal of segregation in the North, too.

■

Erle Johnston learned that lesson when he and other members of the Sovereignty Commission went north to tell Mississippi's story. "We'd go to make our talks to civic clubs up there," he said, "and we found out that the civic clubs were all segregated. There weren't any blacks. We went out to Port Jefferson, New York, and the Boy Scout troops were segregated. *Long Island!*"

Johnston is one of those people who might be called politico-journalists — people who see no problem with drifting back and forth across the line that ordinarily separates journalism and politics. He was a reporter for the *Grenada* (Mississippi) *Daily Star* and then the *Jackson Clarion-Ledger.* Later, he bought, edited, and published the *Scott County Times* in Forest, a small town between Jackson and Meridian. He was mayor of Forest from 1981 to 1985. At the same time he worked as a publicist and strategist in the political campaigns of some of Mississippi's more notable racists — Ross Barnett, James Eastland, John Stennis. Johnston also joined the Mississippi Sovereignty Commission in 1960 as its publicity director, and became the commission's director three years later. His years on the commission are not mentioned on a business card that Johnston hands to visitors (which does provide detail on his years of newspaper service), nor on the dust jacket of Johnston's respectful political biography of Ross Barnett, who was the governor during some of the Movement years, titled *I Rolled with Ross.*[8]

On those trips to the North, said Johnston, he and other commission members tried to defuse the notion that Negroes in Mississippi were totally downtrodden. The point was, he said, "that, yes, we were segregated, in the sense that our schools were segregated, and public rest rooms and even our theaters, you might say — the blacks went upstairs and the whites went downstairs. But we tried to dispel the notion that blacks didn't have a chance. I mean, blacks owned their own farms. Blacks owned their own businesses. Blacks were tradesmen. They had white people as their customers. Black electricians and plumbers. So they had their own niche, and they worked side by side in the plants."

Johnston said the commission grew out of political leaders' convictions that a state agency "might be necessary to stop what was considered then to be the federal usurpation of states' rights. . . .

"The Sovereignty Commission was an attempt at the state level to thwart the federal government from its continuous takeover of states' rights. That was just about the feeling of that era. Frankly, it was more psychological than it was physical. I know when I was director, we had three ladies. We had a bookkeeper, my secretary, and a filing clerk. And then we had three investigators, and they did not carry arms. All they were doing was go out and get information, that's all.

"And some guys from the North would come down here and say, 'I want to see the Sovereignty Commission.' I'd say, 'Here it is.' An office here, an office over here. 'Is that all there is to it?' I say, 'That's all there is to it.' And they were looking for something like an FBI, you know, with typewriters clicking and clacking, and interviews, and all like that. So I think maybe it was a psychological reaction, because the Sovereignty Commission really had no power. It did have subpoena power, but when I was director we never did use it."

Johnston was asked what kind of information the investigators sought.

There was a long pause. "Well, I'll give it to you one way, and that's the only way I can give it to you: information about scheduled events that might cause problems unless steps were taken to try to keep them from happening. Now you figure that out."

But "steps were taken" could mean anything.

"Okay, I'll give you one example. If we found out that a march was planned in a city, we would alert the law enforcement officers there, so . . . they could . . . just make sure that they were out there and be seen so that they would avoid any kind of racial clashes between whites and blacks."

Presumably, then, in such a situation the police didn't have that information already. Does that mean that you got it from informants?

"We had contacts that gave us information."

Contacts in the black community?

"Contacts in the civil rights community, which could mean either black or white."

The commission's work was more psychological than physical, said its former director, not because the agency actively sought to control people's emotions but rather because white Mississippians were grasping at anything that they thought might preserve segregation. "People would say, 'Well, the Sovereignty Commission will take care of that. The Sovereignty Commission will keep the schools segregated.' That kind of stuff. We didn't say that. At least, *I* didn't say that."

In the wake of the *Brown* decision, he said, "whites were clutching at straws: 'What can we do to keep this from happening? What can we do?' Eastland was making speeches up there in Washington. Stennis was making speeches. John Bell Williams was making speeches. And the governor, Governor Coleman, who was considered a moderate by most of the standards, he was making speeches, too, that we're not going to integrate our schools. So it was kind of like, 'What can we do?' "

In Mississippi, said Johnston, "the hope always existed that there would be a way found to retain states' rights, which, in the long run, would have retained local control over education and other things that presumably had been guaranteed in the Tenth Amendment. But there were some, of course, in Mississippi that felt like it was a losing battle. A lot of them said, 'Let's defy. Let's defy. Let's defy, to the last gasp, let's defy.' There were a lot of people who said, 'Well, I don't like it, but what can I do about it?' So we had all kinds of opinions. We even had whites that felt like the time had come to integrate. Those people, if they spoke out that way, they got pretty well ostracized, because that was not the thinking of the day."

■ ────────────────────────────

There were other observers who argue that the Sovereignty Commission was not as benign an organization as Erle Johnston remembers. "Everybody knew it was a criminal arm of state government," said Henry Kirksey, a black man who in the 1980s was a member of the state legislature. Kirksey, in a telephone interview, said the commission employed a private detective firm to do much of its dirty work, and he further alleged that "there is no question in my mind that the Sovereignty Commission ordered the death of Medgar Evers, and possibly others." Evers, the NAACP field secretary in Mississippi, was murdered outside his home in Jackson on June 12, 1963. A white man, Byron De La Beckwith, was tried twice for the crime. Both trials ended in hung juries.

In 1989, the *Jackson Clarion-Ledger*, Erle Johnston's old newspaper, reported that in 1964 investigators from the Sovereignty Commission had assisted the De La Beckwith defense in screening prospective jurors. A Jackson city councilman charged that the commission had subverted justice, and he introduced a resolution asking the state and county to reopen the murder case. The city commission passed the resolution.

Earlier in 1989, a federal district judge ordered that the defunct commission's records, which the legislature had ordered sealed until the year 2027, must be opened. Details were slow in surfacing, however.

The governmental and quasi-governmental forms of resistance were supplemented, as they always had been, by acts of a less official nature that broadcast throughout the Southland the message that segregation would not die easily. In Poplarville, Mississippi, Mack Charles Parker died in April, 1959, in a lynching that was publicized around the nation. The young Negro, charged with the rape of a white woman, was taken from jail by a white mob two days before he was to go on trial, beaten and murdered, and thrown into the Pearl River. No arrests were ever made. The Federal Bureau of Investigation entered the case at the request of Governor Coleman and presented evidence to a grand jury. But the jury refused to act on the matter or even to acknowledge that a lynching had occurred.[9] And Negroes throughout the South felt whites' anger after the Montgomery bus boycott began. Local law enforcement became harsher. The message was clear and it was an old one: Don't step out of line. Even though some members of your race are going into courtrooms and winning victories, and closing down bus companies with their boycotts, stay in your place, for you still live and die at the whim of the white South.

The segregationists were clearly concerned that the principles and passions unleashed by *Brown v. Board of Education* would spread into other areas. And well they might be concerned. *Brown* helped break down the reluctance of the Negro community to file suits and serve as plaintiffs in efforts to desegregate other components of the life of the segregated South: private education, higher education, government facilities other than schools, transportation, housing, and employment.

In the area of public accommodations, blacks brought suits to desegregate amusement parks, hotels, restaurants, beach clubs, cemeteries, barbershops, and a number of other areas, causing the segregationists to pass laws requiring separation in "public assemblages." (It was said that Virginia's version of the law was so strict it would outlaw an interracial gathering at a League of Women Voters political forum in a school auditorium.) When blacks won a federal suit requiring the desegregation of public parks in Montgomery, the city closed several of them because, according to the city's resolution, keeping them open "poses grave problems involving the welfare and public safety of all the citizens of the City of Montgomery."[10] Meanwhile, in the North, Negroes who were obviously aroused by the actions of their Southern counterparts fought segregation in restaurants, taverns, hotels, and private clubs.

There was little change, in the last years of the fifties, in Southern segregation patterns in housing, employment, and courtroom justice, although everyone involved knew that it was only a matter of time before those areas, too, would come under attack. There were stirrings of interest in voting rights and transportation, particularly after the Montgomery boycott began. Overall, however, resistance was successful in forcing a decline in Negro voter registration. States rushed to enact legislation, if they didn't have it already, requiring segregation in transportation within their borders.

And there were other, miscellaneous acts of resistance. The South Carolina Supreme Court ruled in 1957 that publishing a statement calling a white person a Negro was actionable defamation. Mississippi declared that all common-law marriages that took place after the date of the legislation, 1956, were null and void and any children issuing therefrom were illegitimate.[11] Such liaisons were probably more commonplace among blacks than whites.

And in Georgia, Governor Marvin Griffin, a pluperfect racist, signed an executive order in the summer of 1958 setting himself above the U.S. Supreme Court, the president, and anybody else from the outside world of the United States of America. "No order, command, or directive from the Government of the United States or any officer thereof to the Militia of the State of Georgia will be obeyed," announced Griffin, "until the Governor of Georgia certifies in writing to the Adjutant General of the State of Georgia that such order, command or directive is constitutional."[12] He was, in a sense, declaring himself the be-all, end-all Great Constitutional Lawyer of all time.

————————————————— ▪

In the plantation land of Mississippi, L. C. Dorsey noticed a difference. Before the resistance became so hardened, black people were able to subsist, she said, to stay alive on the little money they got from working on the plantations plus the country foods they could obtain. "There were rabbits, and you got food from hunting and fishing, and from gathering nuts from the pecan trees over on the levee and selling them during the wintertime, and from practically every house having a little place to raise vegetables."

But then the change came. "There was the big purge from the plantation. Forcing people out. Really cutting back. And tightening down, without any rational correlation to anything that blacks were doing.

"And I think white folks, who controlled this state at that time, sensed some slipping away of the total control they had over people, and it was met with a hardening of their hearts toward black folks.

"Shortly after that, it was no longer possible for you to go and pick pecans up off the levee. That got to be a no-no. Just all other kinds of things happened. The next thing I knew, people were subsisting on commodities. I mean, people who had never seen commodities before were standing in lines to get surplus commodities to live through the winter, you know. It was these kinds of little things.

"There were fewer lynchings that we knew about, but an incredibly high number of arrests and sending them to Parchman [the state penitentiary], and being leased out to farmers to work off their debt. There was even more control up at Parchman. Parchman used to be a place where, if you were a hardworking fellow and you wanted to go home and visit your mama or your family, you just told your captain, 'Sergeant, I need to go home,' and you went. And he said, 'Be back Monday so you can go to work.' All that changed.

"There was a subtle, gradual tightening down, tightening the screws on people without any apparent effort by blacks. After the Montgomery bus boycott, there was this whole different air. . . . You started going through the countryside, and you saw empty houses sitting out there because people had been let go, encouraged to leave, or work had been tightened up so that they couldn't afford to live anymore, and they had fled to the cities or moved into towns with relatives or what have you. There was this whole move to starve people out."

■ ——————————————————————————

PART FOUR

SOUL FORCE

TWELVE

■ ─────────────────────

HATE AND HISTORY COMING
TOGETHER

─────────────────────── ■

The sit-in at Greensboro, like the rebellion on Montgomery's buses, was not just a spontaneous, unpredictable event. This style of protest went back many years and was not limited to Negro demands for rights and respect.

But there was something different about this one. A great portion of the white community certainly *thought* that the demonstration had come out of the blue, even though Negroes had been preparing for such a day for decades, if not centuries, and their preparations had not gone on in secret. Perhaps this was because the whites had been devoting so much of their resources to the resistance against school desegregation that they had overlooked the wide-ranging nature of the blacks' grievances. Whatever the reason, the demonstration and those that followed struck the white South like an unexpected tornado. And its significance spread through the Negro community with equal force.

Among those who were caught unawares by the events of February 1, 1960, in Greensboro, North Carolina, were the daily newspapers of the nation. The acknowledged leader of American journalism and newspaper of record, the *New York Times*, missed the story on the day it happened. It was not until February 3 that the *Times* carried the story, on page 22 and under the single-column headline "Negroes in South in Store Sitdown." The article had been written and distributed by one of the two major wire services, United Press International. As is often the case with newspaper reports on events to which the reporters arrive late or not at all, the UPI story published in the *Times* was fuzzy about when the demonstrations actually started. Under a February 2 dateline, UPI wrote that "a group of well-dressed Negro college students staged a sitdown strike in a downtown Woolworth store today and vowed to continue it in relays until Negroes were served at the lunch counter." The article omitted the fact that the sitdown strike had actually started the day before, and that February 2 was the second day of demonstrations.

The *Times* quickly recovered, however. By mid-February the newspaper's much-traveled and perceptive Southern correspondent, Claude Sitton, reported on the front page that, while the demonstrations "were generally dismissed at first as another college fad," now the protests were raising "grave questions in the South over the future of the region's race relations." Sitton wrote, "A sounding of opinion in the affected areas showed that much more might be involved than the matter of the Negro's right to sit at a lunch counter for a coffee break."[1]

The demonstration in Greensboro occurred against a backdrop of growing interest everywhere in segregation, along with increased attempts to undo it. Deep South states were just beginning to fight on the public school desegregation battlefield, and voting rights was becoming more and more an issue. As the sit-ins started, Congress was debating a civil rights bill that, among other things, would authorize federal judges to appoint referees to assist Negroes in registering and voting, at least in federal elections. Southern white supremacists, led by Senator Richard B. Russell of Georgia, promised to filibuster, or drag out the proceedings with near-endless speechmaking that, they hoped, would exhaust the bill's proponents. Those who favored the bill were a bipartisan bloc that included Lyndon Johnson of Texas.

But suddenly, with Greensboro, the game changed.

Four black students from North Carolina Agricultural and

Technical College, known as A&T, inaugurated the new era when they entered the downtown Woolworth's store, bought a few items, walked over to the lunch counter, and requested service. The students, all freshmen and all eighteen years old, were Ezell Blair, Jr., David Richmond, Franklin McCain, and Joseph McNeil.* When Blair asked for a cup of coffee, the white waitress replied, in a statement that soon was to be echoed throughout the South, "I'm sorry. We don't serve Negroes here." One of the students pointed out, politely, that the store had already served them by accepting their money for the items they had bought. The waitress replied, "Negroes eat at the other end," indicating a stand-up counter where Woolworth's sold food to black people. A Negro worker behind the counter fussed at the students and called them "ignorant." Eventually the store closed and the students left.

The store manager, C. L. Harris, was not surprised that the demonstration had occurred. Some years before, he had asked his regional office what he should do if blacks sat down and refused to leave when told to. His superiors agreed with Harris's suggestion that it would be best to do nothing, on the theory that the demonstrators would eventually grow tired and depart. Thus an arrest, with accompanying publicity, could be avoided. Although no one with Woolworth's was quoted as saying so at the time, the chain and others like it had a large Negro clientele and were quite vulnerable to economic pressure from blacks. In many Southern cities the central transfer points for bus lines were situated downtown, where the dime stores were, and Negroes passed through twice daily on their way between employment in the white community and their homes on the black side of town.

The students had discussed a possible sit-down demonstration for weeks. A local clothing merchant, Ralph Johns, had urged Negroes for years to stage some sort of protest. Johns, who was white, was the son of Syrian immigrants and was committed to fighting segregation. He also had been known in earlier years as a professional gate-crasher who specialized in getting his picture taken with celebrities, particularly those from the boxing world. Since 1949 Johns had been suggesting to students who frequented his

---

*Blair has since changed his name to Jibreel Khazan.

store that they test and attack segregation at Woolworth's. He and the students met in the rear of his store to discuss the youths' moves. He promised to cover their bonds if they were arrested. (In recent years there has been some disagreement over the degree of Johns's contribution. At a ceremony in Greensboro on February 1, 1990, commemorating the thirtieth anniversary, Johns, now a resident of California, commented that "I started" the demonstration. Franklin McCain remembered that Johns played a less central role.)[2]

The students were not arrested, however. On the second day, Woolworth's continued to allow the youths, their number much larger now, to remain at the counter. A district superintendent made the preposterous statement, "We haven't refused anybody. Our girls have been busy and they couldn't get around to everybody." Ezell Blair, back for his second day, told reporters that black adults had been "complacent and fearful," and that the students had decided to "wake up and change the situation." On the fifth day, a group of white teenagers and a number of Ku Klux Klansmen showed up at the store and tried to prevent the Negroes from getting seats at the counter. On February 6 the Woolworth's store, along with a nearby S. H. Kress & Company store that also had been visited by students, closed their doors. Woolworth's management said it had received a telephoned bomb threat. The students, whose numbers now included young people from Bennett College and Dudley High School, proclaimed victory. At a mass meeting that night they agreed to suspend demonstrations for two weeks to give store officials time to institute desegregation policies.[3]

On the night of February 2, with news of the demonstration flying through the Negro community, the Greensboro chapter of the National Association for the Advancement of Colored People voted to back the students any way it could. On the same day, the students had visited Dr. George Simpkins, a local dentist and NAACP chair, and he had promised to help. Dr. Simpkins did this by sending a postcard not to NAACP headquarters but to the New York office of the Congress of Racial Equality.

That act has been cited by Movement people and others who were chronically critical of the NAACP's "legalistic" approach as evidence that, in a moment of need, even one of its own officers sought help elsewhere. Dr. Simpkins has rejected that interpretation, explaining that he had been reading a CORE pamphlet about its successful effort to desegregate a Baltimore restaurant and thought the organization might be more experienced at the sort of operation under way in Greensboro.

────────────────────── ■

Gordon Carey received the postcard at the cramped and cluttered CORE headquarters in New York City.

Carey, who is white, was born into the pacifist-nonviolence movement in 1932 in Grand Rapids, Michigan. His father was a Methodist minister, a member of the Fellowship of Reconciliation, and chair of the CORE chapter in Grand Rapids. When Gordon was nine or ten years old, his family went to a summer encampment. James Farmer was one of the speakers, and he later stayed at the Carey house. Farmer was to joke in subsequent years about how he had literally bounced Gordon Carey on his knee when he was a child.

Later the Careys moved to southern California, and Gordon eventually succeeded his father as chair of the Pasadena CORE chapter. At that time, in the fifties, CORE's popularity had declined from the level it had enjoyed a decade earlier when it was protesting and demonstrating for equal public accommodations in the North. The reason was success; much of the North had become at least nominally desegregated.

It was a CORE tradition that the second highest elected officer came from the West Coast. So when Carey showed up at a national convention representing the California delegation, he was elected CORE's national vice chair. "I thought that was really big stuff," he said in a 1988 interview. "There were about twenty people at the convention."

At the time, Carey was knocking around from job to job, working as a truck driver, in a manufacturing firm, at a woodworking shop. He spent a year in federal prison as a conscientious objector to military service. He went to Okinawa as a worker on a ship carrying goats.

"I was like a lot of young kids," said Carey. "I used to drink too much and screw around, and so on. I had very strong beliefs, but I also probably didn't act like it a lot of times. The reason I really got interested in CORE was that it was so frustrating to be a pacifist because you can't do anything about it. You read Thoreau, and you know that one man can make a difference, and in a sense, you can. In a long, historical sense, you can be very important. But in the immediate time it's very difficult to affect world affairs." The movement for desegregation, he said, suddenly offered a way to turn pacifist ideas into action. "You could get down and actually do something very specific, so that's what I did."

Carey's work on the West Coast impressed CORE's national office, and when the leadership decided to add full-time field secretaries to the staff, they asked Carey if he would like to sign on. "That was like asking me if I wanted to go to heaven," he said.

Carey had the title of field director in early February, 1960, when the message from Dr. George Simpkins arrived from Greensboro in the New York CORE office.

"It was a little postcard addressed to CORE," he recalled. "It must have been dated around February second. It said something like, 'We'd like some help.' So I picked up the phone and called him. And George said, 'Gee whiz, can you come down? Come and give some support like they did for Baltimore?' I said, 'Sure.' So I hopped on a bus to Greensboro." He recalls thinking of the trip as a fairly routine one. News accounts of the event certainly didn't make it out to be of momentous importance; furthermore, Carey knew that the protests were just examples of the techniques CORE and other groups had employed and advocated for decades. He assumed that his contribution would be to teach anyone who would listen about the values and methodology of nonviolent direct action. By that time, he recalled later, the technique was down to "a science."

Carey was diverted from his destination. By the time he arrived in Durham, where he was to meet the lawyer and CORE loyalist Floyd McKissick, the Greensboro sit-ins had wound down, due to Woolworth's decision to close its lunch counters. But things were happening elsewhere. The spark that was struck in Greensboro lit fires all over the South, particularly in communities where black students congregated in colleges and universities. "Things began to pop in other places," said Carey, "and I never got to Greensboro. I did eventually, but for the time being I just started organizing."

■ ————————————————————

There was no rule book, no operator's manual for the sit-ins. The young people seemed to know exactly what to do: how to reconnoiter a store, how to gravitate toward the lunch counter at a predetermined time, how to behave. Especially how to behave: The demonstrators were almost universally described in press accounts as being "polite" in their dealings with store employees, and as wearing "neckties and jackets." Some carried schoolbooks, perhaps to emphasize the fact that they were college students but also so they could get some work done during the long and usually fruitless waits for service. They were prepared to tolerate abuse both verbal and physical, which usually came, when it occurred, from young white toughs who voiced threats or dumped ketchup or squirted deodorant on the silent students. As they gained experience, and some found that the official response would be not to ignore them but to throw them into the paddy wagon on charges of trespass or loitering, they learned to tuck toothbrushes into their pockets.

Nowhere were the students as ready for the sit-ins as in Nashville, Tennessee. Some veterans of the era will argue even today that the fact that the modern sit-ins began in Greensboro on February 1, 1960, at 4:30 P.M., is a mere chronological aberration, and that they really started in Nashville some months before. For several months, students at the predominantly black colleges in Nashville, with some support from whites at Vanderbilt and other schools, had been carefully working their way toward sit-in demonstrations or something quite similar. They had been brought together, inspired, and guided by a young black man named James Lawson.

Lawson's background was similar to Gordon Carey's: A native of the North, he was the son of a Methodist minister. He went to prison as a conscientious objector during the Korean War. Released on parole to the Methodist missionary agency, he went to India and studied the methods of Mohandas K. Gandhi, who had taken the practice of using nonviolence to achieve political change to the level of artistry. Lawson had been a member of the Fellowship of Reconciliation since his college days. When the Montgomery bus boycott was about to achieve its goals in the fall of 1956, Lawson traveled to the Alabama capital and met Martin Luther King. In

1957 he arrived in Nashville, as the fellowship's first Southern field secretary. He was twenty-seven years old.[4]

In 1958 Lawson and the Reverend Glenn E. Smiley, a prominent FOR staffer who was white, ran a workshop on nonviolence for the Nashville Christian Leadership Council, the local affiliate of the Southern Christian Leadership Conference. Lawson enrolled in the Vanderbilt school of theology and conducted similar workshops there and in the black college complex across town.

The workshops involved a great deal of talk about the theory behind nonviolence, to be sure, but they also dealt with the practical side of the technique. There were discussions on how to bring about a confrontation with the practitioners of segregation; how to negotiate; how to defend oneself if attacked. Perhaps the most significant aspect of the workshops was that they built on the change that had begun to occur in the Movement with Montgomery: a shift from dependency on courtroom attacks on segregation to the use of direct action. Although some of the elders of the Nashville black community were not greatly in favor of direct action — for one thing, they feared for the safety of the younger Negroes just as parents always do — most of the participants in the Nashville events recall now that the established black leadership there was unusually supportive. This was not to be the case everywhere.

The workshops attracted a small but devoted number of students from diverse backgrounds who would become, in the next few years, the backbone of the younger, more assertive wing of the civil rights movement. Diane Nash, an English major at Fisk University, was a black woman from Chicago, a Catholic who once had planned to become a nun but who was, she said later, talked out of it by a priest. James Bevel, who later would become Diane Nash's husband, was a student at a Baptist seminary. So were John Lewis, the son of an Alabama farm family, and Bernard Lafayette, who had been a member of the NAACP Youth Council when he was a high school student in Tampa, Florida.

-- ■

"The meetings were once a week," said John Lewis. "They were on Tuesday nights when they first started. We picked Tuesday or Thursday because those were the days you didn't have many class hours. They would go an hour and a half to two hours, and sometimes much longer. They took place in a little Methodist church near the Fisk University campus. We would sit in circles in a very small group.

"At first, we didn't talk about segregation and racial discrimination. We didn't talk about racism and what was going on in the South. It was almost a philosophical discussion. But after we learned and talked about the meaning of nonviolence, the meaning of passive resistance, the meaning of civil disobedience, then we studied what Gandhi did in India and what he attempted to do in South Africa, and we brought it up to what Martin Luther King, Jr., did in Montgomery and what was happening in our own country. And we talked about how some of the citizens of Europe tried to resist the Nazis in the forties.

"All of that was discussed, but it was all discussed in the context of the power of nonviolence, the relevance of passive resistance and nonviolence. But Jim Lawson apparently knew what he was doing. He knew where he was leading us, preparing us to get involved in what we got involved in. When I look back on it, I think we had the feeling that we were going somewhere. We were going to do something. But it's strange: We were very patient."

Lewis said the Nashville students were not resentful when they learned that their contemporaries in Greensboro had beaten them to the punch. "More than anything else," he said, "it was something that none of us had any control over. It was something out there tracking people down. It was hate and history coming together. The spirit of history just tracked us down and used us, really. We didn't have any control over it."

■ ────────────────────

The meetings included field work as well as classroom discussion. Starting in the fall of 1959, the participants went to a number of segregated eating places in Nashville. When they were refused service, they sought to engage the managers in discussions about segregation. Then they left, with the intention of returning later for full-fledged sit-downs.

Greensboro altered the Nashvillians' timetable. Sit-ins began in Nashville on February 6. Merchants at the variety stores downtown employed a diversity of means to show that their lunch

counters were closed to the demonstrators. Woolworth's sent waitresses home; at McClellan's, the staff asked whites who were already sitting at the counter to inform waitresses when they
planned to leave, so other whites (and not Negroes) could be ush-
ered onto the stools. One store pretended to close, but the students
noticed that the restaurant's steam table was still operating, so
they stayed. A few days later, management tried stacking trash
cans, flowerpots, rugs, and lamp shades on the counter in front of
students to make reading more difficult. Grant's and Woolworth's
turned out the lights in the lunchroom sections of their stores. In
several cases, after whites heckled and beat the students, the police, who until then had remained in the background, moved in
and made arrests — of Negroes, for "disorderly conduct." Bond for
the arrested students was placed at one hundred dollars. When the
students refused to make bond, the court authorities lowered the
sum to five dollars. They obviously did not want the negative publicity that would accompany a jail full of well-mannered, articulate
college students. The students still refused, and bond was eliminated entirely. They then were released into the custody of their
college deans.

Nashville mayor Ben West appointed a committee to study
the situation. On March 30, 1960, the committee released its recommendation: that merchants should open half their lunch
counters as integrated facilities, half as segregated. The students
rejected this idea, which sounded a lot like the earlier suggestion
by the city board of education that three sets of schools — integrated, white, and black — be established. Sit-ins resumed, with
more arrests. Students and their elders successfully promoted an
effort to stay away from downtown merchants in advance of the
Easter buying season. This was a move that was not lost on the
white business community, which received an estimated $10 mil-
lion annually from Negroes.[5] In mid-April, the home of Z. Alexander Looby, a black city councilman and attorney, was
dynamited, with much damage but no deaths. Thousands of Negroes marched on city hall and confronted an uncomfortable Mayor
West on the building's steps. And on May 24 the desegregation of
most of the stores began.

There was little question during the Nashville protest about the support of the black colleges and universities, which, though nominally autonomous, nevertheless were at least partially dependent on whites for financial and political freedom. President Stephen J. Wright of Fisk declared on February 28, 1960, as dozens of his students were being refused service, attacked, and arrested downtown:

> I approve the ends our students are seeking by these demonstrations. From all I have been able to learn, they have broken no law by the means they have employed thus far, and they have not only conducted themselves peaceably, but with poise and dignity. As long as this is true, I have no present intention of instructing them to discontinue their efforts. The point at issue, it seems to me, is not how to stop their efforts but rather to find better alternative ways to end segregation in the public eating places of the city.[6]

───────────────────────── ■

Diane Nash, a native Midwesterner, knew about segregation in the South, but she did not experience it firsthand until 1959, when she transferred to Fisk from Howard University. She had felt anger when she saw the pictures of the murdered Emmett Till in *Jet* magazine, and she had felt compassion for the Little Rock Nine. But her family had always sheltered her from segregation's harshest effects.

"My stepfather was a waiter on the railroads," she said years later, "and he had to make trips to the South. He would tell about the segregated facilities down there. I believed him and listened to the stories, but I think that it was an intellectual understanding. But when I actually got down there and saw signs, and it hit me that I wasn't, quote-unquote, 'supposed' to go in this rest room or use a particular facility, then I understood it emotionally as well." Nash was particularly wounded by this because it was a time, she said, when she was "growing and expanding," exploring the world around her as college students often do, and now she found that world a restricted one. At Howard she had enjoyed going with a friend to downtown Washington to window-shop and have lunch; in Nashville there were constraints on this. It was "stifling," and she resented that.

"I remember that I got really outraged. I had a date, and we went to the Tennessee State Fair. The guy was from the South. I started to use the ladies' room, and those were the first signs I had really seen in Nashville, and they were 'WHITE WOMEN' and 'COLORED WOMEN,' and I just got furious. It really hit me." Nash's date asked her if she was truly serious about her anger, and she assured him that she was.

Nash began looking around for other people who were equally outraged. At first, she said, "I got so many 'no' answers, and the attitude of the students I talked to on campus was so resigned — that that's the way it has been and is going to be. I really had started coming to the conclusion that they were apathetic." But then she ran into a white exchange student, Paul Laprad, who told her about James Lawson's workshops, which were being held in a church a few blocks from the campus.

Lawson was an inspiring teacher, but Nash was skeptical. "I kind of reserved judgment," she said. "I remember thinking, after attending several workshops, that this stuff is never going to work. But it was the only game in town, and so I said, 'Well, I'll go with it because my choice is either to do nothing about segregation or to work with them.'

"But then after using nonviolence, I was really impressed with its effectiveness. It really did work. And there were glorious things about it — things that I found out about myself that I didn't know. I found courage in myself that wasn't there, and I found beautiful things in people who would care enough about other people to put their bodies between another person and danger. A lot of things started making sense to me through the learning of nonviolence as well as the practice of it. And I developed it as a way of life."

When the sit-ins started in Nashville, Diane Nash was elected to chair the activists' central committee. Now she had her organization of equally outraged people, and she had access to courage that she hadn't known before. But she also had fear.

"After we started, I was consumed with the goal we had set for ourselves, which was desegregating the lunch counters in Nashville — specific lunch counters in Nashville — and also consumed with being scared to death. I remember coming back to the dorm the night they elected me chairperson of the central committee, and I was so afraid I could hardly stand up. I said to myself, 'This is Tennessee, and white people down here are *mean.*' And I said, 'We are going to be coming up against men who are white Southern men who are forty and fifty and sixty years old, who are politicians and judges and owners of businesses, and I am twenty-two years old. What am I *doing*! And how is this little group of students my age going to stand up to these powerful people?' "

One day Nash was going from store to store to check on demonstrators. Her photograph had been in a Nashville newspaper. At one of the stores a large number of whites had gathered outside, and she had to squeeze her way through the crowd. "And I heard one young guy in a group of teenagers say, 'That's Diane Nash. She was in the paper. She's the one to get.' And I realized somebody could stab me or something and not even be seen.

"I got terrified. And so I made a deal with myself. I'd take five minutes during which I'd make a decision that I was going to either put the fear out of my mind and do what I had to do, or I was going to call off the sit-in and resign. I really just couldn't function effectively, as afraid as I was. And I found the courage to put the fear out of my mind and keep functioning."

After the dynamiting of Z. Alexander Looby's home, Diane Nash was at the head of the march that ended on the steps of city hall in the confrontation with Mayor West. She recalled later that Rev. C. T. Vivian, a local minister and member of the SCLC affiliate, had made his presentation and Mayor West was replying with "the typical thing that politicians do" — declaring that he was the mayor of all the citizens and pointing out what he had done for the Negro community.

"He was making a political speech," she said, "and I remember feeling like, 'This is not getting us anywhere. What can I do? What can I say?' And, boom, this logical set of questions occurred to me."

The main question Nash asked the mayor was whether he, as a human being, felt it was wrong to discriminate against someone solely on the basis of race or color. It was a simple query, but this time it was being asked on the steps of city hall with a great deal hanging in the balance.

Mayor West later recalled the exchange this way: "They asked me some pretty soul-searching questions, and one was addressed to me as a man. I replied that I could not agree that it was morally right for someone to sell them merchandise and refuse them service. . . . It was a moral question and one that a man has to answer, and not a politician."[7]

The marchers applauded his reply. Diane Nash was surprised, she said later, but she felt a great deal of respect for Mayor West. Three weeks later, the lunch counters were desegregated in Nashville.

■ ───────────────────────────────

THIRTEEN

■

THIS WAS OUR TIME

■

In communities all across the South, young Negroes participated in sit-ins. In many cases the demonstrations were held, as they were in Greensboro and Nashville, at downtown businesses that happily accepted blacks' money for merchandise but refused them equal treatment at the lunch counter. But the technique spread to other places of public accommodation — movie theaters, which in the South segregated Negroes into balcony seats; public libraries; courtroom seating; and full-service restaurants.

In most cases, the students and their lawyers based their actions not only on the moral issues that Diane Nash and Mayor West discussed on the steps of Nashville's city hall but also on the presumption that once the owner of a private business invites the public in, he may not deny any segment of that public access to the facilities inside. The merchants and white government officials based their replies on the notion that the owner of a private business, on private property, has the right to determine who shall enter and, once they enter, who shall be allowed to use the facilities. A private business, like a man's home, was deemed to be the operator's castle, to be run as the operator saw fit.[1]

In many places, sit-ins resulted in relatively quick desegregation, without protracted argument of the legal or moral issues, clearly because the matter was so closely tied to downtown merchants' income. Furthermore, citizens who were in sympathy with the demonstrators mounted picket lines and organized boycotts at Northern and Western outlets of the chain stores that resisted in the South, bringing even more intense economic pressure for quick settlements. A survey by Vanderbilt law school showed that by August, 1960, demonstrations had led to desegregation of some eating places in Alexandria, Arlington, and Richmond in Virginia; Austin, Corpus Christi, Dallas, Galveston, and San Antonio in Texas; Chapel Hill, Charlotte, Winston-Salem, and Salisbury in North Carolina; and Chattanooga, Knoxville, and Nashville in Tennessee. Further evidence of the success of the sit-ins was found, said the survey, in the fact that both major political parties spoke approvingly of the technique in their 1960 campaign platforms.[2]

Augusta, Georgia, was another example of the white community's eventual acceptance of the sit-in demonstrators' aims. Silas Norman was a freshman at Augusta's Payne College, a Methodist institution, when the wave of demonstrations started in Greensboro. Payne students planned a strategy for Augusta in consultation with interested representatives from the faculty. James Lawson visited from Nashville to talk about Gandhian nonviolence. Norman, who became involved in the demonstrations, said the students started with two dime stores downtown and broadened the effort to include other stores that had large black clienteles.

First they sought to negotiate with the merchants. Then they sat in and picketed. During the campaign they met with the city's mayor, who listened politely to what they had to say, and they held meetings with some of the managers of the stores they were boycotting. Norman remembers one negotiating session with the operator of a shoe store who did not want the general public to know he was negotiating. "We met in the attic," said Norman in an interview, "sitting on some boxes back in a corner of his inventory. But he did talk to us." Norman and his fellow students gradually grew to understand that discussions with elected officials might be important, but that many of the real decisions affecting race relations in Augusta were made by the leaders of the business community.

There was little white and no black violence in Augusta. When the demonstrations started, some elements of the black community were leery about becoming involved with the younger activists. At first the students found that they were not welcome to hold their mass meetings in all the black churches, but as the campaign gained support, this changed. "We were increasingly invited to other churches," recalled Norman. "There developed a kind of pride and competition as to where the mass meetings were going to be."

Sit-ins brought comparatively peaceful change in some places, Augusta among them, but in others there was plenty of resistance. In Virginia, within one twenty-four-hour period, Governor Lindsay Almond requested and the legislature passed three antitrespassing statutes designed to deal with sit-ins. Late in February, Negro students from Alabama State College conducted the Deep South's first sit-in when they visited lunch counters in Montgomery. Governor John Patterson replied in what had come to be his characteristic fashion: He threatened the students with expulsion from school, and he conjured up visions of violence if demonstrations were allowed to persist — or, as he put it, if Negroes were allowed to "continue to provoke" whites.[3]

There were the usual allegations of "outside agitator," which any impartial observer could have seen were not true. Of all the segments of society that misjudged the importance of the sit-in movement until it became well established, the stereotypical "outside agitators" — the Northern-based radical and Marxist organizations — were high on the list. They were slow to comprehend the significance of the Southern demonstrations, and when they did head south to get involved, there was little for them to do. Even the nonradical but Northern-oriented groups such as the Congress of Racial Equality saw that this was, at least for the time being, a Southern show.

■

Gordon Carey does not take lightly assertions, from Southern politicians at the time or anyone since then, that the demonstrations were inspired by non-Southerners such as himself. Once the direct action era of the Movement had begun, the Congress of Racial Equality tried to teach its methods of nonviolence to anyone who would listen, just as it had been doing since the forties. But CORE never tried to force its campaign on anyone who wasn't interested in it.

"The whole notion that everything was caused by outside agitators was crap," said Carey later. "The 'outside agitators' were being pulled along by the kids. It was purely spontaneous. That's not to say that there weren't people like me and others around who were helping, but we were not leaders; we were followers."

When Carey was diverted from his intended destination of Greensboro in February of 1960, he headed for nearby Chapel Hill, where teenagers had started sit-ins. Chapel Hill was the home of the University of North Carolina, which had a long-standing tradition of liberalism but whose student body was almost all white and whose faculty and administration were completely so. The college town of Chapel Hill was populated by liberal professors and retired academic people, but it was still a segregated place, with few exceptions, among them the Community Church and the administration of the campus Young Men's Christian Association. Gordon Carey was invited to go to Chapel Hill to teach nonviolence to the black high school students, who had been engaging in fist-fighting with the white hecklers who came to their demonstrations.

"I was supposed to turn them around," said Carey with a smile. "I was supposed to train them. I'm sure they were a little skeptical of me."

Carey started with what in those days was just beginning to be called sociodrama — the use of dramatic playacting to explore and cope with group and intergroup tensions and conflicts, using the members of the group themselves as the actors. James Lawson had used similar techniques in the Nashville workshops, assigning half the group to act as participants at a sit-in, the other half to revile the "demonstrators" in the role of thugs and policemen.

"We had some of them play the part of the restaurant owners or waitresses," said Carey, "and in one evening I drilled into them the whole theory of being nonviolent, to prepare them for the next day. You have people switch roles, and you have them throw a few things, and someone hits someone and tries to pull him off the lunch counter stool or whatever. And they react in a certain way, and then you stop the drama and talk about what happened. You have them evaluate each other and explain why they acted in certain ways.

"However, we also did some tactical things. These kids were going to the same restaurant at the same time of day, every day. Naturally, the white kids also showed up at the same lunch counter at that same time. The white kids would start taunting them, and somebody would throw a fist. It happened every day. So the first thing I told them was, 'Aha. We'll act like we're playing jujitsu here; catch them off guard. You don't go to that restaurant. You go to a different lunch counter, okay?' And with these little tactical changes plus one evening workshop, there was no more violence in Chapel Hill. People thought I was a genius."

Carey's true genius may have been in selecting the toughest member of the group, a young man with the reputation of a ruffian, and placing him in charge of making sure the entire group stayed nonviolent. "He probably told them that if they didn't act nonviolent, he'd knock the shit out of them." Carey laughed. "But it worked."

A reporter wrote a piece about Carey's techniques, and he received an inquiry from a New York organization formed to advance psychodrama and sociodrama. "They wanted to know how I knew about it," said Carey. "I didn't remember how I learned how to do it, but I did it anyway. We'd been doing these kinds of things consistently from the time I joined CORE." The professional organization asked Carey to give its members classes in the technique.

■ ————————————————————

The demonstrations did not reach Jackson, Mississippi, until more than a year after Greensboro. In March, 1961, students from Tougaloo Christian College entered the main city library. The police promptly arrested them after stating that "there's a colored library on Mill Street. You are welcome there." Two days later, when the students were tried on charges of refusing a policeman's order to disperse, the police prevented a crowd of blacks from attending the trial in the municipal courtroom by beating them with clubs and encouraging two German shepherd police dogs to attack them.

Meantime, in the trials, the students' attorneys argued that the demonstrators had conducted themselves in an orderly manner. But the judge, James L. Spencer, said the Negroes were guilty anyway, because their conduct, even though it was orderly, could have touched off a breach of the peace by someone else.[4]

Twisted courtroom logic, German shepherds, threats of expulsion, and violence by gangs of white toughs were but a few of the tools used by white supremacists in attempting to cope with the sit-ins. At first, the authorities relied on time-honored, all-purpose municipal stock charges to arrest the demonstrators. "Disorderly conduct," "public disturbance," "breach of peace," and "failure to obey an officer" were the usual devices. When the waves of demonstrators kept coming, though, authorities moved to statutes that promised harsher penalties — laws denoting offenses such as "criminal trespass" and "conspiracy to interfere with trade and commerce." None of this made much of a dent in the Movement, however. The threat of being thrown into jail may have served well in the past to keep Southern Negroes "in their place," but now, as John Lewis of Nashville put it, jail time had become a "badge of honor."[5] Furthermore, the less adventurous Movement figures who favored the legalistic approach to fighting segregation felt obliged to put their courtroom talents into getting the younger demonstrators out of jail and to defeating the laws that put them in there.

─────────────────── ■

Constance Baker Motley and other civil rights lawyers felt, until the sit-ins started, what she called "great reluctance on the part of the black community to come forward" and serve as plaintiffs in antisegregation actions. And the sit-ins, she said, came about because students were just behaving like students. "The students were doing what the adults had counselled them not to do because of the virtual certainty of arrest or a violent response."

Suddenly now, for whatever reason, the students were producing willing plaintiffs. But they were also providing the NAACP lawyers with some interesting problems.

"Here were these students sitting in," said Motley. "I'll never forget: Thurgood Marshall was away. He had been in Africa. He had been asked by Kenya to help them with their constitution. So he had been away for several months, and [Inc. Fund staff attorney] Jack Greenberg and I said to Thurgood when he got back, 'Oh boy, there's a brand-new day.' He said, 'What do you mean?' We said, 'These students are sitting in, and doing things that we would never have advised them to do' — knowing that they would be arrested and surely would go to jail — and we knew we couldn't get them out because the law was you couldn't go into a privately owned place. The Fourteenth Amendment didn't apply.

"So they were doing things that we would never counsel anybody to do, or agree to represent them if they did it. But we had to. That's how we knew — or at least *I* felt — that there was this revolution coming. Because here at last were black people on their own who understood that the Supreme Court was behind them."

"We certainly wouldn't have counselled people to march down the street and defy the city officials. But they did it. And once they did it, we had to represent them. That's why I felt this was a real revolution: because now the people themselves were involved."

The backing Nashville students received from the older and more established members of the city's Negro community was not always forthcoming elsewhere. In Atlanta, the established black leadership did not approve at all of what the youthful demonstrators from the Atlanta University Center were doing.

"It was our suspicion of them, I think, more than any real friction," said Julian Bond, recalling the students' attitude toward the elders. "For example, when the sit-ins started we went to a lawyer and asked him if he'd represent us in case we got arrested. We didn't know what would happen. And he was not an NAACP lawyer. He said sure; he said it would be about five thousand dollars. We were just astounded — first, that anybody would charge that much money for representing people on what couldn't have been a serious charge to begin with, and secondly, that he would charge anyway. You know, we thought he'd say, 'Sure, I'll be glad to do it. It's for the Movement.' And so we went to the NAACP, which we hadn't wanted to do."

The NAACP lawyers were Donald Hollowell, a longtime stalwart of civil rights in Georgia, and Austin T. Walden, the legendary and somewhat elderly pillar of the black Atlanta establishment. When Bond was arrested, Walden drew his case. The day for Bond's trial came.

"He was asleep," said Bond. "He was asleep on his feet in the courtroom. I said, 'Oh my God, I'm going to jail for the rest of my life.' And then the judge asked me how how do I plead and I didn't know what to do. Hollowell whispered, 'Not guilty, you fool.' I was lucky I didn't say, 'Not guilty, you fool.' "

Bond laughed. "So a lot of it was suspicion that these people, because they disapproved of the methods and the techniques we were using, would try to derail us. And they did try to. M. L. King, Sr., did." Bond explained that the elder King and others in the establishment forced the students to join something called the Adult-Student Liaison Committee. And when the Atlanta sit-ins produced a desegregation agreement with white merchants, the adults demanded that the students sign an agreement stating that they would take advantage of the compact only if Atlanta's token school desegregation, then pending, occurred peacefully.

The elders also insisted, said Bond, that when desegregation day came, only a few Negroes would apply to test the agreement. The whole idea was to keep segregationist whites from getting overly riled — a desire shared by the older black leaders' white counterparts in city hall and in the Atlanta Chamber of Commerce. "And of course when the day came, all these adults shouldered us aside to go down to the lunch counters in their mink coats. This looked so peculiar — these matrons who wouldn't have eaten at the lunch counter in the first place, but they're dressing up in their finest daywear to eat at Woolworth's." Bond did an imitation: " 'I believe I'll have the split,' or, 'The grilled cheese looks good today,' or, 'How's the chili dog today?' "

Student-adult tensions reached the point where a mass meeting had to be called. The students attended and called "Sellout!" at Daddy King. "It took M. L. King, Jr., to calm the crowd down," said Bond.

"I remember: He lifted them up and he let them down." Bond described the formula by which black Southern preachers led their congregations through the rhythmic journeys of call, response, and elation that are their sermons. It was a technique at which Martin Luther King, Jr., was practically perfect. "He was making a speech on leadership and how you have to trust your leadership, no matter what it does," said Bond. "He lifted them up and he let them down, and then he lifted them up, and then he let them down, and then he stopped. People said, 'What happened? We're not angry anymore.' "

■ ─────────────────────────────

Older Southerners who had yearned for and worked toward a civil rights revolution quickly recognized the importance of Greensboro and the subsequent rapid spread of direct action protest. The Southern Regional Council issued a report at the end of February, 1960, declaring that the demonstrations showed the South "is in for a time of change, the terms of which cannot be dictated by white Southerners. . . . The deeper meaning of the 'sit-in' demonstrations is to show that segregation cannot be maintained in the South, short of continuous coercion and the intolerable social order which would result." The council, in another report issued a year and a half after Greensboro, found that all Southern and border states, and more than one hundred cities in them, had been affected by protest demonstrations. Some thirty-six hundred demonstrators had been arrested, and at least seventy thousand persons had taken part in protests. "A solitary instance of spontaneous rebellion," said the council, "has now become a movement of truly massive proportions which has stirred the conscience of the South and of the nation."[6]

───────────────────────── ■

In Charleston, South Carolina, civil rights had been a preoccupation of Harvey Gantt and his family ever since the *Brown* decision. NAACP meetings, protest gatherings, antisegregation speeches, all became a part of the household's life. When Harvey started playing high school football, his father led a group of parents in an effort to force the school board to abandon the black school's dilapidated stadium and use the one at the white school. The attempt was successful, and "that made an impression on me," Gantt said later.

"They petitioned for a change that people said they'd never get and the school board gave it up and gave us the right to use this facility. The next year my NAACP youth group decided that if the kids in Greensboro and college can sit at lunch counters, then maybe we can do it. So I led a group of two or three Negroes, and we sat down at the lunch counters. It was about six weeks before we were to graduate from high school. Much to the consternation of my mother and other parents, we all got sent to jail.

"But then we really didn't go jail. I mean, they put us in the courtroom and locked us up and told our parents to come get us. They said, 'Your kids are down here raising hell.'

"It caused a stir, but it fired my imagination for what possibly could be done, and it gave me a sense of responsibility. A lot of other people felt the same way: 'We ought to do something to change the system.' " Gantt met Matthew Perry, a black lawyer who handled civil rights litigation in South Carolina (and who now is a federal judge). Harvey and his high school friends were impressed with the work the lawyer was doing.

"And so," said Gantt, "what lived in my own mind was having seen this glimmer of light that said there was some hope. And most interesting of all, there were those of us who believed that it could change, and we weren't afraid to talk about the change. I think that was a substantial difference between the younger people back then and the older people — who, in fact, were the ones who helped us to go and sit in those meetings and listen to Roy Wilkins and the NAACP and Jim Farmer and other folks talk. It was that they were a little bit fearful, and we knew no fear."

––––––––––––––––

CORE was different from the NAACP and the Southern Christian Leadership Conference in that its national office existed largely to raise funds to support the work of its local chapters. The chapters were autonomous organizations, free to do pretty much what they wanted, as long as they adhered to what was called CORE Discipline, or the CORE Rules of Action. This was a ten-step set of guidelines that insured CORE would remain nonviolent and would never engage in direct action without first attempting to hold negotiations. As part of its support for the troops in the field, national CORE sponsored summer workshops in nonviolence. One of them was held in 1960 in Miami. Gordon Carey ran it.

"The object was to train people in the techniques of nonviolence so they could go back to their communities and do it right," said Carey. On the very first day of a three-week workshop, Carey would send teams of students out into Miami to determine which places of public accommodation, recreation, and transportation were segregated. Then, on subsequent days, the teams would attempt to negotiate desegregation; if that failed, direct action followed. The last step of the process, Carey hoped, was resolution of the problem. About twenty people took part in the training in 1960.

Bernard Lafayette, the Tampa resident who had been a participant in James Lawson's workshops in Nashville, came to Miami that summer for the CORE project. His team went out to test segregation at a restaurant. The plan had been to sit in until the students were asked to leave. Then they would depart quietly and return to their classroom to discuss what had happened, what their options had been, and how they could have done it better.

The team leader, Lafayette remembered, turned out to have more tenacity than the script called for. "This fellow decided not to move," he said. "When the police came and ordered him to move, he still didn't move. They said, 'Well, we might as well take you to jail.' And he was being very stubborn about it and said, 'Well, we'll go to jail.' That was very admirable, but that was not the purpose. So we ended up staying in jail ten days rather than having a workshop."

Dorothy Miller was twenty-two years old, white, and a senior at Queens College in New York when she heard about the Greensboro sit-ins. She was sitting at a lunch counter in New York City in early February, having a cup of coffee, when she read in a newspaper about the students in North Carolina who were trying to do the same thing. "And I remember thinking, 'This is fabulous,' " she said. "People were doing things that I had always read about and talked about. I was just carried away by these events. I was in college, getting ready to graduate, and I didn't know what I was going to do with myself. And this was thrilling, completely thrilling."

Dorothy Miller came from a long line of leftists, political activists of the Union Square variety, and she was in total sympathy with the goals of the Southern students. She wanted to take part in the Movement but wasn't sure how to go about it until she met someone who worked at CORE national headquarters and learned about the Miami workshop. "And I said, 'This is for me.' I applied and was accepted."

In Miami, "We did the usual — nonviolent workshops and getting arrested and all of that. And even though I had come from the left all my life, this was my first real exposure to the whole black social environment. I mean, I had never even heard of Ray Charles. I remember they all fell on the floor and died when I told them I didn't know who Ray Charles was.

"It was my first exposure to black culture, and *certainly* my first exposure to ministers, to religious people. And they couldn't understand me!" Miller spoke, and still speaks, in what can only be described as a New York accent. "Everybody was the same age. And I was totally taken with everything, with everybody."

Charles Jones had become active in student affairs at Johnson C. Smith University in Charlotte. For several years, he was among the Smith students who attended the North Carolina Student Legislature in Raleigh, a gathering at the state capitol of student government leaders from a number of colleges and universities. The delegates "introduced" and "passed" bills and learned about the legislative process. A fair number of the delegates — the white ones, at least — could be counted on to become active in state politics in their later years.

"I met a number of enlightened white students — my peers — from the University of North Carolina," said Jones. "And I found that many of them were going through a part of the same struggle that I was, but from a different perspective." He recalls that one bit of student legislation that caused a stir among the real legislators was a proposal, jointly sponsored by UNC and Johnson C. Smith students, that would have repealed the state's laws on interracial marriage.

Through his interest in student government, Jones fell in with a group of students who wanted to attend the Seventh World Youth Festival in Vienna. Previous festivals had been pretty thoroughly controlled by students who were sympathetic with communism, and the U.S. delegation had been made up of young people from the far left. This time, in 1959, the United States National Student Association wanted to send a second delegation to counteract the leftist propaganda. (Later it would be revealed that these efforts to neutralize the communists' manipulation actually were backed by manipulators from the U.S. Central Intelligence Agency.) Charles Jones, who had just graduated from Johnson C. Smith and was about to continue his education there in its divinity school, was one of those selected to attend. He took out a personal loan to pay his way; there was a small bit of financial help from a Chicago-based private group about which Jones knew little.

Jones and others from the NSA-backed group did try to present the "other side" of America to the festival. It was a side in which Jones very much believed: that the American system, with all its faults, was still the best there was; that segregation was an awful thing, but that recent events, such as the *Brown* decision and the Montgomery bus boycott, proved that the system worked, that it was capable of change. Jones was very much aware that the leftist students were trying to win over the representatives of Third World countries, and he directed his pitch at the same targets.

"It was a rather lively exchange," he recalled. "I was feeling pretty strongly positive about being black, so the dialogues turned out to be quite interesting and drew hundreds of students. The *Charlotte Observer* ran articles on it. The theme was basically 'Black Southern Student Defends Democracy,' with pictures. When I got back home, everybody was so proud of this colored boy, right?"

One of the actual headlines in Jones's hometown newspaper was "Charlotte Negro Shows World American Way of Life." The article, which ran on August 6, 1959, described Jones as "a champion of Americanism" who, fellow delegates reported, "held his own" in debates with delegates from communist nations. It quoted Jones as warning his fellow members of the "Chicago group" before the festival started: "Don't walk in unprepared for a Communist propaganda campaign. And be prepared to find distortions of the American way of life, particularly our most crucial problem, the race problem." Jones was further quoted as saying "progress has been made" in the United States "on the racial problem," though much more needed to be done.

In early February, 1960, Jones went to Washington to testify as a friendly witness before the House Committee on Un-American Activities (HUAC). The committee, which flourished during the communist-hunting years of Senator Joseph McCarthy, was examining what it called "Communist training operations." As its chairman explained, the "Communist conspiracy" sought to "soften up and condition" sympathetic American students and cultivate potential "hard-core, disciplined conspirators." The communists also sought the "subtle indoctrination of students." The committee was interested in learning from Jones what had gone on in Vienna.

Jones explained that past festival delegations from the United States had not given the "whole truth of the American way of life," and that he and others in the counter-delegation had tried to remedy that, with some success. Jones steered his way deftly through the hearing, avoiding any statements that might make him sound like a red-baiter. His message was simply that even with its troubles, democracy offered more opportunity than the communist alternative. He added:

"We found at the festival that it is much easier — much, much easier — to be anti-Communist than it is to be a good responsible American. You can point at all the shortcomings of the Communist system, but it is another matter when you get down and begin to attempt to get people to vote and you attempt to understand for yourself what we believe in, and attempt to work in a rational manner within our system."[7] Later, Jones recalled his appearance as one in which he was billed as a friendly witness but one in which he declined to toady. Again, he said, the press recorded his testimony along the lines of "Black Student Defends Democracy."

He was driving home to Charlotte when he heard on the car radio a report of the sit-ins in Greensboro. It was about two o'clock in the morning.

"It was like the feelings I had when I first heard about Dr. King," he said; "the feelings that I had when I heard about the 1954 school desegregation ruling. All of a sudden there was a handle to getting at this stuff, and I knew — intuitively I knew that this was our time.

"I came home. I was vice president of the student council at Smith at that point. And I ran into the mayor on the street uptown, and he said, 'Mr. Jones! Boy, we're proud of you. You're a credit to your race. You're a credit to Charlotte, too.'

"I went up to the student council and said, 'Listen: Tomorrow morning I'm going down to Woolworth's. If you want to come, fine.' "

Jones rounded up some other students and said there was going to be a sit-in and that it would be a nonviolent one. Then he went back to his room and got some sleep. When he showed up on the campus the following morning, "There were three hundred students ready to march. I said, 'Okay, guys, showtime!' I'll never forget the feeling of raw power. And then we all started going downtown."

Leadership for the demonstration sort of "emerged," said Jones, though he was certainly one of those most in charge. He was leading a spillover group from Woolworth's to start another demonstration at Kress's when some reporters spotted him and started asking questions. "Of course, they were familiar with this colored boy who was defending democracy," he said, laughing. In the middle of it all, "the mayor came walking down the street. I never will forget this. He looked at me with the most puzzled look on his face.

"And the headline this time was, 'Johnson C. Smith Student Disrupts Downtown Sitting In at a Lunch Counter.' "

"Negroes Extend Sitdown Protest" was the headline on the Associated Press dispatch that ran February 10 in the *New York Times*. The story (which placed the turnout at 150) quoted Charles Jones as saying, "I have no malice, no jealousy, no hatred, no envy. All I want is to come in and place my order and be served and leave a tip if I feel like it." The article noted that Jones had recently testified before HUAC about "his efforts to counter anti–United States propaganda at the Communist-sponsored World Youth Council."

■ ────────────────────────────

FOURTEEN

■

A GLORIOUS OPPORTUNITY

■

The sit-ins by Southern black college students and their sympathizers led to a gathering of demonstration leaders for the purpose of discussing techniques, accomplishments, and goals. All over the region, local leaders such as Charles Jones of Charlotte and Harvey Gantt of Charleston had heard about sit-ins elsewhere and had put on their own demonstrations, which had met with varying degrees of success.

In some places, the merchants and political leaders seemed quite willing (if not anxious, given the economic incentives) to make the change. In others, as in Jackson, Mississippi, the response was billy sticks and police dogs and jail sentences. But in terms of long-range achievement, the demonstrators could not have been more successful. They mobilized the youthful Negroes whom Diane Nash had found to be "resigned" to segregation; they tapped a source of energy and devotion that hardly anyone had known was there. They mobilized, too, the elders of the black community, who had their own problems with resignation. The demonstrators discovered a dramatic way to get their case before the American public at large; the insistence by sit-in leaders that participants be well dressed and polite was a masterstroke.

Perhaps the demonstrators' most important tool in the quest for public sympathy was their use of nonviolence in the demonstrations. Where there was violence, it was provided by the all-too-willing white youths and younger men, neither well dressed nor polite, who strode up behind the Negroes at the lunch counters and poured ketchup on them or dragged them off their stools, and who invariably resembled the stereotype of the Southern white racist at his worst — the grinning, ignorant redneck and the cracker. They were straight out of central casting, and they could not have helped the Movement more. The demonstrators succeeded, too, in taking the matter of desegregation a step beyond the legal issues of equal protection or freedom of association. In the sit-ins, as Constance Baker Motley of the NAACP Inc. Fund observed (and thousands of white supremacists agreed), private and not public property was involved. The demonstrators, in bringing the Movement inside dime stores and restaurants, were insisting that America consider the *moral* implications of segregation as well as the legal ones.

Ella Baker, the executive director of Martin Luther King's Southern Christian Leadership Conference, recognized the significance of the sit-ins. She was quick to see the need for the various student leaders to communicate with one another. So she arranged a meeting for Easter weekend, 1960, the students' first opportunity to get away from their colleges and universities. SCLC contributed eight hundred dollars toward the expenses of the conference, which was held April 16 through 18 at Shaw University in Raleigh, North Carolina. Shaw was Baker's alma mater.

The meeting's organizers expected as many as a hundred students to answer the call for a Southwide Student Leadership Conference, but more than three hundred showed up. In addition, there were observers from more than a dozen Northern-based organizations.[1]

From the beginning it was clear that officials within SCLC — notably Dr. King; second in command Ralph Abernathy; and Wyatt Tee Walker, who had been a member of the SCLC national board

since 1958 and who was chosen King's chief of staff in 1960 —
were hoping that any formal group that grew out of the sit-in
demonstrations would belong to SCLC. It would be a sort of youthful affiliate group to function in concert with, and support the actions of, SCLC's existing leadership, which was older, male, and
deeply rooted in the black church. Ella Baker, who was not afraid
to speak her mind within whatever organization paid her salary,
argued against such an approach on the grounds that the student
movement was too new and too fresh to be co-opted by anyone.
What the young leaders needed, rather, was more independence.
James Forman, who in a few months would become the director
of the new student group, later wrote that Baker wanted to protect the students and their ideals from SCLC's "leader-centered
orientation" and that she "felt that the organization was depending too much on the press and on the promotion of Martin King,
and was not developing enough indigenous leadership across the
South."[2]

After discussions became so heated that Baker walked out of
a conference in disgust, the SCLC leaders backed off and allowed
the student gathering to develop at its own pace. On April 17 the
students rejected any organizational affiliation and established a
group to be called the Student Nonviolent Coordinating Committee (SNCC, pronounced "snick"). It would, they said, be a temporary organization (and, in fact, its original name was the Temporary
Student Nonviolent Coordinating Committee).

James Lawson, who had led the workshops in nonviolence in
Nashville, was the conference's keynote speaker. He talked of the
power and value of nonviolence in showing white Southerners the
evil of their system, but he also spoke critically of the "legalistic"
approach to fighting segregation as practiced by the National Association for the Advancement of Colored People. Before he left
the conference, Martin Luther King, Jr., urged more study of nonviolence, regionwide demonstrations to involve the federal government in the fight against segregation, and a nationwide "selective
buying campaign" to economically punish practitioners of segregation.

On the penultimate day of their meeting, the students adopted a "Statement of Purpose" that clearly reflected the thinking of Lawson and the Nashville group. It said:

> We affirm the philosophical or religious ideal of nonviolence as the foundation of our purpose, the presupposition of our faith, and the manner of our action. Nonviolence as it grows from Judaic-Christian traditions seeks a social order of justice permeated by love. Integration of human endeavor represents the crucial first step towards such a society.
>
> Through nonviolence, courage displaces fear; love transforms hate. Acceptance dissipates prejudice; hope ends despair. Peace dominates war; faith reconciles doubt. Mutual regard cancels enmity. Justice for all overthrows injustice. The redemptive community supersedes systems of gross social immorality.
>
> Love is the central motif of nonviolence. Love is the force by which God binds man to Himself and man to man. Such love goes to the extreme; it remains loving and forgiving even in the midst of hostility. It matches the capacity of evil to inflict suffering with an even more enduring capacity to absorb evil, all the while persisting in love.
>
> By appealing to conscience and standing on the moral nature of human existence, nonviolence nurtures the atmosphere in which reconciliation and justice become actual possibilities.[3]

Ed King, a Nashville student, was chosen as the interim administrator of the group. The new organization agreed to hold monthly meetings, and then the participants returned to their campuses, to final exams, and to more demonstrations. By this time, the word "movement" was being widely employed to describe the effort to break segregation in the American South.

Martin Luther King had been preaching nonviolence for several years, of course. Organizations such as CORE and the Fellowship of Reconciliation had done their own preaching far longer, and the concept was certainly not new to persons interested in the Movement. But the sit-ins marked the first time nonviolence was used on a wide-scale basis throughout the South, and in sympathy demonstrations in the North, Midwest, and West as well. The sociodrama employed by James Lawson, Gordon Carey, and others found a place in classrooms and church meeting halls from Virginia to Texas.

In later years, some of the participants in the Movement would assert that they never really believed in nonviolence as anything more than a tactic. James Forman, SNCC's most durable executive director, is prime among these; his discussions of nonviolence in his memoir, *The Making of Black Revolutionaries*, border on ridicule. He writes, "Nonviolence was always a tactic as far as others and I were concerned, and not the ultimate weapon of liberation." Forman said that he advocated nonviolence in the sixties because, although he actually thought a revolution was necessary, the people weren't ready for one. Revolutions, he writes, "are not made overnight. They take time and people must be willing to sacrifice all, their lives especially, before revolutions can happen. A mass movement to heighten consciousness would be the first step." That would produce a "sacrificial group" which, through its practice of nonviolence, would "develop the mass consciousness."[4]

Nonviolence worked marvelously, as Diane Nash had discovered in Nashville. For every practitioner who felt with her that the technique had become a way of life, there were dozens of others who may well have thought of it as a tactic but who were *behaving*, at the time, as if it influenced their every waking deed.

The SNCC "Statement of Purpose" did a good job of defining nonviolence as it was being discussed and practiced in the early sixties. Central to the concept was the notion of redemptive suffering, or the belief, based on the story of Christ's death, that suffering for others' sins redeems both the sinners and the sufferer. Also fundamental was *satyagraha*, the concept of "soul force" that Charles Jones and many others had discovered in the wake of the Montgomery boycott.

■

In 1988, when veterans of SNCC gathered at Trinity College, there was much talk of the old days but also discussion of how the lessons and techniques learned in the sixties could be applied to the situation today, which almost everyone agreed was one of an unfinished civil rights revolution.

Diane Nash, now back in school in Chicago but still working for social change (she was studying the psychology of the oppression that manifests itself in those identified as the "underclass"), was one of the speakers at the conference. She addressed her remarks not to those who had been through the segregation wars with her but to the large number of younger people in the audience, most of them black, who had come out of curiosity or who were involved in present-day activism on their own college campuses.

"Our goal," said Nash, "was to reconcile, to really heal, and to rehabilitate; to solve problems, rather than to simply gain power over the opposition. And it really comes to the question of, Do you believe that human beings can be healed? Can be rehabilitated?"

Nash explained the Gandhian origins of the Movement's brand of nonviolence, and she paid tribute to James Lawson's work in Nashville. Then she listed some of the "basic tenets underlying the philosophy" as it was practiced then.

"First, we took truth and love very seriously. We felt that in order to create a community where there was more love and more humaneness, it was necessary to use humaneness and love in terms of trying to get to that point that ends do not justify means — that, as Gandhi said, everything is really a series of means.

"We took truth very seriously. In fact, I guess this has been very important to me in living my whole life; I'm sure I've lived an entirely different kind of life as a result of having been exposed to the philosophy in those early years. Truth now, for me, has very little to do with being good or doing what's right. It's more relevant to me in terms of providing oneself and people around us with accurate information on which to base our behavior and base our decisions." Students of the natural sciences understand this principle well, she said, when they are solving mathematical problems or conducting laboratory experiments. This, she added, might explain "why in the natural sciences we're in the space age, and in the social sciences we're in primitive stages." In the social world, nations lie to nations; whole institutions such as the Central Intelligence Agency and the Federal Bureau of Investigation are devoted to lying. "Governments of countries lie to the citizens; in male-female relationships, boyfriends lie to girlfriends, girlfriends to boyfriends, husbands and wives to each other.

"I think another fundamental quality of the Movement is that we used nonviolence as an expression of love and respect of the opposition, while noting that a *person* is never the enemy. The enemy is always attitudes, such as racism or sexism; political systems that are unjust; economic systems that are unjust — some kind of system or attitude that oppresses. . . ."

One of the lunch counter managers in Nashville, she said, was the students' enemy in the first year of sit-in activity. But in the second year he became an ally and encouraged other store managers to desegregate, advising them, "It sounds really difficult, but it's not so bad."

"Another important tenet, I think, of the philosophy," said Nash, "was recognizing that oppression always requires the participation of the oppressed. So that rather than doing harm to the oppressor, another way to go is to identify your part in your own oppression, and then withdraw your cooperation from the system of oppression, and guarantee if the oppressed withdraw their cooperation from their own oppression, the system of oppression cannot work.

"An example of that would be the Montgomery bus boycott. For many years, Montgomery blacks assumed that Alabama whites were segregating them on buses. But in order to have segregated buses, it was necessary for the blacks to get on the bus, pay their fare, and walk to the back of the bus. When Montgomery blacks decided that there weren't going to be segregated buses anymore, there were segregated buses no more. It didn't take *any* change on the parts of whites when the blacks decided that there would no longer be segregated buses.

"So then you have to ask yourself the question, 'Well, who was segregating the buses all this time?' I think there's a thin line between what's known as 'blaming the victim' and identifying appropriate responsibility. And I think that when you do identify your own responsibility in an oppressive situation, it then puts you in a position of power. Because then you are able to withdraw your participation and therefore end the system."

Then Nash explained to the young people the five steps in the process of nonviolent direct action. The steps were employed, successfully, in community after community across the South — even, eventually, in hardest-core Mississippi and Alabama. To most white observers, including the press, there appeared to be only one step — demonstration. But actually overt action came close to the end of the list.

"The first step was investigation," explained Nash, "where we really did all the necessary research and analysis to totally understand the problem. The second phase was education, where we educated our own constituency to what we had found out in our research.

"The third stage was negotiation, where you really approached the opposition, let them know your position, and tried to come to a solution. The fourth stage was demonstration. The purpose of demonstrations was to focus the attention of the community on the issue, and on the injustice. And the last stage was resistance, where you really withdraw your support from the oppressive system. And during this stage would take place things like boycotts, work stoppages, and nonsupport of the system."

Some of the students who had come to the SNCC gathering were taking notes furiously. Diane Nash finished up.

"I think that the philosophy that started in Nashville that was borrowed from India, that was the philosophy of the Student Nonviolent Coordinating Committee in its early days, has a great deal of merit. Everything considered, there was a considerable amount of social change. There were some deaths, a number of injuries, but in looking at the efficiency of that struggle and comparing the number of casualties, I think that the philosophy that Gandhi developed works. It appears to me to be more efficient than many violent struggles. And I would really urge you to do some studying of the history of nonviolence and some reading, perhaps, of how it works. I think it's got great potential for today."

———————

Julian Bond joined up with SNCC and became its communications director. His attitude toward nonviolence was probably representative of many of the Movement's participants:

"At one time I thought I was just all-around nonviolent. This was going to be my way of life. I thought that whatever I did in the future, I'd try to resolve conflicts in this fashion. I thought this for a brief period, but mostly I thought it was a technique, a tactic. And there was no chance of violence of any kind — defensive or offensive. There was just no chance of *that* working."

John Lewis saw the pledge to nonviolence as one that grew largely out of religious commitment. It was no surprise to him, he said, that Southern Negroes took to the philosophy more readily than some of their Northern counterparts. Many, perhaps most, of the demonstration leaders in Nashville and elsewhere were in the process of becoming ordained ministers. Even Diane Nash, an English major, moved easily to nonviolence because she was a devout Catholic, he said.

"The whole idea of nonviolence was based on the love ethic of the New Testament, really," said Lewis. "We really believed in that whole idea that you don't go out hating people, you don't go out using people, killing people, beating people. We really accepted what the great teachers said: Turn the other cheek, and be willing to accept the beating, to suffer, because it's redemptive. It can change the oppressor, but it also can change you and help, in the process, to change the larger society."

As the Movement grew, and as resistance grew harder and people of differing backgrounds and ages took up the struggle, the devotion to love and nonviolence declined. Some people never had it. In SNCC, said Lewis, "Jim Forman was a decent, good person, but I don't think Jim really ever understood the philosophy and the discipline of nonviolence. And I think it was difficult for young blacks and young whites who've grown up in New York or Chicago, outside of the South, without a religious foundation, to come to readily accept this strange message."

Bernard Lafayette was one of the Nashville group, a student at what then was named American Baptist Theological Seminary and a leader of the sit-ins there. He saw nonviolence as "a fulfillment of my whole ministry, my calling."

The idea of redemptive suffering may strike some people as a difficult doctrine to practice, said Lafayette long after the sit-ins, but he disagrees. "In the physical sense, it's easy to do. A lot of people say, 'Oh, I couldn't stand it if somebody hit me.' But that's not difficult. Football players get hit all the time; that's part of the game. They're prepared for it. It's just a matter of being psychologically and physically prepared for it. If you don't want to do that, then you don't get involved. Some people don't get involved in sports because that's part of the game."

Lafayette said one of the reasons he joined the demonstrations was to test himself. "I was curious to know how I would feel if I were struck physically for standing up for what I believed was right. I was more concerned about what was happening on the inside of me — what my reaction would be. How would I feel about that person? Could I in fact find a place in my heart to love someone, not to hate someone, who was physically abusing me and abusing my friends, and my colleagues, my schoolmates?"

As the Movement continued, Lafayette had many opportunities to satisfy his curiosity. His first reaction to being physically attacked, he said, was to acknowledge to himself that he didn't really have to be there absorbing the abuse of segregationists. "It was a choice that I made. I could have removed myself from the situation. But, no, I deliberately chose to be there. The next thing that happened to me was that I felt a great deal of sympathy for the person who was attacking me, because I had the opportunity to be able to stand up for what I believed in. And I also knew, ultimately, that what I was standing for was going to prevail."

The young minister thought of what was going on as a "misunderstanding," he said, and he regretted the fact that, under the circumstances of a lunch counter confrontation or an attack with billy sticks on a courthouse steps, "there was no opportunity to really sit down with them and to discuss this thing back and forth and listen to them express how they felt — the anger, the fear.

"You see, they were afraid. I was not. That was the misfortune there. They were threatened by my presence. They did not threaten me at all, even though they used physical force. So I felt stronger, in a sense."

Lafayette knew it was possible that he would be killed. It had happened before to Negroes who challenged the white system in far less threatening ways than the direct confrontations that were now occurring. But he believed he was prepared to die: "If my life was lost, the thing that they were trying to protect they would lose ultimately," he said. He also knew that if he were killed, the news of his death would advance the cause. "It only becomes fuel for the Movement, in that sense. No one wanted to die. I mean, I didn't. I love to live, okay? But if it had befallen my lot to have made the supreme sacrifice, as others did in the Movement, then that would've been an honor — to have given my life for something that I believe in. Something I feel worthwhile, as opposed to getting run over by a car or getting killed in Vietnam.

"And when you think about all the people who died senseless deaths — blacks who were caught in the wrong place on a dark road at night, a no-name person, the many black bodies they fished out of the rivers in Mississippi when they were looking for the three civil rights workers who died there — those lives were lost, for no cause, simply because they were black, maybe. Those who killed them probably didn't even know their names. So to take some deliberate action to change these conditions was a glorious opportunity."

Henry Schwarzschild, a white man, did not believe in the idea of redemptive suffering, although he admired those who did. He believed in something else that, in the end, was equally strong and motivating and that was his own glorious opportunity.

Schwarzschild was born in Wiesbaden, Germany, in 1925, to a family of Jewish intellectuals who traced their name back to the Frankfurt ghetto of 1425. He moved to Berlin in 1931. His home was filled with the comings and goings of politically, intellectually, and artistically active people. "Even as a young kid," said Schwarzschild, "it was impossible to avoid being made enormously, prematurely conscious of the world around one." A terrifying aspect of that world was the rise of Hitler and Nazism; the family and Henry fled to Paris in early 1939 and moved on to New York City later that year.

Schwarzschild's early experiences left him, he said later, "very sensitive to issues of political liberty." It was a condition that would influence his entire life, but especially so when he returned to Europe at the end of the war as a U.S. counterintelligence agent during the occupation.

Schwarzschild was not a spy, he hastens to point out, but rather a soldier who interrogated war prisoners and worked in the "denazification" effort. And as he talked and dealt officially and personally with the people whom he had last seen in 1939, he discovered a terribly obvious fact: "That the difficult moral problems" in dealing with Germans "were not raised by people who'd been, for example, concentration camp guards.

"That wasn't a moral problem. That was very easy. The *difficult* issue was, What do you do about people who were Germans, who lived in Germany, who had families, who had jobs, who wanted nothing so much as to somehow survive and make it, and who — though they knew precisely what was going on (because everybody did; the notion that that was hard to know, or impossible to know, or unknown, is of course a laughable and melancholy illusion) — themselves may not have been guilty of laying a hand on anyone, but who sat by while it was all going on? *That* seemed to me to be the great moral and human dilemma.

"And so the one thing that I concluded was that I would not want to say to myself at the end of my life that when there were enormously significant things going on in my society, I did nothing. The one unforgivable sin would be to stand by and let them happen and do nothing about them. That I would have to say to myself, as I thought Germans at the very best could say to themselves, that I let it go.

"And I realized, and I certainly realize in retrospect, that it is a rare historical luxury that historically significant events in one's own lifetime will come along where the merits are so utterly and abundantly clear that it isn't a matter, as it is in most political and existential things, of 'on balance' thinking you're probably doing the right thing. With most things, it's sort of fifty-one to forty-nine; and if you think you ought to be on the fifty-one percent side, then you do that vigorously; but you're also very conscious that there are forty-nine percent whose merits lie somewhere else, and you sort of do the best you can. That's how we navigate through life, because the luxuries of radically clear, black and white issues are very rare.

"It seemed to me that the civil rights movement was, after the experience of Hitler and the Holocaust, sort of the closest to that that was liable to come down the pike."

Although Schwarzschild had been prepared for something like the Movement all his life, he remembers being "peculiarly unsophisticated and blindly unaware" of the problems of segregation in his early years in America. But by the time he was in basic training at Fort Benning, Georgia, in 1944, he was ready to put his feelings into action. He was attending a Passover service and meal at the fort for Jewish soldiers, who had been released from normal duty for the evening. The commanding general and the chaplain sat at the head table with people from the local Jewish community.

The first part of the service was held, and then the meal was served. Henry Schwarzschild noticed something wrong. "Here we had been given the evening off, freed from duty," he said, "and who was serving these Jewish GIs their meal at the feast of liberation from slavery in Egypt? It was a bunch of black GIs who were doing extra duty." Outraged, Schwarzschild called the chaplain over and pointed out the irony. "And he threatened me with court-martial. He said if I didn't go back to my seat and sit down and shut up, he — he was an orthodox rabbi from Detroit, I remember — he would court-martial me.

"I left the hall then. I didn't participate in this thing. I was very much outraged by that. I wasn't an activist, and I probably didn't know a single black person to talk to, and never had — but those were my sorts of impulses out of that whole experience of persecution and exile and immigration and readjustment."

It was Easter weekend in 1960, the same weekend when the black student activists were gathering at Shaw University to discuss the future of the sit-ins, when Henry Schwarzschild and his wife, Kathy, then living in Chicago, were visiting Kathy's mother in Richmond, Kentucky. Schwarzschild, who has said he never quite understood Southern whites, managed to marry one — a socially conscious woman who had attended Berea College, a school begun by abolitionists for the education of Kentucky's mountain people, regardless of their color.

The Schwarzschilds drove over to Berea to see one of Kathy's old English professors, who took them to a meeting of the American Civil Liberties Union that he was chairing. "It was a very tiny group," recalled Henry, "including four or five heavy-set, middle-aged black ladies from Lexington who had come down to tell about the sit-ins that were going to take place tomorrow, Saturday, on the main drag of Lexington at the McCrory's and the Woolworth's and the other five-and-ten-cent lunch counters."

Lexington was on the way home to Chicago, and the Schwarzschilds were planning to head home on Saturday. "And we looked at each other and said, 'One cannot drive through Lexington and act as if these sit-ins weren't happening.'

The Schwarzschilds stopped off in Lexington on Saturday. They had a baby with them, so Kathy stayed in the car. "I proceeded to join the demos outside the five-and-ten on the main drag in Lexington," said Henry. "We were not arrested. We only carried sandwich signs outside the store. The vivid memory I have of that is all the people from the country walking along the main street — Saturday being the great shopping day in a place like that, when all the country folks come in to do their shopping — and then stopping, amazed at this spectacle and lip-reading the signs. I remember seeing their lips sort of mouthing the words, unaspirated: 'Don't Buy at This Store,' or 'Racial Justice,' or whatever it was, and with great difficulty figuring out what this was all about.

"I was there for a couple of hours, marching up and down the street with a bunch of black folks from Lexington, and we didn't even, as I remember it, enter the store, and we were certainly not in that sense technically a sit-in. It was more a sympathy demonstration with the sit-ins. And there were no arrests while I was part of that group."

Henry Schwarzschild finished his picket duty, turned in his sign, and went back to the car, and he and Kathy and the child returned to Chicago. Before long he was engaged in a correspondence with the Congress of Racial Equality. He was looking for ways he could help with the Movement that had started.

■ ─────────────────────

FIFTEEN

■

A HANDLE THAT WE COULD USE

■

The Movement was growing rapidly now, its techniques of nonviolent direct action attracting adherents who never before had seen roles for themselves. Through the summer of 1960, the new Student Nonviolent Coordinating Committee met and talked about what to do next and how to do it. The participants were aware that they had a power that never before had existed. They did not at first know how difficult the struggle would be, or how long it would take.

When SNCC held its first formal meeting after the Shaw University conference, in mid-May, it was at Atlanta University, not far from its new office. Ella Baker had provided a tiny, temporary working space in the headquarters of the Southern Christian Leadership Conference. Perhaps even more important, she arranged for the students to use SCLC's mimeograph machine and mailing facilities. One of SNCC's first acts was to publish a newspaper, *The Student Voice*. In the first issue, Julian Bond had a poem. Marion Barry, a graduate student in chemistry at Fisk University, became SNCC's interim chair.

Nineteen-sixty was also a presidential election year. As summer approached, the nation's attention was focussed not only on antisegregation demonstrations, but also on the race between Democrat John F. Kennedy and Republican Richard M. Nixon. More than in any other election since Reconstruction, Negroes and their preferences on election day played important parts in the campaign. While only 28 percent of Southern voting-age Negroes were registered, more than 60 percent of those in the North were signed up.[1] This meant the rules of national elections were being redrawn; the census of 1960 revealed that for the first time in the nation's history, more than half the nation's black population (which made up 10.5 percent of the total population) lived outside the Deep South. Given the right candidate, and the proper motivation to vote for that candidate, the black vote from places such as Chicago and New York and Philadelphia could conceivably make an enormous difference.

Politicians could hardly fail to notice that if Negroes were assured the right to vote in the South as well, they could produce profound and rapid changes in the system. And Negroes did want to vote, despite all sorts of repression. In Fayette County, Tennessee, black tenant farmers attempted to register that year even when they were run off their land by whites and refused credit by local merchants. The dispossessed Negroes then moved into tents in an open field and continued their efforts. After much hardship and white violence, the federal government finally intervened and secured the Negroes' right to register and vote.[2]

SNCC joined other civil rights groups in sending representatives to the major political parties' platform-writing sessions to ask for help with the desegregation struggle. The Democratic party platform urged "equal access for all Americans to all areas of community life" and promised to use existing civil rights acts to secure the right to vote, to eliminate literacy tests and poll taxes, and "to ensure the beginning of good-faith compliance" with the six-year-old *Brown* decision. The Republican party platform condemned racial discrimination as unconstitutional, immoral, and unjust, and said, "As to those matters within reach of political action and leadership, we pledge ourselves to its eradication." A sixth-grade education, said the GOP, should serve as acceptable proof of literacy for voting registration.[3]

The politicians and the rest of white America were offered evidence that not everyone played by the rules of nonviolence. After ten days of sit-ins in Jacksonville, Florida, in August, a riot occurred. An estimated fifty people were injured, and both whites and blacks were beaten. When black people conducted a "wade-in" at a Gulf of Mexico beach in Biloxi, Mississippi, whites rioted, and ten blacks were wounded by gunfire. In Orangeburg, South Carolina, whites (including policemen) reacted violently against demonstrations by a thousand Negroes.[4]

At a gathering in October, SNCC became a permanent organization. A significant aspect of this meeting, as SNCC historian Clayborne Carson has noted, was the presence of a number of observers "from groups advocating Marxist ideas and interracial coalitions."[5] These included the Socialist party, the Young People's Socialist League, and Students for a Democratic Society. SNCC's attitude then, and throughout most of its existence, was that it would accept help from anywhere, anyone, and any organization, regardless of philosophy, so long as the help came with no strings attached. This policy provided SNCC's enemies with abundant opportunities to accuse the organization of being the pawn of communists or extremist "outside" factions. But through the years SNCC was able to maintain its autonomy as well as any other civil rights group, although its positions on militancy and nonviolence did change a good deal. (SNCC's policy on outside help was set down in a version of its constitution published in 1962. "Informal relationships" between SNCC and "various student groups in the North," said the document, had proved helpful in establishing communications and exploring mutual problems, in inspiring Northern students to attack problems in their region, and in raising money for the Movement. The policy, therefore, was to invite such groups to become "associates" of SNCC. "Representatives from associated groups," said SNCC's constitution, "may be invited to attend meetings of the Coordinating Committee, although without vote.")[6]

In November, the nation got, in John Kennedy, the first chief executive who might reasonably be expected to be a "civil rights president." It became possible, wrote Harold Fleming, "to speak meaningfully of a federal civil rights strategy, however rudimentary, for the first time in living memory." All Kennedy had to go on in the field of race relations when he came into office, said Fleming, was "a legacy of piecemeal legislation and executive actions." He certainly inherited a climate in which change was expected. The new president (and his brother Robert, whom he installed as attorney general) could — and would have to — formulate a civil rights policy.[7]

Kennedy's campaign showed that he was aware of this. When he courted New York's Liberal party in the summer of 1960, he said that he hoped to win the Democratic nomination at the convention without a single Southern vote (all Southern convention votes were cast by white people then), and that he considered the civil rights issue to be a moral one. Kennedy appeared before the party's policy committee at a time of intense national preoccupation with race; on the same day the candidate spoke, the regional Hot Shoppes restaurant chain allowed Negroes to eat in its Virginia outlets. Accounts of both events made the front page of the *New York Times*. In his Liberal party visit, Kennedy said, "The next Democratic Administration must offer a new liberalism for the sixties — a liberalism which reaches beyond the era of the New and Fair Deals to the problems of a new age."[8]

Kennedy had clearly promised to be an activist in the field of civil rights. In the summer before the election he declared, "The next president of the United States cannot stand above the battle engaging in vague little sermons on brotherhood." And before that he had said, "In the decade that lies ahead . . . the American presidency will demand more than ringing manifestoes issued from the rear of battle. It will demand that the president place himself in the very thick of the fight."[9]

Much could be accomplished, Kennedy felt, by enforcing existing legislation and by executive initiatives, rather than seeking new laws, which would mean tangling with Southern white supremacists in Congress. He offered as a campaign example the fact that "the president could sign an executive order ending discrimination in housing tomorrow." This became known, no doubt to Kennedy's rue, as his "stroke of a pen" promise. The president didn't keep it until almost two years had passed and civil rights activists had mailed numerous bottles of symbolic ink to his office as reminders. Even then, the executive order was shy on substance.

Kennedy also pointed out in his campaign that the executive branch could make sure that companies doing business with the government did not discriminate in employment. And it was clear that both Kennedys thought that insuring the right to vote was the key to peace and progress in the civil rights arena.

And then there was the matter of the telephone calls.

When Martin Luther King, Jr., moved from Montgomery to Atlanta to participate full-time in the operation of SCLC, he was slow about exchanging his Alabama driver's license for one from Georgia. Even though the law was ambiguous about how much time an immigrant was allowed in which to obtain Georgia certification, the diligent police of DeKalb County, Georgia, arrested King for driving without a valid license. Although it was contiguous to Atlanta and part of the metropolitan area that people meant when they referred to Atlanta, DeKalb had a leadership that reflected small-town and south-Georgia thinking and behavior. A DeKalb criminal court judge, Oscar Mitchell, found King guilty and placed him on probation. By this time Movement leaders and participants expected such actions in court, and nobody viewed the DeKalb conviction with much alarm.

In the fall of 1960, student sit-ins started in Atlanta. Partly in order to defuse the tensions between the demonstrating students from the Atlanta University Center and the entrenched black establishment, of which his father was a charter member, King offered support to the students. He went with them to the Magnolia Room at Rich's department store, a place frequented by proper white shoppers who liked tea and little sandwiches without crusts. The black visitors asked for food. The store, whose owner was thought of as one of the city's "moderates" on race relations, but who also had a lot of white customers, had King and the students arrested. They sang "We Shall Overcome" as high police officials politely escorted them down to the ground floor in elevators and off to jail.

King pretty much had the run of the Fulton County (Atlanta) Jail, getting his hair cut by an inmate barber who also offered him a shoe shine (King declined). But in DeKalb County, Judge Mitchell swung into action. He decided King had violated the terms of his probation on the license conviction, and he ordered the civil rights leader into state prison. This turned out to be another in the long series of actions through which whites who opposed the Movement would bless the struggle with assistance that could not have been bought with gold.

John Kennedy took time out from his campaigning and called King's wife, Coretta, to express his concern. Robert Kennedy telephoned Judge Mitchell, a fellow Democrat, during the probation hearing. He wanted, he said, to express his own interest and that of his brother, who just happened to be running for president at the time. Mitchell told reporters about the call, giving the story much more publicity than Robert Kennedy could have achieved himself. On the next day, King was released on bail. Soon after that, John Kennedy won the presidency. A major factor in his victory was the Negro vote. On the Sunday before election day, black preachers around the nation urged their congregations to vote for Kennedy. King himself came close to endorsing the candidate, and some 70 percent of the Negro vote went to the Democrats.[10] Decades later, blacks who had become thoroughly disenchanted with government in general and the Democratic party in particular would nevertheless speak kindly of Kennedy for what he had done.

Even though the sit-ins were dramatic and produced quick results — or perhaps because of that — the activists in the reenergized Movement began experimenting with new techniques. This offered further evidence that, while the Movement may have seemed to many to be just a collection of unrelated dramatic events, it was actually far more evolution than revolution.

Robert Moses, a Northern Negro, went to Atlanta in the summer of 1960 to work with SCLC on a voter registration project, but he quickly became more interested in SNCC's efforts. Moses (who later would become a SNCC staffer of almost mythical reputation) went off to the Deep South to recruit black leaders for a SNCC conference to be held in October, 1960. Along the way he met Amzie Moore, the NAACP leader in Cleveland, Mississippi. Moore impressed Moses with his arguments about the importance of the ballot in the hard-core South. He convinced the younger man of the value of a project that would send volunteers into Mississippi not to test discrimination at lunch counters or on municipal buses but to help with a registration drive.

And when the October, 1960, SNCC meeting was held, James Lawson asked for another refinement in the technique of protest. He urged students to conduct their demonstrations on a "jail, no bail" basis. Refusing to post bond and staying in jail to serve out sentences for "loitering" and "breach of peace" would dramatize the situation, clog the unjust system with warm bodies, and draw increased attention from the press, which Movement leaders now recognized as essential to their success. Declining the bond option would amount to refusing to cooperate with one's oppressors. And there could be an added benefit: If more and more Negroes and their white sympathizers went to jail, blacks' fundamental fear of incarceration could be shaken and, possibly, shattered. The system's strongest hold on the Negro, terror, might be weakened.

Jail, no bail got a field trial in Rock Hill, South Carolina, at the end of 1960.

Students at Rock Hill's Friendship Junior College, many of them members of the Congress of Racial Equality, had held sit-ins shortly after the Greensboro demonstrations. They had been arrested, and the facilities they had visited remained segregated. The black community of Rock Hill inaugurated a boycott of segregated businesses that lasted through the fall.

In December, 1960, some Rock Hill students who had attended a CORE workshop decided they should demonstrate again, this time refusing to bail out if arrested or pay fines if sentenced. On January 31, 1961, a group sat in and was arrested. The head of the State Law Enforcement Division, South Carolina's version of the Federal Bureau of Investigation, was on hand personally to participate in the arrests. On February 1, the first anniversary of Greensboro, a judge found the demonstrators guilty of trespass and sentenced them to thirty days in jail or hundred-dollar fines. Almost all the students chose jail. The word went out that Rock Hill needed an infusion of demonstrators.[11]

A group of SNCC members — those who functioned as a kind of steering committee — heard the call while at a meeting in Atlanta and responded. They included Ruby Doris Smith, from Atlanta's Spelman College; Diane Nash of Fisk; Charles Jones of

Johnson C. Smith; and Charles Sherrod of Virginia Union University. The SNCC members went to Rock Hill, sought service at a segregated downtown soda fountain, and were promptly arrested on trespassing charges and sentenced to thirty days in jail. Though the protesters had hoped their decision would set an example and bring large numbers of demonstrators to Rock Hill to get arrested and snarl the system, few others were ready to buy themselves guaranteed tickets to jail. But an important precedent had been set.

——————————————————— ■

Charles Jones, fresh from leading the sit-ins in Charlotte, attended the Easter weekend meeting at Shaw University and became a charter member of the Student Nonviolent Coordinating Committee. There he met, for the first time, other student leaders — Diane Nash, James Bevel, Charles Sherrod. Just as the news of the *Brown* decision and then the Montgomery bus boycott had opened Jones's eyes to possibilities he had not seen before, the Shaw meeting and the sit-ins that precipitated it showed him yet another direction. "It was kind of a spontaneous, exciting time," he said, speaking of the demonstrations that started with Greensboro. "At first, there was no communication. The thing that happened to me in my mind and my spirit when I first heard it I'm sure happened to everybody else: All of a sudden there was a handle that we could use."

Back home in Charlotte, Jones found a good deal of encouragement from the black community, but he also heard from those people who wanted to discourage him from taking risks. "They were frightened, worried," he said. "They were the older black women who know that you're going to get killed because they've seen it before; they know the system well enough to know that something's going to happen to you. That was one level. And there was the loving protectiveness of the mothers. . . . I think when you're young, you don't know anything about mortality. I never was afraid. I never feared death. I didn't deal with it."

Opposition to the cause came from another group within the Negro community, as well. A Negro minister who ran a radio station, said Jones, invoked biblical characters as he lectured the students against demonstrating. "He was the only token colored allowed to have a position of authority" in Charlotte, said Jones. "He was saying, 'Y'all ought to be ashamed of yourselves. These white people have been good to you. You need to go home and study, and be quiet.' And we threw some of the prophets back at him.''

When the request came for assistance in the Rock Hill demonstrations in early 1961, Charles Jones went. When he and Nash, Bevel, Smith, and Sherrod got the appeal, ''it kind of caught our imagination. We decided that we would join the students to broaden the context of the Movement.''

The SNCC members, once arrested, declined to post bond and went to jail. Jones refers to his incarceration as being on the ''chain gang.'' At that time, prisoners in the York County, South Carolina, system were not actually chained to heavy metal balls or to each other, but they were sent out each day, under the eye of guards carrying shotguns, to work under miserable conditions on the public highways. Not long after he entered the county jail, Jones had a visitor. It was his father, the Presbyterian minister, formerly of Chester, South Carolina.

''My father, who had seen a lynching or two himself, or was aware of them as he grew up, came down to the jail. He was told that he couldn't come in.'' Jones's recounting of this was slow now, the words spoken with spaces between them, as if his recollections were heavy with tears.

''And that man stood there and said, 'Well, I'm going to see my son, so do whatever you're going to do.' And they let him in. He grew up in South Carolina, about eight miles from the place. And him doing that gave me a lot of inspiration, I suppose. . . . And we spent our thirty days on the chain gang.

''It was not chains, not literally. They had had chains up until, oh, two or three years before this. But we wore all the garb. And we called it the chain gang, because that's what it was known as. There were guards with guns. Sometimes they were on horses. Sometimes they were in trucks. Sometimes they walked along with the shotgun.

''It was interesting: The guards were generally the good old boys who couldn't get a job anyplace else and who didn't totally understand the nature of what they were involved in — that they were basically pawns and tools for the political system which really didn't care much about them individually.

''Charles Sherrod and I worked on one of the guards with our nonviolence, and he ended up being not only right pleasant but wanting to give us kind of little special privileges. That was the way the system worked. And we wouldn't accept the privileges. And he didn't quite understand that, but then he did come to understand it. When we left, he looked around to see if anybody was watching him, and he said, 'Good luck. Bye.'

"But we spent thirty hard days. I mean *hard* days. I gained thirty pounds. I was fit as a mule. We were working from sunup to sundown. We were doing highway work. We were making concrete ditch drainage pipe — two-, three-foot pipe — and we were digging ditches, putting in the pipe on the road. We were basically a road crew. We'd be out working and people would come by and honk their horns and wave. And black folks were saying, 'We're with you. Right on.' We got a certain inspiration. But we were on the chain gang; there's no question we were at hard labor. We weren't actually literally breaking rocks, but we were doing everything else. It was good experience. That began the regional, national movement of students through SNCC. We got a tremendous amount of publicity, which motivated a number of people and also educated a lot of people in the country. It did some interesting legal things. We still appealed, but we went to jail, too. It saved bond money, which became an incredible tool. Setting exorbitant bail was one of the tactics that the resistance used to effectively tie us up a lot of times. And it galvanized us a lot more. And all we had done was sit down and ask for Coke and a hot dog."

Jones was later to be shot at and otherwise harassed during his career in the Movement, but he was aware at the time and remains aware now that although they functioned in an environment that was laced with danger, relatively few of the activists were killed or seriously wounded.

"Some of the other folk would say that God was taking care of us," he said. "I think there was, perhaps, a spiritual dimension that even the hardest redneck was aware of. Whether that controlled his behavior or not, I don't know. But I think he knew that we were not fighting with guns, that we were very vulnerable; but also that we had the press looking at what was happening." In such a situation, he said, the white leaders could see that killing someone might bring down more trouble than it was worth. Exceptions would be Mississippi and Black Belt Alabama, where those who murdered civil rights proponents could be relatively certain that they would never go to jail. But in most other places, said Jones, "the resistance pretty much took control. I mean, the guard at the York County Jail was fairly much uninformed about what was going on. He was given his orders directly, and the political structure that was making decisions was aware that it would create more problems than it would solve" if it allowed slaughter.

———————

Charles Jones did his time on the chain gang and returned to Charlotte and to Johnson C. Smith University, whose president, Rufus P. Perry, had been defending him from attack by the local Selective Service office.

As long as he was a divinity student in good standing, Jones had been deferred from the draft. But when his residence changed temporarily to the York County Jail and his occupation became involuntary highway laborer, the draft board declared him no longer a student and started the wheels turning toward his induction. President Perry intervened. He told the board *he* determined who was and was not a student, and that Jones was one.

The school's position, said Jones later, was, "We've been teaching these students for seventy-some years self-respect and dignity, and giving them tools, and to turn our backs on them now that they're acting out what we taught would be a contradiction of everything we've said."

So when Jones arrived in Charlotte, he went to see President Perry and thanked him. Jones recalls that the president said, "You understand that I had to protect you. I had to protect the school. I will work with you to make sure that you are back in classes. Now cover me by covering yourself, by producing." Jones promised that he would. He worked hard, taking makeup tests and churning out term papers — in one case nine of them in one month.

Charles Jones completed his second year at the Johnson C. Smith divinity school in 1961. He finished his last test at noon one day in May, and at one-thirty he and a friend were on a bus, heading toward Alabama. CORE had started the Freedom Rides.

■ ————————————————————

PART FIVE

CONFRONTATION

SIXTEEN

AN ABSOLUTELY AWFUL DAY
IN ALABAMA

By the end of May, 1961, according to one informed estimate, well over a hundred towns and cities outside the Deep South had undergone desegregation of soda fountains, restaurants, and other facilities. But in much of the region, the political leaders, law enforcement authorities, officials of the courts, press, church, and the white population in general behaved as if the transformations that they witnessed every night on the television news did not affect them. To Jackson, Mississippi, or Birmingham, Alabama, or Albany, Georgia, the spectacle of Negroes and whites peacefully drinking coffee in a Woolworth's might as well have happened on another planet. Even the black residents of some of these places (not Birmingham, though) acted as if the wave of change sweeping the nation was not destined to reach them. The terror was that strong. Then the Congress of Racial Equality began its Freedom Ride into the Deep South.

The ride was seen at the time as a dramatic event (and it was, thanks to the white violence that greeted it), but the format was not at all new. Bayard Rustin and other members of the Fellowship of Reconciliation and CORE had conducted their Journey of

Reconciliation by interstate bus in 1947. In it, Negroes sat at the front of buses and whites sat at the rear to test the 1946 Supreme Court decision that states did not have the power to establish segregation rules regarding interstate passengers. That ride, however, was aimed not at the Deep South but at the upper-tier states of Virginia, North Carolina, West Virginia, and Kentucky. (Its mid-South status, though, did not prevent North Carolina from arresting the riders and putting them on a chain gang for thirty days.)[1]

The 1961 ride was designed to challenge any interstate transportation segregation that might be found in bus terminal facilities along a route extending from Washington, D.C., through the Carolinas and Georgia, Alabama, and Mississippi. Diverse rulings of the Supreme Court and the Interstate Commerce Commission made it clear that such segregation was illegal, although the practice in the Deep South was to the contrary. The plan was to end the ride in New Orleans on May 17, the seventh anniversary of the *Brown* decision.

In mid-March CORE announced that it would hold the ride and invited participants to apply. Participants would be both black and white, and they would ride the scheduled buses of both major interstate lines, Greyhound and Trailways. In April CORE wrote to President John F. Kennedy, advising him of its plans. The organization held workshops in nonviolence in Washington for the riders. Gordon Carey's sociodrama techniques were used. A lawyer explained the current laws on interstate transportation. A social scientist talked about the attitudes of the inhabitants along the journey route, and a veteran of social action talked about the possibility of injury and death.

The ride began on May 4, 1961, with thirteen passengers of varying ages, seven of them Negro. Some left and others joined during the ride. One who went all the way was James Peck, an old CORE hand who had been on the original Journey of Reconciliation of 1947. James Farmer, CORE's director, was on board, as was John Lewis of Nashville and SNCC. Farmer likened the ride to a sit-in on wheels. "If there is arrest," he said, "we will accept that arrest, and if there is violence, we are willing to receive that violence without responding in kind."[2]

There were no major problems as the buses rolled through

Virginia, North Carolina, and Georgia. In Rock Hill, South Carolina, John Lewis and another rider were attacked by local thugs while a policeman watched. After an overnight stay in Atlanta, local Movement people saw the bus off from the terminal on May 14, Mother's Day. Everybody was in good spirits except the highly conspicuous photographer from the Georgia Bureau of Investigation who always showed up on such occasions, trying unsuccessfully to assume the protective coloration of the press.[3] The entire group left Atlanta for Birmingham in two buses, one Trailways and one Greyhound. The Justice Department, which had kept tabs on the ride from the beginning, warned Birmingham police that the riders were coming and that it had picked up reports that there might be violence. (Actually, as it will soon be seen, the Federal Bureau of Investigation knew there would be violence and had no plans to prevent it.)

In Anniston, Alabama, on the road to Birmingham, a white mob met the Greyhound bus and prevented its passengers from getting off. The group of about one hundred men, among them members of the Ku Klux Klan, also slashed the vehicle's tires. The bus rolled along anyway until about six miles outside Anniston, where the tires went flat. The white mob, which had been following, tried to board the bus but was repelled by an investigator for the Alabama state police, Ell Cowling, who had joined the ride in order to collect intelligence on the participants' plans. Cowling pulled his gun and displayed his badge and backed the klansmen off. Someone threw a flaming device through one of the bus windows. The vehicle was destroyed by fire. It is likely that if Agent Cowling had not done what he did and if two highway patrolmen had not fired their guns into the air to further disperse the crowd, the passengers would have been trapped on the burning bus. As it was, twelve of them were admitted to a hospital, most for treatment of smoke inhalation.

When the second bus, the Trailways, arrived in Anniston, the mob beat its passengers. The riders continued on to Birmingham, where another mob, which had been waiting for several hours, attacked them. James Peck, who was especially conspicuous because he was white, was beaten unconscious; it took fifty-six stitches to close the gashes on his head. Neither in Anniston nor in Birmingham did the local police protect the riders; in Anniston, policemen stood and watched the violence, and in Birmingham, the police didn't arrive until after ten minutes of rioting. (When the Birmingham Young Businessmen's Club criticized the city's public safety commissioner, Eugene "Bull" Connor, for this, he replied that he was sorry about the attack, but a big part of the police force was off for Mother's Day.)

———————————————————— ■

Isaac Reynolds was a student in Detroit when CORE began organizing the ride. Reynolds had joined CORE back when the sit-ins had started, and he had walked picket lines at Woolworth stores in Michigan in support of the Southern movement. When James Farmer came to Detroit one night to deliver a speech and recruit people for the Freedom Ride, Ike Reynolds signed on. Except for basic training in the army in Missouri, it was the first trip to the South for the muscular young Negro.

Reynolds sat next to Dr. Walter Bergman, a white man who had retired from a teaching position at Wayne State University. Bergman's wife, Frances, sat farther back in the bus. When the violence began in Anniston, Reynolds saw that the attackers were especially vicious in their assaults on the white riders. Frances Bergman watched in horror as her husband was beaten into unconsciousness and then literally thrown over the bus's seats to the rear. James Peck was also beaten savagely. Local police stood by and did nothing. Only after the beatings ended did an Anniston policeman board the bus and say to the Freedom Riders: "I didn't see anything, I can't prove nothing; anyone want to swear out a warrant?"[4]

"Every Freedom Rider on that bus was beaten pretty bad," said Isaac Reynolds later. "I'm still feeling the effect. I received a damaged ear. My father was somewhat against my coming south. I guess he feared my injury or death, and he probably also didn't believe that I could adhere to the nonviolent philosophy.

"At that point, I had no doubt that I could. Of course, it was like a soldier about to go into combat who's never been there before. Not knowing what to expect, he just goes in with the belief. And my belief was that I could do it. And I did."

■ ————————————————————

Greyhound's drivers refused to take the group to Montgomery, the next way station on their interstate journey. When President Kennedy asked Governor John Patterson to provide protection, Patterson agreed, but on the following day he changed his mind, declaring: "The citizens of the state are so enraged I cannot guarantee protection for this bunch of rabble-rousers. I refuse to take the responsibility to guarantee their safe passage." He ordered the removal of the highway patrol car assigned to guard the bus.[5] The original Freedom Riders abandoned their bus trip, which would have taken them to Montgomery and Jackson before the final run to New Orleans, and made plans to fly to New Orleans. Their first attempt to leave Alabama was thwarted by a bomb threat, but they finally made it safely out of the state.

From the beginning, it seemed, the energies of the Justice Department had been focussed not on protecting the riders as they exercised their rights, but on trying to talk them out of riding. After the Anniston and Birmingham violence, but when it still looked as if the trip would continue by land, Attorney General Robert F. Kennedy (who only a week before had promised in a Law Day speech that the government would enforce civil rights statutes)[6] urged the riders to take the most southern route to New Orleans, thereby avoiding Jackson. It was as if he didn't understand the purpose of the demonstration. William J. Simmons of the Citizens Council in Jackson promptly wired Kennedy his congratulations: "With your continued help in keeping the agitators away, Mississippi will continue to enjoy peaceful race relations within the historic pattern of our segregated social order."

The original ride ended in New Orleans with a meeting in a church. The Southern Regional Council, in a report published at the end of May, commented, "The mobs and official hostility broke the back of the first Freedom Ride."[7] But the second one was quickly at hand.

--- ■

When CORE put out its initial call for Freedom Riders, both John Lewis and Bernard Lafayette applied. The two were veterans of the Nashville sit-ins, and they had become committed to taking part in

any direct action that seemed useful in advancing the Movement.

CORE insisted that all the riders be at least twenty-one years of
age, however. Lewis had turned twenty-one the previous February, but
Lafayette would not make the grade for another two months. So Lewis
went on the first ride, and Lafayette stayed behind in Nashville and
finished taking his final exams. (As it developed, the age rule fell into
disuse.) But he did not stay long. After the violence in Anniston and
Birmingham and CORE's cancellation of the remainder of the trip, Lafayette joined a number of other Nashville students and headed for
Birmingham.

A fundamental philosophical difference between the CORE and
Nashville groups, said Lafayette later, revolved about redemptive suffering. Those who planned the original ride, he said, were "very much
concerned that there was no protection." They were committed to using
their nonviolence as a tactic, while "*our* view of nonviolence says that
unearned suffering is redemptive. It was that no wall of violence or
avalanche of violence would ever stop us. That somehow when the tidal
wave of violence is high and strong, then we need only respond with a
greater power." In other words, it didn't matter whether the Nashville
group received protection or not. "Those of us who were committed to
nonviolence as a way of life, we were not dependent on any kind of
protection. In fact, the very people who were talking about providing
protection, the Southern police, were folks who we felt considered us
their enemy."

Diane Nash, one of the leaders of the Nashville group, talked with
James Farmer of CORE about continuing the ride. Farmer's father had
died while the original ride was on its way to Alabama, and he had left
the demonstration and flown home for the funeral. There was, Farmer
has said, an unwritten agreement that SNCC and CORE would not in-
trude on each other's projects without consultation and permission. Although Farmer was unenthusiastic at first about the dangers involved in
SNCC's taking over the ride (and, as he later acknowledged, about the
possibility that "CORE's great new program" would "slip from its grasp
and be taken over by others"), he agreed with Nash's argument that if
the Movement now allowed itself to be halted by violence, it would die
in its tracks.[8]

"There were about twenty of us," said Lafayette. "We decided that the climate was right for us to continue. We divided the group up into two different sections. We would send the first ten and see if they would survive — or get arrested or stopped or whatever. And then we would send in the second group. I was a spokesman for the second group out of Nashville."

■ ───────────────────────────

The second wave arrived in Birmingham on May 17, a bus carrying fresh riders from Nashville (and one not-so-fresh one; John Lewis returned to Nashville from the carnage of the first journey to take an exam at his seminary, then came back to Alabama with other veterans of the Nashville sit-in movement). When the bus arrived at the terminal, a mob was waiting. The police jailed the riders, eight blacks and two whites, for what they called "protective custody." Fred Shuttlesworth, the Birmingham minister and Movement leader, was also charged with "conspiracy" with persons unknown to cause a mob to gather and with disturbing the peace. Some of the riders made bail and left, but most remained in jail.

On May 19, Alabama state circuit judge Walter B. Jones approved a request by Governor Patterson and his attorney general to enjoin CORE and anyone else from "entry into and travel within the State of Alabama, and engaging in the so-called 'freedom ride' and other acts of conduct calculated to provoke breaches of the peace." The police, with efficiency they had not shown in coping with white peace-breachers, stopped buses entering the state and read the injunction, proclamation-style, to the passengers. During most of this time, both President Kennedy and Attorney General Kennedy were trying to reach Patterson to ask him to restore law and order to Alabama. But Patterson would not come to the phone.

Early that same morning, Bull Connor put into action his own plan for dealing with the Freedom Ride. He went to the jail, introduced himself to the young riders, and told them: "You people came here from Tennessee on a bus. I'm taking you back to Tennessee in five minutes under police protection."

A rider asked: "Do you mean to say you're taking us back without our consent?"

Connor said, "Yes, and if you argue, I'll have no other course but to turn you loose now." "Loose" almost certainly meant into the hands of the Klan, whose members enjoyed close relationships with members of the Birmingham police department. When the students demanded to see their lawyer, Movement attorney Len Holt of Norfolk, Connor said Holt wasn't licensed to practice in Alabama. The police drove the seven students away in a black limousine with three unmarked police cars as escort. More than four hours later they stopped at Ardmore, a hamlet on the Tennessee-Alabama state line. Connor put the students out and advised them: "This is the Tennessee line. Cross it and save this state and yourself a lot of trouble." To which one of the students replied, "We'll see you back in Birmingham about noon." He was off by only a couple of hours.

■

When Connor's "escort" had departed on its return trip to Birmingham, the Freedom Riders found the home of a Negro who had a telephone (not an easy task in the tiny community) and called Nashville. Bernard Lafayette sent two cars to Ardmore to pick up the stranded riders, while other Nashvillians left for Birmingham by train and car. They avoided buses because they knew the Alabama authorities would be looking for them there. "The main thing we wanted to do was get to Birmingham to continue the ride," said Lafayette. "We rendezvoused at Shuttlesworth's house. We regrouped. We got our tickets — Shuttlesworth had bought them — and we went down to the bus station in Birmingham."

Whenever the students tried to board a bus for New Orleans, their interstate destination, by way of Montgomery, that bus would be cancelled. So Lafayette and the others stayed at the Birmingham bus station through the night of May 19–20.

"That was my first physical contact with the Klan. They had the whole place surrounded, and they had the sheets on, the hoods, the robes." Lafayette remembered one high-ranking Klan official who was there. "He had a black robe. Very impressive, you know. And had this huge, you know, reptile of some sort embroidered on the back. I found out he was a Baptist minister under that robe." Lafayette said he thought about the wide range of clerical activities represented there: "So, well, Baptist preachers: We were having sit-ins; we were leading the Klan." He laughed.

"We stayed there overnight. The policemen had these long night-sticks, and there were these ceramic tile floors — train station, bus sta-tion–type floors. You'd hear a big twanging sound, and you'd know one of these nightsticks had dropped on the floor because the policemen were sleeping standing up. And everybody could tell who it was because he had to pick up the nightstick. It was embarrassing. I also remember that we all went to the rest room in a group because no one wanted to get caught in the rest room alone. We couldn't use the white rest room because it was in the white side of the bus station. We started toward the [black] rest room, and these whites, the Klan members and such, they would surge forward. We didn't know what to expect out of the policemen, because they didn't stop the Klan from coming around and stepping on our feet and throwing ice water on us when we were asleep.

"So we all went together to the rest room. There were so many of us. The Klan rose up, and then the policemen did. They didn't want a conflict inside the rest room, so they stopped the Klan from going in. Some of the policemen, I imagine, also were Klan members, but they just had different uniforms on at the time. On duty, off duty, you know. But that was to be expected."

During one of the group's attempts to board a bus bound for Montgomery, the driver stood on his vehicle's steps and asked the crowd, "How many of you are from CO'?" Nobody answered. "How many of you are from the NAACP?" Although nobody answered that either, the driver said, "Well, I have one life to give, and I'm not going to give it to the NAACP or CO'." He picked up his traveling bag and walked off. Not long afterward, after a flurry of telephone conversations between the bus company and the attorney general's office, an agree-ment was worked out. With a company supervisor on board, the bus took off for Montgomery. The driver was the man who was particular about how he gave up his life.

When Farmer left the ride to bury his father, he called Gordon Carey in New York and asked him to hurry to Alabama and join the riders. "Which I did," said Carey. "I flew down to Birmingham. Scared to death. God, was I scared! Most scared I've ever been in my life. This was after the bus had burned and all that. And Jim calls me in my flat up in New York and tells me to go down there, and this little white boy's gonna go down to join the Freedom Ride, you know. Jesus Christ! Anyway, I got to Birmingham and I stayed with Shuttlesworth in his house; in the same bed, as a matter of fact. The polite thing to do when you have a small house and you don't have a place for guests is you ask your wife to go sleep on the couch, and your guest sleeps in the bed. So Shuttlesworth and I were sleeping in the same bed. And he had rifles all over the place. He told me not to worry about a thing."

Diane Nash had served thirty days in the county jail in Rock Hill, and she had gone back to Fisk, but getting an education just wasn't the same. The Movement was consuming more and more of her time. "The Chaucer classes became unbearable after Rock Hill," she recalled. She withdrew from school just before the Freedom Ride. "I felt that the Movement needed the services of a full-time person."

When Nash heard about CORE's abandonment of the original ride, she phoned James Farmer and asked permission for her group, a combination of SNCC and Nashville student activists, to continue it. She was aware, even before Farmer reminded her, of the potential for violence, injury, and even death. She was afraid.

"But you know what?" she said later. "I was afraid *not* to continue the Freedom Ride. If the signal was given to the opposition that violence could stop us . . . if we let the Freedom Ride stop then, whenever we tried to do anything in the Movement in the future, we were going to meet with a lot of violence. And we would probably have to get a number of people killed before we could reverse that message."

■ ───────────────────────

From Birmingham, the riders in their Greyhound bus rolled to Montgomery, about a hundred miles south, under escort from the highway patrol. The state officers left when the bus reached the capital city. Although the FBI had informed Montgomery officials of the possibility of violence and the local officials had said they could handle the situation, Police Commissioner L. B. Sullivan had no officers on hand. An enraged mob of a thousand whites attacked the riders, Negro passersby, reporters and photographers, and John Seigenthaler, Attorney General Kennedy's personal representative on the scene. It was a full ten minutes before the local police arrived. Commissioner Sullivan, asked about his department's performance, replied: "We respond to calls here just like anyplace else. But we have no intention of standing guard for a bunch of troublemakers coming into our city and making trouble." When he was asked why an ambulance was not summoned for Seigenthaler, who was left lying on the pavement for twenty-five minutes before a policeman put him into a car and took him to the hospital, Sullivan responded: "Every white ambulance in town reports their vehicles have broken down." The local sheriff's mounted posse, which had been formed for riot control, arrived seventy-five minutes after the riot started.

Rioters grabbed one Negro walking along the street near the bus terminal, poured an inflammable liquid on him, and attempted to set him afire. At one point, ten to fifteen whites were beating one Negro who was lying on the ground. When an ambulance arrived to carry off the injured, the mob chased it away. John Lewis was among those who were seriously injured.

In the shocking spectacle offered by local law enforcement officials (and by Governor Patterson in his simultaneous running commentary), there was one striking exception. Floyd Mann, who as Alabama's public safety director was the head of the highway patrol, started protecting the victims of the mob as soon as he arrived on the scene. Running to the side of one Negro who was being beaten, Mann pulled his gun and ordered the mob to back off. "We are going to keep law and order," he said.

A few blocks away at the state capitol, John Patterson was alternately issuing statements and avoiding telephone calls from President Kennedy and the attorney general. Patterson's position changed rapidly, but on balance it seemed to be that violence would not be tolerated; no help was needed from the federal government; the state could not and would not "escort busloads or carloads of rabble-rousers," bent on challenging Alabama's laws, about the countryside. And, it was clear, any violence would be blamed on those who challenged Alabama's overruled laws, not those who attacked the challengers with ice picks, lead pipes, chains, and firebombs. On the day of the Montgomery debacle, the state ordered the arrest of the Freedom Riders for their alleged contempt of its May 19 injunction against putting on a "so-called 'freedom ride.'" In one statement, issued not long after the mob had ended its two-hour reign, Patterson declared, "We are a peaceful, hospitable, God-fearing people, and we welcome visitors from all other states." Roy Wilkins of the NAACP issued a statement suggesting that Alabama secede from the Union.

Robert Kennedy sent Patterson a telegram, noting that he had been unable to reach the governor by telephone, that Patterson had been wrong to promise that federal intervention was not needed, and that the attorney general was taking a number of steps. Kennedy asked the federal court in Montgomery (which likely meant Judge Frank Johnson) to enjoin the Klan, the National States Rights party, and "certain individuals and all persons acting in concert with them from interfering with peaceful interstate travel by buses." He asked the FBI to send more investigators to Montgomery. And, most important, he arranged "for United States officers to begin to assist state and local authorities in the protection of persons and property and vehicles in Alabama," by which Kennedy meant he was sending four hundred U.S. marshals and other federal officers to the scene. They were dispatched to Alabama that day under the same authority that had been used to send troops to Little Rock.[9]

On Sunday, May 21, the day after the mob attack, U.S. marshals began to arrive in Montgomery. James Farmer came from his father's funeral to the Alabama capital. Martin Luther King, who had not participated in the ride but had given it his blessing, flew in from Chicago, where he had been on a speaking engagement.[10] The Freedom Riders and their out-of-town sympathizers, meantime, stayed in Montgomery, many of them with members of the black community who had been active in the bus boycott.

During the day, Patterson stepped up his verbal attack on federal intervention. By now he had received messages of support from several of his fellow Deep South governors, including Ross Barnett of Mississippi, and he was riding on the crest of segregationist rhetoric. He told Byron R. White, the U.S. deputy attorney general (later to become a Supreme Court justice), that if any of the federal officers sent to Montgomery "encroach on any of our state laws, rights, or functions . . . we'll arrest them." Patterson accused Washington of sending marshals in "to help put down a disturbance which it helped create," and he added that he thought communists were behind the Freedom Ride. White replied that he didn't know of any communist infiltration, "but no matter what this group's connection may be, if any, that is no reason why they shouldn't be assured of the right to travel peacefully by bus." Patterson also declared what he termed "qualified martial rule," which involved calling up the Alabama National Guard. This was necessary, he said, "as a result of outside agitators coming into Alabama to violate our laws and customs" and causing "outbreaks of lawlessness and mob action." Once again he tried to place the blame on anybody but the rioters: "The federal government has by its actions encouraged these agitators to come into Alabama to foment disorders and breaches of the peace." In the meantime, Judge Frank Johnson signed the injunction requested by the Justice Department, restraining the Klan and others from interfering with interstate travel. The judge also asked the department to protect him and his home from possible violence.

Later in the day, and for reasons that were not clear, the state changed its tune dramatically. Floyd Mann asked the federal government for all the help it could send. "This is an ugly situation," he said. And he was right.

As the Sunday evening fell, some fifteen hundred Negroes and white sympathizers gathered in a mass meeting at Ralph Abernathy's First Baptist Church.* King was the main speaker, and from this moment on, many Americans, including much of the press, began thinking of the events of that spring as Martin Luther King's Freedom Ride. As King spoke, a white mob formed outside the church. And as King conferred nervously by telephone with Attorney General Kennedy in Washington, the federal marshals and state policemen, along with a few local police officers, managed to keep the rioters out of the church. On the marshals' advice, the occupants of the church stayed there all night rather than risk being caught outside by members of the white mob. Again, Floyd Mann directed his state policemen to overrule what may have been their personal feelings about race and to protect the besieged

---

*The press referred to Abernathy's church in Montgomery as "the Negro First Baptist Church," presumably so it would not be confused with "the White First Baptist Church."

antisegregationists. The Alabama Associated Press Association singled Mann out as "the one notable example" among the state officials, the one man who carried out his duties.

———————————————— ■

In June, 1959, when some of his colleagues were still outwardly nervous about a Northerner and a Catholic in the White House, John Patterson had been the first Southern governor to support John Kennedy for the Democrats' presidential nomination. While Patterson may have caught some flak for his action, Kennedy probably caught more. Northern liberals were concerned about his being endorsed by a man as openly racist as Patterson. After Kennedy's election, the new president made matters even worse by appointing a Patterson crony, Charles E. Meriwether, as a director of the Export-Import Bank, despite Meriwether's reputation among some as what one account called an "ardent segregationist linked with White Citizens Councils."[11]

Patterson, reflecting now on the events of that May, downplays the notion that he should shoulder the blame for what happened.

"As far as the Kennedy administration and the press was concerned," he said, "I came out pretty bad in that thing. But the truth of the matter is that that was a law enforcement problem more than anything else. . . . The Freedom Ride, you know, was a mixed group — mixed sexually and racially. They started up there in Washington and came south, and the publicity preceded them. It was a bad time, of course, in Alabama, and it was all through the South.

"Now, when the Freedom Riders got to Birmingham, of course, it became the city of Birmingham's responsibility, and [Bull] Connor got involved in it. And he just did a miserable job of handling that goddamn thing. Then, of course, they came on down to Montgomery. By that time, Robert Kennedy had got involved in it. He and I were having arguments over the telephone about all this. He was insisting that we escort these people around and permit them to do whatever they want to do. And this was a pretty big order.

"They were not really bona fide interstate travelers. They wanted to go to lunch rooms and waiting rooms and toilets and things that were segregated; they wanted to go and test the local people on whether or not they would enforce those customs and, in some places, ordinances. I was willing to do everything I could to protect them, like anybody else. But I really didn't want to escort them around to permit them to violate laws.

"Anyway, when they got here, the city of Montgomery had indicated that they could handle it and that they didn't need any state help. . . . If you're the governor you have to let the city do their thing if you can. If you step in there and say, 'Wait a minute; you're not doing this right,' they'll dump the thing on you and go home. It's a very ticklish situation.

"They let us know here that they would handle it, and when the people got to the bus station, a mob suddenly materialized down there. And the city police were not there. And I think Floyd Mann will tell you that we think that the [Montgomery public safety] commissioner at that time — he's dead now, and he can't defend himself — but we think that he had let the Klan know that he'd give them a few minutes to work on the riders a little bit. We think probably that's true. We can't prove it, but we think it's true."

Patterson said Mann didn't completely trust the city's assurances that it could handle the situation, and he kept some of his state troopers nearby. When it became clear that the situation was out of control, Mann moved in. "Floyd and his assistant saved the Freedom Riders down at the bus station there; no question about that," said the former governor. "And then he brought our people in real quick and broke it up real quick, and that was the end of it."

Patterson said that even as events unfolded, he knew he was in for a lot of criticism. "I was very much concerned about that," he said. "I knew that this was a losing fight, as far as I was concerned. I mean, I didn't want this thing, and I kept trying to get Robert Kennedy to get these people to behave themselves or to get them to go home. But I couldn't prevail on him. He was intent on seeing that they got to do their thing."

Next, said Patterson, Martin Luther King came to town. "And man, that heated it up sho-nuff! And then every nut and crank in the United States began to float in here. I'm talking about [George Lincoln] Rockwell's Nazis showed up, that sort of people.* Great big bozos walking

---

*George Lincoln Rockwell was the head of an organization known as the American Nazi Party. It was headquartered in northern Virginia.

up and down the street here from California and places like that, and who have no earthly idea of what they're doing in town. You'd say, 'What are you doing here?' 'Well, we just come over to see what's going on.' Oh, Lord.''

Patterson recalled the night of the siege at Ralph Abernathy's church. The federal marshals, he said, were mostly nice people, but they were "really process servers" and not trained for riot duty. It was actually Mann and the Alabama National Guard, he said, who "broke that thing up very quickly. I declared a limited martial law in order to protect them. You have to have some type of legal process to protect the [law enforcement] people in a martial law situation, otherwise they'll all get sued.

"I was sitting in my governor's office with all this [information], and I had liaison people there with me, and all the papers [for the martial law declaration] had already been drafted hours before, and it was just like that" — Patterson snapped his fingers — "and it was all over, and that was the end of it. And two or three days later, we escorted the bus over to the Mississippi line and turned them over to the Mississippi authorities, and that's the end of it.''

Patterson said that actually the federal government was directly implicated in the Freedom Ride violence. He said an FBI informant who was a member of the Ku Klux Klan was "instructed by somebody in the Justice Department" to take part in the violence at Anniston and Birmingham.

Patterson paused a moment. "You know," he said, "hindsight's a wonderful thing. 'If I had only known that then!' God! If I had it all to do over again, I'd do a lot of things differently.''

The former governor of Alabama said that throughout the crisis he retained his admiration for the president he had helped elect. "I liked John Kennedy. He was a fine fellow in every respect, and I had high regard for him, and still do. I think he understood problems down here probably better than his brother did. I think it might have been a more peaceful transition if he had lived.

"But Robert, now, is another matter. I never could get along with him, and we finally got so we just couldn't converse without getting mad. Everything he did was based on what was best for him politically, I think. He didn't give a damn about our problems, and we had our problems, too. I had political problems in this thing; that was of no interest to him at all.

"In fact, I told Ross Barnett he'd better be damn careful with him, and if he made any deal with Robert, he'd better get it in writing." Patterson laughed.

———————————

On the night of the mass meeting, Wyatt Tee Walker was one of those trapped inside the First Baptist Church. He felt a fear then, he said, that was like what he felt when he went out of town and worried that "somebody would do something to my wife and children."

But Dr. King, whom Walker called Leader in private conversations, did not seem afraid. "We were trapped in Ralph Abernathy's church," he said, laughing. "And Martin Luther King said, 'The only way we're going to appease this crowd is we who are leaders, we've got to go out and give ourselves up.'

"And I said, 'Sheee-itt! Every man for himself!' "

———————————

Bernard Lafayette, who was there in the church and there in the riot, remembers Floyd Mann as a decent white person. "He was Southern," said Lafayette, "but I don't think he had the same kind of passion for preserving segregation at any cost as some of his colleagues. I think he was a Southerner with maybe a greater sense of humanity. Maybe he was caught in a system where he had to perform certain duties, but he wanted to do it in the most humane way."

Mann says now that he knew there were going to be problems on the Freedom Ride, given the prevailing political atmosphere. That's why he dispatched Ell Cowling, his investigator, to join the ride in Atlanta.

"He boarded that bus in Atlanta with equipment that he could determine what route they were going to take when they got to Alabama," said Mann, who still lives in Montgomery. "He was on the bus when they got to Anniston to keep us informed, so we could try to secure that bus. He had listening devices to see what the discussion was of the people on that bus — to see what route they were going to take when they got to Alabama." Mann was, even after all those years, reluctant to go into great detail about the eavesdropping equipment, but he acknowledged that it was some sort of a microphone that was highly directional in its ability to pick up sound.

"He was there on that bus to give us intelligence about what that busload of people was going to do when they got to Alabama. And, of course, it turned out to be that the greatest purpose of it all was he saved all of their lives. They'd've burned to death if he hadn't been on that bus. He had to pull his gun and show his badge to make those klansmen back away from the bus so they could get those Freedom Riders off the bus."

After the violence in Birmingham, Mann arranged a heavy escort for the bus to Montgomery. "I had sixteen highway patrol cars in front of that bus and sixteen behind it, and a helicopter running reconnaissance in front of the bus to make sure there weren't any bridges blown up between Birmingham and Montgomery. The atmosphere — I just can't tell you — it's just unbelievable today, remembering how hot it was."

His purpose, said Mann, was "to protect those people; to get them through Alabama." Did he disagree with the riders' aim of testing and attacking segregation? "I wasn't involved in that," he said. "My purpose was law enforcement, trying to make certain that nothing tragic happened to those people while they were in Alabama."

Mann received word that the Montgomery police would not show up at the bus station, despite their assurances that they could handle any problems at their end. So Mann called in seventy-five state troopers and billeted them at a state facility nearby. His planning proved priceless; the troopers were badly needed. In the minutes before the troopers arrived, Mann and his assistants stood beside downed and beaten riders and waved their guns to drive the mob back.

"It was an absolutely awful day," said the former public safety director. "My clothes were almost torn off of me, and my assistant director, too, where we had to get in there and get kind of ugly with some of those folks. One fellow that was standing over one of the blacks with a baseball bat, I just had to stick my gun in his ear and just tell him if he swung that bat one more time, I'd kill him."

Mann said he had "really mixed emotions" about the arrival of federal marshals because he knew they were not schooled in riot work and because their presence could "aggravate the whole situation." But he kept his feelings in check. His discipline did not extend to some of his own employees, however. "I had problems with some of those troopers, including some in pretty high command. They didn't like it at all. In fact, with one of the top officials of the troopers, I had to almost relieve him that day."

Mann's own rule was simple: "During my career in law enforcement, what I've always tried to do is try my best to train those people, discipline those people to treat every citizen in Alabama the way *they'd* like to be treated, regardless of their color." It was a rule that Mann's parents had taught him when he was growing up back in Alexander City, in southeastern Alabama, along with the general rules about race relations that the system taught. "We grew up in a society where it was just kind of instilled in you that you're different from black people. You didn't associate socially and what have you. You didn't ever go to school with them. But I grew up in a family that believed in treating people right. My parents would've got on me so quick for mistreating somebody like that" who was black, he said. "It was just as bad as mistreating a white."

John Patterson had said that in the end, what happened in Alabama during the Freedom Ride was a law enforcement issue. Floyd Mann, Patterson's chief law enforcement agent, says it was a political issue.

"It could've been a much easier way that it could have been done," he said. "If the elected officials in the city and the state had just taken this position that 'this is a situation where we're going to have to offer protection and go along with it, and we don't want any mob at this place,' they could've done a lot of things that weren't done. . . . I feel sure that some of the elected officials knew that this was a situation that was probably going to end the way it did end, but they were trying to capitalize on it politically."

∎ ───────────────────────

If Floyd Mann's advice had been followed, it is possible that the white violence that greeted the Freedom Ride would have been avoided or minimized. It is likely, too, that if the Federal Bureau of Investigation had done its job properly, the incidents at Anniston and Birmingham would never have happened. The FBI knew of the Ku Klux Klan's conspiracy to attack the riders — one of its own employees was an influential member of the terrorist organization — and it knew that high-ranking members of the Birmingham police department were collaborating with the Klan. Yet the agency did nothing to prevent the violence it knew would occur.

Twenty-two years after the Freedom Ride, in 1983, a federal

district judge in Michigan handed down his decision in the case of *Bergman v. United States.*[12] Walter Bergman, one of the original Freedom Riders who had been brutally attacked in Alabama, had filed suit in his home state against the national government and against six present or former agents of the FBI. Bergman's complaint was simple: The government knew that there was a conspiracy among Klan members to attack the Freedom Riders when they got to Alabama; the government did nothing to prevent the violence; and, therefore, the government was liable for the injuries the riders sustained.

The case was made difficult by the Justice Department's refusal to supply needed information, on the grounds that it would reveal the identities of informants to whom it had promised confidentiality. District judge Richard A. Enslen excoriated the government for this and — when the defense did eventually come up with documents — for producing versions that "seriously mischaracterize the events." The judge wrote:

> The obligation of the Federal Bureau of Investigation cannot "transcend" the interests of this lawsuit where that obligation would thwart and denigrate the interests of justice under this nation's system of laws. . . . Our constitutional system of government works because we want it to — we pay more than lip service to the rule of law. In this case, the FBI has not only argued the propriety of its refusal to disclose, but also wants to sit in judgment upon that refusal, thus ignoring the cornerstone of our system of constitutional government, the separation of powers.

In the end, the FBI handed over the documents.

The evidence revealed was shocking, even to cynical observers of the civil rights struggle. Barrett G. Kemp, an FBI agent in Birmingham, recruited Gary Thomas Rowe, Jr., as an FBI informant in May, 1960. Rowe came to the Bureau's attention because he had been accused of impersonating an FBI agent. Though such a background raised obvious questions about Rowe's stability and veracity, the Birmingham FBI office put him on the payroll, Agent Kemp testified in the Bergman suit, because (in the judge's words) he "expressed an interest in law enforcement and because Rowe said he had been approached about joining the Klan." The FBI had been on the lookout for informers to place in the Klan. Rowe was also a violent man, and the FBI knew it when it hired him. In one incident known to his FBI handler, he had assaulted an elderly couple in their home.

Rowe would come to national attention in 1965 when he testified against fellow klansmen in the murder of civil rights activist Viola Liuzzo in Selma, Alabama. But at the time of the Freedom Ride, he was known only to the FBI, the Klan, and the Birmingham police department. A Birmingham police sergeant, Thomas Cook, was among those officers who expressed sympathy toward the Klan and gave the terrorist group confidential information, according to Rowe's testimony.

Rowe served as a spy for the FBI about Klan plans and actions, but he also informed his masters about the intimate involvement of the Birmingham police department in the work of the Klan. Thus in the early spring of 1961, wrote Judge Enslen, "the Bureau had excellent reason to believe that the Birmingham officials, vested with the responsibility for enforcing the law, extolled instead the principles of the Klan." CORE's announcement of the Freedom Ride provided this collaboration with an opportunity to put its principles into action.

According to the judge's reconstruction of the events, Rowe attended a meeting in April, not long after CORE announced it would conduct the ride, with Robert Shelton, the imperial wizard of the Alabama Klan,* "and 'Bull' Connor 'and his boys.' " The "boys" included Sergeant Cook of the Birmingham police. Rowe said Cook told the Klan that the police would allow a quarter-hour of violence when the riders arrived at the bus depot. Rowe quoted Cook as saying: "We're going to allow you fifteen minutes to beat, bomb. . . . You can beat 'em, bomb 'em, maim 'em, kill 'em, I don't

---

*"Imperial," in Klan language, denoted a national office. The imperial wizard was the president and chief executive officer of a national Klan organization — in the case of Shelton's group, the Knights of the Ku Klux Klan, United Klans of America, Inc. State affiliates, known as realms, were headed by officers called grand dragons. Other national officers had titles such as imperial klabee (treasurer), imperial kladd (secretary to the president), imperial klonsel (legal adviser), and imperial kludd (chaplain).

give a —— . . . . There will be absolutely no arrests. You can assure every Klansman in the country that no one will be arrested in Alabama for that fifteen minutes." Rowe reported this immediately to his FBI handlers. The Bureau received confirming information about these plans from Rowe after subsequent meetings, as well as from at least one other informant. By May 12, two days before the ride crossed the Alabama state line, wrote Judge Enslen, "the FBI knew or reasonably should have known that the Freedom Riders would encounter violence at least as early as Anniston, at the hands of the awaiting Klansmen, and with the approval of the local and state police." The agency "had developed a full and complete knowledge of the precise nature of the conspiracy between the Birmingham police department, the Alabama Klans, and others."

But the FBI did not quash the conspiracy. "The Bureau did not stop Rowe's participation," said Judge Enslen,

> nor did it prevent or hinder the carrying out of the conspiracy. Not only did the government fail to prevent the violence on May 14, but its own informant, Rowe, was one of the attackers on the Freedom Riders in Birmingham. Indeed, a photograph introduced in evidence shows Rowe beating a man who appears to be Freedom Rider James Peck. While Rowe had been cautioned about partaking in the violent activities of the Klan, the Bureau concluded after a brief period of time that if information were to be gained about violence then Rowe would have to do what had to be done.

Nor did the FBI inform the Justice Department's civil rights division of the conspiracy until after the Mother's Day violence. And afterward, at least according to Rowe, the Bureau exerted pressure on its informant to deny that he had taken part in the Birmingham violence.

The government compounded its guilt by introducing arguments at the trial that showed its eagerness to evade responsibility. It said the FBI was just an investigatory agency. Judge Enslen swept that argument aside, noting that the Bureau didn't even inform the Department of Justice that a crime was being committed. Furthermore, said the judge, "nowhere in the history of [federal legislation concerning the duties of the FBI] does it provide that the government may sit idly by when a federal crime has been detected and when an operative of the government has immersed himself and an executive department of the United States government into an illegal scheme."

Enslen batted down Washington's other arguments: that its duty to maintain law and order is discretionary; that Rowe's information was mere hearsay (the FBI considered it reliable at the time); that the riders' own "negligence" had contributed to their injuries; that the plaintiffs had assumed a risk that placed them in way of a "known danger."

The district judge in Michigan examined all the propositions set forth by the government of the United States, and he came up with a simple and devastating conclusion: "The United States' failure to carry out its duties was a primary moving cause without which the physical injuries to the Freedom Riders would not have occurred." The government was guilty of "dereliction of duty and negligence." He awarded Walter Bergman thirty-five thousand dollars in damages.

SEVENTEEN

A LIMIT TO LIBERALISM

The Federal Bureau of Investigation did nothing to stop the ambush it knew had been planned, but eight days after the violence in northern Alabama it arrested four men, white residents of Anniston aged nineteen to forty-three, and charged them in the bus burning. The Congress of Racial Equality, meantime, announced that it would resume the rides. Others sympathetic to the cause who were not CORE members started heading south to test transportation segregation. State troopers vainly read Judge Jones's injunction on buses entering the state.

One group of riders, arrested while eating at the Montgomery Trailways terminal, included Wyatt Tee Walker and Ralph Abernathy of the Southern Christian Leadership Conference and Fred Shuttlesworth, the Birmingham leader. Some of those arrested promptly filed suit against the state, asking that its laws requiring segregation in the terminals be invalidated. Another group rode into Montgomery and was arrested. It included the Reverend William Sloane Coffin, Jr., the chaplain of Yale University; other prominent white academics; and Charles Jones of Charlotte. After a night in custody, the academics went home; Jones stayed in jail.

The *New York Times* ran a story about Diane Nash's part in continuing the original ride with demonstrators from Nashville and titled it "Negro Girl a Force in Campaign; Encouraged Bus to Keep Rolling." The article said a Justice Department official "attempted to have her delay the trip" on the grounds that it would be "dangerous and irresponsible." The official, whose name was not given, was quoted as saying, "It was as if I were talking to a wall. She never listened to a word." By now, Nash, who was twenty-two, had been in jail in Nashville and at Rock Hill. She did not ride a bus in the Freedom Ride, but was chosen by her fellow demonstrators to be the "executive officer" of their protest. She and Fred Shuttlesworth arranged a code for relaying information about riders by telephone. The *Times* article quoted Nash as saying, "They beat us, and we're stronger than ever."[1]

The *Des Moines Tribune*, meanwhile, reported that the Alabama advisory committee of the U.S. Commission on Civil Rights had told the commission it had found a link between the Klan and Alabama police — presumably the connection that would be revealed later in the *Bergman* case. The FBI, it also was learned later, had set up three vans, loaded with equipment for making moving pictures, near the riot at the Montgomery bus station, but all their film was reported to have turned out bad. And a group of Birmingham ministers met and pledged to "make efforts to reestablish better communications between the races." One of the ministers pointed out that the group was all white. When he learned there was a reporter present, he asked that his name not be used.[2]

Montgomery had quieted down considerably by May 23. Governor John Patterson blamed the riot at the First Baptist Church not on the white mob but on the federal marshals, but it was clear that the segregationist governor's rhetoric was losing some of its punch. Attorney General Robert Kennedy issued a request, one of several he would make during his time in office, for a "cooling-off period." He said, "It would be wise for those traveling through these two states [Alabama and Mississippi] to delay their trips until the present state of confusion and danger has passed and an atmosphere of reason and normalcy has been restored."

Implicit in Kennedy's announcement seemed to be the assumption that reason and normalcy would result if the riders stopped riding — an assumption that was valid only if segregation and state-sponsored disobedience to federal laws were considered reasonable and normal. Kennedy also seemed to be saying, as did editorial writers for segregationist newspapers, that the riders were somehow responsible for their own predicaments. Kennedy said, in his "cooling-off" statement, that "besides the groups of Freedom Riders" then on the road, there were those who were "curiosity seekers, publicity seekers, and others who are seeking to advance their own causes," along with those who were simply traveling from one place to another. "In this confused situation, there is increasing possibility that innocent persons may be injured. A mob asks no questions." The attorney general seemed to be putting the riders and "others seeking to advance their own causes" (which were, in fact, the same causes as those of the U.S. Constitution) into the not-innocent column.[3] The nonsegregationist press engaged in this blame-the-victim thinking, as well; a *New York Times* headline declaring, "Freedom Riders Held Blow to U.S." actually was a report on the United States Information Agency's statement that the nation had been getting a bad press around the world because of the racial violence — none of which had been caused by the riders themselves, of course.[4]

The demonstrators rejected Kennedy's request for a suspension of activity. The feelings of many of them could be summed up in a telegram that activist Uriah J. Fields of Montgomery sent Robert Kennedy: "Had there not been a cooling-off period following the Civil War, the Negro would be free today. Isn't ninety-nine years long enough to cool off, Mr. Attorney General?"[5]

On May 24, 1961, the day after Martin Luther King, James Farmer, Ralph Abernathy, Diane Nash, and John Lewis announced that the travels would continue, a group of riders ate a desegregated breakfast at the Montgomery bus terminal and left by bus for Mississippi, under heavy escort by the Alabama National Guard and the state patrol. When the convoy reached the Alabama-Mississippi line, the Alabama troops peeled off and Mississippi authorities took over. Although there had been rest stops in Alabama, the officials in Mississippi allowed none in their state, and by the time they got to Jackson the riders were sorely in need of rest rooms.

They were not to use them, however. When the twenty-seven riders stepped off the bus in Jackson, city police captain J. L. Ray arrested them, one by one, on charges of "breach of peace" and "refusing to obey an officer." Two days later the riders were convicted, fined two hundred dollars each, and given suspended jail sentences of sixty days each. Municipal court judge James L. Spencer displayed a mastery of Mississippi logic when he sentenced the riders: "They were not traveling for the purpose of traveling but were traveling for the purpose of inflaming the populace. . . . Their avowed purpose was to inflame the public, which will only result in those things which an inflamed public do [sic]."⁶ (This was the same Spencer who had convicted sit-in demonstrators on the grounds that their orderly protest might have provoked someone else to commit violence.) The riders spurned the court's offer of suspended sentences and elected to stay in jail. James Farmer of CORE, who was among them, called for an expansion of the rides to include railroad and air terminals.

There was unusual unanimity within the civil rights movement, at least at first, on the need to continue the demonstrations. Roy Wilkins of the National Association for the Advancement of Colored People urged Negro college students, who were ending their spring semester, to return home on a "nonsegregated transportation basis" and to "sit where you choose on trains and buses." Wilkins also rejected Robert Kennedy's call for a cooling-off period, declaring, "There can be no cooling-off period in the effort to obtain one's citizenship rights. The effort must go on continuously by all feasible methods."⁷

As small groups of protesters continued to arrive in Jackson, a few of those arrested made bond and left town. But a significant number chose jail rather than bail. In New Haven, Connecticut, William Sloane Coffin preached a sermon in which he revealed that the attorney general's office had asked his group "to reconsider our decision to make the trip." And in Washington, the political pressures generated by the ride produced results: The attorney general asked the Interstate Commerce Commission to issue regulations banning segregation in interstate bus terminals. Six years before, the commission had outlawed segregation in rail transportation, but it had done nothing about bus terminals. The agency had brought only one complaint against bus lines themselves for segregation, and that ended in a hundred-dollar fine. The Supreme Court had already ruled segregation illegal in bus terminal restaurants; Kennedy's request was believed to be aimed at making enforcement easier.

———————————————— ■

After the original Freedom Ride bus had been burned in Anniston, the riders had gone to the Birmingham home of Fred Shuttlesworth. When Diane Nash was planning the second wave of riders, she called Shuttlesworth to make the arrangements. They spoke in an elementary code. "Rooster" meant young man, "hen" meant woman, and "chickens" meant the fresh troops from Nashville. Then Robert Kennedy's phone calls to Shuttlesworth started.

Kennedy's calls, as Shuttlesworth remembers them, were all directed at minimizing the demonstrators' exposure to possible violence. The attorney general repeatedly proposed that Shuttlesworth convince the riders that they should accept police escorts, first out of Birmingham, then to Montgomery. Gradually, with Kennedy phoning Bull Connor in Birmingham and John Patterson in Montgomery and then Shuttlesworth to confirm the riders' agreement, a travel plan was organized. As Shuttlesworth recalls it, the attorney general required some educating in group dynamics.

"Patterson finally agreed to escort us to Montgomery," he said later. "So Kennedy calls, and he was happy about that. I said, 'Well, where do we go from Montgomery? We're heading for Jackson, Mississippi.' He said, 'Well, can't you go through to New Orleans?' I said, 'I thought you weren't in the way of telling people where they go, Mr. Kennedy.'

"Then he called me again, and he said, 'Well, I'll tell you what, Mr. Shuttlesworth. I arranged it so that you can go to New Orleans if you want to.' I said, 'Well, I just told you, we don't *want* to go to New Orleans. We're going to Mississippi, see.' He says, 'Wait, I'll call you back.' He called the governor of Mississippi. And the governor of Mississippi agreed to escort us from the state line to Jackson.

"Bless his heart. I respected those boys. When he got the agreement, he said, 'Now you can go either to Mississippi or to New Orleans.' I said, 'Well, we'll be going to Mississippi.' Then he asked me a question. He said, 'Well, now, *you* aren't going to ride, are you?'

"I said, 'Mr. Kennedy, don't you know I'm a battlefield general? I lead troops into battle. Especially here. Don't you know the record of Birmingham?' I said, 'It was I who's been abused, and yet I've always led the troops into battle.' And he said, 'Well, I respect that. But you don't have to ride, do you?'

"I said, 'Well, why would I ask anybody *else* to ride? Yes, I'm going to ride if the buses roll.' And do you know it wasn't thirty minutes after that before I was arrested."

Shuttlesworth's theory — actually, it is a certainty in his mind — is that Kennedy, worried about the outspoken minister's life expectancy if another mob of klansmen attacked the Freedom Ride he was on, called Jamie Moore, the Birmingham chief of police (and a far less volatile man than his boss, Bull Connor), and asked that Shuttlesworth be arrested.

"To keep me from being killed," explained Shuttlesworth.

Shuttlesworth, unaware of these manipulations, went to the bus station, bought a ticket, and started walking toward the bus to Montgomery. Then he heard his name called.

" 'Freddie Lee?' It was Chief Moore. He always called me that. 'Freddie Lee? Where you going?'

"I said, 'I'm going to the bus.'

"He said, 'No. I'm giving you an order not to get on the bus.' I said, 'What you mean, I can't get on the bus? I have my ticket. You can't stop me from riding.'

"He said, 'Well, no. But I can get you for refusing to obey the lawful order of a policeman. And I'm telling you to go home.'

"I said, 'I ain't going home.' He said, 'You refuse to go home?' And I said, 'Yes.'

"He said, 'I'm arresting you for refusing to obey a lawful order.' I said, 'But you can't arrest me when I've got a ticket to ride.' He said, 'But that's what I'm arresting you for.' So I was in jail when the bus took off. And as I look at it now, I'm sure that they would have killed me. I'm sure if I had ridden that bus, my life would've ended in Montgomery."

Henry Schwarzschild was one of those arrested in Jackson and convicted by Judge James Spencer. In his billfold now he carries his tattered Jail Commitment Certificate from Jackson, along with a police mug photo of himself. The certificate declares Schwarzschild to be a "white male," and it certifies that Judge Spencer has committed him to the Hinds County Jail "for the crime of breach of the peace." Schwarzschild was sentenced on June 21, 1961, to four months in jail or a two-hundred-dollar fine. He stayed in the jail for a week and then paid his fine. When he had returned to Jackson for his trial, he badly wanted his mug shot for a souvenir. "I called [a high official in the Jackson police department, now dead] to get a copy," he said. "We exchanged presents. He was waiting outside the courtroom to testify against me, but he slipped me this little brown envelope, and I gave him something. I can't remember exactly what. We made believe it was costs of reproducing the mug shots. It was money." Schwarzschild thinks it may have been five dollars. "It reminded me of what they used to say about the Austrian civil servants: You can bribe them for so little money, you can almost call them incorruptible."

Schwarzschild left jail on the day that Martin Luther King returned to Atlanta after a meeting in Jackson on whether to continue the Freedom Rides. The two men were on the same airplane, one of several Delta Airlines flights that hopped among Atlanta, Birmingham, and Jackson and that served as the Movement's logistical lifeline. They talked awhile, and Schwarzschild asked King to inscribe his Jail Commitment Certificate. The civil rights leader wrote, "Your courageous willingness to go to jail for freedom has brought us closer to our nation's bright tomorrow. Martin Luther King, Jr." In his billfold Schwarzschild also carries a dried and pressed flower that hung with many others outside the door of the motel in Memphis where King was murdered in 1968. And there is a cloth Star of David that he got in Germany at the end of World War II. The Nazis forced Jews to identify themselves by wearing the stars on their left breasts or as armbands.

After he returned to Chicago from the trip to Kentucky at Easter, 1960, where he carried a picket sign at a dime store, Schwarzschild continued to participate in Movement activities. Like Will Campbell, he clearly understood that the Movement had to be run by black people; he offered his help whenever he could, but he never tried to take over. When he heard about the Freedom Ride a year after the sit-ins began, he asked around and learned that more riders were needed. After the initial burst of bus trips into the hard-core South, a decreasing number of volunteers were willing to invite almost certain arrest, conviction, and incarceration, and possible injury as well.

Schwarzschild left Chicago with a few others by bus for Nashville. There he met Diane Nash, who impressed him with her sternness on the subject of who and what the Movement was all about. "I was reproached," recalled Schwarzschild, "for having referred to Martin King — whom, of course, at that point I had never met — as *the* civil rights movement, and I was told that he was the *symbol* of the civil rights movement and please not to refer to him as its leader — a lesson which I have never forgotten, nor have I ever violated it."

Because of logistical problems, the volunteer riders were sent to Atlanta, where others were waiting to start a trip. His group, Schwarzschild remembers, consisted of four whites and three Negroes. The Greyhound bus from Atlanta to Montgomery was escorted by all sorts of official hardware — police cars, emergency vehicles, and the occasional Air National Guard airplane, with changes of the guard at state lines.

"There was all this even though we were on a regularly scheduled bus, and seven harmless people sitting together, black and white, in the middle of the bus.

"The politicians, I think, at the time still wanted the drama. Even these dumb jerks knew that we certainly were not going to engage in violence. They probably justified to the public and maybe even their own minds this array of military power by saying that we were going to create so much turmoil that they were in effect protecting us. But I've never been clear in my own mind why they wanted to make it so big. I mean, here were seven people sworn to nonviolence. Sworn to be killed on the highways rather than lift a finger against any of these people, civilian or uniformed. And yet there was this great need to make enormous crisis drama out of it by the state agencies."

Though he had served in the military in the South, had been naturalized as an American citizen in the South, and had married a Southern woman, Schwarzschild had little familiarity with the place he was visiting with such fanfare. As the bus purred through the Black Belt and he stared out the window, Schwarzschild realized, he said later, that "I knew nothing about the region. And I still know very little about it — about the social texture of the South. It's not so much that I wasn't concerned; it's that I really gained essentially no access to it.

"In that period it was, after all, the lovely heyday of the Movement when, to a white man involved in the civil rights movement in the South, what was out there in the society was unremittingly hostile and dangerous. The only place you were welcome, at home, safe, loved, well received, was the black community, in whose bosom you lived and who loved you for being there. It was really kind of a love feast, and that's not said casually.

"The only white Southerners I met were people who were marginally or directly involved in the civil rights movement affairs, whether it was in Atlanta with the Southern Regional Council, or the press, and people of that sort. People like Chuck Morgan [Charles Morgan, Jr., a white attorney from Birmingham who became a civil rights lawyer at a time and a place when even moderates were in danger]: dissenting, fascinating, significant, courageous, terribly knowledgeable and sophisticated people. But the general society of the South was then and is now, in effect, a closed book. . . ."

The riders in Schwarzschild's group anticipated being arrested, and they carried a change of underwear, an extra shirt, and a toothbrush. In Montgomery there was a gathering of white toughs, but by now the local police had started showing up for such events. Their presence, however, did not prevent Schwarzschild from experiencing a sensation he had last felt in Europe before fleeing the Nazis in 1939: "I had the sense of the imminence of being killed under the open sky by somebody. And it was the first time in my life that I experienced that the old phrase about your knees knocking out of fear is literally true. You are so tense that your muscles really shake, and my knees really did knock together. It was a very odd experience of terror."

It didn't help that a young reporter for the *Montgomery Advertiser* walked over to interview the riders and mentioned in passing that local segregationist sentiment was so high that if *he* walked across the street into the mob, *he* would be immediately beaten, and *he* lived there. "You can imagine what they'd do to *you*," he said. Then Schwarzschild and others went to spend the night at Fred Shuttlesworth's house. "It had been bombed, I think, a week before," said Schwarzschild. "Fred and his wife were up in Chicago, taking their kids to safekeeping there. But we stayed at their house. That was also a little worrisome."

When the bus arrived in Jackson, there was no time to wonder about a white mob. Schwarzschild and the others stepped from the bus into the "white" waiting room and then immediately into the arms of Captain Ray, who arrested them. "We were taken to a waiting paddy wagon, which again, with a roar of sirens and a dozen police cars, sped off a half a block down the street to the Hinds County Jail and police headquarters," said Schwarzschild.

Schwarzschild was represented in court by a courageous and dedicated Negro lawyer, who told his client that he had failed the bar examination twice. "And I said to myself, 'Jesus Christ! He's my lawyer!' I could have lived very nicely without knowing all that."

Henry Schwarzschild knew that he would soon be leaving the jail, but he was not prepared for the feeling that descended on him as soon as the heavy doors clanged shut. "It took me only a day or two to become all but numbed almost insensible by a kind of prison psychosis," he said. "I remember very well, somewhere in that week — and that's all it was for me — looking out through the window of that jail cell to the streets of Jackson, which were down below — we were up in the third or fourth or fifth floor — and seeing somebody, an ordinary person, walk down the street and at the corner, cross the street and turn left and go on the next side street. And I remember the sense of utter strangeness; of disbelief that one could, in this world about whose reality I seemed to remember *nothing,* turn left and go down the street if one wanted to turn left and go down the street. In a few days it had sort of evaporated as a reality. I was utterly numbed by the sense of being in here. One didn't know what would happen to one; you didn't know whether you could get out."

■ ───────────────

Governor Patterson's appeal to racism did not sit well with all white Southerners or with all white Southern newspapers.[8] A letter to the editor of the *Montgomery Advertiser*, published shortly after the Anniston, Birmingham, and Montgomery violence, said: "Gov. Patterson referred to the freedom riders as 'rabble rousers.' He is entitled to his opinion, but is Alabama to glory in the fact that it has furnished sufficient rabble to be roused?"

The *Tuscaloosa News* wrote, in an editorial: "Failure of public officials to provide intelligent, courageous leadership is the principal reason for the current crisis in our state." In North Carolina, the *Charlotte Observer* declared that "the people of the South will continue to live under tension and suffer anguish until they support a different and a better kind of public official. Our region has been led by false prophets since the Civil War and especially since the 1954 Supreme Court decision. By their policies, by their own angry, emotional statements on race, they have contributed substantially to building the kind of climate favorable to raw and ugly violence." And the *Tampa Tribune* noted that the Freedom Riders had "obtained the full cooperation of the Ku Klux hoodlums and thick-headed politicians who are the South's greatest liability. . . . A South moving steadily forward in racial progress could deal readily enough with its enemies — if it were not constantly tripping over the native numbskulls who profess to be its friends."

There was a tendency in other quarters to follow the politicians' lead and blame the victims. In Mississippi the *Columbus Commercial Dispatch* roared: "The senseless defiance of tradition by the crackpots riding on the so-called Freedom Ride gave the South a slap directly in the face and were rewarded [*sic*] for their impertinence by a sound beating. Good enough for them. The action by the citizens of Alabama is entirely understandable."

Other newspapers seemed to want it both ways. South Carolina's *Charleston News and Courier*, a stridently anti-integrationist newspaper, tempered only slightly its criticism of those who tested the segregation customs. "CORE sent its agents south in the expectation that some might become martyrs in the cause of racial mixing," said the paper. "In such cases, guilt must be shared by both sides." On one day in May, the *Birmingham News* wrote that the citizens of Alabama let Governor Patterson "talk for months in a manner that could easily say to the violent, the intemperate, that they were free to do as they pleased when it came to the 'hated' integrationists. . . . We, the people, asked for it." But on the very next day, it published an editorial, addressed to Attorney General Kennedy, arguing that it was as important "to stop those who provoke violence as it is to stop those who commit violence" and adding that "the right of peaceful assembly has its limitations, just as has the right of freedom of speech. The performances of Fred Shuttlesworth in Birmingham have long deliberately abused these guarantees of the Constitution."

The *New York Times* editorial writer seemed not to understand the purpose of the Freedom Ride or the reason it had to be held in the way that it was. Ignoring the fact that travel facilities had remained segregated despite court and regulatory agency rulings, the paper declared, "Non-violence that deliberately provokes violence is a logical contradiction." Although somewhat more polished, the reasoning seemed similar to Judge Spencer's tortured analysis in Jackson municipal court.

The Freedom Rides marked a transition in the Movement, just as the sit-ins had done in the previous year. The sit-ins incorporated the experiences of the Montgomery bus boycott and moved the effort a significant step forward — from depending on arguments in the courtroom to throwing down a moral gauntlet before the perpetrators of segregation, and doing so with the rest of the world looking on. The sit-ins were the essence of passive nonviolence; all the demonstrators had to do was walk into a place of public accommodation and sit down, and the system did the rest. The system's most difficult problem at that point became trying to answer coherently the question Diane Nash asked Mayor Ben West on the steps of Nashville's city hall: How can you justify selling merchandise to these people while refusing to sell them a cup of coffee?

The Freedom Rides were different. They dealt with a question of law, and they dealt with the moral question of public accommodations, but in a much more aggressive manner. The demonstrators compelled their tormenters to pay attention to their demands. They rode into a community — "invaded" was the term the segregationists used, and it was not all that far off the mark — and, striding past the signs and symbols that the community had long ago erected to separate the races, they insisted on their rights. Furthermore, they did so in full knowledge — in *everybody's* full knowledge — that their tormenters might explode with violence.

To a lot of people, South and North, including liberal journalists and government officials, that was the sticking point in the Freedom Rides: If you asked for violence, and you got it, then you had nobody to blame but yourself. This analysis overlooked the fact that the demonstrators never really did ask for violence; they just took risks that might reasonably be expected to elicit violence from others. The segregationists were completely free to behave without violence. This analysis also ignored the fact that blacks had done it the other way — the way that many whites said they favored, the way that assumed fair play and decency and sportsmanship on the segregationists' part — for decades and decades, with disastrous results. Once the initial layers of racial injustice had been peeled away — when the border states that valued education managed to find ways to desegregate some schools; when economic wisdom dictated the desegregation of lunch counters in some communities; when the federal government had clearly indicated that it would not actively participate in the desegregation process — then there was no other instrument left save the "creative tension" that Martin Luther King and the other proponents of nonviolence were advocating. Actually, there *was* another instrument: violence. And even in 1961 there were some black Americans who were talking about the futility of treating the system politely any longer — about advancing their struggle by taking up arms.

Two organizations, the Southern Christian Leadership Conference and the Southern Regional Council, attempted after the Freedom Rides began to explain all this to the general public. SCLC was quoted in a comprehensive *New York Times* article on passive resistance:

> SCLC believes that the American dilemma in race relations can best and most quickly be resolved through the actions of thousands of people, committed to the philosophy of nonviolence, who will physically identify themselves in a just and moral struggle.
>
> It is not enough to be intellectually dissatisfied with an evil system. The true nonviolent resister presents his physical body as an instrument to defeat the system.

Through nonviolent mass direct action, the evil system is creatively dramatized in order that the conscience of the community may grapple with the rightness or wrongness of the issue at hand.

The nonviolent resister has no alternative but to disobey the unjust law. In disobeying such a law, he does so peacefully, openly and nonviolently. Most important, he willingly accepts the penalty for breaking the law. This distinguishes SCLC's position on civil disobedience from the "uncivil disobedience" of the racist opposition in the South. In the face of laws they consider unjust, they seek to defy, evade, and circumvent the law. But they are unwilling to accept the penalty for breaking the law.[9]

In a detailed report on the rides issued May 30, 1961, the Southern Regional Council noted that some observers were calling the riders "extremists," and commented: "It would be more intelligent to realize that they are pointing out to the South what must be done, and done quickly, if we are to forestall the emergence into power of real, genuine extremists." Such advice, while eminently sound, must have seemed almost unintelligible to Southern governors such as Patterson, who had invested great energies and wads of taxpayers' money in trying to outlaw the NAACP, one of the least extremist of the black organizations.

On June 1, 1961, the protest began to pay off in Montgomery. The *Times*'s Claude Sitton discovered that Greyhound had "quietly desegregated its terminal" in the Alabama capital.[10] The nationwide call went out, meantime, for more volunteer riders. On June 2, federal judge Frank Johnson in Montgomery took an action that caught everyone by surprise. He issued a temporary injunction restraining the Freedom Riders from conducting further tests of segregation in Alabama. He asserted that the rides had put "an undue burden and restraint on interstate commerce." In a sense, Judge Johnson had bought the argument that doing something that brings violence on yourself, even if you're perfectly within the law, is itself a violent act.

The riders' actions, wrote Judge Johnson, "may be a legal right," but "the right of the public to be protected from the evils of their conduct is a greater and more important right." Johnson said his order did not apply to people engaged in "bona fide" travel, who did not have sponsorship or funding for the specific purpose of testing desegregation. He also found that the Montgomery police and municipal officials had demonstrated "willful and deliberate failure" to protect the riders and forbade them to do so again. And he enjoined the Ku Klux Klan and others from interfering with such "bona fide" travel.[11]

The reaction from the Movement was not surprising. Marvin Rich, CORE's community relations director, said, "We feel that the right to travel on interstate vehicles cannot be abridged, nor can it be limited." Martin Luther King said, "I think we have revealed through many experiences that we have no fear of going to jail and staying to serve time when necessary." Movement leaders said they would try to overturn the injunction.[12]

The Justice Department seemed surprised by Judge Johnson's ruling. A spokesman hastened to point out that the department did not approve of the injunction against riders, and on June 9 the department filed a brief with the judge objecting to the decision and noting that no previous cases could be found "in which the exercise of lawful, peaceful, constitutionally protected activity has been proscribed because such activity was expected to arouse unlawful violence by others."[13] On June 12, Judge Johnson allowed his temporary order to lapse.

The administration in Washington, meanwhile, was trying other ways to convince the Movement to end the rides voluntarily. Burke Marshall, the assistant attorney general in charge of civil rights, said at a Fisk University seminar in late June that localities had jurisdiction in matters of arrest, and that the Justice Department was powerless to stop the local authorities when they arrested people as they had been doing in Jackson. He added, however, that he thought the arrests would be found invalid by the courts.[14] The department filed suit for the first time to end segregation in airport terminals. The target was the airport at New Orleans. And, as will be seen in the following chapter, the administration was dangling another carrot before the Movement in its effort to cool off the demonstrators.

The Freedom Ride and subsequent forays into the South's transportation centers were of tremendous importance to the civil rights movement. They forced a discussion of just how angry and provocative Negroes could be in demanding an end to segregation. They brought the federal authorities into the struggle in ways far more complicated than had Little Rock or earlier court decisions. They put white liberals and moderates on the spot and required them to decide how much militancy they were willing to accept (a choice that would be repeated several times as the Movement and the resistance to it grew). In doing so, they showed Negroes (if they needed showing) that the commitment of many of their white friends had limits. They encouraged the more conservative black organizations, such as the NAACP, to reendorse direct action. They revealed the hypocrisy of Southern elected officials better than most earlier attempts. They took elements of past protest efforts and blended them into a new strategy that worked reasonably well. They established young Negroes as the most aggressive element of the Movement — quite a step, since the youth only a year or so previously had been firmly relegated to the back of the Movement bus by their elders.

The rides also illuminated a number of other factors that were important, or would become important, in the Movement: They showed that the time-honored practice of blaming the victim was alive and well in American society. They demonstrated that the racists' own violence actually helped the cause of integration (another lesson that would be repeated many times). They revealed (hardly a surprise) that the resistance listed red-baiting in its arsenal of weapons. (T. B. Birdsong, the head of the Mississippi highway patrol, said the rides were "directed, inspired and planned by known communists," and that American students had gone to Havana and learned, from nine Soviet officials, "how to make sit-ins, walk-ins, kneel-ins and Freedom Rides.")[15]

The rides produced techniques by which the Movement could force the federal authorities to get involved, even when they didn't want to. They demonstrated that the white press would always pay more attention to the even mildly uncomfortable predicament of a prominent white person (such as the Reverend Mr. Coffin of Yale on his night in an Alabama jail) than the most devastating calamity that the system could visit upon almost any black person. They showed that the one black person who would be an exception to the above rule was Martin Luther King, Jr. Although King had relatively little to do with the Freedom Rides, once he did become involved the media and the rest of the nation cast him in the role of mastermind and sole leader. And the rides also revealed the role — both pro and con — that could be played by the federal judiciary (and in one example by the same member of the federal judiciary, Frank Johnson, with his unusual injunction against the Freedom Riders).

Most important, the rides showed that the hard-core South was immune to moral arguments that might have had some weight elsewhere. Sit-ins could trouble the conscience of a mayor in Tennessee and the bank accounts of the downtown business elite in Atlanta, but in deepest Alabama and Mississippi, and much of Louisiana and south Georgia, the whites who ran things showed no inclination toward reform, no spasms of guilt. If a Negro wanted to ride a bus into their town and undergo a little redemptive suffering, that was fine with them.

But when it was all over, and the presence of a black person in a "white" waiting room was no longer unusual, the demonstrators had failed to achieve a complete victory. They had not won the support of whites as they had done with the sit-ins. This was not their fault; the whites' reactions just showed that the white "moderate" and "liberal" and "Northern" communities also had lines that they would not cross — or, as some of the most cynical Movement people were beginning to put it, that they were racist just like the rest of American society.

The existence of this philosophical line was evident in the way the editorial writers reacted to the riders' arrival in Jackson. There, the segregationists had devised a simple system, a triumph of public relations: Rather than let the Klan enjoy its ten minutes of uninterrupted violence against the integrated groups that arrived at the bus station and airport, thus inviting the wrath of the nation and intervention by the federal government, the rule was simply to arrest everybody as they got off the bus. It was neat, nonviolent, and unconstitutional. Almost as soon as Jackson started using the technique, the press started praising it. The *Milwaukee Journal* commented, "They were politely received. There were no mobs. When they entered rest rooms they were just as politely arrested." Said the *Detroit Free Press:* "The state of Mississippi has kept its defense against desegregation on a civilized plane. . . . Mississippi, in arresting them for alleged disobedience of an officer, breach of peace and incitement to riot, has met their challenge in an orderly way."[16]

The press also reflected the notion at large in the white community that it was one thing for residents of a community — full-time residents, or even students there for the academic year — to mount protests, but quite another for outsiders to ride interstate buses into a city and conduct a similar protest. The *New York Times* quoted a "white leader who has played a prominent role in the civil rights struggle," but whom it did not name, as saying "for persons just to test and challenge is too much like baiting. They don't appeal to any underlying sympathy among Southerners. This becomes a dare, not a protest."[17]

The dare was much more productive, however, than appeals to the sweet reason of the system's keepers. On September 22, 1961, the Interstate Commerce Commission issued a regulation in response to Robert Kennedy's request, which in turn was a response to the pressures exerted by the Freedom Rides. The regulation, scheduled to become effective on November 1, prohibited carriers of interstate passengers from having anything whatsoever to do with "any terminal facilities which are so operated, arranged, or maintained so as to involve any separation of any portion thereof, or in the use thereof[,] on the basis of race, color, creed, or national origin."[18]

EIGHTEEN

■ ─────────────────────

WHERE'S YOUR BODY?

─────────── ■

It was clear that the leaders of the national administration were among those who disapproved of the sort of direct action exemplified by the Freedom Ride..Robert Kennedy had tried repeatedly to convince the demonstrators that they should accept "cooling-off periods." He had urged the rerouting of the ride to avoid central Mississippi. He or his aides had suggested to prominent Northern liberals that they not go on the rides following the original one.

The attitude in Washington reflected the paternalism that had always marked the national government's position toward Southern Negroes and their cause. It also attested to a desire to avoid confrontation with Southern racists, who, through their seniority, controlled Congress. This was confirmed in an article that appeared in the *New York Times* late in May, 1961, soon after Robert Kennedy had made one of his "cooling-off" requests and as he was attempting long-distance traffic management with phone calls to governors, demonstrators, and heads of interstate bus lines.

The article was written by Joseph Loftus, a journeyman reporter with excellent access to the Kennedys. It bore all the markings of the prototypical Washington story generated by politicians seeking to achieve a specific end: A reporter who is known to be not unfriendly is offered information on an exclusive basis, on the condition that names not be used. The politician who plants the story gets a point across without personal risk, and the reporter gets a piece of information all to himself or herself. Loftus attributed his information to "high sources in the administration," which almost certainly meant *very* high. Those sources, he wrote, "made clear that they were not trying to dissuade the Freedom Riders from traveling. This policy, they believe, is quite different from positively encouraging such travel. Their position is that if citizens choose to exercise their rights it is the function of government to safeguard those rights. At the same time, the administration is trying to avoid any suggestion of interference with state and local agencies."[1]

President Kennedy and his administration had already demonstrated their willingness to tolerate racism in several areas — the president's failure to eliminate housing discrimination with a "stroke of a pen" was but one example. Their reaction to the Freedom Rides indicated to the Movement, to all Americans generally, and to the entrenched resistance just how aggressive a role the administration was willing to take.

As the rides continued, another indicator emerged on June 16, 1961. But few in the media or the public at large recognized its importance. On that date, the attorney general and some of his assistants met in Washington with some of the civil rights leaders who were active in the testing of Southern transportation segregation. The Associated Press reported on the day of the meeting that several leaders had "called on" Kennedy, "reportedly to ask for help in stopping arrests of the demonstrators against segregation." The attorney general's office was quoted as saying afterward that "there was a frank exchange and the meeting was a useful one" — the stock comment a government agency uses when it wants to say nothing.[2]

Later versions of the meeting differed dramatically. According to one newspaper report, the one now believed to be most accurate, Kennedy called the leaders together and urged them to change their strategy from direct action to voter registration. This account, published in the *New York Times*, said the attorney general had "told the group of six Negroes and one white person that he felt the bus riders had made their point on travel facilities and there was no further advantage to be gained in continuing them [the Freedom Rides] as a protest against segregation." Those in attendance, said the article, included James Lawson, who served as the leaders' spokesperson; Gordon Carey of the Congress of Racial Equality's national office and Lolis Elie, a CORE activist and lawyer from New Orleans; Charles Sherrod, who had just been hired as the first field secretary of the Student Nonviolent Coordinating Committee; and Wyatt Tee Walker of the Southern Christian Leadership Conference. A later report included Diane Nash in the list. James Farmer, who ordinarily would have represented CORE at such a meeting, was in a Mississippi prison at the time, having participated in one of the rides himself. The article, which was apparently written after a reporter talked with Justice Department officials, did not describe the leaders' reaction to Kennedy's proposal.[3]

Not everyone agrees on this attendance list, just as not everyone agrees on what was said at the meeting. Gordon Carey, for example, now says he did not attend. On two points there is general accord. One is that Kennedy argued that the right to vote was fundamental to all the others sought by the Movement, and that the leaders should concentrate more on registering voters in the South and less on direct action. The other is that the attorney general said if the Movement were to redirect its attention toward a voter registration drive, he would try to secure foundation backing for it.

There is widespread disagreement on another aspect of the meeting. Several of those from the Movement felt afterward that Kennedy had assured them, if not in so many words then surely by implication, that if they undertook a voter education campaign they would receive federal protection. They would, after all, be assisting the victims of illegal repression to exercise a constitutional right. The more cynical of them noted, too, that the right almost surely would be exercised to the advantage of the Kennedy administration; that newly registered voters would not forget who helped them secure the franchise, just as black voters in 1960 had remembered who made the telephone calls to Georgia on Martin Luther King's behalf.

The meeting produced intense discussion among the Movement's activists — almost enough to precipitate a split between
those who favored continued direct action and those who wanted
to move into voter registration. The debate took place against a
background of lessening interest in the Freedom Rides. Claude Sitton of the *Times*, in a front-page article from Nashville, reported
that a forthcoming conference of Movement leaders was expected
to agree that the trips should be suspended, although there was
opposition to this from some participants, notably Diane Nash.
The reasons for the expected halt, said Sitton, included the fact
that the Justice Department had asked the Interstate Commerce
Commission for a ruling outlawing the bus station segregation that
the riders were protesting; the increasing difficulty in obtaining
funds; and a decline in the willingness of Southern Negroes to
participate in the rides. Also cited was the failure of the rides,
conducted largely by Northerners, to "generate much sympathy for
desegregation among Southern whites."[4]

Sitton had excellent sources for his prediction, but he had not
counted on CORE's dedication to the rides. When the meeting, a
private one, was held to discuss the future of the rides, Gordon
Carey emphatically announced that CORE would continue them,
no matter what. The leaders of the other groups then agreed to
align themselves with CORE's position. The debate between continued direct action and other tactics — in this case, voter registration — was relatively minor, and it certainly did not produce the
headline writer's dream word, "split." But it was a hint of the deep
discussions that were just beginning in the Movement about what
should be done next. And it was a prelude to the establishment of
one of the era's most important institutions, the Voter Education
Project.

James Farmer heard secondhand about the Kennedy meeting, from
his jail cell at Mississippi's Parchman Penitentiary. Some of the
Freedom Ride prisoners had been transferred to Parchman, purportedly because of overcrowding in the Hinds County Jail. According to his autobiography, Farmer's interpretation of the
meeting was that Kennedy said, "If you'll cut out this Freedom
Riding and sitting-in stuff, and concentrate on voter registration,

I'll get you a tax exemption." The young activists at the meeting, wrote Farmer, "gasped at the statement and considered the suggested trade-off to border on bribery. They also thought that it revealed a lack of sensitivity to the indignities imposed by segregation, which had to be addressed *now* and could not wait until free access to the ballot box could bring about change."[5]

James Forman, SNCC's executive secretary, saw the administration's move as strictly political. In his autobiography he wrote that "policy makers in the Kennedy administration were pondering how the energies of black students could be used to help line up Southern black voters for the Democratic Party," and they produced the voter registration scheme, in conjunction with liberal foundations. "The Democratic Party and friendly foundations, especially Field and Taconic, were together interested in using tax-exempt money to register Democratic voters."[6]

–––––––––––––––––––––––––– ■

Julian Bond agrees with this reasoning. The Kennedys, he said, were "basically decent people who, for one reason or another, just couldn't control this monster" of racism, "and for political considerations, didn't want to. Bobby didn't want to hurt Jack's chances of getting re-elected — didn't want to lose the white South for Jack. That's why they wanted us to go into voter registration: because they thought it would be nonthreatening activity, and that the blacks who registered would replace the whites who defected — never realizing that the struggle to register the blacks *by itself* would make the whites defect."

––––––––––––––––––

For Lawrence Guyot, a SNCC worker who became strongly identified with voter registration work in Mississippi, the voting scheme was "set up, really, by Robert Kennedy to stop public demonstrations."

––––––––––––––––––

Diane Nash remembers that when Kennedy invited the civil rights activists to his office, "we had quite a session.

"We had a conversation with Robert Kennedy, and then with Burke Marshall, and it was made clear to us that there would be all these thousands of dollars available through the foundations if we would do voter registration." The person who made it clear, she said, was not Kennedy. Her recollection was that it was Marshall, the assistant attorney general in charge of civil rights. "It was direct and clear that money would be made available from foundations for SNCC to do voter registration. Thousands of dollars."

Nash, who by now had left Fisk University to devote all her time to the Movement, does not recall that the activists responded directly to this overture. "But shortly thereafter, when the fact was considered that this money would be made available, I remember a number of people suddenly deciding that *they also* needed to drop out of school and work full-time for the Movement." She laughed.

Nash said she was worried that accepting the Kennedy plan would put the federal government "in control of the Southern black movement. And I knew that if they were making thousands and thousands of dollars available, then we were in real danger of that happening." She said she made up her mind to keep an eye on those people who suddenly decided, after hearing about the availability of large sums of money, to go into the voter registration field. "I didn't make judgments about them," she said, "but I decided that I'd watch them."

John Lewis was in prison at Parchman, along with James Farmer, when the meeting with Kennedy took place. When the suggestion came that activists should redirect their attention toward voter registration, said Lewis, "I think most of us in SNCC and in the Movement had the feeling that the Department of Justice would provide the necessary protection. We thought that the FBI, rather than just coming down and taking notes and pictures, would be there to protect us."

Wiley A. Branton was a black civil rights lawyer from Pine Bluff, Arkansas. He had been the counsel to the plaintiffs in the Little Rock school desegregation case, and later he would head the largest and most successful voter registration effort in the region. In an interview not long before his death, in 1989, Branton recalled that he had attended many meetings with administration officials on the subject of registration, and "they implied that the Justice Department would be there backing us up in any legal way that they could." Asked if that was the way it turned out, Branton said, "Oh, hell no. No."

Charles Jones, speaking of a later meeting with the attorney general, recalled: "Generally there was an agreement that they would, as best they could, protect us" while voter registration work was going on. "There are different versions of what was said," he added. "Just suffice it to say that there was an understanding — unwritten, but there was an understanding — that if we were going down there to the front lines and fighting the war for democracy, that we would get some protection."

Jones said this assurance came from Burke Marshall, but that other SNCC members had heard the same thing from Robert Kennedy. Furthermore, he said, "there was an understanding that we would not be inducted, either." The military draft was still in effect then; international tensions were high as a result of the downing in 1960 of an American U-2 reconnaissance airplane in the Soviet Union and the administration's disastrous attempt in 1961 to invade Cuba at the Bay of Pigs. Males of Jones's age who were finishing college or taking time off from their studies might find themselves without student deferments.

"Let's just say that my understanding was that assuming we followed the route of conscientious objectors and appealed any decisions that denied our [immune draft] status, that it would eventually go to the president" on appeal, he said, "and that, everything else being equal, our position as conscientious objectors would be reinforced." Although this left open the question of whether the activists could be inducted anyway and assigned to noncombat duties, as conscientious objectors had been in the past, Jones said, "Let's just say that when I went down [to register voters], it was with an understanding that the administration would do whatever it could within the framework of given statutes to leave us free to work toward voter registration."

■

The federal government's rendition of the voter registration–direct action discussions is mute on the subject of draft deferments. But it is clear that Robert Kennedy strongly urged the Movement's leaders to shift their attention to the vote and that he thought Washington could be more supportive of the Movement if they did. It is not clear that the attorney general made a hard-and-fast promise of federal protection for voting rights workers, but he did imply a strong degree of cooperation.

Kennedy was interviewed extensively in December, 1964, on his and his brother's actions in the civil rights arena by *New York Times* columnist Anthony Lewis. The former attorney general explained in the interviews, among other things, why he had urged a voter registration campaign. First, he said, "this was the area in which we had the greatest authority; and if we were going to do anything on civil rights, we should do it in that field where we had the authority." Second, the vote would produce the "most good" and influence change in other areas of life: "From the vote, from participation in the elections, flow all other rights far, far more easily." Finally, voting was an apple-pie-and-motherhood issue. "I felt that nobody really could oppose voting," Kennedy told Lewis. "How could anybody, really, get very mad because you're making an effort to make sure that everybody votes?" Because voting was an issue that would generate "less internal struggle and strife," reasoned Kennedy, there would be less need for agents of the federal government "coming down into Southern states and telling them what they should do. They could do it themselves."

During the Freedom Rides, said Kennedy, he had several meetings with civil rights leaders — the June 16 gathering was apparently not the only one — to make his case for "going down and registering people to vote." In one such meeting, the attorney general proposed the idea to Martin Luther King. "I think that they rather resented it," he told Lewis. "That's not what they wanted to do, and that's not where they were going to focus their attention."

Kennedy stated during the meetings that money could be obtained from foundations to finance such a voter drive, and he recalled that "I think I suggested that they set up an outside organization and that the money that could be given to it would be tax free. . . . I was able to work out with Mort Caplin for them to receive a tax [exemption]." Mortimer M. Caplin was the commissioner of Internal Revenue. Kennedy also said that he had never talked with his brother John about the political implications of increased black voting in the South. Rather, he told the interviewer, he doubted that the president's endorsement of black

voting would have made "that much of a difference" in his anticipated 1964 campaign for reelection, "compared to the fact that we
were alienating so many people." Presumably the attorney general
was referring to white Southern segregationists and other white
supremacists.[7]

Kennedy's assistant for civil rights, Burke Marshall, who sat
in on the sessions with Anthony Lewis, had delivered a series of
lectures in the same year the interviews were conducted in which
he declared that the administration was wary about offering police
protection to civil rights workers because of constitutional limitations on the powers of the federal government. Marshall also
complained of "an immense ignorance," shared apparently by most
everyone but himself, and "apparently untouched by the curricula
of the best universities, of the consequences of the federal system."
Robert Kennedy supplied the foreword for the published edition of
Marshall's lectures and agreed that federal involvement "would
lead inevitably to creation of a national police force." But Kennedy,
in the interview recalling his conversations with the Movement
leadership in the summer of 1961, revealed that a promise of protection *was* part of his pitch for a voter registration campaign. He
said he argued that "this was the area where we had the authority.
We didn't have the authority to give protection or to move in some
of these other fields. But we did have authority in voting, and we
could do something about that."[8] If that statement correctly reflected what Kennedy said to the activists at the time, they could
hardly be blamed for believing that he was promising them federal
protection, something they already knew they badly needed and
that those who had been to Mississippi knew they would need even
more.

As it happened, the administration did not provide active protection, and the Southern states certainly did not welcome the voting rights issue as one that promised "less internal struggle and
strife." Nor did they undertake to "do it themselves," as Robert
Kennedy continued to naively believe. In the clear vision of hindsight, none of that sounds surprising. But until that stage of the
civil rights movement's development, everyone outside the government was unsure what commitment Washington would make.
Indeed, the administration itself did not know; its civil rights pol-

icy was one of reacting to events, not trying to provide leadership
for them. Many Negro activists, possibly the majority in the summer of 1961, remained convinced that the system they were trying
to change *worked*. They believed that it would respond to their
legal demands and that the nation's constitution would be enforced
by the federal administration. Bit by bit, though, the national government was delivering the messages that the system was still a
white one and that there were limits to Washington's involvement.
And as these messages were delivered, the Negro's conviction
withered and his alienation grew.

What the Kennedy administration did believe, apparently, was
that it should take action in civil rights matters only if its own
constitutional authority were challenged by a state or other lesser
jurisdiction. If individuals or groups of individuals did the challenging, the federal government would almost certainly not act,
even though the challenges amounted to clear defiance of the Constitution. The term for this in vogue at the time was "private action." If a state passed a blatantly unconstitutional law or thumbed
its nose at a federal court order, that was a public action and the
administration would be expected to respond. But if a group of Ku
Klux Klansmen who were in league with a local police department
murdered a civil rights worker, even one who was clearly exercising a constitutional right, such as registering voters or seeking desegregated interstate transportation facilities, then that was a
private action. The state government, and not the federal, held the
responsibility for enforcing the laws against *that*.

The difficulties with this thinking, which was widely promoted by Burke Marshall, were several. For one thing, how could
the federal system function in a situation, commonplace in the
South at the time, in which the state abrogated its responsibility
to enforce the law or, worse, collaborated in illegal "private actions"? The system was effective only as long as all its constituent
groups played by the rules, which is what the thinkers in the
administration seemed to assume — unrealistically — they would
do. But that is not the way it was in the real world. For another
thing, it was clear (and would become clearer) that the Kennedy
administration was quite selective in deciding which public actions to protest. For decades the states had been fully engaged in

the business of denying Negroes the vote, equal education opportunities, equality in housing and employment and, especially, justice. Public funds and public offices were used, with virtually no
complaint from Washington, to perpetuate segregation and discrimination. The segregated jury system was one of the more scan-
dalous examples of this. Surely these were nonprivate actions that
could and should be dealt with by Washington, even under a strict
reading of Burke Marshall's federal system. But Washington did
little until it was prodded, embarrassed, and goaded into action by
Movement volunteers who placed their lives on the line. The Freedom Rides were a prime example of this.

The meeting with Robert Kennedy in the summer of 1961 amplified a debate that had been going on within the Student Nonviolent
Coordinating Committee about which direction its actions should
take. One group, primarily the Nashville activists, held to the belief that nonviolent direct action, as exemplified by the sit-ins and
the Freedom Rides, was an important technique that had not out-
lived its usefulness. Another group, which included Lawrence
Guyot, Charles Jones, and Charles Sherrod, thought that voter registration offered the best hope. It was not, the participants asserted,
a question of employing one technique to the exclusion of the
other, but rather a matter of whether SNCC's limited resources
should be stretched to include a registration program.

Diane Nash understood as well as anyone that the vote would
be a powerful tool in the emancipation of the South's Negro population. But she also harbored the fear that participation in a voter
registration campaign, and one funded by foundations friendly to
the Kennedys, might give the administration too much control
over the Movement in general and SNCC in particular. She and
the others debated the issue throughout the summer at SNCC staff
meetings. Entertainer Harry Belafonte, who was a loyal supporter
of the Movement, sponsored an informal gathering in Washington
at which the issue was thrashed out. There was further thrashing
at a seminar on student leadership held in Nashville. Finally, at a
meeting in August, SNCC's senior advisor, Ella Baker, brought the
dilemma close to solution by proposing that the organization sup-

port two distinct campaigns, one concerned with voting and headed by Charles Jones, the other dedicated to direct action and run by Diane Nash.[9]

In the end, all the debating may have been unnecessary, except as a device for sharpening SNCC's decision-making skills. (One characteristic that set SNCC apart from other civil rights organizations was its willingness to convene lengthy staff meetings to discuss issues as completely as possible — or, as some exasperated members put it, to talk them to death.) As the summer wound down, SNCC worker Robert Moses and other volunteers excused themselves from the debate and started working on voter registration in Mississippi. They discovered almost immediately that in the hard-core South, securing the right to register and vote for black people was direct action of the most forceful sort. To the racists of Mississippi, Alabama's Black Belt counties, and south Georgia, a Negro voter was far more of a threat than a busload of "outside agitators" rolling into a Greyhound terminal. As Bernard Lafayette recalled it, "Eventually, all of us got involved in voter registration. No question about it. Because for that section of the country, for that period of time in history, to be involved in voter registration was the most direct form of action, and it was the most threatening."

■

The debate that summer did more than sort out the partisans of direct action from those of voter registration, said Charles Jones. It produced "a notion that separated the serious people from the not serious. The notion was, 'Where is your body?' Talking was cheap. Throw your *body* into the Movement."

All this was discussed, Jones said, at the meeting hosted by Harry Belafonte, who was performing in Washington. Among those who attended, said Jones, were Charles Sherrod, Charles McDew, Diane Nash, Dion Diamond, and Tim Jenkins. McDew had replaced Marion Barry in 1960 as SNCC's chair. He was a Northerner, from Massilon, Ohio, a sociology student at South Carolina State College, a black convert to Judaism, and the proprietor of one of the Movement's more acute senses of humor. Dion Diamond was a SNCC staff member, and Tim Jenkins was a former student at Howard University who was the National Student Association's representative to SNCC.

"We spent about three days analyzing everything about where we were at that point," said Jones, "broadening the whole context of what we were doing, becoming very much more politically aware of what we were doing and why, and starting to define objectives and goals. We had a fantastic time! We were guests of Harry at his hotel, and wined and dined with him. It was great. It was a very unusual transition period. On about the last day, Harry said, 'Well, it's been an interesting discussion. Where's your body?'

"And I looked around at McDew. McDew looked at Sherrod. We both looked at Dion, Diane, Tim. Tim was silent there for a while. I think I said, 'Well, I'm in.' Sherrod said, 'I'm in.' McDew looked at me and said, 'Well, I guess I'm in.' " Jones did an imitation of McDew's voice, which is deep and profound and somewhat theatric, in the manner of the actor James Earl Jones.

"We all looked at Diane, because Diane had been talking all of that stuff. And Diane was saying, 'Well, I don't know. I'm not convinced that voter registration is what we ought to be in, that politics is what we ought to be doing. Gandhi was pure soul force and direct action. He didn't get involved in the politics.' And we were saying, 'Diane, that was the most political thing he ever did. He just used a different tactic, but everything he did was political. It was so political that it changed the entire relationship of England and the entire huge country of India. I mean, that's as political as you can get.' She wanted it to be pure soul force.

"So she said she wasn't ready. See, we were talking about going to Mississippi at this point. Bob Moses had already gone; was in Mississippi. The Klan had started putting folk on their list, and Bob Moses was next on it. We knew that. So it was time to make either some concerted effort to organize SNCC as a functioning organization throughout the South or leave it alone."

That, said Jones, was what "I'm in" meant.

"It meant we were going to commit ourselves full-time. And it meant voter registration, because that went directly to the heart of how decisions are made in this country and on what basis."

When Diane Nash maintained that she wanted to continue nonviolent direct action as SNCC's primary tactic, the activists decided to hold the leadership seminar at Nashville, a meeting that Jones called "a very heated, very intense discussion and debate.

"Everybody who ultimately was central in the evolution of the whole thing was there. And basically what we ended up doing was to establish two groups: voter registration — I became the director of voter registration — and nonviolent direct action, soul force." Bob Moses left his organizing in Mississippi and came to the meeting, recalled Jones. "When Bob came in, we were all kind of quiet, and then everybody embraced him. It was like we knew his life was constantly on edge, but he was still hanging in there. No support; nothing."

"I'm in" also meant leaving school to work for the Movement, said Jones. (In a sense, then, Diane Nash had declared herself "in" before anyone else, since she had already dropped out of Fisk to work full-time in the Movement.) Some of those at the meeting could not disrupt their educations then, and they had to count themselves out of the new campaign. "It was interesting," Jones added, "because there was never any tension between those who went back to school and those who went into the Movement full-time, because it was understood that we were going to be rotating anyway. We'd stay in for a while, take the front line, take that first phase. As we got tired or whatever, others would come in and we'd just go. We were just the ones who said at that point, 'We're in.' "

Belafonte and SNCC scared up some money for those who were "in" to start a registration effort. Jones remembers that late in the summer, he and several others decided to take a brief rest. "We agreed that we would take two weeks and go anywhere in the hell we wanted to. Meet back and then head to Mississippi. And we agreed that we would pay for that out of the pot. So we fanned out to different places in the world. I went to Mexico, to Acapulco. I don't know where the others went."

"It wasn't that I did not want to do voter registration," said Diane Nash afterward, "but that I did not want the voter registration to become SNCC's major reason for being. I didn't want it to be under the control of the Kennedys. . . .

"Ella Baker was very instrumental in the resolution of this problem. She recognized that, even though this was a conflict, by and large we needed to stay together. We had more in common than we did in conflict. And we did come to an agreement where there would be two arms of SNCC — the voter registration arm and the direct action arm. I think that that whole process, the conflict and the resolution, did prevent the thing that I was afraid of — the federal government starting to own and direct SNCC. However, when we did get involved in Mississippi, it became clear that voter registration was a critical issue, and it was volatile also. It really did amount to direct action."

■ ─────────────────────────

By the end of the summer of 1961, less than two years after Greensboro — and thanks largely to the Freedom Rides — nonviolent direct action had become a stock item in the Movement's inventory. That fact alone was not remarkable, for the technique was clearly an effective one. What *was* remarkable was the rapidity with which black Southerners had moved from seemingly passive participation in a system that promised immediate and painful punishment for direct action into active, even joyful defiance of that system.

The strategies that began with Greensboro, growing out of the Montgomery boycott more than four years before, and that were extended and elaborated during the Freedom Rides, were now available to anyone who wanted to change the system, regardless of age, color, race, creed, or national origin. The sit-ins and allied demonstrations, which often were mounted in the firm expectation of arrest and jailing, were especially attractive to young people, who lacked their parents' fear of the jail and what could happen in it. But they were also useful as devices to draw the elders into active protest, since hell hath no determination like mothers and fathers concerned about the welfare of their children. And before long, the elders themselves were using the techniques of direct action to achieve goals they previously might have sought only in the courtroom, or hoped for in the by-and-by.

Direct action also involved the "decent whites," who almost certainly would not have defied segregation laws or carried picket signs themselves but who were able to see bright, polite, well-dressed young Negroes as human beings with names, faces, and aspirations, and who worried, some of them for the first time in their lives, about what might happen to these young people in jail. In Atlanta at the height of the student sit-ins in the fall of 1960, a number of local black teenagers were arrested, as well as students from the Atlanta University Center. The city's white leaders were intensely aware of Atlanta's image on the national and international scenes, and the municipal movers and shakers tended to frame their reactions to segregation challenges in terms of how Atlanta would look rather than what they knew to be morally right. Still, the police continued arresting the demonstrators and putting them in jail, hoping all the while that nothing untoward would happen before bond could be posted.

One Negro teenager, upon being released after a mass arrest, was asked by a concerned white woman how the young people were treated by their arrestors and jailers. "With kid gloves" was the reply the young woman meant to give, but what came out was "With rubber gloves." The white woman immediately got on the telephone to organize a protest of her own against what she believed were unnecessary and humiliating strip searches at the police station. Eventually the terminology got straightened out and the protest was called off.*

At the same time that direct action was becoming almost commonplace for thousands of blacks, it was in the process of becoming old hat for hundreds of others — the young activists of SNCC and CORE who saw political action as the logical next step. It was also at this time that it became impossible to think of the Movement as a series of discrete events. It became mandatory to think of it as a number of intricately entwined occurrences. In truth, it never really had been a chronology that could neatly be classified as "Montgomery," "Greensboro," "Freedom Ride," and so forth, but the classifications were handy nonetheless.

Now, with the advance of the Movement into its most productive years, and with the rapid maturing of some of its newer constituent organizations, the campaign against segregation moved

---

*At the time, much of society considered intimate searches of nonviolent prisoners to be beyond the pale; the procedure is commonplace now.

onto a dozen fronts simultaneously, and in each case the activists were free to draw from the entire stock of tools, from courtroom litigation to boycott (or "economic withdrawal," as the activists preferred to call it, to circumvent local laws prohibiting boycotts) to face-to-face confrontation with the forces of white supremacy. SNCC and CORE could operate a number of campaigns at the same time, and so could the Southern Christian Leadership Conference and the National Association for the Advancement of Colored People. Like Diane Nash and a number of others who had their origins in the student movement, people were going into Movement work full-time.

With the increased activity, there came a change in the nature of the struggle. No longer was it solely a matter of a civil rights organization's confronting the white supremacists and the apathy of "decent whites"; now the organizations were competing with each other as well.

The competition was not restricted to mostly polite efforts to tap the same likely sources of financial support. Black nationalism was on the increase across America, and often its message was that separatism, not integration, was the solution for black people.[10]

Competition of another sort was represented by those Negroes who publicly announced that they themselves were not committed to nonviolence and would defend themselves with arms if necessary. As noted earlier, Robert Williams was suspended by Roy Wilkins as the NAACP chair in Monroe, North Carolina, after Wilkins heard Williams's statement that "the Negro in the South cannot expect justice in the courts. He must convict his attackers on the spot. He must meet violence with violence, lynching with lynching."[11] What was not as widely broadcast as the statement was the belief of many that Monroe, a town between Charlotte and the South Carolina line, was run in as mean-spirited and racist a fashion as any place in the Mississippi Delta. The white community, from city hall to police station to local and regional officials of the Justice Department and FBI, paid scant attention to the polite requests of Monroe's Negro citizens for a redress of their grievances. The Ku Klux Klan appeared to operate against blacks at will.

For good reason, Robert Williams had abandoned hope of such luxuries as equal protection under the law and fair trials. But his brand of militancy and his political preferences (he had visited Fidel Castro's Cuba and liked what he saw) made him a "wild man" in the eyes of the white press. The same organs of communication that could enshrine a protester who displayed the "traditional American values" of a Rosa Parks whose "feet were tired," or a college student who wore a necktie to a sit-in, could with equal facility isolate forever the activist who rang all the wrong bells. Robert Williams never had a chance in the mainstream press after he made his "violence with violence" statement, no matter what the context.

Williams's militancy grew after the NAACP suspension, and in the summer of 1961, he was active with others in seeking integration of municipal facilities and equal opportunity in employment. Whites responded with violence, for which they were not punished. In August, during a particularly tense period, a white couple strayed into the Williams house (as Williams put it) or was kidnapped by Williams and his colleagues (as the couple maintained). Williams fled to New York, followed by an FBI wanted notice that called him "schizophrenic" and warned that he "allegedly has possessed a large quantity of firearms, including a .45 caliber pistol which he carries in his car" (a practice duplicated by a vast number of rural Southerners at the time). From New York, Williams fled into Canada, then to Cuba.

Today, the Williams case is remembered by casual students of social change, if it is remembered at all, as a transitory phenomenon, a mere glitch in the chronology of those years — the exception to the rule. People are far more likely to recall the Monroe "kissing case" of 1958, in which two Negro boys, aged eight and nine, were charged with rape because their white female playmate kissed one of them. They were sent to reform school and would have remained there if a British journalist's account of the case had not got worldwide circulation and caused international outrage. But Monroe showed that there were limits to many Negroes' patience, and to what Martin Luther King called "our willingness to suffer." Not everyone on the black side of town was a member of the redemptive community. In a few short years this would become manifestly clear in rioting that would sweep the black ghettoes of the North and portions of the South as well.

Robert Williams explained it, for anyone willing to listen (and hardly any were), in a thin volume published in 1962, *Negroes with Guns*. He wrote in his prologue that, for the first time,

> American Negroes have armed themselves as a group, to defend their homes, their wives, their children, in a situation where law and order had broken down, where the authorities could not, or rather would not, enforce their duty to protect Americans from a lawless mob. . . . It has always been an accepted right of Americans, as the history of our Western states proves, that where the law is unable, or unwilling, to enforce order, the citizens can, and must, act in self-defense against lawless violence. I believe this right holds for black Americans as well as whites.[12]

NINETEEN

■

IN THE BOWELS OF THE BEAST

■

In its cramped and primitive office on Park Row in New York City, the Congress of Racial Equality was undergoing a spurt of growth. The Freedom Ride had generated new national interest in the two-decades-old organization. With that growth in CORE, and the increasing importance of the Student Nonviolent Coordinating Committee, rivalry became an attribute of the Movement. Battles for organizational turf were sometimes friendly, sometimes bitter.

Each organization except the National Urban League accused one or more of the others of citing accomplishments that weren't theirs in their efforts to raise funds. And the National Urban League charged the press with paying undue attention to the activities of demonstrators and other practitioners of dramatic protest and ignoring the hard, solid work done by Urban League professionals. The rivalry sometimes approached shrillness because each organization — even SNCC, whose members had practically taken vows of poverty — needed to raise money from Northern white liberals, and everyone considered the pool of such support to be finite. CORE accused the Southern Christian Leadership Conference of using the Freedom Ride to seek funds, and SCLC accused

CORE of exploiting Dr. King's activities. The National Association
for the Advancement of Colored People was the most secure of all
the organizations, and might have seemed immune from rivalries,
but its leader, Roy Wilkins, engaged frequently in bitter nonpublic
sniping at Martin Luther King.

————————————————— ■

James Farmer was instrumental in creating the Freedom Ride, and thus
in taking the Movement to its new level. But Farmer was not a hell-for-
leather activist, a Movement fighter who relished the opportunity to
engage in physical confrontations with the enemy. Farmer was an intellectual, a debater, a man who liked to prove his points with logic and
rhetorical flourishes.

"Confrontation is not my style," he said in 1989. He was blind
now, but as alert as ever, living on a bit of farmland in northern Virginia
near a college where he taught. Close to his kitchen door was a small
lake with an island in the center, connected by a bridge and looking
almost like a Japanese garden. On the island was a gazebo where Farmer
liked to sit and think.

"But confrontation is something that I simply determined needed
to be done at that particular point in history, and something therefore
that I felt I had to do," he said. "Contrary to my style, contrary to my
inclinations, contrary to everything. I wished it could be done and then
over with. I wanted to do something to help my people, and I wanted
that down in the marrow of my bones. I wanted to wipe out discrimination. That was the thing that gave my life motivation.

"But somehow I wanted to — this was a contradiction, to be
sure — I wanted to speak and to write. I much preferred to sit in isolation and contemplate my navel, out in my gazebo, on my island. I was
never at home demonstrating. I was always uneasy about that. *Abnormally* afraid." He laughed a deep, wide laugh. "Spitless. I was scared
spitless."

In his autobiography, Farmer had been mildly critical of "several
prominent persons" who "demonstrated thus their solidarity" during
the Freedom Ride "by flying into Jackson to have their encounter with
Captain Ray. They jailed in, bailed out, and returned to their respective

labors." Among the names he mentioned were two black politicians from New York City and Wyatt Tee Walker of SCLC.[1]

Asked about this, Farmer laughed again and replied that he guessed "there *was* a little bit of chiding" involved. "I felt that it was sort of grandstanding. Here we had been risking our necks and getting clobbered, and now the thing was headline news — and now that it was safe, most of all — they knew that nobody was going to get killed. In the earlier stages, we didn't know whether we were going to get killed or not, but now we knew: Nobody was going to get killed, nobody was going to get hurt. So then they flew down and got arrested and bailed out, so they could say 'I was on the Freedom Ride.' And it's in their bios now, that they send out: 'Arrested in Jackson, Mississippi, on the Freedom Ride.' So there was something that seemed a little phony about it."

Farmer was displeased with anything that smacked of phoniness in the Movement, and that extended to some of the interorganizational rivalry that went on. He is particularly upset, he says, when modern-day recollections of the Movement, most notably television presentations, ignore his and CORE's role in the Freedom Ride. The docudramas tend to credit Martin Luther King and SCLC with the demonstrations — an error that was facilitated, said Farmer, by SCLC's own efforts at the time. "They put out a pamphlet titled *The Ride to Freedom.* And here was Martin and Coretta on the front cover page, who took the Freedom Ride, when they *weren't there!* That really ticked me off. But it was such a sensitive issue that I couldn't jump up and down about it."

Farmer said that he once raised the issue with King. He said he told the minster, " 'Martin, you're raising money on the Freedom Ride. You haven't spent a dime on the Freedom Ride. *We're* going *bankrupt* on the Freedom Ride expenses. You're raising money on it. If you're going to continue raising money on the Freedom Ride, you've got to send money to us. Because we're spending it.'

"He said he wasn't aware that they were raising money on the Freedom Ride, and if they were, then he'd see that they didn't do it anymore. He said he'd stop it. But he seemed to recall that back in 1956 — that, of course, was long before I was national director of CORE [Farmer broke into a broad grin] — that during the Montgomery bus boycott, CORE sent out a mail appeal mentioning the Montgomery bus boycott. Well, it was possible that they did; I had nothing to do with that."

Farmer recalled Whitney Young of the National Urban League as a lighthearted man who nonetheless felt the sting of the competitive spirit. "He came in once and looked at me and said, 'Jim, you know, it's awfully hard, running around, trying to be a national civil rights leader without going to jail!' I loved his sense of humor.

"Roy Wilkins was very outspoken, and very sharp. He was always taking Martin to task. Always. He didn't like Martin, it would appear. . . . He didn't *say* he didn't like him, but that was the impression I got." Of the major civil rights leaders, said Farmer, "he was probably the most vocal. Whitney was the mediator type; he was the chairman of the board sort. But Roy always wanted to argue and debate, especially with such persons as Jim Forman" of SNCC.

"I think there was a lot of jealousy there. He did say to Martin once, 'One of these days I'm going to catch you, Martin; I'm gonna catch you.' Meaning in terms of popularity and renown and all of that. After all, the NAACP was a big organization. It was there long before the others were born. And the head of the NAACP ought to be number one. The big number one. And he wasn't."

Farmer made a strategic error, he said, when he failed to press for a merger between his organization and SNCC after the Freedom Rides. CORE had good relations with the younger group then, he said. "I had a good shot at it because I was respected by the SNCC people — after the Freedom Ride, and because of the Freedom Ride. I was there in jail, along with them and the CORE people, and stayed in. And then we sent whatever small checks we could to a lot of the SNCC people who stayed in Mississippi. And SNCC didn't have any money then. . . .

"I think we could have pulled it off. As to whether it would have stayed stuck once we glued them together, I don't know." Nor did he know what the resulting organization would have been like, he said, but it probably would have been active in both North and South, and "it would have dominated the activist wing of the civil rights movement." It also would have represented the merger of "a semistructured organization," CORE, with "an antiorganization organization. SNCC was opposed to having structure.

"The advantages would have been that there would not have been the competition which later developed between the organizations —

competition for the same headlines, same news stories, and for the same buck. That was the big thing: the same buck. And that meant competition for a number of bloodied heads to be shown on the same front pages of the same newspapers. Because that produces money. A cruel fact, but it is a fact of life which both SNCC and CORE understood."

■ ─────────────────

Even as the South and the nation were starting to adjust to the idea of direct action, the Movement was readying a new and potentially far more significant technique: voter registration. The power of the ballot box had been discussed since Reconstruction, of course, but this time it was different. As demonstrated by their refusal to ride segregated buses in Montgomery and their willingness to face jailing in lunch counter sit-ins, Negro Southerners were ready to follow their quest for political equality anywhere it might take them, even into the most dangerous fortifications of racism. The undertaking could be attributed in part to the sticks and carrots that Robert Kennedy brandished after the Freedom Rides. But in another large part the move to voter rights, with the economic and political justice that would follow, was a logical next step. The Movement's leaders were already starting to say that the right to sit peacefully at a dime store lunch counter meant little without the ability to pay for the hamburger and cup of coffee.

As SNCC debated the relative values of direct action and voter registration, one of its number was off on his own in Mississippi, rendering the debate academic. Robert Moses was a Northern black, a high school mathematics teacher who had come to the South during the summer of 1960 to help out at SCLC. Moses quickly joined forces with SNCC instead, and went to Mississippi on a recruiting trip for a conference of black leaders. In Cleveland, Mississippi, he met local leader Amzie Moore, who argued the case for voter registration. Moses promised to come back the following summer and lend a hand.

When Moses did return to Mississippi, he had difficulty finding adequate accommodations in Cleveland for the additional voter registration workers he hoped SNCC would be sending in August. He went instead to McComb, in the southwest part of the state, where he had been invited by a local NAACP leader named

C. C. Bryant. Moses arrived in McComb in July, 1961, made housing arrangements, and soon welcomed two other activists, Charles Sherrod and Marion Barry. By now, those who worked full-time for SNCC were referred to as field secretaries. One of the first things the young men did was to establish clinics, or "freedom schools," to teach voter literacy to prospective registrants, who were required to fill out complex forms and reply to registrars' questions about the state constitution.

──────────────────────── ■

Lawrence Guyot was a member of the SNCC faction that believed voter registration, rather than protest demonstrations, was the key to useful change in the South. In an interview years afterward, Guyot said that he "and the wing that I was in in SNCC took the position that if you're going to make long-term change, it has to be around the vote. It has to be around institutions of power, either paralleling them or controlling them, or proving that they don't work by attempting to *make* them work."

Guyot is a big, intense man whose passion for debate inspired his fellow activists in the sixties to create the verb "Guyotting" to describe his method of ideological argument. He recalled that not everyone in the Movement felt that the vote could be gotten in Mississippi. He said that Bob Moses had once gone to see Roy Wilkins of the NAACP to talk about working in the state. Wilkins, said Guyot, replied that his organization was concerned only with promoting its membership in Mississippi, and that (as Guyot recalls the conversation) "we believe that anybody who tries to organize in Mississippi is crazy. . . . If we had our wishes, we'd cut Mississippi off and let it drift into the sea."[2]

But SNCC was just crazy enough to try it. And SNCC eventually realized that the debate between direct action and political action was academic in the extreme. "It took a long time for SNCC internally to realize this," said Guyot, "that when you're attempting to secure power in the South, it doesn't matter whether you're sitting at a lunch counter or you're attempting to register to vote. The most threatening of the two was attempting to register to vote. If you sit at a lunch counter, you're either served or you're not served, and that's it. But once you get control over the electorate, everything else happens. Everything else flows from that. . . .

"There was never a decision made in Mississippi that wasn't political. The board of supervisors in a Mississippi county is unlike any other government entity anywhere else in the country. It runs every aspect of life in that county: whether or not a plant comes in; whether or not it pays taxes; who gets their road paved; whether or not you get commodities or welfare; whether or not you're generally left alone by the political subdivisions; whether you pay ad valorem tax or don't."

▬

Mississippi was a place of great danger for persons who wanted to change it from a closed to an open society. Officially sanctioned repression, in addition to the less subtle style dispensed by the Ku Klux Klan, Citizens Councils, and other racist organizations and lone operators, made it difficult for a Negro, native or outsider, to speak out — or for a white to do so, either, for that matter. And yet, the seeds of rebellion were there, as they are wherever there is repression. The Mississippians who harbored them were all the more hardy for having withstood the annealing process of the nation's most racist region.

▬

Victoria Gray, now Victoria Gray Adams, was born well before the Movement came to Mississippi. She was raised on her grandfather's farm in Palmer's Crossing, a village near Hattiesburg. She became aware early on, as did all Mississippians, of the differences between white and black.

Victoria was on hand one day when her aunt's white employers gave her a ride home from work. Afterward, she remarked to her aunt and grandmother, "I sure wish we were white so we could be rich." She recalled the incident later: "I guess the thing that impressed me was the fact that they had an automobile. We had a horse and wagon and mules and all that sort of thing. In the South at that time, I guess we were fairly well-to-do, but my thought at that particular moment was that they had a car and we didn't. I remember clearly sensing that I had said something that got their total attention. Thus began my education on the importance of the richness of being what and who God created me to be."

A few years later, Victoria underwent another educational experience. In school one day, her teacher called her in front of the class to chastise her for talking. Victoria had not been talking and told the teacher so. The teacher told Victoria to hold out her hands. She hit the hands with a ruler. The teacher struck Victoria again, and Victoria put her hands down. The teacher demanded that Victoria present her hands again, but the child refused. She swore to herself, she said, that never again would she "passively cooperate with or allow people to punish me for that which I did not do. I'm going to resist."

When Victoria Gray was a teenager she went to Detroit, where her father had gone in search of employment. She stayed a year, and marveled at the "whole new concept of life" she found there. "I was for the first time exposed to an open society," she said later. On the way back to Mississippi, Victoria and her mother had to change buses in Louisville. "We came off the bus, went into the bus station, sat down, waited, and this very lovely little old white-haired lady came over and wanted to know where we were coming from. My mom told her. And then she invited us to go into the other waiting room." The black waiting room.

"And you know, the walk out of that waiting room into the other waiting room was really traumatic. Even after one short year. The turning point that took place in my life at that time was, nobody is ever going to convince me that I am less than anybody else. It was a decision that I consciously made at that time."

Victoria Gray had been taught by her grandparents that self-reliance was a virtue of great importance, that she was largely responsible for her own destiny. When confronted by incidents such as the bus station rebuff, she reacted with indignation, sometimes strongly outspoken indignation. "I was keenly aware of the contradictions around me," she said. "And I didn't have a lot of reservations about sharing that fact." Her elders noticed all this and told Victoria that she would someday move into a position of leadership in her community. But they also feared that her outspokenness would get her into trouble. "I was also told that I would probably self-destruct quite early," she said.

The outspoken Negro girl from Palmer's Crossing grew up, married a career military man, and moved frequently to other states and nations.

She always returned to Mississippi, because she loved the place. "You know," she said, "the problem is not Mississippi. The problem was what went on in Mississippi — and in the rest of the country, too, but especially in Mississippi at that time." She was in the Hattiesburg area in the early sixties, when the Movement first reached into deepest Mississippi. She was in her late thirties. On a radio talk show she heard a woman — a white woman, certainly — call in and complain that people who didn't like Mississippi the way it was should get out. "It was, 'This is the way we are here and if you don't like it here, then you can leave, because this is our place, our state, our whatever.' "

Victoria Gray, as impetuous as ever, was incensed. She wondered, " 'What gives *her* the authority to decide that this is any more hers than it belongs to anybody else who was born and raised here?' So I got on the phone and made it very clear to her that it wasn't like that at all; that she had no larger claim on Mississippi or that particular portion of Mississippi than any other native-born person there — or for that matter, a person who came from outside and decided that they liked it and decided to stay. And that I loved Mississippi as much as she did, I'm sure. But there were a few of the conditions that existed in Mississippi, in terms of how people treat each other, that were not acceptable, and I had taken a position that rather than leave, I was going to stay, and see if it couldn't be changed."

Gray told the woman and the radio audience that she had lived in many other places in the nation and in the world "and I knew that it was possible for people to live differently. I took a stand that said, 'Mississippi is my home, and I'm going to stay here and see why it can't happen here, too.' "

Victoria Gray recalls that her pronouncement drew a lot of attention at the time. White listeners called the radio station wanting to know who she was and whom she worked for. Some of them wanted to know where she got the money to do "all that travelling," as if it must have come from some nefarious source. They talked about everything except the real issues that Gray was raising.

Curtis Conway Bryant, the NAACP leader in McComb, recalls the young activists' arrival in southwest Mississippi not so much as part of their plan as it was a continuation of the long-standing NAACP tradition of registering voters. In 1954, the year of the *Brown* decision, Bryant became president of the Pike County, Mississippi, chapter of the NAACP. He was thirty-seven years old. Pike County was not the sort of place where people bragged publicly about their NAACP membership; the Klan and mob crews were active practically to the point of being in control of government and commerce.

Bryant's father was a barber and presser who, he said, "taught his children to respect the law, but he taught us not to be afraid of any man. He wasn't afraid of anybody. If you bothered his kids, he was going to call you into question." The younger Bryant, too, was an outspoken man. Although whites were harsh in their relationships with blacks after the *Brown* decision, and reserved their especial hatred for the NAACP and its officers, Bryant enjoyed a degree of insulation from harassment by virtue of his job on the railroad and his position as a strong union man. He also operated a barbershop in the black community. Still, during the Movement years he received a steady stream of hate calls and worse. "Some of the first bombs that were thrown were thrown in my barbershop," he said, with what sounded almost like a tinge of pride. "And they threw a stick of dynamite down in front of my house." Bryant says he never thought about leaving. "This is my home, and this is where I intend to live and die."

Pike County in 1960 had about nineteen thousand residents of voting age, about one-third of them Negro. A federal document disclosed that 207 nonwhites of voting age, or 3 percent of the total, were registered in that year. In all Mississippi counties for which information was available, only about 6 percent of voting age Negroes were registered. In thirteen Mississippi counties, no Negroes were registered at all.[3]

One of those who was registered in Pike County was C. C. Bryant. He braved the discriminatory application procedure back in the 1940s and cast a vote for Harry Truman in 1948. "The registrar was very hostile," he recalled, "and we had to go back two or three times before he'd let you register, and interpret the constitution to his satisfaction."

Bryant thinks that the whites who ran Pike County weren't too alarmed by one or two blacks' registering. The trouble came when many Negroes went down to the courthouse to register. "You shouldn't underestimate the vision of the white man," he said. "He knew there was power in a lot of votes. Very few people were voting. They didn't even respect your vote. They didn't even ask for your vote, because you didn't have any. So when we started a drive, *then* the whites saw that that was a beginning of change, and therefore they resisted."

Bryant said he and others in McComb read in a Negro magazine — he thinks it was *Jet* — that some students were coming to Mississippi to spend part of the summer of 1961 working on voter registration. So the local NAACP "provided the contacts and the opening of doors for them," he said. "We printed ballots and we set up voter registration classes to teach people how to vote. . . . This has been a part of the NAACP's program and policy ever since its inception — to get the vote. Inasmuch as we had the students who were accessible, then we utilized them. . . . We took advantage of the student manpower."

■ ————————————————

Getting people registered (and getting people to *try* to get registered) was a slow and sometimes disappointing process in McComb and in Pike County in the summer of 1961, but Negroes in neighboring Walthall and Amite counties asked Moses and the other SNCC workers to establish freedom schools there, too. The whites, in the words of C. C. Bryant, saw the beginning of change there, as well as in McComb, and they moved into action. In mid-August Bob Moses was arrested in Liberty, the seat of Amite County, after accompanying registration candidates to the registrar's office. When he returned a few days later, he was beaten by a relative of the sheriff. In an action that was practically unheard of in that time and place, Moses filed charges against his attacker. A trial was held at the end of August, and the all-white jury acquitted the attacker. But in the meantime, thousands of Mississippi Negroes were treated to the spectacle of a black man openly challenging the system.

———————————————— ■

Charles Jones and the other SNCC people returned from the two-week late-summer vacations they had given themselves, and they started out for Mississippi. They left by car from New York City, stopped awhile in Atlanta at SNCC headquarters, and then set out through Alabama toward Mississippi.

"Right out of Anniston," said Jones later, "a dog ran out in the road. I was driving. I veered to miss the dog, but the dog got hit. We stopped, of course. White lady ran out and said we killed her dog and called the police. Said we purposely intended to kill her dog. We were in *Anniston, Alabama.*

"Police came. Luckily, a neighbor had seen the whole thing and, for whatever reason, stepped up and told the police officers that that's not what had happened. What had happened was the dog ran out in the road. I did everything to avoid it, including almost wrecking the car, and it was just an unavoidable accident. And they said, 'Well, all right. You boys can go on.' " Jones made a sound of relief. "Hummm. For a moment there, I was convinced that they were going to have us right downtown!"

If the Anniston police had taken the young men in, they would have captured much of the leadership of SNCC. In addition to Jones, there were Dion Diamond and Charles McDew, then SNCC's chair. The three resumed their trip in high spirits.

"So we were going on down the road, singing, having a good time. All of a sudden we came to a rise in the road, and there was a sign: 'WELCOME TO MISSISSIPPI.' And we crossed that and for about ten minutes, nothing, no word. Everything was totally silent. Everybody was in their own thing.

"And all of a sudden, the total impact of Mississippi hit all of us. The lynchings, the killings, the whole total disregard for any black folk. Just total silence. Then Charles McDew started singing." Jones tried to duplicate McDew's deep, rich voice: "Ain't gonna le-et Mis-si-ssip-pi turn me round. . . ."

It was one of the Movement's earliest and most stirring anthems, a song that was sung almost as often as "We Shall Overcome." The lyrics were easily modified to accommodate any occasion, town, or adversary. At various times its singers had vowed never to be turned around by Bull Connor, numerous police chiefs, the Ku Klux Klan, and, as in this case, the entire idea of white Mississippi.

" 'Ain't gonna le-et Mis-si-ssip-pi turn me round.' And then we joined in. And we sang from that point almost to Jackson. There was more energy in that darn car. I don't think any of us will ever forget that. It was all of the emotions you could come up with. It was fear, it was resentment of the fear, of having to feel that way, of being totally vulnerable . . . and it was being afraid: literally afraid that some of us were just not going to come back. And we knew that. I mean, that was not academic. We were *now in Mississippi.*"

The singing helped with the fear, said Jones, but "it was hardly replaced. But at least we got back to where we were. Underneath there was still that anxiety, but on the surface we were still strong, in good spirits. Went on down to McComb, where a group of students — high school students — had gone to the lunch counter, gotten arrested.

"We decided to support the students, called a mass rally. And, you talk to people who were there, they will always talk about that mass meeting. There was so much energy there that night. It was the first time anything like that had happened. And we were in just *rare* form. I mean, it was a culmination of all of the Movement up to that point, and we were now in the heart, the *bowels,* of Mississippi.

"The singing, the intensity of that night . . . that was another one of those historic mileposts for the Movement. It was out of that energy that we resolved that we would do it. It was one thing to *say* we were going to take on this beast, this monster, but it's a totally different thing to take it on. In the bowels of the beast, it was different. So we all reinforced each other, and the spirit that night — God! And sure enough, a number of people went down, and everybody got arrested. I was chosen to be the outside contact person. Incidentally, there's probably a warrant still out for my arrest in McComb."

■ ───────────────────────

The young people who had been arrested in McComb were led by two young men from Pike County, Hollis Watkins and Curtis Hayes. When SNCC first arrived in the county, Charles Sherrod and others conducted the by-now standard workshops in nonviolence. Watkins and Hayes attended the meetings, and on August 26, 1961, the two held a sit-in of their own at the Woolworth's store in McComb. The whites immediately charged them with breach of the peace. Other black young people, most of them high school students, joined the protest and expanded it. They, too, were arrested and sent to jail.

In the meantime, the voter registration campaign continued, as did the whites' violent reaction to it. In late September, an Amite County native who had been active in registration work,

Herbert Lee, was shot and killed by a white state legislator. The white claimed self-defense, and a coroner's jury found him innocent of any crime. Afterward, a black man who had been a witness at the inquest told Bob Moses that he had lied but that he would tell the truth about what had happened if he received protection. SNCC asked the Justice Department to protect the man. The federal government denied the request. It later was revealed that the FBI had informed a deputy sheriff about the black's willingness to tell the truth, after which the deputy beat the witness. Two and a half years later the witness was murdered by someone whose identity was never revealed.[4]

On October 4, the students who had been arrested during the McComb sit-ins were released from jail. When they sought to return to high school, their principal refused to allow two of them to reenter. The school authorities also attempted to make the students sign documents saying they understood they would be expelled if they took part in any other demonstrations. When students and SNCC workers responded to this with a march on the McComb city hall, they were attacked. Bob Zellner, a white Alabaman who at the time was SNCC's only white field secretary, was badly beaten. SNCC then opened its own high school as an alternative to the one run by the whites with compliant Negro management.

Later that month, key SNCC workers McDew, Moses, and Zellner, along with local protest leaders, were sent to jail, effectively if temporarily ending the newly mounted voter registration project. In December, when the SNCC field secretaries were released, they left McComb, wiser in the ways of resistance as practiced in the bowels of the beast.[5]

———————————————— ■

Hollis Watkins was twenty years old when SNCC came to McComb. He wasn't a high school student, as often has been reported, but he had not been out of school long. The twelfth child of a sharecropping family that lived just across the Pike County line in Lincoln County, Watkins had paid little attention to the civil rights movement until that summer of 1961. He was in California, staying with relatives and thinking about looking for work there, when he heard about the Freedom Ride. When one news report said that the riders planned to end up in Mississippi, Watkins decided to go home and check it out.

He was back in southwestern Mississippi when a friend told him, erroneously as it turned out, that Martin Luther King "and some other big people" were in McComb, holding meetings and drumming up support for the Movement. Watkins and a few friends went to the county seat, but they never found King.

"I went looking for Dr. Martin Luther King and the other big shots," said Watkins later, "and found Bob Moses. And he told me that he didn't know anything about Dr. King being out there, but he told me that *they* were out there working on voter registration. And he explained to me what they were doing, and asked me if I would be interested in helping them. So I told them that I would.

"I joined SNCC the first day that I talked to Bob. He asked me if I was willing to work with him, and I gave my commitment. From that day on, I continued to come to the SNCC office and work in the community. We were promised — we didn't get it — we were promised ten dollars a week. This was before tax was taken out." Watkins laughed the way all former SNCC field secretaries do when they discuss the payroll that did not always get met. "But you didn't need any support, for the most part, because all you needed was some food to eat and a place to stay. I was still staying with my parents, so I had a place to stay, and if you needed a snack or something to eat during the middle of the day or while you were working, then some of the people in the community were providing food. So it wasn't a matter of your needing a lot of support."

One other organization had already established a record in voter registration — the NAACP — but Watkins was not attracted to it. Because most people (other than its fearless chapter chair, C. C. Bryant) were afraid to be identified with the NAACP, he said, "it was a movement that was in the closet." Watkins wanted something more open, more forthright. SNCC met his need handsomely.

"I think the thing that really drew me to SNCC," he said, "was that here was a group of people that saw that a problem existed and said, 'Hey, look, we're going to go all-out and do what we can to eradicate this problem,' rather than maybe trying to sneak up on the solution." SNCC made no secrets about its aims and methods. It was, said

Watkins, a matter of saying, "We are here. This is our purpose: We're going to get these people registered and we're going to be going from door to door. We're going to be getting in touch with people any way we can to make sure that they become registered voters so that they can become first-class citizens. We're prepared to suffer the consequences of whatever might come down, because this is what needs to be done, and this is what we're about."

Watkins was aware of the ideological differences within SNCC over political action versus direct action, but they had little practical effect on the conduct of the Movement in McComb. "It was obvious that there was a need for both," he said. "If there's someone who's willing to do some of both, the more the merrier."

Watkins spent his days during the voter registration campaign knocking on doors in the Negro community. "You'd walk down the street, knock on the door. Find out whether the people are registered or not. Tell them what you're doing. Ask them to go down to the courthouse and attempt to register. If they needed rides, they could come by the office. If they needed some assistance in filling out the form, they could come by the office. People at the office would teach them how to fill out the form before going down. We'd have a couple of copies of the form there. If they wanted us to go over it with them right there, we'd go over it with them right then. And we'd invite them to come to the mass meetings that we would be having. Generally there would be at least two or three a week."

Many of those who answered Watkins's knocks were reluctant to become involved in the registration campaign. "There were some people," he said, "who were so afraid until when they found out who you were and what you were doing, they would close the door in your face. And you'd have people who would tell you they'd go down and register and wouldn't do it. . . . But the kind of response that I was getting was enough to make me feel good about what I was doing and to feel that there definitely were accomplishments being made."

Soon after SNCC arrived in McComb, Hollis Watkins and Curtis Hayes and others formed the Pike County Nonviolent Movement to expand their efforts from voter registration into direct action. Sit-ins and other forms of direct protest might have become almost passé in some sections of the South, but not in deepest Mississippi, Alabama, and Georgia. SNCC workers warned that there might be arrests and violent

FRED POWLEDGE

When Negroes arrived at a downtown Woolworth's store in Atlanta in the fall of 1960, they found a sign saying "FOUNTAIN CLOSED" and a store employee holding a chain across the lunch counter entrance. They stayed, and eventually the store and others desegregated.

FRED POWLEDGE

Participants in the 1960 sit-ins quickly learned that a favorite tactic of some lunch counter operators was to ignore the demonstrators and hope they would go away. So the students brought schoolbooks to read.

FRED POWLEDGE

At some sit-in demonstrations, white opponents of desegregation tried to occupy lunch counter stools to keep Negroes from sitting down. During this 1960 demonstration in Atlanta, the result was integration, of sorts. But neither black nor white was served.

GERALD HOLLY, THE TENNESSEAN

Diane Nash, a junior at Fisk University and chair of the Nashville demonstrations, with the Reverend Miller Kelly Smith, pastor of the First Baptist Church and president of the Nashville Christian Leadership Council, during the demonstrations in 1960.

FRED POWLEDGE

WHITE CUSTOMERS
WARNING
THIS STORE IS
INTEGRATED

A less-than-subtle prosegregation sticker that was affixed to Atlanta stores that desegregated their lunchroom facilities in 1960.

FRED POWLEDGE

FRED POWLEDGE

Martin Luther King, Jr., in handcuffs as he is transported from jail in Atlanta to a court hearing. King and others were arrested during sit-ins at downtown department store lunchrooms in 1960.

King, speaking at a mass meeting in Albany, Georgia, in the summer of 1962.

Charles Sherrod, of the Student
Nonviolent Coordinating Committee
(SNCC), speaking during a mass
meeting in Albany in July, 1962.

SNCC's Charles Jones, after
desegregating the men's room at the
Albany city park, summer, 1962. A
moment later, a city employee arrived
and padlocked the rest room door.

C. B. King, the lone "lawyer of color"
in Albany, Georgia, rests his head in
his hand during a July, 1962, press
conference with (left to right) Ralph
Abernathy, Martin Luther King, Jr., and
William G. Anderson, leader of the
Albany Movement.

FRED POWLEDGE

FRED POWLEDGE

CITIZENS OF ALBANY!

All Who Believe In The God-Given Rights of Freedom, Justice and Equality Under the Law

COME TO CHURCH THIS SUNDAY

Prepared to Bear Your Cross Like Paul and Silas!!!

Prepared to Help Lift Our City Out of The Present Moral Crisis!!

Yesterday hundreds of our brothers and sisters have walked together to jail for FREEDOM! Their sacrifice is not in vain!

We Negro citizens of Albany have a right to be able to peacefully protest injustice on the steps of City Hall or anywhere else!

Our Ministers are asking YOU to join the FREEDOM CRUSADE at any of the following Churches: (SUNDAY)

Mt. Zion	Mt. Olive No. 1
Shiloh	Mt. Olive No. 2
Bethel A.M.E.	Beulah
Union Baptist	Mt. Mariah
Church of God in Christ	Macedonia

Come to church services with your "Walking Shoes" on this Sunday, July 22nd

"Bless those who persecute you. Live in harmony with one another. Do not be overcome by Evil, but OVERCOME EVIL WITH GOOD."   Romans 12:14-21

This handbill circulated in Albany, Georgia, in 1962 is typical of the large number of flyers, handbills, and posters that could be found in black communities during the Movement years. The reference to "Walking Shoes" reminds prospective participants that they'll be expected to take part in a mass march downtown, and one that would likely result in their arrest.

Albany police chief Laurie Pritchett surveys the line of demonstrators who kneel to pray in front of city hall, July, 1962. In the background are reporters Claude Sitton of the *New York Times* (right) and Bill Shipp of the *Atlanta Constitution.*

ALABAMA DEPARTMENT
OF ARCHIVES AND HISTORY

FRED POWLEDGE

FRED POWLEDGE

FRED POWLEDGE

Far left: John Patterson, governor of Alabama from 1959 to 1963.

Left: Arthur Hanes, mayor of Birmingham, in 1962.

BOYCOTT

THE FOLLOWING MERCHANTS

RICH'S Inc.	DAVISON'S
WOOLWORTH'S	McCROY'S
GRANT'S	WALGREEN'S
JACOB'S PHARMACY	KRESS
SEARS ROEBUCK	KERSGE
H. L. GREEN	NEWBERRY'S
LANE'S DRUG STORES	

These stores have moved to break down the Tradition of the South.

DO NOT TRADE WITH ANY STORE IN THE DOWNTOWN AREA.

White Citizens: Trade with the Local Merchants in Your Residential Area.

To Negro Citizens of Atlanta: Do not Trade Downtown, Trade with the Merchants on Auburn Ave. and W. Hunter St. They need your support.

Citizens of Georgia: Boycott these stores throughout Georgia.

The cover of a pamphlet (c. 1963) soliciting female membership in the Ku Klux Klan. Although the Klan was male run and dominated, substantial numbers of women and smaller numbers of children always took part in cross-burnings, rallies, and leafletting.

This relatively subtle, unsigned segregationist handbill (1960) urges a white boycott of Atlanta merchants who allowed some desegregation of their facilities. For good measure, it advises blacks to stay away, too.

FRED POWLEDGE

FRED POWLEDGE

Klansmen, parading in downtown
Atlanta, 1962.

FRED POWLEDGE

A klanswoman, 1962.

A member of the American Nazi Party
demonstrates outside the 1962 annual
convention of the National Association
for the Advancement of Colored People
(NAACP), which was held in Atlanta.

FRED POWLEDGE

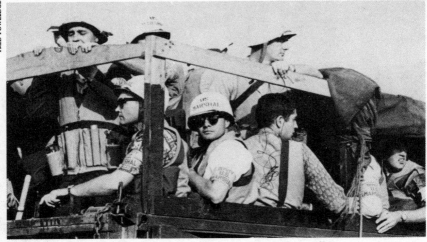

Deputy U.S. marshals and other federal law enforcement officers arrive at Oxford, Mississippi, on the afternoon of September 30, 1962, to enforce a federal court order allowing James Meredith to enter the state university.

FRED POWLEDGE

The marshals line up on the steps of Ole Miss's administration building on the night of September 30, 1962. A few state police officers talk with them. Not long afterward, the state forces disappeared and segregationist students and others attracted to the campus began a deadly night-long riot against the federal presence.

COURTESY OF EDWIN GUTHMAN

Oxford, the morning after. *Above:* Chief U.S. Marshal James McShane (right) replies to a question from the press while Edwin O. Guthman, the Justice Department's public information chief, listens. McShane inscribed this photograph: "For Ed Guthman. It was such a wonderful night — let's do it again sometime!!!" *Below, left:* Federalized National Guard troops patrol the downtown area beneath a tall monument to the Confederate dead.

FRED POWLEDGE

FRED POWLEDGE

A few months after the Oxford riot, Harvey Gantt became the first Negro student to enter South Carolina's Clemson College. There was no violence and even very little verbal abuse at Clemson. Gantt, shown here in January, 1963, attributes the relative ease of his entry to the lessons the South learned at Oxford.

FRED POWLEDGE

FRED POWLEDGE

Above: Part of the audience at the fifty-third annual convention of the NAACP, held in Atlanta in 1962. *Left:* Roy Wilkins, the NAACP's director, in 1962.

Below, left: Harry Ashmore, editor of the *Arkansas Gazette,* in his newsroom during the 1957 Little Rock school desegregation crisis. *Below, right:* L. C. Dorsey of Mississippi, in 1988.

RODNEY DUNGAN, *THE ARKANSAS GAZETTE*

HANDY'S PHOTO SERVICE

Floyd McKissick, in 1966.

The Reverend Will D. Campbell, on the porch of his home in Tennessee, in 1979.

Wyatt Tee Walker, of the Southern Christian Leadership Conference, in Albany, Georgia, in the summer of 1962. He wears a black armband as a sign of mourning over Albany's segregated system.

Ralph Abernathy, of the Southern Christian Leadership Conference, in 1962.

FRANK SIKORA, THE BIRMINGHAM NEWS

FRED POWLEDGE

U.S. district judge Frank M. Johnson of Montgomery, in 1978.

A protester against desegregation in Atlanta, 1962.

ED HOLLANDER

James Farmer of the Congress of Racial Equality (center) leads a march in Bogalusa, Louisiana, 1966.

ED HOLLANDER

Fred Shuttlesworth (left, with microphone) addresses a crowd in Selma, Alabama, after the aborted March 9, 1965, march across Pettus Bridge. James Farmer of CORE is at center.

ED HOLLANDER

Isaac Reynolds of CORE, one of the original Freedom Riders.

COURTESY OF HENRY SCHWARZSCHILD

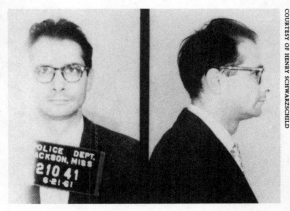

Henry Schwarzschild's police mug shot from the Freedom Ride, 1961.

FRED POWLEDGE

SNCC staff members attend an Atlanta governmental hearing on the Peyton Road barrier controversy, 1963. From left: James Forman, Julian Bond, Jane Bond.

FRED POWLEDGE

FRED POWLEDGE

Above, left: In January, 1963, Atlanta city officials, who had gained much national acclaim for their "moderation" on racial issues, erected a barricade to keep residential Peyton Road from changing from "white" to "black," an action that outraged the city's Movement activists and their sympathizers. On a cold winter day, James Forman, the executive secretary of SNCC, went to the site, lit a homemade "Freedom Torch," and kept a vigil, explaining his mission to curious passersby. *Above, right:* Dorothy Miller Zellner, working in the SNCC office, in 1962.

ED HOLLANDER

ED HOLLANDER

Left: Demonstrators at the Florida state capitol, demanding the vote and equal employment. *Above:* Joseph Rauh argues the Mississippi Freedom Democratic Party's case at the 1964 Democratic National Convention in Atlantic City.

ANN MEUER, COURTESY OF SHARON BURGER TOWNSEND

Sharon Burger in southern Louisiana in the summer of 1964.

Members of the audience sing "We Shall Overcome" at a mass meeting in Albany's Shiloh Baptist Church in the summer of 1962.

At a rally in Brandon, Mississippi, in May, 1965.

reactions from the whites, but the young people already knew that, having lived in Mississippi all their lives. When the direct action started, said Watkins, "we *knew* we would be arrested, and actually we thought we would be beaten, although we weren't beaten the first time."

The whites' reaction to direct action, said Watkins, could be summarized in two words: "Surprise and hostility. I think they were surprised. I don't think they were expecting anything like that to start happening in McComb." The immediate reaction of the whites was to accuse the demonstrators — even Watkins, a native Mississippian — of being "outside agitators." The supremacists used the expression as freely, he said, as they did "the communist term."

When Watkins and Hayes conducted their first sit-in at Woolworth's, it caused little local stir. Although there had been no advance notice, the police were on hand to make their arrests even before the young men arrived, leading Watkins to suspect that his phone had been tapped or that there was an informant in the black community, or both. That really didn't matter, though, he said, because "if they hadn't been there, we knew that they would soon be there." At the jail, he said, whites came by to gawk at the two daring young men and to threaten them with hanging.

By the time of the larger-scale demonstration, when the high school students marched down to the city hall, a large crowd of whites gathered to watch and threaten. But Watkins had the feeling that open mob violence in daylight was not very likely. At the time, he said, the whites "didn't want to be seen outright in the open public attacking and doing something to someone which would have been an obvious violation. But if it was a situation where they caught you in an alley or caught you out on a lonesome road or something, then they would take matters into their own hands, because later on there were many times that we were chased. Once you were seen in a car outside of town you could be chased. And there were other times when, if you were walking, you were literally followed inside of the city limits. . . . There were some instances where you had some fear."

▪ ————————————————

James Forman had left his job as a schoolteacher in Chicago to work in the Movement full-time, and he soon was drafted as SNCC's executive secretary. At about the time of his arrival, in the fall of 1961, SNCC was moving from a position of conformity with what one observer called "white middle-class notions of respectability" to discussions about how to start a social revolution, although there was still a lot of uncertainty about just how to do that. The group was creating and perfecting its organizing techniques, and it was talking more and more about the need to avoid imposing its own leadership on the communities it visited. SNCC should exist, the thinking went, mainly to encourage and support the indigenous leadership.[6]

Forman also observed, and complained about, the "lack of discipline" among the organization's members.[7] It was to be a recurring theme with Forman, who was given to talking in terms of "cadres," the "black bourgeoisie," and the "thin line of contradiction" between cooperating with and opposing the federal government. Some SNCC staffers joked about Forman's frequent demands for organizational discipline, but they also respected him deeply. Everyone knew that Forman was masterful in nurturing SNCC's own thin line of contradiction between being the sort of undisciplined, disorganized group that was just crazy enough to go to a place like McComb, Mississippi, and being the kind of organization that could actually do some good once it got there.

A strict reading of the McComb chronology might suggest that SNCC's initial journey into the bowels of the Mississippi beast was a failure. Results of the door-to-door solicitation of potential voters were not spectacular. The white opposition responded to the slightest provocation with stiff jail terms. As the scorch marks around C. C. Bryant's home and barbershop showed, one element of the opposition was willing to use dynamite and firebombs to maintain the existing system.

But the Movement learned from the McComb experience, as it did from Montgomery and Greensboro and Anniston. It learned that registering voters was every bit as dangerous and important as nonviolent direct action. It learned that some elements of the racist opposition were not moved by appeals to reason, or by the example of redemptive suffering, or even by the opinion of the rest of the nation. It learned that in sending the young and fearless troops of the Movement into the Deepest South it was challenging not only racism but, to some extent, the more conservative civil rights organizations that had been around a long time. Most of all, the Movement learned that there was a Long Haul.

──────────────────────────── ■

The march on the McComb governmental center after that moving mass meeting resulted in the arrest of practically everyone except Charles Jones, who had been chosen to remain outside in order to keep the communications lines up. He wasn't very sure, however, where those communications lines went.

"There was no SNCC office. We were it. No one in Atlanta. No contact with the outside world at all. No organized press relationships, no organized contact with the rest of the world; nothing. I called Harry Belafonte that night and said, 'We're down here and everybody's arrested.'

"Now, the press wasn't covering any of this, which was even another dimension of why we were vulnerable. He said, 'Let me see if I can call Bobby Kennedy. Where are you?' I gave him the number. And he called back and said, 'I located Kennedy out in Hollywood, out in California at a party. Here's the number. You call and you keep trying to get at him, and I'll call.'

"I did contact him, and he referred me to John Doar, of the civil rights division. Got him up. He was living in [a suburb of Washington]. And I said, 'Hey, we're here. We're down here. We need help.'" John M. Doar, one of the few federal officials who receives virtually unrestrained acclaim from Movement veterans, was deputy assistant attorney general in the civil rights division from 1960 to 1964, then head of the division from 1965 to 1967. Doar was almost always accessible, and he was possessed of a courage that even some of the racists admired.

"I said, 'Here's the situation. We had a voter registration rally. Went to the courthouse in McComb. Everybody was arrested. Everybody's in jail. All kind of charges. Bob Moses in jail, and the word we had on the street was that some Klan members had told three people to tell us that they were going to take Bob out of jail and kill him that night or the next. We don't have any support. We don't have any bond money. I'm the only one out. Help.' He said, 'Okay. I'm coming right in.'"

While he awaited the arrival of the Justice Department official, Jones went into hiding. He took refuge in a Negro-owned butcher shop in the building where SNCC held its meetings. "The next day, the police were coming out looking for me," said Jones. "I put on this butcher's coat, and was back in the meat shop murdering, just *butchering,* this meat: I didn't know what I was doing. And outside it was, 'No, sir. Jones? No, sir.' Inside, it was, Wham! with the butcher knife. I must've messed up twenty dollars' worth of meat, whacking on that board with this knife.

"They said, 'Well, you tell the boy if you see him — tell the nigra we have a warrant for his arrest.' And, 'Oh, yes, sir, I sure will. No question 'bout it. I sure will.' They left, and I went back to the office, because that's where our phone was. It was literally our only contact.

"That night, I heard this knock on the door. I opened the door, and John Doar said, whispering: 'Hurry, hurry, close the door.' Now this is the representative of the president of the United States of America. He said, whispering again, 'Close the door. Those people are *serious!* I'm afraid they're going to kill me. They've been snooping around my motel room. What we going to do?' "

Charles Jones released a long, slow "Ahhhh" as he remembered the conversation. It was more a sigh than anything else. "At that moment," he said, "my disillusionment started. I couldn't imagine this representative of the U.S. government coming in that door, scared, closing it behind him, hiding with me. This was the might of the United States of America, the greatest country in the history of the world, quote-unquote, telling me to close the door and keep the light down and talk quiet.

"At that point I knew we were on our own. I mean, that if it was going to happen in the country, *we* were going to do it. That at best, there would be supports and resources, but this man was scareder than me. In McComb, Mississippi."

■ ─────────────────────────────

PART SIX

ALBANY, OXFORD, AND
BIRMINGHAM

TWENTY

■

A WILLINGNESS TO SUFFER

■

Not long after their painful campaign in McComb, some of the Movement's activists went to another Deep South center of resistance. Albany, Georgia, the strategists and field secretaries at the Student Nonviolent Coordinating Committee felt, was the key to change in hard-core Georgia. Albany also was a stone wall of white resistance. The opposition was just as formidable as any that had been encountered to date in the South. It was, at least on the surface, less violent than Mississippi, but that was only because white supremacy could achieve most of its objectives through the political system — through instilling fear in the hearts of Negroes who dared to question the social and economic order. Southwest Georgia and the small city that was its trade center had never hesitated to use violence, however, when the need arose. A joke common to white men around Albany referred to "the nigger who was so dumb that he stole all that heavy chain and then tried to swim across the Flint River with it wrapped around his neck." People used similar jokes to explain lynchings that ended up in the Pearl River in Mississippi.

Events in Albany set important precedents for the civil rights movement, teaching valuable lessons to a leadership that was, after all, just beginning to feel its way through the war against segregation. Neither the leaders nor their followers (nor even the supremacists, for that matter) knew exactly what would happen. They knew that some communities in America had reacted with violence to the demand for change, while others had capitulated almost graciously, if tokenism can be gracious. But nobody was ready for the Albany response, which was to define peaceful, constitutional protest as a violation of the law, to categorize as violence acts that had not occurred and that showed no signs of occurring, and to create a literal police state to suppress protest — all the while claiming to enforce the law. Albany was one of the few places where a black person could be charged with breaking the law just by crossing a certain street.

Albany was a defeat for the Movement where defeat had not been expected. It was a victory for the resistance, and thus it provided a useful model for other communities that wished to maintain segregation. Albany was another test of the Kennedy administration's commitment to integration, and it showed, as did the Freedom Ride, that Washington was at worst not very committed at all and at best confused about what to do and how and when to do it. Washington, with all its talk of federalism and private and public action, couldn't seem to cope with an efficiently run local police state that employed wiretaps, eavesdropping, informants, and fancy word games with the law.

Albany also revealed how difficult it was for local black leadership to evolve and persevere in a system that whites totally controlled for their own benefit — a system that was something like slavery as it existed in the plantation era. Still, there was the amazing fact that the Albany Movement survived at all. And in its defeats and its few successes, it gave the nationwide Movement a greater understanding of the nature of the opposition and better tools with which to fight it.

Albany was one of the early examples of the broad-gauge use of public demonstrations against broad-spectrum racism. Montgomery had provided a public display of people walking and riding in car pools to avoid subsidizing a segregated bus line.

Greensboro was the beginning of attempts by Negroes to receive the same sort of treatment in quasi-public establishments, and the Freedom Ride was a risky, courageous elaboration of this. But Albany was long lines of people marching in twos and threes from the relative security of their all-black neighborhoods across the well-defined dividing line into the white world, into the most public places of a community — the downtown business district, the city hall, the police station — the very centers of the whites' power, to protest the totality of segregation, the enormous insult of racism.

Albany, too, was one of the Movement's first probes into the section of the South where the plantation was still part of everyone's thinking.

And Albany provided evidence that nonviolence could not always be guaranteed. On several occasions Negroes, almost always young males, threw rocks and bricks at the policemen who came to arrest them and keep them on the black side of Oglethorpe Avenue. It was a reminder that perhaps the leaders of the white resistance should have thought twice before refusing to deal with dedicated practitioners of nonviolence such as Martin Luther King, Jr.; that the violent alternative was a lot less attractive. They ignored the reminder, though.

Official, white Albany was trying back in 1961, and still tries today, to keep its feet in both the past and the present. It was incorporated in 1841 and was the trading center for a large area of slaveholding plantations. The abolition of slavery did not mean the abolition of the plantations; the huge farms still produce most of Georgia's peanut crop, as well as papershell pecans and livestock. As always, the owners and overseers tend to be white and the laborers tend to be black. Because it was a financial center, Albany had enough urban accoutrements such as banks, hotels, and eating places to qualify it in the minds of many locals as a cosmopolitan place, particularly when compared with the surrounding area. Albany had Jewish merchants (as did many Southern towns large enough to support dry goods stores), whom some residents offered as incontrovertible proof not only of the place's worldliness but also of its high degree of tolerance. But even a superficial examination would show that, despite its comparatively large population, Albany was essentially a country town, mired in the racial attitudes of the white rural South.

Georgia's infamous county unit system penalized urban voters by virtually equating the strength of rural and urban counties, regardless of population, in statewide Democratic primaries. (The system was ruled unconstitutional in the Supreme Court's 1964 one-man, one-vote decision.) Sheriffs, some of them ancient and firm believers in the philosophy and practice of segregation forever, exercised great control over much of the life and commerce in Dougherty County (of which Albany is the seat) and the surrounding counties of Lee, Worth, Mitchell, Baker, Calhoun, and Terrell.[1] In Albany, the sheriff's office was across the street from city hall, which was governed by an all-white group of city commissioners and a mayor. At the time the Movement and Albany collided, Albanians, as they called themselves, totalled about fifty-six thousand people, of whom some twenty-three thousand were black.[2]

---- ■

C. B. King puffed at a cigar, expertly. Everything C. B. King did, he did expertly.

Chevene Bowers King was the only "lawyer of color," as he put it, in Albany. He was the only one in southwest Georgia, and, in 1962, when he was interviewed, one of the very few lawyers of color in Georgia. He was thirty-eight years old then, a graduate of the segregated Albany public schools, Tuskegee Institute, Fisk University, and then the law school at Case Western Reserve University. He was probably the most articulate human being in southwest Georgia, given to flowery and grammatically elegant speech and prose. He was absolutely unafraid of white people and, it was abundantly clear, not all that respectful of them, either. He died of cancer in 1988.

C.B., as everyone called him, kept a simple office on the second floor of a shabby frame building on Jackson Street, on the black side of Oglethorpe Avenue. His walls were covered with lawbooks; his desk piled high with briefs, bills, books, and letters, many of them handwritten.

"In the thirties," he said, "when I was quite a young boy, there was an experience that stands out quite vividly in my mind. It was during this time that the government was doing everything it could to rehabilitate our economy; pursuant to which you had recreation activities in the communities, directed by persons who had been displaced by the lack of jobs. There was a gentleman who was in charge of the playground — this was a WPA project [the Works Progress (later Work Projects) Administration was a New Deal effort] — it was in a schoolyard in the old Monroe Normal School, where I attended school.

"This was during the summer months. We were all out of school, and the kids would go to the playground and there be supervised by Mr. Johnson. Mr. Johnson was a graduate of Brown, and there was a rather significant amount of pride I took in him as a result of his scholastic achievements. We had such activities as horseshoes, croquet, and swings, and a manually operated carousel. This was something more than what we, as Negroes in the community, had been accustomed to in the way of recreation. We would use this area to play in even if the supervisor wasn't there.

"We were out in the schoolyard, in the playground, swinging in the swings, and all of a sudden there drove up a prowl car of the city police department, in which you had a rookie officer, whose name was Lamar Stewart. He had been the community grocery boy at what was then Grayson's grocery store on the corner of Monroe and Mercer Streets, and had since gotten a job with the police department.

"Of course, we had known him in the past as a grocery boy, and we had simply known him as 'Lamar.' He got out of the car, and it was obvious that he wanted us to show our admiration for, and our deference to, his newly acquired position as a rookie policeman. He sought to make sure of this by jumping out of his prowl car and brandishing his gun. We ran under houses. There was an old folks home in the neighborhood, and I remember distinctly running under it and running a very substantial distance under it.

"Some of the kids were caught; I was not. Some of them were arrested. None of these were teenagers, even. They were arrested and taken down to the city police department, and they were charged with vagrancy. It must have been a difficult proposition for their parents to have extricated them and gotten them back into custody.

"This experience made me to know intuitively, I presume, that there was something wrong with this kind of symbol of the law. This was my first such experience of this nature, and a very traumatic one, too."

(Lamar Stewart remembers things differently. "We had a call from the school about them being over there throwing rocks and knocking out windows and so forth," said Stewart in 1990. "I got the call to go there, and I did, and of course I chased them and caught them." Stewart said he carried the children downtown, where someone called their parents, who came and got them. Stewart remembered delivering groceries to the King home. "I had all the respect in the world for his daddy," he said. Asked about C.B. himself, the former policeman replied, "Well, C.B. always accused everybody else of being a racist, but C.B. was the biggest racist I'd ever known. But he was smart. No doubt about that. . . . It was amazing to hear him talk, you know.")

C. B. King drew on his cigar. "I think of another experience that I had which was to make me know, intuitively anyway, that there was something wrong with it as an appropriate symbol of the law, and that was to see that there were Negroes who owed debts whom I believed honestly could not pay them. But the police authority was being used to enforce the payment of debts to the white merchant, who had allowed or extended credit to the Negroes in the community, and due to some fortuitous circumstance the debtor, the Negro, was not able to pay as he had promised that he would.

"But this understanding was that the policeman — this symbol of the law — would go and arrest him, and of course he would disgorge the money if by no other way perhaps than to get a commitment out of his employer to deduct from whatever pittance he might be making."

All this, said King, combined to convince him that "the greatest fulfillment for me was promised in terms of a legal career in Albany, Georgia. Of course, I'm able to make a livelihood for myself and my family. But I think that almost of equal significance is the consideration that I have the security in believing that I am of some worth to the community, in terms of making them aware, in terms of being its spokesman in regards to what the law means when translated in such a way as it is applicable oblivious to considerations of race."

C. B. King next saw Lamar Stewart, he said, on the island of Okinawa during World War II. Both men were there, fighting the Japanese. "I saw him, oddly enough, in a sick-bay line. Fungus was rampant on the island of Okinawa, and we were all going in to have some fungicide applied to our festering and plasma-exuding areas. I spoke to him, and he inquired as to whether I was not King's son, or boy, or something to this effect. It was rather a sort of rapport, as I remember it — a matter of talking about home, this sort of thing, but this was the first time that I had seen him since becoming an adult. Of course, later I saw him when I first was admitted to the bar." (Lamar Stewart, asked if he had been happy to see someone from home, replied: "You'd better believe it! In fact, if I remember right, I think we *hugged* each other!") After the war, Lamar Stewart resumed his law enforcement career in Albany. Since C. B. King was the only lawyer of color in the same town, and one who not only disliked segregation but actively despised it, it was just a matter of time before the two men would meet, forcefully.

■ ——————————————————————

In October, 1961, the Student Nonviolent Coordinating Committee began a voter registration project in southwest Georgia. Charles Sherrod and Cordell Reagon, a young SNCC staffer, went to Albany, the region's largest town and the logical center for such activity. Soon afterward Charles Jones joined the team. The field secretaries set up shop in the Harlem section, not far from one of the community's most prestigious institutions, Shiloh Baptist Church. Across Whitney Avenue from Shiloh was Mount Zion Baptist Church, another influential center of black life.

Although Albany's segregationist leadership was to make the allegation with great frequency (and still does), these "outside agitators" were not wholly responsible for "stirring up" what whites invariably described as Albany's normally satisfied and happy Negro population. Early in 1961 a group of Negro leaders had petitioned the city commission for a bare minimum of desegregation in some city facilities. The whites ignored the leaders and their requests.

When Sherrod and company arrived, it was with the aim of accomplishing what the political participation wing of SNCC, as well as the attorney general of the United States, wanted to do: They intended to register voters, rather than engage in street protest. But Sherrod quickly realized that the repression in southwest Georgia was too deeply etched into the lives of both blacks and whites. An enormous gulf of fear stood between Negroes and their political freedom.

SNCC's staff workers and volunteers, Sherrod realized, could not begin simply by taking prospective voters down to the county courthouse to register, or even by running workshops in interpreting the state constitution and filling out registration forms. They would have to start at an even more fundamental level. They would have to teach the black people of southwest Georgia to overcome their fear. One way to do that would be to perform an act that few of these Black Belt Negroes had ever seen and that virtually none still alive had done: defy the white supremacist to his face by flouting his rules in public. Not the least of the obstacles in the path of the activists, Sherrod found, was the existing structure of power in the black half of Albany. Negroes who sought change in many Southern communities found that competition among members of the existing black leadership, notably in the clergy, threatened to retard progress. This was particularly so in Albany.

"Our best selling point," wrote Sherrod a year or so later in a paper titled "Non-violence," which SNCC copied and used as part of its manual for organizers, "is that we are students with nothing but our bodies and minds, fearlessly standing before the monsters who [k]illed our mothers and castrated our fathers — yet we stand with Love."[3]

He also wrote that "fear and suspicion" infected both white and black communities, and a dehumanizing tradition of falsehood had developed between the races, making "the potential for mass violence . . . very great." However, he added,

> we enter the situation with an invincible instrument of war — the instrument of nonviolence. Nonviolence as a way of life is a long way off for most of us. The best that can be said is that our great advantage is the work of the church in the South, or lack of the same. For even the hypocrisy of this great fellowship bears the seeds of the ultimate victory of Truth. The point where the church stops must be *our* point of entry.

No activist working in the South could hope for success, wrote the young minister-activist, without including the church in his or her plans. Doing so adhered to the SNCC policy of accepting people as it found them and trying to promote the growth of indigenous leadership. Sherrod wrote:

> The only questions to be asked are: How much suffering are they willing to accept? and How much are we willing to bear in our bodies and in our minds?
>
> We have a choice to make; we can suffer under the brutality of unjust men in the South or we can suffocate in the North — we *must* suffer. It seems good sense, then, to suffer one last time, that all may not have to suffer in the same way that all of us have. Millions in the South feel that they have no such choice to make. We are the last Negroes and liberals; if we are victorious over this system, human beings will be our posterity.

Sherrod also composed a checklist that proved to be a model for Movement organizing in the hard-core South. He wrote that, first, organizers should study the community, making a detailed analysis of existing organizations, including their size, desire to cooperate, and effectiveness. Then organizers must familiarize themselves with changes that had already gone on in the community. They should obtain their information by interviewing people, from railroad and bus station porters ("so close to whites in some ways") to undertakers (who could provide economic information — "prices families are willing to pay for funerals" — as well as "gossip"). The effective organizer must know how to orchestrate a meeting, including the planning of an "emotional peak in [the] meeting or some kind of development — may be intentional development but you may intend to be unintentional." And the activist should not "let the project go to the dogs because you feel you must be democratic to the letter or carry out *every* parliamentary procedure."

Once the organizer was installed in the community, he (Sherrod spoke, and SNCC thought in those days, only in terms of "he," though women played important parts in the organization and in the Movement generally) should "teach the songs of freedom." "We Shall Overcome," which developed from a song of organized labor, had already become the Movement's anthem. There were many others, and nowhere during the Movement years were they sung as robustly as in Albany, Georgia.

The organizer should develop personal relationships with members of the community. This was not difficult for SNCC workers, who were paid virtually nothing and who not only wanted to but *had* to live with families in the community. "We promote the adoption of each of us as their children," wrote Sherrod; "we call them mother, moms, pop — that's home."

Communication was essential. "We speak at the churches," continued Sherrod, "interpreting the proposed action in religious terms." A "propaganda sheet" should be published, in which "no incident goes without note and analysis in terms of what is best for the project." Activists should keep outside media informed, especially the "liberal newspapers of greatest influence in this country and the world." And "all negative situations should be presented to the conscience of the nation." Communication must be incoming as well as outgoing. "We should always know the desire of the community and the extent of their willingness to suffer," he wrote. "At no time should there be a reaction within the community unknown to us."

As for finance, local projects must be self-sustaining, since "there are too many civil rights organizations and too few civil rights dollars." Anyway, said Sherrod, "it is best from a tactical point of view that we are penniless." Mass meetings in places of worship provided one source of income, inasmuch as people were accustomed to giving money in that environment. When conditions got really bad, activists had to be ready to pick cotton and baby-sit in exchange for food and lodging.

Sherrod included a section on dealing with the national government. About the Federal Bureau of Investigation, he wrote:

> These boys are hard to figure out. I must assume that they are basically dedicated to finding out the truth when told to do so by higher authorities. But on the other hand, these boys are in many cases local yokels, and

voice the same sentiments as the opposition. We must take precaution where necessary. A compilation of facts and interpretation of the inefficiencies of the F.B.I. is under way in all of the states where we have field secretaries. We have all concluded that the best thing for those boys is a nationwide expose.[4]

Despite this obvious lack of trust in J. Edgar Hoover's employees, Sherrod counselled organizers to call them "whenever we feel constitutional rights are abridged." Similarly, officials at the U.S. Department of Justice should be telephoned in emergencies, with affidavits and follow-up reports in writing. Activists should try to get to know the officials, and when they came for visits, "drain them of as much information as they are willing to give." Sherrod added: "There is presently an attempt to change the function of the Justice Department from a legal machine to a diplomatic, bargaining, behind the scenes, powerful, fellow-doing-good. This is no judgment for or against — but we must be able to meet the challenge presented in situations arising out of [the] action or inaction of the Department."

——————————————— ■

"Our objective," said Charles Jones, "was to organize the entire region, but starting with Albany — the entire black community. We went in with perhaps fifteen or twenty dollars in our pockets and this notion that the people were their own power and they didn't need individual leaders. They needed a collective leadership process. So we went to the people on the street. We started talking to the members of the church, in addition to the ministers. We had met the Kings."

The Kings here were not the members of the family of Martin Luther King, Jr., or Sr., but rather an influential and multitalented family of southwest Georgians. C. W. King, a well-to-do Negro real estate broker, with his wife, Margaret Slater King, headed a local dynasty that produced seven sons. One of them was Clennon King, whom Governor James P. Coleman had tried to have declared insane in 1958 for attempting to enter the University of Mississippi. Another was Slater King, also in real estate and a powerful member of the community. Slater's wife, Marion, was an equally respected member of the community. And there was Chevene B. King, the lawyer.

"I remember Mrs. King," said Jones, speaking of Margaret Slater King. "Mama King. The matriarch. Oh, I hope history is nice to her. She was the finest embodiment of motherhood. Universal motherhood. She took us in, made sure we had a little something to eat. And put dollars in our pockets, just for little things.

"So we started organizing the people. We took the position that everybody needed to be in the Movement, and we got opposition from the NAACP. We took the position that everybody needed to be a member of NAACP, and NAACP needed to be a member of the Movement. We were showing some very creative leadership at that point, if I must say so.

"Our theology was — " He interrupted himself to backtrack: "And it was literally theology. Both Sherrod and I were divinity students, and we felt that the cross meant that we all individually took it up, and the power was with the people. And, of course, we ran immediately into opposition from the ministers, whose notion basically was that God had chosen them and put them between Him and the masses for the purpose of providing the divine leadership and that any action of any significance had to be led by the ministers.

"And our position was that *everybody* made decisions. The ministers certainly should be a part of, individually, the leadership structure, but the decisions were made by a broad group of leadership, or a group of leaders." Jones laughed as he remembered the clash of the two philosophies. "Many of them said, 'No, if you do that, you can't use our churches.' So we went to the deacons, and the deacons and the elders told the ministers, 'Understand that we have a vote about whether you stay here or not.' So the churches were made available for the meetings. By this time, there was so much interest from the grass roots that the leadership — the traditional leadership — had to either get into the process or try to fight us."

_____

Charles Sherrod says now that he was truly amazed by the level of fear he encountered when he first arrived in southwest Georgia. He soon realized that one way of attacking that fear was to include white organizers in the project, working alongside Negroes.

"I didn't involve white people initially," he said. "But I had come to understand our people a little better. I had come to understand that our people do what white people say. And I'd also come to understand our society. I knew that black people cared for their children. That's how I got people to move in Albany. I found out that, no matter how scared a person was, if you messed with their baby, they'd be willing to die for their children. When I learned that, then I was able to move black people in Albany."

Sherrod and Reagon and Jones focussed their early organizing efforts, then, on young people. They hung out near the campus of Albany State College, a black school whose administration strictly forbade student involvement in sit-ins or any other demonstrations. They played basketball with teenagers on Harlem streets. In the evenings, they held workshops in nonviolence. Gradually, the message got across to the younger members of the black community, and from them it reached their elders.

"But you learn in the Movement," continued Sherrod, "at some point or another, that to continue you've got to create mechanisms which allow for more creativity. If you don't, you stagnate and . . . you get drained. You ultimately get drained anyway. But you'll get drained faster if you don't create these mechanisms that I'm talking about." So Sherrod proposed to SNCC that whites be recruited to help the project.

"I told them that white people don't care anything about us, but they care about their children. White people are human beings, just like black people. They're no different in the human qualities. They are essentially the same. And the point that I was making was that if their children came south, the children of these white people — the good guys, the good thinkers — then money would come with them. New people would come with them.

"Which was my second point: that we needed to expose the bad things that were happening to us." Without white involvement, said Sherrod, the Movement lacked access to the media; it could not easily show influential Americans what the supremacists "were doing to us so they could stop them doing these things to us." When he first presented his ideas to others at SNCC, he said, there was a lack of excitement about them. But his "creative mechanism" was to become the basis for the Movement's campaign in Mississippi in the summer of 1964.

Another thing he learned soon after he arrived in southwest Georgia, Sherrod said, was that whatever happened in race relations in

Albany would spill over into the surrounding counties, which Sherrod and others were starting to refer to with such names as "Bad Baker" and "Terrible Terrell." But he also learned that the reverse was true. "What happens in all these counties will happen in Albany. I saw this whole area as a wheel, and an organism here in Albany in the middle of the wheel. And so I got this bus — a red, white, and blue bus — to do it with. This was the mechanism."

Sherrod would pack the bus full of young people from Albany and take them to an outlying community where fears of reprisal meant only ten Negroes might be expected to show up for a mass meeting. The result was a mass meeting that was attended by fifty people."And therefore the small group would be a big group, and they'd feel the assuredness. It was, 'Oh, yeah, we've got a great meeting.' We sang them great songs, you know, and pumped them up. They'd go out and tell more people to come from their county, you know. Pretty soon we'd have forty from that county coming to the meeting, and therefore we'd have eighty-some folks. Filling up the church, one of those little small churches."

The SNCC activists learned, too, that the white leadership of Albany and the surrounding counties knew the value of instilling fear in black people, whether that fear was justified or not. People in several communities believed, as a result, that no matter how bad the repression in their own county, it was even worse in another. "The sheriffs and the authorities weren't that smart," he said. "But they stumbled upon something, the same thing we stumbled upon: the value of fear." One outgrowth of this was that Negroes, fearing what troubles might descend on them if they ventured into Sheriff So-and-so's county after dark, or if they were seen walking down the main street of Sasser or Dawson or Leesburg, voluntarily curtailed their own mobility.

The Movement everywhere valued contacts in the white community and utilized them where they could be found. They were channels through which information could be sent and received; they were informal means for releasing trial balloons or issuing ultimata. But in a place such as southwest Georgia, there were virtually no such contacts. "I didn't know anybody in the white community," said Sherrod, "until I found this guy. He was going with a black woman who lived in the black community. He was an intellectual, a real smart guy. That was my only link to the white community. So I had no feel for what I could expect from the white community.

"When we started marching, one or two white people from this community came over and marched with us and withstood the ridicule. They were ostracized. They were kicked out of the community. I don't remember anybody who came back."

The whites who opposed change in southwest Georgia often took the position, voiced by supremacists everywhere, that Negroes could vote if they wanted to but stayed away from the registrar's office because of apathy, and that they had been perfectly happy with their lot until outside agitators arrived and stirred them up. Lucius Holloway, a black resident of Terrell County, had some answers for those arguments.

"Terrell County," he said not long ago, "had about eleven thousand five hundred people. And blacks had about sixty percent of that. And we had fifty-two people registered to vote. Fifty-two." It wasn't simple apathy that kept them away, he said. "I would say fear."

The examples were abundant. When M. J. Hall, a Negro farmer who had been a landowner all his life, sought to register to vote, white merchants refused to sell him farm supplies or even fuel. "He had to put a drum on his truck and drive into Americus or Albany to get gas and diesel and seeds." Others who registered could not buy gasoline locally. "Myself, I was with that first group that went down to add on to that fifty-two." It was in the early sixties, Holloway said, at about the time the SNCC workers arrived to encourage voting. On a cold day shortly after Holloway registered, he said, the man who sold him residential propane gas for cooking and heating drove to the Holloways' home when the family was out, clipped the gas lines, and removed the tanks.

"All this was a result of the voter registration drive. That's all we wanted to do at that point — get people to register to vote. Educate them how to vote. Tell them what the vote is about. Our primary and only concern was to get people to have the nerve enough to know that it was their constitutional right to get registered as a citizen." Holloway pronounced the word slowly and precisely: "con-sti-*tu*-tion-al."

Negroes who demonstrated such nerve were particularly vulnerable, in southwest Georgia as everywhere else, to retaliation in the marketplace, which was almost totally controlled by whites. Blacks who worked for the federal government, however, were widely believed to be immune from such repression. Holloway found otherwise.

At the time of the voter registration activity, he served as a substitute custodian at a south Georgia post office. Although the U.S. Treasury issued his paycheck, Holloway lacked the job security of blacks who were members of postal unions. His efforts in the Movement, said Holloway, elicited a constant string of threats from his supervisor. "Day after day, the postmistress said to me, 'Sooner or later I'm going to get you.' "

One day Holloway went to Augusta to attend the state convention of the American Legion. He was the commander of his local post, and he had done an outstanding job of enrolling members. He was invited to the meeting — it was segregated — to receive a pin in recognition of his success.

He was a little late in returning to the post office to sweep up and bring the flag in. Instead of recording his true arrival time, though, he did what everybody else did: He wrote down the time he was *supposed* to have arrived. The postmistress, he says, confronted him with this and fired him. "Plus I had to make restitution to the government. It was less than an hour's worth of work. At that time, I think I was making about four or five dollars an hour. She tried to make the FBI arrest me, and they said they didn't want any arrest. I wasn't much more than thirty minutes or so late."

Holloway thought a moment. "They were turbulent times. It was a time when I was economically squeezed out of Terrell County and Dawson."

Not only did Holloway never think about backing down; repression made him work even harder for the right to vote. He became, or perhaps always had been, the sort of "indigenous leader" that SNCC said it wanted to encourage. "I was not any brave hero," he said. "I was afraid. But I always felt that my being led to do what I did at that time was inspired by God. And I felt like because God inspired me and sent me, He took care of me. But yes, we were scared. We were scared because it was a new venture."

It was also lonely. Not every black person in Terrell County was able to subdue his or her fear as well as Lucius Holloway.

"It was so few of us who got uppity," he said. "The others were scared back real fast. They didn't attempt to get uppity" once they saw what happened to outspoken Negroes such as Holloway. "They were told, 'You see what we did with them.' They were frightened out of being uppity, if you want to use that term, before they got to that stage. They stayed back, and they were good boys and girls."

When Charles Sherrod, Cordell Reagon, and Charles Jones arrived in southwest Georgia with their new ideas and their philosophies of nonviolence and their red, white, and blue bus, Lucius Holloway thought of them as anything but outside agitators. They were additional evidence, he thought, that God hadn't forgotten about Terrible Terrell County. "I believed then, and I believe now, that my actions were inspired by God," he said. "Well, I look at their coming as being a package of that inspiration. Like when Moses was sent to Egypt, he made all kind of excuses, but God sent who along with him? His brother. So therefore, Charles and those coming into Albany were part of that package. I had somebody else to look at, to talk with, who shared the same views that I did to give me that little extra motivation I needed when I was afraid. In other words, I was not afraid. My family and I were not alone. There were other people that were with us who were afraid, who helped make a *crowd* of us who thought the same thing. And we continued to carry on."

■ ————————————————————

TWENTY-ONE

■

THE LAND OF NEVER

■

On the first day of November, 1961, the Interstate Commerce Commission's regulation outlawing segregation in interstate transport terminals became effective. This was the commission's response to the request made by Attorney General Robert Kennedy during the Freedom Ride. It outlawed interstate carriers' involvement in any terminal facilities that were segregated in any way. In many parts of the South, the regulation took effect without much fanfare, and Negroes who sought to use terminal facilities were accepted, if grudgingly. But not in Albany. Albany was the stone wall of segregation, the land of never. Albany's police and city government mocked the law while claiming to obey and enforce it.

Charles Sherrod and others in the tiny vanguard of SNCC's southwest Georgia project (the white volunteers had not yet arrived) organized a test of the facilities at Albany's Trailways terminal for November 1. When Negro students entered the "white" waiting room, they were ordered away by members of the Albany police department.[1]

News of this rebuff, one in a long series in Albany, spread through the black community. This time, perhaps because SNCC had prepared the ground for a local Movement organization, there was a constructive reaction. By mid-November, a group calling itself the Albany Movement had been formed. It was a coalition of members of SNCC, the local chapter of the NAACP (which had been a relatively unmilitant member of the community, but which had to be included for reasons of diplomacy), the black ministerial alliance, and other groups. Dr. W. G. Anderson, a local osteopath, was chosen president; the fact that he was not a preacher meant that he would be acceptable to most factions. Slater King was named vice president, and Marion Page, a retired rail worker, was secretary.[2]

Less than a week later, five Albany State students attempted to visit the restaurant at the Trailways station. This time they were arrested by Police Chief Laurie Pritchett. Pritchett was not the stereotypical Deep South redneck police officer, a fact that was soon perceived by the media and trumpeted far and wide as Albany's crisis grew. Pritchett, who had been a schoolboy football player, had served as a policeman in Griffin and Newnan, Georgia, before being appointed chief in Albany in 1959. He was a Rotarian, an Elk, a Shriner, and a thirty-second-degree Mason.[3] He did not use the word "nigger" in public (though once he was widely quoted as having done so), he did not chew tobacco, and he avoided most of the other crudenesses. He appeared to be patient and mindful of what constituted good police procedure. He seemed to possess a sense of humor, and he got the job done. The job, in Albany at that time, was to coolly arrest and cart off to jail all Negroes who dared to violate the laws, including the illegal laws, or who even acted as if they wanted to violate them.

The arrests distressed Albany blacks, and this time there was a vehicle by which they could express their frustration with the system. The Albany Movement's first mass meeting was held on November 25. Other meetings followed over the next several days. When Negroes marched from Harlem into the downtown area in protest, they, too, were hauled off to jail.[4]

On December 10, an integrated group of SNCC workers rode a Central of Georgia train from Atlanta to Albany to further test the ICC ruling. When they arrived and entered the "white" waiting room, the police ordered them out, and as they were getting into automobiles outside, Pritchett arrested them. He charged them with obstructing traffic, disorderly conduct, and failure to obey an officer. The next day they appeared in Albany recorder's court and the assistant police chief explained why such vague charges had been used. The *Albany Herald*, a profoundly biased local newspaper, quoted the officer as saying the visitors "were asked to leave when it appeared that a disturbance was in the making. A large crowd of Negroes had gathered outside the station, and sizeable groups of white persons were attracted to the scene. . . ."[5]

The city maintained the fiction (and it was acknowledged privately as a fiction by virtually everyone involved, even as it was being accepted publicly as legitimate) that the arrests had nothing to do with race. Furthermore, the city arrested citizens who were peacefully exercising their rights, and it justified the arrests on the grounds that the peaceful behavior might inflame others into breaches of the peace. It was Alabama and Mississippi and the Freedom Ride all over again, but with a bit more restraint. Practically all the segregation-related arrests in Albany for the next year would be — at least officially — for such catchall infractions as "breach of peace," "failure to obey an officer" (even when the officer issued an illegal command), "loitering," "disorderly conduct," and, in at least one case, according to the local newspaper, "tending to create a disturbance."[6]

The city's favorite charge, which it used whenever Negroes walked in groups from the Harlem community into downtown to protest at city hall, was "parading without a permit." It is interesting to note that these arrests almost never took place until the Negroes crossed Oglethorpe Avenue from "their" side, the south side, into the "white" side — a gesture that further reminded Albany blacks of the emotional ghetto in which the whites insisted on imprisoning them. These "parades," which the blacks thought of as attempts at peaceful protest, and which usually included kneeling and praying just before Pritchett's men made the arrests, universally ended in trips down to the city hall–city jail complex for booking and jailing. The prisoners were walked (or carried when they refused to cooperate) down a narrow alley beside the city hall into the police headquarters.

The *Herald* article on the recorder's court trial, written by the paper's city editor, Vic Smith, called the Albany Movement "an avowed local effort to integrate practically everything in the city." Three days later, James Gray, the *Herald*'s owner and editor (a transplanted New Englander who therefore was, in a sense, an outside agitator himself), took to the front page of his newspaper with an editorial, titled "The Passing Storm," that charged local demonstrations were "engineered and palpably paid for by the professional agitators" of the NAACP, the Congress of Racial Equality, the Southern Christian Leadership Conference (none of whom were then really involved), and SNCC. Gray also assured his readers that both white and Negro Albanians prized segregation; they "have ethnic convictions of the rightness of this condition," he wrote.[7]

Thus a pattern was set, and the attitude of a city revealed. In his guidelines on nonviolence, Charles Sherrod later wrote about the need for organizers to ferret out and understand "the cluster of social values on which the way of life in [a] city is based, and around which attitudes are fastened." He was writing primarily about black values and attitudes here, but his point was valid for white Albany also: Life in white Albany was grounded in resistance to all efforts at desegregation, or even negotiations that might lead to desegregation, and the racists were perfectly willing to pervert the law in order to keep things that way.

Thus, while the defiance of a Governor Patterson in Alabama had been theater, in Albany it was theater played out on a particularly cruel stage. The segregationists pretended to be law abiding — to want to "prevent violence" and to avoid a "disturbance in the making" — even if it meant trampling on federally guaranteed rights of freedom of speech, freedom of assembly, and equal protection of the law. Furthermore, white Albany managed to play this game in a way that brought acclaim and support from the federal government itself.

In the process, the white city leadership routinely deceived and misled its citizens. It practiced eavesdropping and wiretapping. It backed away from its previous promises and refused even to listen to citizens who sought peaceful redress of their grievances. The police arrested people who conducted demonstrations on private property even though the owners had not complained and state law required that the merchants themselves must file the charges.

The vehicle by which the city accomplished this oppression was one that United States citizens traditionally have deplored as un-American: The elected leaders effectively abandoned their responsibilities and handed over the power of both martial and political law to the police chief.

Part of the character of white Albany was its almost total refusal to grant any concessions whatever to its Negro citizens. The board of education seemed to make an exception in December, 1961, when it announced that it would build a new Negro elementary school and that this would be the first air-conditioned school in the county system. But it was obvious that the project was designed to deflect Negro demands for desegregation of public education, of which there was none in southwest Georgia.

James Gray's newspaper provided daily evidence of the whites' attitude toward blacks. When it was discovered early in that same December that Negroes were urging voters to write in names in opposition to Mayor Asa Kelley in the coming municipal election, the *Herald* front page screamed: "Negroes to Attempt Steal of Monday's City Election." After revealing the nature of the Negroes' perfectly legitimate campaign, the article gave details of "a counter-movement . . . among white Democrats." It did not describe the counterattack as an attempted "steal," however. In what appeared to be a roundup of plots hatching to the south of Oglethorpe Avenue, the article also warned that Negroes had a plan for "attempting to invade white churches." After the election, the *Herald* proudly reported that "Write-in Rumor Spurs Huge General Election Vote Here," by which it meant that the rumor *it* spread had helped get out the *white* vote.[8]

Discussions of black voters by whites in Albany, and particularly by the *Herald*, always referred to "the bloc vote," a term never applied to white voters. The newspaper specialized in finding the Negro angle in practically any issue. "Chicago Negro Dope Ring Under Probing" was the page-one headline on a wire service story about allegations of a narcotics market in a Chicago post office. Other front-pagers included "Negro Student Lauds Reds" and "Negro Admits Killing Pair," a wire story about a routine murder in Missouri.[9] If citizens of Albany desired an adequate and honest description of what was going on in race relations in America, in the South, or in their own town, they would have to look elsewhere than the local press for it.

—————————————————— ▪

Asa Kelley was not the stereotypical chief executive of a Deep South town, any more than Laurie Pritchett was the stereotypical police chief. As a law clerk and teacher, then as a member of the state legislature, he had spent some time in Atlanta, a place that was regarded by many rural Georgians as a beacon of cosmopolitanism and licentiousness. In the sixties, he became mayor of Albany.

Today Albany's old city hall and jail have been replaced by a modern building, and Kelley's job has changed as well. He is a superior court judge. His thinking about the events of the Movement years seems not to have changed at all, however.

"We were basically trying to enforce the law as we interpreted it to be, and that's what we did," said Kelley. "For example, they never bothered to get parade permits, things of that nature. Of course, integration was not on the books then. It was something you just didn't have. Of course, that's what the chief of police was doing, was to enforce the laws as he understood them to be."

When Kelley said that "integration was not on the books" and that white Albany enforced the law "as we interpreted it to be," he spoke of the *local* books and the *local* law. Actually, the Supreme Court and numerous other courts had interpreted the laws regarding segregation in quite a different way. And the Constitution certainly did not see things the way Albany whites did. The fundamental element of Albany's strategy was its insistence that it was enforcing the local law.

Asked why, then, Chief Pritchett arrested people who were obviously engaged in interstate travel — in situations where there was really only one correct interpretation of the law — the judge replied: "Well, he was arresting them locally." There was the faintest hint of a smile on his face.

But what about the arrests at the bus and train stations?

"May have," said Kelley. "I don't know. I don't remember.

"What you've got to understand is, Albany has always been a very lenient, a very tolerant town. We have been an amalgamation of races here. For example, we've had county commissioners and city commissioners who were Jewish. We've had some that were Catholic, some that were Protestant, some were nothing, as far as religious beliefs were concerned. But everybody respected each other, and the blacks were respected. But they were expected to go by the rules *as we understood them to be.*

"The basic tenet was that we wanted everybody to go by the law. That's what we did. The big complaint, of course, was the failure to get parade permits. That was the basis of the big, massive lockups."

Kelley confirmed that the city's elected officials willingly handed over their powers to the police chief. "That's the way it turned out," he said. "I don't know it was determined by a vote or anything like that. . . . But we more or less turned the handling of the matter over to him, subject to guidelines established.

"He was on it twenty-four hours a day, and he proved to be quite capable in doing it, too. Of course, my interest was the same that the president and the vice president of the United States [expressed]. All of us agreed that the idea was to avoid conflict and personal violence, and that's what we attempted to do. I think quite successfully."

On one occasion, however, President Kennedy declared at a press conference that he found it "wholly inexplicable why the city council of Albany will not sit down with the citizens of Albany, who may be Negroes, and attempt to secure them, in a peaceful way, their rights."[10] When he was asked about that complaint, Kelley replied: "I think my response was that I think it's wholly inexplicable that we had intruders coming in, making demands which were unrealistic, not in conformity with the law as we understood it. . . . Not in conformity with the law *as we understood it to be.*"

One law that the city of Albany understood incorrectly involved the arrest, in August, 1964, of two Negroes — one of whom was the Reverend Samuel B. Wells — on charges of "circulating insurrectionary papers." Chief Pritchett further charged Wells with inciting insurrection. Both charges were serious state offenses; the inciting insurrection allegation was a nonbailable charge, and the Reverend Mr. Wells spent thirteen days in detention. The arrests grew out of the Negroes' distribution of handbills protesting what they called the police murder of a black man; any first-year law student knows such a protest is a constitutionally protected exercise of freedom of speech.

The problem with Albany's actions, however, was that the U.S. Supreme Court had ruled in 1937, more than a quarter-century before, that the inciting insurrection statute was unquestionably unconstitutional. Even a federal court judge who was blatantly sympathetic to the city's position acknowledged that.[11]

Furthermore, the illegality of state-ordered segregation in transportation, which was plainly what Albany was practicing, was well established. The Supreme Court declared on February 26, 1962, in a case involving Mississippi, that "we have settled beyond question that no state may require racial segregation of interstate or intrastate transportation facilities."[12]

Much about white Albany troubled the Reverend Samuel B. Wells. What troubled him most was the attitude, expressed by white leaders such as Asa Kelley, that the local Negroes were well off and happy until they were stirred up by outside agitators. While Wells is no great friend of the former mayor's, he does place some of the blame for that attitude on the black community as well as the white.

"I don't think any slave on earth made a better slave, a quieter slave, a satisfied slave, a cooperative slave," said Wells not long ago, "than the black slave of America." He paused to let his statement sink in, and then explained:

"We made the best slaves in the world, and so Judge Kelley got that message. We showed a Judge Kelley and the Kelleys of that time that we were happy. Now, sixty percent of our happiness came through our religion. This religion had the philosophy of the scripture, where Paul says, 'You honor your master, those who are over you.'[13] We felt like we were serving the Lord. And fighting back was out of the question, because we are Christians. Jesus was nonviolent, and Jesus didn't fight back. And He didn't pick up the sword. And He didn't 'Burn, baby, burn.' And so we felt, and still feel, that we are closer to Jesus through nonviolence. So now this could give our white sisters and brothers a feeling that slavery didn't bother us — that we weren't bothered about not being free. We were all right. We were 'happy.'

"But there is one thing they leave out. Aside from the religion that kept us intact and kept us our sanity, you know, in all kind of hardships, the fact was that they were lynching our brothers and they were lynching our sisters. And that goes back all the way through the history of our experience of three hundred years. It goes *all* the way back." Wells slipped effortlessly into the rhythm of the black Southern sermon, although he was not standing in the pulpit but sitting at his kitchen table in an apartment just south of Oglethorpe Avenue. He lifted and lowered his voice almost as if he were singing. "And so they used fear. So, when they say we were happy now, it seems to me that they ought to reach back and also say, 'Now, I lynched your father, and I made his children look on. And I snatched him out the door when his wife was standing there crying.'

"He didn't say anything about that. And that fear that they instilled in us made the helplessness, you know. We were helpless and weak."

Albany's whites easily controlled the blacks, he said, by means other than fear of violence, too. They doled out small favors, picked and chose which Negroes they would negotiate with, which supplicants they would comfort.

"A hungry dog will eat anybody's crumbs," said the minister. "Now, that's the way racist America has kept us crawling on our bellies and quiet: by keeping us poor and keeping us living from hand to mouth, where everything that comes into our hand goes straight to our mouth. And if it rained that week, we may not eat tomorrow. *That's* how racist America has been able to use us, like a mechanic picks up a tool. A mechanic can pick up a tool and use it when he gets ready."

After Okinawa, C. B. King saw Lamar Stewart next in Dougherty County Superior Court. The time was somewhere in the fifties. King was a practicing lawyer now, and Stewart was chief deputy sheriff of the county. "We exchanged pleasantries about fungus infection and this sort of thing — something very casual — and this consideration of where I would be seated became a problem of the moment," said King. The courtroom, like everything else in Albany and Dougherty County, was rigidly segregated. The question of where a Negro lawyer should sit had rarely, if ever, been raised.

"I recognized and was sympathetically disposed toward this as a problem in terms of what a man and his system are like," said King, in a 1962 interview. "I thought, and still think, that Mr. Stewart felt that he was being of assistance to me in terms of avoiding as much embarrassment as possible to me, and perhaps avoiding any future problems for me. He offered me a seat, which I summarily rejected, for this to me is the symbolic mold [in] which the Negro has been cast — special treatment, special this, special that, generally in a derogatory vein, but always special, and not necessarily assistance, but always special." (Stewart remembered that C.B. had chosen to stand by the window, "and, of course, we didn't let anybody stand in the window. We made them sit down.")

"And I saw this as a symbol which I could not accept. I said that I preferred to stand, and I did stand, for a good period of time, in my sympathy toward what the situation was obviously like — and I had some misgivings as to what would be the situation when I *did* decide to sit down, because this I would, but I planned to sit down as any other attorney would sit down, and where he would sit.

"So it turned out that I stood." King explained that, while the court operated with a docket, or list of cases to be tried, the order in which cases were heard was generally not known in advance. A lawyer was expected to be on hand whenever his or her case was called, even if that meant waiting around for hours. "So I found myself standing. And there was about two days of it.

"So I said, Well, I might as well be seated. So I found what I considered to be the least offensive seat in this area the attorneys used that I could possibly find. And there I sat. . . . There were white lawyers who looked at me. There were many caucuses that were held. Stewart was in the courtroom, and he caucused with the others, but he didn't say anything. The judge didn't say anything. So on the day following, we went back to the court. The sheriff was there." The sheriff was Cull Campbell, an ardent segregationist.

That morning, said King, one of the cases involved a counsel who was from Ohio and who was working in association with a local lawyer. "I am a member of the Ohio bar," said King, "so this afforded me some alien contact with a memory which had long since passed. So after he was introduced and after the hearing on the motion was concluded, I went over and indicated that I, too, was a member of the Ohio bar . . . and a member of the Cuyahoga Bar Association. I don't think we were alumni of the same school, but I did indicate that I was a graduate of Western Reserve University, and we exchanged pleasantries, and I went back to my seat.

"Of course, almost instantaneously the sheriff comes over and he says, 'You get up from here, boy' " — King mimicked a redneck dialect — " 'and you go back there. Sit down with them other colored folks.' So I said, 'What did you say?' He says, 'I said you go back there and sit down there with them other colored folks. What the matter, you think you better than they are?'

"I says, 'No, I don't think I'm any better than they are; however, as an officer of the court I feel it to be my privilege to sit where any of the other attorneys sit.' So there was a momentary pause to attempt in a very awkward sort of way to assess where my greatest responsibility is — to this client, whom I would be representing, who was being charged with assault with intent to murder of two police officers, carrying a gun without a license, carrying a concealed weapon, and maybe one other count against him, or whether I should challenge this and thereby, by calling this to the court's attention and disrupting the whole proceeding, draw to the attention of all the jurors my private battle with the local sheriff of the county of Dougherty. Or whether I should let this go by the board and subsequently challenge.

"I decided to vacate; however, not without the idea of pursuing it again. I went outside. I walked around. It was a hell of a traumatic experience; you can bet your boots on that. It tore me up inside.

"So eventually the case is tried, and my client is acquitted on all counts except one." The key to the verdict, said King, probably lay in the jury's inability to believe the policemen. Both said they had fired in self-defense while the defendant was coming toward them with a pistol. But King put his client on the stand and had him remove his shirt and show "that the point at which the officer's bullet made contact was in the back, so he was obviously in flight at the time they fired upon him."

When the case was over, King returned to the courthouse and sat down again where the other lawyers sat. "As I anticipated, the sheriff came and whispered in a rather gruff voice: 'Boy, I done told you once to go back there and sit down where you belong. Did you hear that, boy?'

"I said, 'Well, I am an officer of the court, Mr. Campbell; I consider it my right to sit where the other attorneys sit.' He said, 'Did you hear what I said, boy? You want me to hit you?'

"Really, not knowing what to expect, I said, 'Well, I expect that's what you'll have to do. This is the only way that you will move me.'

"He said, 'Goddamnit, I'll give you about five minutes to get up. Because you think you're better than the other colored folks.'

"I said, 'No, it's a matter of my identifying almost absolutely [with them]. However, I have a function as an officer of the court which permits me to sit here.'

"So he left, and during the interim my imagination went wild. I speculated that some of the deputies would be out there waiting for me. But there was a fierce determination on my part that this was right. Certainly there was a desire to defend my position. Anyway, he returned in about twenty minutes. He said, 'Goddamnit, you haven't got up yet.' He said, 'Now get up here, I done told you once.' I said, 'For the last time, Mr. Campbell, I have indicated to you that I do not propose to leave. And the only way that I actually plan to leave voluntarily is if the court orders me to do so. In order to avoid contempt of court I would leave, but only with the idea of subsequently gaining a determination of whether this is correct.'

"So he rushed up to the bench, and he spoke to the judge. And he gesticulated frantically in my direction. I don't know what the judge said, but I know that he — the sheriff — afterwards dropped his head rather despondently and sauntered out of the courtroom."

It was a victory. A thin, grim smile spread across C. B. King's face as he ended the story of his confrontation with Sheriff Cull Campbell. He took a long, careful draw on his cigar. "However," he added, "there have been repercussions in other areas. He has done everything he can to make it as inconvenient for me as possible."

■ ────────────────────

The Albany approach might have gone unrecognized by the national media if the Albany Movement had not gotten a visit from Martin Luther King, Jr.

W. G. Anderson, the Albany Movement president, invited King and Ralph Abernathy to the southwest Georgia town to help out. Anderson and King had been classmates in Atlanta twenty years previously, and he and Abernathy had gone to Alabama State College together.[14] The charismatic leader of the Southern Christian Leadership Conference would provide just the spark to enable the local movement to burn brightly, thought Anderson. The SNCC workers believed otherwise: Long, steady, hard organizing

in the black communities was what was needed, not instantly supplied jolts of charisma. King, whose entire career as a civil rights
leader was marked by an unwillingness, perhaps even an inability,
to hoard his talents or let down those who depended on him, had
little choice but to accept the invitation.

King arrived in mid-December, 1961, and spoke at a mass
meeting at Shiloh Baptist Church. There was singing, of course,
and among the songs was one that ran: "Jordan River's chilly and
wide; get my freedom on the other side." Afterward, King and Abernathy led a march downtown, across Oglethorpe Avenue, Albany's own Jordan River, into the hands of Chief Pritchett's men. By
then there had been 737 arrests.[15]

Part of Pritchett's plan had been to make sure that the Movement could not snarl Albany's legal system by filling the jails. He
quickly farmed his prisoners out to neighboring county jails, where
communication was difficult and where the officials' attitudes
were considerably cruder than Pritchett's. When Sheriff Z. T. Mathews of Terrible Terrell County encountered Charles Sherrod on
his county premises, he hit the young man in the face and told
him, "I don't want to hear nothing about freedom."[16]

After the jailings, Pritchett represented the city in one of its
few meetings with the Movement leadership. The upshot of the
gathering was that the Negroes believed they had reached a verbal
agreement: that the jailed demonstrators would be released after
posting property bonds, not cash; the city commission would hold
a hearing on the black demands; and, therefore, demonstrations
would stop. The blacks kept their part of the bargain. As Christmas
approached, the demonstrations ended, much to the relief of downtown merchants, who feared any disruption of the seasonal buying
tradition. Reporters referred to the situation with the all-purpose
cliche "uneasy truce." The *Herald* ran on its front page a story
written by the Associated Press that could only be described as
fawning. Albany's "racial history is one of unusual harmony,"
went the article, which was distributed far beyond the reaches of
southwest Georgia, "dating from the Confederacy, remnants of
which still linger in the huge, sprawling plantations in this area."
The piece, at least as it was edited and printed in Albany, quoted
several whites but no Negroes.[17]

A few days later, James Gray unfurled another signed editorial, which was also the text of a speech he gave over his television station, WALB-TV. He railed at the "cell of professional agitators" that had descended upon Albany, and he accused Martin Luther King of trying to make "the fast buck," though he failed to provide the details of such a financial scheme.[18]

With the "uneasy truce," which was based on the Negroes' belief that the white city would negotiate with them in good faith, the Albany Movement lost momentum. Then the white city backed off its verbal agreement to negotiate at all.[19]

Throughout the Movement years, the press and much of the public tended to view events in terms of one crisis followed by another. Usually, the crises were assigned the names of cities: Montgomery and Greensboro, for instance. After Martin Luther King came to Albany, that town's name was added to the list.

There was good reason for this method of accounting for Movement activities. The Movement did progress in a kind of unplanned way from one crisis to the next, and the crises usually could be assigned geographical names. The public's attention then, as now, was limited, and it tended to focus on only one crisis at a time. But it is important to remember, too, that there was a great deal else going on in American race relations. In virtually every town or city or county seat in the South, there was a Movement of some kind at some stage of development: an embryo of one, or one about to come to term, or perhaps just a couple of black ministers who had politely called on the courthouse, seeking change, and who had been rebuffed, and who now were considering what to do next.

For every crisis in the South, there were efforts by black Americans in Northern urban centers, or Midwestern cities, or West Coast communities, to make their own statements about segregation and racism. Sometimes these were demonstrations staged in sympathy with the Southern struggle. But just as often, if not more so, Negroes outside the South seemed to be assessing the conditions that surrounded them and deciding that *their* situation needed improvement, too. For decades, a New York or a Chicago or a Los Angeles had been celebrated by Southern Negroes as the place at the end of the bus or train ride where freedom could be enjoyed; where a decent job could be found; where there were actual laws that prevented segregation. But now, with the Southern movement illuminating so clearly the pervasiveness of racism, blacks outside the region began expressing their own disgust with the social environment. They began counting the number of Negroes in well-paid trades and crafts and wondering if perhaps the unions weren't part of the problem and if the business community couldn't be influenced by a picket line or a boycott.

There was increased activity in the Southland, too. More than ever before, white communities across the region were recognized as having adopted (influenced, almost always, by the actions of their elected leaders) either a hard or soft line in matters of desegregation. Atlanta, for example, tried to project a reasonableness and cosmopolitanism that would attract talent and investments to its rapidly growing downtown. In 1962, *New York Times* reporter Claude Sitton quoted William B. Hartsfield, who had just retired after more than two decades as Atlanta's mayor, as saying, "Regardless of our personal feelings or past habits, we're living in a changing world. To progress, Atlanta must be part of that world." But Sitton also noted that only eight Negro students attended the Atlanta high schools that had once been all white. In that same year, the Metropolitan Opera made its annual journey to Atlanta. The opera, from chorus to carpenters, always arrived with a dramatic flourish by special train and played before hordes of Atlantans dressed to the teeth. Now, for the first time, the Met performed to an integrated Atlanta audience. The self-congratulations were more deafening than the applause. When entertainer Harry Belafonte came to town for a benefit concert, however, he and his retinue were welcomed at the registration desk of one of the city's gaudier hotels (simulated Roman sculpture dotted its driveway), but they were refused seats in the restaurant.[20]

Mississippi, as usual, embraced neither cosmopolitanism nor reasonableness. A state legislator complained that white and Negro children were using the same facilities at University Hospital in Jackson. The hospital director responded that it was difficult to keep black and white children from playing together in the pediatric wards. He said hospital officials "discourage this practice," and he welcomed suggestions as to how to stop it.[21]

Political white supremacists stepped up their efforts to stamp out dissent in state institutions of higher education. Alabama governor John Patterson complained that the president of Alabama Agricultural & Mechanical College, an all-black institution near Huntsville, had allowed members of CORE to come on the campus to solicit for contributions and members. Furthermore, said Patterson, about one-third of the Negroes arrested in recent sit-ins in Huntsville had been students from A&M. This, said the governor, "leaves something to be desired . . . in the financial operation" of the school. The state board of education got the message, went into "emergency session," and ordered the college president to take a leave of absence that would last until his retirement date later that year.[22]

In December, 1961, some two thousand students at Southern University in Baton Rouge, Louisiana, the nation's largest Negro college, took part in demonstrations against lunch counter and employment discrimination. The police used violence and tear gas to break up the protest, and CORE student activist Ronnie Moore was charged with "criminal anarchy," an offense that could bring up to thirty years in prison. Campus tensions rose and the university president ordered all students to leave. The school would have temporarily closed for midterm vacation anyway, but the president required each of the 4,344 students to reapply for admission, a process that, he apparently felt, would weed out the instigators. The trouble, said the president, was caused by a "small segment of disgruntled students." In February, when the school reopened, the president suspended some students and refused to readmit others. Students mounted a boycott, and the police arrested one of their leaders, SNCC activist Dion Diamond. In March, when SNCC's Bob Zellner and Charles McDew visited the campus and attempted to see Diamond, they were arrested, first on charges of "suspicion of vagrancy," then on charges of criminal anarchy. McDew and Zellner were released on ten-thousand-dollar bonds, raised by the Movement, and when they failed to return for their trials the bonds were forfeited. Most of the legal charges raised against Movement activists were later dropped, thrown out, overruled, or just forgotten, but at the time they served the segregationists well as warnings against dissent and as welcome sources of bond money. In the case of McDew and Zellner, a considerable sum of money was involved. (McDew said in an interview in 1990 that he promised God he would never set foot in Louisiana again, lest he be seized for jumping bond. "I've strayed in all the other promises I've made," he said, "but that's one I can hang on to." Once when McDew was flying from New York to Mexico, his plane developed engine trouble and landed at New Orleans. Rather than stay in Louisiana while the plane was repaired, he took the next plane back to New York.)

The supremacists continued to justify segregation by maintaining that Negroes were biologically inferior to whites. The state of Louisiana put on its schools' required reading lists a book by a former airline executive, Carleton Putnam, titled *Race and Reason — A Yankee View*. Reputable scientists had repeatedly asserted that there were no data to back up claims of race-based inferiority; Putnam called this a "pseudoscientific hoax" that was "part of an equalitarian propaganda typical of the left-wing overdrift of our times." In Virginia, political boss Harry F. Byrd liked the Putnam thesis so much that he sent copies to friends. And the Virginia legislature, which maintained a sharp and continuous lookout for even centrist overdrift, pondered a resolution asking the state board of education to determine if Putnam's book should be studied in public schools.[23]

In several states and communities, whites and Negroes gathered, sometimes under formal auspices, sometimes informally, and sometimes in utmost secret, to explore ways to improve communication and reduce tensions between the two races. By the mid-sixties these groups would be fully operational throughout the South, even in the hard-core areas. They were typically called councils on human relations, and their work was usually sufficiently low key to escape the notice and finger-pointing of politicians and the racist groups. The Southern Regional Council sponsored many of these councils. Often, when a community managed to produce peaceful change, close examination would reveal the behind-the-scenes work of one of these groups.

Opponents of segregation provided numerous incentives for communities to seek ways out of their racial dilemmas. The economic boycott, executed to perfection in Montgomery, now was part of the Movement's repertoire almost everywhere. No downtown business leadership could afford to ignore Negro demands for long, although some, as in Albany, certainly tried. A survey in the spring of 1962 by the Center for Research in Marketing, Inc., warned the business community that *un*organized boycotts were a greater cause for alarm than the announced, organized kind. Individual blacks across the country, said the center, were aware of retail stores' attitudes toward them, and tended to stay away from those whom they perceived to be unfriendly. "Many of these stores are not even aware that they have incurred particularly poor relations among the Negro community," said the center's top officer, who pointed out that Negroes were achieving increasing economic importance in urban areas.[24]

Mississippi took a dim view of boycotts of any sort, or at least those conducted by Negroes. When blacks in the Clarksdale area issued leaflets and spoke in public in favor of desegregating downtown stores, five of them were convicted on charges of "conspiring to hurt public trade." It was, said the state's prosecutor, an organized attempt to ruin downtown business. The five were fined five hundred dollars each and given six-month jail terms.[25]

There were occasional reminders — perhaps fewer than might reasonably have been expected, given the provocations — that not all Negroes were committed to nonviolence, and that there were limits to blacks' patience. After members of the NAACP Youth Council in Augusta, Georgia, finished a picketing session outside a supermarket in the Negro community that did not hire black employees, someone threw rocks at a Negro woman who had bought groceries at the store, and then at policemen who arrived to put down the disorder. A few nights later, three white youths driving through a Negro neighborhood were shot at, and one of them was killed. The survivors said they had become lost, but the police chief said rocks and an air rifle were found in the whites' car.[26]

The emerging emphasis on confrontation at lunch counter, bus terminal, and sidewalk provided a distinct change from the traditional courtroom challenge to segregation practices. But litigation had not become passé. On the contrary: Because of arrests in sit-ins and street demonstrations, civil rights lawyers were busier than ever. By mid-1962, the NAACP Legal Defense and Educational Fund, Inc., had brought twenty-nine cases before the U.S. Supreme Court in its current term — more actions than had been brought by any other organization except the federal government itself. Almost half the cases had grown out of the sit-ins. The Inc. Fund also had more than one hundred cases pending in courts other than the Supreme Court.[27]

Voter registration had become, by early 1962, a permanent entry in the Movement's agenda. Robert Kennedy's talks with Movement leaders in the summer of 1961 had developed into a project facilitated by Stephen R. Currier, the president of the New York–based Taconic Foundation. Currier had asked organization leaders how they would use hefty sums of money if they were made available for voter registration projects. The outcome was the Voter Education Project, a two-and-a-half-year effort to coordinate the registration activities of the major civil rights organizations and local groups. Under the skilled guidance of Wiley A. Branton, the Pine Bluff, Arkansas, lawyer who had represented the Little Rock Nine, VEP was successful where previous registration campaigns had failed.

Although organizers such as Charles Sherrod in southwest Georgia and residents such as C. C. Bryant in McComb had discovered otherwise, the feeling of many influential Americans, including the president and the attorney general, was still that voter registration would be a relatively noncontroversial way to further the cause of desegregation. Anthony Lewis, then the legal correspondent for the *New York Times*, reported the thinking of the administration when he wrote, in a Sunday think piece early in 1962, that Washington believed "there is no more effective way to end racial discrimination in the South than to increase the number of Negro voters." The officials, said Lewis, thought that voting campaigns would "meet less resistance in the South and from Southerners in Congress than action in other fields. . . . [I]t is morally difficult for even the most dedicated white supremacist to make a frank argument that Negroes should not be allowed to vote." As it turned out, the hard-core segregationists were not interested in the gentleman's sport of making "frank arguments." Flaming crosses, economic intimidation, reprisals, and murder were their weapons of choice.[28]

The constituent organizations of the Voter Education Project, which was set up under the wing of the Southern Regional Council, were successful in a number of ways, which will be discussed later on. It is hard to find a comparable effort with a greater return on investment. In all, the Taconic and Field foundations, the Edgar Stern Family Fund, and smaller contributors put $870,371 into the project. Between April, 1962, and November, 1964, the time when the VEP was in operation, approximately 688,000 Negroes registered to vote in the eleven states of the South — the largest increase since the 1944 death of the white primary. And the project's effect on every other area of Southern race relations can hardly be calculated. A case can be made, for example, that the national Head Start program of early childhood development should be traced to the work of persons registering voters for VEP.[29]

As the opponents of segregation turned their strategies and actions more toward economic and political issues, other important changes were taking place in American race relations. The migration of Negroes from the South to the Northeast, North Central, and Western parts of the country had accelerated. And for many Negroes who remained in the South, there was migration within the region — from the Black Belt and plantation counties into the growing urban centers. The U.S. Bureau of the Census looked at its figures for the 1950–60 decade and estimated that an average of some four hundred Negroes left the South each day. The movement by blacks into urban areas, be they Atlanta and Birmingham or the big cities of the North and Midwest, meant that a restructuring of political power was in the making. Southern whites whose vision was not obscured by racism could see, too, that a realignment of economic power was likely. As in the migration that accompanied World War II and the growth in Northern defense industries, the South stood in danger of losing its traditional supply of cheap labor.[30]

Some whites whose vision *was* obscured by racism delighted in the idea of Negro departures. Citizens Council members in New

Orleans came up with the idea of buying one-way bus and train tickets for Negroes who wanted to leave the segregated South and move to New York, Detroit, and other cities in the North. Northern liberals denounced the plan as cruel and heartless. The supremacists replied that they just wanted to demonstrate what the situation was in the North. Some of the first Negroes to arrive said they were happy to take advantage of the offer.[31]

TWENTY-TWO

■

YOU RELIED ON LOCAL HELP

■

Once the "truce" in Albany evaporated (if it had existed at all in the minds of whites), the city's pattern for dealing with dissent in the Negro community was clearly established. Early in January, 1962, some Negro students walked into the Carnegie Library and asked for library cards. The librarian refused them and told them to go to the "Negro" library. The police came and questioned the students.[1]

Two days later, a citizen named Ola Mae Quarterman sat down near the front on a local bus. In Albany the bus line was operated by a private company. The driver ordered the young black woman to move. She replied, "I paid my damn twenty cents, and I can sit where I want." The driver called the police, who arrested Quarterman on a charge of "vulgar language."

At the trial, the city set about showing that its reverence for politeness and order — the same reverence that placed such great value on parade permits and potential breaches of the peace — extended to the spoken word. Ola Mae Quarterman was found guilty not of violating the tradition of transportation segregation but of using "obscene language," presumably a companion violation to "vulgar language."[2]

The Negro community, which had already started a boycott of the bus line, intensified its action, and soon the buses stopped rolling. White businessmen, worried about the boycott's effect on trade, met with Albany Movement and bus company officials. Under the agreement they negotiated, bus service would resume on an integrated basis, and the company would accept applications from Negroes who wanted to become drivers. This sort of agreement was getting to be almost commonplace in Southern communities where Negroes decided to withdraw their economic support of segregation. But in Albany there was a hitch: The negotiators asked the city commission for written assurance that the city would not interfere with the plan by enforcing a municipal ordinance (one of those local laws so beloved by the whites) requiring segregation. The city commission refused and, instead, sent a sharp message to the bus operator that its own policy was not to negotiate under duress "and we recommend that the bus company officials follow the same policy." Mayor Kelley was the sole commissioner voting against the position, noting that "there is no harm in the city commission allowing the bus company to operate as they wish." The boycott continued.[3]

By the end of January, Albany's public transportation service was gone. The company announced that it would sell the fifteen buses and its other assets and leave town.[4]

The Albany Movement, in the meantime, continued trying to redress its grievances through the commonly accepted channels. It petitioned the city commission, asking, among other things, that bus and train stations be open "at all times without police interference" and that a biracial planning group be established, with three members appointed by the commission and three by the movement. The commission replied a week later with a lecture straight out of slavery days: "The demand for privileges will scarcely be heard, wherever and whenever voiced, unless . . . arrogance, lawlessness, and irresponsibility subside." Black leaders could "earn acceptance for their people . . . by encouraging the improvement of their moral and ethical standards."[5]

Again, Asa Kelley dissented from this insulting, white

supremacist sermon. Kelley, whom the press tended to classify as "reasonable" despite his essentially hard-line approach, at least recognized the need for some dialogue. He said Albany "has got to recognize that it has a problem and cannot solve that problem by sticking its head in the sand and ignoring that problem. No solution can be reached unless there are lines of communication."[6]

Arrests continued whenever blacks tried to exercise rights guaranteed by the Interstate Commerce Commission. When Charles Sherrod and Charles Jones sought service in the restaurant at the Trailways terminal, Chief Pritchett charged them with loitering and commented, "We don't allow people to go in there and just make it their home." And trials began for those previously arrested. Martin Luther King, Jr., came first. When he and Ralph Abernathy appeared in recorder's court on February 27, 1962, to answer charges of parading without a permit, the city, as usual, denied the arrests had anything to do with race. The defense asked for the city's definition of "parade," and Chief Pritchett said there was none. It was anything he wanted to call it, said Pritchett. The court said its decision would be rendered later; it would be four months before the ruling came down. During that time, King and Abernathy continued free on bail.[7]

Decisions were made more expeditiously in other cases. Charles Jones, Cordell Reagon, and others were sentenced to sixty days for trying to buy food at a drugstore lunch counter. When the SNCC train riders were tried in county court, sheriff's deputies beat and dragged from the room those who tried to sit in the courtroom in a desegregated manner.[8]

───────────────────── ■

C. B. King represented the group. "They had been charged with a conspiracy of sorts to violate the laws of the state of Georgia," he said. "This was late in March. On this particular morning the defendants filed into the courtroom and observed a row of seats which was toward the front and vacant, and decided that they would sit together. There were roughly eleven defendants. This was an area which was by tradition and custom reserved for whites. So the chief deputy, Mr. Lamar Stewart, immediately took the matter in hand.

"He emotionally shouted to one of the Negroes, Reverend Charles Sherrod, to go to the back of the courtroom. Sherrod inquired why. Stewart just had an emotional outburst. He slammed the man to the floor and pushed him, and he and another officer grabbed him and picked him up and took him to the back of the courtroom. And then you have the white defendants, who were sitting up front, but who now tried to absent themselves from those seats and go to the back and attempt to sit back there.

"This, of course, further confused the officers. One of the white chaps was rather fiercely attacked by this man, all the way to kicking and dragging across the seats. They dragged his wife across the seats and pulled her out."

His reaction, said the attorney, "for the lack of a better description, was traumatic. The impact was terrific. I tried as best I could to translate what I saw, or observed, into writing, and it was extremely difficult. I have since seen it, and it is rather incoherent. I was trying to write in longhand what I was observing, and this is next to impossible to do.

"The judge said nothing."

■ ─────────────────

As Albany's warm spring turned into a punishingly hot summer, the events of black and white were played out against a new background. In addition to the fundamental racism and unwillingness to share that underlay the white city's actions and reactions, there was a gubernatorial campaign in progress. In Georgia and all other Southern states, that meant racism to a dangerous degree. Carl Sanders, one of the candidates, was a lawyer who was generally regarded as a moderate on racial questions (or at least one who would *like* to be a moderate; actually being one was sometimes beyond a Georgia politician's abilities). He was opposed by Marvin Griffin, a racist of the old school whose previous term as governor had coincided with a festival of corruption in state government.

Sanders tried desperately to avoid saying anything that was overly racist, while at the same time avoiding the appearance of being soft on Negroes. Griffin took the low road and trotted out an old-fashioned campaign of demagoguery and impossible promises. "We are going to reverse this trend toward massive race mixing in Georgia," he told one crowd, "and we are going to try to rid ourselves of token integration and we will keep the schools open at the same time." Griffin swore he would be a governor "who is not the puppet of a foreign-owned integrationist press and a bloc-vote political mechanism."[9]

The term "bloc vote" was self-explanatory; it was so well used that it had become part of the political vocabulary, like "farm supports" and "better roads." The reference to the "foreign-owned integrationist press" concerned the Atlanta newspapers, the after-noon *Journal* and the morning *Constitution* (the paper edited by the man the segregationists called Black Rastus McGill). The news-papers were the property of the Cox family, out of Dayton, Ohio, and thus were "foreign owned." They advocated the same sort of cautious moderation in racial matters that Atlanta's downtown leaders saw as good for business. But even more to the point for Marvin Griffin, the papers for years had mined the rich lode of scandal provided by his earlier administration. The *Journal*'s wise and dry-witted political editor, Charles Pou, maintained a large network of state and federal employees who provided tips on strange occurrences in the Griffin administration, and he routinely turned out stories of political malfeasance, many of which he at-tributed, without exaggerating, to "impeachable sources."

In apparent reference to the scandals of his earlier term, Grif-fin in the summer of 1962 seemed to be pledging at least to not try to recycle his old tricks: "I have made mistakes in appoint-ments in the past, but you can rest assured that I will not make the same mistakes again," he was quoted as saying. Charles Bloch, the "great constitutional lawyer" who had met with John Patterson of Alabama back in 1955 to prepare a defense against integration, endorsed Griffin as someone who "will put a stop to what has been going on in our state capital city for the last couple of years, cli-maxed with the occupation of Atlanta by the NAACP." The as-sociation was holding its annual convention in Atlanta at the time.[10]

The *Albany Herald* was very much in Griffin's corner, edi-torially and in its news columns. When the two candidates opened their formal campaigns in July, 1962, the *Herald*'s eight-column, two-line banner was "Thousands Cheer Marvin's Speech; Sanders Crowd Lags in Statesboro."[11] The paper consistently characterized

Griffin's rallies and speeches as drawing many more than Sanders's. This phenomenon did not prevent Sanders from eventually winning, however. In any event, everything that happened in Georgia race relations that summer and fall had to be judged in the additional context of a statewide political campaign.

On July 10, 1962, the recorder's court judge finished his four-month deliberation in the King and Abernathy parading-without-a-permit trial. Judge A. N. Durden, Sr., found each guilty and sentenced both to forty-five days in jail or a $178 fine. When Donald Hollowell, the NAACP lawyer from Atlanta, asked the judge for the legal basis of his decision, Durden said he didn't have any. Rather, he said, the decision was founded on "general research of the law." Durden also was quoted as saying he felt it was the duty of a police officer to break up assemblies of people on the streets or sidewalks "although no violence might be involved."[12]

King and Abernathy chose jail, with attendant national publicity. That night, when policemen drove by Shiloh and Mount Zion churches in the Harlem section, where mass meetings were in progress, their automobile was pelted with bricks and rocks. Inside the car with the city police were two agents of the FBI — "by coincidence," as the *Herald* put it.[13]

Judge Durden's "general research of the law" failed to take into consideration the national reaction to his jailing Martin Luther King on a patently transparent charge. Soon the telephone lines were humming between the Justice Department in Washington and Mayor Kelley's office in Albany. In a reenactment of the 1960 DeKalb County call that may or may not have been conscious, Burke Marshall called King's wife, Coretta, to promise that the department would, as the *New York Times* reported it, "use whatever influence it could to obtain his release."[14]

————————————————— ■

Henry Schwarzschild had become increasingly involved with the Movement since his release from jail following the Freedom Rides. Now he could be counted on to show up at any major Movement event. Albany was no exception. Schwarzschild kept in touch with SCLC, and when King went to Albany, he called the office in Atlanta and asked if his help was needed.

"They said, 'Yes, we need help,' " said Schwarzschild. "So I flew down to Atlanta by Southern Airways DC-3 and was picked up by Wyatt because Martin and Ralph were in jail, and Wyatt was sort of running things.

"I did the kind of thing I always did: I swept out the office and I wrote press releases and that kind of stuff. And Wyatt took me down to the jailhouse. Nobody could get in, but he got *me* in. He was a minister, so they let him in. That's Southern courtesy, right? They'd address him as 'Reverend' or as 'Preacher,' but they wouldn't address him as 'Mister.' He was a minister so they let him into jail. And he got me in by pretending, though he knew better, that I was a rabbi from New York.

"They opened up the cell door, and there was a top and a bottom bunk, and on the bottom bunk, reclining in repose, was Ralph reading a Bible, and on the top bunk, sitting with his legs dangling over the end of the bunk, was Martin in blue silk pajamas with a crease in them. So help me God, I remember the crease in these blue silk pajamas.

"He said, 'Hi, Henry, what're'ya doing here?' "

▪ ————————————————————————

On July 12, someone paid King's and Abernathy's fines and the men went free. Or *had* to go free, since they had not authorized or wanted the action. It was revealed much later that the fines were paid by Mayor Kelley's law partner (who, of course, was white) after a hurried trip to Washington and consultation with people at the Justice Department. Everyone with knowledge of the incident twisted the·truth into Gordian knots in explaining what had happened. Chief Pritchett, who was in on the scheme, said at the time that he had been "told" that an "unidentified, well-dressed black man" had paid the fines. (Pritchett still maintained as late as 1989 that technically a white man didn't pay the fine: "A black man brought the money," he said with a smile. "It was a white man that *gave* the black man the money.") Asa Kelley, asked who had paid, at first said "I don't know" and later settled on the strange statement, "I have no communicable knowledge of who posted the money." It is a phrase that he was still using in the summer of 1989, with a twisted little grin as he spoke it. King spoke of "subtle and conniving tactics used to get us out," and pointed out that Pritchett must have known about the trick, because he had ordered King and Abernathy to trade their jail clothes for their own street clothes and to come to his office *before* the time when the fine was purportedly paid.[15]

Although the city secretly conspired with Justice Department officials to reduce its embarrassment over the King jailing, in public it attacked the department over the presence in town of one of its employees. Gordon A. Martin, Jr., was supposed to be a federal observer of the Albany situation, said Mayor Kelley, but he actually spent his time "collaborating and conspiring with the leaders of the Albany Movement and the outside agitators in an effort to aid, abet, and assist the Negroes in planning strategy to violate existing ordinances of the city of Albany." Burke Marshall was reported to have assured Kelley that Martin had been sent to observe only. In the meantime, the city commission rejected several requests from Albany Negroes for meetings to discuss the racial problem on the grounds that it would not meet with "law violators." The Albany Movement began preparing lawsuits to challenge the city's enforcement of segregation. When Charles Jones led Negroes in efforts to use public facilities — the library and a municipal park — they were ordered to leave. Pritchett was quoted as saying, "They seem to be trying to aggravate us."[16]

Late in July, white supremacist Albany got some help from a segregationist federal judge. J. Robert Elliott, a recent Kennedy appointee, issued a temporary restraining order against what he called the Albany Movement's "unlawful picketing, congregating or marching in the streets . . . participating in any boycott in restraint of trade . . . ," and "any act designed to provoke breaches of the peace." The defendants in the city's request for an injunction, wrote Elliott, "threaten to continue and intensify their acts of mass picketing, demonstrations, parades, boycotts, and riotous conduct which threatens the good order, public peace, and tranquility of the city of Albany." And: "Such acts threaten mob violence and tend to deny other citizens of the city of Albany equal protection of the laws, and . . . such injury is imminent, immediate, and irreparable."[17]

The injunction, which would stay in effect until July 30, when arguments were to be heard on a permanent order, forced the Albany Movement to call off a planned Saturday demonstration. But when Saturday night came, some 160 people, many of them teenagers, walked from Shiloh Church toward city hall and were arrested. The Reverend Samuel B. Wells was one of the march's leaders. The arrest was attended by Chief Pritchett's force, state troopers, and county police. FBI agents stood by taking notes. The *Albany Herald* had a field day with the event, mocking Wells's praying as he was arrested and labeling its article "Children Led into Uprisal [sic]."[18] Chief Pritchett shipped his prisoners, children and all, out to a jail in Camilla in Mitchell County. When Marion King, a prominent member of the Negro community and the wife of real estate man Slater King, went to Camilla with other women to take food to a friend's jailed daughter, two deputy sheriffs ordered the women, whom one of them called "niggers," away from the jail fence. Mrs. King, who was six months pregnant, had her three other children with her. She carried one of them, a three-year-old, in her arms. A deputy told her she was not moving fast enough. She turned to talk to him, and he knocked her to the ground and then beat her on the head until she was unconscious.[19]

Martin Luther King announced that he would obey Judge Elliott's temporary injunction. King offered a convoluted explanation; he thought it was proper to "break an unjust law which has an air of permanency," he said, but this one was a temporary ruling "which will last for only a specified period." He did call the order "unjust and unconstitutional," however. His decision dismayed SNCC activists in Albany, who saw it as a capitulation not only to a clearly unconstitutional order by a segregationist judge but also a caving in to federally instituted racism. There was plenty of evidence around, however, that by this time King regretted having gotten involved in the Albany situation at all. There was not enough structure and not enough planning in the movement in Albany; what King had agreed to do as a favor to an old friend had become a burden that he could neither shed nor control.

The injunction allowed King and the SCLC to extricate themselves from the Albany problem. Federal district judge Elbert

Tuttle of Atlanta, a member of the Fifth Circuit Court of Appeals, quickly overthrew Elliott's temporary order, agreeing with Inc. Fund attorney Constance Baker Motley that it was a denial of free speech and peaceful protest. Tuttle, an Eisenhower appointee, pointed out the elementary fact that the Fourteenth Amendment, which Elliott cited as a basis for his order, was not designed to protect the state from its citizens, but the other way around. Pritchett and Kelley warned that if violence occurred now, it would be Tuttle's responsibility.[20]

On July 27, King, Abernathy, and others went to city hall to seek an audience with the city commission, but Pritchett arrested them for "causing a disturbance." This time no mystery man turned up to pay the fine, and King and Abernathy stayed in jail. The next day, attorney C. B. King visited Dougherty County sheriff Cull Campbell, across the street from Albany City Hall, to check on the condition of William Hansen, a white SNCC worker who had been beaten unconscious by one of the sheriff's jail trusties. Campbell picked up a walking stick and beat C. B. King's head bloody. The sheriff said he would do it again if necessary, because "I'm a white man and he's a damn nigger."[21]

Judge Elliott, his temporary restraint dissolved, moved on to a hearing on the request for a permanent injunction. Chief Pritchett, who had been quoted two days earlier as saying that Albany was calm, testified in court that "racial tensions have reached a boiling point."[22] The judge said he would have to consolidate all the racial cases in Albany — the city's request for a permanent restraining order against protest, as well as the Albany Movement's suits demanding the dismissal of Albany's segregation laws and policies. As the legal proceedings dragged on, King and Abernathy were released from jail. At about the same time, the city commission said it would agree to hold talks with local Negroes who were "responsible" and "law-abiding." By the city's definition, this excluded practically anybody who had even thought of being a member of the Albany Movement. King adopted the view that if he could help get negotiations rolling by getting out of town, he would be happy to do so. He thus effectively ended his stay in Albany.

Some demonstrations continued, with the predictable arrests on all-purpose charges and a few new twists (the city padlocked its library and park facilities), but the Albany Movement turned its attention to voter registration — which was what Charles Sherrod originally had come to southwest Georgia to promote. Some seventy-five ministers and rabbis came down from the North to help out. They were refused admission to the city's white churches, and when they went to city hall, Pritchett arrested them, first lecturing them on the need to "clear your own cities of sin and lawlessness." By early October, black youths who crossed Oglethorpe Avenue wearing tee shirts with printed messages that urged shoppers not to patronize Albany merchants were picked up and questioned by the police. White Albany's police-state efforts to control the minds and behavior of its citizens were as strong as ever.[23]

---------------------------------- ■

Charles Jones was opposed to obeying the federal injunction, and he told Dr. King so. "By obeying it," he explained later, "we would have to stop all of the movement, all of the demonstrations. If we defied it, then we were, quote, breaking the law. Dr. King was in touch with the president and Bob Kennedy, and he talked to a number of advisors. It came down to a discussion in the back of Slater King's house on a Sunday afternoon between Dr. King and myself.

"I'm basically representing the notion that, 'Martin, we have to defy the order. We have told people, motivated people, got people involved, got people in jail, got their whole lives and fortunes and livelihoods and resources tied up in fighting the system, defying the use of the legal process to control and contain the community and maintain the system of segregation. You have said that evil laws should be broken and we should accept the consequences of them. If we do not defy the order, at this point, we will be forever controlled by the legal process,' which at that point clearly, clearly favored the maintenance of the status quo. 'You will tie up all this energy and take away our most potent weapon.'

"He said, 'Chuck, I promised that we would not violate the injunction. The president is going to take this case all the way up to the Supreme Court, and we will be vindicated, but we will not be viewed as lawbreakers.'

"I said, 'Martin, by the time this gets to the Supreme Court, all these people who are in jail' — at this point, we were talking about twenty-some hundred people, spread out throughout southwest Georgia — 'the momentum would be lost, the credibility is going to be lost. You will have to, at some point, challenge the national leadership.' And we discussed this for about an hour.

"Everybody else just sort of backed off into the background because, at that point, the dialogue came down to those basic points of view. He and I had been working together a lot in different places. We had a trusting, respectful relationship. So I wasn't hollering and screaming at him. It was just that we had gotten down to the political, theological discussion. And so we sat there — it must've gone on an hour or so — he and I, chatting. He finally said, 'I decided; I think we ought to obey the order.'

"I was very disappointed. I was a little hurt. And you know what happened after that. He did pull out. There was a so-called compromise, and they went on someplace else, relieved that they had gotten out of that situation. And of course the rest of us stayed there and picked up the pieces."

■ ────────────────────────────

Albany proved that there was a form of white resistance that would withstand attack and that, like Captain Ray's methodical arrests of the Freedom Riders as they arrived in Jackson, would actually win praise from segments of the American population that thought of themselves as enlightened and liberal. It also proved once again that the dedication of the Kennedy administration to civil rights had definite limits. John and Robert Kennedy, it was said at the time, demonstrated far more interest in producing peace than in insuring justice. They were, in fact, willing to trade justice for peace in Albany — or at least what the white community called peace; for continued repression and segregation and perversion of the laws in the black community certainly could be defined only as chaos, not peace.

They were able to get away with this largely because the press had become enamored of Chief Pritchett (and, to a lesser extent, Mayor Kelley) and thus had lost its taste for demanding, as it had done in Anniston and Birmingham and Montgomery, that the federal government step in and do something. Thus, Robert Kennedy felt quite justified in telephoning Mayor Kelley, as he did in December, 1961, at the time of the announced "truce," to congratulate him on avoiding violence. Kennedy also sent a congratulatory telegram to Pritchett.[24] The attorney general and other Justice Department officials held meetings in Washington with city officials, including Chief Pritchett, who says Kennedy offered him the job of chief U.S. marshal for Georgia.

Not long before, the Justice Department had opposed Judge Frank Johnson's injunction during the Freedom Rides on the grounds that there were no precedents for proscribing peaceful activity "because such activity was expected to arouse unlawful violence by others." Now, this same agency was congratulating city officials who had arrested Americans for constitutional actions that caused violence from others.

Negroes were aware of the administration's seemingly two-faced civil rights policy. A local group in Little Rock, the Women's Emergency Committee for Public Schools, staged a protest in March, 1962, against the Kennedys' nomination of a new U.S. marshal for Arkansas. The nominee, they said, had helped to arrange a large rally for segregation in 1956. Robert Kennedy replied blandly that allegations against the man "were fully investigated," that "I talked to him personally," and that he believed the man would "meet his responsibilities and fulfill the obligations of his office." At about the same time, Kennedy's office was the site of several sit-ins by activists, among them members of SNCC, who said they wanted faster and better protection of Negroes' rights. In May, Secretary of Commerce Luther H. Hodges spoke to an all-white business group in Birmingham. The apparent exception to the administration's rule against allowing cabinet members to address segregated groups came, according to an Associated Press dispatch, "because Mr. Hodges is considered an expert on desegregation and set up the first token desegregation in North Carolina while governor." A few days later, Martin Luther King, Jr., said in a speech, "I believe segregation will end in my lifetime," but he added, "I do not feel that President Kennedy has given the leadership that the enormity of the problem demands."[25]

Nowhere was the Kennedys' lack of true commitment more

clearly revealed than in their selection of federal judges. Robert and John Kennedy appointed a number of judges who were racist, white supremacist, and wholly unqualified, and they did so strictly for political reasons — to placate and curry favor with the Herman Talmadges and James Eastlands of the South. The Kennedys could talk all they wanted about the practical and moral need for desegregation; they could propose all the legislation in the world to integrate transportation facilities and classrooms and public accommodations. But by appointing one racist federal judge, they could undo all this good. And they appointed several.

Clearly the worst of these was Judge W. Harold Cox of Jackson, an out-and-out racist who used the term "nigger" on the federal bench and who once compared a group of Negroes who were seeking the right to vote to "a bunch of chimpanzees." Close behind was J. Robert Elliott, the man who issued the restraining order in the Albany case.

Elliott was an old-fashioned Georgia segregationist, a white supremacist of the Herman Talmadge persuasion. A Columbus lawyer and former member of the Georgia legislature, he had labored to build the state's pyramid of segregation. In 1947, he and Roy Harris of Augusta, an extreme racist who published a virulent broadside that made the Klan's written screeds seem almost tame, had worked together to try to keep the primary white. In 1952, Elliott was quoted as saying, "I don't want these pinks, radicals, and black voters to outvote those who are trying to preserve our own segregation laws and other traditions." In January, 1962, President John Kennedy nominated Elliott to be a federal district judge for the middle district of Georgia. (Actually it was a matter of Senator Herman Talmadge's choosing Elliott and Kennedy's agreeing.) During Robert Kennedy's time as attorney general, Elliott ruled against Negroes in more than 90 percent of the civil rights cases that he handled.[26]

In 1964, when he was interviewed for an oral history by newsman Anthony Lewis, Robert Kennedy was asked about the Elliott appointment. At first he could not remember the name of the judge he and his brother had appointed two years before — it was "that fellow from Georgia." With Burke Marshall jogging his memory,

Kennedy recalled that Elliott had "made some statements about Negroes," but that he had been backed by "the Negro leadership of the South, or the leadership of the Democratic Negroes." By this he meant that Herman Talmadge had got the ancient Austin T. Walden, of "Colonel" Walden fame, to call and speak on Elliott's behalf. Walden, though accorded the respect due a figure of historic importance by the Atlanta black community, could hardly have been called "the Negro leadership of the South," except perhaps by a politician who didn't really know much about Southern Negroes.[27]

■

When Judge Frank Johnson of Montgomery was asked if he thought the federal judiciary had done a proper job of discharging its responsibilities, he replied:

"In most instances. In some instances it didn't. You had some district judges that accepted the position of a United States federal judge, and took an oath, who absolutely refused to give relief in any of these cases. The most egregious example of that came out of the Mobile area, where you had a district judge that handled a school case . . . against the Mobile Board of Education. And that district judge set a record for reversals. He was reversed in that case fourteen times." One way that judges and others in the judicial system score one another's abilities is by the number or percentage of the times that higher courts reverse their decisions. This method assumes, of course, that the higher courts are "right." During the Movement years, there was no question that the higher courts were "right" in terms of cutting through obfuscation and contortion in matters of civil rights.

"Judge Cox in Mississippi . . . he wasn't able to put aside his prejudices and discharge his duty as a federal judge. That was pretty obvious. And that's what you have to do."

And Judge Elliott?

Judge Johnson thought a moment. "Yeah. J. Robert. Columbus, Georgia. Well, I would say that his record indicates he was very reluctant, very reluctant. Judge Elliott has a not good record on appeal. That's about the nicest thing I can say. He has a very bad record as far as the appellate courts are concerned."

Edwin O. Guthman was Robert Kennedy's special assistant for public information in the sixties. He was trusted by reporters who covered the Movement because, although he clearly wiggled and squirmed on occasion to avoid giving a direct reply to a question, he never lied. It is a science and art that has since fallen out of favor among top government spokespersons. Guthman disagrees with arguments that the Kennedy brothers were unduly influenced in their civil rights actions by a desire not to lose the white South — that they winced as they walked the line between supporting the Movement and catering to the supremacist politicians.

"We certainly know that John and Robert Kennedy were politicians to the core," said Guthman not long ago at his home in southern California. "But in the discussions that I participated in about what we were to do in the South, it always revolved around two things. One was, What does the Constitution require; what does the court require? Two, How do you avoid violence?

"I never heard anybody say, 'Well, if we do that, we're really going to get the Mississippi Democrats or the North Carolina Democrats angry,' or whatever it was. I don't have any question in my mind that Bob and Jack, in the privacy of the White House, discussed the fact that this was not a political issue that they were going to win on. But this never penetrated any of those discussions." When important decisions were made by the attorney general's people, he said, "then they would go over to the White House and tell President Kennedy what they were going to do," rather than ask him if it was all right to do it. Guthman said he never witnessed any discussion other than, "What was this work we have to do? We have to see that the orders of the court are enforced and we're going to do this to prevent violence."

■ ————————————————

Another element of the American judicial system was represented by the Federal Bureau of Investigation. Until the Movement years, the FBI had enjoyed among many Americans a proud image — one of a corps of highly skilled "G-men," doing battle with machine-gun-toting John Dillingers, sniffing and snuffing out plots by the Godless Communist Conspiracy to overthrow the American Way of Life. At the top of the image, and largely responsible for it, was the venerable Mister G-man himself, J. Edgar Hoover, the FBI's director.

The FBI was great on solving bank robberies and catching interstate thieves, but as the Freedom Rides proved, it had its own agenda on civil rights issues. There was a perception — a fact in the minds of most Movement people and sympathetic observers — that the highest levels of the FBI were spiritually, philosophically, and practically on the side of the segregationists. With virtually no agents or executives who were not white males, the agency had no experience with blackness or black people, except those it hired for the contemptible job of informer. It was easy for the FBI to think of outspoken blacks, even those whose outspokenness was in support of fundamental, constitutional rights, as troublemakers and radicals. It was easy for an agency that knew nothing about Negroes to conclude that they lacked the intellectual ability to formulate the positions they espoused and were, therefore, directed by others who were, of course, white. It was but a small leap from there to "communist dupe," a leap the agency took frequently and, it seemed, joyfully. It was the FBI's version of the "outside agitator" cry. Influencing all of this was the strange personality of J. Edgar Hoover himself, who fairly glowed with white supremacism and who combined a dirty-minded little boy's penchant for spying and bending the law with a master bureaucrat's ability to cover his actions with memos and self-serving paperwork. The result was that the FBI was one of the civil rights movement's biggest enemies. It was, in sum, un-American.

In Albany and other centers of Movement action, criticism of the FBI centered on two issues. First, agents on the scene (they were easily identified, since Hoover believed in a strict dress code, even in the heat of a south Georgia summer) were perfectly capable of standing by — indeed, were under orders to stand by — and watch while the most serious crimes were committed against the Constitution, *if* they involved civil rights. The same agents would go into instantaneous, G-man action if they heard of a bank robbery in progress, or if they were on the trail of a suspected interstate auto thief.

The nation's laws actually empowered them to make arrests on the spot, without warrants, if a felony or a misdemeanor was committed in their presence, or if they had reason to believe one had been committed. But the police of Albany or Jackson or Birmingham could deprive citizens of their rights of free speech and peaceful assembly and generally turn the Constitution into mincemeat, and the FBI could be counted on to stand on the sidelines. The agents always took notes on what they saw, but if the notes ever were put to good use that fact was well concealed.

The second flagrant problem with the FBI was that its agents were invariably chummy with the local police, who were themselves almost always integral parts of the problems of segregation and racism. This, like the note taking, could have been changed in an instant with a policy order from headquarters, but one never came. Martin Luther King brought down a ruckus during a 1962 trip to New York City when he was quoted as saying that one of the problems with the FBI in the South was "that the agents are white Southerners who have been influenced by the mores of the community. To maintain their status, they have to be friendly with the local people and people who are promoting segregation. Every time I saw FBI men in Albany, they were with the local police force."[28]

The FBI's and Hoover's response was an angry one (Hoover could never abide criticism), and it was almost totally directed at refuting the statement that "the agents are white Southerners." Cartha D. DeLoach, known as Deke, the assistant to the director, accused King of "deceit, lies, and treachery."[29]

King was wrong about white Southern agents in Albany. Only the most senior of the six agents there, Marion Cheek, was a Southerner, and Cheek had travelled widely enough to have lost the veneer of the white Southerner to which King was clearly referring. Cheek was not a cracker or a redneck, but a professional policeman, with the policeman's essentially conservative philosophy. His professional skepticism for anyone in the public spotlight, integrationist or segregationist or in between, was pretty healthy.

King was absolutely correct, though, in his assessment that the FBI agents were overly friendly with the local people and his statement that every time he saw them in Albany, they were in the company of local policemen. FBI agents in Albany routinely sat and travelled in cars with Chief Pritchett's men. When they were seen chatting with the local police, the conversations were animated and obviously friendly; when they spoke with members of the Movement, or even black people in general, they turned formal and suspicious. Their bond with the local police should not have been surprising. Reporters from national newspapers and news magazines who came to Southern towns to cover civil rights stories developed similar friendships with local reporters who shared their assumptions about life and politics and segregation and whom they felt they could trust.

An obvious question was, Why didn't the Kennedy administration, with its oft-stated belief in the aims of the civil rights movement, order J. Edgar Hoover to change the ways his agents operated? In the sixties, such a question would have elicited belly-thumping guffaws. It was widely believed — by white politicians, black activists, local policemen, and reporters — that John and Robert Kennedy (and everybody else in important public office) didn't dare irritate Hoover because they believed Hoover had damaging information on them, gathered from wiretaps, electronic eavesdropping, and informants. The degree to which this suspicion was true, as opposed to generated by guilt, has not yet been determined, although historian David Garrow has provided detailed glimpses of Hoover's spying on one prominent figure, Martin Luther King, Jr., in his books *The FBI and Martin Luther King, Jr.* and *Bearing the Cross.*[30] Certainly there was much in John Kennedy's life, part of which was spent in the company of women other than his wife, that might arouse a bureaucrat who thrived on snooping and who had a fixation on protecting his turf. But it is also likely that the widespread *belief* that the director had massive secret dossiers on practically everyone, whether he actually did or not, was sufficient to produce the behavior that Hoover desired. The Kennedys kowtowed to him. They kept him in office long past normal retirement time; they praised him to the point where knowledgeable people would have to avert their eyes in shame; they let him run the FBI as he wanted. They showed every evidence, in sum, of being terrified of Hoover. Author-editor Victor Navasky writes that at Robert Kennedy's Justice Department, "getting along with the FBI, although not perceived as an 'issue' at the time, had as high an operational priority on the RFK-JFK list as solving the problem of the Negro."[31]

■

Ed Guthman maintained a healthy skepticism about the FBI from the time he left Seattle, where he had won a Pulitzer Prize for investigative newspaper reporting, to go to work for Robert Kennedy.

Before he departed Seattle, three local FBI agents whom he knew took Guthman to a farewell lunch.

"We had a nice lunch," Guthman recalled. "And at the end of the meal, two of them get up and say, 'We're going to go pay the bill.' And the other guy says, 'Let's finish our coffee.' And then he puts his hand under the table, and he hands me a piece of paper. He says, 'Take that piece of paper. There's three names on there, and you watch out for them when you get to Washington.' And one is Deke DeLoach. So I had an idea what I was going into."

During his first week on the new job, Guthman said, DeLoach took him to lunch. The assistant director of the FBI offered to include Guthman in a scheme whereby FBI officials purchased their meat at wholesale prices. Guthman said he wouldn't have accepted the offer anyway, but that he was especially leery after having been warned about DeLoach.

Guthman thinks Hoover did amass information on public officials, including the president and attorney general. "But I don't think that he ever threatened them. I don't think that's the way Hoover worked.

"He let you know that he had information. But I don't think that was what motivated the Kennedys in their dealing with Hoover. I think that the deep impression that they felt in this period of time was that it was important to try to get along with him, and as best you could. Now, you have to understand that it was not an easy relationship."

The Justice Department, said Guthman, had "found out during the Freedom Ride that we couldn't depend on the FBI for intelligence from the South." The department began relying more and more on the investigative work done by John Doar and the lawyers who worked under him.

Hoover's own employees felt a great need to get along with the boss, as well, said Guthman. "If they didn't give Hoover what he wanted, rather than what it *was*, they'd end up in Butte or someplace." (The FBI office in Butte, Montana, was legendary as the place where Hoover dispatched agents who displeased him.)

Guthman said that Robert Kennedy spoke of wanting to turn Hoover out to pasture in his brother's second term as president, and Guthman believes the attorney general was serious about it. The key was winning that second term. "It wasn't like Jack Kennedy was sitting there with a great, grand mandate to do whatever he wanted. He had a Congress that was fighting him all the way on a lot of things. He had a lot of opposition, and he was looking to 1964, and I think that discretion was the better part of valor.

"In hindsight we can see that the brave and the courageous and probably the right thing to do would've been to kick his ass to Iceland or someplace, but in that time and in that atmosphere, you couldn't do it. The thing that happened was that over the course of those four years, those of us who operated at any kind of a level [of dealing with Hoover] came to totally disbelieve anything that he said."

Marion Cheek, the sole FBI agent in Albany who fit Martin Luther King's definition of the white Southerner, was born in Atlanta. In 1958, after service in the naval air corps and as an assistant U.S. attorney in Tennessee, he was in Washington, serving as the supervisor of the FBI's major case squad there, and he was doing well in the FBI scheme of things. "I had about as good a job as you could get in the FBI," said Cheek not long ago. "Had my own squad and stenos and clerks and this, that, and the other. And interesting cases. I met cabbages and kings on a day-to-day basis. And then to come down here, to the boondocks, really." Cheek grew to enjoy the boondocks, though. After retirement, he stayed on in Albany.

He came to southwest Georgia in late 1958 because his mother, who lived in Atlanta, was suffering from a terminal illness. On a Wednesday Cheek went to see J. Edgar Hoover to tell him about the illness. Two days later he got a transfer to the Atlanta office. Atlanta, a division office in the FBI, maintained several suboffices, known as resident agencies. There were openings in Columbus, with the adjacent Fort Benning military reservation; Dalton, a textile center; and Albany. "I picked Albany because I knew the other two," said Cheek. "I didn't want Fort Benning, and I didn't want to speak chenille. And so I came to Albany, and it was close enough to the Gulf and the Atlantic, and I love fishing. And I love hunting. But I felt kind of lost when I first got down here, because there wasn't a whole heap going on.''

Cheek and his five agents covered twenty-four counties in southwest Georgia. "We had the normal cases," he recalled, "the thefts from interstate shipment, the interstate transportation of stolen motor vehicles, an occasional white slave case, an occasional bank robbery, an occasional extortion case. We managed to carry on an average of about thirty cases at all times." Then, in December of 1961, the civil rights movement came to southwest Georgia. Things became quite busy in the Albany resident agency. Cheek and his agents worked literally night and day on civil rights matters, investigating allegations of police brutality and, in the violent counties around Albany, church burnings and shootings. And they took notes on everything they saw.*

Cheek was aware of the criticisms of the agency's civil rights record. He countered with his own criticism of Robert Kennedy's Justice Department. Investigating a typical complaint involved elaborate dealings with Justice, he said.

"You had to have the authority of the assistant attorney general in charge of the civil rights division in order to work a civil rights case. When you got a complaint, you sent a Teletype in to Bureau headquarters in Washington. And you requested permission to conduct an investigation.

"They'd come back and tell you to conduct a preliminary inquiry, limiting it to the following: Interview John Smith, Tom Brown, what have you. *Or* conduct a full field investigation. *That* meant there were no holds barred and Katie bar the door, and let the chips fall where they may. Occasionally, they sent down a lawyer from the civil rights division to supervise the investigation. This went over like a lead balloon with the U.S. attorney's office in Macon, who was a political appointee of the senator from this area. Herman Talmadge appointed the U.S. attorney in the middle district of Georgia. He got the middle district and the

---

*Cheek said, in his interview, that he certainly had collected enough material during his years with the FBI in Albany to fill a book, but that he had signed an agreement with the agency promising not to write one. He added that it was FBI policy for its agents to burn their notes. Part of the ritual of running the Albany residency involved collecting all those notes that FBI agents were always taking and driving out to the marine corps base north of town and putting them into the incinerator.

northern district, and the junior senator got the southern district, which was Savannah. But that's the way civil rights cases worked. Now, we didn't have to have anybody's authority to go out and work a bank robbery, a straight criminal case."

The procedure was unwieldy, and it obviously grated on a policeman who thought of himself as a professional and who long ago had developed a healthy contempt for political appointees and their bosses. "Yeah, I'd criticize the Justice Department. I'd have to first criticize the White House, because the White House at that time *was* the Justice Department. When your brother is the attorney general and you're the president, the White House is the Justice Department. And the assistant attorney general in charge of the civil rights division during most of that period of time was Burke Marshall. He wouldn't have crossed the Kennedys for all the tea in China. And you were dealing with an extremely sensitive political situation, and the Kennedys did not want to write off the South."

When Cheek spoke of some of the civil rights figures who came to Albany in those years, it was with a degree of distaste. But he expressed a certain admiration for Dr. King. "We had no problems dealing with Dr. King down here. He called me many a morning at two, three, four o'clock in the morning. I've gotten out of bed and gone down to see him and listened to his complaint. Handled the situation. And that's not to say that it didn't put us through literal hell." The hell lasted well past King's departure from Albany in the fall of 1962. Until about 1965, rural southwest Georgia was the scene of a good deal of violence, most of it directed at proponents of equality.

"We covered all those towns out of here. I had as many as seventy agents working out of here during the height of the racial turmoil. We rented motels, the whole motel. We brought down stenographers and clerks from Atlanta. Atlanta would call *us* up and try to borrow agents to handle some of *their* work.

"I had to talk to Washington four times a day to give them a 'summary Teletype' over the telephone. Dictate to the steno up there on the phone, four times a day. Starting at eight o'clock in the morning, and the last call being at midnight. And if anything materially happened during the middle of the night, call them again. We had every news medium in the country represented down here. All the TV networks were here. Some of the news really happened, some of it was created."

Cheek said, with the air of a cop who has seen it all, that "a certain network" staged demonstrations that produced violence. "They weren't reporting the news. They were creating it." The purpose, he said, was to give the network prior knowledge, and therefore exclusive coverage, of sensational action footage. Although the retired FBI man supplied the name of the network that he accused of "staging news" and "paying people to put on a demonstration," independent confirmation of the charge was not available in 1990, and persons who were on the scene could not recall that the reporter named by Cheek even covered the Albany story.[32]

When Marion Cheek was wakened in the middle of the night by a telephone call, he said, in most cases it would be a complaint of police brutality. He would jump into his clothes and head out the door to investigate the allegation that might, or might not, excite further attention at the Justice Department.

"I'd go to the alleged victim, take a signed statement, take photographs. For example, C. B. King, the civil rights attorney here, was hit on the head by Cull Campbell, Sr., and I was standing on the police department steps. He came over and he said, 'Mr. Cheek, I have just been brutally assaulted by the sheriff of Dougherty County.'

"And I said, 'C.B., you need to see a doctor.' He said, 'I need to make my complaint first. I want you to take pictures.' So I took the pictures and took his statement, and the wound was very superficial, but it bled a lot. Most skull wounds do. Did we get an indictment? No, we didn't get any indictment. Cull Campbell could've shot him down on the courthouse steps, and they wouldn't have indicted him."

In a more typical investigation, Cheek would interview witnesses. Then he would send a summary of the investigation to date to Washington, by Teletype, and ask for instructions from the civil rights division. A typical police brutality summary would run three to five double-spaced, typewritten pages.

"Usually within forty-eight hours, we'd get an answer. They never said no." There was one exception, he said. It involved the proposed indictment of a person active in the black community. In that case, said Cheek, "they said not only 'No,' but 'Hell, no.'

"But never in a civil rights case did they say a flat 'No.' They came back and limited you to a preliminary investigation, where they told you to do specific things. The very first thing you always had to do was to notify the head of the agency involved. If it's a policeman, you had to notify the chief of police that 'we're conducting an investigation at the request of Mr. Burke Marshall, assistant attorney general in charge of the civil rights division, who has requested we interview John Brown, one of your officers.'

"Sometimes it was, 'You're not going to interview Brown. I'm not going to let you interview him.' Most of the time they did let you. But you told them the parameters of the investigation you'd been ordered to conduct. Or if the civil rights division came back and said do a full field investigation, you still had to comply with step one. You weren't going behind anybody's back."

What about the allegations, Cheek was asked, that were often made about the FBI in the South? That its agents were white Southern in their thinking and overly friendly with the local authorities?

"We had one Southern agent in the Albany office — me. I was born in Atlanta. I moved from Memphis, Tennessee, to Chicago in 1947. From there to New Orleans. From there to New York. From there to Washington. And in '58, in December, I returned to Georgia. I'd been back in Georgia less than two years when all this mess started. I'd lived in the North. I'd been a naval officer. I was a carrier-based fighter pilot in the Pacific in World War II with sixteen months of combat. I've lived in Seattle. And I had worked with blacks throughout my FBI experience from '47 on."

His fellow agents in the Albany office, said Cheek, "had all been in the South a lot longer than I had, were a lot closer to Southern law than I was, a lot more attuned to the way of thinking down here than I was.

"Were we friendly with the local police? Of *course* we were. We worked with them on a daily basis. . . . When you have five men, you're covering twenty-four counties, you're working some hundred and sixty federal violations, who are you going to get the help from? . . . You asked them to go out and put their lives on the line with you, because you had nobody else to ask to go along with you but that deputy sheriff. And you ask him to go along because you sure as hell couldn't afford to take another agent with you. He had seven or eight counties to take care of himself. You relied on local help. You had to."

Sometimes the federal agent was more than professionally close to the local officers. Ed Friend, one of two detectives Laurie Pritchett assigned to keep watch on Martin Luther King and the Albany Movement, was "a very close personal friend of mine," said Cheek. The two men went fishing together. When Friend had to enter an Atlanta hospital for open-heart surgery, Cheek drove him there. Cheek handled Friend's business affairs, paying his bills by completing blank checks that Friend had signed and handed to him.

And sometimes, said Cheek, the local police were definitely not friendly. "I remember getting a call on a house shooting and burning up in Sumter County at the height of their problems up there, from the reddest-necked sheriff in the state of Georgia and reddest-necked GBI agent I ever met." (The notorious Georgia Bureau of Investigation was the state's investigatory agency; in those days it was a direct arm of white supremacy.)

"And I had a boy with me, an agent from Minnesota. We parked our car, and their car was blocking the one lane into the house. And you could still see the smoke smoldering. I started in, and these guys blocked the way with arms akimbo and both with their hands on their gun butts and said, 'You're not going in there.'

"I said, 'Yes I am.'

"I got my little gold badge out, and I said, 'My gold badge is as big as your damn gold badge, except mine's made out of gold.' And I says, 'I could outshoot both of you. And get your damn hands off your gun butts or I'm going to stick them up your ass.' "

Cheek paused and added, in a somewhat softer voice, as if he were divulging an important secret: "I don't know what I'd have done if they hadn't. But they took their hands off their gun butts and I walked right between them. And made a point to brush both of them with both shoulders. And my other agent followed right in behind me."

Cheek had nothing but praise for the two men who governed Albany during its race relations crisis. The city was "blessed," he said, to have Laurie Pritchett running its police department "with an absolute iron hand." Cheek added: "If I had to single out two men in this town responsible for keeping this from turning into a real bloodbath, it'd be Asa Kelley and Laurie Pritchett."

He had less enthusiasm for members of the Albany Movement, although Cheek probably spent as much time with them as he did with

Pritchett and Kelley. (Attorney C. B. King was once quoted as saying about Cheek — and the statement could probably be honestly applied to FBI agents all over the South — "The only people who are relevant to him are white people.")[33] When he recalled Charles Sherrod, who stayed on in Albany, Cheek's warm tone evaporated and he spoke the name "Charles Melvin Sherrod" as if he were writing it in a Teletype to Washington. (Asked about this, Cheek smiled and said, "I *have* written that name, a thousand times.") Cheek said he never doubted Sherrod's motives. Others who came, though, particularly whites from the North, "were here to agitate, to raise hell, to cause trouble, to create as much of a stink as they could create."

Marion Cheek said he had enjoyed his years in the FBI. But the time in Albany was painful.

"If I could eliminate three years of my experience, it would be those three years. They were not enjoyable, primarily because of the working conditions, of the pressures you got from all sides of the fence. It's no fun to go to work before seven o'clock in the morning and not get home till after midnight. It's no fun not to have an off day for six months. It's no fun to live in a hotel for a couple of months and have your wife come see you and bring you some clothes."

But through it all he remained a Hoover man. J. Edgar Hoover was unfairly accused of being opposed to the aims of black Americans, said Cheek. "Where he got the reputation for being anti–civil rights, I don't know. We in the Bureau looked on him as being pretty liberal. . . . Hoover's house was staffed by two blacks, a black major domo, so to speak, who ran the place, and one who took care of the yard and the shopping and the odd chores." Another Negro, the outer guard in Hoover's office for thirty years, "was an agent, and Hoover hired black agents before you had to hire black agents. Did he hire a preponderance or in proportion to the population? Hell, no, he didn't.

"I found the man very gracious. I think he's a great American, and I hate like hell to see people who didn't have balls enough to knock him in life attack him in death."

▪ ————————————————————

TWENTY-THREE

■

A FAILED SUCCESS

■

After Martin Luther King, Jr., extricated himself from Albany, and from a situation not entirely of his own making, there were, indeed, as Charles Jones had observed, many pieces left to pick up.

The work of the Student Nonviolent Coordinating Committee continued, as Jones said it would. Young white people, carefully screened by Charles Sherrod, arrived from the North to help challenge fear in Dangerous Dougherty and Terrible Terrell and Bad Baker.

Some of the college-age volunteers stayed with Lucius and Emma Kate Holloway, often as many as eight or nine at a time in the Holloways' two-bedroom house. Holloway was young himself then, only about thirty, but "I looked at them as being young kids, and they looked at me in kind of a daddy fashion." The Holloways were impressed by their visitors' willingness to serve in positions subordinate to local black people and to fit into the community. "They were like average people used to being without and willing to sacrifice to get the job done that they'd come to do," said Holloway in an interview. "They did not act scornful or say, 'We need three meals a day,' or 'We need something special to eat.' They ate what was there. When there wasn't anything there, they didn't eat or they went out and they scrounged something to eat. And they took care of their hygiene and stuff like that. They had nothing fancy to wear. And that's how they did. Just fell right in line. It made a good team."

Lucius Holloway headed the voter registration drive in Terrell County. One night in that summer of 1962, he was chairing a meeting at the Mount Olive Baptist Church, in Sasser, Georgia, when about fifteen white men walked in. As the tension grew, Charles Sherrod led the meeting participants, black residents and white volunteers, in a recital of the Lord's Prayer. Sheriff Z. T. Mathews of Terrell County stalked in, along with the sheriff of Sumter County and two deputies. Mathews warned the participants that "my people are . . . getting disturbed about these secret meetings. . . . We are a little fed up with this registering business." The atmosphere was charged with the electricity of impending violence. Mathews went on: "We want our colored people to live like they've been living." At the time, Mathews and all other county officials were under a federal court injunction to refrain from interfering with voter registration.[1]

A deputy demanded a list of the names of the Negroes present. Mathews, at the front of the chapel now, went on about what a great friend of the Negro he had always been, and how the "outsiders" would soon depart, leaving the local people as before. Pat Watters, then a columnist for the *Atlanta Journal,* one of a handful of newspeople who were there that night, reported that as the sheriff continued his harangue, the Negroes started humming the tune to "We Shall Overcome." And when the humming turned into the words of the anthem's stirring line, "We shall o-ver-come some-day-a-ay-a-ay," the whites "retreated then, to the back of the church." Eventually they left the building. The singing continued. A few nights later the church was one of three in southwest Georgia that were burned to the ground. Night riders shot into the homes of several Negroes who had been active in voter registration. The Justice Department had responded to most such incidents with statements that it was "investigating" and "watching the situation closely," but this time it asked the federal court for an order prohibiting local police from intimidating potential voters. The federal court, unfortunately, was Judge Robert Elliott. He said he saw no immediate danger for those involved.[2]

———————————————— ■

Marion Cheek investigated the church burnings for the FBI, and he did not like what had happened at all.

"We investigated each and every one of them," he said. "But we had some problems. I had three church shootings and burnings, which were motivated by their having been used for voter registration meetings. We had signed confessions, witnesses. Couldn't get an indictment from the grand jury." And that wasn't just on civil rights cases, said Cheek. "We went for a period of two and a half years in Americus, Georgia, which was a division of the middle district of Georgia, where no federal agency won any case at all. We lost bank robberies with eyewitnesses. We lost assault on federal officers with eyewitnesses. Half the time, we couldn't even get an indictment.

"The time was not apropos for some of the things that very advisedly were pushed on the populace. You have to understand what the Deep South was in 1960. It was redneck. They would've voted for a klansman quicker than they would for the Pope.

"You had the so-called blue-ribbon grand juries then, which were a hundred percent white. You just about had to be a property owner to be on them. The clerk of U.S. district court actually investigated everybody who got on it. Checked them out with the leaders of the community. 'Would Mr. So-and-so be a good grand juror? Does he own property here? Has he got a business? Is he married? Got any children? Is he active in his civic clubs?' That sort of thing. That's what went behind your being on a grand jury.

"Well, if you can't get people indicted, you can't convict them of anything, period. And the criticism of no convictions and of [activists'] being lynched in Mississippi and Alabama: Yeah, they were murdered, and nothing was done about it. And the [Jewish] Temple in Atlanta was bombed, and nothing was done about it. And churches were bombed in Birmingham, and nothing was done about it. And churches were bombed in Sasser, Georgia, and up here in Lee County, Georgia, and Smithville, Georgia, and nothing was done about it. But did we investigate it? You bet your bottom dollar we did. Did we find out who did it? We solved every last damn one of them."

Was he saying he had airtight cases?

"You can't get much more airtight than witnesses, and signed confessions, and fingerprints on gas cans."

■ ————————————————————

The federal government did get involved a year later, but not on the side of the Movement. In its first civil rights prosecution of the decade, the department got a grand jury to indict nine Albany Movement leaders on grounds that they were "conspiring to obstruct justice." The leaders had picketed a store, situated in the Harlem section of Albany, that was owned by a white man who earlier had served on a jury that had dismissed brutality charges against a sheriff.[3] The indictment eventually went the way of much anti-Movement legislation and judicial decision making, but it served to inform blacks in Albany, the South, and the nation once again that the system they were challenging did not stop at Mason and Dixon's Line.

———————————————————— ■

The Reverend Samuel B. Wells was working at the marine corps base when the indictments came down. He was one of the nine. "Marion Cheek's the one who came on the base to talk to me about it," he recalled. "They flew in here like flies. Like a swarm of bees, for the indictment.

"And they went arresting us like flies, because of the white power structure. I've got an old piece of car, and we rode all the way to Washington, D.C., one time, during the demonstrations, and sat down with John Doar. He was the assistant to Kennedy, you know. We sit down with John Doar. Say, 'They're putting us in jail, Mr. John Doar, every time we hit the street.'

"John Doar said, 'Well, the voting rights law is spelled out in detail more than [the law pertaining to] picketing and demonstrations,' and this and that, and so we came back empty-handed. But came the time when the white power structure said, 'The niggers are out here violating federal laws,' and they landed in thirty seconds. They landed on us all out on our jobs, like bees. And put us in jail. And they carried us to court."

■ ────────────────────────────

Marion King, the pregnant woman who had been beaten and kicked by Mitchell County policemen when she visited jailed demonstrators in Camilla, came to term late in the summer of 1962. Her baby was born dead. Not long afterward, she spoke at a conference of SNCC activists in Nashville. She told them that she had been certain, during "the many days and the sleepless nights of labor," that "the baby would not make it." But she said she wanted to "thank you young people of SNCC for starting something that will not die and that cannot be stopped."[4]

──────────────────────────── ■

Police Chief Laurie Pritchett's popularity was undiminished, at least among white people and white institutions in Albany. As he looks back now on the events of the early sixties, there is little he would apologize for, little he would do differently.

Albany, he said, was a "cosmopolitan city," a place dedicated to obeying the law, a place whose police officers believed in applying the law equally. But it was a city whose white leaders believed in segregation. If there were any partisans of racial integration in Albany's power structure, he said, "they never mentioned it."

The people who came to Albany by train and bus in 1961 and 1962 to test the city's attitudes were surprised by what they found. "We were told when they were coming, and some of what they intended to do. And we had enough time that we could prepare. I think they felt they were coming into a little sleepy town — that they could walk in there one day and the next day the town would turn around and they'd walk out and everything would be different. I think Dr. King was told and thought that he could walk in there, into a lazy little Southern town, and spend the night, and say that he was going to break down the walls of segregation, and the city leaders would do a backflip. And it just didn't work. The whole city — the leaders, merchants, everybody — was behind the police department.

"And the police department was a well-trained police department." He knew that Martin Luther King espoused the Gandhian philosophy of nonviolence and the creation of tensions to challenge the system. "King's philosophy was, 'Fill the jails and they've got to give in to us.' And our plan was *not* to fill our jails; to ship them out as soon as we loaded up. And the men were well trained. They knew the demonstrators' philosophy, and if they were hit they would not retaliate."

Pritchett said that he realized, probably a year before the first outside demonstrators arrived, that Albany's system would be challenged. He said he went to see Mayor Asa Kelley and the city commissioners and told them: " 'Now, look, this is coming. This is coming. We are prepared for it.'

"They were hesitant," recalled Pritchett. "They said, 'Well, can we cope with it?' And I said, 'Yes, I think we can.' And so when it did happen, they had a council meeting. It was closed; it was an executive session. And Asa said, 'Can you handle it?' And I said, 'I can handle it, but I don't want any interference. Now, if I'm going to handle it, it's going to be my responsibility, and I don't want any second-guessing. Because if it goes good, then it's going to be fine. If it goes bad, I'm the one that's going to be hung out.' And he says, 'All right.'

"And, unknown to me, Asa had given the college permission to come up and march. And I didn't know it until just before it happened. Asa came up and said, 'I have given permission.' And I said, 'You mean you have given permission to come up here?' " By "up here," Pritchett meant coming across Oglethorpe Avenue into white Albany and downtown to the city hall.

"He said, 'I told them they could come up and go around the block twice.' And I said, 'Asa, at the end of that two times, they're not going to quit.' They came, and they just kept going and they kept going. . . .

"That was the first little run-in that Asa and I had. I went in, and I said, 'Asa, you put me in a bad situation. My people had the understanding that there would be no marches. Now if you're going to run it, you run the damn thing. I'm not.' And that's when they said, 'You have executive power. Nobody tells you what to do — city manager, the mayor, city council, nobody.' And so they put it on the books, and I guess it's still there. I had the right to close down, open up, do anything that I wanted to do."

The knowledge that he had virtually unlimited power, at least within the borders of Albany, Georgia, made the chief a bit apprehensive, he said. "Later, when we closed the swimming pools down, and we closed the library down, I'm the one who did it. And it was an awesome feeling." But Pritchett said he knew that he was using that power to "keep the peace" and defuse the "potential" for violence. "It gave me the knowledge and the strength to go to my men and say, 'Look, we're running this whole deal now. Nobody's going to interfere with us anymore. We won't have any interference. We're going to do it like we said we were going to do it. And nobody will interfere.' " Once during a particularly tense period, said Pritchett, Governor Ernest Vandiver called and offered to send in the National Guard. Pritchett said he told the governor, "If we need you, we'll call you." Mayor Kelley heard about this and suggested that Pritchett be less harsh with the governor. But Pritchett replied, "Well, if I need him, I'll call him."

Pritchett's recollections conflict with the city's often-repeated statements (and Asa Kelley's comments even now) that the whole thing was a matter of blacks' not obtaining parade permits. Even when the mayor himself had issued such a permit, Pritchett's "executive power" took precedence. The chief's recent comments about who came up with the "executive power" idea also seem at odds with an interview he gave in 1971 to Paul Delaney of the *New York Times*. Pritchett had left Albany to become the chief of police at High Point, North Carolina, where he lives in retirement now. Delaney quoted Pritchett as saying then that he had been just the tool of the Georgia city's rulers: "The power structure in Albany made the law, and I had to enforce it or quit. I enforced the law, but not their philosophy. I didn't agree with their philosophy. The power structure saw the handwriting on the wall but refused to admit it. That was unfortunate. The whole thing could have been done in 1961, and we would not have spent all that time, all that money, and all that energy fighting it."[5]

At any rate, said Pritchett, Martin Luther King arrived and "was arrested. As he told me later, he didn't plan it that way. He didn't plan on coming down. And then when it happened, he had to try to save face. And so he said, 'Well, I'm moving Wyatt Tee Walker, Andrew Young [another top SCLC official, later to become U.S. ambassador to the United Nations and mayor of Atlanta], the whole thing down to Albany.' And that's when we really started going at it."

Pritchett said he was mindful, in the exercise of his extraordinary powers, to stay on the right side of the law. "Everything I did was within the law," he said. "And people can criticize, but when the final chapter's written, they're going to say, 'Chief Pritchett enforced the law. He did not violate any laws. He did it aboveboard. There was no violence. Dr. King left there not an enemy of Chief Pritchett, he left there as a friend.' "

■ ─────────────────────────────────

The police chief also maintained that the arrests he made at the bus and train stations had nothing to do with enforcing segregation. "Never anyone ever proved that I enforced the law to keep Albany segregated," he said.

The evidence contradicts this. The author was present in a combination variety store–pharmacy on the white side of Oglethorpe Avenue in 1962 when one of Pritchett's motorcycle policemen drove up, entered the store, and announced excitedly, "The niggers are coming." Three well-dressed Negroes entered and walked toward the lunch counter. The pharmacist said nothing. The policeman ran in front of the Negroes and extended his arms to block their way. "You're all under arrest," he said. "State trespass law." In what appeared to be an afterthought, he asked the pharmacist if he wanted the blacks arrested. State law required that the operator of the store, not the police, file the complaint. The pharmacist thought a moment and said, yes, he did want them arrested. The policeman called for the paddy wagon.[6]

Pritchett's and the city's use of the "breach of peace" scheme to arrest people who were not breaching the peace at all but who the police claimed might cause *others* to get excited was also firmly discredited. In June of that summer, the U.S. Supreme Court ruled in a Louisiana case that four Negroes who had been arrested under similar circumstances in a bus terminal waiting room had been unconstitutionally convicted. The presence of nonviolent Negroes in a "white" waiting room, even when the Negroes were there by preconceived plan, was not sufficient evidence to sustain a charge of breach of peace, said the court.[7]

■

Chief Pritchett acknowledged that the laws he used to arrest demon-strators were catchall, all-purpose statutes. "They were arrested on what they call white-collar laws," he said. "They were laws such as failing to obey a police officer, blocking traffic, impeding traffic. It was simple laws."

But, he was asked, wasn't that a "trick bag" — a ruse, a subter-fuge?

"I know that is," he replied.

At times in the sixties, Pritchett seemed to be mocking those who, with considerable courage, marched across Oglethorpe Avenue and vi-olated his "simple laws," sometimes by falling to their knees and praying in front of city hall. He also was not averse to playing devious games with his opponents, though he prefers another term.

"We used psychology," he said. "Lot of times I'd tell Ed Friend," the detective assigned to the Movement, to collect another officer and go on a special assignment. "I said, 'Look, y'all go down to Shiloh.' I'd say, 'Go down there, and take your black bag, walk around to the back, like you're slipping up in through there.' And I said, 'Go up under the church, fool around, and then come on out.'

"He said, 'What do you want to do that for?' I said, 'Just do it.' They went down there, and they come back, and, boy, the phone started ringing. 'You put something under the church.' The FBI called: 'They reported that your detectives are over there wiring up the church.' We used psychology on them."

Why? Wasn't that beyond the call of duty?

"No. As I say, we were using psychology. They were trying to second-guess us, and we kept them where they couldn't second-guess us."

Pritchett seemed proud that, after that busy summer of demon-strations and arrests, he received a call from the attorney general of the United States, inviting him to Washington — or at least that is his version of the matter. "At first," he said, "I couldn't figure out what I was there for, why he wanted me up there. Had chauffeurs driving me around, and the head U.S. marshal was there. . . . And finally the attorney general says, 'What do you think your people will do when the public accommo-dations bill is passed?' I said, 'You're referring to the people in Albany.

Because that's the only people I have any say-so with.' And he said, 'Well, yes, because whatever you do there the rest of them are going to follow.' I said, 'I can only speak for Albany, Georgia. When that bill is signed, the president signs it, they'll obey it. But otherwise they won't.'

"And he says, 'I want you to go to work for me.' He says, 'You can go to Jackson, Birmingham — all those Southern cities — and you'll be welcomed.' And I said, 'Yes, Attorney General. If I went as Chief Pritchett, I'd be welcomed. If I went as an FBI agent, or a United States marshal, they'd tar and feather me.' And he laughed. I said, 'I can't work for you.' " On a wall of Pritchett's summer cottage by a lake in North Carolina there is an inscribed photograph of the former attorney general. The inscription reads: "For Laurie Pritchett with best wishes. R. Kennedy." (Edwin Guthman recalled that it was Pritchett, not Kennedy, who initiated the discussions about a job change.)

Pritchett paused in his recollections of the summer of 1962. He thought a moment, and said: "I don't deny and I wouldn't change a minute of it. And it wasn't Pritchett against integration or Pritchett preserving segregation. It was Pritchett enforcing the law as it was on the books at the time." And, he said, it was a matter of Pritchett's non-violence versus the Movement's nonviolence. He said he told his officers, "They're going to spit on you. You don't hit them. They're going to do everything to you. You don't do anything." And it worked, he said. When the demonstrators clashed with the Pritchett police force, "nothing happened. And King could not stand it." And he went home.

The Reverend Samuel B. Wells has a somewhat different version of the way Chief Pritchett's nonviolent army fought its battles.

One day after Dr. King had gone on to other crises, and even many of the SNCC workers had moved on, Wells led a march downtown. By then he was the head of the Albany Movement. Dr. W. G. Anderson had stepped down, and Slater King had taken over the leadership for a while, and then he handed it to Wells. A lot of the activists were tired and discouraged, said Wells, "but I was just as determined then as I was when I first started."

Pritchett's policemen intercepted the march about a block and a half from the municipal building. They placed the marchers under arrest and walked them to the jail.

When the group got to the alley that led from the street back to the jail entrance, the demonstrators stopped moving. They refused to cooperate with the police, a common practice in the civil rights movement by then. "So at that point," said Wells, "we went limp. And so the police — the police had me like this."

He illustrated by placing a hand on his upper thigh.

"And he dragged me out of the sight of the people, the people who were watching, you understand? Then he grabbed me here. You understand what I'm saying?" Wells indicated his testicles.

"And he dragged me into the jail."

Why did he think the policeman had done that?

"Well," said Wells, "he was just trying to be cruel. He was trying to be cruel."

■ ──────────────────────────────

For those who were willing to think beyond the fictitious stereotypes of "outside agitator" and "bloc vote," Albany provided many lessons for and about the nature of the evolving Movement and the resistance to it. One of these concerned the degree and nature of the white community's obsession with spying on the Negroes in its midst who wanted to change the system. Albany, with its emphasis on tight police-state control, afforded a prominent example of this predilection for information gathering. Even at the time, reporters who covered the Albany situation were aware that telephone conversations were not always just two-way, and that informants were constantly on the prowl within the Negro community and elsewhere.

The more experienced members of the Movement assumed that their phones were tapped by the police. They gave the impression, as they conducted their affairs, that dealing with this sort of surveillance was just part of the job description. (Indeed, the FBI had been keeping Martin Luther King under surveillance for years, and in 1963 would start extensive tapping of his telephones at work and home, with the approval of Robert Kennedy and others in the Justice Department.) But in Albany, as Samuel Wells had said, the situation was so bleak that "a hungry dog will eat anybody's crumbs." As Pritchett understood when he sent Detective Ed Friend burrowing under Shiloh Church, the issue of informants and eavesdropping was a volatile one.

At a 1962 mass meeting in one of the Harlem churches, Albany Movement president W. G. Anderson referred to the problem of spies and spying in one of his rousing speeches about the need to sustain the boycott of the city's segregated bus line: "The way is clear but uncharted, with temptation prowling in the shadows. . . . They're down there at the police station offering you five dollars for some information. When they ask you for information about the Movement, you tell them the information is God and unity. We've got to stay together, stick together, keep the faith. That's all it takes. Stay off that bus. Stay off those buses even if they're trimmed in gold."

Now, a quarter-century later, some of those who benefited from the spying are willing to talk about what they did. As often is the case with Albany whites, they seem to feel no need to apologize.

———————————————————————— ■

"I had paid informants going to every damn meeting and tape-recording everything that was said at the churches where King was preaching," said Marion Cheek in 1989. "I knew what the hell they were planning. I knew when the demonstrations were going to come off. Sure I did. I met with the informants till twelve, one o'clock in the morning every damn morning.

"From February until October the fifth of 1962, I did not have one day off. My minimum day was from before seven A.M. until after midnight. One two-month period I stayed at the New Albany Hotel downtown, and my wife would bring me clean clothes about twice a week. I wasn't even permitted to leave town. I had a room right on the front where I could see everything that went on at the police station across the street. Hell, we had informants in the police department who told us what was going on there."

His fishing buddy, Detective Ed Friend, was one of them, said the former FBI agent.

"I had some newspapermen, too." Cheek mentioned the name of a reporter from out of town — not from one of the national newspapers that covered Albany — and he confirmed the suspicions of other reporters at the time that the FBI fed selected exclusive information to this man. It was obvious during the Albany crisis that the reporter received special treatment from the agency and that he found the Movement's aims distasteful.

There were others, said Cheek, in the Ku Klux Klan and in the Albany Movement who received money for their assistance. "I wouldn't tell you the name of a criminal informant for anything on earth," he said. "Those who were in the Klan, I couldn't afford to. And those who were in the Albany Movement, I couldn't afford to. Some of them are still here. And some of them could still get hurt."

During the busy summer of 1962, when mass meetings were being held almost every night, sometimes at both Shiloh and Mount Zion churches to handle the large crowds, Cheek would sit outside in an Albany police car with Ed Friend and his partner. "When the meetings were over," he said, "they'd meet their snitches and I'd meet mine." He added that a white reporter for the *Albany Journal,* a newspaper that circulated in the black community, served as one of his informants. The man "wore a wire into meetings," including mass meetings, said Cheek. In those days the FBI equipped its informants with small, easily concealed wire recorders, which they wore close to their bodies. The machines, which were first used by Nazi Germany during World War II, ran for only thirty minutes, then had to be rewound. "We made them in our lab from the German models," Cheek said with pride. "We used them for our top informants." He spoke with admiration for the local white informant, who is now dead. "He had the balls of a burglar."

Cheek said the FBI eventually conducted surveillance and electronic tapping and eavesdropping — what the Bureau called "technicals" — on King, SCLC, SNCC, CORE, the Ku Klux Klan, "on anything that wasn't pretty well dead center. Hoover wanted informant coverage on everything."

Hoover, it would later be revealed, prized the results of his agents' spying on King because they showed that he was engaged in dalliances with various women — information that Hoover used in his unsuccessful attempts to discredit and silence King. But Marion Cheek said the secretly gathered information on the Movement had another practical value as well.

"It was a help for one reason," he said. "You had a logistics problem. Bear in mind, you're chief of police. You can't give off days. You've got a hundred and fifty men. And to cover a whole town, you've got a hundred of the hundred and fifty tied up on something they're normally not tied up on. You don't have anybody left to work traffic. You've got a few detectives working crimes. Logistically speaking, if you can know when the next demonstration is going to be, if it's two hours from now, you can tell the guys to go take a nap. I'd say if for nothing else, those techs worked to our benefit for that.''

Were the results of the spying shared with Chief Pritchett?

''Some of them were, some of them weren't. Those that would help him logistically, we shared. Those dealing with personalities, we didn't.'' The fact that So-and-so was arriving on the five-thirty Piedmont flight from Atlanta, he said, was an example of intelligence that he would not share with the local police. The fact that a demonstration was going to take place at six P.M. was shared.

What about the information that Martin Luther King was coming to town?

''They knew when he was coming, because he'd call. That was one thing King did. He called you when he was coming. I'd get a call from him at the office before he was leaving Atlanta. And who he was coming with.''

''I had informants in all the meetings,'' said Laurie Pritchett. ''Nothing went on in those meetings I didn't know about.

''I had people wearing wires. They'd come to my room at the hotel, and we'd sit down — me and other members of my staff — and we'd listen to it and then plan. You know, they [the Movement leadership] never could understand. They'd plan to be someplace to demonstrate. When they'd get there, we'd be there.'' He said Movement people then began searching visitors to their meetings. ''But unknown to them, we had people in their organization.''

Who were they?

''Well, I'd rather not say.''

But it's been a long time.

''I know that, but they're still living, and some of them are active, still active, and they carry the reputation as being civil rights fighters, and they were playing both sides of the street.''

The chief's corps of snitches, he said, included some members of the press. Many reporters provided information involuntarily; their telephone conversations passed through the switchboard at the local Holiday Inn motel, which Pritchett acknowledges having monitored. "We knew what was going on," he said. "Everything that went through the switchboard, we knew about."

Pritchett said he didn't have to worry about "most" of the reporters, "because most of them would come over to my hotel room." He named a reporter for the Associated Press who was suspected by several other reporters of being overly friendly with the segregationist forces. Pritchett's interviewer mentioned this fact.

"Oh, he was," said the former chief. "He'd come over there. We'd have drinks. He'd put on my hat, you know, and get up and say, 'Keep moving!' . . .

"All of them . . . they'd come up and give me information. A lot of times I'd play my recording and they'd play their tapes."[8]

Pritchett seemed pleased, even after all these years, with his cleverness. "You know, if it happened that night, the next morning it was all dictated out and copies sent to the mayor. . . .

"I never will forget when we were in federal court [the city's policies were being challenged in a lawsuit], and this fellow come in with black-and-white shoes on and filed a brief as a friend of the court from the Justice Department. We knew when he came in. He flew in. He went downstairs into the airport, rented a car with a Justice Department credit card. As soon as he did, the man that rented the car to him called me. Says, 'He's here. This is his name. He's with the Justice Department. He wanted to know where C. B. King's office was. He was going there.' We put a tail on him."

The man at the car rental agency was not a regular informant, said Pritchett, but rather a concerned citizen. "When somebody came in there using a credit card from the Justice Department, he said, 'Hell, he don't need to be down there. We don't need none of them folks.' So he called." Pritchett said he telephoned Robert Kennedy, demanding to know what the man was doing, visiting Movement leaders and "using public money to haul them around." He laughed and recalled another spy story.

"Charlie Weeks was head of the FBI in the state of Georgia. He was their chief agent. He came down one time, and we were friends — all of us were friends with the FBI. He says, 'Chief, I want to ask you a question. Do you have all these telephones bugged, tapped?' He said, 'We're getting reports that you've got everybody in this town influential's telephones tapped.'

"I said, 'Are you asking me if *I* do?' He said, 'Yes.' I said, 'No, I don't.' Now," said the chief with a sly grin, "he didn't ask me if the *department* did."

Did it?

"Yeah, we had them tapped. And most of the time we didn't have to, 'cause people would tell us, you know."

■ ──────────────────────────

The stone wall that had been fabricated out of local racism and strengthened by federal indecisiveness remained solidly in place, and many of the warriors in the civil rights movement moved on to other challenges. Some — almost all of them the young field secretaries and volunteers of SNCC — stayed. They included the Charles Joneses and Charles Sherrods, those who had signed on for the Movement full-time back when they had believed "full-time" meant a few years. Now they saw otherwise, and they grew weary. "You ultimately get drained," Sherrod was to write.

It was not the arrests and jailings or even the beatings that seemed to bother them so much, but the day-in, day-out grinding effort to accomplish something that they once thought was an American right that, once demanded, would be granted. They had believed a few short years before (though now it seemed an aeon ago) that once America discovered the injustice that infected her system, she would move quickly to eliminate it. Now they saw that America was not much interested in making the change. Some Americans, virtually all blacks and many whites, wanted improvement. But not enough of them to change the system. The federal government itself could not be counted on to support the Movement. Into this void came black nationalists with the message, See what nonviolence has gained you! And out of this void came exhaustion.

Out of it also came a good deal of clinical scrutiny (some of the most exhausted called it postmortem examination) of what Albany meant and how its lessons could be applied to the rest of segregated America. The examination goes on even today; much of it is aimed at debunking the idea, which has wide currency, that Chief Pritchett simply "outsmarted" Dr. King by throwing his own brand of "nonviolence" at him. Those who were the younger activists of the sixties are mildly outraged now at the popular notion that Albany was Dr. King's show, to begin with.

───────────────── ■

Wyatt Tee Walker, King's chief lieutenant in Albany, was and is no great friend of SNCC, but even he agrees that when King answered Dr. Anderson's invitation, he came into a situation over which he had little control.

"We jumped in the fire somebody else had made, reluctantly," said Walker. "Dr. King said, 'I can't refuse to go.' And he went. And then, when he would say something, or his people — me — would say something about how we should do something, it got vetoed.

"We bring in the national press, we bring in the dollars, we bring in the attention, and then the Leader gets vetoed by some youngsters who ain't wet behind the years? *Bullshit!*"

SNCC, he said, "didn't have the organizational discipline. They didn't have any plan. They just went and did things. I called them the Student Violent Noncoordinating Committee." He laughed.

"Oh, they were brave — senselessly brave, in my view. But you look at the age group. They had no mortgages, no car payments, no families. Shit, they could get up and go. I told them, 'I can't do that. I married my wife in 1950. I got a commitment I made to her before this movement got started.' They couldn't understand that.

"I learned in Albany that we made a tactical error. Morally, we were right: Attack evil — segregation. But this was the first time we'd ever been in a revolution. We made a tactical error of assaulting too many things."

─────────────

"Albany was one step in the process no one could figure out," said Julian Bond. "I think it was a defeat. It was a loss.

"I think it was a loss for King, and it was a loss created by their lack of leadership development. They sent all the leadership to jail, and they didn't have a real plan. Albany seemed to be kind of — this is all hindsight — sort of a make-it-up-each-day-what-to-do thing. And then

Pritchett was able to modulate the police response so you didn't have an enemy."

"I think Pritchett was winging it a great deal," said Henry Schwarzschild. "I don't think he was always as foresighted and as insightful as he now claims to be."

Pritchett was aided, said Schwarzschild, by the fact that Albany was a failure for the Movement. "Who was it who said what we ought to do about the Vietnam War was declare victory and leave? Martin tried to do that about Albany, and it was transparently false, and everybody sort of knew it was false. Martin was a little bit too much of a taboo subject for people to say it out loud.

"But I at the time said, 'It's a very bad mistake to declare Albany a victory. I think what you ought to do is go public and declare Albany a defeat. That's more honest and everybody knows you're lying about it right now, and that's not good for us, and because it's a very important way of moving developments along; to say, "Listen, we put everything we had into Albany and the jerks were too strong for us." '

"Now, you know, that's a very important thing to say. It is not chiseled in stone that you're going to win every campaign. Here you invested a great deal and you lost. That's a good thing to say, not a bad thing to say. Your defeats will help you as much as victories."

"The technique varies from situation to situation," said SNCC's executive secretary, James Forman, back in 1962. "We don't really have a formalized approach. . . . It was an experiment. And it worked."

If Negroes in southwest Georgia had had the vote back in 1962, said Laurie Pritchett, "there probably wouldn't have been any of this."

"Down through the years," said Charles Sherrod, who stayed on in Albany, "the only thing that Albany is going to be remembered for, perhaps, is the place in which King failed. The place that got King.

"But I ask the question: How can the Movement have failed when all of the goals that we had in 1962 were accomplished? How can we have failed when we're no longer segregated? How can we have failed when we are sharing the power? Not to the extent that we want to share it, but there's nothing happening in Albany, Georgia, that some black folk don't know about. Or we may not have the economic strength to stop it or promote it, but certainly you got to say that we are in on everything now. They can't ease nothing in here that we don't at least know about. One or two things, maybe, but not a whole lot. Because we've got people everywhere."

Charles Sherrod, in fact, has served several terms as an Albany city commissioner.

"Albany," said Charles Jones, "was the first time we developed a broad grass-roots and total black community involvement in a process that systematically looked at every facet of discrimination and developed programs to deal with them. Its strength was the masses of people — individual people — who committed themselves to freeing up the society."

Martha Prescott Norman was a SNCC field secretary in the sixties. Now an instructor in Afro-American history at the University of Toledo and Wayne State University, Norman was one of many Movement veterans who attended a conference of SNCC activists in 1988. She was particularly interested in seeing that history did not record Albany as a defeat.

"Here it was that a Black Belt community showed the level at which it was going to struggle for civil rights," she said. "When Albany, Georgia, citizens marched to the courthouse by the hundreds in 1961, they said, 'We're going for broke. We're not worried about oppression, we're not worried about our jobs, and we *really* aren't worried about our lives.'

"They were the first to do such. They were the model. They created the mold on which the rest of the civil rights movement was based. Their numbers and their seriousness served notice that the South could no longer maintain its system of racial oppression — because that's all they had to uphold it, the threat of arrest, of beatings, of economic reprisals. When Albany, Georgia, citizens went to the courthouse, they announced that these threats weren't going to work anymore. And I can't see that as anything but a victory."

■ ------

Martha Norman was right. Albany brought an end to what Charles Sherrod had seen when he first visited southwest Georgia: the fear Negroes had of those who would be their masters. When the troubled summer of 1962 ended and many of the Movement people moved on, something was different. Sheriff Zeke Mathews was no longer invincible. Nor was Sheriff Cull Campbell. Asa Kelley and Laurie Pritchett were no longer completely in charge. It turned out, in the words of Wyatt Tee Walker, that Albany was a major failure not for the Movement but for the segregationist white South.

■

Charles Jones, son of a minister, student at a seminary, had been destined to become a preacher himself. But what he saw in Albany changed him.

"In Albany," he said, "one of the 'key' ministers had gone to the mayor and said, 'Please, sir, if you don't mind, we've been good and faithful and we're not like all the rest of them, but if you could just give me and some of my folk a little help, we'd appreciate it.' " Jones's imitation fairly dripped with scorn.

"And C. B. King said" — and here Jones shifted to King's marvelously deep and dignified voice — " 'May it please the court, I represent these people who've been *charged* with trespass. Pursuant to the decision in so-and-so and so-and-so, the actions of the police chief here are totally unconstitutional, and I move that they be dismissed.'

"When C.B. spoke, everybody listened. Whether they liked it or not, they listened. They respected him. Because he had the language of the power, the system, which is what the law is all about. When I heard C.B. talk, and when I saw how he was respected — whether he was liked or not — I knew the way to function effectively in the system was to learn the language of the power. And it was clear in my mind that my best resources were going to be in learning the law and practicing it."

Jones was also dead tired. Although he remembers now that in 1962, in Albany, he was still full of that youthful optimism that denies not only the likelihood but also the possibility of death, some of the tension was getting to him. Once, when he was riding from Americus to Albany, shots were fired at him. "It got my attention," said Jones. "After that, I made sure I was always in the presence of someone else, particularly the press, when we did things. Because people got lost. People got missing."

So Charles Jones left the active Movement for a while. In September of 1963 he entered law school at Howard University and started training for what was to become his present career. But before that, he left Albany and dropped out. He went back to Mexico, where he had had a pleasant time once before, "and just cooled out for a while.

"When I left Albany, I was a hundred and forty-five pounds, I was taking Miltowns, ten milligrams, smoking a pack and a half of cigarettes a day, no appetite, emotionally shot, intellectually drained, spiritually drained. I mean, in that kind of movement, that kind of intensity, you gave everything that you had ever learned or felt. You gave it all. And I was just absolutely drained. Physically, emotionally drained.

"I found, in the native tourist section, a hotel room with a balcony, kitchen, bedroom, living area, cooking facilities, for seventy-five cents a day. Go out to the markets in the morning and get the tortillas, fruit. I'd spend two pesos — eight, sixteen cents. Communicated with people just on an intuitive level.

"I had a terrible toothache. This old lady, *old* lady, just looked at me, and she gave me some whole cloves. She told me to put it in the tooth. I put it in the tooth, and in about fifteen minutes, zap, no pain. And I looked at her. She smiled and walked on.

"For me it was a dimension beyond race, which was very unusual, because you were totally preoccupied in this country, America, with race. Totally."

■ ————————————————

TWENTY-FOUR

∎

A MISSION AND A NERVOUS STOMACH

∎

The next big moment for the civil rights movement, the next big place-name on the road toward freedom, was Birmingham. The Movement organizations needed a Birmingham badly as an antidote to what was widely regarded as the defeat of Albany, and the strategists of the Southern Christian Leadership Conference had barely unpacked their bags from the Albany experience before they began planning their campaign in the Alabama city.

But before Birmingham would come the most dramatic confrontation of the Movement so far — one in which control of events was completely beyond the reach of the civil rights organizations. What happened in Oxford, Mississippi, in the fall of 1962 was the product of the actions of a racist governor, an extraordinarily determined and courageous black man, a handful of federal judges, and, in the end, another handful of uncertain and inexperienced officials of the Justice Department. James Meredith's entry into the University of Mississippi was proof that the Movement belonged to no single organization or group of organizations, nor to any charismatic leader but, rather, to everyone and anyone who had become disgusted with the segregated system and who was willing to exert energy to change it.

James Howard Meredith was a native Mississippian, from Kosciusko in Attala County, in the central part of the state. He returned to his native state in the summer of 1960 after serving nine years in the air force. He then applied for admission at the University of Mississippi.

Meredith is a complicated man, one who does not fall easily into the usual categories. As his ordeal progressed (and it could be nothing but an ordeal for a Negro to attempt to attend the all-white university of the most hard-core segregationist state in the Union), Meredith's nature confounded his enemies, perplexed his allies, and probably saved his life a dozen times.

When he drove home in 1960, Meredith explained later in his memoir of the events, it was with a feeling of "Divine Responsibility . . . a personal responsibility to change the status of my group."[1] He had returned, he wrote,

> to fight a war. . . . A soldier must at all times be ready, without hesitation or question, to die for his country and his cause. That the Negro American was to become legally and officially free and equal was no longer a question in my mind. I was sure that it would become a reality. Whether or not the Negro would become actually and effectively free was not so certain, and it was for this I was prepared to fight. What most Negroes and their organizations were fighting for — the principle of equality, the idea that "I am not inferior to you" — was to me a foregone conclusion. . . . My objective in this war was total victory: victory over discrimination, oppression, the unequal application of the law, and, most of all, over "White Supremacy" and all of its manifestations.[2]

At the time, white supremacy in its most flagrant Mississippi manifestation could be found in Ross Barnett, the governor. Barnett was sixty-two years old in 1960, just starting his term as the state's chief executive officer. Barnett had worked his way through college by selling life insurance policies to — among other classmates — his girlfriends. After graduation, he became a lawyer. According to the *Hartford Courant*, when he was in Connecticut in 1950 trying a damage suit for a construction worker, Barnett became incensed when he discovered that a Negro was eating in the same restaurant with him. He demanded that the owner throw the Negro out. The owner refused, and Barnett, said the newspaper, became so abusive that the proprietor called the police, who took Barnett into custody. He was released without charge after apologizing to the restaurant owner.[3]

Barnett had been defeated in the 1955 campaign by James P. Coleman. In his second run, however, Barnett successfully courted the white supremacist vote; one of his campaign buttons declared "NEVER, NEVER." As Mississippi's chief executive, Barnett devoted some time to seeking industry for his state, and he became the first in his office to appoint two Miss Americas to his staff as honorary colonels. But his major contribution as governor was to insure that white Mississippi became synonymous with racism.

Barnett believed, he said, that "voting is a privilege, not a right," and he placed himself in the camp of the brain-weight fringe by declaring that Americans had been slow to consider the "scientific facts on race and human genetics" because they believed those facts would be "unkind to the Negro." However, Barnett told a Florida Citizens Council meeting, "charity does not include the sacrifice of our children and grandchildren on the altar of mongrelization." His first speech after becoming governor was to a Citizens Council group. The councils had been among Barnett's strongest campaign supporters.[4]

Barnett gave every indication of being a hard-core Southern racist politician, one whose actions were not merely theater, as with John Patterson in Alabama, but rather those of one who truly believed in gut-level white supremacy. Yet when the showdown came, as it would in the Meredith case, even Barnett would reveal himself as willing to sell out his stated principles in a charade designed to please the racists in his audience while masking his collaboration with the federal forces of "usurpation." Barnett's turn on the stage of racial politics included an attempt to make white Mississippians think that he was physically preventing Meredith from entering the university and that he gave in only when forced to by federal armed might. The result was a terrible riot in which 2 persons were killed, an estimated 375 wounded, and a university's reputation shredded.[5]

─────────────────────────── ■

Former governor James P. Coleman is no friend of the late Ross Barnett, who died in 1987. "He's dead, and I don't care to speak evil of him," said Coleman, who went on to speak in terms certainly unflattering.

Barnett got elected, recalled Coleman, on the claim "that I had not done enough, by any means, to preserve segregation." Coleman said he had done a good job of preventing racial violence in Mississippi, and that trouble started only after Barnett took over. "That whole thing at the university could've been avoided easily if they'd done just what I did in the King case, except it had to have been a little bit more stringent." He referred to the case of Clennon King, whom Coleman had tried to have declared insane in 1958 for attempting to enroll in the University of Mississippi.

Coleman said he never would have employed Barnett's trick of seeming to physically bar Meredith's entry, and he expressed scorn for Barnett's attempts to force the federal government to arrest him so he would "become galvanized in public office as long as he lived." The incident at Oxford, he said, "came as near as could be to destroying the state of Mississippi. If four or five coeds had been killed up there, the state of Mississippi would've burned off like a broomsage pasture all the way from Tennessee to the Gulf. It would've been horrible. Thank the Lord, it just didn't happen. And Barnett wasn't up there trying to contain it."

The former governor did not mention that he had publicly backed Barnett at the time. According to a newspaper account, Coleman said he was supporting "the governor and all elected and appointed officials in this matter."[6]

■ ───────────────────────────

Another group of actors in the drama at Oxford included the U.S. Justice Department, its attorney general, and his brother the president. At first, Justice did not consider itself directly involved. But, as was the case in so many civil rights crises, it became drawn into the matter when the decisions of the federal courts were challenged.

The setting for the action was the pleasant-looking college town of Oxford, in north central Mississippi, and the college campus that was Oxford's chief industry. Ole Miss, as the place is called, was typical of many Southern state universities at the time: attractively landscaped, shaded by tall oaks, sleepy looking, not particularly distinguished academically, overly interested in football; the place the sons (rarely daughters) of the state's politicians and business leaders were expected to go before starting their own professions or taking over the family business. Ole Miss was where aspiring lawyers and business managers went. A former professor once described the university's primary national image, though one that was "not entirely of its own making," as "that of a producer of Miss Americas and football teams."[7] The university also was the site of an annual summer school for baton twirlers.

There had been abundant precedent for desegregation of higher education in the South. Black graduate students had been going to formerly all-white schools for some time, and many state-supported universities had bowed to lawsuits and desegregated their undergraduate colleges as well. In some cases the bowing had occurred only in the face of crises and after violence occurred. In January, 1961, two young Negroes entered the University of Georgia under a federal court order to desegregate. The state legislature had relied on a 1956 appropriations act it had passed that ordered the cessation of funds to state schools upon their desegregation. But a federal judge had overruled that law.

It was just as well, some white Georgia politicians said privately at the time. They didn't want the state university — which was the training ground for political and business leaders, teachers and lawyers, and home of the football team that bore the state's honor — shut down. Governor Ernest Vandiver, who had promised to close schools before they desegregated, backed down, uttering the usual lines about federal usurpation — but only after a night of violence had forced the two Negroes, Charlayne Hunter and Hamilton Holmes, to leave the campus briefly. When they returned, they had become the first members of their race to desegregate any level of the state's public education system.[8]

Desegregation in Georgia had come after a good deal of discussion among whites, both in private circles and in government. Even hard-line members of the legislature, which was in session at the time, agonized over the choices they were making. By contrast, the desegregation crisis at Ole Miss took place with virtually no public debate and very little in the way of public discussion. So airtight was Mississippi's closed society that there appeared to be only one point of view, at least in the white community. There were a few exceptions — a group of white clergymen in Oxford heroically spoke out in favor of reason — but by and large, little stood in the way of Ross Barnett's leading "the state toward public insanity," as one observer put it.[9]

Ironically, the event that Barnett and other racists were trying to prevent had already happened. During the height of the crisis at Ole Miss, an extremely light-skinned Negro named Harry S. Murphy, Jr., revealed that he had attended the university in 1945 and 1946 as a participant in the navy's wartime V-12 program, which put students through intensive training leading to their commissioning as naval reserve officers.[10]

Meredith's initial application, which he sent to Ole Miss in January, 1961, was uneventful. He wrote the registrar, asking for application forms. He received the forms promptly, along with a friendly letter from the official, Robert B. Ellis, which said, "We are very pleased to know of your interest in becoming a member of our student body."[11]

The situation changed dramatically a few days later, when Meredith, who conducted all his affairs with great precision and attention to detail and common courtesy, returned his completed forms, along with a note. It started out:

> I am very pleased with your letter that accompanied the application forms you recently sent me. I sincerely hope that your attitude toward me as a potential member of your student body reflects the attitude of the school, and that it will not change upon learning that I am not a white applicant. I am an American — Mississippi — Negro citizen. With all of the presently occurring events

regarding changes in our old educational system taking place in our country in this new age, I feel certain that this application does not come as a surprise to you. I certainly hope that this matter will be handled in a manner that will be complimentary to the University and the state of Mississippi. Of course, I am the one that will, no doubt, suffer the greatest consequences of this event, therefore, I am very hopeful that the complications will be as few as possible.[12]

With the news that Meredith was not white, the registrar's attitude changed with the suddenness of a Mississippi tornado. Ellis sent a telegram:

J H MEREDITH FOR YOUR INFORMATION AND GUID-ANCE IT HAS BEEN FOUND NECESSARY TO DISCON-TINUE CONSIDERATION OF ALL APPLICATIONS FOR ADMISSION OR REGISTRATION FOR THE SECOND SEMES-TER WHICH WERE RECEIVED AFTER JANUARY 25 1961. YOUR APPLICATION WAS RECEIVED SUBSEQUENT TO SUCH DATE AND THUS WE MUST ADVISE YOU NOT TO APPEAR FOR REGISTRATION.[13]

After repeated attempts to work out an agreement with the school, Meredith filed suit in the U.S. District Court for the Southern District of Mississippi. In a class action that sought judicial relief not only for himself but for all others who found themselves in similar situations, Meredith argued that his rejection was based solely on his race and color. The NAACP Legal Defense and Educational Fund, Inc., which handled Meredith's suit, assigned Constance Baker Motley to it. Meredith later praised the choice: "Her assignment is the best possible thing that could have happened. I do not believe that anyone else could have survived two and a half years of Mississippi courts." He also wrote, "I was not apprehensive over the fact that my chief lawyer was a woman, since it was Mrs. Motley." The *Meridian* (Mississippi) *Star*, meantime, wrote that the suit was an "opening wedge" that would surely lead to intermarriage between the races and "the emergence of a tribe of mongrels."[14]

The district judge, Mississippian Sidney C. Mize, was not a white supremacist of the Judge Cox style, but he was no integrationist. Mize, a Franklin Roosevelt appointee, once said in a school case that "differences between Caucasians and Negroes are genetically determined and cannot be changed materially by environment." He ruled on February 3, 1962, eight months after the Meredith suit was filed, that "the evidence overwhelmingly showed that the plaintiff was not denied admission because of his race. . . . The proof shows, and I find as a fact, that the University is not a racially segregated institution." This incredible finding was apparently based on university officials' sworn assertions that segregation did not play a part in their decisions.[15]

Meredith, still hoping to enter the school in the current semester, immediately filed an appeal and a request for an injunction.

The Fifth Circuit Court of Appeals reviewed the case, after repeated courtroom delays by the state, and decided at the end of June, 1962, that Meredith should be admitted.[16] Judge John Minor Wisdom, who wrote the decision, destroyed Mize's decision: "A full review of the record leads the Court inescapably to the conclusion that from the moment the defendants discovered Meredith was a Negro they engaged in a carefully calculated campaign of delay, harassment, and masterly inactivity. It was a defense designed to discourage and to defeat by evasive tactics which would have been a credit to Quintus Fabius Maximus."

Judge Wisdom criticized the state's delay and Judge Mize's part in it, and accused the state of trying to postpone action until it would be meaningless. In the fall of 1960, Meredith had entered Jackson State College, a traditionally Negro state institution in Jackson. Wisdom said the state wanted to drag things out until Meredith, who had accumulated some academic credits in the air force, became a senior at Jackson State and graduated. "It almost worked," wrote the judge.

During the trial, the state had tried in a number of ways to support its position that race had nothing to do with its decision. Housing at the school was overcrowded, they said. Meredith's credits from Jackson State weren't acceptable because the school wasn't an accredited member of the Southern Association of Colleges and Secondary Schools (no Negro schools were). Meredith wasn't trying in good faith to get an education; instead, he was "a man who has got a mission in life to correct all the ills of the world." He didn't have the requisite certificates of good character from Ole Miss alumni. (The state's board of trustees of higher education started requiring such certificates after the *Brown* decision. Meredith, noting that his race made it practically impossible to comply, had supplied recommendations from nonalumni.)

Another reason the school didn't like Meredith, said the state, was that "all letters received by [the registrar] from plaintiff were sent registered mail return receipt requested." And, said the state and the university, James Meredith was "a trouble maker" who had "psychological problems in connection with his race."

This last was purportedly based on a psychiatry report from Meredith's air force service. The young man had voluntarily sought counselling several years before to help with problems he had been experiencing. The counsellor who saw him had started his report this way: "This is a 26 year old negro S Sgt who complains of tension, nervousness and occasional nervous stomach. Patient is extremely concerned with the 'racial problem' and his symptoms are intensified whenever there is a heightened tempo in the racial problems in the U S and Africa."

Judge Wisdom's ruling barely concealed his scorn. He wrote: "It is certainly understandable that a sensitive Negro, especially one overseas, might have a nervous stomach over the racial problem. There must be a good many Negroes state-side with similar abdominal reactions. . . . Meredith's record shows just about the type of Negro who might be expected to try to crack the racial barrier at the University of Mississippi: a man with a mission and with a nervous stomach."

The state's effort to delay the decision into oblivion came close to working. Time dragged on, and Meredith feared that he would graduate from Jackson State without even wanting to, thus rendering moot his application for undergraduate status at Ole Miss. As graduation day approached, the only barrier between him and a degree was the $4.50 fee for a cap and gown. Meredith didn't pay it, and remained an undergraduate.[17]

July, 1962, brought an extended game of cat and mouse. District judge Ben F. Cameron of Meridian, a member of the court of appeals, tried to undo what the remainder of the court had decided. Cameron stayed Judge Wisdom's order pending the state's appeal to the Supreme Court of the United States. When the appeals court set aside the stay, Cameron wrote another one. After Cameron had done this four times, purchasing two months of time for the white supremacists in the process, Supreme Court justice Hugo L. Black reviewed the whole mess, consulted with his colleagues, and told Cameron he was wrong.

It was now September, 1962. A new semester was starting. The nation's highest court agreed that James Meredith should enter Ole Miss. The final round of deadly games began.

On September 4, the Board of Trustees of State Institutions of Higher Learning met and transferred all powers and authority from university officials to itself. A little more than a week later, Judge Mize, acting now in accordance with the higher courts' rulings rather than his own initial one, ordered university officials to admit Meredith. On the same day, Governor Barnett dragged out the old, discarded rhetoric of interposition. He issued a proclamation ordering all state officials to obey state laws in the face of "direct usurpation" attempts by the federal government "and to interpose the State Sovereignty and themselves between the people of the State and any body politic seeking to usurp such power."[18]

Now rulings of the federal courts were being defied. The Justice Department finally entered the case, on September 18, as amicus curiae. At about the same time, federal officials started planning Meredith's entry. They, as well as just about everyone else, based their strategy on the possibility of violent resistance by the state and by individual citizens, and they began thinking in terms of using U.S. marshals to accompany Meredith. Justice officials conferred with state executives — the enemy — about providing protection, to the point that Meredith, whose fearlessness had been monumental, began to be concerned about his safety. He wrote later that he understood the nature of Mississippi whites well enough to know that "I would be doomed the minute [the marshals] withdrew." The fact that President Kennedy had federalized the Mississippi National Guard, a device that would insure that the guard could be employed quickly to do the national government's, rather than Barnett's, bidding, did not make him less apprehensive.[19]

Meredith, who was across the Tennessee state line at Millington Naval Air Station in Memphis, where the United States was staging its operation, discussed this with Nicholas deB. Katzenbach, the deputy U.S. attorney general. He got little response. "I made it unequivocally clear that this was the item of number-one importance, but I was thoroughly convinced after talking to Katzenbach that the federal government would do nothing that it was not forced to do," wrote Meredith. He started wondering if the rumors he had heard about a deal between the president and the governor were true. One version was that Barnett would allow Meredith to enroll if he was accompanied by marshals. Then the marshals would withdraw, and the student would find it impossible to stay in Mississippi. "Under this plan, everybody would have gained, except me and the rest of the Negroes," said Meredith.[20]

The state played one of its remaining cards, the sort of pseudo-judicial trickery that had worked so well in the past. After Meredith had applied for admission, he had registered to vote in Hinds County when he moved to Jackson to attend Jackson State. The state claimed that he was actually a resident of Attala County and thus had engaged in "false swearing." Now, on September 20, the state legislature passed, and Barnett hurriedly signed, Senate Bill 1501, declaring that a person would be ineligible for admission to a state institution of higher learning if he had a conviction or a "criminal charge of moral turpitude pending against him in any court of the State of Mississippi or in any federal court." That same day, a Jackson justice of the peace tried and convicted Meredith in absentia on the "false swearing" charge.[21]

The freshly enacted law, thought the "great constitutional lawyers" in the legislature, would keep Meredith out of Ole Miss because of his conviction. The bill's drafters were clever enough to exclude from its provisions those whose charges or convictions involved traffic laws, violations of the state fish and game laws, and "manslaughter as a result of driving while intoxicated or under the influence of intoxicants." (This last exception was inserted specifically to cover an undergraduate white who had been in a bit of trouble and who wanted to get into the school of law.) The federal courts immediately demolished the "moral turpitude" law.[22]

It was a busy September 20. The state board of trustees met and gave Barnett "the full power, authority, right, and discretion of this Board to act upon all matters pertaining to or concerned with" Meredith's registration, admission, and attendance. Barnett sped to Ole Miss, confronted Meredith in a university office, and read a proclamation turning the student away. The document was festooned with the Great Seal of the State of Mississippi. "When he had finished reading it, he handed it to me," wrote Meredith. "I was finally given a piece of the show, and at least I would have a souvenir to pass on to my children and their children and their children's children."[23]

Meredith said that he had thought, as his convoy of federal vehicles sped from Memphis to the meeting in Oxford, "how utterly ridiculous this was, what a terrible waste of time and money and energy to iron out some rough spots in our civilization. But realistically I knew that this action was necessary. I knew change was a threat to people, that they would fight it, and that this probably was the only way it could be accomplished." Chief U.S. marshal James J. McShane, the giant of a policeman who stuck closest to Meredith, asked the young man how he felt when their car passed the "WELCOME TO MISSISSIPPI" sign. Meredith replied that his home state was the most beautiful in the world, at least in "natural beauty," and McShane was surprised.[24]

The federal courts began finding university and state officials in contempt of court for their behavior. The university officers were let off the hook after they agreed to enroll Meredith, but Barnett was found in contempt, as was Lieutenant Governor Paul B. Johnson, who stood in for Barnett during another confrontation. Johnson got his picture taken shaking a fist at James McShane. Shortly thereafter, the two men shook hands. Johnson used the picture the following summer when he successfully campaigned for governor against James Coleman. At another of their meetings, this time in Jackson, Barnett drew laughter when he was approached by Meredith, McShane, and John Doar, and cracked, "Which one of you gentlemen is James Meredith?" Then he let fly another proclamation, one that "interposed the sovereignty of this state . . . to hereby finally deny you admission to the University of Mississippi."[25]

On the morning of September 26, James Meredith woke early and wrote his last will and testament. He gave it to Constance Baker Motley. It began, "In this time of crisis, I feel it is appropriate for me to clarify my position as to my intention, my objectives, my hopes, and my desires. . . ." Meredith wrote what many of his white detractors could not believe — that his prime object was to "receive the educational training necessary to enable me to be a useful citizen of my own home state of Mississippi" — but he also wrote that the future of the nation and the region depended on "whether or not the Negro citizen is to be allowed to receive an education in his own state." If the answer was no, he wrote, "then democracy is a failure." And: "The price of progress is indeed high, but the price of holding it back is much higher."[26]

––––––––––––––––––––––––––––––   ■

The Freedom Ride had arrived in Mississippi just a couple of days before Constance Baker Motley, in May, 1961, walked into Judge Mize's courtroom to force Ole Miss to admit Meredith. To her, Mize was a "liberal," at least by Mississippi standards. He called the black lawyer "Ms. Motley," while others in the judicial system in Mississippi referred to her as "Constance."

"He couldn't say 'Mrs.' to save his life," recalled Motley. "He said 'Mizz Motley.' He was the first person I ever heard say 'Ms.' "

When Judge Mize finished the case he was trying, he invited Motley into his chambers. "He sat down," she remembers, "and he said to me, 'Why did you have to come now?' The Freedom Riders had come two days before, and Mississippi was aflame. So I said, 'Judge Mize, we don't pick the day.'

"And I'll never forget when the case was all over, and we'd been to the Supreme Court, and the university had been ordered to admit Meredith. I went in with the motion to hold the governor in contempt for calling on all Mississippi officials to resist.

"We were down in Meridian. Judge Cox" — the one who called Negroes "chimpanzees" — "had just been named a judge. Judge Mize was about to take senior status [a form of semiretirement for federal judges]. They were both sitting at the table. We had done these papers very hurriedly because time was running out.

"And I handed a paper to Judge Mize. Judge Cox took it. It said 'Order' instead of what it should have said, which was 'Motion.' That was because my secretary had put the wrong paper on top — the order that he was supposed to sign, rather than our motion.

"Judge Cox threw it across the table at me and said, '*Look* at this: It says "Order." ' And Judge Mize put his hand on Judge Cox's hand and said, 'Judge Cox, it's all over.'

"Actually, it wasn't. It was just the beginning, because the governor then called on everybody in the state to defy it. But Judge Mize was saying to Cox, 'Look, we're federal judges. They've won. You can't fight them. You're the judge. You can't do this.' "

■ ————————————————————————

Unbeknownst to most people, the deal between federal and state officials that James Meredith had smelled was a real one.

As the crisis moved toward its conclusion, Ross Barnett tried to arrange a bit of playacting that would allow the federal government to have its way — enrolling Meredith in the University of Mississippi — but that would certify Barnett as a hero to the state's other white supremacists. The Justice Department's transcripts of telephone conversations between Barnett and Robert Kennedy reveal the governor's true nature in shocking detail. Barnett and his lieutenant were fully prepared to back down and allow Meredith into the university, to change "never" into "right now."

All they wanted was for the federal agents to pull their weapons so they could boast to their constituents that they were forced to desegregate at gunpoint. And Attorney General Kennedy was willing to go along with the theatrics. All *he* wanted was an assurance that the state's highway patrol would prevent any eruption of violence. As it turned out, neither side got what it thought it was bargaining for.

On September 27, the day that the Justice Department planned for Meredith's entry, Kennedy was on the phone to Barnett. The group would arrive at the campus around 5:00 P.M., the attorney general said, and Barnett agreed. (Meredith did not like this idea. Five o'clock was getting toward twilight in the Southern autumn — "lynching time," thought the young black man.)[27]

Kennedy summarized the terms of the deal:[28] "I will send the marshals that I have available up there in Memphis, and I expect there will be about twenty-five or thirty of them; and they will come with Mr. Meredith and they will arrive wherever the gate is, and I will have the head marshal pull a gun and I will have the rest of them have their hands on their guns and their holsters. And then as I understand it he will go through and get in, and you will make sure that law and order is preserved and that no harm will be done to Mr. McShane and Mr. Meredith."

"Oh, yes," replied Barnett. But then the governor, who referred to Kennedy as "General," added:

"General, I was under the impression that they were all going to pull their guns. This could be very embarrassing. We got a big crowd here, and if one pulls his gun and we all turn, it would be very embarrassing. Isn't it possible to have them all pull their guns?"

Kennedy: "I hate to have them all draw their guns, as I think it could create harsh feelings. Isn't it sufficient if I have one man draw his gun and the others keep their hands on their holsters?"

Barnett: "They must all draw their guns. Then they should point their guns at us and then we would step aside. This could be very embarrassing down here for us. It is necessary . . . [inaudible] everyone pull your guns and point them and we will stand aside and you will go right through."

Kennedy: "You will make sure not the marshals but the state police will preserve law and order?"

Barnett: "There won't be any violence."

Lieutenant Governor Johnson: "It is absolutely necessary that they all draw their guns. . . ."

Later in the conversation, Barnett appeared anxious that word of the deal might leak out. Kennedy assured him, "There's not going to be any mention of it from here." Barnett said he had already heard a man predicting that the supremacists — that is, he himself — would compromise. Kennedy jollied the governor along, saying, "You are not compromising. You are standing right up there."

Then Barnett and Johnson started waffling on whether they would be able to assure that law and order would prevail when Meredith entered the campus. "We got a few intense citizens here," said the lieutenant governor.

Barnett asked for more time. "If half a dozen people got killed," he said, "it would hurt me, you, the lieutenant governor, all of us. . . ."

Then Barnett tried to talk the attorney general into using his influence with the courts, which would rule on his contempt citation the following day, to postpone their action for thirty days. Kennedy said he had no control over the courts; he continued to press for promises of law and order. Barnett and Johnson seemed far more concerned that they would be revealed as compromisers; that they might be "embarrassed" by large-scale slaughter.

As the afternoon turned into evening and the Meredith caravan sped down the highway toward Oxford, the Justice Department picked up reports that Barnett's state policemen planned to depart once Meredith was on the campus, leaving his protection strictly in the hands of a few marshals. Already a sizeable crowd of mean-looking white men had gathered around the campus.

Barnett told Kennedy he was worried. "We don't know these people," he said, referring to the crowds. Kennedy said he now believed he should call off the entry attempt. Barnett spoke once more of his personal stake in the drama, as if nothing else mattered:

"There is liable to be a hundred people killed here," said the governor of the state of Mississippi. "It would ruin all of us. . . . There are dozens and dozens of trucks loaded with people. We can't control people like that. A lot of people are going to get killed. It would be embarrassing to me." Kennedy told the caravan to turn around and go back to Memphis and try again another day.

On the next day, the court of appeals found Barnett in contempt, and a day later it similarly cited Paul Johnson. Barnett, said the court, "shall be committed to and remain in the custody of the Attorney General of the United States and shall pay a fine to the

United States of $10,000 per day." The findings were never enforced.[29]

On September 29, a Saturday, as Kennedy and his assistants wrestled with a revised date for bringing Meredith to the campus, Barnett appeared at an Ole Miss football game in Jackson and waved the bloody flag. "I love Mis-si-ssip-pi!" yelled Barnett. "I love her people! Her customs! And I love and respect her heritage!" An Ole Miss political scientist later wrote, "The response was reminiscent of Nazi rallies thirty years earlier."[30]

On Sunday morning, President John F. Kennedy read a proclamation of his own. He called on all persons engaged in the "obstruction of justice" against Meredith's entry to cease and desist and "to disperse and retire peacefully forthwith." He also issued an executive order directing the secretary of defense to take steps to enforce the rulings of the federal courts.[31] The lone student's attempt to enter his state university had grown into an order of the nation's highest courts. The federal government now, finally, was fully involved. Meredith's entry was imminent. Reporters from around the world flew into the Memphis airport, then rented cars for the hundred-mile trip past the "WELCOME TO MISSISSIPPI" sign through rolling countryside to Oxford.

■

It was the kind of lazy, early fall Sunday afternoon that is especially lovely on a college campus. But not this one.

Enormous military airplanes touched down at the tiny Oxford airport, a few miles from the campus. They took practically every inch of runway to land. Then they disgorged federal marshals, border patrol officers, and prison guards. The men carried white helmets and billy sticks that looked brand-new, and they wore side arms and were equipped with tear gas masks and canisters. (It would not be generally known until later that the guns were not loaded, on orders from the president and the attorney general. The federal officers kept their bullets in their pockets or in their hands.) As the officers made their way to Ole Miss, James Meredith, John Doar, and James McShane drove onto the campus and went to Baxter Hall, a men's dormitory. The officials installed Meredith in a two-room suite (a federal man would be staying with him), and Meredith turned in for the night. He said later that he did not hear the disturbance that followed.

The central object of the Ole Miss campus, architecturally, is a grassy oval, thick with old oak trees. At the top, or twelve o'clock, of the oval (which is known as the Circle) is the Lyceum Building. The administrative offices were there. Every college campus has a symbolic center of attention, and the Lyceum served this purpose. This handsome old building with six white columns had served as an emergency Confederate hospital during the Civil War. Now the officials from the Justice Department installed themselves in the Lyceum and set up a command post. Around the perimeter of the oval were other campus buildings, most of them nondescript, as if they had sprung up at odd intervals without much concern for one another.

There were few students in the Circle at first; many of them apparently were still returning from the football game in Jackson the day before. By contrast, hundreds of people had gathered a short distance from the foot of the Circle on University Avenue, where a railroad underpass marks the beginning of the campus. Several highway patrolmen maintained an outpost at this point, passing onto the campus only a few of those who applied. Among the crowd were dozens of reporters and young people, male and female, who appeared to be students.[32] There were others, too: males who were too old to be students, and dangerous looking. Local people had noticed that many automobiles with licenses from other Southern states — Alabama, Georgia, Texas — had been coming into Oxford all day, and that some of the cars contained three, four, or five men. The mood was expectant and angry and noisy, but mostly it was excited, charged with a current of anticipation.

The reporters urged the patrolmen, as reporters always do, to let them onto the campus. At first the answer was no. Then, as if by a prearranged command, the troopers seemed to melt away. Everyone surged up the short block to the foot of the Circle, then hurried, some running, across the grass and past the monuments to the Lyceum.

There the crowd found its target. Many of its members may truly have believed that James Meredith was inside the administration building, and truly may have wanted to pass the marshals to get to him. But it is far more likely that the crowd's needs were satisfied by the marshals themselves. They stood there along the Lyceum's steps in their white helmets, looking apprehensive and scared and touching their billy sticks as if to make sure they were still there. Some wore suits; others wore windbreakers. All of them wore the uniform, invisible but unmistakable, of Federal Power.[33] In front of the marshals was a line of olive-drab all-purpose military vehicles, ten-wheeled trucks with removable canvas covers over their beds that had been used to carry the marshals from the airport to the campus. Beyond the trucks was a handful of Mississippi highway patrolmen. Just beyond the patrolmen, on the edge of the Circle, the mob gathered.

At first there were taunts. Then the crowd threw a few harmless objects at the marshals. Then the harassment became more serious, almost in direct proportion to the increasing darkness. People in the crowd threw burning objects at the federal officers. The yelling got louder, the insults sharper. The tension was palpable. One young man who looked like a student asked a white reporter where he was from. When the reporter replied, "Atlanta," the young man shouted, "Let's get this nigger-lover," and slugged him. When a motion picture photographer, Gordon Yoder, and his wife drove along the perimeter of the Circle, they were stopped by hundreds of rioters and their car was attacked. Highway patrolmen helped the Yoders escape. One of the military trucks burst into flames. The reporter from Atlanta looked around and realized that the highway patrolmen were no longer standing between the mob and the marshals. Before long, the state officers had disappeared entirely. Now there was a full-scale riot in progress.

The marshals had stood firm in the face of attacks by rocks, soft drink bottles, and lighted torches, and now the abuse got worse. Shortly before 8:00 P.M., Chief Marshal McShane gave the order for the marshals to use tear gas. The federal officers put on their gas masks — a sure warning that they were about to use the substance — a full ten minutes before the first canister was fired. But the mob did not back away. Rather, it got bolder.

The first eccentric spirals of smoke shot across the top of the Circle, and they were followed immediately by the odor and eye-piercing sensation of tear gas. Some members of the mob retreated, but then they surged forward again. Claude Sitton, of the *New York Times*, knew that his deadline was approaching. He had to leave and get to the telephone in his room at the Ole Miss Motel. Sitton gave the keys to his rental car to the reporter from Atlanta and asked him to drive the car over to the reporters' motel when the mob calmed down. The car was parked at about ten o'clock on the Circle, between some of the rioters and the marshals.

Inside the car, the reporter was relatively protected from the sickening fumes of the gas, although he felt danger from the mob swarming around him. The men in the crowd were calling now for the destruction of anyone who was not obviously one of them. The reporter wondered what he might learn if he turned on the car's radio. He slipped the key into the ignition and clicked the radio on. The dial light was soft, and it did not give away the reporter's position.

He was amazed to hear the voice on the radio was that of the president of the United States.[34] John Kennedy was telling the nation that "The orders of the court in the case of *Meredith versus Fair* are beginning to be carried out. Mr. James Meredith is now in residence on the campus of the University of Mississippi. This has been accomplished thus far without the use of the National Guard or other troops — and it is to be hoped that the law enforcement officers of the state of Mississippi and the federal marshals will continue to be sufficient in the future. . . ."

Outside, the tear gas formed a thick, nauseating cloud across the top of the Circle. The "officers of the state of Mississippi" were nowhere to be seen.

"All students, members of the faculty, and public officials in both Mississippi and the nation, it is to be hoped, can now return to their normal activities with full confidence in the integrity of American law. . . ."

An old fire truck, loaded with rioters, drove up the middle of the grassy oval and headed, like a battering ram, directly at the marshals. For some reason, it veered off, sputtered, and stopped short of its goal.

The president continued with his speech, which he was delivering live but obviously in ignorance of the true situation on the Ole Miss campus. Actually, it was more of a defensive lecture than anything else: an explanation of how the case had been brought; how the federal government had *had* to be involved once its courts' orders were defied; how Kennedy regretted the fact that any action by the executive branch was required, but that "other alternatives and avenues" had failed. The president carefully named the fifth circuit judges involved in the Meredith decisions, pointing out in each case their home states — Georgia, Texas, Alabama, Florida, Louisiana. He spoke of the university's "great tradition" of "honor and courage, won on the field of battle and on the gridiron as well as the university campus."

Having covered all the bases believed to be of any importance to white male Mississippians — war and football being prime among them — Kennedy ended his statement. "The eyes of the nation and of the world are upon you and upon all of us, and the honor of your university and the state are in the balance. I am certain the great majority of the students will uphold that honor."

"Kill the nigger!" a young man yelled on the Circle. A tear gas grenade, resembling a child's twisted pinwheel, its red paint singed off, shot across the tenuous, narrow gulf and exploded at his feet. The young man tried to pick it up and throw it back at the marshals. He was absolutely enraged.

■ ─────────────────────────────

When it was over early in the morning, two persons had been killed. Paul Guihard, a reporter from France, was shot in the back at about 9:00 P.M. Ray Gunter, a local man, was shot at about 11:00 P.M., apparently while watching the riot. Their assailants were never arrested. Hundreds of others, most of them deputy marshals, border patrol officers, and federal prison guards, were wounded. The Lyceum once again served as a military field hospital. Snipers fired during the night at the marshals and virtually anything else that moved. Some of the shooters did not even seek the traditional concealment of snipers; they stood on open ground and fired away at their targets. Two bullet holes in the trim around the Lyceum's massive front door were visible a quarter-century later, though efforts had been made to cover them with wood filler.

During the night, the Mississippi National Guard moved onto the campus to assist the federal officers. The majority of the guardsmen must have personally deplored the idea of a black man's entering the university, but the federalized units performed as they were ordered to.

In the morning, federal officers woke James Meredith and told him what had happened. They escorted him into the Lyceum, through the back door, to register for the fall semester. Both entrances to the Lyceum are on the grand scale, and Meredith said later that if he had known he was going in the back door, "I would have had to confront the question of whether this was a concession to the Mississippi 'way of life.' "[35]

Behind a desk was Robert B. Ellis, the registrar who had changed moods so quickly when Meredith informed him he was a Negro. Meredith recalled that among those in the administration building — there were wounded marshals, as well as rioters awaiting interrogation by the federal forces — "he was a lone stand-out, the only man on the scene with spirit — a spirit of defiance, even of contempt, if not hatred." John Doar explained the little group's purpose, and Ellis pointed to a pile of forms that Meredith would have to fill out. At 9:00 A.M. James Howard Meredith attended his first class — in colonial American history.

That night, October 1, 1962, Ross Barnett, apparently still concerned about personal embarrassment, went on statewide television and said the violence at Ole Miss had been caused by trigger-happy federal marshals. The marshals, he said, deliberately started the riot as an excuse to bring in army troops. The governor's lie could be, and was, refuted by any number of people who had been on the scene.[36]

───────────────── ■

A few weeks after the riot, Justice Department officials assembled several of those who had represented the federal government, including marshals and border patrol officers, and conducted a critique of the operation.

"Our conclusions," said Ed Guthman later, "were that we had contributed, either by negligence or mistakes, to what happened down there." There was much, he said, "that we had failed to do [and] things that we might've done in hindsight that would've made a hell of a difference."

For example, said the former press aide to Robert Kennedy, the federal forces knew little about the physical layout of the campus. Only John Doar had spent sufficient time in Oxford to know how to get around the place. "We didn't know a goddamn thing," said Guthman. "We were just put in there on a Sunday. We were running out of tear gas and there was more tear gas at the airport. But if John Doar hadn't been there, none of us would've known how to get to the airport. It was that simple. We didn't have any medical equipment with us. We didn't have a Band-Aid with us. The United States took four and a half hours to come sixty miles."

Guthman was referring to the military's extremely slow response in moving troops and equipment into Oxford. "Anybody who's been in the service knows they always have these wonderful plans," said Guthman. "You cross the line of departure at eight-oh-five and at eight-thirty-three you reach such-and-such a point. Well, you know it never happens." Barnett's double cross was part of the problem, as was the fact that the Mississippi highway patrol "evaporated in the night." And, said Guthman, it is important to understand that in 1962, the term "high technology," if it existed at all, certainly did not mean the sophisticated communications and computer equipment of today. The Justice Department used government-issue pencils and yellow legal pads and ordinary telephones to conduct most of its business. Particularly telephones.

"We're in the Lyceum Building," said Guthman, slipping into the present tense. "We'd put the marshals in. What is the first thing we do?

"We put a dime in a phone, and we rang up the Justice Department. We opened up another phone in the office where Nick [Katzenbach] was — that was to the White House — and we never let those phones go.

"We got instantaneous communication with the White House, so Nick is telling them what's going on. And meanwhile, [Defense Secretary Robert] McNamara's sitting over in the Defense Department getting *his* information, and he's calling over to the president and saying, 'The troops are arriving,' and Kennedy knows they're not there. McNamara's information is all coming from the [army] signal corps, which is forty-five minutes behind what's really going on.

"Anyway, about four days after the riot, the president wanted Nick and me to come up and brief the cabinet on the whole thing. So they sent a JetStar down to Oxford, and we went out to the airport, and there's a two-star general from the signal corps there. And he asks Nick, 'Can I get a ride back to Washington?' Nick says, 'Sure.'

"So we're on the plane, and the general says, 'I'm General So-and-so from the signal corps. I want to tell you, Mr. [Deputy] Attorney General, that this is the most embarrassing experience of my life. I've just had my ass chewed out. Every time we reported something to the

Pentagon, they would come back and say, 'You're half an hour late, and the president already knows that. Your information is wrong, whatever it is.'

"He says, 'You guys had tremendous communication. How in the hell did you do it?' And Nick reaches into his pocket and he takes out two dimes."

■ ───────────────────────

After he entered Ole Miss, James Meredith was harassed everywhere he went on the campus. He was always accompanied by Justice Department personnel. He believed that they and the Inc. Fund were conspiring to make sure that whenever he left the campus he also left Mississippi, preferably for the safer precincts of Memphis. Although the university maintained that it was "outside agitators" who had caused most of the trouble on the night of September 30, it was clear that students set off the fireworks in his dormitory and students jeered at him on his way to class. Back in Kosciusko, the home of Meredith's parents was shot up by night riders.

The university found itself under fire from the Southern Association of Colleges and Secondary Schools, which was alarmed at the blatant way in which the school had allowed politics to interfere with its conduct of academic affairs. The association threatened to withdraw Ole Miss's accreditation unless there were assurances that such meddling had ended and would not happen again. On November 15, 1962, a few days before the association was to consider the case, the school turned out a self-serving report making the case for "outside agitators" and engaging in syntactical acrobatics over the difference between "political interference" and "political pressure." In the end, however, the school never dealt seriously with the issue of punishing students who rioted or engaged later in harassment.[37]

On January 7, 1963, Meredith, always a man for surprises, announced that he would not register for the coming semester unless "very definite and positive changes are made to make my situation more conducive to learning."[38]

Segregationists were overjoyed; this meant their harassment techniques had paid off. People in the Movement were appalled, along with those in the Justice Department who had put so much effort into getting Meredith in and who now feared it would have to be done all over again. Meredith thought the matter over. On January 30 he announced his final decision at a crowded news conference.

"I have concluded that the 'Negro' should not return to the University of Mississippi," he said. A white radio newsman from Jackson broke into applause.

"However," added the young black man, with his impeccable timing, "I have decided that I, J. H. Meredith, *will* register for the second semester at the University of Mississippi."[39]

On August 18, 1963, in the middle of Mississippi's high summer, James Meredith gathered with 440 other Ole Miss students in the university's library, where federal officers had bivouacked during the previous fall. A Negro employee of the university tugged at a rope, and chimes started ringing from the bell tower. Meredith and the others, wearing black caps and gowns, marched double-file through the Lyceum Building, down the steps, past the place where the marshals had stood off the attack, and onto the shady, grassy grove of the Circle. The minister of an Oxford Methodist church delivered the invocation. "We live in a difficult time," he said, "when it is apparent that men do not love one another." He called for "love out of hate, hope out of despair." One by one, the graduates stepped forward to receive their diplomas. When his turn came, Meredith received his degree, a bachelor of arts in political science, from Chancellor J. D. Williams. In the audience, with only a few empty folding chairs around them, were Meredith's wife and young son and his parents, Mr. and Mrs. Moses Meredith of Kosciusko.[40]

Meredith, a man to whom symbols meant a lot, that day wore the same clothes that he had worn on the afternoon he entered. Beneath his flowing graduate's gown, he wore a Ross Barnett campaign button, the one that said, "NEVER, NEVER." Meredith wore it upside down.[41]

TWENTY-FIVE

■

NOT ANOTHER OXFORD

■

The debacle at Ole Miss, like the other crises in the era of civil rights, provided some lessons of incalculable value.

Once again, the Movement and the rest of America saw how far the federal government would go and how forcefully it would act to bring equal rights to all its citizens. Unfortunately, it was not nearly so far and forcefully as possible or necessary.

The Kennedy administration's reluctance to get involved until it was pushed was revealed this time in public statements. The president, in his oddly timed address to the nation as the riot was mounting, heaped praise on Mississippi whites and came close to apologizing for having to enforce the decisions of the federal courts. It was those courts, he said, that required him to act: "My responsibility as president was therefore inescapable." Robert Kennedy, reviewing the administration's actions two years later, said he and his brother sent federalized troops to Oxford "because there was a violation of a court order."[1]

The scene at Oxford also demonstrated that the administration was continuing to think of Southern white supremacist politicians as honorable, honest public servants — as people who would treat the volatile, raw-nerve issue of segregation as if they were playing a game of croquet on the grounds of the Kennedy family compound in Hyannis Port, Massachusetts, with devotion to the rules of the game and handshakes all around when it was over. Boston Irish politicians such as the Kennedys should have known better. But they and their advisors insisted on adhering to what author Victor Navasky has called "the code of the Ivy League Gentleman," a doctrine that included "the assumption that negotiation and settlement are preferable to litigation" and that "reasonable men can always work things out."[2] By 1962 there was such an abundance of evidence to the contrary that an observer would have been forced to consider whether the Kennedys wanted to be fooled by the Southern racist politicians, or whether, while not being fooled for one moment, they feared for the votes the racists controlled.

Worst of all, the administration was continuing to show that it preferred to play the role of follower, not leader, in the civil rights struggle despite the moral mandate with which it came into office. The administration's stance was reactive — a term that could easily be translated into "timid."

Ole Miss provided some glimmers of hope, as well as causes for alarm. Events preceding the riot showed that even white Mississippi had limits beyond which it hesitated to go. Despite his deceptions, Ross Barnett demonstrated, by his very willingness to cut a deal with the federal authorities, that he lacked total commitment to the racism of "Never." He showed he was only another Southern white supremacist politician who, like the John Pattersons and Ernest Vandivers, was willing to playact before his constituents.

Of course, many of the constituents believed the rhetoric and conducted themselves accordingly — hence the Oxford riot. Still, if a politician could bend his beliefs in one direction, he might be moved to bend them in others, as well. Perhaps even more significant was the way in which officials of the University of Mississippi, the trustees of higher education, and others who valued learning in the nation's most backward state scurried around trying to prevent the loss of their school's accreditation.

The affair also showed that one determined Negro could make

a big difference. James Meredith proved that the Movement did not always require the combined efforts of thousands of people, arrayed beneath the banner of this or that civil rights organization. The banner could be carried by anyone — provided he or she was brave enough to risk death. It could be carried even in the face of the formal Movement's reluctance. (Robert Kennedy, in 1964, said the Inc. Fund's Thurgood Marshall had told him Marshall "had tried to discourage" the Meredith suit.)[3]

Ole Miss was different from other milestones in the Movement's history. Here was organized, deadly violence, condoned and augmented by the actions of the state's chief executive and tolerated by almost the entire white community. But even this had its positive side (although that might provide small comfort for the friends of the dead and wounded). Officials and leaders of opinion in other communities started talking about not wanting to become "another Ole Miss" or "another Oxford."

It is easy to forget that violence in 1962 was far less prevalent than violence in the 1990s. Mississippi and the South (and, for that matter, the nation) were dangerous places in the sixties, but the violence was not as commonplace as it would be in later years. The builders of the Civil Rights Memorial in Montgomery, which was dedicated in November, 1989, counted nine persons who had been killed "during the struggle for equality" between May, 1955, and the Ole Miss riot.[4] By the violent standards of the late eighties and nineties, that would have to be referred to as *only* nine deaths.

The era of assassinations had not yet begun. Candidates for president, and even presidents themselves, felt free, and even obligated, to plunge into crowds to shake hands and kiss babies. The presidential security detail, the Secret Service, broke into cold sweats at such activities, but the assumption was that American society was too open for them to be prohibited. Bulletproof vests were not yet standard issue for public figures. People had not yet become inured to accounts of violent deaths in the dozens or hundreds; a good argument could be made that society placed greater value on human life then. The fact that two people were killed in the Ole Miss riot was truly shocking for many Americans, as was the fact that one of them was a reporter. So the events at Oxford were regarded by many other communities in the South as something to avoid — and the more intelligent leaders saw that the only way to avoid an Ole Miss was to desegregate. Ross Barnett's "Never" helped many other political and business leaders say "Now." Unfortunately, these lessons, though valuable to the majority of the South, were largely lost on white Mississippi itself.

In the South outside Mississippi at the end of 1962, there were signs here and there that the resistance was beginning to crumble. The smarter political figures knew that change was coming, or that it had already arrived, and they started remaking their personalities. To be sure, they did not all proceed at the same pace; in some places they did not proceed at all. And in most communities, the progress did not occur in a straight line. Rather, it happened sporadically, some of it voluntary and some only after agonizing direct pressures from the Movement and the courts. It was as if the region were going through a particularly difficult first labor; it was giving birth to an idea, a new entity, that was at the same time inevitable, painful, and frightening.

Frequently, the change occurred in communities where a measure of progress had been made before, only to be followed by a lull. This produced an effect that some people referred to as the "second wave." There was one example of this in Nashville. Mayor West's conversation with Diane Nash on the steps of city hall in 1960 had resulted in a few accommodations between the city and its Negro residents, but there was much more to be done.

The second wave of confrontation and negotiation in Nashville occurred around 1962. The students from Fisk and the other black schools who had brought the sit-ins to Nashville were gone now, many of them to centers of Movement activity in Georgia and Mississippi. But the job they had started back home had not been finished, and a new generation of activists, combined with local residents who were still fed up with segregation, replaced them.

Although the variety and department stores had desegregated their lunch counters, many public accommodations remained segregated. Negroes were becoming angry about the slow pace of change. There were boycotts, and there were fistfights. Will Campbell, the white Baptist minister who was a pilgrim to the Movement, remembers that the city was "in a state of near chaos" when the assistant chief of police roared up to his little house one day, red lights on and siren blaring, to deliver the mayor's plea for help, terrifying the neighbors in the process.

Ben West had been succeeded as mayor by Beverly Briley, and Briley wanted Campbell, who was drawing a small stipend from the National Council of Churches, to head a new city human relations committee. The job would pay nothing and Campbell's directorship would not be announced, which was fine with the preacher, who by now was certain he could do more good by operating from a low profile.

Campbell and the assistant chief rode downtown, where tense demonstrations were in progress. Mayor Briley presented his new troubleshooter with the list of the new committee's members. It was the day of the steeplechase, an annual event in Nashville.

"He said, 'What do you think of my human relations committee?' There was every major insurance company president and every bank president. I said, 'Well, I notice you don't have any ministers on this committee.' And he called me over to the window, and he said, 'Do you see that restaurant down there?' He pointed to a place down the block. 'It's been in business eighty years. And it's been segregated every day of those eighty years. If the preachers had done their job, I wouldn't be up here on Saturday getting these bank presidents and insurance executives off the golf links and away from the steeplechase. I'd be out there watching the horses race. They haven't helped me, and now they can't help me and they can't hurt me, so fuck 'em. I don't need 'em.' And that was the end of that. And he was right."

Campbell says he believed the mayor thought of him less as a preacher than as "someone who he thought understood the black community. He thought that I had more influence in the black community than I really did, and I didn't tell him any different."

Members of Nashville's white establishment, Campbell learned, assumed that the Movement had a leader, a single person who spoke for the entire community. No amount of explaining otherwise could make them abandon that notion. Eventually the committee dissolved, but in the meantime Campbell did what he could. "They would say, 'Who do we talk to?' and I would say, as I did on a few occasions, 'Talk to your chauffeur.' Or, 'Talk to your housekeeper. *They* come to the rallies and the mass meetings that are being held in churches all around the city every night.' ''

_____

It was about this time that Will Campbell received word that he had better not go home to see his parents in Mississippi anymore. He had visited from time to time on important occasions — funerals, weddings, holidays — and now he heard from his father that there were people back home who were enraged over Campbell's activities on behalf of integration: '' — that if I came home, I would never leave.''

A young man who knew the elder Campbells had overheard his own father confessing tearfully to his mother that the decision had been made to kill Will Campbell. As the story was relayed to Nashville, the informant had said, ''Pappa was crying and about half drunk and was telling momma that he and ———— had to kill Will, and he was crying because he didn't want to.''

''There was no real personal hatred of me,'' said Campbell as he recalled the incident. ''It's like if my little dog goes rabid, I have to take him out behind the barn and shoot him because he is a danger and a menace.

''And I had gone rabid. I was a traitor to the community, to the South, to the family, and to the faith. I was a communist, in their mind. They were going to kill me, really, out of a broken heart.''

_____

Campbell never thought of himself as a crusader, but rather as someone who was merely doing what he thought his Christian faith required. He learned early on that not everyone in his calling felt the same way. ''I'm not a very religious person,'' he said. ''I'm a Christian, but Christianity is not very religious.''

While the Movement hardly could have been what it was without the black church, Campbell feels, ''ninety-nine and forty-four one-hundredths percent of the white church was uninvolved and ineffective. It didn't really try. Now, I understand that. It has to do with the nature of institutions — that they're not going to do anything that threatens the harmony and the growth or, in essence, the life of the institution. By then it exists for its own purpose, for its own self, for self-perpetuation.''

There were prominent exceptions to the rule of noninvolvement by white organized religion. One of the most valuable was the American Friends Service Committee, which maintained a small staff in the South that worked hard to facilitate communication among the various factions. Another was the Episcopal Society for Cultural and Racial Unity, founded in early 1960 to move the Episcopal church into a more active role in the Movement. The society received little help from the formal church, however.

"If a white minister started rattling the cage in which he was existing," said Campbell, "he's not going to receive approval and adulation. He's going to receive rejection: 'Let's get rid of him.' So that when I say that the white church was ineffective and uninvolved, I'm not passing a judgment on my white brothers and sisters who were caught up in that. I'm passing the judgment on the institution. The nature of religious institutions is like all other institutions. Now, the institution of church, even the white institution of church, I think, could *produce* the crusaders, the radicals. But then it would reject them when they tried to practice within the household that had produced them."

■ —————————————————————

Ernest F. Hollings served as governor of South Carolina from 1959 through 1963. In those years and the several that preceded them when Hollings was a local-level politician, he managed to avoid the image of the hard-core, Barnett-type white supremacist. Hollings's name did show up, however, in accounts of Southern governors' gatherings where resistance was discussed, such as one held in 1961 in Jackson to plan "a positive program of economic and governmental cooperation" against "the enemies of the South." Hollings also appeared on films produced by the Citizens Council, and, as a legislator, in 1951 he sold the idea of a sales tax to benefit education as a device to continue segregation. But it was clear that Hollings knew the true score. He knew, furthermore, that the South's racial animosities were hindering progress that the region badly needed to make.[5]

On January 9, 1963, Hollings delivered his farewell speech as governor to the South Carolina legislature. Hollings (who later would go on to become a popular U.S. senator) reiterated some of the points he had often made as governor — the need for South Carolina to improve her educational system, to harvest what he called "the space age forest," and, above all, to recover from "the hangover of a hundred years of poverty." At the end of his address,

Hollings came, as a Southern politician must, to the central question of the region. He said, as Judge Mize had told Judge Cox in Mississippi, that it was all over:

> We have all argued that the Supreme Court decision of May, 1954, is not the law of the land. But everyone must agree that it is the fact of the land. Interposition, sovereignty, legal motions, personal defiance have all been applied. . . . And all attempts have failed. As we meet, South Carolina is running out of courts. If and when every legal remedy has been exhausted, this general assembly must make clear South Carolina's choice — a government of laws rather than a government of men. As determined as we are, we of today must realize the lesson of one hundred years ago, and move on for the good of South Carolina and our United States. This should be done with dignity. It must be done with law and order. It is a hurdle that brings little progress to either side. But the failure to clear it will do us irreparable harm.[6]

———————————————————— ■

Among those South Carolinians who read the governor's remarks with interest was Harvey Gantt. After leading the sit-ins in his hometown of Charleston, Gantt had decided to become an architect. As the winner of a National Merit Scholarship, he could have entered almost any college with a school of architecture. A handful of traditionally black schools offered architecture, but Gantt's counsellors thought it wise for him to attend an integrated school. That, of course, meant a school outside the South.

Gantt agreed. "I said to myself," he explained later, "that clearly this is one of those professions in which by far the predominance of the practitioners were white. It made some sense to me to go to a school where *they* were going, where they were getting *their* education. And I needed to get out of the South." In 1961, Gantt entered Iowa State University.

"I chose the Midwest primarily because I'd been a football player in high school," he said. "I was always enamored of the Big Ten and the Big Eight and those big power football conferences, and I got the mistaken notion that this was probably an area of the country that was probably more democratic than anywhere else. There were probably lots of black kids on these campuses, and the state schools were reasonable in trying to get out-of-state students.

"Plus South Carolina was very generous" — he smiled — "in offering help to its black students who wanted an education, in the areas that were not available in the black institutions. They would give you the difference between the in-state and out-of-state tuition, and one round-trip ticket."

An unfriendly roommate helped Harvey Gantt discover on his first day in Ames that the Midwest was not a racial paradise. "I found out that there were lots of different kinds of 'niggers.' People with black skin were 'niggers'; Catholics were 'niggers.' In other words, people were prejudiced, and there were second-class citizens in the minds of a lot of folks, other than just blacks — whereas in the South, I thought we were the only group that was being discriminated against." He also discovered that in many cases, the black athletes from Midwestern schools whom he had seen on television were the only blacks on those campuses.

"So it was lonely. And it was cold, and it didn't make sense. And it didn't take me long to figure out that I didn't like that situation." Gantt also discovered that his idea about joining an old-boy network of architects worked only as long as he remained in Iowa. His classmates were headed toward Des Moines and Davenport, and they would stay in touch with each other. A state university, he realized, produced educators, lawyers, and architects for that state — people who would use the connections formed in college for the rest of their lives, as long as they remained within the boundaries of that state. But Gantt had no plans to stay in Iowa. He wanted to go home.

About then, he read that Clemson Agricultural College, as it was known then, had one of the twenty best architectural schools in the nation. Clemson was in South Carolina. "It was like that," said Gantt, snapping his fingers. "It made sense to me. But it made even more sense to me because I had been introduced to the civil rights movement in 1954." Gantt remembered his experiences with segregation in high school, and the logic of it all struck him face-on: "Why should I be out here in Iowa going to school, when I could be in South Carolina? One thing led to another, and I applied."

Gantt's initial dealings with Clemson paralleled James Meredith's experiences with Ole Miss. His letter of inquiry in January, 1961, brought a quick and courteous reply, but when the color of his skin became known he got a rejection notice. Gantt waited a year and applied again. Nothing happened. So he and the Inc. Fund, with the indefatigable Constance Baker Motley and South Carolina civil rights lawyer Matthew Perry in the front lines, brought suit in July, 1962. When Governor Hollings told the legislature on January 9, 1963, that South Carolina was running out of courts, he was correct. A federal district judge from South Carolina who lacked even the learning to capitalize the word "Negro" had ruled against Gantt's entry, but his decision then went before the court of appeals. One week after Hollings's speech, that court ruled for Gantt, declaring that South Carolina's practice of shuttling Negro students to out-of-state colleges was not only illegal under *Brown* but also violated even the spirit of separate but equal.[7]

When Gantt entered Clemson on January 28, 1963, the nation and South Carolinians could think of only one thing: Ole Miss. But by the end of the first day, Clemson had become the example of proper school integration, and Ole Miss the aberration. Gantt, surrounded by a swarm of reporters and a huge number of state policemen, both in uniform and plain clothes, entered without incident. He stayed there two years, worked hard, earned his degree, and became an architect.

The state's police presence seemed to melt away almost immediately after he entered Clemson, but Gantt discovered otherwise one day. "We played a joke," he recalled. "Some kids from the architecture school and I were heading back from lunch to the school, and we faked a fight just to see what would happen. A couple of people who looked like students came out of the woodwork and said, 'What's going on here?' So then we knew that we were being watched fairly closely by unobtrusive security people."

Gantt had some theories about why his experience was so remarkably different from James Meredith's (or, for that matter, from those of Charlayne Hunter and Hamilton Holmes in Georgia and Autherine Lucy in Alabama). One factor was the school's decision to deal firmly with any students who harassed Gantt — a dramatic contrast to the near-total lack of discipline at Ole Miss. Since Clemson was seeking accreditation as a university, it had something to lose. Combined with that was his classmates' tendency to accept his presence on the campus, once they realized that he was a serious student. His first semester grades were A's and B's.

Another theory has to do with South Carolina's fundamental nature.

"South Carolina was one of the thirteen original colonies," Gantt said. "And it always was a state dominated by the planters from Charleston: country gentlemen, polite. I always said you could appeal more to their manners if you couldn't always appeal to the morality of a situation. It was manners over morals."

It occurred to Gantt, as he watched his suit being tried in the federal courts, that mixed in with the state's arguments about the unconstitutionality of *Brown* was a "kind of casual conversation that went on between counsel from both sides about the inevitability of this whole thing. It was a little deceitful to a young eighteen-year-old listening to some of this. It suggested that all of the so-called opinion makers in that state, the policy leaders, understood that it was just a matter of time.

"There's no question in my mind that they considered themselves aristocrats: stiff upper lip, don't like it a damn bit; we're gonna fight it to the end. And that's all that whole charade of the trials was. It was: 'This is the way we demonstrate to the rednecks that we're sincere.' Constance Motley brought that out. She asked, 'How many dollars are you spending to fight this young man going to school here?' And [the state replied], 'We're going to fight this and exhaust every available remedy that's legally available to us.' Once that was done, then they could sit back and say, 'Now we're not going to do what Mississippi did.' "

This theory was supported by the history of the Southern resistance movement. But Gantt still wonders about one thing: "There's a question always in my mind," he said, "as to whether my theory of the manners-over-morals issue would have come to play had Mississippi not occurred.

"Meredith's situation in Mississippi was the worst thing that had ever happened with regards to the civil rights movement. The kind of thing that happened on the Oxford campus just sent a message right on through the whole structure of Southern leadership, in my opinion.

It was, 'Jesus Christ, you know, we don't really want that kind of thing to happen.' "

His colleagues at Iowa State who knew that Gantt was seeking a transfer to Clemson watched the events in Oxford and told him, " 'You've got to be crazy to want to do that. How are you going to study something that's as difficult as architecture in that kind of environment?' And I kept saying, 'Something tells me it'll never happen that way in South Carolina.' "

▪ ─────────────────

Elsewhere in the South and nation, examples of progress were almost invariably accompanied by steps backward. Leroy Johnson, a black man from the Atlanta area, was elected in 1962 as the first Negro to serve in the Georgia legislature in close to a century. His election contrasted with the puzzling behavior of Atlanta's mayor, Ivan Allen, Jr., who was widely thought to favor peaceful desegregation and who had been put into office by the city's downtown power elite (with support from the black voters) to do just that. In that year he welcomed the NAACP's annual convention to his city with a promise that Atlanta "will have the courage to face these problems" of race "that have hovered over us so long."[8] But in January of 1963, Allen erected a barricade across one of the city's roads in an effort to maintain the status quo in housing. White families lived on one segment of Peyton Road and blacks on the other, but the city made the division between them glaringly real by building the wall. James Forman of the Student Nonviolent Coordinating Committee showed up at the barrier one cold day to light a "freedom torch," constructed of Sterno and aluminum foil, and Mayor Allen's mistake quickly became known as Atlanta's Berlin Wall.

───────────────── ▪

"It was such a dumb move," said Julian Bond, who was active full-time in SNCC in Atlanta at the time. He had skipped his final semester at Morehouse College in the spring of 1962 and was SNCC's communications director. "It was so incredibly dumb. What was it Mayor

Hartsfield [Allen's predecessor] said? 'Never make a mistake they can photograph.' "

Bond said that Atlanta's movers and shakers, despite the image they promoted of themselves as progressive minded and eager to escort the city safely past the issues of race into an era of economic abundance, were nonetheless reluctant to face change.

"They portrayed themselves as people caught in the middle," he said, "and they made plays for our sympathy. It was, 'We want to do it; we'll be willing to do it. It's just these wild klansmen out here who will cause the trouble.' I think they much exaggerated the strength of that group of people. I don't think they were any real kind of threat. I remember when we locked the Klan up in the Krystal downtown, and they were afraid to come out."

Bond was referring to a demonstration in downtown Atlanta at a popular fast-food restaurant called the Krystal. The Negro demonstrators were inside the Krystal when a phalanx of Ku Klux Klansmen, resplendent in white muslin robes, trooped into the place. The Negroes left and picketed outside the entrance, and the klansmen seemed afraid to leave. "You could see these middle-aged guys in their hoods and stuff — they didn't have masks on — and they looked like, 'I mean, you know, we didn't *count* on this.' "

■ ───────────────────────

In Alabama, conditions worsened. George Wallace had undergone a racism transplant since he had campaigned unsuccessfully, with NAACP support, against John Patterson in 1959. Now, in 1962, Wallace was opposed by former governor James Folsom, a six-foot eight-inch man of gargantuan appetites who railed against the people the common folk of Alabama loved to hate: the "big mules" of industry and finance. Folsom tirelessly and correctly accused these powerful people of deliberately pitting race against race, class against class.[9]

Big Jim, as he was predictably known, might have done well against Wallace, who had been his campaign manager and speechwriter in 1954, and who now was calling himself "the fighting little judge from Barbour County" who refused to kowtow to the federal usurpers and mongrelizers. But on the eve of the election,

Folsom appeared on statewide television in a state of almost knee-walking drunkenness. Wallace rolled over him.

In his inaugural address in January, 1963, delivered at practically the same moment that Ernest Hollings was telling South Carolina the fight was all over, Wallace was shouting that it had just begun. "I draw the line in the dust and toss the gauntlet before the feet of tyranny," he screamed, "and I say segregation now, segregation tomorrow, segregation forever."[10]

It became more apparent, as the Movement passed its formative years and headed toward a sort of maturity, that there were distinct differences among its numerous organizations and personalities. Within the Movement itself, the arguing could be quite forceful, as it would be in any collection of people engaged in a tense, dangerous battle. And, just like military commanders, the leaders of the Movement did not want their arguments reported in public.

One wide-open secret was the fact that Roy Wilkins of the NAACP did not like the way either the Southern Christian Leadership Conference or the Student Nonviolent Coordinating Committee conducted their business. The leaders of these groups tended to classify Wilkins's objections as simple jealousy. While SNCC, which would have felt unfulfilled without criticism, seemed to accept Wilkins's sniping as part of its way of life, Martin Luther King and SCLC tried to make peace and minimize the friction. Said Wyatt Tee Walker in later years: "Dr. King made a summary decision that we wouldn't be a membership organization simply because Roy Wilkins got nervous that if we went to membership, it would cut into their funds. Dr. King always took the back seat." King also went out of his way to help the NAACP and repair interorganizational rifts whenever he could. When the organization held its 1962 convention in Atlanta, King was a speaker. He warned about "outside forces" who might stimulate discord among the rights groups, and added: "The demands of today are too great and the issues are too serious for any of us to be involved in ego-battles and trivial organizational conflicts."[11]

Except for the reluctant enforcement of federal court orders, the national government pursued civil rights objectives in fits and starts. When once again it was discovered that edicts ordering armed forces desegregation that dated back to Harry Truman had accomplished far from enough, President Kennedy appointed a commission to study the matter. By 1962 Negroes were about 11 percent of the national population, but they made up only 3.2 percent of officers in the army, 1.2 percent in the air force, 0.3 percent in the navy, and 0.2 percent in the marines. On the other hand, some 13 percent of all federal employees were black.[12]

Shortly after the Kennedy administration had taken office, the executives of a number of private corporations, all of them defense contractors, signed a pledge that they would work affirmatively for equal employment opportunities. Kennedy called it "an historic step forward." But when a reporter checked on how the signatories' Atlanta offices and facilities were doing more than a year later, he saw that Plans for Progress, as the program was called, might have brought some change on the national level, but in the South it was more publicity stunt than sincere effort. Some regional executives had never heard of the program. One said, "They don't mean regional divisions like us." Another justified his lack of participation by explaining that he ran "a sales and service office. We don't have any manufacturing in Atlanta" — a clear indication of the sort of employment for which he thought Negroes were fit. An official at a Ford assembly plant acknowledged that there were no Negroes among the plant's 250 salaried workers. A Pan American Airways executive explained, "Even though we're an international firm, we have to be localized in Atlanta." A manager for Kaiser Aluminum said, "It would strike me as rather ridiculous to hire someone [such as a Negro] for an outside sales responsibility. . . . If we had a lot of Negro customers, we would have a Negro salesman."[13]

President Kennedy sent voting rights legislation to Congress in early 1963, but at the same time his civil rights expert and resident federalism scholar, Burke Marshall, explained to Leslie Dunbar of the Southern Regional Council why the president could not ask Congress to set a deadline for school desegregation: "I am afraid that the problems of enforcement in some places . . . are almost insurmountable under the federal system." At that time, less than 8 percent of all Negro pupils in seventeen Southern and bordering states and the District of Columbia attended integrated classes.[14]

In Washington, there were hints from the veteran activist A. Philip Randolph that a march on Washington might help things. There were noises from the administration that such a demonstration would be inadvisable.

Although segregationist federal judges at the district level, some of them Kennedy appointees such as Robert Elliott in Georgia and Harold Cox in Mississippi, continued to serve blatantly as part of the white opposition, the federal courts on balance moved toward making the Constitution available to all Americans. The appeals courts, and in many cases the lower ones as well, stepped up the process of overruling state and local courts' convictions of Movement participants on various charges. They also endorsed Negroes' efforts to get past the obstacles to desegregation that had been erected by local school boards and other official bodies. They threw out the charge of "interfering with police in the discharge of official duties" in Charleston, South Carolina. They enjoined the commissioners of Harris County, Texas, from running a segregated park. A federal court declared Georgia's bus segregation laws to be unconstitutional. One particularly effective district judge was Elbert Tuttle of the Fifth Circuit Court of Appeals in Atlanta.

Predictably, the state courts and the "great constitutional lawyers" were hard at work trying to postpone the day when desegregation would finally come. A court in Louisiana allowed the city of New Orleans to deny Negroes permission to hold a meeting in the city's auditorium. The Maryland court of appeals affirmed the convictions of demonstrators on criminal trespass charges. In Alabama, a circuit court permanently enjoined the NAACP from doing business in the state. But there were bits of hope even here. The Georgia court of appeals reversed a lower court's conviction of demonstrators for "parading without a permit." Slowly, very slowly, the South was changing.[15]

Or much of the South. The hard core continued to draw the line in the dust and toss the gauntlet and scream, "Segregation now, segregation tomorrow, segregation forever," even when it knew that the fight was over, the battle long ago lost.

TWENTY-SIX

MISSISSIPPI: CAUGHT UP IN THE TRADITION

White Mississippi, having furnished the horrible example of Oxford, seemed determined to be the last place to benefit from it. Except for the university's frantic scurrying to protect its accreditation, there was little evidence that the people in power felt any need to change their ways. There were, of course, whites who didn't have much power who nevertheless did what they could, through their limited bases in religious groups and the like. But white society in Mississippi was so closed that these people always travelled a fine line between being able to speak their minds and having to flee the state in the middle of the night. Those who were in power showed every sign that they still believed they could hold back the tide with the old standbys of legislative and administrative smoke and mirrors, "interposition" rhetoric and other political fantasy, and intimidation and violence against those who dared not conform.

Yet there was a hint there of a white Mississippi that could change — or, as the optimists saw it, of the Mississippi that would exist *after* the change. That wisp of hope was invisible among the state's rulers — the elected and appointed officials, the Sovereignty

Commission members, the Citizens Council "elite" — but it did surface every now and then among the ordinary citizens, the people in whom change would have to occur if it were to be meaningful. It was these people who best expressed what L. C. Dorsey, the young woman who had been raised on plantations, called Mississippi's essentially contradictory nature.

———————————————————— ■

There had always been, in the Negro community, the notion of the "good white man." It was an important, perhaps crucial distinction to be borne in mind by a black person, who could suffer mightily from a chance confrontation with the obverse of that coin, the bad white man. L. C. Dorsey and her then-husband were chopping cotton in a plantation field in the spring of 1959 when a white man told them how to make sure a lynching victim's body would disappear.

The white man, like all members of his race in Mississippi's system, was clearly the Negroes' superior — at least as designated by the system — but he was hoeing in the fields alongside the blacks. Mack Charles Parker had just been lynched in Poplarville.

"What they did, ordinarily, was put people in the bayou," said Dorsey. "They could weigh you down with cinder blocks. And I learned from this white man that we were working with how to make sure they never came up. I mean, we were all in the field chopping cotton together, and he was explaining to my ex-husband how you made sure they never surfaced again. You put the cinder blocks around them and you also slashed their stomach. So there's no gas bubbles.

"Now, I'm grown at this point. It's 1959. And I remember thinking, 'Here this man is out here talking to us, and he's the only white person in this field.' The rest of us had weapons — those hoes. And we could've chopped him up. But he was telling us how, if *he* had been in the crowd that got Mack Charles Parker, the body never would've been found."

Perhaps the man was just showing off; indulging in some perverse form of braggadocio?

"No, no indeed. This was a *good* white man. He was not showing off. No, no, no. He was just saying the guys who did it were stupid. They didn't know to let the bubbles out of his stomach. No, he was making a technical observation about the procedure of how you do stuff. And he was not making some complicated point. He was an uneducated person. I think we can say that he was caught up in the tradition.

"He would never have been out there for the lynching, but if he *had* been out there, he certainly would've done it right. This is how you have to interpret that conversation. And this is the guy, incidentally — when my house caught fire and we were in the field with the kids at home alone — this was the guy who went to the house and went into the burning house and made sure all my kids were out. So it's part of that complexity that is the Southern life."

Another facet of the complexity was the knowledge, shared especially by those who were bad white men but also understood by the good ones, that at some distance beneath the surface — and they never knew how far down — the mistreated Negro had the power to strike back. It was a danger with which guilty whites lived constantly. And in the societies where the most repression went on, as in Mississippi, the danger was greatest.

L. C. Dorsey's father got caught one time picking cotton on somebody else's plantation. "He would slip off early in the morning before it was light," she recalled, "and go to another place where he was picking cotton to earn money so we could eat. That place was paying more money than we were getting on our own plantation." But the rules, she explained, were that you worked only on your home plantation. "That was standard procedure on the plantation. You belonged to the people while you were on the plantation. You didn't go and work anyplace else.

"Somebody told the boss man that he was doing that." The boss man drove to the farm where Dorsey's father was working, she said, and brought him back. "He planned to whip my daddy. He was going to take him down to the shop, where the tractors and stuff were, 'cause that's where he whipped people. At first, he brought Daddy back to the field and told him, 'Now you get out there. If you want to pick cotton, you pick cotton for me.' But then he changed his mind and said, 'Get on in this truck. I'm going to take you to the shop.'

"We *saw* all this. We were in the field. We saw this happening.

"Daddy never said a word. He turned right around, got back in the truck, and in getting in the truck — See, he carried a pocketknife, a little

Barlow pocketknife. He opened the blade of the pocketknife, and he said later that his plans were that before they killed him at the shop, he was going to stab this man, and he was going to throw sweeps at everybody.

"You know what a sweep is? It's like a plow, but it's just a blade part that you attach to a piece of iron bar that you hook behind the tractor. You attach them with screws, big screws, long screws with nuts and stuff. And you had them all stacked up in the shop, because you took them apart so they could be sharpened. They took those things off at the end of the cultivating season and got them cleaned up and ready for using next time.

"And Daddy said he intended to do nothing but just walk in there with them and when they reached for him he intended to grab a bunch of sweeps and start throwing and hitting people with them.

"He knew he could've been killed. He anticipated his death. 'Cause he wasn't one to take a whipping."

But Dorsey's father did not have to throw the sweeps. The truck started off toward the shop, but then it stopped and Mr. Dorsey stepped down from it.

"The white man stopped the truck," said Dorsey. "He drove about as far as from here to the door, stopped the truck, and told him to get out and go on out there and pick cotton.

"I'm sure he sensed that Daddy's response was too quick, and he thought, 'This is somebody I'm going to have to kill.' I'm sure he was thinking, 'If I do this with him, I'm going to have to kill him.' And he just decided it wasn't worth it, and he put him out. And I'm thankful he did, 'cause Daddy would've been killed. And perhaps this man would've been killed. And we would've had trouble, then, the rest of our lives.

"So that's the only time I know of that anybody messed with Daddy."

▪ ————————————————————

Through the summer and fall and winter of 1962, the hint of hope that white Mississippi would change was a tiny one indeed. In black Mississippi, though, there was excitement and enthusiasm nonetheless. The young organizers, most of them from the Student Nonviolent Coordinating Committee, spread optimism wherever they went, even though their presence always brought with it risk and danger. They worked in tandem with local leaders, many of them affiliated with the National Association for the Advancement of Colored People, and under an umbrella program known as COFO.

The Council of Federated Organizations had existed before as a loose coalition of organizations working on civil rights in Mississippi. In April, 1962, the Voter Education Project was formed to coordinate voter registration work and to manage the foundation money that Robert Kennedy had helped to gather. VEP chose COFO as its vehicle for distributing funds in Mississippi.[1] The arrangement sounded efficient and effective. Wiley Branton, VEP's director, was a lawyer who worked well with people of diverse backgrounds and philosophies. The project had the backing, not to mention the money, of respectable and prominent members of the foundation world. The reputable Southern Regional Council served as VEP's general overseer. The attorney general of the United States had helped found the effort. But for the campaign to produce any results, people had to go out on the highways and dirt roads, to the plantations and Deep South courthouses, and risk their lives.

By the end of 1962, the issue of federal protection for civil rights workers, including those whose work consisted of trying to register the voters whom the government said it wanted to register, was clearly settled. Washington would not provide protection. It might file some suits to restrain white officials from denying black people the right to register and vote, and it certainly would enforce the decisions of its own courts when they were flagrantly challenged. But the activists who had gathered to hear Robert Kennedy urge a swap of provocative demonstrations for voter registration, and those who followed them into the bowels of the beast, were very much on their own.

--------------------------------------- ■

Hollis Watkins quickly became familiar with danger. He liked to say that *any* Negro in Mississippi was in danger, but the sort of work Watkins did — registering voters, conducting demonstrations right on the steps of the state's meanest courthouses — put him in a special category.

It also put him in jail a lot, which in the Deep South meant danger indeed. Watkins was asked if he felt, at the time, that he was risking his life. He recalled a time when he was being questioned by the police in McComb City Hall. "Three men in plain clothes walked into the room with a rope that had the hanging noose in it, and says to me, 'Okay, get up, nigger, let's go. We going to have a hanging here tonight, and you going to be first.'

"So I looked at them, and they came a few steps, and they looked at me, and they turned around and left. So, now, is that coming close to losing your life? You don't know. I have no idea why they left. I have no idea.

"And the time when they moved me from the city jail in McComb to carry me down to the county jail in Magnolia, they led me down through the mob of people. But was that close? I was only kicked a couple of times, in the ankle."

There was another time, when Watkins and some other SNCC workers were travelling to Atlanta for a meeting. They stopped for gasoline and used the rest rooms at a service station. The owner of the business met them on the way out with "a long .38" revolver and shouted, "Git, nigger, git." And there were the times klansmen and Citizens Council members chased the activists in pickup trucks, and there were the people who followed them everywhere in unmarked cars. "So I knew something could happen to me," said Watkins. "I knew the possibilities were there. But I tried to carry the whole thing of what I was doing to another level, which was a spiritual level, because I believed that what I was doing was part of the work of God.

"I had that kind of faith and confidence in the Creator that because I was doing part of His work, I would be able to come through it. Now, I felt that even though I would come through it, there would be times when I perhaps might be beaten or what have you, but generally what I would do in each situation was just ask for the protection and ask for the knowledge and guidance as to what to do, when to do, and how to do it in those situations." Watkins believes this faith "prevented a lot of things from happening that normally could've happened."

One example, he said, occurred while he was in the county jail in Magnolia. "The jailer told me that they were going to let me out, let me go, because I hadn't done anything wrong. He said that they had looked at the laws and saw that I had not broken a law because that law was not constitutional, and that they were going to let me go. And something within me asked the jailer who was it that put up my bond, and where was my lawyer."

The jailer didn't have ready answers to Watkins's questions, and that made the young man suspicious. "I told him I needed to make a phone call, because I needed to stay there until somebody came and picked me up. And then he told me that, no, he was going to put me back in jail. But before doing that he told me to look around the corner. I looked, and they had some bloodhounds that they were going to turn loose on me had I walked on away. They were going to say that I was trying to escape. And that could have led to my death."

One other time, the white authorities tried the ancient trick of manufacturing an incident in which an outspoken black man could be punished by the judicial system if the lynch mob didn't get there first. Watkins was confined in a cell with others when a white woman appeared in front of the cell door. The woman, who appeared to be drunk, told a story of having been beaten by the police. She raised her dress and showed Watkins "deep bruises and scars up near her vagina."

Watkins didn't believe the woman was drunk, and he didn't believe her story. He assumed that the plan was for the woman, acting in league with the police, to claim that the Negroes in the cell had raped her through the bars. Watkins went to the rear of his cell and stayed there.

These attempts did not surprise Hollis Watkins or the other activists, nor did they succeed in advancing the whites' goal of intimidating black people into the perceived servility of the pre-Movement days. Watkins does not think his tormenters were particularly intelligent. "I knew about prejudice and how it existed in the hearts of a lot of the whites," he said. "And I think that the whites really felt that the blacks would crumble under just the pressure of being in jail. That's what they were really hoping and banking on. As far as their overall intelligence was concerned, naturally it was not something that was great. Most of the officials we saw were not well-educated people. When we looked at the county registrars across the state, a lot of them didn't have eighth-grade educations. And then you had the people like the jailers, the sheriffs, and the police.

"I think they definitely underestimated our motivation and our ability to endure and our willingness to fight until the change comes about.

I think they really figured that they would arrest a few people and perhaps beat a few and possibly kill one or two, and that would turn everything back around. Because that's what they were used to. You know, if you're used to doing something, then you stick with what has worked for you in the past."

The whites clung tenaciously to their position, he felt, because they had profited greatly from the racist system and wanted to keep it. "And I think they were convinced that once they arrested a certain number of us that they called the leaders, then nobody else would take up the initiative. Then in a little bit of time everything would die down. You got the leaders in jail and you've scared off the followers through some acts of violence and burning of a cross or burning of a building. And by the time that the leaders get out of jail, they'd have no followers, so you've destroyed the whole movement.

"See, the jail was a place that people subconsciously and consciously feared and were afraid of. That was a place you definitely didn't want to go, because there was a history of once you get in there, of sometimes having to stay there for years and years and years. And then when you're in there, you're subject to being beaten. You're subject even, ultimately, to being killed. So that's a place you don't want to go. So the thinking was, 'We can throw them in that place where they don't want to go, and start arresting a whole lot of them, and then that's going to put fear into the minds of the other folks that's out there. And if they fear that their turn is coming, then they'll back off of it.' "

■ ───────────────────

The technique did not work, however. Hundreds, thousands of people who once had been terrified of what could happen inside a jail deliberately took actions that they knew could put them behind bars. Veterans of the Movement are in almost total agreement that the major source of this fearlessness resided in blacks' intense commitment to religion. As Charles Sherrod had found when he went to southwest Georgia, anyone hoping to advance the Movement had to take the black churches into serious consideration. Sometimes, though, as Sherrod had also found, a community's existing church structure was not ready for the Movement, or it actively fought change.

■

"The courage was already there," said Watkins. "I think the courage was born in them, you know. All of the hardship that blacks had gone through had helped to build that courage. I think it was just a matter of motivating blacks to the extent that they saw that something was worth fighting for and really standing up for. And they saw that for the most part nothing could happen to them that wasn't already happening. So if can't any more happen to you than is already happening, and by you taking a stand you can bring about the possibility of changing things that would lead to the betterment of your condition, the condition of community, county, state as a whole, then, hey, we might as well go ahead and stand."

That was the message Watkins and others relayed when they went door to door in the Negro community, and at mass meetings, which invariably took place in churches. "You put it in a religious context," he said. "You related it to things in the Bible."

This could be difficult. The black church traditionally had taught the lesson of there'll-be-a-better-time-in-the-by-and-by, which ran precisely counter to the Movement's argument that improvement could be had right now. "Naturally, you had to fight that," said Watkins. "And in a lot of cases you didn't have the minister. But you had the people, you had the physical building to hold your meeting in, and you had a certain percentage of the congregation that you could deal with. And you had to fight against some of those things. But it was not that hard. The problems you had to fight had come about as a result of the ministers' teaching certain scriptures in the Bible without going to some of the *other* scriptures. And you could lay the Bible open yourself and deal with the scriptures. The people know the Bible; they know the scriptures. It's just that they hadn't thought about it. It had never been said to them. So you said it to them. You talk about the other scriptures, and you do more motivating. And your motivation is genuine because it has a great purpose rather than the motivation of a lot of the ministers. Their motivating purpose really was to get some money out of the people and keep them subjected to the point that they will continue to do that."

Watkins said that, in some cases, the ministers declined to make their churches available for mass meetings. Then the activists would go to the congregation members themselves, who would exert pressure on their pastors to open their churches to the Movement. Once that happened, the Movement was installed in a community. "Once you got up in the mass meeting," said Watkins, "you definitely had equal status, or greater status than the minister."

■ ————————————————

Hollis Watkins was one of those who spoke in 1988 at the Hartford gathering of former SNCC activists. He told his audience that one of SNCC's greatest contributions when it went to places such as southwest Georgia and Mississippi was its effort "to educate, motivate, and inspire people from those different areas to get up and do something and take some initiative upon themselves."

One of those places was Hattiesburg, a town in southeastern Mississippi that sorely needed a voter registration campaign. Watkins remembered that when he and fellow activist Curtis Hayes set off to organize Hattiesburg, "we had reached the level of being a SNCC field secretary — proud, determined, prepared to take on the world if necessary. Had a little money in our pocket — SNCC gave us fifty dollars to go to Hattiesburg to set up a three-months' voter registration." His audience laughed at the idea. But such shoestring ventures were the rule, not the exception, in the Movement days.

———————————————— ■

When Hollis Watkins and Curtis Hayes got to Hattiesburg with their fifty dollars, they found Victoria Gray, the black woman who had caused a stir when she phoned a radio call-in show to point out that Mississippi was *her* home, too.

"They came in with the understanding that they would be talking with people in the different churches and that sort of thing," said Victoria Gray Adams later. "And unfortunately, NAACP, in its determination to protect its turf, as it perceived it, had . . . sent word . . . that [local leaders] were to make sure that these guys didn't get into any of the churches.

"What it all boiled down to was that these two young men all of a sudden found themselves with a message but no place to give it. And they'd been given all the information about where they had to go in order to get into the black community. 'You have to get through this preacher, because if you don't get through him, you ain't going to get in, because he controls the black community.' " To further complicate matters, said Gray, one of the black ministers was widely suspected of being an informant for the Citizens Council. "He was *the* person who, whatever he said, is what the people in the black community would do," she said. "And that was true about a certain portion of the black community, but it wasn't a portion which I moved around in.

"Anyway, it was brought to our attention that Curtis and Hollis had no place to go. I said to them, 'I'm quite sure you can do it at my church.' My church was in Palmer's Crossing. It was called St. John's Methodist Episcopal Church, at that time. So my pastor and some members of his official board met and said, yes, we could use St. John's. And so that's how it started. That's where the Hattiesburg movement started."

There was no doubt, she said, that voter registration was what was needed in Hattiesburg and in the state generally in 1963. "In Mississippi it was the only way to go. That became vividly clear very early. I always say, if you're going to try to do something to change things, just look for something meaningful, something radical, *really* radical, something that *really* could bring change. And voting was in that category. Absolutely. There is no question about it. Without that, you have nothing else, you know."

Voter registration did not begin in Hattiesburg with marches down to the courthouse, but with citizenship education classes. SNCC and other Movement groups active in the vote drive had learned by now that such classes were an important way to prepare people intellectually for the grueling process of trying to register, to minimize their well-placed fear, and to confuse the local white leadership.

"In the beginning," said Victoria Gray, "we held these meetings under the guise of adult education classes." At the same time, people who had attended the classes were going down to the courthouse to register, but the whites did not immediately make the connection. "And I would imagine that by the time they made the connection, everything was full swing."

There was fear, she said, as always. But the unity and the singing helped black residents of Hattiesburg control that fear. "I can remember the first night in my very first class. We always sang 'We Shall Overcome.' And this was the first night of the first class and here we were, hands together, about six of us. I was the teacher. And I looked around that room and I thought, '*We* shall *overcome?* This is the most ridiculous thing I've ever seen. What do I *mean,* We shall overcome?' What were we going to overcome? I looked at the people: two or three who were learning their ABC's, for all practical purposes; another two or three who were just a little bit further on than that, and I said, '*We* shall *overcome?* I don't believe this.'

"But these very same people were there when the big deal started to roll. Many of them had limitations in terms of what they could do, but whatever they could do, you could depend on it. Some could drive people to town, some could meet people and get them to different places, others were good cooks. And so I organized that community, my community, around meeting people wherever they were. It was, whatever it was that they have to give, let's use it."

Basic literacy was one of the most important parts of the citizenship education courses, said Gray. "In many, many cases we were actually teaching people to read and write. But we taught them to read and write their names, their addresses, their social security numbers, segments of the constitution of Mississippi — and then talk about that, explain it. That's the way it was done.

"One of the things that I used to do that I really did enjoy was that, after they had learned to write, I'd ask them, 'What would you like to write? Now that you're writing, what is the thing you most want to write?' And then, whatever that was, then that's what I would work with with that student. Because the classes were always small enough to give that individual kind of attention. I remember a relative who said to me — and I've always remembered this — 'I want to write Ralph a letter.' Ralph was his first cousin who lived in New Orleans. I said, 'Do you really?' He said, 'Yes, I want to write Ralph a letter.' I said, 'Okay, then let's get with it.' So he told me what he wanted to say to Ralph, and I wrote it down. Then I gave it back to him and he wrote it. And then he read it. And that was just about the happiest moment of his life. He sure enough got *that* letter in the mail to Ralph! And after that you couldn't stop him."

■ _____

SNCC, with native Mississippian Sam Block, started a voter registration effort in Greenwood, a hard-core county seat in the Delta, in the early summer of 1962. The Voter Education Project supported the effort financially. Although Negroes of voting age far outnumbered whites, only about 2 percent of the blacks were registered, while 95 percent of the whites were on the rolls. Whites harassed the workers almost constantly, and as winter approached and the cotton season ended, county officials voted to end participation in the federal commodities program, through which surplus food was made available to low-income residents. SNCC organized its own food drive, importing truckloads of staples from contributors in the North. The contributions were coordinated by newly established SNCC and Friends of SNCC offices in Northern cities. As was so often the case in the hard-core South, the attempts at repression in Greenwood actually fueled Negroes' willingness to take risks, and voter registration activity picked up.[2]

By the beginning of 1963, hundreds of Negroes were trying to register at the Leflore County courthouse in Greenwood. The white response to this was increased violence. In February, segregationists burned four black-owned shops to the ground, and the police responded with the old trick of arresting the victim: When Sam Block alleged that the burnings were arson, he was charged with "making statements calculated to incite the breach of the peace." When Block was tried, the whites offered him a deal: a suspended sentence in exchange for his promise to end his activism. He refused. A few days later, as Bob Moses, Randolph Blackwell of VEP, and Jimmy Travis of SNCC were driving from Greenwood to Greenville, a group of whites followed them in a car with no license plates. The whites pulled alongside the Negroes and fired a weapon that appeared to be a machine gun. Travis was shot in the neck, but he survived.[3]

Wiley Branton, the Atlanta-based head of the Voter Education Project, announced a "saturation campaign" to register voters in Greenwood and Leflore County. In a prepared statement, Branton showed how angered he was by the white violence:

The state of Mississippi has repeatedly thrown down a gauntlet at the feet of would-be Negro voters, not only by the discriminatory practices of the registrar, but also by the economic pressures, threats, coercions, physical violence and death to Negroes seeking the right to vote. The time has come for us to pick up the gauntlet. Leflore County has elected itself as the testing ground for democracy, and we are accordingly meeting the challenge there.[4]

The harassment continued. When Negroes paraded to the courthouse in late March, the police threatened, arrested, and turned dogs loose on them. Two other SNCC workers were shot at. Someone fired a shotgun into the home of a citizen who had been active in the vote drive. The COFO office was set ablaze.

After many telephone calls from Wiley Branton to Burke Marshall and others at the Justice Department, requesting federal protection for the registration workers, the department finally responded on March 31, 1963, by going into federal court to seek a restraining order against local officials. The government wanted guarantees of protection for those who sought to register and vote, the release of activists from jail, and cessation of all harassment of the campaign and of Negroes who wanted "to exercise their constitutional right to assemble for peaceful protest demonstrations," as well as protection for them "from whites who might object." It was one of the few such actions by the Justice Department; authors Pat Watters and Reese Cleghorn wrote that "Greenwood was the only place where the Justice Department moved at all to protect constitutional rights as such, except for enforcing compliance with court orders, in the whole movement history from 1960 to 1966."[5]

Even the Justice Department's intervention in Greenwood turned out to be a hollow one. A few days after it sought the restraining order, the department made a deal with local officials. It would drop the request for an injunction if the whites promised to protect Negroes — *if* the blacks stopped marching to the courthouse.[6]

■

Wiley A. Branton had a good deal of practical knowledge about the way Leflore County and the U.S. government operated. Branton was a very light-skinned Negro, a successful lawyer in Pine Bluff, Arkansas, who had family ties to Leflore County. His great-grandfather was Greenwood Leflore, a white plantation owner for whom both Greenwood and Leflore County were named.[7] When Branton was the lawyer for the Little Rock Nine, the students who had sought to enter Central High School in 1957, lawyers from the Justice Department had tried to get him to use his influence to talk the students into withdrawing their applications for a year to allow things to cool down.

"I just took the position that the Constitution ought to mean what it says," recalled Branton in 1988, shortly before his death, "and that we expect you to back it up."

Branton was thirty-seven years old when he was summoned to Washington from Arkansas to be interviewed for the job of general counsel of the U.S. Commission on Civil Rights. At the same time he got a call from Burke Marshall, asking if he would drop by the Justice Department when he was in town. Branton did, and he met Robert Kennedy. The attorney general asked if Branton wouldn't rather head the newly established Voter Education Project. Branton flew to Atlanta, talked with Leslie Dunbar of the Southern Regional Council and others, and became excited about the possibilities of a regionwide registration campaign.

Branton was widely acknowledged to be a master in orchestrating the talents and resources of a number of civil rights organizations, some of which by now were almost openly contemptuous of one another. "By and large," he said later, "they cooperated. But I think I had to do the extra effort to get that cooperation. And frequently I would do things that *required* them to cooperate.

"For example, I would frequently make an assessment as to what organization I thought was best equipped to work in a particular geographic area, and would make a grant for voter registration support to a particular organization based on that and would let the other organizations know exactly what I was doing. And let's say that there was an area where NAACP was strong and SCLC just had a little program. I would try to get the local SCLC to work closely and in cooperation with the NAACP with the full understanding that the grant was going to the NAACP, and take another town where SCLC was stronger, and try to get NAACP to do the same thing. In a lot of instances I was able to get them to do that.

"Sometimes when I could not work it out, if there were serious competition between the big five groups, I would go in and help organize a truly local group that would have among its membership people who were active in those other organizations. Nine times out of ten, you're talking about the same people." The Council of Federated Organizations, the Mississippi umbrella group, was an example of that.

The Student Nonviolent Coordinating Committee was the least conventional group with which Branton dealt. Some of its members were far less devoted to voter registration, which was permissible under VEP's tax-exempt charter, than to direct action, which was not. SNCC was never one for detailed financial record keeping, and Branton had to read the riot act a few times. But the VEP director liked the youngest and feistiest civil rights organization. "They seemed to be genuinely interested in voter registration," he said. "But they also wanted to be provocative in terms of *all* the issues of civil rights — which didn't bother me at all. I know they were upsetting to some of the more traditional civil rights groups."

Branton was less appreciative of the federal government. The Kennedy administration "assisted in finding ways for tax exemption," he said, and Robert Kennedy said at the outset that Branton should let him know if there was anything he could do to help. "But beyond that, I must say I was disappointed at what they did. I think there were a number of things that they could have done and should have done on the legal front that they simply did not do. They just kowtowed to some of those reactionary Southerners down there. They seemed very fearful of the senior senator from Mississippi, Eastland." It was James Eastland, he said, who successfully prevailed on the Justice Department to back off from its attempt to get a restraining order in Greenwood.

"And some of the worst federal judges that we encountered were Kennedy appointees." Branton named a few: Cox in Mississippi; Walter P. Gewin of Tuscaloosa, Alabama; E. Gordon West of Louisiana. He, like Robert Kennedy in his oral history, had difficulty remembering the name of "the judge in south Georgia," Robert Elliott, who had done such a thorough job of retarding civil rights in that state.

Branton also deplored the Justice Department's unwillingness to provide legal protection for voter registration workers, despite the implied promise that it would. And the behavior of FBI agents in the South rankled him: "Such things as, for example, FBI agents sitting outside meetings, making notes, and people being intimidated and even shot following those meetings, with the FBI knowing full well that something's going to happen to some of them."

He complained to Washington about the FBI's intimate relationship with local police. "I pointed out that the FBI works closely with local police and sheriff's departments on auto thefts and things like that," Branton said, "and in these small towns there's sort of a buddy-buddy relationship, and they're not likely to either report or pursue actions that might cause problems for the local police. I recommended that they send in outside FBI agents, and not assign these matters to local agents who had been assigned to that territory and had been working there for a while." The agency ignored this request at the time, but in more recent years it has adopted just such a policy.

"I was in frequent contact with Burke Marshall," said Branton. "I said, 'Burke, you know, you ought to send people down here, you ought to do this, you ought to do that.' And his reply was always one of these plaintive pleadings, saying, 'Well, we can't. We'd like to do it, but if we do this or that it will precipitate this or that.' "

■ ———————————————————————

The experiences in Mississippi in 1963 helped convince the activists on the front lines, if any of them needed convincing, that the federal government was at best a reluctant partner in assuring the right to vote. Charles Jones had learned this after his chilling experience in McComb, when John Doar's hushed visit revealed that a high-ranking white representative of the U.S. government could be fearful for his own safety in Mississippi. The lesson taught by the federal officials, said Jones, was that those people who wanted to change the system have "got to do it ourselves. We counted on using them as we can, but we cannot depend on them to basically protect us."

But there was something else that could be done. "Now we had to try to maneuver them into the position of *having* to protect us," said Jones. Hollis Watkins saw it in a similar light. "Initially," he said, "we thought that the federal government was on our side, all the way. As time began to go on, we saw and felt that the federal government, from the Washington level, was on our side, but they had begun to rely too much on the Southern officials, who we felt were on the side of our oppressors. And then we started to feel that the federal government in Washington was really beginning to get the cold feet, because the big Southern officials had begun to put pressure on them.

"So at that point we felt that this whole monkey is on *our* back, and the only help we're going to be able to get, even from the federal government, is going to be based on how much pressure we can put on them. In other words, it's in our hands. And if we don't force it to come about, then it's not going to come about."

TWENTY-SEVEN

■

PEACE IN THE VALLEY

■

Mississippi, in the eyes of those who worked for equal rights, was a place that lent itself easily to expressions such as "beast" and "bowels" and "darkness." It was dangerous. It was deadly. Anyone who was involved in the Movement in those days, and who entered the state on one of its main highways, almost certainly has an everlasting memory of that "WELCOME TO MISSISSIPPI" sign and of the feelings it generated. For many, the emotion was a mixture of fear — itself a ferment of base-level apprehension and barely controlled terror — and love for the place. Mississippi was, as James Meredith explained, a place of great beauty. You could almost feel the warmth of the moist, fecund earth as you drove down one of its roads; you could almost hear the vegetation send its vines and leaves out to take over anything that stood in its way, from telephone pole to abandoned tractor. You could almost touch the enormous orange sun that took so long to set along the flat horizon of the Delta. The ache of love for the place was only intensified by the bitter knowledge that so much injustice went on there.

But Mississippi was not the only area where darkness had taken control. There were similar places all through the South.

States that enjoyed reputations as centers of progressiveness, such as North Carolina and Tennessee, harbored pockets of meanness and unrestrained hatred. Louisiana, as the Congress of Racial Equality discovered early and often, could be a cauldron of malicious enmity. And Alabama came closest to being another Mississippi.

People in the Movement whose work took them into all the Deep South states were heard to say in those days, and they repeat now, that they felt their lives were in danger every bit as much in Alabama as in Mississippi. Some of them tried to enunciate the not-too-subtle distinctions between the neighboring states. In Mississippi, they said, the segregationists seemed to feel that they needed some legal pretext for harassing or murdering the nonconformist. They would arrest him on a phony charge and then shoot him while he "tried to escape." But in Alabama, the reasoning went, the haters felt no need for a pretext. They would shoot from ambush, or leave a few sticks of dynamite. In Mississippi, the elected officials in most cases at least mouthed the cliches of law and order, but in Alabama, once George Wallace became governor, it was clear that the political leadership was an active part of the terror.

Birmingham was a major contributor to Alabama's rapidly emerging reputation as a citadel of hatred. And it was Eugene Connor who was largely responsible for Birmingham's notoriety. Connor, a former radio sports announcer who was known as Bull, was one of the three members of Birmingham's governing commission. He was a devout racist who had been seen to literally foam at the mouth when he got excited about Negroes, which was much of the time. One of Connor's more notable public statements of his feelings about race relations was, "We're not goin' to have white folks and nigras segregatin' together in this man's town."[1] Connor was the commission member in charge of public safety and education, and in 1962 and 1963 he was widely thought to have his eye on the governor's mansion, which George Wallace would have to vacate in 1966 under the state's one-term rule.

Birmingham's other commissioners were J. T. "Jabo" Waggoner, in charge of public works and improvements, who was heard from infrequently on racial matters, and Arthur Hanes, the mayor, and president of the commission, who ran Birmingham's parks, airports, and city services. Hanes, an ex-FBI agent and employee of Hayes Aviation, a Birmingham firm with secret ties to the Central Intelligence Agency, was less outspoken on race than Connor, but only by Birmingham standards.

Official Birmingham had had many opportunities to address itself to the inevitable, but it had avoided them all. The almost-constant agitations of Fred Shuttlesworth somehow were ignored, as were the warnings of the few white voices of moderation. When Harrison Salisbury wrote in the *New York Times* that the only thing shared by Birmingham's blacks and whites was "a community of fear," the city sued him. When the Greater Birmingham Council on Human Relations issued a statement in January, 1961, that among other things criticized the failure of local media groups to report on race relations, those local media groups also failed to report the statement. Birmingham banned a schoolbook because it had black and white rabbits in it.[2]

The municipally assisted violence that erupted when the Freedom Ride came to Birmingham caused some members of the downtown business community to become openly concerned. Birmingham was getting to be one of those places, like Oxford, that other cities didn't want to be another of. The boosters of Atlanta, some 150 miles away, who competed with Birmingham in southeastern regional matters, liked to point out to potential investors and factory builders that "they make the steel in Birmingham and we sell it in Atlanta." Birmingham, they hinted, was a roughneck, redneck place. The downtown elite of the Georgia capital also liked to boast that Atlanta was "the city that's too busy to hate."

The competition for business was real and intense, and Atlanta and Birmingham were locked in an ongoing contest to see which city would win the title of marketing and distribution center of the South (or the New South, as the boosters had been putting it since the days of the Old South). Any public occurrence could be thought of as ammunition in this battle, particularly if it was photographable. When the white rioters attacked the Freedom Riders in Birmingham, they also went after photographers. One of their victims was a cameraman for the *Birmingham Post-Herald*. The rioters broke his camera but did not have the presence of mind to remove the film. The result was a picture of violence that made front pages all over the world — including Tokyo, where a group of Birmingham businessmen were attending a convention of the Rotary Club. Incidents such as this counted for a great deal in the city-image game.

Sidney Smyer, the president of Birmingham's chamber of commerce, showed at the time of the Freedom Ride that he was aware of all this and wanted to do something about it. His city's business leaders, reported United Press International, "were concerned that recent racial violence might adversely affect the city's economy." Smyer said there had been reports that businesses had been having trouble getting their supervisors to accept transfers to their Alabama installations. Those whose jobs might take them to Alabama also were concerned that the state would abandon public education in order to continue segregation.[3]

Perhaps the biggest contributor to Birmingham's bad reputation was the city's history of virtually uninhibited violence. The police department under Bull Connor and his chief of police was one of the meanest in America, Gestapo-like in its seemingly random cruelty against the minority. It has been proven in court that there were connections between the department and the Ku Klux Klan. And Birmingham so richly earned its reputation for midnight dynamite attacks that critics referred to the place as "Bombingham."

Between January 1, 1956, and June 1, 1963, according to a survey by the Southern Regional Council, there were at least 138 race-related bombings in the eleven states of the South. As the council's Barbara Patterson pointed out in a 1963 article, the bombings seemed to be clustered in time and place around incidents of "the strongest Negro assertions of rights: Little Rock during school integration in 1960 and 1961; Tennessee during school integration in 1956 and 1957; the Atlanta area around school integration time in 1961; Alabama and Mississippi during voter registration activity in 1963."[4]

Thirty-two of the bombings and attempted bombings occurred in Alabama, with the greater number of those in Birmingham. The bombers there attacked the homes of Negroes, a synagogue, a motel, and, most frequently, Negro churches. To be a black person in Birmingham who spoke out against segregation was to risk being dynamited.

───────────────────────── ■

The white violence in Birmingham was almost always connected directly with progress by Negroes. It was as if the bombers were commenting editorially on the gains made by their enemies. The racists assumed that black attorney Arthur Shores was behind every federal court order that was favorable to Negroes, even when other civil rights lawyers were more directly involved.

"One day the federal court issued an order for the public schools here in Birmingham to be desegregated," said Shores. "And that night, one end of my house was blown off. Two weeks later, when the first black entered Phillips High School, they blew off the *other* end of my house.

"I received a call — my telephone is unlisted, but I knew there were some klansmen who worked for the telephone company — and the fellow said, 'Shores, it serves you right. You got your just due.' " The lawyer said he told his caller that he had not worked on the lawsuit. But the caller insisted, "You were behind all of it, and you received your just due."

When the desegregation of Phillips High School approached, Shores said, he had doubted that he would be attacked again. "But I thought, 'The old saying that lightning doesn't strike the same place twice may be all right, but I'm going to take my Winchester and kind of get out on this porch and watch what's going on.' And the moment I approached the entrance, the door was blown in. If I had stepped a step closer it would have caught me full in the face.

"In a few minutes I guess I had two or three hundred blacks there. They were outraged. They wanted to kill that man right there. Blacks were shooting, whites were shooting, police were shooting. But blacks were shooting. They had armed themselves. It was quite a situation."

─────────────

C. Herbert Oliver was a Negro who was raised and educated in the Birmingham system and who decided to fight it. Oliver, who was born in 1925, left the city long enough to go to divinity school. He returned in 1948 to be the minister of the Christian and Missionary Alliance

Church. That year, Oliver conducted a church service in violation of one of Birmingham's segregation ordinances. He allowed three white people to enter his church and sit with black people; the law required signs announcing that the races would be separated, even in church. Bull Connor arrested C. Herbert Oliver for this violation.

After the arrest, no one in Birmingham, white or black, would give Oliver a job. He left Birmingham, entered a Presbyterian seminary in Philadelphia, got advanced degrees in theology, served a white congregation in northern Maine for almost six years, and returned home in 1959. Within a year Bull Connor had arrested him again.

"This time I was hauled out of my house with only a robe and no shoes — nothing on but a robe — and taken to jail that way. They charged me with violation of Code 866. Whatever that was; I don't know. It just covered everything." Some students at a local black college had held sit-ins. They had been arrested, then released and returned to the campus. Oliver visited the campus and consulted with the students, advising them to get an attorney. When the president of the college heard about this, said Oliver, he called the police and asked them to arrest the minister. "I was told by some of the students that he told the police not to arrest me on campus but to wait until I left campus," said Oliver.

"So a police car actually came and parked right by the building where I was and stayed there about an hour while I was in the building. Then the car went to the edge of the campus. Students let me know that the police were there. I stayed there; I didn't go out. The car moved farther away, and I simply decided that I would spend the night there. So I spent the night on the campus.

"The next morning I left and went on about my business and served my church. Came back home, and that was when they came to the door and asked me if I was Reverend C. Hubert Oliver. I said 'I'm Reverend C. *Herbert* Oliver.' They said, 'Well, we're going to take you to jail.' So I said, 'What is the charge?' They said, 'Never mind that,' so I said, 'I'd like to know what you're arresting me for, and do you have a warrant for my arrest?' And one officer simply grabbed the screen door and yanked it open and reached me and grabbed me by the shoulder and flung me out the door and hustled me to the car.

"My wife rushed out and asked them, 'What are you doing?' and they told her to mind her own business. So she told them to let me get some clothes. They said, 'No, we're taking him like this,' and they took me to jail. So I spent the night in jail. And I really don't know what the charge was, but the charge was dropped. The charge in 1948 was dropped, too."

The sit-ins built sentiment in Birmingham's black community for an all-out attack on segregation, and that produced an ongoing attack by the city's police department on Negroes generally. Every Monday night, C. Herbert Oliver attended meetings, chaired by Fred Shuttlesworth, at which the Movement was discussed and at which citizens came forward with accounts of police harassment and intimidation.

"I began to document cases of alleged police brutality, mainly in the Birmingham area," said Oliver, "and to circulate those around the country and around the world. When we would hear of anyone who had been mistreated or brutally handled by the policemen, we would document the story."

The "we" was a group of about a dozen ministers, known as the Birmingham Inter-Citizens Committee, that gathered information on the cases, including sworn affidavits from victims and witnesses, and sent reports to local officials (including Bull Connor), to influential members of Congress, to the Federal Bureau of Investigation, to interested persons around the world and at the United Nations, and to members of the press. The committee turned out its reports, approximately one hundred of them, over a period of five years. "Out of that hundred," said Oliver, "four officers were brought to trial. But they were exonerated. No one ever got any justice out of that." But he credits publicity from the reports with producing a gradual decrease in brutality, to the point that there were no complaints at all in 1965. "The good thing about the system was the freedom of the press, freedom of speech," he said, "and I think our freedom to tell what happened was the thing that exposed these wrongs and was the most powerful thing in bringing them to a halt."

Harrison Salisbury referred to some of the cases in his *New York Times* article on Birmingham. "The press was very instrumental in pinpointing and showing the world what was really happening there," said the minister. "But I make a distinction between the local press and the national press. The local press was a source of danger, because if you wrote a letter to the editor in those days, the newspaper would print it, but also print your name and address. And then the Klan would come after you. And the Klan came after me. I wrote several letters and expressed my views without biting my tongue.

"At first they started by calling me at my home. Threatening calls. Saying such things as 'What kind of fertilizer do you want your little nigger children to be made into?' I never responded to that; I'd simply hang up. And I told my wife, 'If you ever get any of those, just hang up.' But quite a few of those were coming.

"When we'd have interracial meetings in Birmingham, the police would go and get the license numbers of everyone. Then those names would appear in the newspaper as people who were at this meeting, and they were harassed. White and black."

On the night after one of Oliver's letters appeared in the newspaper, a pickup truck containing several white men came and parked in front of his house. "And this was a totally Negro neighborhood.

"I looked out the window and I knew this was something that was seriously wrong. So I switched out all the lights in my house. I called my neighbor across the street and told him, 'There's a load of white men sitting out here in front of my house,' and they turned on their front porch light. I called my neighbor next door; he turned on *his* front porch light. I called my neighbor on the other side; they turned on *their* front porch light. Then the truck drove off.

"The next night, the men in the neighborhood called a meeting and decided that this would not be allowed in the community, and that in case anybody else came again like that, there was going to be some shooting. They said, 'Reverend, you stay out of this; we're not going to allow this.' But the people never came again. This was a one-time event."

Oliver was pleased with the national press's reaction to his Inter-Citizens Committee documents, but he deplored the reception they got at the FBI. "They should have shown some sort of strength to curb this sort of activity," he said, "but they didn't. The head man of the FBI [in Birmingham] was furious that we were finding all these cases." A neighbor who spoke often with the federal agent quoted him as demanding, " 'Where is Oliver getting them from?' He was furious with me for coming up with all those cases, because it did embarrass the FBI," said Oliver. "But they didn't do anything about them."

■ ————————————————————

The documents that were assembled by Oliver's committee were straightforward narratives of the brutality that occurred in Birmingham — almost dry, like legal depositions; but at the same time full of pain and emotion. Some excerpts:

> After the policemen had gone I went into the Travis home.... It looked like they had a hog killing in the house. [Part of the sworn statement of Willie Travis, concerning the warrantless police invasion of a home in Birmingham on October 27, 1961. From Inter-Citizens Committee Document No. 20.]

> They [two Birmingham policemen] said they were going to take me to jail, but instead they made me lie down on the floor of their car and they took me to a wooded area. When they told me they wanted me to submit to them, I refused. But one of them said to me, "How are you going to get out of this?" One had his gun out, not pointing it at me, but playing with it. I thought of another Negro woman who was found dead one night by the railroad tracks and I knew the same thing could happen to me. So against my will I was forced to submit to them. [Part of the sworn statement of Creola R ——. From Inter-Citizens Committee Document No. 21.]

> They drove away with me. When they got near the ball diamond on Huntsville Road, the officer ... began beating me with the stick.... I ... was pleading for mercy. But they had none. When I would lean down to avoid the blows in my face, the officer would strike upward hitting me in the face with the stick. I was crying and hollering and pleading but he kept beating me. He hit one place on the back of my head about ten times. Each blow seemed to make everything go black with pain. My hands were still handcuffed behind me. A car came by and he stopped beating me until the car passed. Then the officer in the front said it was his time to beat me, so he

got in the back and continued beating me while the other
one drove. [Part of the sworn statement of James Eddie
Steele. From Inter-Citizens Committee Document No.
68.][5]

When the lawsuits against segregation finally made it up the judicial ladder, Birmingham was faced, like the other communities
of the South, with legally enforceable orders to change. The elected
leaders of many other cities had gotten to this stage and made the
preparations for desegregation. Indeed, some had secretly welcomed being pushed to this point so they could declare the rhetorical ordeal over and done with and could start addressing the
region's more serious problems of inferior education, health, and
employment opportunity. It helped some of them to phrase the
decision in terms of a choice: either desegregating or going without. The Georgia legislature chose to allow two Negroes into its
state university rather than face the ignominy of having no university at all (or, for some of its members, the greater disgrace of
having no football team). A county commission, under legal attack
to desegregate its courthouse cafeteria or have no subsidized food,
often would decide that a little integration wasn't all that bad.
Walking was, for many, clearly inferior to having a municipal bus
system.

But this was not the way it was in Birmingham. When a federal court issued an order desegregating Birmingham's public
places — more than one hundred parks, playgrounds, swimming
pools, and golf courses — the city's governing body decided to close
them instead. When the deadline was reached, on January 15, 1962,
the city would close everything except the football stadium, the
zoo, and two parks. Those exceptions, reasoned the troika that
ruled Birmingham, were "stand-up" places, where vertical race
mixing would do the least harm.

To Art Hanes, the mayor, it was a simple decision. When he,
Connor, and Waggoner were elected the previous spring, said
Hanes at the time, the voters were giving him a mandate to keep
the city segregated. So Hanes, Connor, and Waggoner padlocked
the parks, stored the sliding boards, and filled the holes on the golf
courses with dirt.

Hanes explained his position in an interview in December, 1961. Yes, he said, Birmingham was coming in for criticism, but

we'll have more trouble and create a worse image if those parks are open. This is what the press around the world is waiting for — something to happen. They're sitting around waiting, like a bunch of vultures. The real issue isn't integration. The main thing is the overriding principle of people's rights to determine something for themselves. It is the idea of the Communists to destroy every tradition and symbol that this country has ever stood for.

I feel that men should progress by their own ability and gain by their own effort and not by the passage of laws. If they merit acceptance, it will be given naturally, just as night follows day.

Hanes recited most of the white supremacist's litany, leaving out only mongrelization and the bloc vote. "I will never negotiate with Communist Negroes, Negro radical groups," he said. "They have nothing to negotiate with. . . . The Negroes in Birmingham have always been treated with kindness, generosity, and warmth. But with their present attitude, this could change."[6]

Hanes, it turned out, had placed too much value on his mandate. The plans to padlock the parks, added to Birmingham's well-documented reputation for official violence and repression, gave more of the city's well-placed white moderates an opportunity to speak out. It is doubtful that many of them would have suffered personally from the closing of the parks, for they surely all lived in Vestavia, Homewood, Mountain Brook, and other suburbs outside the city limits. But it is certain that all of them were well aware of the impact of the closings on Birmingham's status with national and world leaders of industry and finance.

For once, white *moderate* Birmingham spoke out. The chamber of commerce indicated its desire to keep the parks open. So did the Jaycees, the Birmingham Committee of 100, the Young Men's Business Club, the Downtown Improvement Association, the Woman's Club of Birmingham, and, after practically everybody else, the *Birmingham Post-Herald* and the *Birmingham News*.

Fourteen Episcopal ministers called the park-closing plan "folly." The minister at Bull Connor's Methodist church delivered a sermon in which he recalled that Jesus Christ "taught us to love one another as brothers and sisters" and suggested that "if Christ is our savior, surely we can be friends with each other." One of Birmingham's few certified white liberals, attorney Charles Morgan, Jr., asked publicly for his fellow residents to contemplate "how high a price we are willing to pay" for segregation.[7]

The answer to Morgan's question, at least as far as Hanes, Connor, and Waggoner were concerned, was "Anything." The citizens disagreed, however. The troika's actions in closing the parks helped solidify resentment against them, and the citizens obtained more than eleven thousand names on a petition (seventy-five hundred were needed) to call a special election in November, 1962, to change Birmingham's form of government.

-- ■

David Vann was a lawyer in Birmingham, a white man who thought of himself as a "moderate activist." A native Alabaman, he had gone to school in Washington, D.C., and had clerked for Supreme Court justice Hugo Black at the time of the *Brown* decision. Back in Alabama, he quickly became known as one of the handful of white lawyers — of whites of any calling, for that matter — who understood and sympathized with the plight of Negroes. C. Herbert Oliver recalls that when he asked Vann for help in filing the incorporation papers for the Inter-Citizens Committee, Vann agreed. But the lawyer, who at the time worked in a corporate firm, suggested that they meet in a car in the black neighborhood. "That's how nervous *he* was at the time," said Oliver.with a smile.

Vann had good reason to be nervous. "The white population that differed with the system was probably more intimidated than the blacks," he said recently. "If you expressed sympathy for desegregation, I think you'd just be fired. If I went to a Negro church to meet with a group, as I did, my picture would be in the Ku Klux Klan paper, and my phone would ring, and they'd threaten to blow up my house and do all kinds of things to me." (Of course, Oliver's affidavits showed that black Birminghamians clearly suffered from harsher intimidation.)

It was worse, Vann said, for white people who lacked his access to the legal process. When a young man attended a meeting on race relations at a local Methodist church and expressed dismay at those who supported segregation, Bull Connor's men went to the man's workplace and arrested him on a charge of vagrancy. "Vagrancy meant having no visible means of support," exclaimed Vann. "And they arrested this kid on his *job*!"

Vann became a key member of the group of business and civic leaders who wanted to get rid of Bull Connor and his colleagues. But one of the first obstacles such a movement faced was the attitude of the business community itself.

Segregation, said the lawyer, was "a system that was seen by your business element as a way to maintain peace — that if you get whites and blacks separated, there wouldn't be fighting; that that would be the best way for the two races to live together, to live 'separately but equally,' although 'equal' was never *equal*.

"What the businessmen really wanted was peace in the valley. Peace in the valley lets you have a place where you can make money. If you have disturbances, discord, that's against business." It did not matter, he said, that much of Birmingham's industry was owned by corporations from the North — the most glaring example (literally) being U.S. Steel's open-hearth furnaces, which gave the city's nighttime skyline a fiery glow. But, said Vann, "the policy of the out-of-state owners was always, 'Do whatever the local people do. Follow the local customs. Have peace in the valley. We're here to make money. We're not out to change the world, but to make money.'"

The businessmen did not arrive all on their own at the conclusion that separate but equal, the doctrine of *Plessy v. Ferguson*, was acceptable. They received confirmation from a Supreme Court that had, until very recently, endorsed that doctrine. "That opinion was reflected in almost everything they read in the newspapers," said Vann. "It was reflected in what they were taught in school. They were taught that the Civil War wasn't about slavery, but that it was about states' rights."

The business leaders (and other whites) saw a situation in which a strong central government was trying to impose its will on a democracy, Vann said, and they felt that "the way democracy is supposed to work, you take a vote and how the majority votes is how it ought to be." That may be a "primitive idea of what democracy is," he added, but those who hold it fail to note that America's brand of democracy also has a constitution that limits the power of government, so that individual rights might be protected. "And that ours is the most unique democracy that ever came into existence, in that the will of the majority is *required* to be thwarted. . . .

"So here we had this terrible burden of trying to overturn a system that was emplaced by the will of the majority, in a democratic country, and the system had been blessed by the Supreme Court of the United States, supported by the churches; all legitimate opinion pointed to it. Now, how do you get from A to Z in that kind of situation? It was one of the toughest problems that a democratic government faces."

Vann and the others got to Z by making use of a law that gave a municipality the power to change its form of government through initiative. If a specified number of voters petitioned for a referendum on a change, the referendum would be held. Bull Connor and company had helped matters immeasurably by their behavior during the Freedom Ride in 1961. The businessmen started to realize that "they were causing *un*peace in the valley," said Vann. But there remained the difficult job of collecting the names, exciting the voters, and slogging through the street-level work of turning the referendum into a reality.

Charles Morgan, Jr., and other young lawyers were fighting a state legislature reapportionment battle at the time, and a court had ordered a special election for August, 1962. Vann had the bright idea of setting up a booth across the street from every polling place on the day of the special legislative election and snagging voters for the local petition as they left the polls. That way, he said, "I could avoid all the usual problems of petitions," which included not having as many signatures as you thought you had, forged or otherwise incorrect names, petitions snatched away by the opposition, and the like.

The businessmen convened a meeting to hear Vann's scheme. Their first reaction, said the lawyer, was to hem and haw — to say they needed to think it over and consult. But a representative of organized labor, whom Vann had insisted on bringing to the meeting, interrupted. Vann quoted him as saying: "I represent a hundred and fifty thousand members of organized labor, and I think instead of wondering *should* we do all this, why haven't we done this before? Why did we let this thing go so long?" The businessmen agreed. Now, they said, they needed a handful of respected people — citizens with impeccable reputations, known for their devotion to charity and civic progress — to publicly sponsor and inaugurate the initiative. The group drew up a short list of twenty-five candidates and asked for volunteers. None stepped forward. So Sidney Smyer of the chamber of commerce suggested that sponsorship be open to anyone, with a goal of five hundred names. Within a few days, a thousand had signed.

Then came the collection of names for the petition itself. As political petitions go, this one was a marvel of efficiency: six copies on snap-apart carbon forms, with a column for telephone numbers so precinct captains could get out the vote later, when the actual election was held.

Vann said city officials threatened to fire any municipal worker who signed the petition. So the committee announced it would remove any employee's name upon request, or provide him or her with a lawyer to fight dismissal. From an unidentified proponent of reform came a tape recording on which the existing city administration promised fire fighters, who were under Bull Connor's control, a pay raise if they voted against the initiative. The committee publicized the tape widely. When the August legislative election was held, a week after Vann's plan had been put into operation, the committee came away from its petition booths with more than eleven thousand names, a guarantee of a November referendum, and a shot at genuine city reform.

■ ————————————————

The reformers won the referendum, and another election was set, for April, 1963, to select the city's new leaders. Bull Connor ran for mayor under the new system, but he lost to Albert Boutwell. Boutwell was one of the men who had met with John Patterson in 1955 to plot a delaying strategy for *Brown*, and he was the architect of Alabama's pupil placement law. But in the context of Birmingham at that time, he was considered a moderate on racial matters — not the sort of man who plugged up golf courses, who allowed the Klan to have its sport with Freedom Riders, or who foamed at the mouth at the sight of Fred Shuttlesworth.

Connor et al. refused to leave office graciously, arguing that they should be allowed to serve out their terms, which would not expire until 1965. The new government was forced to sue the old one. Still, it was beginning to look to white residents as if Birmingham was calming down. Then, in the spring of 1963, Martin Luther King, Jr., came to town, and all hell broke loose in the valley.

TWENTY-EIGHT

SO NICE TO HAVE YOU IN BIRMINGHAM

It was widely accepted within the Movement, and especially in the Southern Christian Leadership Conference, that Dr. King and his organization sorely needed a victory after Albany. The stay in southwest Georgia, while it advanced the Movement and its aims in some ways, nevertheless was viewed by much of the public and some activists as a strategic loss. Just as Diane Nash had seen the halt in the original Freedom Ride as an interruption that must not be allowed to damage the Movement's momentum and reward the segregationists for their violence, King and others feared that setbacks would occur if the Movement did not win a decisive victory soon.

From the viewpoint of the wounded Southern Christian Leadership Conference, Birmingham was the perfect candidate for a next victory. It had a loyal, fully functioning affiliate of SCLC, the Alabama Christian Movement for Human Rights. The affiliate's leader, Fred Shuttlesworth, was more predictable, at least in the eyes of SCLC workers, than W. G. Anderson had been in Albany. Furthermore, Shuttlesworth was a fearless leader. He would willingly stride into an arena jam-packed with hungry lions, as long as he knew that the lions believed in segregation. Little friction with other groups, notably the Student Nonviolent Coordinating Committee, could be expected there. Best of all, Birmingham had Bull Connor. Bull was not like the officials in Albany. He could be counted on *not* to read up on Gandhian nonviolence, *not* to go to great pains to appear to be enforcing the law equally, *not* to pull Bobby Kennedy and Burke Marshall into his plans and thus acquire the appearance of legitimacy. Bull functioned on the visceral level of truncheon, jail cell, shotgun, and brute force. He was as predictable as the headstrong animal whose namesake he was. If it nurtured him properly, the Movement could get a great deal of unwitting assistance from him and, as one activist put it, in the process "turn Bull into a steer."

Much has been said about King's need for a victory and his selection of Birmingham as the battleground site, but it also is true that King and the Movement had not only a right but an obligation to go to the Alabama city. First, Shuttlesworth had invited his friend to come. More important, Birmingham was a place where a civil rights leader *should* have gone in those days. The city was a powerful symbol of defiance to the desegregation effort. It was an urban center and thus could be expected to influence other Southern cities by its actions. It had an active, dedicated black community. It had much that needed to be changed. It was, as King would later remark, "probably the most thoroughly segregated city in the United States."[1]

▪

The issue in Birmingham, said Fred Shuttlesworth, was simple: "The system said, 'No, no, hell no, a thousand times, no.' And we said, 'Yes, yes, hell yes, we must go. We *must* do it.' " Part of the issue — and this was particularly true in Birmingham, but it also was a feature of almost every Southern community's showdown with segregation — was the virtual absence of communication between white and Negro communities. Whites in Birmingham certainly knew who Fred Shuttlesworth was, but few of them, even those who were regarded as moderate or even liberal, ever got around to meeting with him and asking him what he wanted and how he wanted to get it. That situation changed dramatically, however, in 1962, when Shuttlesworth invited Martin Luther King to come to town.

"I didn't have a whole lot of conversation with them," said Shuttlesworth of his dealings with the downtown whites. "They talked to me periodically. I knew they were trying to change the form of government, and so forth and so on. But I didn't have a lot of conversation with David Vann or any of the white people, really. I think it was a mistake for them not to have talked to me more. The very first time I met with the power structure of Birmingham was in '62 when I had invited Martin Luther King to come over from Atlanta. We had threatened demonstrations before Christmas, and they wanted to meet to know how they could keep Dr. King out of town."

The influential and moneyed whites first consulted those they considered their counterparts in the black community, the prominent and wealthy Negroes. The list included A. G. Gaston, a millionaire with several local business interests who, they assumed, had influence with the black community. The well-to-do Negroes referred inquiries to Shuttlesworth. "Gaston told them, 'You have to talk to Fred. Fred's got the folks,'" said the minister. "And they had to. I never will forget this scene. They called me Doctor, and I said, 'I'm not a doctor. Neither am I a bright boy or somebody you can use. I've been bombed twice, and I never heard anything from you. I never met you. So I couldn't be a doctor, and I couldn't be your boy.'

"I said, 'So my problem is, what do you want?' They said, 'Well, we want to know how to keep Dr. King out of here.' I said, 'You can't keep him out. I have invited him in on behalf of the Movement.' I said, 'In fact, we think it'd be nice if you put up signs saying, 'We think it's nice to have Dr. King here.' At the time, they had signs all over the place that said, 'It's so nice to have you in Birmingham.'"

The whites' response, as Shuttlesworth remembers it, was a lot of clearing of throats. "I said, 'So we think it's nice to have him. What will you give to keep him out? I'm busy fighting, and I didn't come here just to talk, because I presume you don't have anything to talk with me about anyway. I'm trying to fight for freedom.' They started saying, 'We can't make any promises,' and I said, 'Well, you're wasting our time.'"

That meeting ended without resolution, but another followed shortly. The merchants made an offer. Shuttlesworth says, "They said they would desegregate the water fountains. I said, 'No, we got to have toilets now.' " One of the Negro community's constant complaints was that women were welcome to spend their money in the downtown department stores, but they had to use segregated rest rooms.

The business people mulled that over, and a delegation of white clergymen spoke with Shuttlesworth, who says he gave them equally stern treatment. When the merchants returned, negotiations seemed no further along.

"I broke the logjam," said Shuttlesworth. "I said to one of them, 'I tell you what. I've just decided how we're going to win this thing. I've decided that Dr. King, Ralph Abernathy, and myself are going to be arrested in *your* store. And when the police arrest us, we won't walk out. We'll be *dragged* out. Camera'll get all that. And then when we go to jail, we won't eat. We'll fast. Won't shave. Folks will see how bad we're treated, and I'm sure won't nobody be shopping with you.' And so this fellow who had another store, a nice little fellow, said, 'Well, let me make a call.'

"He came back, and he said, 'Listen: I tell you what I did. My maintenance man, he's back at the store painting, and he just messed up a sign.' The sign said 'WHITE.' I told him, 'You're a white man that's got some sense. All the rest of y'all can paint out your signs and we'll just see what happens.' "

The agreement was that the merchants would remove their "WHITE" and "COLORED" signs on rest rooms, water fountains, and the like, and Shuttlesworth would not make a public announcement about it. Sidney Smyer, who led the white group, extended his hand to Shuttlesworth to seal the deal. "He said, 'Doctor, I give you my hand.' I said, 'No, I'm not a doctor. I'm a fighter.' He said, 'Well, I give you my hand. We're going to keep the promise.'

"I said, 'Okay. Fine. Just remember: Atlanta's just one hour from here by plane. We can start anytime, because the war is on. If the sign goes back up, the fight goes on.' "

The deal was on its way to working out when Bull Connor heard about it. "Bull told me he was going to arrest any store [owner] who did that," said Shuttlesworth, "so they had to put the signs back up. When that happened, we threatened to demonstrate." Shuttlesworth said the delay helped his cause, because it pushed events into the Easter season, which was second only to Christmas as a source of profits for the downtown merchants.

Emil Hess owned and operated the Parisian store in downtown Birmingham, a highly successful retail specialty store that his family had controlled since 1920. Hess practically grew up in the store, and when he returned from the Wharton School and the navy he devoted himself full-time to it. Parisian is now a chain that operates across the Southeast.

In the sixties, Hess was one of the businessmen whom Sidney Smyer assembled as part of an ad hoc committee for meetings with Fred Shuttlesworth and other Negro leaders. The migration to suburbia was well under way then, but the regional shopping malls had not yet been built, and Parisian, like other stores, had a single operation in the downtown center. Business was good in downtown Birmingham, supported by a solid core of working-class consumers, many of them black.

"I was asked to serve on that committee, I guess representing the merchants," said Hess in 1989, "although I didn't feel that was my role. Nor did I have their authority to represent them as such, but more as an interested citizen to try to ameliorate some of the problems that were in the community and were being brought to the attention of this group by blacks. Fred Shuttlesworth was on that committee from the black side."

The group met at an Episcopal church, said Hess, "because we considered it neutral ground. . . . Those of us that were white used to have some apprehension about meeting. . . . It was fear, I guess, of what the reaction would be of Bull Connor and some of the folks from city hall. Anyway, we met. We heard some of the complaints from the black community. We met several times, and really all they were concerned about were the indignities they were suffering. They weren't talking about job opportunities, but the indignities they suffered when they went to register to vote, when they went to buy an automobile license or a marriage license. Couldn't we please do something with the people that were working at the county level to at least treat them properly?

"They also were concerned with the way that the employees of the bus company were treating them. Really, it was more concern with indignities they were suffering." The blacks felt that little progress was being made on their grievances, and so they let it be known that they wanted Martin Luther King to come to town and lead a protest "and maybe start to use a little more pressure."

The Negroes, said Hess, assumed that the downtown merchants

were the leaders of Birmingham's power structure. "I don't think that was a realistic assessment," he added. "The merchants were never part of the power structure of this city. The power structure, in my judgment, was more the people at the utilities and the financial institutions." The merchants understood, however, that when pressure for change was brought, "we had to be the ones to acquiesce."

Merchants were "the most visible, and they were the most sensitive to economic pressure. I mean, blacks weren't going to pay off their loans at banks, but they sure could stop shopping at the stores. King came in and organized some marches, and used schoolkids in the marches. To my knowledge, at no time did they ever do any damage in any downtown store. That was not their purpose, from my observation. They merely wanted their presence recognized. Now, what it *did* do, in my judgment, was cause some fear on the part of, maybe, the white shopping community and the reluctance to come downtown. So from that standpoint I think it was effective."

The pressure worked, and the downtown merchants agreed that they would take down their discriminatory signs. Department stores had to desegregate their eating facilities, drinking fountains, rest rooms, and fitting rooms, as well as promise to integrate their sales forces. Parisian was a specialty store and didn't have a dining room, but Hess remembers the entire period of change as one of "trauma," particularly after Bull Connor attempted to sabotage the agreement.

He knew at the time, he said, that what the Negroes were demanding was proper. "Morally, it was right," he said. "But it was still traumatic.

"In retrospect, they seem like such small things that were being asked of us," he said. "But at the time, they seemed monumental, because of the concern we had for the reaction of our constituents. After the agreement was announced, of course it was in the papers. It wasn't the sort of thing that was going to be done quietly and the signs would go. The press took it and reported it, and there it was for the total population to read about.

"I got a few calls. I was listed in the phone book. I got some calls at home. Frightened my wife. They're not pleasant. Profanity and abuse. But I also got a few calls from people who identified themselves as business people. And several of them said, 'I'm more upset about the fact that you're going to put my wife in a fitting room with blacks.' I said, 'Now, wait a minute. That's never happened before, and it's no way it can happen. Each fitting room is occupied by a single customer. There's no way that a fitting room — it's a cubicle — can be occupied by two people at one time, so there never has been and there never will be a time when two women of the same race or opposite race will occupy the same cubicle. Now, what's the problem?'

"Well, they didn't have an answer for that, you know. And you look back at some of these things now and they seem so ridiculous. At the time, they seemed monumental."

■ ————————————————————————

Early in April, 1963, Martin Luther King came to Birmingham, as promised (or threatened, depending on one's side of the racial fence). Demonstrations started at downtown department stores. They were followed shortly by protest marches, sit-ins, and kneel-ins at local white churches. White moderates urged a suspension of demonstrations to give the new government time to be sworn in and act on its commitment to change, but Negroes replied that they had waited long enough already. On April 7, Palm Sunday, blacks marched on a "prayer pilgrimage," and Bull Connor sent officers with police dogs to follow them.

On Good Friday, King was arrested during a march. He was charged with "parading without a permit." President Kennedy called Coretta King and told her the FBI had been ordered to make sure her husband would not be mistreated while in jail. King stayed in jail for eight days before being released on bail.

While King was incarcerated, a number of white Birmingham clergymen issued a statement calling his and the Movement's ac-tivities "unwise and untimely." King replied with a long letter that is his most eloquent explanation of his role in, and hopes for, the civil rights movement. King's "Letter from Birmingham Jail," dated April 16, 1963, and addressed to the seven clergymen, replied to the concerns they and other white "moderates" had articulated.[2]

The clergymen's statement had deplored the demonstrations then under way in Birmingham, noted King, but "did not express a similar concern for the conditions that brought the demonstra-tions into being."

King recounted the numerous times the Movement had postponed its demonstrations to allow the white community to act on its own and to accommodate the change in government. But the wait produced only broken promises and requests for more delays. He patiently explained the concept of "creative tension" to the clergymen: "Nonviolent direct action seeks to create such a crisis and establish such creative tension that a community that has constantly refused to negotiate is forced to confront the issue." And he pointed out that there had not been a single civil rights gain without "determined legal and nonviolent pressure." He expressed his feelings about the need to violate unjust laws. And King confessed to what he called his grave disappointment with the white moderate and with the organized church, which he depicted as a "tail-light . . . rather than a headlight leading men to higher levels of justice."

On the day before King dispatched his letter, Albert Boutwell and a new city council had been sworn in as Birmingham's new leadership. The old troika refused to leave, however, and Bull Connor continued to direct the police department's attack on protesters.

As was often the case after mass demonstrations had been conducted for a few days, the numbers of those who were willing to be arrested and jailed started to decline. Then, at the beginning of May, SCLC sent children, some as young as six and seven years of age, into the streets. Connor arrested nearly a thousand of them, provoking the outraged involvement of their parents and the undivided attention of the media. More children marched the next day, and this time Connor directed high-pressure fire hoses and police dogs at them and the other demonstrators. Photographs of his response appeared in newspapers and on television around the world, producing international revulsion.[3]

His jail full, Connor shifted to a strategy of simply attacking the protesters with water and dogs, rather than arresting and incarcerating them. When some Negroes fought back with rocks and bottles, Connor called in the Alabama state police. The state officers were commanded by George Wallace's director of public safety, Al Lingo, who was almost as wild on the subject of race relations as Connor. Robert Kennedy issued a statement agreeing with the demonstrators' goals but deploring their timing. The president said Birmingham was damaging the nation's reputation. The administration refused to intervene, however, on the grounds that no federal laws had been violated.[4]

On May 8, King agreed to a twenty-four-hour truce, over Fred Shuttlesworth's objections. On the next day, King announced an agreement with the ad hoc white group. It called for the commitment of downtown leaders (but not of city officials) to the desegregation, in ninety days, of some public accommodations; progress in hiring and promotion; the release of arrested Negroes on bond or personal recognizance; and the creation of a biracial committee to get communication going. Deposed mayor Art Hanes called the white negotiators "a bunch of quisling, gutless traitors." The city commission tried to scuttle the agreement, but failed. King said the settlement was "the most significant victory for justice we've ever seen in the Deep South."[5]

--------------------------------- ■

Much of what happened in Birmingham appeared to the outside world to be spontaneous, but to Wyatt Tee Walker, it was the result of months of hard work.

Martin Luther King's right-hand man had started making trips to the Alabama city not long after King pulled out of Albany. "I was hooking it up," said Walker later. "I went to Birmingham and hooked up the wires, and then Dr. King came and pushed the button."

Such work was characteristic of Wyatt Tee Walker. The young minister was possessed of a sharp wit and an equally sharp tongue, but he never complained about subordinating himself to the man he called Leader. Walker was quite capable of successfully occupying practically any spotlight the Movement might shine on him, but he avoided ever intruding into the brilliant beam that constantly illuminated King.

"I take pride in doing things well," said Walker. "I don't care what it is. You know about my ego. But did you know I washed Dr. King's underwear and his socks, shined his shoes? Oh, yeah. Dr. King liked his shoes shined. And we'd be rushing — couldn't get to a shoeshine place coming through the airport. One day I said, 'Doctor, I believe I'll shine your shoes for you.' He said, 'Oh, Wyatt, you don't want to do that.' I said, 'No, I'll do it.' And then he'd say, 'But I didn't bring another pair of socks.' I'd say, 'When do you have to go out again, sir?' I'd say, 'I'll wash your socks for you.'

"There wasn't anything I wouldn't do for Martin Luther King, because I sensed his commitment to that struggle, and I respect leadership. I used to have to tell staff, 'Don't call Dr. King "Martin." He's the President, he's our Leader. You call him "Dr. King" around here.' "

"My mandate," said Walker, "was to run workshops and to recruit three hundred people, so that when we got ready to launch the campaign in Birmingham, we'd have three hundred people ready to go who would spend at least five days in jail. So I'd been in and out of Birmingham — slipping in, slipping out, slipping in, slipping out. Very quietly. The authorities never knew I was there. If you go back through all of those periods, it is difficult to find a picture of me, because I studiously stayed out of photographs. Whenever I had to go into one of these Southern towns, I didn't want the authorities to immediately know that King's man was in town. I did it by design. Like I say, I see myself being very sharp. And it paid off in the long run."

But certainly Walker was well known by the white authorities?

"My *name* was well known. You've got to remember: All niggers look alike to them."

Walker said his scouting efforts virtually ignored the possibility of seeking help from Birmingham's white religious leaders. "We wrote them off," he said. Instead, Project C, as the campaign was called (for "confrontation"), was directed almost exclusively at jeopardizing the power structure's ability to make money.

"We decided that the most effective way to get the attention of the deciders and presiders of Birmingham was to stop the ebb and flow of finance," said Walker. "So we concentrated on the mercantile industry, and we got a big plus. We wanted a boycott that would be fifty percent effective among blacks. It was more than ninety percent effective. You couldn't *find* any black folks downtown. Plus, with the power of those marches and what was going on and the dogs and the water hoses, the white men told their women, 'You stay away from downtown.' We had a stranglehold on downtown Birmingham."

There was one other, and quite essential, element that was needed in Birmingham: a crisis to focus everyone's attention (including the nation's) and to generate a steady resupply of energy for the Negroes who demonstrated and went to jail — to engender the creative tension that King knew was necessary to produce meaningful negotiations and lasting change.

"Back in Atlanta, Dr. King said, 'Wyatt, you've got to find some way to create a crisis,'" recalled Walker.

"I said, 'Yeah, I know, Leader. I don't know how I'm going to do it, but I'll find some way to do it.'"

The way became clear to Walker during a Sunday mass meeting and march that took place not long after the demonstrations had started. Perhaps a thousand people had gathered, said Walker. When the mass meeting was over, hundreds marched out of the church and down the street. After they had walked one or two blocks, the police, who had their dogs with them, made the arrests, as usual. "And the next morning UPI said, "Eleven hundred march in Birmingham. Eleven arrested.' Or 'Twelve arrested.'

"I said, 'Leader, I got it! I got it!' He said, 'What have you got, Wyatt?' And I said, 'We're going to drag the demonstrations out till the people get home from work. And Bull Connor will do something.'" Walker knew that if a demonstration lasted long enough and attracted enough people, Connor would surely swing into violent action. "I knew I had it then. We *presumed* that Bull would do something to help us. We didn't know what it would be. So that's what I did. I just dragged out the demonstrations till the crowd got home, and Bull Connor was predictable. We knew he'd do something. I mean, that was it. We had Huntley and Brinkley every night." (The "Huntley-Brinkley Report" was a popular evening television news program.)

"That dumb-ass Bull Connor!" Walker laughed. "All he had to do was let us go down there and pray, and after four or five days it would be over. See? But as long as he kept going and stopping us, we said, 'We're just going to keep on applying the pressure.'"

After several days of this, the crowd's interest began to wane. But Connor, as if on cue, again performed a valuable service for the Movement. It happened during another demonstration downtown.

"Somebody got to juking at the dogs," said Walker. "You've seen that famous picture of that man." Walker referred to a photograph of a policeman in sunglasses and with what looked like the trace of a smile on his face, holding the sweater of a young black man while a leashed German shepherd buried his fangs in the man's midsection. The picture was transmitted around the world by the Associated Press. The young man, said Walker, "had nothing to do with our movement. He was a spectator." But his victimization became a powerful symbol that reenergized the Movement in Birmingham.

So did the participation of young children in the demonstrations, as did Bull Connor's use of fire hoses against demonstrators. James Forman, of the Student Nonviolent Coordinating Committee, was highly critical of SCLC for sending children into battle and for what he called King's lack of proper leadership in Birmingham. It particularly bothered Forman, he wrote in his memoir, that when demonstrators were on "the barricades" and their demonstration was threatening to get out of hand, King spent the afternoon in the Gaston Hotel eating steak and still in his pajamas. Forman also said that "it was a disgusting moment to me" when he saw Wyatt Tee Walker and Dorothy Cotton, an SCLC official, "jumping up and down, elated" at learning that Connor had turned dogs and fire hoses on the demonstrators.[6]

Asked about this, Walker replied that Forman was "a liar." On the question of sending people into a demonstration in the knowledge that they would be dealt with violently, he said: "In a war, you have casualties. . . . Why would we have workshops on nonviolence? . . . We conducted workshops, we told them that this can happen to you, but you must not fight back. In the workshops we spit on people. We put cigarettes on them. We called them vile names. That had been going on for years in our movement. So the potential was already there."

And the black people of Birmingham, he said, were ready and willing to take risks. "They believed in God," he said. "They believed in Dr. King's leadership. And they were tired of being humiliated as human beings. The most important thing that happened in that whole period was that people decided that they are not going to be afraid of white folks anymore. Dr. King's most lasting contribution is that he emancipated black people's psyche. We threw off the slave mentality. Going to jail had been the whip which kept black folks in line. Now going to jail was transformed into a badge of honor."

"If you're going to talk about the attack we mounted, you'd have to figure two stages," said Fred Shuttlesworth: "Number one, the stage before the massive demonstration. That was purely economic. We stayed off buses and other things, too. You see, seven years before Martin

Luther King came to Birmingham, we had actually legally won the battles, but they were Pyrrhic victories. If we went in the parks, they closed the parks down. We'd win the right to go to the libraries; they'd close them down. And so we came to the confrontation, the raw, direct challenges. And then you must remember, also, the SCLC needed a victory. They did not get a victory in Albany."

In Albany, said the minister, the opposition was intelligent enough to keep its jails from being overburdened by shipping demonstrators off to neighboring counties. There was no similar problem in Birmingham, where Bull Connor *wanted* to fill his jails. This was fine with Shuttlesworth.

"We knew Birmingham wasn't going to do anything. We literally intended to fill the jails. We *intended* to have confrontations. Fill up the jails, override the system, make the system take care of it. We knew that we had to fill Bull Connor's jail, because Bull Connor thought that the jailhouse was sacred," a place that struck terror into the hearts of Negroes. "He told us he'd fill the jails up with us. So that's what we wanted."

Connor quickly complied. "At one time," Shuttlesworth said, "we had over four thousand people in jail. And the way I knew that we were sure enough breaking the system and about to break the barriers was one day when I was arrested and I went down before Judge Brown, and he said to me, 'Mr. Shuttlesworth, I regret that due to the overcrowded conditions in the jails, I cannot sentence you this morning.' I said, 'Your Honor, we're making progress.' "

Perhaps recognizing that Birmingham was failing where Albany had succeeded, Bull Connor hired Laurie Pritchett as a consultant.

The former Albany police chief said that Connor's police chief, Jamie Moore, had visited Albany during the Georgia city's crisis and was impressed with what he saw. He said Moore recommended to Connor that Birmingham adopt the Albany approach.

"So Bull called Asa Kelley and said he wanted me over there as a consultant. He said, 'We'll pay him,' so Asa said, 'Go on over there, Chief. Spend some time with him. And give him a good deal.' So I went over there. I'd never seen Bull Connor. I walked into the office, and he was sitting in a chair with his back to me, big old chair. And when he turned around, there was a little man with a big voice. He said, 'We're glad to have you over here, Chief. I was just talking on the phone to the recreation [department]. They're trying to integrate the golf courses. I really messed them up. I put concrete in all the holes.' And I'm looking at him, and I said to myself, 'Man, how damn stupid can you get?'

"See, he was an opportunist. He was doing this with the idea that he was going to be the next governor. And he was a fool."

Plugging the holes on the golf course, said Art Hanes, the former mayor, was "just an act of rebellion," and besides, they were filled with dirt, not concrete. "I guess at the time a little politics entered into it, too. Southern politicians had to take a stand one way or the other."

Hanes had taken stands *both* one way and the other. As often happened in elections in the one-party South, in the initial campaign he went after voters of all sorts — even Negroes. Once the field was narrowed down for the runoff, he deliberately focussed his appeal to whites, accusing his opponent of being overly friendly with Negroes. George Wallace had done the same thing.

After Birmingham's Negroes overwhelmingly endorsed Hanes's opponent in the runoff, Hanes said, "I had a prominent black man call me and tell me, 'Mr. Hanes, you've always been fair to everybody that's ever known you. And I'm going to tell you this. Unless you yell, "Nigger, nigger," in this runoff, they're going to beat the daylights out of you.' And I said, 'Thank you, thank you, Doctor.' And so I just took a stand."

The stand Hanes took was decidedly a segregationist one. But Hanes denied that white supremacy was ever a consuming interest of his.

"I grew up in the South and never thought about it," he said. "We never talked about that thing. We used to play ball on Saturday against the black team from across the streetcar tracks. It never lasted past two innings because it always ended up in a rock battle. Nobody ever got hurt. And we both used the old swimming hole. Blacks would come down there and catch us in the creek and take our clothes and run with them. Or we'd go there when they were there, and we'd take their clothes and run down to the creek, tie knots in them, and put rocks in them, and throw them back in the creek. This was just a way of life. Nobody ever thought much about it . . . .

"It was nothing vicious, and of course I never thought *that way* about blacks or anything. You just took it for granted. You just grew up that way in the Deep South."

Hanes said that during the time Sidney Smyer and the downtown business leaders were meeting, none of them ever called on him for help. "I was never contacted by any of the black leaders or the white leaders," he said. But, he added, "I knew at the time that it was explosive."

When the explosion came, though, according to Hanes, it wasn't as bad as the public was led to believe. "When all the demonstrations started," he said, "they made a lot out of the police dogs. We just had old moth-eaten hound dogs here. That's all we ever had. You show me one person that had a skin break, I'll buy them a double-breasted Kuppenheimer suit. Just show me one person. . . ."

Nonetheless, the picture of the "moth-eaten hound dog" that looked remarkably like a German shepherd made the front page of virtually every newspaper in the country. The Reverend C. Herbert Oliver and his Inter-Citizens Committee published a signed statement by Henry Lee Shambry, a Negro who swore that the police "put two dogs on me and I was bitten on my left arm, my left leg and my right hip. I had to go to the doctor for treatment." The affidavit contains three photographs of a man, identified as Shambry, being attacked by two dogs whose leashes are held by white police officers. In one, a German shepherd is tearing off a leg of the man's pants. Shambry concluded his statement with the words. "This experience has made [me] more determined than ever to be free."[7]

"That picture's a fake, though, the one I saw," said Hanes. "We didn't have uniforms like that, dogs and all that. I didn't take that too seriously, because nobody got hurt." As for the fire hoses, the former mayor of Birmingham said, the Negroes actually enjoyed them. "They would take off their blue jeans and they had swimming suits, bathing suits on. And they just ran and played in the fire hose and all that.

"I've seen some *real* violence as a PT boat skipper in the South Pacific. I sailed in the face of a Jap task force and fired my torpedoes at point-blank range at the Jap navy cruiser and battleships. One of the greatest navy sea battles of all time. So that didn't upset me too much."

■ ────────────

On the Saturday night after the May 9 announcement of the Birmingham settlement, the Ku Klux Klan held a rally on the edge of town. Afterward, during the night, a dynamite explosion ripped through the Gaston Hotel, where King had been staying (he was away from Birmingham at the time) and where SCLC had its Birmingham command post. Another blast struck the home of the Reverend A. D. King, the leader's brother. An estimated twenty-five hundred Negroes poured out of their homes and into the streets. Some of them rioted, setting police cars afire and breaking department store windows and looting. Emil Hess's store, Parisian, was among those that were damaged. In some cases, blacks pulled passing white motorists from their cars and beat them.

Al Lingo's state troopers went on a rampage, clubbing Negroes and in some cases hurling them through locked doors. Art Hanes, who maintained he was still mayor pending a court's resolution of the two-governments issue, was quoted as saying: "Martin Luther King is a revolutionary. The nigger King ought to be investigated by the attorney general. This nigger has got the blessing of the attorney general and the White House." Of Attorney General Kennedy himself, Hanes was quoted as saying: "I hope that every drop of blood that's spilled, he tastes in his throat, and I hope he chokes on it."[8]

President Kennedy moved toward federalizing the Alabama National Guard, but it turned out not to be needed. Members of the Black Muslim religion, meantime, were urging a more aggressive confrontation of white racism.

Before the end of May, the Supreme Court of the United States decided that the newly elected city government was the only legitimate one, and the Boutwell administration finally took office. The court also ruled that all of Birmingham's segregation ordinances were unconstitutional.[9] David Vann thought of the first decision as "the coup of history, of a Southern city changing its policies by democratic process."

■

Laurie Pritchett was in Birmingham, serving as Bull Connor's consultant, on the night of the riot.

"I told Bull Connor,* I said, 'Bull, you got the Ku Klux Klan just over the mountain here holding a meeting. They're going to blow King up. And if anything ever happens to him, wherever he's at, the city's going to burn.' I said, 'Cities all over this United States are going to burn.'

"He says, 'Let them blow him up. I ain't going to protect him. They would've killed him that night, but the Klan didn't have sense enough to know to pack the dynamite. They just laid it up against the building [the Gaston Hotel]. And the resistance knocked it out instead of in. And then they tore up every car that the city of Birmingham had that night. The next morning I went in and told Bull, 'Man, I give you advice. You're paying me well. You don't take the advice. I'm going home.' "

———————————

Isaac Reynolds of the Congress of Racial Equality was in Birmingham, staying at the Gaston Hotel, that night. "When they bombed the hotel," he said afterward, "it was my room that really got bombed, because King's room was above mine. There was a hole on the back part of my room in the ground that I could've stood in and couldn't have looked up out of it." Bull Connor was searching for him that night, said Reynolds, and he had to flee the hotel and find refuge in one of A. G. Gaston's other enterprises. "They had to hide me in the Gaston undertaking parlor," he said. "I slept for about a week in a casket every night. He stored his caskets up on the second level, and I would look out at the Birmingham police and the state troopers looking for me. Prior to that time, I really didn't care for funeral homes."

■ ———————————

After the settlement and the resulting violence, Birmingham's Negroes seemed less patient about the sort of white harassment that had been commonplace in the days when C. Herbert Oliver's Inter-Citizens Committee was compiling its documentation. When a

———————————

*Actually, Pritchett referred to the Birmingham official as "Bull Connors." Several other people interviewed for this book, both black and white, made the mistake of adding an *s* to Connor's name. It is ironic that the former public safety commissioner of Birmingham should be remembered not just for his racism but also for the inadvertent contributions he made to the civil rights movement *and* that those remembering him should get his name wrong.

spate of dynamite blasts followed the purchase by Negroes of homes in a formerly all-white neighborhood — one where Arthur Shores lives now — the Negroes hired a white private detective to infiltrate the Ku Klux Klan. He learned, said Shores, that on a particular night a certain house would be burned or dynamited.

"About a dozen blacks with shotguns, rifles, and pistols secreted themselves across the street from that house," said the lawyer. "And right on time, the whites gathered there. And before they could do anything — set the house afire or bomb it — the blacks fired on them. Killed one, wounded one, and the rest of them fled.

"They never found anybody to prosecute. Well, that broke up the bombing and burning of houses that blacks were moving into."

Everything that happened in the Movement, from the decision in *Brown* to Bull Connor's actions in Birmingham, contained a large measure of experimentation. Few participants in the struggle, be they segregationists, black activists, or government officials, could be certain of what the next step would be. The same could be said of those observers of the Movement who transmitted the news that it made to the front pages, radios, and television screens of the nation.

The written media had covered long-running stories before, of course. Wars had provided plenty of experience for that. Newspaper reporters were accustomed to working on beats, or specialized fields of interest, so it was second nature for editors to designate certain reporters to cover the Movement. In the majority press, this almost always meant white reporters, for the mainstream press had few black newsroom employees.

Still, the experience was a new one for the newsgatherers of the South and nation. This was an ongoing story in which the traditional centers of respectability and power — the governors, legislatures, school boards, judiciary — often were cast in the role of lawbreaker and arrogant defier of the law of the land. Some newspapers covered the Movement as they would any political story, such as a legislative session or gubernatorial campaign, because the featured actors were the same. Some papers relied on the wire services, the Associated Press and United Press International, for their coverage. Often the local coverage was atrocious, as at the

Albany Herald and some of the papers in Mississippi; sometimes it was heroic.

Television news in the sixties was, if not in its childhood, at least in its prepubescence. Technical advances that in a few years would be taken for granted, such as lightweight videotape cameras and instantaneous transmission by way of satellites, were unknown on the hot, dusty streets of Albany and Birmingham. The people who reported the news from the field for the television and radio networks, many of them, were different as well. They were experienced reporters who had gotten their training, as likely as not, in the print media. They were selected for their jobs because of their reporting competence, not for their on-air presence and good looks. Some were almost as homely-looking as newspaper reporters. All of them — reporters from newspapers, the weekly newsmagazines, radio networks, television, and the categories that were called "the foreign press" and "the Negro press" — shared an uncertainty about what might happen next and an intense desire to be there when it did happen.

———————————————— ■

Like several of his fellow reporters, Claude Sitton of the *New York Times* started covering the civil rights movement at Little Rock. The 1957 school desegregation crisis was the first big story that grew out of the *Brown* decision. Sitton, the newspaper's chief Southern correspondent, stayed in Little Rock for six weeks, with no time off. His wife, Eva, flew over from their home in Atlanta for one weekend. Before long, extended absences from home had become commonplace. "One time I came back from having been on the road for some time," said Sitton, "and I noticed that my older son was talking. I said to Eva, 'Clint's talking.' She said, 'Well, what you mean is, he's been talking for three months.' Wives had to put up with a lot."

Sitton, who was born in Atlanta in 1925 to a schoolteacher and a railroad man, soon became the member of the press corps who could be counted on to show up at any significant Movement event. Reporters from other publications used his presence or absence to measure the importance of an occasion. Once in Alabama, a reporter from another newspaper was seen standing behind Sitton as he typed out his story, making notes on the paragraphs as they emerged from the platen.

Sitton's typewriter, and the machine of choice for reporters covering the Movement, was a lightweight Olivetti 22 portable, a tiny workhorse that travelled in a neat zippered case and that was, unfortunately, also a dead giveaway that the owner was a reporter. Sitton found that there were times when it was helpful to be known as a newspaperman, but there were others when it was best to look like something else.

"I rented white Pontiacs in Mississippi," he said, "because the Mississippi highway patrol had white Pontiacs. I also wore a London Fog raincoat and a hat because it provided a little protective coloration." Segregationists were likely to assume that a stranger dressed like that was a federal agent, and therefore (at least in the minds of some of them) someone to leave alone. Once Sitton and a reporter from *Time* were in the bus station diner in McComb, Mississippi, waiting for Freedom Riders to arrive. They were hoping not to be identified as reporters. "We were sitting there in the cafe, drinking coffee," said Sitton. "Both of us had on London Fog raincoats and hats. The bus pulled up at the front door." The first rider into the cafe was jumped by a local oil-field worker and a brief but spirited one-way fight ensued. "The next day, the *McComb Enterprise Journal* reported that two FBI men had sat in the bus station and watched the riot and had not turned their hands to do a thing."

Sitton popularized a device that made life safer for dozens of reporters and that remains in wide use now: the Claude Sitton Memorial Sawed-off Notebook. Formerly, most reporters took their notes in stenographic notebooks — the wide, spiral-bound books that are used to take shorthand notes in offices. The books were too wide to carry in an inside pocket, and they clearly marked the bearer as a reporter. This could be decidedly unhealthy in places where the press, with its penchant for bearing tidings whether they be good or bad, was routinely despised.

"We were immediately identified by these notebooks," Sitton said. "So what I did was, I would take one of these paper knives [a heavy-duty hydraulic cutting device, found in print shops] and cut the notebook down, so it would slide all the way down into your jacket pocket. Sometimes if things got real tight, well, you'd just take your pen and you'd take notes inside your pocket." One day Sitton was walking past an office supply store in Richmond when he spotted commercially made narrow notebooks. He bought a few, liked them, and ordered a case. The store, Stationers Incorporated, was clever enough to print its address and telephone number on the notebooks, and soon reporters from all over the South were ordering them. "Stationers really should give me a dividend," joked Sitton.

Edwin Guthman worked at the Justice Department, but he was enough of a lifelong newspaper reporter to keep his notes, too, in a notebook. Guthman was keenly aware of which publications were in worst odor in white Southern communities, and which ones were acceptable to the segregationists. "In Birmingham they'd see the notebook and they'd say, 'You from the *New York Times*?' Or 'Are you from *Time* magazine?' And I'd say, 'I'm from *U.S. News & World Report*,' and they'd leave me alone."

Guthman recalled the way Jack Nelson, then the *Los Angeles Times* reporter who covered the Movement, got important information after the police fired on demonstrators at Orangeburg State College in South Carolina. Survivors of the rampage were taken to a local hospital. "He goes to the hospital, and he walks right in, and he wants to get the medical records," said Guthman. "He says, 'I'm Nelson of the Atlanta Bureau,' and they hand over the goddamn records. It showed that every one of those kids who were in the hospital had been shot in the back." Guthman teaches a journalism course now at the University of California, and he said he uses the reporter's implication that he was from the FBI, rather than the Atlanta bureau of a newspaper, as an example of an "ethical question." But he clearly admired Nelson's resourcefulness.

Charles Quinn got his training in journalism at the *New York Herald Tribune*. Quinn covered Little Rock for the newspaper, then went to the National Broadcasting Company in 1962. He was born in 1930 in Utica, New York, but he had strong roots in the South. His father was a native of south Georgia, and Quinn grew up in a home that had a portrait of Robert E. Lee on the living room wall.

"We used black-and-white film," recalled Quinn of his television news work, "and sixteen-millimeter cameras. We used small, hand-held cameras called Filmos that would carry a hundred feet of film. It was silent. Then we had the Auricons, the bigger cameras, that had four hundred feet with sound." Often the smaller cameras were used in tight, fast-moving situations where the larger machine, which rested atop a heavy tripod, would be too cumbersome. A television news crew would usually consist of the reporter, a camera operator, a sound technician, an electrician (who handled the lighting), and a driver. Sometimes, when conditions got really rough, a network would include an armed guard to protect the crew. Later on in the Movement years, the Columbia Broadcasting System added another crew member, a field producer, who handled logistics.

There were many logistics to handle. A crew had to either get its film to a friendly or affiliate television station by late in the afternoon for processing, or it had to hand the undeveloped film to a trusted airline pilot or flight attendant who, for a few dollars, made sure it got into the hands of a network courier at Atlanta or New York City. All this had to be accomplished in time for the film to be edited and matched with sound, which was recorded separately, then squeezed into the evening news show, which then lasted for only fifteen minutes. Charles Quinn's reports went to the "Huntley-Brinkley Report" in the evening and the "Today" show in the morning. He was also responsible for phoning in hourly audio reports to the network's radio news division and for sup-plying news for other radio shows. Once Quinn was in Birmingham at the end of a particularly tiring day. He had gotten the film in, done the hourly news shows, and had one more program to do. He sat in his hotel room, phoning in the report, and when he got to the end, he signed off: "This is Charles Quinn, NBC News — ." He had forgotten where he was.

Quinn was especially mindful of accusations that the press, partic-ularly the visual media, "staged" or otherwise contrived news events. Early in his career in television (and early in television's career in covering the Movement and live news generally) he saw occasional examples of film crews who crossed the line into directing the people they were photographing. Quinn intervened a couple of times to stop the practice, he said.

"I'm not going to mention the network," he said, "but once in Americus, Georgia, there was a racial story. A white kid had been shot. And a reporter — I use the word loosely — from another network got with the head of the local black community and said, 'Why don't you get organized and have a memorial march down to the bridge where this boy was shot and throw a wreath into the water to show that you're sorry?' " Quinn said he threatened to do a report not on the march but on the competing television crew's attempt to manipulate the news, and the crew backed down.

Often, said Quinn, Movement strategists would offer to restage some event that the NBC crews had missed, but each time he refused. He was mindful, he said, that the presence of a television camera causes people to do things they otherwise might not have done. "We all knew that we provoke stuff," he said. "Everybody acts a little differently" when they know they are on camera.

"A lot of people would accuse us of being used by them. They'd say it wouldn't have happened if we hadn't been there. But I can cite to you dozens of stories where we weren't there and where all holy hell had broken loose the night before, and we had to go in the next morning and pick up the pieces. It would've happened anyway. I just think that television dramatized it in a way which newspapers couldn't. You could write about it. You could write two columns, but to see the state policemen and the sheriff's deputies attack the marchers and demonstrators — I mean, that was the ball game."

■ ────────────────────────

It looked for a time as if segregation — hard-core segregation, of the variety practiced so earnestly in Birmingham — had been dealt a heavy blow. Even George Wallace seemed to have lost some of his steam. On June 11, 1963, Wallace appeared on the campus of the University of Alabama in Tuscaloosa, with Al Lingo's state troopers very much in evidence, and carried out his promise to "stand in the schoolhouse door" against integration. Two young Negroes, the first since Autherine Lucy, were entering the school under federal court order. When the order came down late in May, Wallace replied, "I am the embodiment of the sovereignty of this state, and I will be present to bar the entrance of any Negro who attempts to enroll at the University of Alabama."[10]

But the "fighting little judge," who half a year before had promised "segregation now, segregation tomorrow, segregation forever," actually came up with "segregation yesterday." In a carefully scripted performance that was staged literally in the doorway of a campus building, Wallace first denied the demand by Assistant Attorney General Nicholas Katzenbach that the students be admitted, then stepped aside and let them in. The desegregation of the university's Huntsville campus took place with even less drama.

On the same day, President Kennedy announced he was sending a comprehensive civil rights bill to Congress. "The events in Birmingham and elsewhere have so increased the cries for equality that no city or state or legislative body can prudently choose to ignore them," he said. "We face, therefore, a moral crisis as a country and as a people. . . . Next week, I shall ask the Congress of the United States to act, to make a commitment it has not fully made in this century to the proposition that race has no place in American life or law." The Southern Regional Council said the proposal for legislation, which covered public accommodations, schools, voting rights, and equal employment, was "the strongest ever made by a president on Negro rights."[11]

But the veterans of the civil rights movement knew by now that there could be no gain without some sort of counterreaction. It was the racists' way of doing things. On the day after Kennedy sent his bill down the long road to enactment, Medgar E. Evers was killed in Jackson. The Mississippi NAACP leader was shot from ambush in front of his home.

PART SEVEN

OTHER FRONTIERS

TWENTY-NINE

THE MARCH

In the summer of 1963, after Birmingham, street protests spread throughout the South. A Justice Department study counted 758 demonstrations in 186 cities during the ten weeks after the Birmingham crisis. By the end of that year, the Southern Regional Council estimated that there had been 930 protests in 115 cities in the 11 Southern states, with more than 20,000 arrests, at least 35 bombings, and 10 deaths that were directly related to racial protests. There were demonstrations in the North, as well, most of them tied to complaints about unequal employment opportunities and about public education that might be integrated de jure, "by right," or under the law, but that were segregated de facto, in reality.[1]

In the spring, the Congress of Racial Equality had enlarged its Freedom Highways program, which had begun the year before. Foreign black diplomats who traveled U.S. Highway 40 between Washington and New York City had often encountered segregation in eating and lodging places along the way, and CORE had conducted demonstrations at businesses operated by chains such as Howard Johnson's, with some success. Now CORE extended the campaign into the southeastern states, especially North Carolina.[2]

The Student Nonviolent Coordinating Committee, which was largely edged out of the SCLC's Birmingham campaign by Wyatt Tee Walker, mounted its own protests in Nashville and Knoxville, Tennessee; Pine Bluff, Arkansas (where Albany veteran William Hansen was especially effective); Gadsden, Alabama, which had been a center of police brutality; Atlanta and Savannah, Georgia; Jackson, Mississippi; and Greensboro and Raleigh, North Carolina. Charles Sherrod's southwest Georgia project continued, with its interracial staff of eleven and its willingness to count success in terms of dozens, rather than thousands, of Negroes registered to vote.[3]

A SNCC project that summer in Cambridge, on Maryland's Eastern Shore of the Chesapeake Bay, was seen by many observers as a confrontation of personalities. The most compelling of those personalities was Gloria Richardson, the leader of the Cambridge Nonviolent Action Committee. Richardson was by no means an outside agitator; she came from one of Cambridge's oldest Negro families. Her grandfather had served for half a century on the city council until his death in the forties. "The council had a banquet once a year," recalled Richardson in 1963. "They sent my grandfather's meal to his home by way of police car."

SNCC came to Cambridge early in 1962 on one of the Freedom Rides that spread through the South in the wake of the original ride. Richardson, then the manager of a patent medicine store, became the Nonviolent Action Committee's president and led what she called "mild protests" against segregation — by which she meant the condition that was maintained not only by Cambridge's white leadership but also by Negroes who, she felt, had been co-opted by the whites. A program of voter registration followed, and some blacks were elected to city and county offices. After the elections, when the committee asked for changes in the way the government treated Negroes, negotiations bogged down. Militant demonstrations followed, with children on the front lines, as in Birmingham.

In Cambridge, there was violence by both blacks and whites. The Maryland National Guard came and stayed a month. Three days after the guard left, violence broke out again, with roving bands of Negroes and whites turning the main thoroughfare, Race Street (once the site of buggy races), into a battle zone. Violence begat negotiations, and eventually, painfully, there were some breaches in the system of segregation in Cambridge.

Danville was even tougher.

The underlying facts were painfully familiar. The city, with a third of its population Negro, maintained segregation in everything from public accommodations to hospitals — and especially in the public library. The main library in Danville, a mill town in southern Virginia, was in fact a memorial to the Confederacy, the site where the rebels' last full cabinet meeting was held, in April, 1865, before Robert E. Lee announced his surrender to the Union forces. One early goal of the antisegregation campaign in Danville had been the opening of the library to blacks. A 1960 court order forced the desegregation of the facility, but its operators closed it for several months. When the library reopened on an integrated basis, all the seats had been removed and a fee was charged for a library card.[4]

Out of the library campaign grew the Danville Christian Progressive Association, which became an affiliate of the Southern Christian Leadership Conference. A key aim of the Negro movement in Danville in 1963 was equal access to municipal jobs, including those of firemen, policemen, clerks, and meter readers. When the city was slow in responding to polite demands, demonstrators sat in at the city hall. The city replied to that and other demonstrations with brute force of Birmingham caliber. Policemen kicked in the door at a Negro church and arrested the organizers inside. They used fire hoses on protesters and clubbed them. On June 10, 1963, known in Danville as Bloody Monday, sixty-five protesters were injured.

The city's legal response to dissent was about as heavy-handed as its police reaction: Fourteen people, including SNCC workers who had come to town at the invitation of the Reverend Lawrence Campbell, a Baptist minister, were charged with "inciting the colored population to acts of violence and war against the white population." White Virginians had passed the statute after the 1831 Nat Turner Rebellion, in which the Southampton County slave led an uprising that resulted in the massacre of some fifty whites. Turner was captured and hanged. The statute had been used in 1859 to hang abolitionist John Brown after his raid on the federal arsenal at Harpers Ferry to seize weapons for use in freeing slaves. When the municipal judge heard the 1963 cases, he had a gun strapped to his waist. When the demonstrators' attorney started to argue their cases, he, too, was arrested.[5]

■

After her participation in the CORE workshop in Miami in 1960, Dorothy Miller returned to New York City — reluctantly, because she wanted to stay in the South and become part of the Movement — and got a job in the welfare department. She remembers that, as part of their training, she and others were given large case folders on recipients — or "clients," as the bureaucracy calls them — to study. One of the recipients, she said, was constantly referred to as "a Puerto Rican man who doesn't work." Miller's territory was Harlem, and she and other caseworkers were expected to make frequent "home visits," to "make sure that there were no secret men" visiting the female recipients "and that they truly were in poverty, and that kind of thing." A supervisor told her to visit the Puerto Rican man who didn't work.

"I found out that he had one arm," she said. "They had not mentioned it for years. For years they would complain that he was not working, and he had one arm." This was one reason Miller did not like being a part of the welfare bureaucracy, but she was resigned to staying — until she got a call from Atlanta. The Southern Regional Council wanted to hire her as a research assistant. "I was determined to get to Atlanta," she said, "because I knew that's where the SNCC people were. So I went."

She lived in Atlanta "on the white side" until she met Jane Bond, who also had been hired at SRC. Jane's brother was Julian Bond. This provided Miller with an excuse to do something she had been afraid to do: visit SNCC. "I was there for four months before I got the courage to go over to the SNCC office," she said. "Because in my mind they were these unbelievable heroes, and I was totally awestruck.

"Forman was there. And Forman, of course, latched on to me immediately. Forman was, in my opinion, an organizational genius. He could find out in five minutes what you knew how to do, and in his mind he had a place for you to be. He was phenomenal. He asked me the fateful question, which I teased him about many years later, which was, 'Can you type?'

"It turned out that I am a totally self-trained typist, from the time I was twelve. Three fingers on each hand and *very* fast. A lot of mistakes, but very fast. So he was thrilled that he had me. He soon put me to work in the evenings. My first job was to type the affidavits from the field secretaries coming back from the field.

"That was trauma city. These unbelievable people were sitting next to me saying, 'I took Mrs. Smith to the courthouse in Liberty, Mississippi,' and I'm sitting there typing the whole thing up! I was verbatim typing as they spoke.

"Then one day I said to Forman, 'You know, in addition to typing, I know how to write.' And of course he was totally thrilled. He decided that I should work with Julian. And we started working on the newsletter, *The Student Voice.*"

From then on, Dorothy Miller was a confirmed and loyal SNCC person. Although she did not join the staff officially until the summer of 1962, she was from the beginning one of the valuable half-dozen people who kept SNCC running. She and Jane Bond rented an apartment, on the black side this time, and she spent long hours at short pay turning out press releases, newsletters, appeals for funds, and urgent telegrams to the Justice Department.

When Bob Zellner became SNCC's first white field secretary, Miller took a liking to him. The liking had developed into something far more serious by the summer of 1963, when both Miller and Zellner went to Danville. Miller wrote a substantial SNCC research document on the city, but her role as noncombatant did not immunize her from police violence. "I had the usual experiences in Danville," she said. "Beaten up by a cop. 'Beaten up' is a little exaggerated; he hit me in the head with a club.

"Just once. I actually saw stars. I didn't believe that you can actually see stars. Everything started flashing. I'm sure it ruptured some blood vessel or something. But the thing I didn't forget was that I was on the ground when he hit me in the head. The water hoses were on us, and we were utterly helpless. So it was just out of meanness and vengeance."

By then, she and Bob Zellner definitely wanted to get married. "But I was always away, or Bob was arrested, or something was happening to prevent it." In this case, it was a matter of Dorothy's leaving town in a hurry. She was one of those named in indictments for "inciting the colored population to acts of violence and war against the white population," and there was a warrant outstanding for her arrest. She fled the city on a plane, using a fake name.

The Danville movement, said the Reverend Lawrence Campbell, was primarily interested in improving economic opportunities for Negroes, both in private and public employment.

"It was a two-pronged thing," he said. "We were talking with the mayor and city council about giving to us employment as water meter readers, secretarial positions, and all that kind of thing, with them. Then we were talking with enterprises about hiring blacks and integrating the lunch counters. We organized the Danville Christian Progressive Association because we were not pleased with the way the NAACP at that point was doing things. We felt that the NAACP should have been more adamant in terms of seeing that the city would've complied with that [*Brown*] ruling. It was just a feeling that they just were moving too slow. They didn't want to disturb the status quo."

When Martin Luther King, Jr., came to Danville to address the group in 1963, the demonstrations started. "We had given to the city council a position paper on how we felt about employment, boards of commissions, that sort of thing," said Campbell. "But they ignored us."

On Bloody Monday, however, the ignoring turned to violence. The city had deputized its white garbage collectors and stationed them at the city hall–police station complex. As in Albany, an alley separated the two offices.

"And . . . these fifty marchers, who were walking in this corridor to pray for the people who had been incarcerated that day as a result of demonstrations, they got caught in the alley. The city had the fire hoses and dogs, and these deputized garbage collectors just started whipping heads. My wife was one of those who was beaten.

"Prior to that time, we had not really gotten the majority of black people involved because they were afraid. This was really almost a total agrarian community, except for Dan River Mills. We did not have Corning Glass, did not have Goodyear, did not have Gypsum, any of these other industries that we have here now. And people here were largely seasonal workers. The professionals here were typical of what you would see in any black community — the preachers, teachers, and undertakers. And they were reluctant to participate. But after the people were beaten, it sort of solidified the community."

It was, said Campbell, like Bull Connor and Birmingham all over again. "Had there not been a Bull Connor, you probably would not have had a Martin Luther King. The way I look at it, had there not been a Judas, you may not have had a Jesus. I think you needed that counterpart."

■ ────────────────────────────────

Observers of the Movement began to detect among Negroes, after Birmingham, what they called a "new militance" — or at least that is what white observers called it. The term was hardly heard among the Movement's practitioners themselves, probably because they did not see their demands as being new or especially militant at all. There were several reasons why the demeanor of Negroes who demanded their rights may have appeared to be more intense: For one thing, the relatively mild positions they had taken before — demands for biracial committees and for the desegregation of public accommodations and the like — had been dealt with in relatively peaceful (if token) fashion by white power structures in such places as Atlanta, Nashville, and Raleigh. The same moderate demands seemed much more militant, though, when they were addressed to hard-core, "never" places like Oxford and Birmingham and Cambridge and Danville.

Another factor in the change was the postponement of school desegregation. With every year of delay, additional thousands of Negro children were deprived of equality. Parents became increasingly angry at seeing another generation of black children consigned to segregated schools, all those years after *Brown*. There were also other reasons: The formerly bright promise of federal participation in the struggle for civil rights was now tarnished, and some activists were saying it was blemished beyond repair. Proponents of black nationalism, such as Malcolm X and Elijah Muhammad of the Nation of Islam, proclaimed loudly that militance was the only thing that white America would understand.

When the NAACP held its 1963 convention in Chicago, there was a clear split between delegates who favored a continuation of restrained protest and those who wanted nonviolent direct action. When Mayor Richard Daley rose to welcome the delegates, he was booed off the platform.

In some places, "militance" consisted only of blacks' trying to vote where none had voted before. In West Feliciana Parish, Louisiana, the Reverend Joseph Carter became the first black person to register since 1902. A white mob gathered to keep him from entering the courthouse, but Carter went in the back door and got his name on the books. Slater King ran for mayor of Albany. It was obvious that not enough blacks were registered there to elect him (or, as the *Albany Herald* might have put it, that the "Negro bloc vote" wasn't powerful enough), but King said his candidacy "helps the Negro to think politically" and made it harder for whites to take Negroes for granted.[6]

In a number of places, Negroes sought redress of their grievances by peaceful means and then, when they were rebuffed, did not demonstrate a "willingness to suffer" or a total commitment to nonviolence. This had happened in Birmingham, and later it occurred in Cambridge, Savannah, and a number of Northern cities. In Jackson, at the funeral for Medgar Evers, some of the mourners reacted violently against the white police who were present. John Doar of the Justice Department probably averted a real riot by stepping into the middle of the street and taking command of the situation.

There was increased, if not new, militance on the part of the hard-core segregationists, as well, and that certainly helped to fuel black militance. A gubernatorial campaign was under way in Mississippi, guaranteeing a higher and meaner level of racial rhetoric. Former governor James P. Coleman was opposed by Lieutenant Governor Paul Johnson, who had shaken his fist at the chief U.S. marshal at Oxford. On Mississippi's scale of moderate-to-rabid segregationist, Coleman, who boasted that "I know how to handle niggers," was considered a moderate. He lost.[7]

In Mileston, Mississippi, the home of Hartman Turnbow, the first Negro to try to register in that community, was firebombed. When Turnbow and his family ran from the house, someone, presumably the firebombers, shot at them. Turnbow shot back. On the next morning, the authorities charged Turnbow with arson.

Later, under pressure of a federal lawsuit, the charge was dropped.[8]

The perception of increased black militance helped move the federal government from its position just to the left of dead center on civil rights. Robert Kennedy attended a meeting in New York City arranged by the black novelist James Baldwin in the spring of 1963 and was shocked to hear scorn heaped on him and the administration. That may or may not have contributed to the fact that, by the summer, the administration had filed more than three dozen voting rights suits, eleven of them in Mississippi. The Civil Rights Commission, however, reported that the experience of five years of lawsuits filed under the 1957 Civil Rights Act showed that individual, case-by-case actions had not solved the problems of voting discrimination. But most attention on the federal government's actions was focussed on the president's proposed new civil rights act, which was beginning its long journey through Congress.[9]

In 1963 James Baldwin's most recent book, *The Fire Next Time*, had wakened a lot of white people to the ideas that freedom was not just the ambition of impoverished black Southerners and that nonviolence was not necessarily the only means Negroes might employ to get what they demanded. Robert Kennedy had read the book, and he wanted to talk to Baldwin. A meeting at Kennedy's home in Virginia fell through because of a late airplane arrival, so Kennedy invited Baldwin to assemble a group of interested people for a discussion at his apartment in New York City late in May.[10]

Kennedy apparently expected an assembly of experts on urban and racial problems, scholars who could contribute to the composition of the new civil rights bill. What he got was an apartment full of angry black people, many of them active in the arts. They knew little about how to solve such problems, but nevertheless had a lot of opinions, many of which were uncomplimentary to the Kennedy administration. The attorney general was stunned by what he heard.

———————————————— ∎

"There were people like Lena Horne and Harry Belafonte and Lorraine Hansberry," recalled Edwin Guthman, Kennedy's public relations liaison, who was there. "There were maybe about fifteen people. And, boy, they went at him. There was a young guy from Mississippi who had been in the Freedom Ride, and he'd been beat up. And it's going from bad to worse, and this kid [Jerome Smith, of CORE] says that he would not fight for the United States if the United States went to war with Cuba. And Bob had never heard anybody say that.

"It was a very unpleasant meeting. And Bob came out of there just furious. He was really pissed off. For about three days he's nothing but just pissed off. It's, 'Can you imagine those people . . .?' " Guthman said Kennedy was especially upset because some of those present who could have intervened on his behalf remained silent; a few even apologized to him in private, later. "And then — and this is typical Bob Kennedy — he begins to think that, you know, 'Maybe if I had had the experiences of that guy, I wouldn't want to fight for the United States, either.' And the next thing you know, he's up testifying in front of a congressional committee on some civil rights matter. He's saying to them, 'How can we say to a man that in time of war, you're an American citizen, but the rest of the time you're a citizen of the state of Mississippi, and we can't protect you?'

"There was that kind of evolution all his life. I think he always was still pissed off, because he thought that Harry Belafonte and some of these others should've stood up and they didn't, but they felt that they couldn't or they would be discredited. And that they were sort of making up for the fact that they hadn't been arrested, they hadn't been on the picket lines."

Robert Kennedy and his brother were under enormous pressure, thanks to Bull Connor, Art Hanes, and the police dogs and fire hoses of Birmingham, to produce meaningful legislation on the civil rights front. As authors Charles and Barbara Whalen observed in their history of the 1964 Civil Rights Act (the law that evolved from the 1963 proposals), "Birmingham had swept John Kennedy into the maelstrom. He was fully aware of the consequences of a strong civil rights bill. His political instincts told him not to present such a bill. Not only would it fail in Congress, but it would ruin his chance for a second term. Nevertheless, he had sworn to defend the Constitution."[11]

Guthman remembers that the attorney general's reaction to the need for such legislation was also "typical Bob Kennedy."

Birmingham had cooled down substantially, and Guthman and

several high-ranking Justice Department officials were returning to Washington on an airplane. "They were talking about how they had to have a civil rights bill. They outlined the basis of a bill. We got in on a Friday night, and they went to see Bob. On the next day he was going down to Asheville, North Carolina, to make a speech. So everybody goes down to Asheville with him. And on the plane going down, they tell Bob, 'You've got to have a civil rights bill, and it's got to have public accommodations and education and voting' — they went through the whole four main parts of the civil rights bill.

"And he said, 'Why not? Let's do it.' They stayed at the airport, on the plane, and worked on a draft of the civil rights bill. Bob and I went to this old hotel in Asheville, and he makes this speech.

"It was a luncheon meeting. He made the speech, came back, got back on the plane, and flew back to Washington. By the time they got back, they had it pretty well roughed out. And I think that it was that night or the next day that he went over to the White House and talked to President Kennedy about introducing the civil rights bill. Now, President Kennedy was feeling that because of the television pictures from Birmingham, and the dogs and everything, with public opinion what it is, there's a chance of getting the bill through. So then they started working on really drafting a bill.

"One of the things about both the Kennedys was they didn't like to tilt at windmills. They wanted to do something and have a chance of getting it done."

■ ———————————————————————

There was another source of pressure on the Kennedys: the March on Washington.

A. Philip Randolph, it seemed, never tired of proposing marches on Washington. When the respected black labor leader suggested this one early in 1963, it met with resistance from the White House that was not all that different from Roosevelt's reaction in 1941. Elected officials are always uncomfortable with the idea of large numbers of citizens seeking redress of grievances. Their stated reason for this usually is concern over possible violence.

When it became obvious that the march would take place with or without the administration's blessing, the Kennedys moved to make it *their* march — a demonstration of support for the new civil rights bill. The march's organizers managed to steer a course away from co-optation, however.[12]

Randolph's proposal was controversial within the Movement, as well. Roy Wilkins of the NAACP at first was skeptical about the demonstration, but later went along with it. Wilkins was particularly worried about the man Randolph had chosen to direct the march, Bayard Rustin.

---------------------------------■

Of all the personalities who influenced and were influenced by the civil rights movement, Bayard Rustin probably attracted the most diverse opinions. To Fred Shuttlesworth, Rustin was a "genius." To many who have written about civil rights, Rustin was the Movement's strategist and its tactician, a man whose influence on Martin Luther King at the time of Montgomery was second only to that of Mohandas K. Gandhi. To others, that is fiction. To James Farmer, talk about "strategist and tactician" is "a crock."

"I see no truth in it at all," said Farmer recently. "None whatsoever. I've gone over it from every conceivable angle, and I just don't see how that can be said."

In his earlier years, said Farmer, Rustin was under the influence of A. J. Muste, the noted pacifist. Rustin "pretended" to be a pacifist, Farmer said, "and sounded like one," but shortly after Muste's death, Rustin changed his tune "and became much closer with the conservative wing of the AFL-CIO, with George Meany and the building trades."

Farmer acknowledges, however, that "Bayard made an important contribution to the civil rights movement" by organizing marches for A. Philip Randolph. Before the 1963 march, Rustin handled the Prayer Pilgrimage to Washington and the Youth March on Washington. "Randolph," said Farmer, "was a great man, and one of my real heroes, because I think he was a stalwart figure, a great person, a man of courage, intelligence, and compassion — he was a *grand* person. But he was not an organizer. Rustin was an organizer. . . .

"Randolph proposed the march. Phil had dreamed of having a march since the original demonstration of 1941 was called off when Roosevelt issued the executive order. He came before CUCRL [the

Council of United Civil Rights Leadership, an organization of top civil rights leaders, organized by the Taconic Foundation's Stephen Currier] and requested of Wilkins, who was the rotating chair at that time, that he be allowed to make his presentation to CUCRL. Wilkins got unanimous agreement among CUCRL members. Randolph came in and proposed that we have a march on Washington; that all of the organizations put their resources into it and back it, with staff, and some funds, and other resources, and that Bayard be its director.

"Well, Wilkins objected. First of all, he has a dim view of a giant march as a way to influence legislation; the way to lobby is through professional lobbyists like Clarence Mitchell of the NAACP. However, he's not going to oppose it; he just doesn't think it's the best way to lobby. But he will not oppose it. However, he does think that it's not a good idea to have Bayard Rustin directing it. He didn't say why, but everybody in the room was aware of what his reasons were: homosexuality and the fact that Bayard had been YCL — Young Communist League — in his youth.

"So he says, 'You be the director, Phil, and we'll hold *you* responsible for anything that happens in the planning of this thing. And you can name anybody you want as your deputy.' And so that's the way it was done. Randolph was the director, and he named Bayard as his deputy. And Bayard did what in my opinion was a first-rate organizing job in coordinating the thing. And it was something to coordinate. A difficult task.

"And it came off. And with overwhelming success. I missed it, as you know."

■ ————————————————————————

Farmer had a previous engagement with the jailer in Plaquemine, Louisiana. The CORE director went to Plaquemine in late August, just before the march, to speak at a rally. There was a protest march against police brutality, and Farmer led it. He and some two hundred others were arrested and jailed. Farmer was under considerable pressure to post his five-hundred-dollar bond and fly to Washington to take part in the big march, but he remained in jail on the grounds that CORE didn't have enough money to bail out all the demonstrators, and he should not receive special treatment.[13]

* * *

Some of those who knew him said Bayard Rustin was closer than he should have been to organized labor, which had a far from clean record on civil rights, but few questioned his commitment to the aims of the Movement. Rustin was a native of West Chester, Pennsylvania. He was a football player in high school; when his team visited a restaurant and he was denied service because of the color of his skin, Rustin sat in until he was thrown out. He had been jailed eighteen times on the 1947 freedom ride through the South. And he was a consummate organizer of protests such as the March on Washington. Rustin, who was fifty-three at the time, assembled a tiny staff in a Harlem political hall, the Utopia Neighborhood Clubhouse, Inc., and wore it ragged organizing everything from the precise wording that would be allowed on marchers' signs to the acquisition of portable toilets, from keeping the top civil rights leaders who served as the march chairmen happy and placated to recruiting off-duty Negro New York policemen to serve as marshals for what was officially known as the March on Washington for Jobs and Freedom.

---------------------------------- ■

"Bayard was a master organizer," said Norman Hill, who was a CORE official in the sixties and who now serves as the director of the A. Philip Randolph Institute, which Rustin headed until his death in 1987.

"But I think he was a strategist and a tactician unlike the Movement had ever seen — whether it was in terms of helping King sort out where he was really going with . . . the Montgomery bus boycott of 1955, whether it was in terms of helping King understand and think through how he could develop from there some organizational base and the founding of the Southern Christian Leadership Conference, or whether it was in terms of sitting down with civil rights leadership and trying to help them think through as to what the next stage of the Movement ought to be" after the March on Washington and the subsequent passage of civil rights legislation.

Hill said the events in Birmingham only made the march more urgent. It "sort of sped up the whole civil rights timetable. It pressured Kennedy into introducing legislation and making some response to it, and it catapulted the civil rights leadership to sitting down together under Randolph's chairmanship and saying, 'All right, what do we do now? We've got this whole thrust in the South, we've got Randolph's idea of a march.' Randolph, being the oldest and most respected of the civil rights leaders, could call people together and they would come. And what developed out of that meeting was an agreement to have a march. But instead of being just a march for jobs, as Randolph had originally conceived it, it became a march for jobs and freedom to encompass the Southern thrust and the Southern direct action in which King and others were involved, and SNCC was involved in as well."

Rustin and Randolph set about recruiting march supporters from outside the Movement itself — from labor and white organized religion, particularly.

"A segment of the labor movement joined," said Hill, "but it was only a segment, because the AFL-CIO never endorsed the march. George Meany was uncertain and unsure, was concerned about whether it would be effective and whether there might be violence, and so the AFL-CIO did not endorse the march. But Walter Reuther, who was then president of the industrial union department of the AFL-CIO and the autoworkers, did endorse it and came on the march policy committee along with representatives from the Catholic, Protestant, and Jewish religious segments.

"So with all those groups coming together, it then took the sort of unique character of Bayard Rustin, who could *keep* all those elements together."

■ ————————————————————

No one knew how many people might turn out for the August 28 demonstration. When march headquarters began using the figure 100,000 in its planning, some members of the press discounted the estimate as the usual publicity exaggeration. But Hill (who was on loan to the march from CORE) and others started receiving call after call from around the nation about arrangements for transportation. "We knew that it was going to be big," said Hill. "None of us knew how big." In the end, a crowd estimated at more than 200,000 persons gathered in Washington at the Lincoln Memorial for a demonstration that was to become one of the major events of the civil rights movement, and in all of American history.

Rustin's staff worked on a financial shoestring to coordinate the event. Staff memos were typed on the backs of discarded mimeographed material to save expense. Every logistical contingency was considered. The official march lapel button, which would sell for twenty-five cents, would be 2³⁄₁₆ inches in diameter, with black lettering on a white background. It would prominently feature a label, or "bug," testifying that it was union-made. The captain of every bus arriving for the march would make sure each passenger had an index card upon which would be written the location of the bus and its license plate number. Since Washington can be tropically sultry in August, there would have to be adequate supplies of drinking water. All slogans displayed at the march were to be selected from an approved list ("JOBS FOR ALL NOW," "VOTING RIGHTS NOW") and prefaced with the words "WE MARCH FOR" or "WE DEMAND."

The fact that the modern movement for women's equality had not yet occurred (but it would soon, and as a direct outgrowth of the civil rights movement) was manifestly clear in the committee's elaborate exertions over how to include females on the program. A working paper noted, under the heading "Women":

> Since the Chairmen are all men and since it is imperative that the role of women in the struggle be made clear, Mr. Randolph proposes that the following women be invited to participate:
>
> A) Mrs. Rosa Parks
> B) Mrs. Medgar Evers
> C) Mrs. Daisy Bates
> D) Mrs. Gloria Richardson
> E) Mrs. Diane Nash Bevel
>
> The difficulty of finding a single woman to speak without causing serious problems vis-à-vis other women and women's groups suggests the following is the best way to utilize these women:
> That the Chairman would introduce these women, telling of their role in the struggle and tracing their spiritual ancestry back to Sojourner Truth and Harriet Tubman. As each one is introduced, she would stand for

applause, and after the last one has been introduced and the Chairman has called for general applause, they would sit.[14]

Arrangements had to be made to massage the egos of show business celebrities, some of whom chartered an airplane from Hollywood. Marlon Brando told a reporter that when he got back home, he was "getting some people together . . . to see what we can do about pulling our pictures out of movie houses that are segregated." Brando carried with him a cattle prod, the high-voltage electric device that particularly sadistic Southern white police had used on demonstrators. Agents for a well-known folk singer, a woman who could bring audiences to tears with her rendition of "We Shall Overcome," sent in a bill for $740.10 for transportation expenses. This represented approximately one-tenth of the entire sum budgeted for staff salaries. Rustin, in a plaintive memo to a friend who was an entertainer, asked if perhaps the singer would be happy if just her hotel bill were covered.[15]

The biggest problem, though, was with violence. Not actual violence at the march, for there was virtually none, but the violence that detractors insisted on predicting.

The majority white press assumed beforehand, on both its editorial and news pages, that such a large congregation of Negroes would almost certainly result in trouble. When the day ended without anything that could be called a negative note, editors and writers returned to their typewriters to express their amazement that the demonstrators were, in the words of *Chicago's American*, of "extreme good nature."

U.S. News & World Report pointed out that some of the marchers were "'beatnik' types — bearded young men and young women with hair trailing over their shoulders, wearing tennis shoes and dungarees." James Reston, in his *New York Times* column, growled that the reaction in northwest Washington (then, as now, a white enclave) was "mainly one of annoyance" because people there couldn't buy a drink at a bar (closed for the day), "or get a taxi downtown, or count on the colored cook coming in for dinner." An editorial in the *Wall Street Journal* grudgingly acknowledged the lack of violence, but wondered: "Is a procedure so laden with potential violence, however worthy the goal, a good one to employ in the United States of America?" The paper's reply to its own question was clear. "This nation is based on representative Government," it said, "not on Government run by street mobs, disciplined or otherwise." Of course, one of the marchers' complaints was that the nation was *not* run by representative government, and that the right to vote was still not assured all citizens. And the schoolteachers, social workers, cafeteria helpers, clerks, bus drivers, priests, and cooks on their day off who marched that day hardly constituted "street mobs," except perhaps in the minds of editorial writers who opposed the "worthy goal" of an end to discrimination.

The day was, and will be, remembered as a triumph, not least for the speech by Martin Luther King that ended with the words from a spiritual, "Free at last! Free at last! Thank God Almighty, we are free at last!" But out of the view of the joyous audience was some intramural turmoil of the sort that the Movement was coming to expect.

John Lewis, SNCC's chair, was one of the speakers at the Lincoln Memorial. His speech, as originally composed, was the only one that was critical of the Kennedy administration for its failure to enforce civil rights laws and the Constitution. In his second paragraph, Lewis had written: "In good conscience, we cannot support the administration's civil rights bill, for it is too little, and too late. There's not one thing in the bill that will protect our people from police brutality."

But the official mood that day was one of a love feast, a celebration in which certain shortcomings would be overlooked, at least for the day. Others who were to be on the platform asked Lewis to change his text. After soul-searching, he did, out of a desire to maintain the unity of the occasion. The second paragraph, as delivered, was: "True, we support the administration's civil rights bill but this bill will not protect young children and old women from police dogs and fire hoses. . . ."[16]

SNCC's James Forman went along with the change, but his scorn for the march was almost boundless. Forman wanted to spend part of the day picketing the Justice Department, he wrote later; he wanted the march to be "the forum from which we articulated to the nation a militancy not heard before from civil rights organizations." But the demonstration that was billed as a march for jobs and freedom "turned into a victory celebration for the Kennedy administration and its supporters." SNCC people went to the demonstration, he said, but "we sang freedom songs to amuse ourselves and discussed the hypocrisy of the march." Among the leading hypocrites, he wrote, were labor unions that had never sent money to SNCC, but that now were carrying big signs "for the benefit of the press and the television cameras."[17]

Forman was also critical, at least within SNCC's walls, of Martin Luther King. He complained later that the minister's "emphasis on nonviolence, love, and religion made him a darling of the U.S. State Department," which showed a film of the march, made by the U.S. Information Agency, all over the world as proof that the nation celebrated peaceful change. Forman and several others in SNCC clearly were moving, or already had moved, from supporting a civil rights movement that worked to secure a color-blind America to wanting a total renovation of the nation's economic and political systems. The strains of a life that was subject not only to the pressures exerted by the white resistance but also to conflicts within the Movement itself were showing on Forman. About this time, he acknowledged to friends that he was suffering from a painful bleeding ulcer.[18]

Not everyone within SNCC thought the March on Washington was something between insult and diversion. Julian Bond went and had a good time. "For ninety-nine point ninety-nine percent of the people who went," he said later, "I think it was a great experience. It was marvelous for the people from the rural South, many of whom had never been outside of their home areas. For them, it was incredible."

Despite such dissent as Forman's — virtually none of it public at the time — the overwhelming reaction to the march was favorable, especially when the predictions of violence proved to be without foundation. Columnist Murray Kempton wrote that the event "represented an acceptance of the Negro revolt as part of the American myth, and so an acceptance of the revolutionaries into the American Establishment."[19] Some might quibble with the word "acceptance"; the Negro revolt had *forced* its way into the American myth and into the considerations of the American establishment. The white guardians of the system, from Mississippi county courthouse to racist federal judge to "moderate" downtown businessman to occupants of the White House, had used every device at their command to keep the revolt at bay; "acceptance" came only through sacrifices by thousands of Americans, who (with the involuntary assistance of the Bull Connors of the land) were willing to risk imprisonment, fire hoses, dog attacks, and death to get for themselves what the Constitution promised and the rest of the nation took for granted. And it was clear, and would become even clearer in subsequent years, that much of white America had no desire or intention of accepting the revolt, the revolutionaries, or black people in general.

The march also certified Martin Luther King, Jr., as the Movement's single most important leader. Americans — certainly the white keepers of the system but also the Negroes who never had marched — needed a single person on whom they could fasten their attention, someone who could be counted on to explain "what Negroes want." The media, in particular, historically have found themselves at a dumbfounded loss if they do not have a single "spokesman" for a cause or an event. With his "I Have a Dream" speech at the Lincoln Memorial that August 28, 1963, King's selection was ratified — unanimously so, if the grumblings of James Forman and a few others are overlooked.

James Farmer, who would have relished standing there, making *the* speech that summed it all up, thought King's comments were on a par with Lincoln's Gettysburg Address.[20] Hundreds, perhaps thousands, of Americans, both black and white, went home that day thinking that the Movement had arrived somewhere, had reached a goal. Bayard Rustin and others who had planned the march immediately started discussing what to do next, and the field secretaries and organizers returned to the hard-core Deep South to continue doing what they had been doing all along. For them, the celebration had been just a brief vacation from their nonstop work of dismantling segregation.

THIRTY

---■

YOU ALWAYS HAVE TO WORRY

■ ---

The March on Washington and the weeks of preparation for it provided America with more than symbolism and a certified leader, more than a moment of triumph and reflection for the Movement people who had labored so long in the South. The march also helped focus the attention of Northerners, both whites and blacks, on the fact that the land north of Mason and Dixon's Line was segregated, too. In the summer of 1963, sounds of the Movement were heard in construction projects and on sidewalks outside government offices in the big cities of the North. "We Shall Overcome" became a hymn that was sung in Brooklyn and Philadelphia, too — although sometimes the demonstrators preferred a more militant cry such as "Freedom now!" or "We want jobs!"

It was as if Negroes in the North felt a need to join the movement their Southern brothers and sisters had started; had looked around themselves and realized that for all the antidiscrimination laws that were on the books, and all the pronouncements of brotherhood from their white elected officials, they were still the victims of deep discrimination. They lived, many of them, in crumbling and neglected housing, public and private, that was confined to certain parts of town just as surely as Negroes in Albany and Jackson were confined to the balconies of movie theaters. Their children attended schools that were as segregated as those in the South, with the added insult that few of their teachers and virtually none of their principals were black.

Because of union regulations that favored seniority and nepotism, they were denied employment opportunities even in publicly funded projects. One of the demonstrations mounted in New York City at the time of the March on Washington took place on the construction site for the large Downstate Medical Center, a state-sponsored project in Brooklyn. New Yorkers were used to seeing, and many to being on, picket lines, for the Northeast was heavily unionized. But now the pickets were almost all black-skinned, and the placards they carried were not signed "LOCAL 234," but "BROOKLYN CORE" and with the names of local civil rights groups.

To one way of thinking, then, it was possible to say that the civil rights movement came north in the summer of 1963. But to the observer who had been on the scene in a dozen Southern confrontations, and who now was hearing the chants on Northern construction sites and sidewalks, there were important differences. The Southern movement that had been fashioned in the previous four years out of hope, resistance, trial, error, success, failure, and circumstance did not translate itself smoothly into a comparable movement in the North.

One profound difference was religion. Although churches in Northern black neighborhoods were many, were packed full on Sunday mornings, and fairly shook with the same sort of spirited singing and preaching that characterized the mass meetings of the South, the black church was much less a force in the emerging Northern struggle. Religion was not the emotional, spiritual, and social haven that it was in the more obviously segregated South. The issues that most vexed Northern Negroes were likely to be economic and educational, and there was not much the church could do about these. Individual ministers, however, did get involved.

Because the church was less important, Northern Negroes

seemed less devoted to nonviolence, either as a way of life or as a strategy. The big cities of the North were violent places for everybody, white and black. Someone kneeling in prayer in front of a municipal building or a union hiring hall ran the risk of being mugged by a passing criminal, shoved aside by the hurrying crowds, or, perhaps worse, being ignored completely.

Black-run organizations in the North, other than the churches, tended to be political groups — neighborhood clubhouses that functioned to get out the vote at election time and, if the club's candidate won, to distribute largess after the election. Voting was not discouraged in the North; on the contrary, representatives of political parties, clubhouses, and individual candidates were delighted to show the nonregistered how to sign up, and they provided free baby-sitters and rides to the polls on election day. (In some places, such as politically corrupt Chicago, ward heelers even voted on behalf of members of the electorate, sometimes for years after they were dead and buried.)

The black political leaders who were elected by this process, many of them, might be admired by their constituents, but they did little to truly extricate them from poverty and discrimination. Congressman Adam Clayton Powell of New York was almost idolized by the voters of Harlem who elected him — not least because of his delight in thumbing his nose at his white colleagues — but when he got through, Harlem was still a ghetto. Theodore H. White, the chronicler of presidential campaigns, noted in 1963 that Powell was "the single Negro most strategically placed (as chairman of the House Committee on Education and Labor) to operate on two of the greatest problems of his people: jobs and schooling. Not a hint of creative thinking or leadership in these supremely vital fields has come from Powell."[1]

Another, and critical, difference between the North and the South lay in the nature of the enemy. Time after time, Movement warriors would venture from the Birminghams and Jacksons to the cities of the North and come away complaining that in the South, you knew who your enemy was, while in the North, the opposition was hidden and diffuse.

In the North, the mayor pronounced the word "Negro" correctly. If accused of racism, he could probably whip out a card proclaiming his membership in the National Association for the Advancement of Colored People. Plaques hanging on his office wall, issued by black organizations, certified his sympathy for Negro causes. The corporate leader probably gave money to the Urban League. The police chief could point to regulations forbidding discrimination in hiring, promotion, or in the department's dealings with the citizenry. The newspaper executive wrote editorials condemning Bull Connor and (after it was safely over) lauding the March on Washington, and when he was asked why there were no Negroes on his reporting and editing staffs he could reply, "We can't find any qualified ones."

While the people in the South who were identified by society and themselves as "white liberals" were generally welcomed and appreciated by the Movement leaders there, the term "white liberal" was almost an epithet in the North. To black activists there, it meant someone who paid lip service to the fight to end discrimination but who, when the chips were down, always sided with the forces of segregation. This "white liberal," the Northern blacks felt, was perfectly capable of sending off a check to help Martin Luther King in Birmingham or James Farmer in Plaquemine, but would fight tooth and nail to keep a son's or daughter's elementary school from being consolidated with a black school from the adjoining neighborhood. And the worst part of this was that the white Northerner, confronted with evidence of his collaboration with the forces of racism, would indignantly deny it — would produce the NAACP membership card, the framed certificate from the Urban League, the grateful receipt from the Southern Christian Leadership Conference, and loudly proclaim that under those circumstances, he could not be anything remotely related to a racist.

--- ■

"In New York," said Julian Bond, "you had this black congressman, and black people in Harlem are living in absolute desperate straits. But when you tried to organize people against the government, you found that some of them were *in* the government. Even though they weren't getting anything from it, they were in it. They were a part of it. They were precinct captains, and ward leaders, and ward heelers, and there were little patronage trickles that came down there. They were mailmen and school principals and people like that, who were tied to the existing structure much more so than Southern blacks were. It was just a radically different situation.

"And we didn't know how to deal with it. I don't think we realized the extent to which Northern blacks were *politically* integrated, as opposed to alienated in the South. And it couldn't work. It couldn't work. I'm not saying it couldn't have been done, but it couldn't have been done trying to repeat in Philadelphia, Pennsylvania, what had worked well in Greenville, Mississippi."

James Farmer remembers that after the March on Washington, the Congress of Racial Equality found its Northern enemies harder to confront than the Southern variety, with the result that CORE began to fight with itself. "CORE was a bundle of energy," he said, "and it had to keep in motion. When it tried to turn its focus from an exclusive concentration on the South to a national focus, meaning more Northern, there were no Bull Connors. It's difficult to organize around a campaign when you don't have a devil — a real, live devil. With horns.

"So CORE, not having a Bull Connor, not having a devil to fight against, and having all of this energy pent up, turned the energy inward and began chewing at itself. We had to fight somebody, so we fought each other."

In actuality, he added, there were plenty of devils to fight in the North, "but they weren't personified. They weren't personalized. [A politician would say] 'I'm your buddy, remember? I helped you on this. I contributed to CORE, remember? And I walked in your picket line.' So the thing was kind of diffused and amorphous. It was just not the clear situation that it had been when we focussed on the South and sitting in at lunch counters and riding buses. So we began chewing at each other; that was the easy thing to do."

■ ———————————————————

A striking example of the insensitivity of Northern whites to the issues of race relations — once those issues moved out of Birmingham and McComb and touched their own lives — had been provided in the summer of 1962 by John Fischer, the editor of *Harper's* magazine. Fischer published an essay titled "What the Negro

Needs Most: A First Class Citizens' Council," in which he put on public display what many Negroes meant when they referred to the "racism" of the white liberal or moderate of the North.

The essay's title was certainly one tip-off. Fischer, a white man, was clearly lecturing black people. In his opening paragraph he proposed "a new Negro organization" with the purpose of "the genuine integration of Negroes into the normal stream of American life." Thus Fischer managed to call Negro life abnormal. The new group's slogan would be "Let's Make Every Negro a First Class Citizen."

The "decisive battles" of the civil rights movement, Fischer wrote, "have been won. . . . The rest is a mopping-up operation, like the war in Europe after Bastogne." (This was before the Albany confrontation, before Birmingham, before the worst part of Mississippi, before the Northern riots.) All that remained was for "the average Negro (not just the brilliant exception)" to become accepted by "the average white." (Note that, again, it was the Negro who must be absorbed into the "normal stream.") Acceptance would come, wrote Fischer, once the Negro showed himself able "to carry the full responsibilities of good citizenship."

And now Fisher ticked off what was bothering him most. His list was duplicated in the mid-sixties by educated, seemingly cosmopolitan whites from Manhattan to Marin County — sophisticated, yet strangely unaware of how closely their arguments mirrored those of the Ross Barnetts and George Wallaces. These were the people who deplored construction of the barricade on Atlanta's Peyton Road but who panicked and ran to the white suburbs when a Negro family moved into their neighborhoods in New York City or Boston or Philadelphia.

When Negroes come to a community, wrote Fischer, crime increases. Black families "that can't find money for a bucket of paint or a pane of glass somehow manage, surprisingly often, to drive fancy cars and buy a fifth of whiskey every weekend." Blacks "seem apathetic" about participating in civic activities — an amazing assertion, considering the amount of energy and blood Negroes had invested in making the Constitution a living document. And — as always, it seemed, North *or* South — there was the Sex Problem. Negroes had a "casual attitude" about it.

Once the new organization started doing its work, and the majority of white Americans learned that they had "nothing to fear from close, daily association with Negroes in jobs, schools, and neighborhoods," wrote Fischer, then prejudice would surely disappear.[2]

——————————————— ▪

C. Herbert Oliver left Birmingham and the Inter-Citizens Committee that he had helped to found, and moved to New York City in 1965. His motive was not to escape the persecution he had often endured in Alabama, but to pursue an attractive career opportunity. A Presbyterian church in Brooklyn's Bedford-Stuyvesant section needed a minister to work with young people. Oliver was partial to the parish ministry, and he took the job. After about a year in Brooklyn he accepted a call to become the pastor of Westminster Bethany Presbyterian Church, where he remains today. Not long after he arrived in the North, Oliver became involved in a bitter dispute over community control of public education in Brooklyn.

"For me," he said, "it was just a move from one type of a segregated environment to another," to a place where discrimination differed only in that it was "more subtle."

"In the South, if someone didn't like you, they told you. They'd tell you. 'We hate you, nigger; get back!' You can deal with that, because he's up front. I know where a person is coming from if he tells me that. If I have to fight him, okay, I fight him. If I have to run from him, I run from him. But I know what to do.

"But when someone says, 'We're all brothers, but you stay over here; you should stay in this neighborhood; don't try to get out of this neighborhood — we all *love* you — ' but you see a school system that is segregated; you see a school system where teachers come into the black community and get their tenure, and then move on out to other areas and stay there for a long time, and the black community is constantly being recycled with teachers coming and going — and our kids start making less progress . . . It was really harder to deal with that."

The situation was made even worse, he said, by the unwillingness of many Northern whites to comprehend and acknowledge that what they were doing amounted to discrimination, regardless of what they said their attitudes were. The problem was not limited to individuals. "The *New York Times* was very helpful when they printed those documents of cases of police brutality in Birmingham," said Oliver, referring to reporter Harrison Salisbury's use of the Inter-Citizens Committee reports in one of his Birmingham dispatches. "I think that article helped preserve my life. The fact that somebody would print it, and it would get headlines in a national newspaper, was, to me, very reassuring. Because I was expecting at any time to get knocked off [for] documenting these things and putting the names of policemen down. I had to always move by watching everything, front and back. Never allowed myself to be trailed.

"I had to live like that, and watch my family all the time. That was my lifestyle when I was doing this kind of work. But I felt reassured when, through Harrison Salisbury, that article was printed.

"But then, when the school situation started here, the *New York Times* was totally different. They didn't see the issues. They never saw clearly the issues that we were trying to deal with in Ocean Hill–Brownsville."

■ ────────────────────────────────

Oliver was referring to the crisis that developed later in the sixties over control of the community school board in a Negro section of Brooklyn. In 1967 the New York City Board of Education, with the assistance of the Ford Foundation, created three demonstration districts, one of them in Ocean Hill–Brownsville. Wide-ranging education decisions, on everything from selection of personnel to budget allocations to curriculum, would be made by eleven-member boards. Five of the members would be appointed by the mayor, while six would be elected by the community.

The United Federation of Teachers fought the plan bitterly, as did New York's Central Labor Council. The teachers union, which was largely white and which had many Jewish members, opposed community efforts to install black principals and to control the assignment of black teachers and the dismissal of white teachers whom the community did not like. Charges of racism and anti-Semitism flew back and forth, the media did a poor job of explaining what was really going on, and the central school board, a Byzantine memorial to bureaucracy, failed to exert control.

Before it was all over, there had been a boycott by students and a strike by teachers, fistfights, bomb scares, and false fire alarms. Eventually the city suspended the local board, which was chaired at the time by C. Herbert Oliver. The experiment was succeeded in time by community school boards that became highly politicized miniature versions of the central school board. And true community control still eludes the residents of New York's black ghettoes.

———————————————— ■

Milton A. Galamison was a Negro leader in the North who had no experience in the South or with the Southern movement. He was born in Philadelphia in 1923 to a postal employee and a member of the housekeeping department at Strawbridge and Clothier, the department store. Life in Philadelphia was not one of constant, overt racism, said Galamison not long ago. In fact, race became a factor for him only at those times when he walked through a neighboring Italian community to get to the library — which was often, because Milton loved to read. Fights would break out, he said. "No knifing, no serious violence; just every now and then they'd bang you on the head or throw stones at you and chase you out. And call you nigger."

There were restaurants in Philadelphia that would not serve Negroes, and there were few black policemen and almost no black firemen. "There were very few black schoolteachers," said Galamison. "But in our little world, we lived almost without any racial incident. It was a black community. No racial incidents in the integrated schools to which I went."

Milton Galamison went to nearby Lincoln University and then to Princeton; he became a minister and in 1948 moved to Brooklyn and Siloam Presbyterian Church. He never went south for civil rights activities because, he thinks, "I never felt that I could have dealt calmly with overt mistreatment and violence." Instead, Galamison came in contact with a great deal of discrimination that was not so overt, and that was what got him involved in civil rights causes in the North.

"The thing that started me off on this business," he said, "happened when I and my family were riding out to Indiana, to a Presbyterian conference. This was back in 1952. I had my little boy with me. He was about four or five years old. And we couldn't get a hotel to stay in. We couldn't find a place to eat. We finally turned around and had to come back home.

"I said, 'This is terrible.' My son, who was very fair, said, 'Daddy, I know why they won't give us anything to eat: because you're colored!'

"You see, the difference — this may be elementary to even say this — but the difference between being black and white sometimes is this: If you're white, you don't have to worry about whether you're being discriminated against or not in a situation. If you're black, you *always* have to worry.

"I remember, one time we stopped in a restaurant in Connecticut — we had come off the Connecticut Turnpike — and we sat at this table for half an hour, and nobody waited on us. I looked at the table next to us — there was a white couple sitting there, and they weren't being waited on, either. They were calm, but I was getting ready to throw the sugar bowl through the window when the manager came and confessed that nobody had been assigned to these tables. He apologized.

"I believed him. But the white people, they didn't have to worry. They were sitting there being concerned about poor service. I was sitting there wondering if somebody was not going to give my wife and my child food because we are black. This is the difference: You're constantly paranoid. You're constantly on the defense."

Galamison led the demonstrations in the summer of 1963 at the Downstate Medical Center construction site, and he played a major part in the New York City school desegregation struggle. He, like Oliver, felt betrayed by whites who were so proud of their credentials as liberals. "The resistance in the South was a shameless resistance," he said. "In the North, everybody was polite and everybody was ostensibly pro-freedom, proprogress. But the things we set out to do never really got done because they were defeated largely behind the scenes. And then when the Movement got too close to home, even the most liberal whites began to resist." It was the school desegregation and decentralization battle that brought matters "too close to home," he said.

Galamison had problems during the school crisis with the white media, and he had problems with the established black organizations. The press, with rare exception, covered the school decentralization controversy with great superficiality and a lack of understanding of the true dynamics of the situation — a not surprising shortcoming, since there were few Negro reporters and virtually no Negro editors or other executives on the mainstream newspapers. One day Galamison passed a newsstand and saw a front-page photo of himself, Adam Clayton Powell, and Malcolm X. "The New Triumvirate," he recalls the caption reading. "We were going to burn down the city." He laughed. "We hardly *talked* to each other!" Relations with the media got so bad at one point, Galamison said, that friends told him, " 'Your image is bad' " and sent him to a publicity specialist "to try to turn me into the Man in the Gray Flannel Suit. After having lunch with the guy, I decided I don't want to be the Man in the Gray Flannel Suit.

"But the press did me a great service, too; it wasn't all negative. For years I was in the newspaper every day. I had the wire. People would call just to see what I had to say. So I got my message out. I didn't have many friends," he said with a laugh, "but I got the message out. You can't have both.

"Sometimes the reporters would come by and say, 'Come on, Galamison, let's go have lunch.' They knew that the board of education had issued an arrest warrant for me. And they wanted to be with me at lunch when I was arrested. And I'd probably pay the check, too.

"The captain of the precinct used to call. He used to say, 'Milton, we've got a warrant to arrest you. We'll give you a half hour. You got someplace to go hide?' I got on great with the police. We had good relations, because we tried to be honest with the police. They asked us to control the crowd and whatnot, and we tried to do it. My demonstrations were usually under control. They never had a big problem with us. When we wanted to get arrested, we'd tell them: 'Look, you're going to have to lock us up today, because we're going to do so-and-so.' And then there were other times you didn't feel like going. Like you had a speaking engagement in California or something."

When he started leading demonstrations and speaking out on issues in New York, said Galamison, he sought the help of established organizations such as the NAACP and the Urban League. What he failed to understand, he said, was that "people and organizations usually have to depend on the sources from which they get their income. And the financial sources that back these groups limit the effectiveness of the groups. Now, that's the kindest way that I can put it. . . . My personal experience with the NAACP and the Urban League and CORE, to a degree, is that their mission is to *capture* movements and contain them. In other words, to get in on the ground floor, if they can, but to contain the movement — to see that the movement doesn't really threaten what it set out to correct.

"I can't say that the Urban League's objectives, for example, were not the same as mine. And I cannot say that they didn't take credit. Because publicly they did, for a lot of things that they didn't achieve that were achieved in the grass-roots movement. But they pulled out. And maybe it would be fairer to say that the role is to squelch other black leaders who may be running a competitive effort. Here you are, an individual guy; you've got three hundred dollars in the bank, and this is all you've got to run your movement on. And here are these people with thousands of dollars and a tremendous budget, maybe several million dollars, and you're getting done what they're not able to get done.

"They have to quiet you. You know, it's a competitive society."

Galamison remembered an occasion when he had just gotten out of jail — his number of incarcerations was right up there with many SNCC staffers' — and he was a guest at a luncheon. "I sat on the dais next to Whitney Young, who was then head of the Urban League, and Whitney Young had the nerve to say to me, 'Galamison, when all this smoke is cleared away, the Urban League is going to be in the saddle.'" Galamison roared with laughter.

■ ─────────────────────

A major and obvious difference between the movement that had developed in the South and the one that was evolving in the North was the Northern campaign's emphasis on economics. A. Philip Randolph's original idea had been for a March on Washington for Jobs; the "and Freedom" was appended, almost as an afterthought, in recognition of what had been done in the South. There was a certain arrogance in all this, since a good case could be made that the Northern effort never really caught on until black Southerners showed the way. Some Northern Negroes even betrayed a touch of disdain for their Southern colleagues, as if they thought the Southerners were too primitive to understand the complex economic problems of the Northern black ghetto. There was talk, reaching an audible volume in 1963, that the movement in the South was only a prelude to the *real* issues, most of which had to do with jobs. Many of those who spoke this way were veterans of the labor movement, and they tended to see every issue in such terms. In 1963 their arguments sounded almost incoherent to activists in the South, who saw the real issues as getting the vote, putting down police brutality, conquering fear, and just staying alive.

Bayard Rustin was strongly sensitive to the tribulations of Southern activists (time on a chain gang surely had helped there), but he nevertheless tended to talk about "next steps" for the Movement, as if the current steps had already been taken, which they hadn't. A typewritten, undated transcript remains of a meeting Rustin and others held after the March on Washington, one of several devoted to the question What next? The expression "master plan" came up frequently; those who were present clearly thought it was time for one to be drawn up.

At one point, Rustin stated, "What we should be giving our attention to is what has been referred to as a master plan. Now, first of all, there are two things in mind. When I was talking about a master plan I was talking about an economic and social plan which I humbly said I was not in a position to draw up. When you are talking about the civil rights master plan my argument is that there is [no] such thing — that the civil rights movement can only advance to a certain level unless there is a broader master plan for social change." Rustin's comments made it clear that he thought the labor movement was an important vehicle for such change. He went on to discuss his hope for "masses of unemployed Negro and white adopting the techniques of civil disobedience to get jobs, adopting the dynamic of the Negro struggle."[3]

Rustin's thoughts would be further clarified and presented to the world in February, 1965, with the publication of his essay, "From Protest to Politics: The Future of the Civil Rights Movement," in *Commentary*. The "legal foundations of racism in America" were gone, Rustin wrote, and now it was time for the creation of a political movement that would bring revolutionary change to the American system.

The civil rights movement, he said, was "perhaps misnamed," because its challenge was to "social and economic conditions" rather than civil rights. In any event, what was needed was political power, and any movement that wanted to obtain it would have to be a coalition: "The future of the Negro struggle depends on whether the contradictions of this society can be resolved by a coalition of progressive forces which becomes the *effective* political majority in the United States." The coalition, wrote Rustin, was the same one that orchestrated the March on Washington: "Negroes, trade unionists, liberals, and religious groups."[4]

■

"Bayard was suggesting not that protest be abandoned," said Norman Hill, "because protest against injustice and inequality had been very much a part of his life and Randolph's life. But he was suggesting that if the problem was not simply one of racism and discrimination, but also was one of economics and class, then one had to address it politically." If the nation would not respond to black poverty and would not respond to the poverty of Appalachian whites, then "it would respond, possibly, to a situation in which you were proposing that the country deal with the problems of *all* those in need, regardless of who they were. We were saying that blacks clearly were a part of that strategy, and that was a problack strategy but not an antiwhite strategy, and hopefully a strategy that could bring in the necessary allies to get movement and change."

The resolution of issues such as segregation at lunch counters and the state of Mississippi's refusal to admit a Negro to its university, said Hill, "didn't really cost very much in economic terms, or even challenge the priorities of the country in terms of how money would be spent. But if one talked about the eradication of slums, one talked about providing quality education for all to enable people to maximize their learning potential — if one talked about creating a full employment economy and how and on what basis one would do that — those were demands of a much greater dimension. And they encompassed both the South and North."

■

Meanwhile, back in the South, it was not so obvious that the big battles had been won and that the Movement was ready to pursue a broader, national agenda. White Mississippi discovered that great constitutional lawyers and governors who promised "Never" were no longer totally effective against the wave of "agitation" that was directed against the state, and the state increased its use of violence against those who challenged the system. In November, 1963, the Voter Education Project announced that it was reluctantly cutting off funds for registration campaigns in Mississippi because more money had been spent there, with fewer results, than in any other state. Also, the Justice Department had been unable to win voting rights lawsuits in the state.[5]

The spirit of the Movement in Mississippi was not daunted, however. Unregistered Negroes in a number of Mississippi communities tried to vote anyway in the August party primaries under provisions of a state law that had been unearthed by summertime volunteers from Yale University. None of the votes was accepted, and some of the "voters" were arrested, but the action set the stage for a mock election, held in the fall, simultaneously with the regular election, in which some eighty thousand people participated. "Freedom candidates" ran for office in a clear demonstration that Negroes would vote in Mississippi if they were allowed to.

In Alabama, the good feelings left over by the March on Washington and the partial victory over a repressive political system were destroyed on September 15, when another bomb exploded in Birmingham. This time the dynamite went off at the Sixteenth Street Baptist Church, a center of Movement activity, on a Sunday morning. Four young girls who had been attending a Sunday school class were killed. Two of them were fourteen years old, one was eleven, and one was ten. Dozens of others at the church were injured.

White Birmingham held its breath and waited for a violent reaction from the black neighborhoods. It did not come. But white youths that day shot a Negro boy who was riding by on a bicycle, for no apparent reason, and the police killed another black youth who, they said, ran when they told him to halt.

Charles Morgan, Jr., the white civil rights lawyer, went the next day to the Young Men's Business Club luncheon, a group he described as "the future leaders of Birmingham, concerned about tomorrow." He delivered a speech that was to be much quoted in Movement history. He recalled the litany of Birmingham's segregated past and answered the question "Who is guilty?" with the words "Each of us." Birmingham, said Morgan in a statement that probably cut closest to the thoughts of the white businessmen in the room, "is not a dying city. It is dead." When Morgan sat down, a member moved that the club admit a Negro to membership, but the motion died for lack of a second.[6]

Al Lingo of the Alabama highway patrol announced the arrest of three men who had Klan connections on charges of illegal possession of dynamite. They went to court, were convicted, and got six-month sentences and hundred-dollar fines.[7]

Undoubtedly because of what was perceived as the Movement's increased militancy, especially in the North, white liberals and others started expressing more concern about what they termed efforts by communist organizations and individuals to infiltrate and take control of the Movement. One reason for this was the information J. Edgar Hoover had been feeding Attorney General Kennedy about the influence a Northern white lawyer, Stanley Levison, allegedly had over Martin Luther King. Levison, asserted Hoover, was a "secret member" of the Communist party's United States hierarchy. Kennedy believed this, according to his former press aide, Edwin Guthman.

Said Guthman in a 1988 interview: "The whole thing about Stanley Levison was accepted by Bob and Burke [Marshall] and the president, and I don't think there was ever any question that . . . what [Hoover and the FBI] claimed was accurate. What Bob Kennedy was told was that Stanley Levison was a secret member of the presidium of the Communist Party U.S.A., and the fact that the FBI knew that was a matter of the top sensitivity. Top national security." Guthman said that "as much as we got to distrust Hoover later on," when the administration officials heard this, they had "really no reason to doubt it. And saw that as a serious threat to the civil rights movement." This was the feeling, said Guthman, despite the fact that by the time of the civil rights movement, everyone who was aware of the situation knew that "the Communist party was pretty well destroyed."[8]

The administration seemed to be suffering from the same inability displayed by Southern white racists to believe that the Movement could be doing everything it did on its own. The supremacists, who were always seeing the hand of "outside agitators" and secret NAACP types, never could understand that Southern Negroes were capable both of becoming enraged at the system that persecuted them, and of formulating plans for destroying it. When red-baiting became national in scope in 1963, it sounded very much as if the big brains in the Justice Department and elsewhere were saying that those poor Southern Negroes must have had the help of scheming white men. J. Edgar Hoover was delighted to supply "confirmation."

On the basis of Hoover's data, which have never been authenticated, Robert Kennedy authorized taps on Martin Luther King's telephones. Guthman recalls that when he asked his boss why, the reply was, "I don't know how to settle it any other way. . . . If I don't do this, Hoover's going to block the civil rights bill." Kennedy gave Hoover permission to install the taps for one month.

On November 22, 1963, John Kennedy was assassinated in Dallas. In the confusion that followed, the attorney general's limited permission for the telephone taps was forgotten. The FBI continued to eavesdrop on the man who had become the acknowledged leader of the civil rights movement.

White liberals and others were worried about SNCC, as well. The organization had steadfastly refused to reject help from anyone because of his or her political convictions, including lawyers who were known in the North as dedicated left-wingers. This turned on a red light in the minds of many government officials and journalists. Writer Theodore White, who had a high degree of access to the thinking of the Kennedys, wrote in the fall of 1963 that "sinister groups," including "the Communists," were "interested in direct action." A "serious penetration by unidentified elements" of SNCC had been attempted in Jackson and in Birmingham, wrote White, who offered no supporting evidence.[9] SNCC snorted at such attacks, which, it said, were just more proof of the racism of American society. They did hurt fund-raising, however.

SNCC, in the meantime, started making plans for 1964. There was evidence, from Charles Sherrod's experiences in southwest Georgia and from the Freedom Election in Mississippi, that the use of young white volunteers, particularly from the North, would help the campaign in the hard-core places. Majority America might be wholly unconcerned about the jailing and beating and even the murder of a young black voting rights activist, but wherever its white sons and daughters went, intense interest would follow. The staff started putting together plans for a summer, 1964, project in Mississippi.

——————————————————— ■

Dorothy Miller and Bob Zellner, both safely free of Danville, managed to find a moment when both were out of jail and in the same town, and they got married.

The wedding took place in Atlanta, at the home of a Negro minister. "At midnight," said Dorothy, "because that was the only time we could get together.

"I remember it was midnight, because when it was over I called my parents at two o'clock in the morning to tell them I was married. Casey [Sandra Hayden, a SNCC stalwart] and Julian [Bond] were our witnesses.

"Of course, they all thought it was riotous. By the time we got into the place, there were all these people who were tipsy and carrying on, and we were in a minister's house. And, of course, I terrorized him because I told him we wanted it 'long on brotherhood and short on God.' He got a little upset at that. Of course, I didn't say 'brotherhood and sisterhood'; that was back then.

"So then we left right away. While the ceremony was going on — Bob, of course, did not believe in locking car doors — half of his clothes were stolen out of the car. So then we left and we went on this incredible whirlwind honeymoon to California, and turned right around and came back in time for the March on Washington."

Afterward, they moved to Cambridge, Massachusetts, and Bob entered graduate school at nearby Brandeis.

"Forman said 'Fine; that's the beginning of a SNCC office in Cambridge,' " recalled Dorothy. " 'You run the SNCC office.' " She opened the office and started raising funds and, later, interviewing applicants for the summer project in Mississippi.

■ ———————————————————

THIRTY-ONE

THE EDUCATION OF
SHARON BURGER

The Movement — that is, the sum total of the endlessly energetic wave that swept across the South, and not necessarily each of the individual people who gave it that energy — had started only a few short years before with the belief that the disease of segregation, once exposed to the cleansing oxygen of national scrutiny, would simply disappear. White Americans, once they saw the infection, would be prompted by guilt and common decency to remove it. It did not take long for even the most idealistic Movement participants to realize, as Fred Shuttlesworth had said in Birmingham, that a rattlesnake doesn't commit suicide; that white America might be willing to change some, but not if it meant giving up power. So now the Movement tried a different tactic, one more cynical than before, but still an approach that acknowledged the hope that a multiracial society was worth having. The Movement brought the whites' children into the battle.

The approach had worked well in Birmingham with the children of the black community, and the white and black volunteers in Charles Sherrod's project in southwest Georgia had understood and used it for a couple of years. Now, with the need so obvious for a breakthrough in voter registration in Mississippi, the hardest of the hard-core states, the plan seemed amazingly simple: Gather the sons and daughters of Northern whites together, train them in self-preservation, and send them to the Deep South for the summer of 1964 to do voter registration and other work.

They would be, by and large, articulate people, "smart" by the standards of the mainstream society, and they would be working with men and women who were poor, illiterate, and conditioned to see the white person as master. But the young volunteers would have to understand that they were not missionaries who had been sent to deepest Mississippi and Louisiana to "save" the poor savages. The light shade of their skin would not automatically confer leadership status on them. For starters, they would be working under the supervision of blacks who were not from their Ivy League colleges, or any college at all. It was an impossible undertaking, and it worked.

The organizers of Freedom Summer, 1964, were mostly from the Student Nonviolent Coordinating Committee and the Congress of Racial Equality, gathered under the banner of the Council of Federated Organizations. In a report called "Prospectus for the Summer," SNCC's staff wrote:

> It has become evident to the civil rights groups involved in the struggle for freedom in Mississippi that political and social justice cannot be won without the massive aid of the country as a whole, backed by the power and authority of the federal government. Almost no hope exists that the political leaders of Mississippi will steer even a moderate course in the near future; in fact, the contrary seems true: As the winds of change grow stronger, the threatened political elite of Mississippi become more intransigent and fanatical in their support of the status quo. . . . Negro efforts to win the right to vote cannot succeed against the extensive legal weapons and police powers of local and state officials without a nationwide mobilization of support.
>
> Therefore, a program is being planned for this summer which will involve the massive participation of

Americans dedicated to the elimination of racial oppression.[1]

The project was a broad-ranging one, although its major aim was the registration of voters. COFO sought out teachers, clergy, artists, and lawyers to staff freedom schools, community centers, and a repertory theater. An estimated six hundred young people went south that summer. Most worked in SNCC-run projects in four of Mississippi's congressional districts, while the rest participated in a CORE effort in another district. CORE put on its own registration projects in Louisiana. All the volunteers had been chosen with great care. Dorothy Miller Zellner, who was in charge of SNCC's recruitment in the Northeast, worked with Kate Clark (the daughter of Kenneth Clark, of the *Brown* decision's Footnote 11 fame) to weed out inappropriate volunteers.

There was a myth that developed during the summer, said Zellner later, that many volunteers went south for the sexual experiences that seemed inevitable in such a tense, tomorrow-we-may-die atmosphere. Although healthy American citizens in their early twenties who *weren't* somewhat preoccupied with sex might be cause for alarm, the myth was a greatly exaggerated one. Still, Dorothy Zellner did her best to filter out any applicants who weren't, in her words, "able to adapt and who didn't have the discipline that we thought was necessary to behave there." In the process, she said, the SNCC operation collided with an effort run by Allard Lowenstein. Lowenstein, a white who had developed a taste for liberal Democratic politics while at the University of North Carolina, had participated in the mock Freedom Election in Mississippi in 1963, and had been critical of SNCC for its unwillingness to take a firm no-communist stand. SNCC's leadership was distrustful of Lowenstein, who, some felt, was trying to capture the organization for the forces of liberal white accommodation. Lowenstein's friend and associate Barney Frank clashed with Zellner over the control of recruiting, she recalled, and SNCC's main office finally had to explain that she was in charge.[2]

The COFO volunteers for Mississippi gathered in mid-June, 1964, on the campus of Western College for Women in Oxford, Ohio, for a week of orientation and training. Some of their instructors were concerned about the white volunteers' capacity to submit themselves to the discipline and supervision of Negroes. Other members of SNCC had been doubtful about the usefulness of the project altogether. SNCC historian Clayborne Carson referred to the "complex interplay of resentment and compassion" that influenced the relationship between the staffers and the white volunteers at the training session and through the summer.[3] But everyone who was involved knew the painful truth of the inestimable value of the volunteers: An America that would, at best, yawn over the news of a Mississippi Negro's arrest on unconstitutional charges, his beating by a sheriff, or his murder at the hands of a gang of klansmen — this same America would pay close attention if a young, articulate white college student from Yale or Harvard or Berkeley were thrown into jail or roughed up for supporting the right to vote.

The summer project received help from a number of lawyers and attorneys' groups, one of which was the Lawyers' Constitutional Defense Committee. LCDC was formed by a number of civil rights and civil liberties organizations to provide legal services for the summer. Henry Schwarzschild was more or less drafted to coordinate the program, which worked out of offices donated by the American Civil Liberties Union in New York City. Schwarzschild's main job was to find lawyers who would spend their summer vacations in Mississippi. One of his recruits was a young man with political ambitions named Edward Koch, who later would become mayor of New York City.

Schwarzschild recalls that at the time Koch received his assignment, LCDC needed lawyers to staff its Memphis office, which provided services for northern Mississippi. So Koch was asked to report to Memphis. But before the date came, Schwarzschild said, he got a call from Koch:

"Would it be possible to reassign me to the Jackson office in Mississippi?" Schwarzschild remembered Koch saying. "I said, 'Well, it's difficult. The plans are all made. It's a very complicated schedule.' And he gave me to understand very clearly that it would be politically very much more useful for him to have been in Mississippi than to have been in Tennessee. He was very conscious that, though it was a great thing to do and a courageous and decent thing to do, he also wanted to get his political mileage out of it, and it would sound a great deal better if he spent a few weeks as a volunteer civil rights lawyer in Mississippi than in Tennessee. . . . It's an interesting sort of early glimpse of Ed the manipulative politician."

———————————————————— ■

Sharon Burger, now Sharon Burger Townsend, was living a sort of aimless, lackadaisical life in 1964. Born in Mishawaka, Indiana, she had attended Indiana University for a year, dropped out, reentered the following year, and then dropped out again. She went back to Mishawaka, where her parents lived, and found an apartment with a roommate to share the rent. She became a long-distance operator for the telephone company.

Sharon Burger was white. She did not dislike or fear Negroes. "I'm an only child," she recalled, "and in raising me, the center of the universe, my parents were very careful not to teach me prejudice. They didn't go the *other* way: They weren't putting things in. They were just making sure that certain things were removed. Like I knew that it was terrible to say the word 'nigger' — that that was a bad word and no one should ever say it. They tried to be very careful not to teach me prejudice, but on the other hand, they weren't trying to instill a liberal attitude or making me feel I had any responsibility to do anything about all that.

"Anytime I expressed an opinion, my father would take the opposite opinion, to try and get me to argue it so that I would learn to defend what I believed and make sense of my argument. I don't think he was successful, but he tried, anyway."

When Burger was a freshman in high school, in 1957, she saw prejudice close up when she watched television coverage of the Little Rock crisis. "I remember seeing a white girl who was probably fourteen and probably a freshman in high school, with tears streaming down her face, saying she would rather not go to school than 'go to school with niggers.' I remember that vividly. That had great impact on me, first of all because I'd never seen anyone on the news who was my peer, and secondly because I could not believe that she would say that. I always thought that racism was something that belonged to the older generation, and that all us kids were growing up without it. My parents succeeded in making me devoid of racist feelings, but it never occurred to me that anyone else had them who was my age and my generation."

Burger learned more about the nature of racism during her year at Indiana University. Some of her friends there were Negroes. A distant cousin who was also at the university went to some pains to search her out, she said, "to tell me how concerned he was that I had friends who were black and some of whom were male and what that was going to do to my reputation and my future and all."

Meantime, Sharon Burger had other concerns about her future. She spent her days connecting long-distance telephone callers and her afternoons doing volunteer office work at the local Urban League office, but she had no clear idea of where she was heading. Her inability or unwillingness to stay in school was one manifestation of her feeling that life just wasn't all that interesting. "I didn't have any idea of what I wanted to do for the rest of my life, who I wanted to be, what kind of future there might be for me. I went through a period of trying to figure out what mattered to me. Was there anything that was important enough to live for?

"I could have been very dramatic and tried to think if there was anything that I would *die* for, but what I was really searching for was something that was important enough to *live* for. And what did I really believe and what did I hold important? And what were my values?"

This feeling of almost suicidal listlessness — a popular word among social scientists in those days was anomie, and the term seemed to fit Sharon Burger's behavior — extended to her lack of interest in world and national events. She rarely watched the news on television or read newspapers. Rather, she read the women's magazines to which her mother subscribed. One day — she thinks it was in 1963 — she ran across an article on the Congress of Racial Equality. The article, she said, helped her conclude her "period of introspection" with the decision "that the one thing that *was* important to me, and the one thing that had some meaning outside of myself, was that everyone ought to have an equal shot. Not that everyone was created equal. I don't believe that. But everyone ought to have an equal opportunity to be whoever they were going to be and do whatever they were going to do."

The decision was enough, she said, to make her put aside any ideas of life's unworthiness. It didn't make her an enthusiastic participant in the living process, but "it was enough to make me think I'll explore this a little further — stick around awhile and see what happens then."

The magazine article, as Burger remembers it, "concerned a young man in a Southern state who was white who had gone with a bunch of buddies to watch a demonstration of some kind — probably to disrupt it. The demonstrators were attacked, and there was passive resistance, and he'd never seen anything like that, and the passive resistance really transformed him. He couldn't understand it, was very curious about it, went to a local CORE office, started talking to the people there, and then became involved in the Movement.

"And I thought, 'I wonder if *I* could do something like that.' Then I thought, 'What is CORE? Where is CORE?' Went to the library, got a Chicago telephone directory, found a CORE office, and called and said, 'I want to know if there's some way that I can work for you.' I had no idea what that might mean — what they did, what I might be able to do, where that might take place. And whomever I spoke to talked to me for a little while and said, 'You're white, aren't you?'

"I said, 'Yes,' and I felt, 'Well, that must mean there is no place for me.' But he said, 'We're having a summer project, and we'll send you an application.' So I got the application form. I filled it out and mailed it off and didn't hear anything for a couple of months."

Burger put the application into a corner of her mind and continued with the rest of her life. She went to work at the telephone company in the mornings, and she stuffed envelopes at the Urban League in the afternoons. The next item of any significance on her calendar was a party that a friend was throwing early in the summer, in June. A small crisis occurred when Burger's roommate moved out of town to take another job, and she knew she would have to give up the apartment. About that time, Burger quit her job at the telephone company, with no prospects for new employment. Anomie was a big item in her life.

"People would say, 'Well, what are you going to do?' Of course, my parents were very concerned, too, since I didn't seem to be doing anything, and people kept saying, 'What are you going to do?' And I kept saying, 'Well, on June second I'm going to a party.' Because that was the only thing that I had in the future that I knew about. And after that, I had no idea what I was going to do."

A telephone call from CORE provided the answer.

"They said, 'Be in Plaquemine, Louisiana, on this date, and have enough money to support yourself for the summer. You'll be a volunteer in a voter registration project.' Well, I had no idea what that meant. I had no idea where Plaquemine was." (Plaquemine is a few miles south of Baton Rouge, on one of the many bends of the Mississippi River.)

Burger didn't go to the library and look the place up. "I just got a map and figured out how to get there. But I needed the money for the summer, and I didn't know what to do about that, either. So I asked at the Urban League office if they had any suggestions. The director there got in touch with a group called the Algonquin Club, which is an organization of black businessmen in South Bend, Indiana. Through him, it was arranged for me to meet with this group of men and explain to them what it was I was going to do and that I would like them to fund me."

This was difficult, she said, because she didn't have the slightest idea what she was going to do. "And I had no idea what 'fund me' meant — how much money I would need, and all that. But they did, in fact, give me money for the summer."

Burger was on her own for transportation. Fortunately, she said, "I owned a car. Another remarkable thing about my father: When I quit school for the second or third time and came home, he had just traded in a car that he had driven for years and gotten a new one, and as soon as I got home, he went and bought back the one that he had traded in, which I drove for about three months. And then it was my birthday, and on my birthday, when I came home, my mother said, 'That car is now yours. Your father's giving it to you for your birthday.' So, when he came home and I went to him to thank him, I said, 'Why did you do that? Why are you giving me a car?' And he said, 'Well, I know that you're not going to want to stay around here, and when you get ready to go wherever you're going to go, you're going to need a way to get there.' Well, it had never occurred to me to go someplace or leave. But, in fact, I had a car, so I had transportation. It was a '55 Oldsmobile. A ship of the highway. It was a big, square car.

"The Algonquin Club gave me the money with the understanding that I would come back at some point and tell them what it was I had done. Isaiah Jackson is the name of one of the men in that club, and he was fantastic with my parents. I think that he had a much better idea of what it was I was going to be involved in than — certainly than I or my parents did. But he came to my home and talked to my parents some and tried to reassure them. He was really an exceptional man and very supportive, not just of me, but very supportive of my parents."

So Sharon Burger now had something to live for. "CORE was my lifeline," she said. "Almost by accident, through this magazine article, I had learned of CORE. For some reason I didn't understand, they had decided that I would be allowed to participate in their activities, whatever those might be. So I now had something to do other than go to the party."

■ ───────────────────────────

On June 21, 1964, three young civil rights workers were reported missing in Neshoba County, Mississippi. They were James Chaney, a twenty-one-year-old black CORE worker from Meridian; Michael Schwerner, twenty-four, a white social worker from New York City who had been a member of the CORE staff in Meridian for six months; and Andrew Goodman, twenty-one, a student from New York. It was Goodman's first day in Mississippi as a COFO summer project volunteer.

The three had driven to Neshoba County to investigate the burning of Mount Zion Methodist Church, which they had hoped to use for a summer freedom school. On their way into Philadelphia, the county seat, they were stopped and arrested by a Neshoba County deputy sheriff, Cecil Price, on charges of speeding and arson. (It was by now commonplace in Mississippi for the authorities to charge the victims of anti–civil rights crimes with the crimes themselves.) Price jailed the three, then released them late at night. The young men had not driven far before they were stopped again, this time by Price and a number of Ku Klux Klan members.

The klansmen took the men to a rural area and shot them to death, then buried their bodies in an earthen farm dam that had been under construction.

The murderers may have thought that their deed amounted to just a routine reaction to the "invasion" of Mississippi by "outside agitators." But the nation and world thought otherwise. This time, it was not just a case of another black man's being missing in Mississippi. Two whites — Northern whites — had disappeared.

The FBI at first showed its usual reluctance to move past the note-taking stage, but President Lyndon Johnson changed all that. He met with the mothers of the white youths, and he dispatched J. Edgar Hoover to Mississippi to set up an FBI office in Jackson. (Previously, the entire state had been serviced by agents from Memphis, on the north, and New Orleans, on the south.) Hoover, who was a politically astute man, apparently knew that this time he would have to take orders from the president.

Before long, hundreds of FBI agents were drafted from other offices around the nation and sent to Mississippi. Their numbers were augmented by scores of searchers from a naval installation at Meridian. The contrast between the federal government's vigorous concern now, when Northern whites were involved, and its faltering actions in the past, when "only" Negro lives were at stake, was amazing for some, saddening for others. John Lewis of SNCC commented: "It is a shame that national concern is aroused only after two white boys are missing."[4] The FBI spread informant money around the state, and for thirty thousand dollars it bought the information it needed. On August 4 the agency took a bulldozer to the earthen dam and uncovered the three bodies.

Although it was widely known who the likely murderers were, it also was widely assumed that under Mississippi's peculiar brand of justice, they would never be convicted of murder. Only after Movement activists goaded the Justice Department into action did the U.S. government formally charge nineteen men with a federal violation: conspiracy to deprive the three of their civil rights. (Murder is not a federal offense in the United States.) In 1967 seven of the defendants, including Deputy Sheriff Cecil Price, were convicted and sentenced to prison terms of from three to ten years. Three others were acquitted, and three were freed by a hung jury. The conviction, even in federal court and even on a conspiracy charge, was a first for Mississippi.[5]

Other breaks in the racist armor occurred, but they were rare. From time to time, a woman who identified herself as the wife of a klansman called one of the SNCC offices in Mississippi to warn the activists of imminent attacks. Sometimes she would have to end the conversation abruptly, saying "I can't talk anymore; he's in the next room." The biggest break, though, was the one that was provided by the three martyrs in Neshoba County. White America was horrified at what had happened, and national political leaders felt the pressure. For the first time since the Movement had started, the federal government actually made its presence known. For the first time, a racist who was planning violence against civil rights workers would have to factor in the possibility of an interview with a federal official, or maybe even an arrest. But while civil rights workers now could assume there would be a thorough investigation if they were murdered, they were still on their own in the matter of staying alive.

■

"I think fear was an aid," said Isaac Reynolds, the CORE worker. "If you had fear, then you had to maintain your sharps. Because it was dangerous.

"You had to be sharp at all times, because we were in a war. And we didn't have any guns, and the other side did. We didn't have the law with us. The other side did. In many places before things really would explode, we did not have the press with us. So we had to be alert at all times." The Neshoba County murders, he said, happened because the three young men had let their guard down. When they left the county jail, "there was no way in the world they should have stopped," regardless of the fact that a county policeman had summoned them over.

"That was the general belief throughout the South," said Reynolds, "that if you were out there on the highway, and particularly at night, then you don't stop for anybody. You stop when you get where you're going."

Reynolds, whose work involved making many trips to CORE offices in Louisiana and Mississippi, improved his chances of not having to stop by driving a souped-up Plymouth Fury that, he said, was capable of going "about a hundred and thirty miles an hour."

Once, he said, he was cruising at less than top speed but considerably above the posted limit when the police did manage to stop him in Woodville, Mississippi. Woodville, in Mississippi's southwestern corner, is on a highway that serves as a convenient shortcut between northern and southern Louisiana.

"And I mean I literally got stopped," said Reynolds. "The highway patrol had blocked the highway. I really wasn't going *that* fast. They told me I was exceeding the speed limit, which I was, and that I had to go to jail. I told the man I wasn't going to jail. And he didn't argue or anything. He went over to the radio, and in a few minutes the highway's just full of sheriff's deputies and highway patrolmen, and he came back and asked me, 'Now, nigger, are you going to jail?' And I told him, 'I guess I am.'

"The jail was at a farmhouse in the edge of Woodville. The barn was the jail, and they had a number of other black folks in there, and I asked them why they didn't just walk off. There were no bars, no locks or anything. And their only response was, 'We're in jail.' The justice of the peace was a lady, who was very cordial and began to try to extract a fine from me, which I refused to pay until they got down to twenty-five dollars, and I told her I could write her a check for that. At that time in the trunk of my car I had something like two hundred thousand dollars in cash that CORE had sent me to bond people out of jail around Opelousas.

"The justice of the peace wanted to know if the check was good, and I assured her it was good and everything. And they released me, and I crossed the state line and stopped in Saint Francisville at Mrs. Smith's house, who was a staunch supporter of us over there. I called the bank in New Orleans and put a stop on the check."

Reynolds once took a break from the tensions of the South and went to New York City for a few days. The national CORE office had been holding his checks at his request (life in the Movement afforded him scant opportunity to spend money), and when he went by to pick them up, someone suggested that he take it easy for a while — do some speaking to interested groups around the city at fund-raising events. Reynolds agreed.

"I went back to my room," he said. "I was staying at the Harlem Y. I got in bed, and when I woke up, it was two days later. And it scared the shit out of me. I could remember thinking of those kinds of situations I had been in, and saying, 'A person'd have to be crazy to go back into that.' Once, my room had been bombed. I had been bombed out of my bed. The wall had collapsed. My glasses were broke. I had seen Wyatt Walker's wife's head split open. Had come close to being killed by Bull Connor."

He forced himself to go back anyway. Reynolds left New York

and drove back to the South, almost nonstop. The longer he stayed there, he found, the harder it was for him to go elsewhere and take breaks from the tension. He knew that if he got away from the pressure for a while, he would have time "to sit down and reflect on what you were doing and what the situation was, and it was always terrible.

"The only place I'd feel sort of comfortable going to in the North was Chicago," he said, "because Chicago was so tense. In Chicago I never would let my guard down."

Back in the South, Isaac Reynolds's guard stayed firmly in place. He almost always slept on the floor, out of the range of a shotgun blast through a window. Circuit-riding Movement activists such as Reynolds were frequently the guests of sympathetic citizens on their out-of-town trips, and Reynolds was always offered a bed and breakfast. "People would give me these great big beds and everything," he said, "and they'd come in in the morning and the bed would never have been slept in. I got to the point where I'd just ruffle the cover and the sheets because some of the ladies looked hurt by the fact that I had not slept in the bed."

Reynolds had other protective mechanisms.

"At one point I began to carry a gun. Like I say, many times I'd be on the highway by myself. Now, I would not take a gun on any kind of demonstration or any other kind of project, but I would if I was travelling between cities. There were sheriffs who got to know me and would threaten me about what they were going to do if they caught me on the highway at night. And I would let them know that if they caught me, they stopped me on that highway at night, then I would start shooting. If you stand out there, I'm going to run over you. And if you block the road, I'm going to outshoot you if possible."

Did he have a handgun or a rifle?

"I had a .38," he said. He thought a moment and amended his statement: "I had a .38 and a .357. So I went prepared."

Sharon Burger arrived in Plaquemine, at the CORE project headquarters, on schedule early in the summer of 1964.

In all, there were thirty-six people at the headquarters, most of them summer volunteers. The staff's first job was to teach the newcomers the arts of passive resistance and nonviolence — the same techniques that Gordon Carey's sociodramas had brought to dozens of communities in the South and North.

"The people who were doing the training knew what they were talking about," said Burger. "They had very recent experience with some of this. We learned how to lie in a fetal position, covering your head with your arms. Women with pierced ears were advised not to wear earrings. If you were picked up and put into a paddy wagon, you had to be limp so you wouldn't be hurt.

"All of that was totally unreal to me. We did some role-playing and were taught to be alert. Even where we were in Plaquemine, in what was called the Quarters, which was the black neighborhood, we were taught to never be out by yourself alone, night or day; to always be aware, if there were cars coming down the street, who was in those cars. All of that was totally foreign to me."

Training lasted for two weeks, and then the volunteers were assigned to communities to work in voter registration projects. Burger was aware that neither she nor her colleagues possessed specialized skills for the job ahead of them; she understood that she had probably been chosen because "I was white, Midwestern, middle class, with the attendant concerns that followed me into the South, where a lot was happening." Nor were any of the volunteers particularly *un*suited to the work that lay ahead, though she remembers one person who obviously "had come to lead the poor black people to freedom."

"I learned that I would be going to Pointe Coupee Parish, which was about sixty miles from Baton Rouge and from Plaquemine," she said. "I would be staying with the family of Sergeant Caufield, and I would be working with Kathy Cortez, who was black and who had come from New York as a summer volunteer, and with Peggy Ewen, who was white and had come from the Midwest. The three of us would be a team, and our job for the summer would be to talk to as many black people as possible about voter registration, to ask them to complete voter registration forms, to set up little clinics or classes in churches or homes or wherever we were able to do that, to talk to people about the voter registration form, about what happens when you register to vote, to help prepare people to go to register to vote.

"That would be the activity for the summer, culminating in going to the courthouse with a group of people who would attempt to register to vote and with all of the registration forms that had been filled out over the summer — trying to get the registrar simply to accept those forms."

In some of the summer projects, particularly those staffed by experienced activists, daily trips down to the registrar's office were planned. But in Pointe Coupee Parish, the effort was just to familiarize local people with the intimidating voter registration form and to determine whether the registrar would accept properly filled-in applications in bulk, at the end of the summer. Pointe Coupee Parish was not by any means one of the worst of the Deep South communities in terms of voter registration. Statistics compiled by the Louisiana secretary of state after the summer ended showed that about 29 percent (1,515 persons) of the parish's nonwhite voting-age population was registered, compared with 72 percent (4,384 persons) of the white population.[6]

The Pointe Coupee Caufields consisted of the widely respected patriarch, Sergeant Caufield; his wife, who appeared to be in ill health and who was not seen very much; and two sons and a daughter. The teenaged daughter, Thelma Caufield, soon became the volunteers' guide, confidante, and expert advisor. Thelma knew whom to see, how to get there, how to obtain permission to hold meetings in churches, and almost everything else. She and her family lived in the town of Lettsworth, a few miles from the Mississippi River. The father and sons worked during the week in Baton Rouge and came home only on weekends. Burger remembers Sergeant Caufield as a man who was "treated with respect wherever we went. I remember him as being a large man, a quiet man, and a very kind man. We went to church together on Sundays, and he treated these three young women who were in his home as part of his family. Every Sunday morning he would give us a dime for the collection plate."

The volunteers, with Thelma Caufield, went from door to door in community after community, explaining the project and inviting people to meetings. Burger is skeptical about how much she was actually able to accomplish.

"It took a lot of effort just to communicate," she said. "And I often had the feeling when we talked to people, particularly older people — we would walk up to someone's porch and start talking, and everything that I said was agreed with. Everything that I asked was complied with.

I'd say, 'We'd like for you to come to a meeting . . . ' They would say, 'Yes.' I don't think there was a lot of real communication going on between me and the people that I was talking to. There were people who would come to the church or the home or wherever we were going to be, but I think probably Thelma was arranging most of that. She knew everyone, and her father was someone who was looked up to in the community."

Churches could be, and were, extremely helpful in making space available for meetings. But some ministers "didn't want us to come near their churches," said Burger. "In one community there was a bar. That was the only place in that community where we could have a voter registration class. We had it during an afternoon. Word spread quickly that these four women — two of whom were white — were going to be in the bar that afternoon, and there was just so much curiosity about us. And there was everything going on *except* voter registration, so we decided we couldn't do *that* anymore."

When people did come to learn how to fill out the forms, the volunteers concentrated on simple mechanics: dotting the *i*'s and crossing the *t*'s, the kinds of things the white registrar might be expected to examine closely. "We taught them that for 'color of eyes,' the answer was 'brown,' no matter what color your eyes were. We knew that anything else would flunk the test. It was, 'This is the question, and the answer is "brown." ' "

(Louisiana changed its voter registration laws in 1965, obviously in an attempt to erect one more barrier against Negroes. The application form included certification as to whether or not the applicant had ever been convicted of a felony; had been convicted and sentenced on two or more misdemeanors — other than traffic and game violations — in the previous five years; had "lived with another in 'common law' marriage"; and had given birth to or fathered an illegitimate child. The form also required the applicant's race and eye color, mother's maiden name, occupation, and employer's name, allegedly "for identification of voters at the polls by commissioners, if necessary.")[7]

Burger heard about the murders in Neshoba County, but they didn't seem to affect her one way or another. She never felt terribly afraid, she said, and she rarely had anything that could be termed confrontations with the white resistance. Once she walked down the road from the Caufields' house to a pay phone near the post office to call her parents. She was talking to her mother when she was attacked by insects. "I said, 'I have to hang up, because I'm just covered with mosquitos, and I've got to get back inside. I can't stand out here talking to you.' And a male voice came on the line and said, 'Then why don't you just go home?'

"So obviously people knew that we were there. The house that we stayed in was set back off the road a little, but Thelma knew every car that travelled that road, and as soon as she could hear a car, she could tell you who it was. And she also recognized those that were not from that area, that were just going past at high speed and didn't need to be of concern. But I don't ever remember feeling threatened."

Her father, she said, had been upset over her decision to go to Louisiana, and he had gone to some pains to tell her that "if I were going to do this, then I was on my own." Her mother was "worried sick," and she slipped Sharon twenty dollars on the day she left and asked her not to tell her father. During the summer the parents came to Louisiana for a weekend. They met Sergeant Caufield and saw where Sharon was staying. Burger thinks they left still not understanding why she was there. The confusion was not diminished, she said, by the fact that during the summer she had written articles for her hometown weekly newspaper about the summer project. Some of her father's fellow factory workers came up to him and said things like, "You must be very proud of her," and "You certainly did a good job of raising your daughter." This bothered him, said Burger, because "he didn't think he deserved any credit for that, because he thought I was crazy for doing what I was doing." Others had a more negative reaction, which they expressed in terms that graphically illustrated the old supremacist preoccupation with interracial sex.

Late in July the *Mishawaka Enterprise* carried an article written by Sharon Burger, titled "Canvassing in Louisiana." She described her work, both its frustrations and its joys, and she concluded with these words:

> Loria [a fellow volunteer] and I are canvassing Montpelier this afternoon and holding a clinic in a chapel there tonight. I have been soaked with sweat since I've been here. I don't remember how dry clothes feel. The work is hard — a

lot of walking in a lot of sun. My patience is really developing — everything takes a lot of time — especially teaching the minute details of the [registration] form.

But I wouldn't be anywhere else doing anything else for anything. I really feel — for the first time in a long time — that there's some reason for me to be living and that what I'm doing really matters.[8]

The day came, toward the end of the summer, when the participants in the CORE voter registration project in Pointe Coupee, Louisiana, went down to the courthouse with their collection of applications. It was a special day.

"Sergeant Caufield did not go to Baton Rouge to work that day, and it was a weekday," Burger recalled. "My main memory of that day is that we went to the courthouse and we were standing outside, waiting for everybody to get out of the various cars and to get organized and to make this approach. We had the forms that had been filled out over the summer of all the people whom *we* had registered to vote. And now the object was to get the registrar to accept those. And Sergeant Caufield was the spokesman and the representative of this group that was going into the registrar's office.

"And what I remember most about it was Sergeant Caufield himself. Sergeant Caufield, in my eyes, was a giant. He was a large man, quiet, kindly, well respected. And he was shaking. That's what I remembered about it: that I could see his fear, and I didn't expect him to be afraid of anything.

"I didn't go in. And I remember that they were not inside for very long, and that when they came out they still had the forms, that they had not been accepted, and that no one had registered, and that that was it. Very anticlimactic. But the forms were going to be sent to the Justice Department as documentation that these people wanted to register to vote.

"I had not felt threatened in Pointe Coupee Parish over the summer. I had felt very secure in the black community and within the Caufield family. And since Sergeant Caufield, even in his absence, was my protector, it was extraordinary to see him in a situation in which he was not secure. That was the education of Sharon Burger. This whole period was the education of Sharon Burger. The opening of the eyes of the babe."

■ ————————————————————————

During Freedom Summer, about seventeen thousand Negro Southerners attempted to register to vote. Of that number, some sixteen hundred actually were registered. At the same time, thousands of them signed up as members of the Mississippi Freedom Democratic Party, an organization formed to challenge the regular, or supremacist, state Democratic party for seats at the party's national convention. The convention, which was to be held at Atlantic City, would choose the Democrats' candidate for president. More than two thousand children attended forty-one freedom schools in Mississippi and learned, as they never would in the segregated state-operated schools, about drama, journalism, and black history and culture. The schools continued after the summer ended and represented, in the words of one observer, "one of the first attempts by SNCC to replace existing institutions with alternative ones."[9]

———————————————————————— ■

Hollis Watkins, who had joined SNCC in Pike County, Mississippi, back in 1961, was the COFO project director for Holmes County in the summer of 1964. A Civil Rights Commission examination of voting patterns, using figures from early 1964, showed that 0.2 percent of the nonwhite residents of Holmes County were registered to vote. For reasons that were not explained in the report, *more* than 100 percent of the voting-age whites were registered. Of a total voting-age population of around 13,500, close to two-thirds were nonwhite.[10]

Watkins had been opposed to the idea of bringing in large numbers of non-Southern whites for the summer.

"I was against it," he explained, "basically because I felt that we had reached the point where we were making pretty good headway in getting local people from Mississippi involved and getting local people to take the initiative. And I felt that to bring in Northerners who had no knowledge of the South and who had no prior experience in dealing with people from the South, who would come in with a certain attitude, a certain mentality — that that would ultimately lead to squashing this initiative that the people in Mississippi had just begun to take. And I felt that once it was squashed, then it would leave those of us like myself who were from Mississippi, who would forever, for the most part, be here, with just that much heavier burden in trying to get people restarted all over again.''

Watkins said he was not worried about outsiders per se, but ''a massive number of outsiders. I felt that outsiders could be brought in, but in small numbers where they could be placed with people and they could, if necessary, for a period of time be watched and monitored. So it wasn't an objection to outsiders' being brought in. It was to a large number of outsiders' being brought in at one time and overshadowing and taking over — stifling the local leadership.''

Watkins's objections did not prevail, however, with the result that a lot of the indigenous leadership *was* quashed. ''To a great extent it did happen,'' he said, ''but we have to accept the fact that a lot of good did come out of the '64 summer project.'' The freedom schools were one brilliant example of that.

Watkins's project, he said, was not typical of all the local COFO operations because of the way he ran it. ''I violated one of my principles,'' he said with a smile, ''because I became a complete dictator. I didn't allow any recourses. What I said went.'' As far as the volunteers were concerned, the rule was definitely not SNCC's cherished ''Let the people decide.'' Watkins said he took this approach in order to protect the volunteers, most of whom were ignorant of conditions in the Deep South, but mostly to protect the community.

''There were certain rules that I put out, that I laid down, that were not even questionable. And there were other things that I was willing to discuss. A couple of examples: I knew that, from up at orientation in Ohio, some of the folks who were coming down would drink a beer or so, and liked to go do a little dancing and what have you on weekends. So I laid a couple of laws down stating that for the three-month period that people would be working in Holmes County, there would be no drinking on the project, period. With one exception. And that was that the people who were living with someone, if *they* had some beer or what have you in their home that they were drinking, that it was all right for the volunteers to drink it. But not to go out to anyplace. So there was basically, for the most part, no drinking at all on the project."

Watkins also set strict schedules for the registration workers and freedom school volunteers, with meetings morning and night, that effectively deprived them of enough free time to get into trouble. His dictatorship, like many totalitarian enterprises, proved to be extremely efficient. Of the twenty-three volunteers who came, Watkins had to send away only one. She was one of the four Negroes on the project. Asked why she had to leave, Watkins laughed and replied, "She broke the law." It was clear he was referring to *his* law.

Watkins had more success with one of the other volunteers, a young college student from California. "Mario was a good worker," recalled Watkins. "He was very intense. He seemed to be willing to learn any- and everything that he possibly could. He seemed to be the kind of person that wanted to be sure about the moves that he was getting ready to make, and if he felt the least little bit of uncertainty about it he would always consult me. He realized that he was in virgin territory as far as his knowledge was concerned — that he had little to no knowledge of the community, and they had little to no knowledge of him."

Watkins was particularly pleased when, at the end of the summer, as the young man was preparing to return to school, "he told me that he was going back and he was going to give them hell." He kept his promise. The young man was Mario Savio, and he was credited with starting the Free Speech Movement among students at the University of California at Berkeley that fall. That campaign was one of dozens whose ancestry can be traced directly back to the movement that was begun by Negroes in the segregated South.

Dorothy Miller Zellner spent the summer of 1964 in Greenwood, Mississippi, "totally terrified out of my wits."

She and Julian Bond had attended the COFO orientation session in Ohio, instructing volunteers who would serve as local project communications workers. "I remember saying, 'When you have people going out in a car and they say they'll be back at nine, and they don't come back at ten minutes after nine, start looking.' We told them how to call the police, to call the hospitals. And that's exactly what they did the very next day. They did it to the letter." It was the next day that the three young men were reported missing in Neshoba County.

There were some laughs that summer, too.

"Forman had gotten Harry Belafonte and Sidney Poitier to come down to Greenwood to throw their support behind the voter registration project and the Freedom Summer.

"Now, Bob and I had started out in Greenwood living with this very old black lady who lived far away from the office. And finally I told Forman, 'We have got to move; you have got to get us another place.' Because this woman felt that if we were going to be living there, she had to cook for us and she had to do for us. I could not convince her otherwise, and I could not stand it.

"So Forman got us another place to live, right near the office. So Harry and Sidney were supposed to come down. And I said, 'Harry and Sidney have to know how people are living here; they should go in a place like this lady's,' who was unbelievably poor. At the new place where we were staying, they were not rich, either, but they were a little more comfortable. I think it was a minister's home. Forman said, 'No, and not only that, but Harry and Sidney have to stay in your bed. And *you* will have to find another place.'

"So we grudgingly moved out, and Harry and Sidney stayed in our bed. There was a big mass meeting. Harry and Sidney were going to appear. You can imagine the excitement in the black community there. They started this concert, or mass meeting, or whatever it was, and people were milling around. And Forman didn't know exactly how to start this. And he said, 'This is Bob Zellner. Sing!' He made Bob sing. I mean, here we had Harry Belafonte! So Bob started singing some freedom song.

"It was an incredible mass meeting. The roof practically flew off. Harry sang and Sidney spoke, and it was wonderful having them.

"So after that, we went back to the office. Now, one of my jobs was being on the receiving end of a walkie-talkie arrangement that we had with people in their cars. It was like a CB radio. I went back earlier, and Harry and Sidney and the whole crowd of people came into the office later. This was at night. I was sitting there listening to this truly desperate thing that was going on on the radio, and they all stood around and listened.

"There was this thing coming over like, 'I'm driving in Tallahatchie County and they're following us and we'll have to get back to you later.' And then silence. And: 'We made a left turn but they made a right turn.' It was that kind of stuff. And Harry and Sidney stood there listening, completely terrified.

"And they slept in our bed. I think they actually slept on the floor all night. They kept hearing sounds. That was the biggest fun I had that summer. That one was funny, but most of it was unrelieved terror."

■ ────────────────────────────

The terror was widespread. According to one accounting, there were six murders in connection with Freedom Summer. White violence resulted in thirty-five shootings, in which three persons were injured; thirty homes and businesses were bombed; thirty-five churches were bombed or burned; and there were at least eighty beatings.[11]

──────────────────────────── ■

J. Edgar Hoover, recalls Jim Ingram, had received President Johnson's order to open an FBI office in Mississippi and had told his people, " 'I want the FBI office not completely staffed with Southern-born FBI agents. I want to send in some good investigators from all over the country.' They transferred many, many agents in here. I was one of them."

James O. Ingram had been working in the New York office, then considered a prize assignment for its variety of crimes and criminals. Not all the agents who received transfers to Mississippi were happy about them, but Ingram was. "I would not take anything for the years that I spent in Jackson, Mississippi," he said. "That was a tremendous, dynamic time." After his term in Jackson ended, Ingram served in Washington, New York, and Chicago, and as agent in charge at the last two cities. But when he retired after thirty years in the Bureau, he moved back to Jackson, where he works now as the director of security for a large bank.

Ingram became the chief of the FBI's civil rights desk in Jackson, under Roy D. Moore, the agent in charge. It did not surprise him that the disappearance of Chaney, Goodman, and Schwerner produced intense action on the part of the president and Hoover. "There was so much pressure by all types of groups, including the families," he said. "The Schwerner and Goodman families came out to talk to the president. There was a lot of pressure on President Johnson. . . . So when the president made up his mind that he was going to do everything possible, he wanted to be advised all the time. And I must say, I admired him [for] the way he handled it. When he said, 'This is what we're going to do,' then he did place the full presence of the federal government in on this thing."

Ingram said he was not surprised, either, that Hoover, who was thought by his critics to be the sort of bureaucrat who gave orders *to* a president, rather than the other way around, snapped to attention when Johnson decided to bring the federal government into Mississippi. Working for the director had taught him, said Ingram, that "Mr. Hoover knew the importance of important cases, and he knew that this was something that not only the American citizens were concerned about, but the high government officials" as well.

Michael Schwerner, a young, bearded CORE worker who had been active in Meridian for several months, had been targeted by the Klan for some time, said Ingram. "They called him the Goatee. And they had earmarked Goatee for a violent act. Schwerner was very active in creating a movement in Philadelphia [in Neshoba County] and getting the blacks registered. He was good at it." Several local Klan organizations showed interest in Schwerner, he said, but they were warned off by klansmen in Meridian, who told the others, " 'Please — hands off. Bigger things are planned for him.' I think they actually meant at that time that he was going to be eliminated. Because he struck at the very heart of the system."

Ingram said he doubted that the violent racists were concerned that their acts might hurt their cause more than help it — that their violence would outrage the rest of the nation or move an impulsive president to send in hundreds of FBI agents where before there had been hardly any. "Based upon what we saw in the community and what we later found out from FBI informants, no way were they concerned about what would happen in the future. They had been able to control their situation for years and years. With Medgar Evers's being assassinated here in Jackson in 1963 — that didn't change things to a great degree. They had killings in Natchez and other places; they'd had problems in McComb, Hattiesburg, and other places, and they'd been able to withstand all of that. I really don't think that they said, 'Hey, if we do this, we're going to bring down the full presence of the government.' I don't think that bothered them one bit. All they wanted was, 'Let's get rid of Schwerner.'"

After the Neshoba County murders and the resulting national outrage, the federal government seemed far less nonchalant than before about dealing with complaints of civil rights violations — although people on the Movement's firing lines certainly would not agree with such an assessment. Ingram said the FBI checked out every complaint of police brutality that followed a mass arrest. His agents were constantly on the go, "working the bombings, the beatings, the burnings. We had explosions everywhere. Dynamite was easy to obtain in Mississippi.

"We had some prominent people that came down here from New York that handled legal matters." These were the volunteers from Henry Schwarzschild's Lawyers' Constitutional Defense Committee. Activists who were attacked called the LCDC, which would call the FBI. So would private citizens from around the state, and so would observers who had been sent to Mississippi by the Justice Department's civil rights division. In each case, said Ingram, "we would have to send two agents out immediately. Many times we'd have people missing. Ever since Schwerner, Goodman, and Chaney were missing, every time we had some civil rights workers that were not reported back — they had their own communications system — we would be alerted, and then we would have to go into action.

"We would have a certain length of time to investigate that matter, to go get all the facts and to send our reports to Washington, D.C., to the Justice Department. In those days, we had a three-day deadline and a seven-day deadline. It depended upon the priority. We'd have to interview the people, get the facts, send our Teletypes, and then the Justice Department would look at it and say, 'Okay, we feel the facts warrant further investigation,' or 'Hey, there's nothing here. We can't substantiate a violation under [the civil rights] statutes. FBI Jackson, Mississippi, cease and desist. Don't do any more.' Or they'd come back and say, 'Hey, we are considering presenting this to a grand jury, and for possible prosecution. Continue doing your investigation. And report within seven days the results.' Everything had a deadline. Everything was rush, rush, rush."

It helped in these investigations, he said, that the Bureau enjoyed good relations with local police departments. "The allegations were that the FBI worked too closely with the police. We worked closely with them for several reasons. We needed them, and they needed us." Ingram contends that the relationship helped some local departments "upgrade" themselves. The local police leaders, he said, shared one view: "They didn't want violence."

The investigation of the murders in Neshoba County, said Ingram, put the Ku Klux Klan "on notice" and sharpened its anger at the FBI. The terrorist organization "put out the word that 'you do not have to take anything from these Federal Bureau of Integration agents,' as they called us. And that 'they cannot come upon your property. If they do, you have a right to shoot them.' "

He and another agent, Ingram said, went to visit a klansman in Laurel, Mississippi, who had been boasting that " 'I'll shoot the first FBI agent that comes on my property.' We went out to see him, and he walked out with a shotgun in his hand, pointed at both of us."

Ingram moved to the right, and the other agent moved to the left, so the klansman could not hit them both with one shot and they had him in a crossfire pattern. "I said, 'Mr. So-and-so, we did not come here looking for trouble, but if you raise that shotgun, you *will* be dead. We will defend ourselves.'

"And the guy started crying. Oh, he started crying and shaking, because he was one of the big tough guys. And the sad part about it, his wife was there and his children. We didn't see the children when we first walked up to his farmhouse. About that time his brother drove up. And his brother said, 'What in the world is going on?' And I explained to the guy, and I said, 'Your brother has indicated that he was going to kill the first FBI agent that set foot on his property. And we came out here to talk to him.' And he said, 'Well, he would do it.' And I said, 'Well, we're not backing down.' And he said, 'Well, my brother's crying. I can't believe this.' And I said, 'Why don't you take him with you and we'll follow you and we'll go talk about this thing?' He got into the truck. We followed them. And we stopped and talked and, actually, we never had any problems.

"Now, it was not what you call a *friendly* conversation. But at the same time we told them that we would not be intimidated and that we intended to visit all the klansmen who had made threats. And it helped.

"He said, 'You should not have embarrassed me in front of my wife and children.' . . . He never said he was sorry. And his brother did not, either. His brother said, 'Any other time, I think he'd a killed you.' And I said, 'Well, any other time, we had him in a crossfire.' "

Whenever a civil rights crime was solved, as it was in the case of the Neshoba murders, it was likely that informants played a major role. Informants provide leads and names and places, without which investigators may be left with only physical evidence and speculation.

"It was very difficult to infiltrate the Klan," Ingram said. "But as time went on, some of the individuals could see that, hey, violence was not the answer. And we kept going back, going back, going back, talking to these people. You have to ingratiate yourself. You have to be a good old boy to develop an informant. You've got to be able to be trusted yourself, and you've got to convince them that what they're doing is wrong. You've got to work from within. It's got to be from within, almost all the time." This was particularly difficult with the ritual-obsessed Klan, said Ingram, because "they took the old blood oath literally, and the signs and everything else. They were very devout in their thinking, so you had to keep just trying to drive that wedge. Once you could drive that wedge, then you got a good relationship."

Ingram's informants came from all areas of Mississippi life. There were "listening posts" in each community, people who could be counted on "to overhear something that would be of interest." Some were merchants. The Anti-Defamation League of B'nai B'rith, which maintained an extensive intelligence network, cooperated with the FBI; it was, said the former agent, "very, very helpful to us." Factory workers supplied information on Klan movements. "We had informants in the blacks," said Ingram. "I had some of the best black informants in Mississippi.

"It's amazing how many people want to help. Many people, they sit at home and say to themselves, 'I saw something. I want to do something.' "

For some people, money provided a strong motive for helping out. The FBI paid its regular informants fees that were considered modest by most standards, but probably not by those of working-class Mississippians. Jim Ingram maintained, though, that money was not everything. "You've got to remember," he said, "that a lot of it is the relationship between the agent and the individual. It's got to be a trust. Money talks, but at the same time, a lot of people say, 'Hey, I just can't take this anymore. I can't stomach this violence.' And that happens today. People will say, 'Hey, all right, Mr. FBI. You've been after me for years [to help]. I'm ready to help you.' "

Isaac Reynolds resented the fact that the FBI obviously had informants within violence-prone organizations such as the Ku Klux Klan but did not make proper use of the intelligence they furnished. "They had enough information that they probably could've saved some people's lives or stopped some of the violence that occurred," he said. "And they chose not to on the basis that to do so would reveal their informant. I think they didn't balance things off very well."

Reynolds said he was approached by an FBI agent, a former schoolmate, while he was working in the CORE office in New Orleans. A few weeks after the initial approach, another agent showed up, "wanting to know if I'd be interested in helping them. And I asked him, 'Well, what do you mean? Help you do what?' And that's when he went into his pitch about keeping them informed of our movements and things. I told him I had no interest in that whatsoever."

L. C. Dorsey was ready for the Movement when it came to Shelby, Mississippi, in 1964.

"I had dropped out of school and got married," she said. "I had all these babies. I had six kids living. Another was a preemie that died five hours after he was born. My husband — now my ex-husband — was making thirty-six dollars a week, so I really needed to find work. But I couldn't find work. They had this term: unemployed and unemployable. I was in that category.

"We'd been forced off the plantation. The plantation owner said that it had become uneconomical to have tenants. There was a big shift in agriculture during that period. The whole idea was to use mechanical pickers, and there was a new herbicide that everybody was experimenting with. I think it all had been precipitated by the activities in the early sixties."

So Dorsey and her family moved to Shelby, a town in the Delta north of the all-Negro town of Mound Bayou and south of Alligator. She commuted out to plantations to pick cotton, all the while looking for work in town. Finally she landed a job interview with the couple who ran the clothing store in downtown Shelby. "With almost a high school diploma," she said, "I was one of the more educated people in town." She was sure she would be hired to clerk in the store, and her hopes were raised when the couple asked about her ability to write and her efficiency with the telephone.

The interview had not been going on long when Dorsey realized that she would be working some in the store and some in the couple's home. And then there was an argument between the husband and the wife about whether she would be allowed one day off a week. What it boiled down to was that they wanted a housemaid, and they wanted to pay her nineteen dollars for seven days' work a week. Dorsey turned down the job and went back to catching the early morning truck to the cotton fields.

"But then the Movement came," she said. "And when it came, there were a lot of us who were ready for a change." A COFO worker named Patricia King came to Shelby.

"They came and knocked on my door and said, 'We're going to have a mass meeting such-and-such a night at Shiloh Missionary Baptist Church. Would you like to come?' And I said, 'Yes, what time?' I and a friend of mine walked over to the church for the meeting, and when we got there, we found the place was locked. The pastor had given his permission for us to have the meeting. But the deacons, fearing that the church would be firebombed, had locked the church and said we couldn't have the meeting inside. But these young people were not put off by that. We had the meeting on the outside.

"And I was just in a tither. It was wonderful. I mean, freedom was really here, and it was white folks standing up telling us what we needed to do about voter registration and all of this stuff, and it was just marvelous. There was no elaborate discussion about what voting meant and what it would change and how our lives would be better. I don't even think anybody asked those questions. It was, 'It's dangerous. Some of you may lose your jobs. Some of you may lose your credit. Some of you may get harassed. But that's what we're here to do, is to help you register to vote. All of you who want to, meet us at such-and-such a place, or we'll come pick you up, and we'll take you down to Cleveland [the seat of Bolivar County] and get you registered.'

"And people were ready to go and register. There was nobody

saying, 'Why should I bother? What will it benefit me? How will my family progress? How will I feed my kids?' There were no questions like that asked at that meeting."

Why not?

"I think we were just too anxious. We really had this idea that something magical was going to happen if we could just get past that hurdle.

"I'll never forget what happened when I went to register. I remember this white guy — he was the clerk or somebody — saying, 'You know, L.C., y'all didn't have to go get these folks to come in here and register. You could've been doing this all the time.' I don't think we could have, of course."

———————

Toward the end of Freedom Summer, 1964, the volunteer-staffed voter registration project in Pointe Coupee Parish wound down. But Sharon Burger did not go home to Indiana. She decided to stay with the Movement. She went on the CORE payroll, which meant twenty-five dollars a week, before taxes. She received a new assignment, to Monroe in northern Louisiana.

She had seen her hostess, Mrs. Caufield, very little that summer. "She was like a shadow that would pass through the room in the back," recalled Burger. The woman did not take her meals with the rest of the family at the weekend gatherings. It was at the end of the summer, and Sharon Burger was packing.

"I was in the room where I had slept by myself," she said, "and I remember Mrs. Caufield coming into the room and telling me that it had been an honor for her to have me there that summer. Those are the only words I ever remember hearing her say. . . . "

■ ———————————————————

THIRTY-TWO

NO PLAN, NO PROGRAM

The summer of 1964 was a tumultuous time for the Movement and for American race relations generally. While COFO volunteers and staff members were risking their lives in Mississippi and Louisiana and other places in the South, thousands of Negroes in Northern cities rioted.

The Harlem riot in New York City, which started July 18, became something of a model for the outbreaks of urban violence. Black people, confined by segregation to neighborhoods that received lower-quality government services than their white counterparts (they — and, soon, the social scientists and journalists — called them "ghettoes"), struck out violently against the symbols of their repression. As often as not, it was the arrest or shooting of a black person by a white policeman that set off the violence, although it was clear that almost any provocation would have sufficed. In Harlem, the rioting started after an off-duty police lieutenant shot and killed a fifteen-year-old boy.

The rioters used firebombs and hand-thrown projectiles as their weapons. Their particular targets were businesses in the ghetto that were owned and operated by whites — pawnshops, furniture and clothing stores, groceries — and that Negroes had long suspected of gouging them on price and quality. Looting of these places was widespread. The police (who were predominantly white, despite decades of Northern proclamations of equality in government employment) were also prime targets, along with the fire fighters who came to hose down the burning buildings. Individual whites, such as reporters sent to cover the violence, were ordinarily not attacked.

Typically, a riot would move a community's chief elected white official to express surprise and amazement and to comment that *this* was not Birmingham or Jackson; that equal rights were assured here. The mayors and governors came perilously close, in fact, to saying that "our Negroes are happy" — something that many Southern politicians had learned by now not to say. The white leaders displayed near-total inability to understand black grievances or to identify those black leaders with whom they might discuss a solution. When the Harlem riot occurred, New York City mayor Robert Wagner called Martin Luther King, Jr., for advice. King, while he was considered a hero by New York Negroes just as he was by Southerners, had few connections and no organization in Harlem.

The riots generally lasted a few days before petering out with promises by the white leadership to appoint blue-ribbon committees to discuss problems, which usually included the familiar areas of employment, education, and housing. There is little indication that the committees accomplished anything beyond producing a period in which black tempers cooled down and whites got back to business as usual. After Harlem, there were riots in Brooklyn's Bedford-Stuyvesant section, Rochester, and a number of New Jersey communities across the Hudson from New York — Jersey City, Union City, Elizabeth, and Paterson — as well as Philadelphia, Pennsylvania, and Dixmoor, Illinois. The FBI reported that the riots were "'a senseless attack on all constituted authority'" and showed an "increasing breakdown across the nation in respect for the law."[1] At the same time, the FBI, the symbol of that law, was tapping the telephones of its political opponents and circulating scurrilous accusations about the sexual proclivities of black civil rights personalities.

This period, which some Northerners were calling "the long, hot summer," was made even warmer by the presidential campaign that was under way. President Lyndon Johnson, who had assumed office upon John Kennedy's death the previous fall, was seeking election on his own; his selection by the Democratic National Convention in late August was a foregone conclusion, but who would be his vice presidential running mate was not. (It turned out to be Hubert Humphrey.) More than a month before, the Republicans had given their nomination to an extreme conservative, Senator Barry Goldwater. The Arizona Republican, who had been campaigning for the job for four years, delivered the most memorable line of his career when he said, in his acceptance speech, "Extremism in the defense of liberty is no vice . . . moderation in the pursuit of justice is no virtue."

Goldwater devised what was called his Southern strategy for winning the election. He courted Southern whites, particularly Democrats who were angry at President Johnson for his accommodating posture toward Negroes. The idea was that Goldwater could win the presidency by capturing all of the South and ignoring the Northern states, with their black and white liberal voters.

A few days before Goldwater's nomination, Congress had passed and Johnson had proudly signed the Civil Rights Act of 1964, the legislation that the Kennedys had drafted following the September, 1963, Birmingham church murders. The act insured and facilitated the right to vote in national elections; made it easier to get relief from discrimination in places of public accommodation; allowed the Justice Department to sue to desegregate public facilities; authorized Justice to bring suit on behalf of individuals to desegregate public education; extended the life of the Commission on Civil Rights; created the Equal Employment Opportunity Commission and made it more difficult for firms to discriminate in hiring; outlawed bias in federally assisted programs; and established the Community Relations Service to help resolve desegregation disputes.[2]

Presidential politics had become more racially polarized than ever with the entry of Alabama governor George Wallace into the field of battle. Wallace took part in presidential primaries in Wisconsin, Maryland, and Indiana, and did well. In mid-July he withdrew from the race, claiming that he had fulfilled his mission of making both of the major political parties more "conservatized."

Some of the civil rights organizations feared that what was being called a white backlash against Movement gains and demands and against the Northern riots might manifest itself in votes for Barry Goldwater. Roy Wilkins of the National Association for the Advancement of Colored People, acting on a suggestion from Johnson himself, in late July called for a moratorium on demonstrations, with a shift instead to political action. He got support from Whitney Young of the Urban League, Martin Luther King, Jr., and A. Philip Randolph. Opposition, predictably, came from the Movement's trench fighters. James Farmer of the Congress of Racial Equality and John Lewis of the Student Nonviolent Coordinating Committee opposed the ban, and Wilkins had to modify his position.[3]

One of the presidential nominating conventions was of special importance to the Movement. Concomitant with the summer voter registration effort in Mississippi had been the creation of the Mississippi Freedom Democratic Party, or MFDP. As COFO workers had gone out into the towns, hamlets, and plantations of Mississippi to explain the rules for getting one's name on the voting lists, they also had been signing up members for an alternative political party that, unlike the state's regular Democratic party, did not discriminate against Negroes.

Early in August, MFDP held its convention in Jackson and selected sixty-eight candidates, sixty-four of them Negro, to go to the Democratic National Convention in Atlantic City to challenge the regular slate of Mississippi delegates. "Selected" is the correct term here; although SNCC's guiding principle was "Let the people decide," there is evidence that the staff didn't trust "the people" on the matter of whom to send to the convention. Author and journalist Paul Cowan, who spent the summer as a volunteer in Vicksburg, wrote that he discovered that the local slate "had been chosen by a group of SNCC workers . . . the night before the state convention in Jackson. The organization decided which local people should be rewarded for their loyalty and then rigged the convention accordingly. They were afraid that too many middle-class Negroes would be nominated in an open convention."[4]

The leaders of the challenge wanted to unseat the regular state delegation at Atlantic City, arguing before the party's credentials committee that the regular delegates, who barred Negroes from taking part in their deliberations, were not faithful to the ideals of the national party, while the Freedom Democrats were. Furthermore, the argument went, Democrats who were members of the state's congressional delegation opposed many of the programs of the Democratic president and were actually supporting Barry Goldwater.

However touched Lyndon Johnson may have been by this apparent declaration of loyalty, he did not support the challengers. Johnson feared anything that might jeopardize his support among white Southern Democrats. He told Governor Paul Johnson of Mississippi that the challengers would not be seated. He asked J. Edgar Hoover to keep him informed of the MFDP's actions and plans when its delegates came to the convention. Hoover installed taps on MFDP's Atlantic City phones and supplied the resulting political information to Johnson.[5]

As the convention began, most of the MFDP people knew that the credentials committee would reject their arguments. But they hoped that their sympathizers on the committee would force a minority committee report to the convention floor, where open debate and a vote could take place.

Joseph Rauh, who was the counsel for MFDP, first suggested to party officials that a compromise be worked out: Both delegations would be seated. The leadership liked the idea, but Johnson did not. Then Rauh went before the credentials committee to present a detailed brief he and others had compiled and to argue the challengers' case. President Johnson, who was known as a headstrong politician who would stop at practically nothing and stoop to practically anything to get his way, demonstrated his feelings about the challenge on August 22. Fannie Lou Hamer, a member of a Mississippi sharecropper family who had become active in the Movement to the point that she was one of its undisputed heroes, was testifying to the credentials committee about the time, in June, 1963, when police had sadistically beaten her and others who wanted to vote. In the midst of her moving testimony, which was being televised nationally, President Johnson called a spur-of-the-moment press conference, obviously to detract attention from her presentation.

Johnson was, however, sufficiently rattled by the good press the challengers were getting to send out word that he was willing to compromise. MFDP delegates could come to the convention and they could speak out, but they would not be allowed to vote. MFDP rejected the plan. The Johnson forces came up with another scheme: MFDP's top leaders, Aaron Henry and Ed King, would be admitted to the convention as at-large delegates, while the remaining delegates would be reclassified as "guests" of the convention. At the next convention, in 1968, the party would refuse to seat any state delegation that practiced discrimination.

Rauh took the proposal to the challengers. There was a spirited discussion, and there was pressure from outside Mississippi — specifically, from Martin Luther King and Bayard Rustin — to accept the plan, which everyone referred to as "the compromise." To further complicate matters, Congresswoman Edith Green of Oregon suggested another plan: There would be seats for every member of either delegation who would sign a pledge of loyalty to the party. Mississippi's votes would then be divided proportionately among those who signed.

On August 26, the MFDP delegates rejected the two-seat compromise, despite a strong recommendation from counsel Rauh that they accept it. When the full convention got formally under way, it accepted the two-seat plan. But by then the Freedom Democrats were bitterly charging that they had been sold out, not only by the party generally and by Hubert Humphrey (who, they said, wanted the vice presidential nomination so badly he exerted pressure for the compromise), but by their own lawyer, Rauh.

John Lewis spoke, as he almost always did, philosophically: Atlantic City, he said, showed that "when you plan the game and go by the rules, you still can lose, if you don't have the resources, if you're going to disrupt the natural order of things."[6]

——————————————— ■

"We thought we had built a pretty good case for exclusion of the regulars," said Julian Bond. He didn't go to the convention — he was left behind in Atlanta to mind the SNCC office — but Bond's impression was that a good many people from the Movement and from Mississippi expected the challenge to accomplish more than it did.

"I was not very surprised," he said. "I didn't think it would work, although I think a great many people did, or at least thought more would come out of it than the compromise that was offered. I thought more would result than just this offer of two seats. There was really no way people could have taken *that*." As for Joseph Rauh, said Bond, "he sold us out. I think he intended to do so from the first."

The crisis over the challenge caused an "enormous disillusionment, or the solidification of disillusionment, with establishment liberals," said Bond. The germ of such disenchantment had been there all along. It was "this feeling that these people not only don't share our politics but they're so removed from the reality of what we're doing. If you're a liberal legislator from Wisconsin, you're dealing in one set of realities. If you're working in rural Mississippi, it's like being in a different world. It *is* a different world.

"And there was the discovery that these were people who just could not be trusted; that they would always guard their own interests, and their own interests and our interests were not the same. Could not be the same. Before Atlantic City, we thought that there were some parallel paths we were on. Both wanted to see expanded democracy, wanted to see black Southerners vote. We thought that the white South might have been drifting away from the Democratic party. If you're going to have liberal as opposed to conservative administrations, you had to have a base for it, and this was one way of insuring that base would continue while at the same time living up to the promise that everybody's equal and that everybody has a right to vote.

"And we thought that these people were willing to sacrifice this power they had — let this go, to protect their own interests." That did not happen, said Bond.

"The National Council of Churches turned against us," said Lawrence Guyot, the chairman and one of the major strategists behind the Mississippi Freedom Democratic Party and the challenge. "Roy Wilkins turned against us. Bayard Rustin turned against us. Joe Rauh, our attorney of record, turned against us. You name it."

Victoria Gray, of Palmer's Crossing, outside Hattiesburg, was one of the Freedom Democratic party delegates.

Since the days when she had responded to a statement on a radio call-in show, and when she had secured a church so that Hollis Watkins and Curtis Hayes could hold mass meetings, she had become absorbed in the Movement. "When the Movement finally reached that little corner where I was," she said, "it was simply a formal move for me. Because I was always fighting."

Through a SNCC worker, she was introduced to the Southern Christian Leadership Conference's leadership training workshops, which were held in Dorchester, Georgia. The workshops, which consisted of a week of concentrated work, were conducted by Andrew Young and Dorothy Cotton of the SCLC staff. Gray returned to Mississippi and started setting up citizenship classes on her own. When the summer of 1964 began, she went to Ohio and taught Freedom Summer volunteers. Then, when she was chosen as a delegate on the challenge slate, she went to Atlantic City.

She really expected, she said, that the delegation would get more than the two seats it was offered.

"You know," she said, "when you spend the better portion of your life in Mississippi, and you eventually come to a point where it looks like you have discovered what is necessary to become first-class citizens, to eradicate all of the negatives, you take those rules and you do exactly what you're supposed to do with them, according to what's written there. And why should you expect anything different as a result?" Once she and the others realized that "this was a game, a big game, there was no way under heaven I would have accepted those two seats."

The enemy, she said, was not just the regular Mississippi delegation or even Hubert Humphrey's messengers of compromise. It included the established black leadership, as well, which did not seem to understand that the challengers really wanted "to represent the Mississippi delega-tion." But in the end, she was able to look back on the experience and see that turning down the Atlantic City compromise was helpful. "I have thought about this many, many times. I always had a real sense of the fact that we were only creating an atmosphere back there so things can really begin to happen. I remember thinking that this is a long and ongoing activity that is going to take several generations to really do . . . because it has taken much too long for this thing to get to where it was, and is." To accept the compromise, then, would have damaged the chances of creating that atmosphere. "That would have been a regression."

Joseph Rauh, the warhorse of liberalism and counsel for the Mississippi Freedom Democratic Party, does not think he sold out his clients. Rather, he thinks, as do many of his colleagues, that he did precisely what a lawyer should do: He devoted total loyalty to his clients, offering them his advice on the best possible deal he could get for them.

Rauh was under considerable pressure from another of his employers to accept the compromise. President Johnson, whom Rauh remembers as "paranoid" about the election, dispatched Walter Reuther, the head of the United Auto Workers union, to order Rauh to compromise. At the time, Rauh was also counsel for the UAW. Reuther, said Rauh, "gave me an order to accept" the two-seat settlement, which he refused. "I wasn't thinking in terms of compromise," he said. "My compromise was to seat them both." Johnson told Reuther to get the challenge delegation to accept the compromise, said Rauh. "And the only thing he could think of was muscle. Johnson's idea was, 'Every man has a price.' So what does he do to neutralize me? He gets my biggest client, Walter Reuther, to call me. Not subtle.

"And my greatest friend in politics, Hubert Humphrey. It got so the two of them would call me if they'd see me on the tube. This was before the convention, and I'd be saying something that would get on television, and I'd get two calls. I'd get one from Reuther, just blowing my behind off. I'd get one from Hubert saying, 'Joe, can you give me something to tell the president about why you said that thing yesterday?' But he'd say it in such a nice way that you couldn't get mad at him."

Reuther, said Rauh, would say in his telephone calls, " 'Joe, you're losing the election.' I said, 'Walter, they've nominated *Goldwater. I* could get elected on the Democratic ticket. *You* might be able to.' I tried to lighten it up a little bit. I said, 'There's no danger. That's not what's at stake here.' He says, 'Well, the president and I think there's a real backlash in America.' I mean, they were paranoid."

Hubert Humphrey, on the other hand, did not serve as a lackey for Johnson. "Humphrey wouldn't play that game," said Rauh. "The most honorable guy in that whole fight was Hubert. Every night before I went to bed during that whole convention, and I wouldn't go before four or five A.M., I would stop by Hubert's place. He never once said, 'Look, Joe, we've been together a long time. This is my chance to be vice president. This is our chance. You're the only thing that obstructs it.' And that was what his people were all saying."

Rauh thinks the outcome of the challenge, and the Mississippians' attitude about that outcome, might have been greatly altered if the party had not dictated the terms of the two seats. If the challengers had been able to choose their two delegates, he feels, or if Fannie Lou Hamer could have been one of those seated, the bitterness might have been avoided.

Things might have turned out better, too, he said, if a false report had not gone out of the credentials committee meeting that he, Rauh, had agreed to the two-seat compromise. He was bound by a promise to his clients to approve nothing without checking with the challenge leadership. By the time he was able to deny the report, he said, COFO's Bob Moses "was going around screaming" that "I'm a double-crosser."

In one of his conversations with Hubert Humphrey, said Rauh — one of those times when Humphrey called to ask what he could tell the president about Rauh's unwillingness to cave in to Reuther's pressures and sell out his clients — Rauh suggested that " 'You tell the president I'm just a goddamn ornery son of a bitch, that nobody can handle me.' Humphrey says, 'The president wouldn't understand that.' " The future vice president was saying, Rauh thinks, that Lyndon Johnson would not understand that every man doesn't have his price.

"Well, maybe every man does. Maybe I *have* got my price, but it hasn't been paid yet."

■ ────────────────────────

After Atlantic City, and after most of the summer volunteers returned to their homes and college campuses in the North, the work of the Movement continued in the South. For the activist portion of the Movement — the SNCC field secretaries and CORE workers, the young people who had signed on for a year or so and who had stayed on and on, through crisis after crisis — something had changed.

In the eyes of many, Atlantic City was the final break between the organized Movement that had set out to win Americans over by tapping the goodness that was within their hearts and the Movement that realized that power was what counted. Goodness had been tried; redemptive suffering had been used; soul force had flowed in great abundance. The Movement had played by the rules, even by the rules that white America had written. But when it came down to a question of political power, as it certainly had at Atlantic City, the Movement and black Americans were once again rebuffed.

Or, more correctly, the *formal, organized* Movement felt this break. All across the South, there were Negroes who had not been part of that Movement but who were receiving the benefits of the marches, the demonstrations, the lawsuits, the challenges, and who were making progress in eliminating discrimination. They certainly had made progress in vanquishing fear. These were the people who were not Movement full-timers. They may have marched and demonstrated from time to time, or even gone to jail, but they did not do these things on a steady basis. They called themselves not field secretaries or activists but schoolteachers, day-care workers, housemaids, yard men, mechanics, file clerks, or unemployed. All along, as the full-timers had risked their lives and confronted their crises and broken away the brickwork of segregation, the lives of these people had improved, bit by bit. There was little evidence that they were strongly affected one way or another by what happened at Atlantic City.

But the Movement regulars were. As the summer ended, the most active of the activists found themselves in a peculiar position: There was still plenty of segregation and discrimination all around them, but they had little or no program devised for dealing with it. On top of that, they had less faith than ever before in the white liberals who had always been considered their allies.

——————————————————— ■

Julian Bond noticed that people in SNCC were asking each other, "Didn't what happened in Atlantic City turn you against regular politics?" and they were answering, "Yeah, yeah, it did."

"But I think it did more in retrospect than it did at the time," he said. "It became more of a justification for what followed than what it actually was."

What followed was the disillusionment, the alienation that the activists felt for liberals in the establishment. And in the alienation, SNCC found it had no real plans for what to do next.

"We cast about for a program because we hadn't had a program anyway to follow this," said Bond. "So had the challenge succeeded absolutely, had Mississippians been seated, the others thrown out, and everything gone on and Johnson won — we had nothing to do anyway. We had no other plans. So we were not only casting about for something to do in order to have something to do, but casting about for something *new* to do when this other thing had not worked."

■ ─────────────────────

SNCC held marathon staff meetings, sometimes at an unused seminary in Atlanta, sometimes at a church retreat on Mississippi's gulf coast. (A student of behavior might have remarked the tendency of SNCC, one of the least churched of the rights groups, to remain close to organized religion.) There the staff and field secretaries argued and presented papers and drank copious amounts of wine.[7] As much of the argument, or more, was about SNCC's internal problems as about the external threat of segregation. Women within SNCC were starting to talk then about the unequal ways in which they were treated by male staffers. Bond remembers going to one such retreat with his then-wife and lying in bed at night, fascinated as he heard, through the thin wall, a group of SNCC women discussing the possibility of a "sex strike" to call attention to their grievances. Some Negro staffers began questioning SNCC's interracial makeup; perhaps, they wondered, it would be better if SNCC were an all-black organization. Whites had plenty of opportunities to organize in their own communities, they argued. A phenomenon called "floating" began to manifest itself at SNCC. Field secretaries would drift from project to project, never settling down on anything.

───────────────── ■

"Atlantic City did something," said Dorothy Miller Zellner. "That was the change, I think. Up until then people were riding pretty high, and the moral force of people like Mrs. Hamer was very strong. And people were not prepared for Joe Rauh; they were not prepared for those incredible internal politics of the Democratic party. And after that the feeling was, these people will beat you every time. After Atlantic City, people realized how incredibly difficult this was going to be. There was a different quality — a feeling that things were going to be a lot tougher, that even if we won some of these things, there was still so much to be done.

"Before that, I thought that SNCC was going to last forever. I had made a lifetime commitment. There was no question in my mind. SNCC was going to last forever; we were going to be in it forever. There was no doubt in my mind that we would be victorious — whatever that meant."

■ ────────────────────────────

The Congress of Racial Equality, in the meantime, continued the process that James Farmer had called "chewing at itself." A flap occurred at the group's convention over the proposal that Alan Gartner, who was white, should become the national chair.

Gartner, who later said that "CORE and work within CORE was the central essence of my life," was deeply hurt when Farmer withdrew his support for Gartner's candidacy. But in CORE, as in SNCC, a move away from white leadership, or leadership shared with whites, and toward all-black control was starting. Floyd McKissick became the national chair.

Farmer charged, too, that there were groups out to "capture" CORE — by which he referred to Norman Hill, then the organization's program director. The plan, according to Farmer, was for Hill to create parallel CORE chapters and use them to oust Farmer and install Bayard Rustin in his place. Hill, asked about this recently, said it was not that he wanted to oust Farmer but that he wanted to strengthen CORE by bringing Rustin, who had no organizational foundation, into the structure. When the coup failed, Hill departed and the A. Philip Randolph Institute was created to give Rustin his base, according to Hill.

What the Movement needed, and did not have, reflected Farmer later, was the opportunity or inclination to sit down after the end of Freedom Summer and figure out what to do next. "We had no time," he said, "to do any long-range planning. So after we succeeded in our initial, short-range goals, the Movement didn't know where it was going. There was no plan, no program."

The Movement should have gone into retreat, he said, and come back with strategies and objectives. "It would have been a long process, but we should have gotten started on it, anyway, taking our scholars with us, so we'd have some baseline data, so it wouldn't be just batting the breeze and brainstorming out of ignorance."

Not everyone was exhausted and confused and consumed by internal strife. All around the South, the people who had been inspired by the Movement were busily extending the aims of the campaign — teaching literacy, filing complaints and lawsuits, and, most important, registering to vote and causing elected politicians to think twice before mispronouncing the word "Negro." Some people of color were saying that even when correctly pronounced, "Negro" wasn't the correct term anymore. The term was "black." It was as if an entirely new definition of Negro were being born, and in honor of the change a new identifying term had to be created.

Victoria Gray Adams came back to Mississippi from Atlantic City as dejected as any of her fellow delegates. But for her the letdown did not last long. "For some people," she said, "they said, 'Forget it; there is no more.' But then there were others of us who said, 'No, no, no, no. We're going to keep going.' As long as there is reason for things to be made right, the civil rights movement, the human rights movement, will continue. There will always be those who refuse to give up and quit."

She, for one, was in that category. "Absolutely," she said. "For as long as I breathe."

PART EIGHT

VICTORY

THIRTY-THREE

SEGREGATION IS BROKEN

Freedom Summer turned to autumn. The experience of political reality at Atlantic City showed the younger Movement activists, who saw the challenge outcome as a defeat and an insult, just how weary they had become. It was a weariness without respite; there was so much more to be done. Every gain, it seemed, served to reveal just how deeply etched racism was in the American system. The Movement that had been so joyously celebrated with the March on Washington, that by its sacrifice of human life had finally gotten a modicum of involvement from the federal government in Mississippi, that had moved one of the major political parties to at least a compromise on elementary political justice — that Movement could see now, more clearly than ever, that the tasks ahead were still monumental.

The hard core, the Black Belt, was desperately hard to break. Some of the border states that had desegregated their schools or public accommodations with relative ease were now resegregating them. The liberal, progressive North was being revealed to be as stubborn as any place in the South — it just had a more sophisticated vocabulary. And everywhere white America shared political power, when it shared at all, only when it was forced to. The job of securing the vote, which once had sounded simple and non-controversial enough ("Nobody really could oppose voting," the attorney general of the United States had said), now seemed as difficult as desegregating America's schools had seemed in the late fifties.

For some of the older organizations, such as the National Association for the Advancement of Colored People and the National Urban League, business went on pretty much as usual. These were the long-haul groups; they had learned decades ago to treat every setback as a temporary one. This was not so in the younger, more high-pitched groups that thrived on activism, such as the Congress of Racial Equality and the Student Nonviolent Coordinating Committee. For them, life changed after the summer. Some members — almost invariably they were those who had started out with the sit-ins or even earlier, and who were the old-timers of the younger activists — began drifting away from the most militant organizations, almost always into related fields. Some returned to the college campuses they had "temporarily" abandoned two, four, five years before.

Diane Nash had married James Bevel, whom she had met back in Nashville at the nonviolence workshops. Both went to work for the Southern Christian Leadership Conference. Charles .Sherrod left southwest Georgia after the summer of 1964, at least for a while, and entered Union Theological Seminary in New York City. John Lewis remained at SNCC, but he was under increasing attack by others, such as James Forman, who dismissed him as "young, inexperienced, from a small Southern town," a person who had "fine qualities as a symbol of black resistance" but who was lost among the "overpowering, tricky infighters" from the other civil rights organizations.[1]

Several of the older activists had left to join, in one way or another, the "war on poverty" that President Lyndon Johnson had declared, in his first State of the Union address to Congress on January 8, 1964. As originally advertised, the "war" had a significant provision for community organization and activism; for many Movement veterans it sounded like a logical extension of what they had been doing, with the important difference that salary would amount to considerably more than twenty-five dollars a week. But the system, through its elected leaders and the permanent bureaucracy that engulfs and suffocates any innovative governmental campaign, quickly made it clear that it was not willing to go along with any program, even one heralded as a "war," that required a redistribution of power.

Johnson's domestic war (he was fighting one in Vietnam, too) included battles to improve education, child health and welfare, and employment for the nation's poor, and it established a corps of domestic volunteers. It also provided for community action programs, which local communities might think up and execute in response to their own conditions and needs. The legislation for this stated that such programs would take place with the "maximum feasible participation of the residents of the areas and the members of the groups" involved. However, when those residents started trying to participate maximally, or even minimally, bureaucrats and politicians raised an enormous hue and cry, claiming that the legislation didn't at all mean what it said it meant. Political scientist and occasional government advisor Daniel P. Moynihan, one of the loudest of the squawkers, said the law meant that previously excluded people would "participate in the *benefits* of the community action programs."[2] Before long, community people were effectively squeezed out of policy-making positions in the war on poverty, but not before many of them became disillusioned, just as SNCC's weary field secretaries had become, with government's willingness to improve the system.

Martin Luther King, Jr., stayed, of course. The press and the rest of white America had become even more firm in their insistence that King was *the* Negro spokesman, *the* leader, thus placing King under even more pressure. Furthermore, black nationalism was growing in direct proportion to the Movement's inability to wring meaningful change out of the system, so King was expected to provide an attractive alternative to that, too. Not only did he have to preach to white America that his message was actually moderate, compared to that of nationalists such as Malcom X; he had the added burden of trying to convince his fellow Negroes that it was worthwhile to keep working and suffering for an interracial society, not a separatist one.

In the meantime, the FBI had singled out King for intense scrutiny. J. Edgar Hoover clearly was out to destroy the leader.

Hoover ran a secret and illegal operation called COINTELPRO, for "counterintelligence program," which coordinated covert FBI activities against domestic groups, including those who were exercising their constitutional rights and breaking no laws.[3] A Senate committee later determined that COINTELPRO mounted 2,370 separate "actions" from 1956 until 1971, when an FBI office in Media, Pennsylvania, was burgled and incriminating documents about the covert program were leaked to the press. Those "actions," in the committee's words, were "designed to 'disrupt' and 'neutralize' target groups and individuals," and included efforts that ranged from "the trivial (mailing reprints of *Reader's Digest* articles to college administrators) to the degrading (sending anonymous poison-pen letters intended to break up marriages) and the dangerous (encouraging gang warfare and falsely labeling members of a violent group as police informers)." King was made the target of COINTELPRO operations because the FBI said it thought, in the words of one of its memoranda, he might "abandon his supposed 'obedience' to 'white, liberal doctrines' (nonviolence) and embrace black nationalism."

In one instance of the agency's war on King, William Sullivan, a high-ranking FBI official, wrote in another memo in the summer of 1964 that he had spoken with the general secretary of the National Council of Churches of Christ and had said "that Martin Luther King not only left a great deal to be desired from the standpoint of Communism, but also from the standpoint of personal conduct. . . . I think that we have sowed an idea here which may do some good. I will follow up on the matter very discreetly to see what desirable results may emanate therefrom." Sullivan said the general secretary told him at a later meeting that "steps have been taken by the National Council of Churches of Christ to make certain from this time on that Martin Luther King will never get 'one single dollar' of financial support from the National Council." Sullivan also said the churchman had told him he planned to try to persuade the NAACP's Roy Wilkins "that Negro leaders should completely isolate King and remove him from the role he is now occupying in civil rights activities."

When King won the Nobel Prize for Peace in November, 1964, Hoover and his lickspittles in Bureau headquarters were beside themselves with envy and anger. Hoover had prepared a written account of King's alleged friendships with people the Bureau believed to be subversive, and of his alleged sexual promiscuity, titled "Communism and the Negro Movement — A Current Analysis." As one of his information-gathering tools, Hoover had relied on telephone taps on King that Attorney General Robert Kennedy had authorized.

Hoover started to distribute his written attack within the federal government in October, 1963. But Kennedy, who apparently thought phone taps were one thing but sneaky diatribes quite another (or, perhaps, who could see the possibility of political damage for himself if the taps became public knowledge), ordered that the monograph be recalled. Now, a year later, with King riding high in the view of both Americans and the world, Hoover updated the document. According to the Senate committee, he sent the monograph to Bill Moyers, the special assistant to President Johnson, asking if Moyers thought it should be sent to "responsible officials in the executive branch." Moyers gave permission, and the document went out.[4]

Two attorneys general, who should have known what was going on in the Bureau, pleaded ignorance and naivete when asked later about COINTELPRO. Nicholas Katzenbach, who succeeded Kennedy as attorney general in 1964, testified, incredibly, "It never occurred to me that the bureau would engage in the sort of sustained improper activity which it apparently did." He covered another base by adding that, furthermore, he wasn't surprised that he wasn't told about the acts, since Hoover knew he would not have condoned them.

Ramsey Clark, who headed the Justice Department from 1967 to 1969, and whom Hoover once had called "a jellyfish," said he was too busy to know what the FBI was doing.[5] (Hoover's characterization received some support by an incident reported by Wiley Branton of the Voter Education Project. Branton said, in an interview, that he had invited several VEP leaders to Washington to talk about what was going on in their areas and to receive a pep talk from President Johnson. Branton asked for meeting space in the Justice Department building, and he was assigned an FBI class-room. When Hoover heard about this, said Branton, "he told Ramsey Clark that we could not meet in any of the FBI facilities. And the attorney general of the United States simply told me that we'd have to find another place. . . . I was very disappointed that the attorney general of the United States didn't say, 'Mr. Hoover, since that room is not being used, it *will* be used by this group.' " Such failure, said Branton, "reinforced my thoughts about the failures of the Justice Department down South.")

The one, and perhaps only, cure for all this was by now quite obvious to the entire Movement, to its militants and conservatives, old-timers and newcomers. Political power, gathered through access to the ballot box, could rewrite the script for future Atlantic Citys; it could insure true "maximum feasible participation"; it could even remove J. Edgar Hoover from office. For proof, one needed only examine the almost embarrassingly rapid way in which white politicians had changed their tunes in areas where Negroes *had* been able to vote.

SNCC continued its work to challenge the regular Democrats in Mississippi, specifically by targeting the state's five congressional representatives for unseating. A prospectus for 1965 called this "the most important political event of 1965, notwithstanding efforts to get new voting legislation."[6] There were many places in the Deep South where Negroes would benefit from successful voter registration campaigns, but the Black Belt in Alabama was one of the most attractive. Some within the Movement thought Selma was a logical place to start.

Selma was situated almost in the middle of the Black Belt as it swept across lower Alabama. Once known as High Soapstone Bluff, the seat of Dallas County sat above the Alabama River and on an important east-west land route. De Soto passed by, it is said, in 1540. First a cotton center and slave market, Selma changed dramatically in 1848, when a group of Germans arrived and began casting iron and making guns. During the Civil War, the town's importance as an arsenal and supply depot was second only to that of Richmond. In 1865 Federal forces discovered a large supply of Confederate whisky, drank it, and burned the place down, including all the mules and horses they did not need. One thumbnail account of this notes that the "stench remained long in the nostrils of Selma citizens, making [the] task of reconstruction a difficult one."[7]

Another stench remained even longer in the nostrils of Selma's citizens whose skin was brown or black. The town was a center of Citizens Council activity. The Dallas County sheriff, Jim Clark, was a relentless foe of racial equality, a man in the tradition of Bull Connor who maintained a posse (it would be called a mob anyplace else) and whose followers freely used electric cattle prods against Negroes who demonstrated, spoke out, or showed interest in voting. An effort by the Justice Department to challenge Alabama's discriminatory voting practices and restrain the county registrar and Sheriff Clark did little to improve the situation.

White Selma and its environs showed a pathological fear of letting Negroes vote. While the majority of the citizens of Dallas County, 57 percent, were Negroes, less than 1 percent of the eligible Negroes were registered. Almost two-thirds of the eligible whites were registered. Conditions were similar, or worse, in neighboring Black Belt counties. In Wilcox County, to the south of Dallas, 78 percent of the population was Negro; in Lowndes County, to the east, it was 81 percent. Not a single Negro was registered to vote in either county.[8]

SNCC had been collecting information on Selma since 1962, and had found that a high degree of intimidation and repression awaited Negroes who questioned the system. It was just the sort of challenge that SNCC liked to take on. SNCC worker Mary Varela, meantime, began an adult literacy program in Selma in 1963. In October, 1963, the organization held a Selma Freedom Day to inaugurate a voter registration campaign. Official harassment followed immediately. Local whites took out a full-page advertisement in the newspaper to proclaim that the races had always lived together in tranquillity in Selma, and that they would continue to do so once the outside agitators had departed.

On October 7, one of the two days a month that prospective voters could register in Dallas County, a group of Negroes lined up at the courthouse to get the franchise. Sheriff Clark's men arrested three organizers on the steps of the Federal Building while FBI agents and two Justice Department lawyers watched and did nothing to intervene. The organizers, who had been holding signs that said "REGISTER TO VOTE," were charged with "unlawful assembly." Historian Howard Zinn, an advisor to SNCC who witnessed the spectacle, wrote that he asked one of the Justice Department lawyers, "Is that a *federal* building?" and that the man said "Yes" and turned away.[9]

■

Bernard Lafayette first heard of Selma on the Freedom Ride. The mob of angry whites in Selma was so large, he recalls, that the riders had to bypass the place. He came back in November, 1962, to check Selma out.

Lafayette had been raising bond money for SNCC in the North to get Dion Diamond, Bob Zellner, and Charles McDew out of jail in Baton Rouge, where they had been charged with criminal anarchy. The young minister had been arrested forty-three times himself, he said, and the experience was wearing a bit thin. "I felt that I could get more accomplished outside," he said. He returned to Atlanta and asked for an assignment of his own. James Forman suggested that he join someone else's project — south Georgia, Arkansas, Mississippi — but Lafayette wanted to run his own show for a change (also, there were warrants outstanding for his arrest in Mississippi). " 'I want to take on my own project,' " he said he told Forman. " 'I want to experiment with this thing the way *I* want to do it, and I don't want to end up in jail on somebody else's decision.' I wanted to see what really could be done. My theory was to develop a community to the point where the community was willing to go to jail and take a stand. That's when you get change." SNCC had considered trying to organize Selma, but had dropped the idea because a previous investigation had shown the intense repression made it unlikely that local people would join a movement. SNCC had hung a big map of the South on one of the walls in its cluttered office in Atlanta, but the staff had removed the pin for Selma. "Selma was the only place left," said Lafayette.

So SNCC put the pin back in the map and sent Lafayette to Selma on the first week of November, 1962, with the title of director of the Alabama voter registration project. He found out immediately that the reports he had heard were all true. "Time you hit the community, the police department or sheriff's department was following you. They followed me everywhere I went. How did they know I was in town? Some black folks had to tell them. What people said was there were too many Uncle Toms. The community was so locked up. . . .

"I was curious as to why this condition existed, so I did a couple of things." One of them was to go to Tuskegee Institute, about eighty miles from Selma, and hole up in the library. Lafayette read everything he could find on Selma and Dallas County, including Citizens Council publications.

Armed with this information, Lafayette returned to Selma. "I knew the names of the people who were on the board of directors of the bank, the editor of the newspapers, everybody. And I knew some interesting facts about the history of Selma. Like the capital of Alabama used to be in Dallas County. And there was this feeling and attitude that people had in Dallas County that they had been robbed, because they had probably the best location for the capital. It was centrally located, right in the middle of Alabama. So there was always a feeling that they had been dealt a raw deal."

Lafayette also learned the details about Dallas County's history of black repression. When a group of Negroes petitioned for desegregated schools, the whites "so intimidated the blacks who had signed the petitions until they got all except one or two to take their names off the petitions. Run them out of town, fire their mother-in-law, threaten their children — these people withdrew. They didn't have a petition. The fear was very thick. There were people who had been beaten and chased out of town. It was systematic, and very predictable as to what would happen."

One of Lafayette's most important discoveries was that the people who were labelled Uncle Toms, those who were accused of collaborating with the racists, were invariably those who had previously tried to change the system and who had received no support from the black community. "They came to have such a healthy fear of white people and disrespect for black people and disrespect for themselves," he said, "that they did not believe that things would change. Therefore, they decided to simply try to capitalize on the situation."

Lafayette decided that two things had to happen if Selma were going to change.

"One was that people had to have a greater sense of respect for each other. When I went around talking to people, I would ask them the same questions. I'd say, 'Why is it that Selma is like it is?' And to a person they would say to me, 'This is the worst place in the world. Nothing's ever going to happen here. These people are so backwards and they're so afraid . . . ' And the very people I was talking to, the same thing was being said about them. Everybody was saying the same thing about each other. So there was a lack of respect for each other, for ministers and the other civic leaders."

Very few people in Selma's black community commanded universal respect, Lafayette found. One of them was Samuel Boynton, who had been a local businessman and the head of the Dallas County Voters League, a relatively nonmilitant group. When Lafayette arrived, Boynton was in fading health in a nursing home. His wife, Amelia Boynton, was the person who had originally invited SNCC to come to Selma.

Lafayette's second challenge, he said, was "building a community out of a disorganized, disjunctive collection of people" who were afraid not only of what the whites might do to them, but also of what trouble the outsider from SNCC might bring down on their heads.

"Some people were very fearful that I was going to organize demonstrations and get their kids in jail, and we had no money to get them out. They used to call me the Freedom Rider, because the Freedom Rides were prominent on their minds. So there were some people who were afraid to identify with me and to talk with me. I couldn't find a place to live. One of the schoolteachers said, 'Well, you can come stay in my place.' I stayed in her home until there was an apartment available, which she also owned."

Lafayette, who had been joined now by his wife, Colia Liddell Lafayette, started asking local ministers about using their churches for mass meetings. The reaction was not overwhelmingly positive. But then something occurred to change matters.

"What happened was that Mr. Boynton died. And when he died, we thought it would be befitting to have a memorial service for him. So we printed a flyer which said, 'Please attend this memorial service for Mr. Boynton . . . and voter registration.' It was apropos because he was the chairman of the Dallas County Voters League, and he was a man who had always encouraged people to register to vote and had been their voucher. To register, you had to have a registered voter sign for you. Well, he'd vouch for people.

"The timing was right. If we'd tried to call people together for a mass meeting, it would've flopped because they were afraid. We would have had a struggle getting a church." But no minister could turn down Lafayette's request for a memorial service for a man of Boynton's stature. The pastor of Tabernacle Baptist Church offered his building for the service, but that did not mean fear had been eradicated in Selma. The minister's deacons worried that the church would be bombed and its stained-glass windows broken. A Negro printer didn't want to print the leaflets for the mass meeting. Lafayette realized that he needed something else.

"The first thing you have to do when people are afraid is to give them other models and examples of courage. See, the models and examples they *had* had been people who had been beaten down and killed. People had been run out of town; lost their jobs. It was a consistent pattern. So why should they believe what I said? Well, seeing is believing. So I was beaten in the community and arrested."

On the night of June 12, 1963, the same night Medgar Evers was murdered, a group of white men ambushed Bernard Lafayette and beat him badly. An enormous man struck him repeatedly with the butt of a gun, Lafayette said, and the gang attempted unsuccessfully to put him in a car — for what purpose Lafayette does not know and would rather not speculate on. Lafayette escaped with his life.

"The next day, I got out of the hospital and organized them for a mass meeting. I provided the role model for people; the beating did not stop me from continuing my work." No longer was the outsider denied a place to hold rallies against repression. Bernard Lafayette's voter registration project moved from its research phase into the active stage.

Diane Nash Bevel and her husband, James Bevel, were in Edenton, North Carolina, in September of 1963, working on a voter education drive conducted by the Southern Christian Leadership Conference. They were staying at the home of a local SCLC official when they heard about the church bombing in Birmingham that killed the four children.

"Bevel and I" — she referred to her husband (now her former husband) by his last name, as did most everybody else in the Movement — "were sitting there crying," she said later, "and he expressed the thought — and I agreed — that we could probably find out who did it if we tried. And we considered two options.

"The first option was that we could find out who did it and make sure they got killed. And the second option was that we could get the right to vote for blacks in Alabama, and therefore Alabama blacks could protect their children better. But we decided that we weren't going to let the deaths go unanswered. We were going to pursue one of those two options. We decided on the second option."

Although she had been one of the Movement's more notable advocates and practitioners of nonviolence, Diane Nash Bevel felt nevertheless that the first option was "a clear possibility. We felt that the bombing did have a relationship to the civil rights movement," she said. "And we also felt that those kids were our kids, and that it was being less than a man and less than a woman to let your kids get killed and just do nothing. That would have been pitiful. And I knew I wasn't — and he wasn't, either — willing to be pitiful like that.

"So we said, 'Well, we're going to do something about it. We're going to bring justice to them.' So we chose the second option. That day, we developed an initial strategy. The goal was to get the right to vote in Alabama. We wrote it up and typed it up. Bevel had responsibilities in Edenton with the voter registration campaign, so I was the one available. My job was to take the draft to Martin [Luther King, who was their boss] and encourage him to — insist, in fact — that he call a meeting of SCLC people and decide what to do to address the situation.

"We were going to submit the strategy that we had developed as a draft of one option of what we could do. But the main thing was to decide to do something — even if we decided not to do anything, to have a meeting and make a decision. And so that's what we did. I took off in a plane and did have a conversation with Martin about it."

King turned down the idea of calling a meeting. "He said that he was going to go to talk to the president, and that was the next item on his agenda. I presented the plan to him, and he did not agree to do it. Didn't like it. Said no." She and Bevel tried over the next several months to talk King and his advisor, Andrew Young, into launching a large campaign in Alabama, but "that was not successful." So the Bevels took matters into their own hands.

"We decided that Bevel should take the family car and go to Alabama. That was a big sacrifice, because by then I was pregnant with my second child and I had a toddler. But we decided that he would take the car and go off to Alabama and start organizing, and I would get to work on some research we needed to do in writing a proposed booklet that was called *Handbook for Freedom Army Recruits.* It was just a little pamphlet, a basic kind of thing." The Bevels hoped that James's insubordination would not be considered serious enough to get him fired from SCLC. Still, he took some of his staff with him, and all his actions were taken without King's permission.

"We knew," said Diane, "that if he proceeded to do the organizing and we developed the Alabama movement to a certain point, that the people in Alabama would ask Martin to come over. And he couldn't say no. And that's exactly what happened. We developed a movement. It was a statewide project." She feels now that if "that moment had been seized" after the bombing, when grieving for the young, innocent victims had been so widespread, that "we really could have closed the state down." But the man who could have done the seizing decided otherwise. Nonetheless, Diane and James Bevel kept at their work. "We committed ourselves individually and also to each other that if it took twenty years, we were going to get the right to vote in Alabama."

■ ───────────────────────────

Silas Norman, who had helped organize demonstrations in Augusta, Georgia, after the sit-ins started, graduated from Payne College in 1962 and entered graduate school at Atlanta University. He thought he might want to become a physician, or perhaps teach medicine, so he sought a master's degree in biology. He was absent from a few classes, though. He remembers a valued teacher in the biology department who was understanding about letting his students miss sessions so they could take part in the almost daily marches across the railway viaduct that separated the Atlanta University Center from the segregated lunch counters of downtown Atlanta.

Norman transferred to the University of Wisconsin in the summer of 1963 to study medical microbiology. The following year, as plans were developing for the Mississippi summer project, SNCC's Freedom Singers, a group of mostly Albany veterans who performed at fund-raising and other functions around the country, came to the university.

———————————————   ■

"Madison was a hotbed of political activity," said Norman later in an interview. "It was center or left, mostly left, political activity, and we had a steering committee on civil rights, and there were other groups, a lot of which I'd never heard of." But Norman attended some meetings, and one thing led to another, and he met Mary Varela, who had some connections with SNCC. She asked him if he would like to take part in a literacy training project in Selma, Alabama, that summer. It was important that only the summer be involved. Norman had just about decided that he had to shift his studies to history ("Science was considered not the place to be if you were an activist") and he could not afford to be away from the campus for an extended time.

When he arrived in Selma, the Movement had already made its presence known, largely through Bernard Lafayette's risky pioneering. The city's white leaders that summer obtained a state court injunction against any antisegregation or provoting activity by civil rights groups or anybody else, and the Movement was lying low.

"There were no demonstrations taking place at the time we arrived, nor were you allowed to meet for the purpose of doing what we were doing," recalled Norman. "So we went down sort of in secret, and we worked out of a Catholic mission. Mary Varela lived around in the white community, and we took a place in the black community, and we would come together secretly during the course of the day and sit down and plan our activities." The secrecy, he said, did not bother the young people who were conspiring to promote literacy. "I think we had a sense that we were really involved in the Movement and in some kind of adventure," said Norman.

Literacy tutoring was an important part of SNCC's effort because earlier investigations, by Lafayette and others who had spent days in the Tuskegee library, had shown the literacy rate in Alabama's Black Belt to be quite low. And there was a direct link between being literate and passing the state's voter registration test. "We were specifically there to help prepare people for political activity," Norman said. "Advancing your life and doing all those other things would have been important, but we were strictly at that point trying to prepare people to be involved in the political process."

The volunteers employed a procedure that is widely used in literacy tutoring now: They asked their students about topics that interested them — fishing, cooking, church work. Then the tutors transcribed the verbal comments into written ones and took them back to their students. Since the words and phrases were the students' own, they were able to make the leap between spoken and written language with relatively little pain. The tutors also used as their texts passages that were employed at the voter registration office.

"It took us about a month to blow our cover," said Norman. "We were not supposed to be in contact with the SNCC workers there because that was going to blow our cover. We were not supposed to go down to the SNCC office on Franklin Street, which was across the street from the jail. We were supposed to stay in the mission and mind our business."

Norman's group of noncombatants managed to obey the rules most of the time. But then they received news that the 1964 Civil Rights Act, which included a public accommodations section, had been passed and signed into law. It was, Norman recalled, a Saturday. It was also the Fourth of July.

"We were to be in the mission working that morning. Mary made a mistake of leaving us around lunchtime, and we decided that during lunch we were going to go and test public accommodations. So we went down to a place called the Thirsty Boy, a restaurant. SNCC had just bought a little green Ford, and we drove that car. At first we decided we'd stay in the car, because it was a drive-through. And then we decided, no; we want to go in." The literacy workers, fearing what might happen to the automobile if they parked it in the restaurant's lot, left it instead across the street.

"So we went to the Thirsty Boy, and that's where we met Jim Clark, a few moments later.

"It was the first time we had seen him. We'd heard about him. And we knew about the posse. Everyone had told us about the sheriff's posse. As they arrived — in several cars, as I recall — I remember thinking that there were too many people to justify what three or four of us were doing.

"They had cattle prods. Those are the only weapons they had that I can remember, because they used them on us that day. We were arrested and put in the Dallas County Jail. Two women and another man and me."

The posse members applied cattle prods to Norman's body, though not in the places, such as the genitals, that the racists sometimes favored. "With black females, they sometimes did breasts and female genitals. But mine was arm and body and multiple times, both in the restaurant and on the way up to the lockup. In fact, it was kind of a pleasure to get to the lockup." Norman stayed in jail that time, he recalls, for eleven days.

When he and the others got out, their cover as literacy tutors effectively destroyed, they started to take full part in the Movement's work. Mary Varela, he said, was "a little disturbed with us for having blown the project. She knew it would happen. And she knew that it was going to be difficult to keep us involved in that level of activity when we really wanted to get out and get in the demonstrations."

At the end of the summer of 1964, Silas Norman's three fellow literacy workers went back to their colleges. He attended one of SNCC's marathon unwinding-and-discussing meetings in Atlanta, met James Forman, and went to work full-time for SNCC. His pay, after taxes, was nine dollars a week. He returned to Selma to organize people.

■ ────────────────────────────

Diane and James Bevel went to Selma in the late fall of 1964 to prepare the way for the arrival of Martin Luther King (although King did not know then what they had in store for him). Before long, the Dallas County Voters League invited King to visit. The SCLC leader arrived in January, 1965, and told his listeners, "We are not asking, we are demanding, the ballot." He promised to get the federal government involved in the issue by sending citizens "by the thousands" to the registrar's office.[10]

Sheriff Clark responded just as the Movement knew he would. When 62 Negroes sought to register and refused to enter the courthouse by the alley door, the one commonly reserved for black people, Clark arrested them. The next day, he arrested 150 more, charging them with "unlawful assembly." Martin Luther King was arrested. He spent four days in jail before posting bond.

A federal district judge issued an order prohibiting Clark and others from interfering with registration. SNCC charged that a federal marshal, on hand to enforce the court order, chose to enforce it *against* those who were trying to secure the vote, by denying registration workers "the right to speak to applicants in line or bring them food and water."[11]

When Negroes demonstrated in the nearby town of Marion, the seat of Perry County, rampaging state troopers beat them and shot one, Jimmy Lee Jackson, to death. King, preaching at a memorial service, criticized the federal government for spending millions to prosecute a war in Vietnam while refusing to protect its own citizens' lives. By now, thousands of people had been arrested, and Sheriff Clark's posse was attacking peaceful demonstrators with cold-blooded routine.

Tension — creative tension, as King saw it — was high. James Bevel proposed a fifty-mile-long march, from Selma to the state capitol in Montgomery. Such a demonstration would channel the Negroes' anger and tension into productive lines, and it would certainly focus the eyes of the nation on the Movement. As always, the white resistance had the option of nonviolence. Sheriff Clark, his posse, Al Lingo and his Alabama highway patrol, Governor Wallace — they could stand by and watch, or even assist the marchers in their pilgrimage to the steps of the capitol. Or they could react with violence. The choice was theirs, as it had always been.

On March 7, 1965, more than five hundred Negroes and whites started their march from Selma to Montgomery. The police, some of them on horseback, stopped the marchers at the oddly arched Edmund Pettus Bridge, which spans the Alabama River just east of Selma, and beat them savagely with clubs and whips. John Lewis, one of the leaders of the march, was among those who were beaten bloody. He was there in his capacity as a concerned citizen; SNCC was officially not taking part. King was away from Selma that day, and SCLC was represented by Hosea Williams. Pictures of the attack were flashed around the world, just as they had been during Bull Connor's Birmingham riots, and once again the world reacted with revulsion at what quickly became known as Selma's "Bloody Sunday." Sympathetic people, black and white, headed toward Selma to take part in the next demonstration.

SNCC's head office had been angered when Dr. King's workers came to Selma. It was the old question, said SNCC, of the young activists' doing all the difficult groundwork, only to have

SCLC sweep into town and grab all the glory. Staffers from both organizations at the local level, however, were not concerned with such resentment, and they worked together to plan the demonstration. Eventually even SNCC's office dropped its opposition, and field secretaries from all over the South sped to Selma to take part in what would obviously be an enormous protest. Silas Norman, who had felt resentment enough to sit out the first march on philosophical grounds, changed his mind.

A group of visiting clergymen, who had come to town after the first attempted march, was beaten by a white mob. After one of them, the Reverend James Reeb, a Unitarian from Boston, died of his wounds, there was widespread national outrage. President Johnson telephoned Reeb's wife, and Hubert Humphrey attended the funeral. People in the Movement sadly commented that none of this had happened a few days before when Jimmy Lee Jackson had been killed. Jackson, unlike Reeb, was black.

A few days later, a second march was attempted. District judge Frank Johnson, who had surprised Movement lawyers by briefly enjoining the Freedom Ride, signed an order restraining the march. Martin Luther King said the march would go on anyway. He led a large demonstration to the point where the police were waiting, then turned the marchers around and took them back to town. SNCC leaders, who had complained privately in Albany about King's compliance with federal injunctions, made their feelings known publicly in Selma. They called his action a sellout.

------------------------------   ■

"On the second march on Montgomery," said Silas Norman, "I emptied my pockets and I prepared to offer my body as a living sacrifice." He was speaking at a 1988 gathering of former SNCC workers, most of whom were familiar with his deep, rich voice and his formal, somewhat biblical way of talking. There were young college students in the audience who did not know Norman, however, and from them there was scattered, somewhat nervous laughter, as if they did not know whether he was serious or joking.

"We started the march across the bridge for the second time, and as we got to the end of the Edmund Pettus Bridge, state troopers lined up on every side, I noticed they were not moving *towards* us. But I will remember that Dr. King said — he was a row or two behind me — he said, 'Let us pray.' We prayed. And then the march proceeded to turn around. Well, Jim Forman was close to me. We were all sort of baffled. Jim was saying, 'What's going on? Let's go ahead,' though not quite in those words, and as we turned around and headed back across the bridge, there were hundreds of people behind us asking, 'What's going on? What's happening?'

"We had no idea. We were to discover later that there had been some agreement with [the Justice Department], with government, that that march was not to proceed. Personally, I did not participate in that march again. I felt that we had been betrayed, and I no longer wanted to participate in that, and I felt that I would best spend my energies working with people in the Movement in small groups in Selma."

At about that time, said Norman, SNCC staffers began to arrive from Mississippi and Georgia to take part in the march, and also to take advantage of the new focus of civil rights attention on hard-core Alabama. SNCC had a fleet of Plymouth automobiles with citizens' band radios and tall antennas, called the Sojourner Motor Fleet, and one day Norman looked up and saw Hollis Watkins pull in from Mississippi, leading a caravan of eight or ten of the Plymouths.

"At that point," Norman said, "we were deciding what we were going to do in Alabama. We decided that it was not productive for us to fight with SCLC, so members of the staff then decided to move out, to places where we decided they would not come." The SNCC workers went to Wilcox, Greene, and Hale counties — and to one other, the Black Belt county with a terrible reputation, the county that stood between Selma and Montgomery: Lowndes. "The decision," Norman told his audience, "was that Lowndes County was so bad that nobody would come in there showcasing. And that it was only going to be serious work there. And that we would not be bothered and not be in conflict."

■ ——————————————————————————

Judge Johnson decided that the proposed march was not illegal and could proceed, under certain guidelines.[12] George Wallace refused to provide police protection for the marchers, and President Johnson federalized the Alabama National Guard. SCLC asked people of good will from all over the nation to come and march on Sunday,

March 21. Television crews and print reporters flowed into Selma. SNCC, meantime, sent workers to Montgomery to organize demonstrations. The police reacted predictably, with cattle prods.

The Alabama legislature produced Act 159, a house resolution noting that "many innocent people of Alabama are being led by supposedly religious leaders from other parts of these United States who call themselves preachers," some of whom "have been seen drinking strong drink promiscuously and heard using the most vulgar and profane language on the streets of Montgomery" and had been supplying (in ways the legislature did not specify) "evidence of much fornication, and young women are returning to their respective States apparently as unwed expectant mothers." The legislation commended the local Roman Catholic archbishop, the bishop of Mobile, a rabbi, and assorted Protestant clergymen who "have asked their respective people to stay away from the Selma-Montgomery march and other like demonstrations. . . ."[13]

Governor Wallace requested a meeting on March 13 with President Johnson. Afterward, the president commented, in what actually amounted to a change of policy for the U.S. government: "I have made clear, whether the governor agrees or not, that law and order will prevail in Alabama, that the people's rights to peacefully assemble will be preserved, and that their constitutional rights will be protected."

On March 15, Johnson announced that he would send a voting rights bill to Congress. In a televised address to a joint session, Johnson spoke of the advocates for racial justice and said, "Their cause must be our cause, too. Because it's not just Negroes, but really it's all of us, who must overcome the crippling legacy of bigotry and injustice." Then he shocked the nation by speaking the words, "And we *shall* overcome." The bill went to Congress two days later.[14]

On March 21 the new march began. Although the number of marchers was limited by the terms of Judge Johnson's court order to three hundred on most of the Dixie Overland Highway (also called the Jefferson Davis Highway and Highway 8) between Selma and Montgomery, more than twenty-five thousand people were walking when the trek ended on March 25. Thousands had flown in for the occasion. There were politicians from the North, both black and white, who would boast for the rest of their lives that they "marched at Selma," and there were gangs of television cameras to record the procession and, in the process, turn it into a "spectacular." There were Movement activists whose heads had been laced together with stitches earned while practicing *satyagraha* and soul force and redemptive suffering, and there were ordinary citizens of the Deep South who had been burned with cattle prods and beaten with clubs simply because they wanted to practice democracy.

What there was *not* on the Selma-to-Montgomery march was the deep, pervading fear that had always infected Negro Southerners. If there was any place for a black person to be afraid in America, it was Black Belt Alabama. But even there the fear had been beaten, abolished, vanquished. Segregation had been broken.

Fear was gone, but discrimination and violence, both official and private, had not ended and would not end. As was almost always the case, the Movement's triumph was followed by a tragedy. Viola Gregg Liuzzo, a white mother of five from Michigan who had come to help with the march, was murdered by klansmen as she ferried marchers to and from Montgomery in her car. A day later, President Johnson announced the arrest of four men in the killing.

Three of the four were indicted in an Alabama court. The fourth, Gary Thomas Rowe, Jr., a paid FBI informant and klansman, testified that he had been in the car with the others that night and had seen the murder. Rowe testified against the others. This was the same Gary Thomas Rowe who had been on the FBI payroll at the time he and other klansmen attacked the Freedom Riders. The original trial in the Liuzzo murder ended in a hung jury. The second jury, all white like the first one, found the klansmen not guilty.

The Justice Department then charged the three (that is, the ones who were not on its own payroll) with conspiring to abridge Mrs. Liuzzo's civil rights. A federal jury found the men guilty, and Judge Frank Johnson sentenced them to ten years in prison, the maximum.

Congress passed the Voting Rights Act on August 6, 1965. The relative ease with which the bill became law was seen by many as the clear product of Selma, and of the brutal way in which the white resistance in Alabama had opposed the franchise for Negroes. The new law prohibited the use of literacy and similar tests to screen voting applicants, and it allowed federal examiners to process applications in communities where local authorities had applied the forms in a discriminatory manner. Before long, federal registrars showed up in Selma and throughout the Black Belt. It was one of the first, few clear signs that the government of the United States of America was willing to intervene in an active way to insure the constitutional rights of its black citizens.

THIRTY-FOUR

■

THE END OF TERROR

■

The march from Selma was a majestic moment, television spectacular or not.

It was the nation's last great demonstration against the hideousness of overt discrimination — the discrimination of cattle prods and billy sticks and posses; of indignities and systemic fear; the discrimination that said You must stay where you are because we are better than you, and You cannot even vote in our elections. That was the discrimination that the Movement had started out to destroy. As the marchers ticked off the miles between Selma and Montgomery, the Jim Clarks and Bull Connors and George Wallaces grew smaller and less threatening, until at the end they were revealed as only the weak, harmless shadows of a once seemingly invincible creature that had roamed the Southland.

Of course, the Movement was not over. But an important moment had been passed. The march was one of the last gatherings of the original civil rights movement. Now the groups that together formed the Movement moved further and further apart. The crusade against discrimination went on, but in different ways, at different tempos, with different aims and different agendas. The original campaign — the Movement of *Brown*, of Montgomery, of Greensboro, of soul force and *satyagraha*, of Anniston and Birmingham — was ending. "Never" had died; the Long Haul was here. The real revolution had begun.

Almost before Lyndon Johnson's signature was dry on the Voting Rights Act of 1965, white politicians in the South started courting the Negro vote. Several Southern congressmen who had voted against the legislation when it passed the House changed to "Aye" when it returned from the Senate and it was obvious that the bill would pass. It was surprising even to cynics who were familiar with the Southern white politician's facility for shamelessly adjusting to rapid change. In New Orleans, where only two years before the city had tried to keep blacks from holding a meeting in the municipal auditorium, Mayor Victor Schiro showered Negro voters with promises as he ran for reelection. In Atlanta, Herman Talmadge received and accepted an invitation to speak at the Hungry Club, a lunchtime gathering of prestigious blacks. When rival politician Carl Sanders heard about this, he wangled an *earlier* invitation. He wanted to be first.[1]

Immediately after the law passed, federal examiners arrived in fourteen counties in Alabama, Mississippi, and Louisiana to oversee and facilitate the registration process. Within five months, they were in thirty-seven counties. In twenty months, black voter registration had grown by 430,000 people. The increase was most dramatic where resistance to black enfranchisement had been greatest. In Mississippi, the number went from 22,000 to 150,000 in a few months.[2]

The results were dramatic on election day, too. Julian Bond, running as a Democrat, was elected to the Georgia house of representatives. Lucius Amerson was chosen sheriff of Macon County, Alabama, the first Negro to be elected to that position in the Black Belt since Reconstruction.[3]

There were other, more discouraging events. Less than one week after the Voting Rights Act went into effect, there was a terrible riot in the black Watts section of Los Angeles. The violence, which began after a white state highway patrolman detained a Negro motorist, lasted for six days. Thirty-five people died, twenty-eight of them black. There was widespread looting of white-owned stores. Hundreds were injured, among them many whites. Karl Fleming, a white man who had reported with great courage for *Newsweek* from virtually every dangerous place in the South, and who had been transferred to his magazine's Los Angeles bureau, was badly injured.

There was also a riot in normally placid Tuskegee, Alabama, the home of the renowned Negro institute. Blacks were conducting a voter registration campaign when a white man killed Samuel Younge, Jr., a SNCC worker who had tried to use a "white" rest room at a gas station. The rioting followed the white's acquittal.[4]

By the time the voting bill became law, the Student Nonviolent Coordinating Committee was working in Lowndes County, Alabama, to get the vote for black people. The white rulers of that Black Belt county were working just as hard to prevent this. When one group of activists was being released from the county jail on August 20, 1965, after arrests at a demonstration, a white man shot one of them to death and wounded another. The dead man was Jonathan Daniels, a white Episcopal seminary student from New Hampshire; wounded was a Catholic priest from Chicago. Their assailant was acquitted of manslaughter charges by the usual all-white jury. The killing spurred SNCC to work all the harder on registration. By 1966, blacks had attained a voting majority in Lowndes County.[5]

In Mississippi, a period of relative peace was broken early in 1966 by the burning of some fifty crosses around the state and, a few days later, the firebombing and fatal shooting of Vernon Dahmer, a black grocer from the Hattiesburg area who had supported the voter registration workers when they came to Mississippi back in 1960.[6]

However the Movement might have been defined in the past, it was something else now. Civil rights organizations broadened their scope to take in areas some considered foreign to the Movement, and the federal government started doing some of the work the Movement had once performed. As part of its war on poverty, the federal Office of Economic Opportunity disbursed funds to the Child Development Group of Mississippi to operate centers that would give the children of low-income families a head start in life. The federal Head Start program grew out of this experiment. CDGM took the unusual step of hiring local people as teachers and aides. "Local people" meant blacks as well as whites, and thus the white system's economic power over Negroes, which always had been assured by its domination of the job marketplace, was challenged for the first time since emancipation.

After the first summer of CDGM's operation, the government, fearful of what local control might produce, cut off the group's funds. But CDGM's supporters showed that they were entirely capable of running the program on their own, and so Washington bought its way back in. A year later, another attempt was made to kill the program, and CDGM survived that, too.

In January, 1966, SNCC issued a statement that was critical of U.S. involvement in the war in Vietnam. The declaration anticipated the criticism that surely would follow by stating in its first sentence that SNCC "has a right and a responsibility to dissent with the United States foreign policy on any issue when it sees fit." Murders of Negroes in the South and the killing of Vietnamese abroad, said SNCC, were "no different." The nation, said the statement, "is no respecter of persons or laws when such persons or laws run counter to its needs and desires."[7]

Julian Bond, who was SNCC's communications director at the time, was also State Representative-elect Bond, having been chosen by the voters the previous summer. When the SNCC statement was released, Bond told reporters that he agreed with the statement, and that he admired the courage of persons who burned their draft cards in protest against the war. As a person whose skin color made him a second-class citizen, he said, he did not feel that he should have to support the war. Bond's position would shortly become widely adopted, but in early 1966 many considered it shocking. That included other members of the Georgia legislature, who refused to seat him. Bond carried the issue to court; in December, 1966, the Supreme Court ruled in his favor. He took office in January, 1967.[8]

By June, 1966, James Meredith, the man who desegregated Ole Miss, was a student at Columbia University law school. He began a 220-mile pilgrimage through Mississippi to encourage blacks to register and vote. He was shot from ambush by a white man as he walked along a highway, but was not seriously wounded. Meredith said he had requested federal protection on his trek, but that Nicholas Katzenbach, the attorney general, denied it. Once again, the activist wing of the Movement gathered to take up the march, and once again, the resistance gathered to oppose it with violence. But the marchers prevailed, and thousands of Negroes were encouraged to make the trip down to the registrar's office.

Martin Luther King, Jr., took part in the resumed march. As always, he preached nonviolence. But the media paid more attention to SNCC, which by now was directed by Stokely Carmichael, who had succeeded the nonviolence practitioner John Lewis. The press listened, too, to a catchy phrase that was being shouted by SNCC field secretary Willie Ricks: "Black Power!" To some, its message seemed to be perfectly sensible — that black people wanted a share of the nation's political power, as they always had. But to others, it seemed a chilling challenge, a cast-down gauntlet of racism in reverse.

The whites' fear was multiplied by events in Lowndes County, where SNCC's efforts to insure the vote ran into bitter resistance from the regular Democratic party. The party would not allow black candidates to run in its primaries, so the blacks formed their own party. Its name, the Black Panther Party, sent shudders through many whites, who saw it, like Black Power, as a sign of reverse racism.

———————————————— ■

John Jackson was less than ten years old when the bus boycott started in Montgomery, twenty or so miles from his home in White Hall, a hamlet alongside a railroad track in Lowndes County. He paid close attention to what was happening, and, later, to what happened in Greensboro and Anniston and Birmingham. It was "an instinct from the beginning of birth to be concerned about it," he said not long ago. When the march from Selma to Montgomery came through Lowndes County, Jackson and his friends started thinking about what they could do to make some changes. He attended SNCC's meetings and workshops. He went to Tuskegee as a summer student, and he returned on weekends to work on the Lowndes County movement.

"In 1966 we were beginning to get people registered to vote," he said. "And of course they were turning them down and that type of thing. But we finally got some people to register to vote and began to run people for office.

"They wouldn't allow us in the Democratic party. In Lowndes County there were no registered voters or no black people holding any political positions in this county — no positions at all. No registered voters. No participation. We paid all the taxes. We worked their farms, we took care of their children. So we began to talk to people."

People who did try to register and vote, he said, were often evicted from their rented or sharecropped land. Others gathered around the victims and supported them. Jackson's father, who had ten children to help raise, found that he could not get loans to buy seed so he could plant cotton. The family all chipped in and contributed earnings to keep the farm going. So the Jacksons began to grow their own food. They sold what was left door to door on a truck route. Before long, their father didn't have to depend on loans from white-controlled banks.

After the federal registrars came and Lowndes County blacks got registered, the regular Democrats made it more difficult to run in elections. The blacks brought suit to lower election filing fees. Then somebody discovered a provision in the state law that indicated that they didn't have to depend on the regular Democratic party to get on the November ballot. There could be another symbol on the ballot alongside the Democrats' rooster and the Republicans' elephant.

"We found that we could run on the independent ticket and automatically be on the ballot," said Jackson. The blacks, who functioned under the banner of the Lowndes County Freedom Organization, cast about for a snappy name and easily recognized symbol for their independent party.

"The question came up that black folks still could not read and write. A lot of them were illiterate. They couldn't see the letters on the voting machine and that type of thing. So we said, 'What are we going to do about that?'

"Somebody came up with an emblem. I think it was in an open meeting one day. Somebody says, 'Well, the Democratic party has a rooster, and the Republican party has an elephant, and *we* need an emblem.' And somebody says, 'Well, how about a cat?' People thought that was funny. People were laughing about it. Then somebody said, 'Well, what about a *black* cat?' Black power was what was happening then, and you were trying to raise your consciousness of feeling good about yourself.

"And then somebody sent us about a thousand pretty little black panther cats, stuffed cats, to sell for two dollars to help the party. And that's how it started. I think I've still got one; it's a real pretty cat.

"And so everybody began to feel good about themselves, but then some people started saying that the Black Panther Party was racist and this and that. But that's where it initially started. We used that emblem because we had been in substandard schools, we were illiterate, and we knew a black cat from a white rooster and a red elephant."

One of the side effects of the consciousness-raising that was symbolized by the Black Power slogan was the move by the more activist organizations, notably SNCC, toward all-black membership. SNCC had been heading in that direction for some time, and the Congress of Racial Equality now had black leaders. Most of the veteran white field secretaries understood the change, but that did not make it any easier to accept. No matter how the issue was stated, "black only" meant racial discrimination and segregation — everything the Movement had fought against.

Dorothy and Bob Zellner were away in the Northeast during much of the time that the black-only sentiment was rising within SNCC. When they returned, those who led SNCC were firmly committed to an organization that excluded whites. Whites, they said, could go into their own community and organize. It was an exceptionally cruel thing to say to people such as Bob Zellner, SNCC's first white field secretary, who had risked his life dozens of times and who had never shown the slightest inclination to use his lighter skin color as a means for achieving power within the organization — and who, in fact, *had* spent much of his time trying to bring the white community into the struggle. He and Dorothy proposed, at one of SNCC's retreats, that they stay within the group, organize on the white side, keep their votes in SNCC decisions, and, as Dorothy put it, "retain the privileges, whatever they are, of being on the SNCC staff." The proposal was rejected, eleven to one.

"This was the worst thing that had ever happened to me," said Dorothy Miller Zellner later. She and Bob were now apart, but they remained friends. "It was the worst thing. I understand it and I accept it. But I'm still mourning.

"Looking back, to me it's a tragedy. It was this inevitable, horrible Greek tragedy that was sort of inexorably winding itself along, or down, and there was no way to stop it. But it was just devastating."

The Zellners did not drop out of the changing-the-world business. For years afterward they worked for various causes and various organizations, including efforts to organize white people in Mississippi. And now Dorothy and Bob Zellner are welcome at SNCC reunions and conferences.

Dorothy has noticed that at those meetings, nobody talks about "the black-white thing." Rather, she said, "there's a heavy overlay of nostalgia. There's this yearning to return to that incredibly intense group feeling that SNCC once had."

■ ————————————————————————

Martin Luther King, Jr., continued preaching the gospel of non-violence, but the conditions and events around him caused the details of the message to change. When he exhorted mass meetings to "put on your marchin' shoes, children; don't ya get weary . . . ," the goal was likely to be better jobs or decent housing, rather than a chance to negotiate with city officials for desegregated buses or lunch counters. King, too, spoke out against the war in Vietnam. He took his campaign to the North, where he met with less success than he had had in the South.

He was in Memphis to help out in a campaign for better working conditions for municipal garbage collectors when, on April 4, 1968, he was murdered by a hidden gunman. A white man was caught and convicted; one of his lawyers was former mayor Arthur Hanes of Birmingham. There remains a widespread belief among Movement people that the murder was part of a larger conspiracy that was covered up by the federal government.

*   *   *

In the beginning, the Movement's stated aims included improvements in public accommodations, housing, education, and employment. If an assessment of the Movement's accomplishments thirty years later were restricted to just these areas, the results would be disappointing. Public accommodations are unquestionably desegregated. There is the occasional revelation that a restaurant or swimming pool in such-and-such a town excludes Negroes. Usually the publication of the fact is enough to elicit apologies and at least a promise to change. Other facilities — for some reason, "health clubs" and "fitness centers" are always on the list — seem to require lawsuits or threats of lawsuits before they desegregate. The skimpier the costume, it seems, the greater the likelihood of bias. Professional and academic clubs, those adult equivalents of little boys' tree houses, can almost always be counted on to discriminate; nominees to high government positions are always expressing their amazement, during the confirmation process, at the public's discovery that they belong to all-white or all-male-and-white groups. But it can be said generally that places that invite the public in issue their invitations to people of all colors.

Much housing in America remains segregated. Public education, thirty-seven years after *Brown*, is still far from integrated. Employment presents a mixed picture. White people still run business in America, and they still put black people in lower-paying jobs.* A better-off black middle class emerged because Negroes can now get governmental and allied jobs to which they never had access before. But this also has helped turn the old notion of two societies — one white and one black — into the spectre of three distinct social groups: one white, one comfortable black, and one group, primarily black but also containing many whites, that the others have abandoned to inner-city ghettoes or rural isolation, drugs, nonexistent medical care, inferior education opportunities, joblessness, and homelessness. This third group, at least for the

---

*The eternal rhetorical quest for desegregation in the military, begun by President Truman and seconded by virtually every chief executive since him, continues. The *Washington Post* reported in March, 1990, that the military officer corps was only 6.9 percent black, while blacks made up 20.5 percent of all military personnel.

present, does not have the leadership that could produce a new movement for change.

If the Movement accomplished much less than its stated aims, it also accomplished much more. It changed America, the world, and human attitudes in ways that its directors, its footsoldiers, and even its big thinkers had never foreseen or hoped for.

It held organized religion up under a powerful light and displayed the results for all the world to see. Except for the often heroic contributions of a few individual leaders or renegade groups, who almost always were punished for their actions, white religion was shown to be one of the staunchest opponents of brotherhood that could be imagined. It remains so.

Black religion was revealed to be the religion that worked. The Movement proved that applied Christianity could be practical. The depth of the devotion of the Movement's adherents to Christian ideals is illustrated by the fact that, once the violent phase was over, black people seemed to forgive their former oppressors. Once they achieved political power, they did not treat whites as whites had treated them. Silas Norman — who eventually returned from Selma to college, became a doctor, and now serves as the medical director of a large federal prison in Michigan — says he thinks often of the white people who stung him with cattle prods. "I think I forgive," he said. "I don't hate them. I still believe in all those crazy things we believed in. I've tried to think about ways to hate. Like every other person, I think, revenge crosses my mind when I think about people like that — people who are going around bragging even today about what they've done, and who never have paid any penalty for it. But that feeling doesn't last long. I can't make it last." Arthur Shores's house no longer gets dynamited. The black Birmingham lawyer says if he met Arthur Hanes in public, he would probably shake the former mayor's hand — although "I wouldn't cross the *street* to do it."

Government — the American system — was an embarrassing failure at sympathizing with, furthering, or even understanding the demands and aspirations of America's black population. Throughout the Movement years, as men who thought of themselves as humane and liberal and free of prejudice occupied the White House and the most powerful offices of the nation, the strict rule remained: This is our country, a white country, and you are the outsiders, the supplicants. It was not just the elected officeholders who said this by their words and deeds; the message was delivered also by the business community, the academic world, and the media. With scant assistance from government, Negroes had to carry out their Movement virtually all on their own. They were forced, one might say, to perform as private attorneys general — to use their own resources to bring litigation that enforces a broad compliance with the law. The system ought to be thankful to black Americans for performing this task, for articulating and illuminating and enforcing the Constitution, but there are few signs that it is. The victory would have been much sweeter for America if the majority community had done a better job of participating in the battle.

The Movement, in bringing the vote to Negro Americans, brought black people into politics. It gave them the opportunity to perform better than, as well as, or worse than the whites they replaced. While hundreds of blacks took office and discharged their duties at least as well as anyone else, a few didn't. Marion Barry, SNCC's first chair, became mayor of Washington, D.C., in 1979 and thus had a marvelous opportunity to translate the Movement's ideals into political action, but he failed utterly. Under Barry's leadership, if it could be called that, the residents of the nation's capital suffered from the effects of widespread municipal corruption and incompetence, a high crime rate, and the nation's worst infant mortality rate. Barry ignored his city's poor except in rhetoric, preferring instead to consort with the Big Mules of real estate and development, just as George Wallace had done in Alabama and Marvin Griffin in Georgia.

To compound this tragedy, Barry's administration was punishing a population that was 70 percent black — the very people for whom the mayor had once worked so hard in the segregated South. It was black children who were dying in infancy, receiving inferior educations, and perishing in street violence in Washington. The groups of politically powerful blacks who gathered around some elected officials were just as quick to cut shady deals and sell out as were the courthouse hangers-on of the white supremacist South.

When Barry was criticized about his behavior (which, as was revealed in 1990 by his conviction on a cocaine charge, extended to his use of illegal drugs), his supporters responded by charging that the criticism was racially inspired. Some other black elected officials around the country who were faced with criticism used the racism defense, too. The countercharge seemed to be a convenient way for inept or corrupt public officials to avoid facing up to their transgressions. But there was a nugget of truth in the black politicians' claims: Federal officials (invariably white, as was the Justice Department they served) seemed to be exerting inordinate energies and expending vast sums of the taxpayers' money in trying to indict black officeholders. That was certainly the case in the Barry trial, which followed an elaborate entrapment of the mayor by a squadron of federal officials. Someone who had observed the way in which the white-run system of the fifties and sixties ruthlessly singled out for special punishment the "uppity niggers" — the outspoken black men who dared to question the authority of the white male — could not help but detect in the events of the nineties more than a hint of the old days.

Still, there was a sadness in the realization that once they got the same freedom to vote as their white sisters and brothers, black Americans would probably elect about as many crooks, incompetents, and charlatans as had white citizens. And they would be just about as unenthusiastic about going to the polls on election day. Into this sad picture came, in 1989, an interesting turn of events. In two vastly separated places, New York City and the state of Virginia, black candidates won top elected offices. Neither Mayor David Dinkins in New York nor Governor Douglas Wilder in Virginia had been on the front lines during the Movement years; both had paid their dues instead to the political system and seemed quite willing to live with its shortcomings. Neither had campaigned as a *racial* candidate; they spoke of fiscal responsibility and economic opportunity, and they seemed to wish that the voters would forget they were black at all. Both needed and got substantial white votes in order to win. Each seemed to be about as far removed from the Movement years as it was possible to be; yet it is certain that both of them owed their jobs to the Movement and that their election was, in some sense, one of the more interesting products of the Movement years.

During the sixties it was not unusual to hear observers of the Southern situation comment that Negroes, by freeing themselves of the shackles of racism, were also freeing the whites. White Southerners, particularly the less well-to-do ones, in being forced to support a system that was built on discrimination, were chaining not just their Negro brethren, but themselves, to bad politics and exploitative economics and lifetimes of serving the arrogant Big Mules.

The Movement did not succeed in breaking the whites' chains — or, more accurately, the whites did not succeed in taking advantage of the opportunity that the Movement presented. But it did open a door, and the door is still open. "At the time," said Wyatt Tee Walker, "white people didn't understand: This was as much for them as it was for black folks. When you think about all that white folks had to go through to keep black folks down. . . . I mean, it doubled the size of the school system. And the hatred in your heart. All that has been lifted not only from black folks, but white folks, too."

The Movement disclosed, often graphically, the self-destructive nature of its enemies. It is no longer a joke, but almost a practical proposal, that the black and white activists of those years should chip in and erect memorials to Bull Connor and Jim Clark for the work they did on behalf of desegregation. Perhaps a statue should also be commissioned to commemorate a generic "great constitutional lawyer" or a Southern governor who "just wanted to prevent violence." The lines they spoke and the actions they took, while designed to spin out segregation for as long as possible — particularly past the next election — also hastened the end of "Never."

The Movement wrote the handbook for dozens of other movements, and for movements yet unborn. Women's rights, gay liberation, students' free speech, the Vietnam protests — they all grew out of the civil rights movement. The Movement's influence can be traced also to more recent liberation efforts in South Africa, China, and Eastern Europe.

The most important of the Movement's accomplishments has been the near eradication of fear. Leslie Dunbar, formerly of the Southern Regional Council, more recently summed up the Movement years this way: "*The* main issue in the South was terror. You couldn't make any kind of progress in the South, not from the time blacks were first brought to Virginia, until black life and black claims to life had some civic respect. That was *the* great accomplishment; *the* single greatest accomplishment of the civil rights movement.

"Not that it's completed. But the ending of the sanctioned action of terror to keep blacks in their place in the South is the one indispensable victory. You couldn't get anywhere without it. It was the great victory of the sixties. It's not complete."

That is a commentary on just how far, back in 1960 and 1954 and 1619, the Movement had to go: how much it had yet to accomplish; how repressive the white society was. Teachers and lecturers who tell young Americans today about the Movement years report that children and even college students find it hard to believe that such a system existed — hard to believe that it could be possible for someone to put up a "WHITES ONLY" sign without its being immediately torn down. But that is the way it truly was, thirty years ago.

Could it happen again? Surely it could. White racists could recapture power, and segregationists could regain control of the courts (to the extent that they have not regained it already). White supremacist laws could be passed again, and separate but equal could again be the law of the land. But the segregationists would have to do without the weapon of terror. It is gone, now.

———————————————— ■

Years after the 1964 Democratic convention in Atlantic City, Joseph Rauh wrote Bob Moses a letter. Rauh explained everything that had happened in Atlantic City. He never got a reply. Rauh kept trying. "I just didn't want to die without having talked to him," he said. "I admire Bob."

More years passed. Rauh was invited to Boston to take part in a television debate. He knew that Moses lived in Boston, and he wangled the young man's phone number and address. When he got to town, Rauh says, he called Moses and said, "I'm determined to see you. I'm coming out to your apartment house. You're either going to see me or not. But, by God, I'm going to be out there."

They met on a snowy night and talked for two hours. Moses told him, Rauh said, that he had abandoned the hope that blacks could benefit from the political system, and that he believed community organization was the only possible solution. "We talked and talked," said Rauh, "and I said, 'Bob, let me try this out on you. I believe in the political system very much. I believe it's done a lot of good for blacks. I think we got a lot of legislation that helps blacks. You believe that the only thing that matters is community organization and that there is no hope that we can each persuade each other. But there is no reason why the two of us can't realize that one feels as sincerely in what he believes as the other one.' He said, 'That's all right with me.' So that's the note on which we parted. And as far as I'm concerned, I'm at peace with the thing."

At the thirtieth anniversary of the Greensboro sit-ins, Woolworth's donated the original lunch counter stools to a museum. A black company executive welcomed the original four demonstrators back to town for a reunion and told them that he owed his job to their actions.

In Danville, Virginia, the Reverend Lawrence Campbell, a leader of the bloody 1963 demonstrations there, became chair of the city school board. A few years ago, members of the state legislature's appropriations committee were in town to discuss school funding, and the city threw a luncheon for them in the library that was a Confederate memorial. Campbell said he thought, all through the meal, about "all that had gone on."

The grand dragon of a Ku Klux Klan group was quoted in 1990 as complaining that "these NAACP people . . . want to put white people under their foot and stomp on us."[9]

In Birmingham, David Vann was elected mayor in 1975. Once, he looked out his office window, saw that the Southern Christian Leadership Conference was conducting a protest march against a position he had taken, re-thought his position, went downstairs, and joined the protest against himself.

Jesse Jackson ran for and easily won the 1990 Democratic nomination for one of two "shadow" U.S. Senate seats from the District of Columbia — nonvoting posts that can be used for lobbying for the District. One of the candidates Jackson defeated was James Forman.

John Patterson, now a judge in the Alabama Court of Criminal Appeals, teaches a course in state and local government every Monday night at Troy State University, south of Montgomery. Among his former students who are black are a state legislator and the head of the federal Small Business Administration in Mississippi. "I see the good things that have come of all of this," said Patterson, "and I don't know why in the world it took us so doggone long to do it."

James P. Coleman, former governor of Mississippi, said of the issue that nearly drove his state to ruin: "My own feeling, way, way down and all the way up, is that the people of Mississippi — the white people of Mississippi — are relieved to have it out of the way as a political issue."

Erle Johnston, former head of the Mississippi Sovereignty Commission, said, "It's a lot better because, first of all, we've gotten used to it. And another thing, if you weren't used to it, what could you do about it? So I think the proper word is 'adjust.' The adjustment has been made."

Constance Baker Motley was elected to the New York state senate. In 1965 she left the Inc. Fund and was elected borough president of Manhattan. In 1966 Lyndon Johnson nominated her for a federal district judgeship. Mississippi segregationist Senator James Eastland held up the appointment for nine months, but Motley became a judge in September, 1966. Delay could no longer prevent the inevitable.

John Lewis ran for Congress from an Atlanta district and was elected. His opponent was Julian Bond. The contest was a bitter one. Lucius Holloway, who with his wife provided housing for voter registration workers in their southwest Georgia home, was elected to the Dawson city council. John Jackson was elected mayor of White Hall, in Lowndes County. Harvey Gantt finished Clemson, established himself as an architect in Charlotte, North Carolina, and was elected mayor. In 1990 he ran for the U.S. Senate seat held by North Carolina's right-wing extremist Jesse Helms. Gantt lost.

James Meredith went to work on Jesse Helms's Washington staff. He and the senator believed in the same things, said Meredith. In 1990, Meredith distributed a statement on Helms's stationery that accused many NAACP leaders and other blacks of being controlled by fifteen "liberal elite" whites and of being involved in crime, drug use, and immoral behavior.[10]

"I *live* in the Movement today," said Victoria Gray Adams. The former resident of Palmer's Crossing, Mississippi, would-be delegate to the 1964 Democratic National Convention, and Freedom Democratic party candidate for Congress now is a resident of Petersburg, Virginia. The problems that face black Americans today, she said, are enormous. "But this is a part of the ongoing task. You see, when you talk about change, real honest-to-goodness change versus a peripheral change, this is the part of the Movement where the work has not been done to the extent that it should have been done. I argue all the time that unless you're willing to sit down and begin to develop strategies and programs that will allow those things to happen, you're only changing the complexion of things."

Henry Schwarzschild became the head of the capital punishment project of the American Civil Liberties Union. He took part in protests at the New York World's Fair in 1964, and he went on the Meredith march in Mississippi. In fact, he could be counted on to turn up anytime the Movement needed help. In 1987 Schwarzschild went to a demonstration north of Atlanta in Forsyth County, Georgia, where whites had reacted violently, with Klan leadership, against the idea of equal opportunity in housing. He added his body to the line of marchers, he said, because he still felt, as he had felt in Occupied Germany, that it was wrong not to act.

"It was an obligation," he said. "There was a sense of fatigue; I wish I didn't think it was such a terribly important obligation. But the important thing is not to be there, but to have *been* there."

"There is a satisfaction," said Diane Nash, back in Chicago now. "I was very satisfied. The Voting Rights Act resulted from Selma, and then all those black officials got elected. It's a satisfaction that has to do with the fact that — this isn't modest, but — with the fact that my living has made a difference on the planet. And I love that. I really do."

Charles Jones got his law degree. He moved back to Charlotte, to a house a short distance from the Johnson C. Smith campus, where he had organized Charlotte's first sit-in. He turned part of his yard into a huge greenhouse, where he grows tall banana trees and a jungle of tropical flora — a reminder of the Mexico where he went to regain his energies during the Movement years. Jones practices law out of an office in the house. Much of his practice is given to representing poor people, people without power.

"The *battle* is over," said Jones one day not long ago. "It just evolved into the next natural level of the political process. The registering and education of black citizens has led to tremendous changes throughout society. It goes in my mind directly, *directly* back to McComb, Mississippi; to Selma, to Albany. Those contributions are part of a continuing sort of mosaic, each of which has its own contribution. But for Albany, Georgia, you would not have had a Birmingham. You would not have had a broad voter registration program that now has elected some five or six thousand black people throughout the South who hold very prominent positions. But for Albany, Georgia, you would not have had the broad involvement of people — simple people: not Dr. King, but the simple person and his own evolution of dignity within himself. *But for Albany.*

"So I think we just evolved with the times, and some of us, thank God, survived."

"I wish to God people would get a-moving again," said Fred Shuttlesworth. "Although I don't know whether we could operate a movement that's totally nonviolent, with people's minds the way they are now.

"You know, after a while, the white people wished they *had* been able to understand Martin Luther King, when the burning and rioting started. You see, any time people *talk* about weapons and using them, they're going to wind up doing it. 'For as he thinketh in his heart, so is he.' ''

About the violence of the sixties: Was it possible that Fred Shuttlesworth actually enjoyed the danger in which he constantly found himself?

"Tell you the truth about it, I did," he said, laughing. "Did I get a sort of a joy out of it? Yes. I don't guess I was crazy about going into the danger. I didn't *shun* it. The police could have beaten my head to the fat. Police, Klan, anybody.

"But it was thrilling, in that you were challenging the system, and you knew that something had to move. You didn't know when, you didn't know how, but you knew it had to move. You must remember that God was with us. We knew that God was with us, because you take the religion out of it, it would be nothing."

■ ─────────────

L. C. Dorsey got a job at Head Start in 1966. She continued her own education, went to college, and got a doctorate in social work, with a specialty in criminal justice. Her dissertation was entitled "The Significance of Jealousy and Addictive Love in Acts of Homicide Among Black Women." She serves now as the executive director of the Delta Health Center, a comprehensive, community-based medical care facility in Mound Bayou, not far from the plantation cotton fields where she spent her childhood.

By the time she got to Head Start, said Dorsey, the federal government had completed the program's transformation from its days with the Child Development Group of Mississippi, and it "was not about liberating people." By 1968, Dorsey was leading an economic boycott against merchants in the town of Shelby, and there was also a boycott at the school. Although she swears that she was never a leader in the Movement, always a follower, she managed to make the Ku Klux Klan's most wanted list.

"The Klan called up to the house," she said, "and told whichever one of my children answered the telephone, 'Well, we're gonna kill your mama.' And that was scary. I tried to downplay it for their sake. But it was very, very scary. One night, I heard this noise around the house, and I really thought it was the Klan. I got up and went outside to investigate, because I have this thing about being scared. If you're going to be scared, you have to go confront your fear. You can't just be scared and shaking by yourself.

"My older son, Michael, heard me get up, and he came out to the door also, and when we got outside, there were all these young men there." But they were *black* young men, summoned by a black school principal who had heard about the threats against Dorsey. "They were out protecting our house. The principal had his gun, and he had told these young folks that the Klan was threatening me, and so all these kids had come to guard our house that night. It's a nice memory, a very nice memory.

"You see, if the Klan could have kept me inside that night, they would have kept me inside forever. It was, 'If you're out there to shoot me down, I'm coming out so you can get it over with. Because I can't stand to be in here being scared of you out there in the dark.' "

When the various factions within the Movement momentarily forgot their differences and came back to Mississippi to finish the 1966 march that James Meredith had started, L. C. Dorsey went. She kissed the children and went on the march. "I didn't know if I was going to get back home," she said. "I left the kids behind, because I didn't want them killed, and I didn't know whether I was going to get back.

"But I was scared *not* to have gone. If they could shoot Meredith down, they could shoot all of us down."

A CHRONOLOGY OF
SIGNIFICANT MOVEMENT EVENTS

■ ────────────────────────────

1619   First Negroes arrive in the British North American colonies, at Jamestown, Virginia. They are indentured servants, and records refer to them as "negars."

1857   Supreme Court, in *Dred Scott* decision, declares that Negroes are not citizens.

1861   The constitution of the Confederate States of America, organized at Montgomery, Alabama, declares that Negro slaves shall be counted as three-fifths of a person in transactions involving taxation and representation.

1862   *September 22:*
President Abraham Lincoln delivers the Emancipation Proclamation, to take effect on January 1, 1863, freeing all slaves except those who live in states that are not rebelling against the national government.

1866   The Civil War is officially declared to be ended.

1895   Booker T. Washington delivers his Atlanta Exposition speech, calling for self-help and education as means by which Negroes can achieve independence.

1896   Supreme Court, in *Plessy v. Ferguson*, rules that "separate but equal" is the law of the land.

1941   A. Philip Randolph, president of the Brotherhood of Sleeping Car Porters, threatens President Franklin Delano Roosevelt with a march on Washington to dramatize unequal treatment of blacks.

June 25:
Roosevelt issues Executive Order 8802, forbidding employment discrimination in defense and government industries, and march is called off.

1942   Congress of Racial Equality is organized, largely by pacifists; its members hold a sit-in demonstration at a Chicago restaurant that discriminates against blacks.

1944   Supreme Court, in *Smith v. Allwright*, rules unconstitutional the white primary, by which Southern whites have kept Negroes from voting.

1953   Negroes organize a bus boycott in Baton Rouge, Louisiana, to protest discrimination.

1954   *May 17:*
Supreme Court, in *Brown v. Board of Education*, rules that segregation in education is unconstitutional; the doctrine of separate but equal is dead.

1955   *May:*
Supreme Court hands down guidelines for the implementation of its school desegregation ruling; the rules allow much leeway for continued segregation.

August:
Emmett Till, a fourteen-year-old black child from Chicago, is lynched in Leflore County, Mississippi, because he whistled at a white woman. There is worldwide revulsion over the murder.

November:
Interstate Commerce Commission outlaws segregation in interstate bus transportation.

December 5:
Montgomery bus boycott starts after Rosa Parks is arrested for refusing to give up her seat to a white man. The protest projects a young Baptist minister, the Reverend Dr. Martin Luther King, Jr., to leadership of the Montgomery movement.

1956

The state of Alabama effectively outlaws the operations within its borders of the National Association for the Advancement of Colored People, the nation's oldest civil rights organization and one that had effectively used courtroom challenges to contest segregation. Ban lasts almost a decade.

February:
Autherine Lucy enters the University of Alabama under federal court order. The state soon succeeds in removing her.

March:
Southern politicians publish their Southern Manifesto, a defense of segregation.

December 21:
Montgomery bus boycott ends with a settlement favorable to the protesters. Shortly afterward, Alabama blacks are victims of varied attacks. The home of Birmingham minister Fred Shuttlesworth is dynamited.

1957

January:
The Southern Christian Leadership Conference grows out of the successful Montgomery bus boycott. Martin Luther King is the leader of the group, which represents a coalition of community civil rights leaders in the South, most of them black Baptist ministers.

August 29:
Congress passes a civil rights act. It strengthens Negroes' voting rights, gives greater status to civil rights at the Justice Department, and creates the national Commission on Civil Rights.

September:
With the new school year comes a federal court order to desegregate Central High School in Little Rock, Arkansas. Whites riot, and President Dwight Eisenhower reluctantly sends in federal troops.

1959

April:
Mack Charles Parker is lynched in Poplarville, Mississippi. A grand jury receives evidence in the case but refuses even to acknowledge that a lynching has occurred.

1960

February 1:
Negro students in Greensboro, North Carolina, conduct sit-ins at local variety stores. The technique gains rapid acceptance among students throughout the South, particularly in Nashville. Sympathizers in the North mount picket lines

there, and some national retailing chains scramble to adopt desegregation policies.

April:
Student Nonviolent Coordinating Committee is formed during black colleges' Easter recess. The group grew out of the sit-ins and is supposed to be temporary, but it becomes permanent and is one of the more active of the organizations that make up the Movement.

1961

January:
James Meredith, a young air force veteran, seeks to enter the University of Mississippi. Upon learning that Meredith is black, the school refuses his application, and Meredith files suit.

May:
CORE holds a Freedom Ride via interstate bus through the Southern states. Riders meet with violence in Alabama; those who follow on successive rides are routinely arrested in Mississippi as they step off buses. Later, evidence surfaces that local police in Birmingham and Montgomery were involved in the violence, and that an employee of the FBI participated in the Ku Klux Klan's strategy sessions. The FBI did nothing to stop the violence it knew was planned.

June:
U.S. attorney general Robert Kennedy asks Movement leaders to stop demonstrations such as the Freedom Ride and concentrate instead on voter registration. Kennedy says he'll help line up tax-free financial support. He feels voting rights is a less volatile issue than confrontations over transportation and public accommodations.

November:
Interstate Commerce Commission bans segregation (again) in interstate bus and rail terminals. Movement activists test the new ruling, find it is ignored in several communities. Other places quietly desegregate.

November:
Negro leaders seek redress of their grievances with white officials of Albany, Georgia, but are rebuffed. The Albany Movement is born.

1962

February 26:
Supreme Court rules that state-sponsored segregation in travel is illegal.

April:

The Voter Education Project is begun. It is the outgrowth of Robert Kennedy's effort to get private tax-exempt support for voter registration in the South. VEP soon oversees a project in Greenwood, Mississippi, staffed largely by SNCC activists.

Summer:

Blacks in Albany, Georgia, demonstrate against segregation. The city's white leaders refuse to negotiate and hand over their power to the police chief, who regularly arrests Negroes who march across Oglethorpe Avenue, the dividing line between white and black Albany.

September:

James Meredith wins his suit to desegregate the University of Mississippi. His entry to the campus is accompanied by a large-scale white riot. Two persons die. Federal forces, including a contingent of deputy U.S. marshals, prison guards, and border patrol officers, eventually restore order.

November:

Birmingham voters, in special election, change their form of government to remove Eugene "Bull" Connor and Arthur Hanes, strident segregationists. The ousted politicians try to stay in office anyway.

1963

Voter Education Project and SNCC begin a sustained effort to register voters in Mississippi. It immediately becomes clear that Attorney General Kennedy was wrong when he spoke of the vote as a relatively benign issue.

January:

Harvey Gantt becomes first black student to enter Clemson in South Carolina. His peaceful entry is in sharp contrast to the previous fall's riot at the University of Mississippi.

Spring:

Blacks, led by the Southern Christian Leadership Conference, hold demonstrations in Birmingham. Bull Connor responds with high-pressure fire hoses and police dogs. Photographs of the police-led violence raise international indignation; President John F. Kennedy's administration sees need for additional civil rights legislation.

April:

Martin Luther King, Jr., writes his "Letter from Birmingham Jail," a moving reply to white religious leaders who had criticized him for leading demonstrations. His basic message is that his critics didn't respond to "polite" entreaties, making more dramatic efforts necessary. By now, King has become a master at generating what he calls "creative tension," friction that allows meaningful change to take place. He remains a solid devotee of nonviolence, though some Negroes and their leaders are advocating the use of violence as a means of self-defense.

May:
SNCC, frozen out of the Birmingham campaign by SCLC, begins an effort at Danville, Virginia. The police response there is as violent as Bull Connor's was in Birmingham.

Summer:
Civil rights demonstrations spread to Northern urban centers. They typically concern employment and housing opportunities and inequality in public education.

June 11:
George Wallace, the Alabama governor who had promised "segregation forever," makes a "stand in the schoolhouse door" to deny two Negroes admission to the University of Alabama. Then, in a scripted performance, Wallace steps aside and the students enter.

June 12:
Medgar E. Evers, NAACP leader in Mississippi, is murdered at his home in Jackson, Mississippi.

August 28:
The March on Washington, a day of celebration for the Movement's leaders and their supporters, takes place at the nation's capital. Press and politicians' warnings of violence prove unwarranted.

September 15:
Racists dynamite a Negro church during Sunday services in Birmingham. Four children are killed.

October:
Attorney General Kennedy authorizes FBI to tap Martin Luther King's telephones. The justification is the FBI's stated belief that King is falling under the influence of communists.

1964

Summer:
The Movement sponsors Freedom Summer, a concentrated effort at organization, voter registration, and education in Mississippi and Louisiana. Three workers — one black and

two whites, one of them serving his first day as a volunteer — are murdered in Neshoba County, Mississippi. The killings move President Lyndon Johnson to order stronger federal presence on Southern civil rights battlefields.

July:
President Johnson signs Civil Rights Act of 1964 into law.

July:
Blacks riot in Harlem community of New York City. Urban rioting spreads to a number of other cities outside the South.

August:
When Democrats hold their presidential convention at Atlantic City, an interracial slate challenges the seating of Mississippi's "regular" delegation, which is not very loyal to the Democratic ticket anyway. Party leadership, including President Johnson, rejects the challenge and proposes instead a compromise, which the activists refuse.

1965   *March 7:*
Negroes and whites attempting to march through Alabama's Black Belt from Selma to the capitol at Montgomery are beaten by police at Pettus Bridge in Selma. Once again, much of the nation is outraged; many sympathizers descend on Selma for a renewed march, which does take place on March 21–25. Central theme of the Selma campaign is voting rights.

August 6:
Members of Congress, among those shocked by the Selma violence, pass the Voting Rights Act of 1965. Almost immediately, federal registrars appear in hard-core racist areas and start registering Negroes. A tremendous jump in black political participation results.

August 11–16:
Another urban riot, the worst so far, occurs in the Watts section of Los Angeles.

1966   By now, the Movement is deeply split. CORE and SNCC workers advocate armed self-defense; some former civil rights workers favor aggressive violence. Black nationalist groups attract many who might have joined the practitioners of nonviolence. SNCC and, to almost as great an extent, CORE become all-black organizations; they seem confused over the steps to take next and spend much of their energy on internal fighting.

1967   Martin Luther King, Jr., speaks out against U.S. involvement in the war in Vietnam. The April 4 speech at Riverside Church in New York City loses King friends in the white liberal–labor camp and further separates him from the more conservative NAACP and National Urban League.

August 25:
COINTELPRO, the secret and illegal operation started by the FBI against those it considers America's enemies, adds black-led civil rights organizations to groups it tries to disrupt and destroy.

1968   *April 4:*
Martin Luther King, Jr., is shot to death in Memphis, while trying to secure better employment conditions for the city's garbage workers. A white man is arrested and convicted. Blacks riot after the shooting, most notably in Washington, D.C.

NOTES

■ ──────────────

Interviews

Recollections and reminiscences not cited individually in the chapter notes are taken from interviews conducted by the author with the following persons:

Harry Ashmore: Santa Barbara, California, September 14, 1988
Julian Bond: Washington, D.C., April 25, 1988
Wiley A. Branton: Washington, D.C., May 3, 1988
C. C. Bryant: McComb, Mississippi, June 21, 1988
Sharon Burger (Townsend): New Orleans, August 7, 1988
Lawrence Campbell: Danville, Virginia, October 19, 1988
Will D. Campbell: Mount Juliet, Tennessee, October 27, 1986
Gordon Carey: Burlington, North Carolina, October 21, 1988
Marion Cheek: Albany, Georgia, July 27, 1989
James P. Coleman: Ackerman, Mississippi, August 17, 1988
L. C. Dorsey: Canton, Mississippi, June 20, 1988
Leslie W. Dunbar: Pelham, New York, April 22, 1987
James Farmer: Massaponax, Virginia, November 4, 1987
Harold Fleming: Washington, D.C., May 4, 1988
Milton A. Galamison: Brooklyn, New York, March 19,1987
Harvey Gantt: Charlotte, North Carolina, June 1, 1988

Alan Gartner: New York City, November 13, 1987
Victoria Gray (Adams): Petersburg, Virginia, May 31, 1988
Edwin O. Guthman: Pacific Palisades, California, September 16, 1988
Lawrence Guyot: Washington, D.C., January 5, 1987
Arthur Hanes: Birmingham, Alabama, December, 1961, and August 12, 1988
Emil Hess: Birmingham, Alabama, July 25, 1989
Norman Hill: New York City, November 12, 1987
Lucius Holloway: Albany, Georgia, July 28, 1989
James O. Ingram: Jackson, Mississippi, August 18, 1988
John Jackson: White Hall, Alabama, August 10, 1988
Frank M. Johnson, Jr.: Montgomery, Alabama, July 24, 1989
Erle Johnston: Forest, Mississippi, June 20, 1988
Charles Jones: Charlotte, North Carolina, June 1, 1988, and August 2, 1989
Asa D. Kelley: Albany, Georgia, July 27, 1989
C. B. King: Albany, Georgia, July 10, 1962
Henry Kirksey: Jackson, Mississippi (telephone), June 19, 1988
Bernard Lafayette: Montgomery, Alabama, August 15, 1988
John Lewis: Washington, D.C., July 13, 1989
Charles McDew: Minneapolis (telephone), July 30, 1990
Floyd McKissick: Oxford, North Carolina, November 5, 1987
Floyd Mann: Montgomery, Alabama, August 11, 1988
Constance Baker Motley: New York City, April 30, 1987
Diane Nash (Bevel): Chicago, December 7, 1988
Silas Norman: Detroit, December 10, 1988
C. Herbert Oliver: Brooklyn, New York, March 19, 1987
John Patterson: Montgomery, Alabama, June 16, 1988
Laurie Pritchett: High Rock Lake, North Carolina, August 2, 1989
Charles Quinn: Washington, D.C., July 14, 1989
Joseph L. Rauh, Jr.: Washington, D.C., May 5, 1988
Isaac Reynolds: New Orleans, August 8, 1988
Gloria Richardson: Cambridge, Maryland, summer, 1963
Henry Schwarzschild: New York City, March 17, 1987
Charles Sherrod: Albany, Georgia, July 27, 1989
Arthur Shores: Birmingham, Alabama, June 15, 1988
Fred Shuttlesworth: Cincinnati, December 5, 1988
William J. Simmons: Jackson, Mississippi, June 21, 1988
Claude Sitton: Raleigh, North Carolina, August 3, 1989
Lamar Stewart: Albany, Georgia (telephone), June 5, 1990
David Vann: Birmingham, Alabama, June 15, 1988
Wyatt Tee Walker: New York City, November 12, 1987
Hollis Watkins: Jackson, Mississippi, June 20, 1988
Samuel B. Wells: Albany, Georgia, July 31, 1989
Dorothy Miller Zellner: New York City, March 3, 1988

Proceedings at a conference of former workers for the Student Non-violent Coordinating Committee, held April 14–16, 1988, at Trinity College in Hartford, Connecticut, were recorded by the author.

Some proceedings at a reunion of former Congress of Racial Equality workers, held August 4–7, 1988, at New Orleans, were recorded by the author.

Material was also collected from the author's recorded interviews with Val Coleman, David Crosland, Lolis Elie, William Eskridge, David Hawkins, Tom Hayden, Bea Kaimowitz, Claude Liggins, Leslie McLemore, Robert Mants, Henry Mitchell, Lucy Montgomery, Martha Norman, Penelope Patch, Marvin Rich, Anthony Scotto, and Herman Talmadge.

Abbreviations Used in the Notes

AH   *Albany Herald*

ASNR   Howard Zinn, *Albany: A Study in National Responsibility* (Atlanta: Southern Regional Council, 1962)

BOPNV   Henry Lee Moon, *Balance of Power: The Negro Vote* (New York: Doubleday, 1948; reissued by Greenwood Press, Westport, Connecticut, 1977)

BTC   David J. Garrow, *Bearing the Cross: Martin Luther King, Jr., and the Southern Christian Leadership Conference* (New York: William Morrow, 1986)

CHN   Peter M. Bergman and a staff of compilers, *The Chronological History of the Negro in America* (New York: Harper & Row, 1969)

CJL   Pat Watters and Reese Cleghorn, *Climbing Jacob's Ladder: The Arrival of Negroes in Southern Politics* (New York: Harcourt, Brace and World, 1967)

EOP   *Eyes on the Prize* (Boston: Blackside, Inc., 1988). Television series

FITS   Milton Viorst, *Fire in the Streets: America in the 1960s* (New York: Simon and Schuster, 1979)

FTTF   U.S. Commission on Civil Rights, *Freedom to the Free, 1863–1963: Century of Emancipation* (Washington, D.C.: Government Printing Office, 1963)

IAOM   Russell H. Barrett, *Integration at Ole Miss* (Chicago: Quadrangle, 1965)

IS	Clayborne Carson, *In Struggle: SNCC and the Black Awakening of the 1960s* (Cambridge, Massachusetts: Harvard University Press, 1981)
KJ	Victor Navasky, *Kennedy Justice* (New York: Atheneum, 1971)
LBH	James Farmer, *Lay Bare the Heart* (New York: New American Library, 1985)
MOBR	James Forman, *The Making of Black Revolutionaries* (Washington, D.C.: Open Hand, 1985)
NWG	Robert F. Williams, *Negroes with Guns* (New York: Marzani & Munsell, 1962)
NYT	*New York Times*
OCRM	Aldon D. Morris, *Origins of the Civil Rights Movement: Black Communities Organizing for Change* (New York: Free Press, 1984)
POAD	Anthony Lewis and The New York Times, *Portrait of a Decade: The Second American Revolution* (New York: Bantam, 1965)
PP	U.S. Commission on Civil Rights, *Political Participation* (Washington, D.C.: Government Printing Office, 1968)
RAF	Walter White, *Rope & Faggot: A Biography of Judge Lynch* (New York: Alfred A. Knopf, 1929)
RKIOW	Edwin O. Guthman and Jeffrey Shulman, eds., *Robert Kennedy: In His Own Words. The Unpublished Recollections of the Kennedy Years* (New York: Bantam, 1988)
ROMR	Numan V. Bartley, *The Rise of Massive Resistance: Race and Politics in the South During the 1950s* (Baton Rouge: Louisiana State University Press, 1969)
RRLR	*Race Relations Law Reporter*
TYIM	James Meredith, *Three Years in Mississippi* (Bloomington: Indiana University Press, 1966)
VMR	Benjamin Muse, *Virginia's Massive Resistance* (Bloomington: Indiana University Press, 1961)

Chapter One: The Cost of Oppression

1. *CHN*, 515, 546.
2. Ibid., 212.
3. Booker T. Washington, "Atlanta Exposition Address," 1895, in

Joanne Grant, ed., *Black Protest: History, Documents, and Analysis: 1619 to the Present*, 2d ed. (New York: Fawcett, 1968), 195.

4. *Plessy v. Ferguson*, 163 U.S. 537 (1896).

5. *Missouri ex rel. Gaines v. Canada*, 305 U.S. 337 (1938); *Sipuel v. Board of Regents*, 332 U.S. 631 (1948).

6. *McLaurin v. Board of Regents*, 339 U.S. 637 (1950).

7. *Sweatt v. Painter*, 339 U.S. 634 (1950).

8. *CHN*, 294; U.S. Constitution, Article 1, Section 8; *FTTF*, 134.

9. *Henderson v. United States*, 339 U.S. 816, 824 (1950); *FTTF*, 136.

10. *FTTF*, 181.

11. *FTTF*, 118.

12. *BOPNV*, 7.

13. *BOPNV*, 9. Jim Crowism, a term for officially sanctioned segregation, got its name from a character in a nineteenth-century variety act.

Chapter Two: Race, Creed, Color, or National Origin

1. *LBH*, 154.

2. *FTTF*, 125.

3. Ibid., 127.

Chapter Three: The South's Unique Liability

1. Pat Watters, "Introduction," *New South* (January, 1964), 1.

2. "Toward the South of the Future: A Statement of Policy and Aims of the Southern Regional Council," *New South* (December, 1951), 1.

3. *CHN*, 10.

Chapter Four: The Revolution Got out of Hand

1. *RRLR* (1956), 5.

2. *ROMR*, 54.

3. *Brown v. Board of Education*, 347 U.S. 483 (1954).

4. In 1950, the total black population of the United States was said to be 15,042,286; an estimated 68 percent of Negroes lived in the South. *CHN*, 522.

5. *RRLR* (1956), 11.

6. *CHN*, 540.

7. Ibid., 536.

8. Ibid., 537.

9. Ibid., 542.

10. Ibid., 538, 539.

11. Ibid., 538.

12. Ibid., 535.
13. Ibid., 536, 545.

Chapter Five: Old Black Women Walking in the Sun

1. Rhoda Lois Blumberg, *Civil Rights: The 1960s Freedom Struggle* (Boston: Twayne, 1984), xvii.
2. *CHN*, 540.
3. *BTC*, 11.
4. *OCRM*, 51
5. *BTC*, 14. Robinson is one of those who refuse to allow history to set down an overly simple version of how the Montgomery boycott started. See her *The Montgomery Bus Boycott and the Woman Who Started It: The Memoir of Jo Ann Gibson Robinson* (Knoxville: University of Tennessee Press, 1987).
6. *OCRM*, 54.
7. *CHN*, 540.
8. *OCRM*, 57.
9. *Morgan v. Virginia*, 66 S.C. 1050 (June, 1946).
10. Author's personal experience as a reporter for the *New York Times*.
11. *OCRM*, 58.
12. Ibid., 59, 60.
13. *BTC* 56, 219.
14. *EOP*, part 1.
15. *LBH*, 186.
16. Robinson, *The Montgomery Bus Boycott*, 10.
17. *MOBR*, 77.
18. Ibid., 85.
19. *LBH*, 189.
20. *CHN*, 551.

Chapter Six: Pilgrims

1. *CHN*, 546.
2. *FTTF*, 192; *CHN*, 551.
3. *CJL*, 49.
4. *OCRM*, 102.
5. Ibid., 86.
6. Ibid., 84.
7. Ibid., 91.
8. Ibid., 100; *BTC*, 123.
9. Gayraud S. Wilmore, general editor of the "Christian Perspectives on Social Problems" series published by Westminster Press, writing in

foreword to Will D. Campbell, *Race and the Renewal of the Church* (Philadelphia: Westminister Press, 1962).

10. Will D. Campbell, *Forty Acres and a Goat* (Atlanta: Peachtree Publishers, 1986), 4.

11. Ibid., 5.

12. *CHN*, 561.

13. Quoted in *POAD*, 91.

14. *IAOM*, 33; *TYIM*, 10.

15. *CHN*, 532, 537, 543.

16. Ibid., 547.

17. Ibid., 558, 562.

18. "I remember with some horror," said Gartner in an interview, "that we imported two black guys from Wright Patterson Air Force Base who allegedly knew how to cut hair, and we had our hair cut by them all those years. That was dangerous stuff!"

19. *CHN*, 548.

20. Ibid., 555, 561.

21. Ibid., 559.

22. Ibid., 560.

23. Ibid., 562.

24. John Egerton, *A Mind to Stay Here: Profiles from the South* (New York: Macmillan, 1970), 53.

Chapter Seven: The Power of the Ballot Box

1. *Brown v. Board of Education*, 347 U.S. 483 (1954).

2. *RRLR* (1956), 948.

3. Richard Kluger, *Simple Justice* (New York: Random House, 1975), 256.

4. Ibid., 113.

5. *RAF*, 84.

6. Ibid., 8, 40.

7. Ibid., 82, 48.

8. Ibid., 139; Dr. Charles C. Perkins, Jr., chair of Emory University psychology department, quoted in "Perkins Says IQs of Races About Same," *Atlanta Journal*, October 7, 1962.

9. *RAF*, 201, 264, 98.

10. W. J. Cash, *The Mind of the South* (New York: Alfred A. Knopf, 1941); James McBride Dabbs, *Who Speaks for the South?* (New York: Funk & Wagnalls, 1964), viii.

11. Dabbs, *Who Speaks for the South?*, 288.

12. Ibid.

13. Howard Odum, dissertation "Social and Mental Traits of the Negro," quoted in Kluger, *Simple Justice*, 311.

14. Frank Tannenbaum, *Darker Phases of the South* (London: G. P. Putnam's Sons, 1924; reprinted by Negro Universities Press, New York, 1969), 161.

15. *PP*, 3.

16. Ibid., 4.

17. Ibid., 5.

18. *BOPNV*, 65.

19. *PP*, 8.

20. V. O. Key, Jr., *Southern Politics in State and Nation* (New York: Vintage, 1949), 628.

21. "Rights Unit Asks U.S. Writ for Alabama Voting Data," *NYT*, December 10, 1958.

22. "Patterson Gains Alabama Victory," *NYT*, June 4, 1958.

23. Quoted in Michael Dorman, *The George Wallace Myth* (New York: Bantam, 1976), 23.

Chapter Eight: The Desire to Survive Politically

1. *VMR*, 5, 44.

2. J. Lindsay Almond, Jr., address to special session of Virginia legislature, January 28, 1959; text in *RRLR* (1959), 183.

3. Samuel DuBois Cook, "Political Movements and Organizations," *Journal of Politics*, vol. 26, no. 1 (February, 1964), 131.

4. John J. Calhoun, "Six Works," 1831, quoted in *RRLR* (1956), 468; *RRLR* (1956), 466.

5. *RRLR* (1956), 445.

6. Quoted in *KJ*, 240.

7. *RRLR* (1956), 435.

8. See Dorman, *The George Wallace Myth*, for a discussion of political corruption in Alabama.

9. John Craig Stewart, *The Governors of Alabama* (Gretna, Louisiana: Pelican Publishing Company, 1975); "Negro Bands Barred," *NYT*, December 30, 1958.

10. "Defiant Governor," *NYT*, May 22, 1961.

Chapter Nine: Faith Is Not Enough

1. It is a possibly apocryphal (but nevertheless indelible) part of the history of Alabama politics that Wallace, upon learning of his defeat by Patterson in the Democratic primary in 1958, declared that he had been "out-niggered" by Patterson and that "I'll never be out-niggered again." In recent years Wallace, who claimed to have mellowed some and even to have changed his mind about segregation, started denying having said such a thing. In his *Governors of Alabama*, John Craig Stewart writes that

Wallace "vowed he would never be 'outsegged' again" (p. 214). Although both terms were in wide and interchangeable use in Southern politics in the fifties and sixties, the "out-niggered" one sounds far more authentic and is the one students of the era tend to remember. Patterson, speaking about this in 1988, said he "never heard" Wallace make the comment. Asked if he had, in fact, "out-niggered" his opponent, Patterson replied: "Well, I don't really like the expression. But I was perceived to be stronger on that issue than he was. He was perceived to be liberal on that issue." The former governor laughed. "That's hard to believe, isn't it? Being the attorney general, and having the responsibility for representing the state in what litigation there was concerning that issue, it made it possible for me — and particularly in the NAACP case — almost every day to grab the headline on race relations. Any day I wanted to file something, or appear in court, or say something concerning the race issue, I could get the headlines. I could control the publicity. And I became the Alabama spokesman on that issue, and he was eliminated out of that." Attempts to ask Wallace about all this were unsuccessful, but events surely showed that after 1958, he was rarely "out-niggered" by anyone else in Alabama politics.

2. "Patterson Warns Race Agitators," *Birmingham Post-Herald*, January 20, 1959.

3. Harry S. Ashmore, *Hearts and Minds: A Personal Chronicle of Race in America*, rev. ed. (Cabin John, Maryland: Seven Locks Press, 1988), 231.

4. Cook, "Political Movements and Organizations," 133.

5. *RRLR* (1957), "Race Relations Law Survey, May, 1954–May, 1957," 889.

6. Ibid. (1959), 181.

7. Ibid. (1958), 15; (1959), 182.

8. Ibid. (1957), 805.

9. Letter from L. P. Godwin of Montgomery to Governor John Patterson, in Alabama Department of Archives and History, Governors' Papers, vol. 2, "Race and Segregation" letters file, box 389.

10. Austin Earle Burges, *What Price Integration* (Dallas: Royal Publishing Company, 1956), 5–7, 34, 35.

11. Author's files from *The Daily Tar Heel*. University of North Carolina at Chapel Hill, winter, 1962; Associated Press dispatch published in *Daily Tar Heel*, October 3, 1962; undated paper by W. C. George, circa 1940s; *Atlanta Journal*, October 7, 1962.

12. *RRLR* (1959), 5.

13. Ibid. (1958), "Substantive Civil Rights Under Federal Legislation" survey, 139.

14. Ibid. (1957), 887.

15. Interview with C. Herbert Oliver; *RRLR* (1957), 886.

Chapter Ten: Nothing Personal, You Understand

1. From an opinion written by federal judges Morris A. Soper and Walter E. Hoffman, quoted in *VMR*, 49.

2. *ROMR*, 220.

3. *RRLR (1956)*, 956.

4. Ibid. (1959), 208.

5. *National Association for the Advancement of Colored People v. State of Alabama* [In re: *State of Alabama ex rel. Patterson, Attorney General, v. NAACP*], in *RRLR* (1958), 611; *RRLR* (1959), "Freedom of Association" survey, 208.

6. *RRLR* (1959), "Freedom of Association" survey, 222.

7. Ibid., 226.

8. Ibid. (1958), "Inciting Litigation" survey, 1257.

9. Ibid. (1956), 941, 953.

10. James W. Silver, *Mississippi: The Closed Society* (New York: Harcourt Brace Jovanovich, 1964).

11. *RRLR* (1957), 682.

Chapter Eleven: A Subtle, Gradual Tightening Down

1. In 1960 the party nominated Arkansas governor Orval Faubus for president. He declined the honor. Cook, "Political Movements and Organizations," 142.

2. Mississippi Department of Archives and History, "Citizens' Council Forum Films," Folder MP 86.01.

3. *ROMR*, 169.

4. Cook, "Political Movements and Organizations," 136.

5. *POAD*, 33.

6. House Bill 880, Chapter 365, *General Laws of the State of Mississippi*, approved March 29, 1956; text in *RRLR* (1956), 592.

7. *ROMR*, 180.

8. Erle Johnston, *I Rolled with Ross: A Political Portrait* (Baton Rouge: Moran Publishing Corporation, 1980).

9. For a chilling and thorough account of the murder, see Howard Smead, *Blood Justice: The Lynching of Mack Charles Parker* (New York: Oxford University Press, 1986).

10. *RRLR* (1959), 2, 206.

11. Ibid. (1957), 443; (1956), 434.

12. Ibid. (1958), 1081.

Chapter Twelve: Hate and History Coming Together

1. "Negro Sitdowns Stir Fear of Wider Unrest in South," *NYT*, February 15, 1960.

2. For one engrossing account of how the Greensboro sit-ins started, and of Ralph Johns's part in them, see Miles Wolff, *Lunch at the Five and Ten: The Greensboro Sit-ins* (New York: Stein and Day, 1970).

3. Wolff, *Lunch at the Five and Ten*, 32; "Klan Tries to Halt Negroes' Protest," *NYT*, February 6, 1960; "Negro Protests Lead to Store Closings," *NYT*, February 7, 1960.

4. *OCRM*, 162.

5. *Fisk News* (spring, 1960); *EOP*, part 4.

6. *Fisk News* (spring, 1960).

7. *EOP*, part 4.

Chapter Thirteen: This Was Our Time

1. *RRLR (1960)*, "Legal Aspects of the Sit-In Movement" survey, 935.

2. Ibid.

3. "Virginia Bills Enacted" and "Sitdown Staged in Alabama Shop," *NYT*, February 26, 1960; "Protest Scheduled," *NYT*, May 1, 1960.

4. "Police and Dogs Rout 100 Negroes," *NYT*, May 30, 1960.

5. *RRLR (1960)*, "Legal Aspects of the Sit-In Movement" survey, 936; *EOP*, part 4.

6. "South Is Warned of Time of Change," *NYT*, February 28, 1960; Southern Regional Council, "The Student Protest Movement: A Recapitulation" (September, 1961).

7. "Communist Training Operations," Part 3, *Hearings Before the Committee on Un-American Activities*, House of Representatives, 86th Congress (February 5, 1960), 1451.

Chapter Fourteen: A Glorious Opportunity

1. See, generally, *MOBR*.

2. *MOBR*, 216.

3. "Statement of Purpose," Student Nonviolent Coordinating Committee, adopted April 17, 1960; from a copy obtained at the time by the author.

4. *MOBR*, 106.

Chapter Fifteen: A Handle That We Could Use

1. The proportions of registered voting-age Negroes in the South in 1960 ranged from 32 percent in Texas to 25 percent in North Carolina, 14 percent in Alabama, and a low of 4 percent in Mississippi. *CHN*, 565.

2. *CHN*, 565.

3. Ibid., 566.

4. Ibid., 570.

5. *IS*, 28.

6. "The Student Nonviolent Coordinating Committee," as revised in conference, April 29, 1962, obtained at the time by the author.

7. Harold C. Fleming, "The Federal Executive and Civil Rights: 1961–1965," in *Daedalus*, "The Negro American" issue, part 1 (fall, 1965), 921. Fleming by this time had left the Southern Regional Council, put in some time as deputy director of the federal Community Relations Service, and was serving as executive vice president of the Potomac Institute in Washington.

8. "Kennedy Assures Liberals He Seeks No Help in South" and "7 Restaurants Open to Virginia Negroes," *NYT*, June 24, 1960.

9. "Kennedy Role on Rights," *NYT*, May 24, 1960.

10. Fred Powledge, *Black Power / White Resistance: Notes on the New Civil War* (Cleveland: World, 1967), 61; *CHN*, 567.

11. "10 Negroes Seized in Carolina Sit-in," Associated Press dispatch in *NYT*, February 1, 1961.

Chapter Sixteen: An Absolutely Awful Day in Alabama

1. *LBH*, 186.

2. *NYT*, May 5, 1961.

3. The photographer, who was something of a joke among Atlanta activists and members of the press, carried a huge Speed Graphic press camera with flashbulb attachment. By the early sixties, virtually all real photojournalists were using small 35-millimeter cameras and available lighting in such circumstances.

4. Presented as evidence in *Walter Bergman and James Drummond, Personal Representative of the Estate of Frances Bergman, Deceased, Plaintiffs, v. United States of America; Barrett G. Kemp, individually and as a former employee of the Federal Bureau of Investigation, and four unknown agents of the Federal Bureau of Investigation, Thomas J. Jenkins, individually and as a former employee of the Federal Bureau of Investigation, Defendants;* quoted in decision of U.S. district judge Richard J. Enslen, Western District of Michigan, May 31, 1983 (hereafter cited as *Bergman v. United States*).

5. *NYT*, May 16, 1961.

6. Speech by Robert F. Kennedy, May 6, 1961, at Law Day exercises at University of Georgia law school, quoted in *Bergman v. United States*.

7. Southern Regional Council, *The Freedom Ride, May, 1961* (Atlanta: Southern Regional Council, 1961). The account of the Freedom Ride given in the next few pages is based largely on this report.

8. *LBH*, 203, 204.

9. "400 U.S. Marshals Sent to Alabama as Montgomery Bus Riots Hurt 20; President Bids State Keep Order," *NYT*, May 21, 1961. The authority, which exists under an 1871 federal statute, gives the president the power to use a militia, armed forces, or anything else "to suppress in a state any insurrection, domestic violence, unlawful combination or conspiracy," in the event that a class of citizens is deprived of a constitutional right and the "constituted authorities of that state are unable, fail, or refuse to protect that right."

10. Farmer, in his book on the Movement, recalls that when the original riders passed through Atlanta, King, who was a member of CORE's national advisory board, invited the group to have dinner with him at "an excellent black-owned restaurant," then stuck Farmer with the check. *LBH*, 200.

11. "Patterson Urged Kennedy to Run," *NYT*, May 23, 1961.

12. The following account of the FBI's involvement in Freedom Ride violence is based on *Bergman v. United States*.

Chapter Seventeen: A Limit to Liberalism

1. "Negro Girl a Force in Campaign; Encouraged Bus to Keep Rolling," *NYT*, May 23, 1961.

2. "Rights Aide Silent on Police-Klan Link," *NYT*, May 23, 1961; author's interview with Judge Frank Johnson; "Ministers in South Ask Racial Accord," *NYT*, May 26, 1961.

3. *NYT*, May 25, 1961.

4. Ibid., June 3, 1961.

5. "U.S. Moves for Injunction Against Police in Alabama," *NYT*, May 25, 1961.

6. *RRLR* (1961), 544.

7. "N.A.A.C.P. in Plea," *NYT*, May 27, 1961; "Opinion of the Week: At Home and Abroad," *NYT*, IV, May 28, 1961.

8. Editorial comment on Freedom Ride in the following paragraphs is quoted in Southern Regional Council, *The Freedom Ride, May, 1961*, and "Opinion of the Week: At Home and Abroad," *NYT*, IV, May 21, 1961.

9. Claude Sitton, "Passive Tactics Spread in Rights Battle," *NYT*, IV, May 21, 1961.

10. "Alabama Terminal Drops Racial Curb," *NYT*, June 2, 1961.

11. "U.S. Court Enjoins Freedom Riders in Alabama Trips," *NYT*, June 3, 1961.

12. "Bus-Test Backers to Appeal Ruling," *NYT*, June 4, 1961.

13. "Justice Department Acts," *NYT*, June 10, 1961.

14. "Arrest of Riders Held Local Issue," *NYT*, June 22, 1961.

15. "Reds Called Key to Freedom Riders," Associated Press dispatch in *NYT*, June 30, 1961.

16. "Opinion of the Week: At Home and Abroad," *NYT*, IV, May 28, 1961.

17. "Dr. King Refuses to End Test by Freedom Riders," *NYT*, May 26, 1961. Actually, King had little to do with the ride.

18. *RRLR* (1961), 902.

Chapter Eighteen: Where's Your Body?

1. "U.S. Puts Length of Deputies' Stay up to Alabamans," *NYT*, May 24, 1961.

2. Associated Press dispatch, *NYT*, June 17, 1961.

3. "Bus Riders Urged to Shift Target," *NYT*, June 20, 1961.

4. "Negro Leaders Seek Halt in Freedom Ride Testing," *NYT*, June 25, 1961.

5. *LBH*, 219.

6. *MOBR*, 265.

7. *RKIOW*, 102.

8. Robert Kennedy in foreword to Burke Marshall, *Federalism and Civil Rights* (New York: Columbia University Press, 1964), ix, 4; *RKIOW*, 102.

9. *IS*, 41.

10. *The Chronological History of the Negro* reported that in 1961 there were fifty-one Black Muslim temples and missions in America. Many, but not all, were in the North (p. 574).

11. *NWG*, 63.

12. Ibid., 39.

Chapter Nineteen: In the Bowels of the Beast

1. *LBH*, 22.

2. This recollection cannot be confirmed independently. Wilkins is now dead and Moses, who in recent years cut himself off from many of those who knew him in the Movement years, did not respond to queries.

3. U.S. Commission on Civil Rights, *1961 United States Commission on Civil Rights Report: Book 1, Voting* (Washington, D.C.: Government Printing Office, 1961), 274, 108.

4. *IS*, 48.

5. Ibid., 49.
6. Ibid., 54.
7. *MOBR*, 235.

Chapter Twenty: A Willingness to Suffer

1. Today the tourist division of the Georgia state government publishes a map (jointly with the Georgia Peanut Commission) that places Albany and environs in a region the image-makers call "Plantation Trace." The Trace is just south of "Presidential Pathways" and to the west of "Magnolia Midlands" and the "Colonial Coast."
2. *ASNR*, 3.
3. Charles M. Sherrod, "Non-violence," a working paper prepared for the Student Nonviolent Coordinating Committee, undated, circa 1963.
4. The expose promised by Sherrod did not materialize.

Chapter Twenty-one: The Land of Never

1. *ASNR*, 3.
2. Ibid, 4.
3. "Man in the News: Determined Police Chief," *NYT*, July 23, 1962.
4. *IS*, 59.
5. *ASNR*, 4; "Jail Negro Demonstrators as Trials of 11 Open Here," *AH*, December 12, 1961.
6. "Jail Negro Demonstrators," *AH*, December 12, 1961.
7. "Freedom Riders Face Trials Here," *AH*, December 11, 1961; "The Passing Storm," *AH*, December 14, 1961.
8. "Write-in Rumor Spurs Huge General Election Vote Here," *AH*, December 4, 1961.
9. "Chicago Negro Dope Ring Under Probing," *AH*, July 28, 1962; "Negro Student Lauds Reds," *AH*, December 23, 1961; "Negro Admits Killing Pair," *AH*, December 27, 1961.
10. *ASNR*, 13.
11. *RRLR* (1965), 82.
12. *World Almanac and Book of Facts* (New York: World-Telegram and The Sun, 1962), 52.
13. Paul, in Acts 23:5, says, "Thou shalt not speak evil of the ruler of thy people."
14. *OCRM*, 243.
15. *ASNR*, 4.
16. Ibid.
17. "Albany White People Aloof from Trouble," Associated Press dispatch in *AH*, December 15, 1961.

18. "Albany's Head Is High," *AH*, December 18, 1961.

19. *IS*, 60.

20. "Atlanta's Example: 'Good Sense and Dignity,' " *NYT Magazine*, May 6, 1962; "Atlanta Inn Bars Belafonte Group," *NYT*, June 7, 1962, and author's personal experience.

21. "Segregation Aid Sought," United Press International dispatch in *NYT*, January 20, 1962.

22. "College President Ousted in Alabama," United Press International dispatch in *NYT*, February 14, 1962. The board rejected the proposal that it fire the president on the spot, however.

23. "Virginia Debates Negro Abilities," *NYT*, February 18, 1962.

24. "Advertising: Unorganized Boycotts by Negroes Found," *NYT*, April 18, 1962.

25. "5 Negroes Convicted," Associated Press dispatch in *NYT*, January 4, 1962.

26. "6 in Augusta Held in Racial Outbreak," *NYT*, April 18, 1962; "Augusta Moves to End Violence," *NYT*, April 21, 1962.

27. "N.A.A.C.P. Fund Piling Up Suits," *NYT*, June 18, 1962.

28. "Strategy: Negro Vote," *NYT*, January 7, 1962.

29. *CJL*, 26–27. *Climbing Jacob's Ladder* is the source for much of the information here on the Voter Education Project. It is one of the best-written and most informative books on the civil rights movement.

30. "Big Cities Getting More Non-Whites," *NYT*, April 15, 1962; "The Negro Migration," *NYT*, April 29, 1962.

31. "New Orleans Whites May Send Two Buses with Negroes Here," *NYT*, April 26, 1962; "Negro Father of 8, Sent Here by Whites, Offered Jobs," *NYT*, April 22, 1962; "Negro 'Ride' Plan Stirs New Furor," *NYT*, April 25, 1962.

Chapter Twenty-two: You Relied on Local Help

1. *ASNR*, 6.

2. Ibid., 5.

3. "Albany's Bus Service Ends at Midnight," *AH*, January 31, 1962.

4. "Boycott Closes Bus Service in Albany," *AH*, February 1, 1962.

5. *ASNR*, 6.

6. Ibid.

7. Ibid.

8. Ibid., 7.

9. "Griffin Says Time to Halt Race Mixing," *AH*, July 6, 1962.

10. "Bloch, Bodenhamer Choose Candidates," "From Wire Reports," *AH*, July 6, 1962.

11. "Thousands Cheer Marvin's Speech; Sanders Crowd Lags in Statesboro," *AH*, July 8, 1962.

12. "King, Abernathy Go to Jail Here," *AH*, July 10, 1962; *ASNR*, 9.

13. *ASNR*, 9; "King Languishes in Bastille as Demonstrators Are Halted," *AH*, July 11, 1962.

14. *NYT*, quoted in *ASNR*, 9.

15. Taylor Branch, *Parting the Waters: America in the King Years, 1954–63* (New York: Simon and Schuster, 1988), 604; " 'Somebody' Pays King out of Jail; Mayor Stays Mum," *AH*, July 12, 1962.

16. "Albany's Mayor Blisters Justice Man's 'Conduct,' " *AH*, July 15, 1962; *ASNR*, 10; "Pritchett Says Agitators Plot Harassment in City," *AH*, July 19, 1962. The *Herald* referred to Charles Jones as a "self-styled 'humanitarian' from North Carolina."

17. *ASNR*, 10; "U.S. Judge Halts Albany Negro Marchers," *AH*, July 21, 1962.

18. "Albany Negroes Defy U.S. Court Order, March in City; Children Led into Uprisal," *AH*, July 22, 1962.

19. *ASNR*, 11; Marion King, "Reflections on the Death of a Child," *New South* (February, 1963), 9.

20. "Mayor Says Judge's Rule on Order Is 'Incredible,' " *AH*, July 24, 1962; *ASNR*, 12. James Gray of the *Herald* referred to "the currently popular interpretation of the highly controversial Fourteenth Amendment" that held that minority rights should be safeguarded. "Albany Will Stand," *AH*, July 25, 1962.

21. *ASNR*, 12.

22. Ibid., 13.

23. Ibid., 15.

24. *KJ*, 207. Navasky writes that Kennedy wired Pritchett "congratulating him on keeping the peace (which he did by the simple expedient of jailing the non-law-breaking demonstrators)." Navasky, in his perceptive book on Kennedy's years at the Justice Department, makes the often-overlooked point that the attorney general didn't have a real civil rights program from 1961 to 1963, and that civil rights did not occupy a place high on the administration's agenda. The author places civil rights toward the middle of the administration's early list of priorities, below such issues as antitrust efforts, organized crime, and getting Teamsters boss Jimmy Hoffa, and above crime in the streets. Furthermore, writes Navasky, the Kennedy administration treated each civil rights crisis as a "temporary eruption," as "the random, discontinuous by-products of a society evolving painfully toward racial integration. The trick was to encourage the inevitable integration but never at the cost of disturbing the social equilibrium. [Kennedy's] most visible and most significant civil rights activities were responsive, reactive, crisis-managing, violence-avoiding." *KJ*, 97, 167.

25. "Arkansans Score New U.S. Marshal," *NYT*, March 16, 1962; "R. F. Kennedy Backs Marshal Nominee," *NYT*, March 17, 1962; "Robert Ken-

nedy Target of Sit-in," *NYT*, March 14, 1962; "Federal Action Urged," *NYT*, March 20, 1962; "Hodges Asserts U.S. Must Spur Exports," Associated Press dispatch in *NYT*, May 5, 1962; "End of Segregation Predicted by King," Associated Press dispatch in *NYT*, May 21, 1962.

26. *KJ*, 256, 246.
27. *RKIOW*, 107, 113.
28. *NYT*, November 19, 1962, quoted in Branch, *Parting the Waters*, 681.
29. Ibid.
30. David Garrow, *The FBI and Martin Luther King, Jr.* (New York: Penguin, 1983).
31. *KJ*, 135.
32. Including the author of this book.
33. *KJ*, 122.

Chapter Twenty-three: A Failed Success

1. *CJL*, 165.
2. Ibid., 164; *ASNR*, 25.
3. *IS*, 93.
4. Marion King, "Reflections on the Death of a Child."
5. "Former Albany, Ga., Police Chief Builds a New Reputation in a New Town," *NYT*, March 21, 1971.
6. This incident was originally recounted in Powledge, *Black Power/White Resistance*, 43.
7. *Taylor v. State of Louisiana*, June 4, 1962, 82 S.Ct. 1188, reported in *RRLR* (1962), 333.
8. In the opinion of the author, who was one of the reporters who covered the events in Albany, Pritchett's version of this seems highly exaggerated and may be just part of an effort to appear, in retrospect, as some sort of invincible master of the Albany situation — a role that he certainly seemed to enjoy playing at the time. Journalists who worked on the Albany story regarded some local reporters and at least one out-of-town newsman (the wire service writer) as violators of the unwritten, but ironclad, reporter's rule against collaborating with any of the principals in an ongoing event. Pritchett claims, though, that "all of" the members of the press fed him information. This is not true.

Chapter Twenty-four: A Mission and a Nervous Stomach

1. James Meredith's *Three Years in Mississippi* (*TYIM*) is the authority for much of this chapter.
2. *TYIM*, 20.

3. "A Barnett Disturbance in Connecticut Recalled," United Press International dispatch in *NYT*, October 1, 1962.

4. Johnston, *I Rolled with Ross*, 16; "North Being Sold False Ideas: Barnett," United Press International dispatch in *AH*, January 20, 1962.

5. "Mississippi Gives Meredith Degree," *NYT*, August 18, 1963.

6. *IAOM*, 100.

7. Ibid., 101.

8. Calvin Trillin, *An Education in Georgia: The Integration of Charlayne Hunter and Hamilton Holmes* (New York: Viking, 1963); "2 Negro Students Enter Georgia U," *NYT*, January 11, 1961; Fred Powledge, "Too Much for Governor Vandiver," *The New Republic*, January 25, 1961.

9. *IAOM*, 103.

10. Ibid., 113.

11. *TYIM*, 54.

12. Ibid., 57.

13. Ibid., 58.

14. Ibid., 62, 105, 107.

15. *CJL*, 218.

16. Meredith's appeal and Wisdom's ruling are taken from *TYIM*, 134, and *RRLR* (1962), 423.

17. *TYIM*, 141.

18. *RRLR* (1962), 748.

19. *TYIM*, 180.

20. Ibid.

21. *TYIM*, 183.

22. *IAOM*, 103.

23. *TYIM*, 189.

24. Ibid., 184, 185.

25. Johnston, *I Rolled with Ross*, 102; *RRLR* (1962), 759.

26. *TYIM*, 200.

27. Ibid., 205.

28. Details of the Kennedy deal with Barnett and Johnson are taken from *KJ*, 209.

29. *RRLR* (1962), 761.

30. *IAOM*, 121.

31. *RRLR* (1962), 764.

32. The "dozens of reporters" included the author (the "reporter from Atlanta"), whose account this is.

33. For shorthand purposes, the combined force of federal deputy marshals, border patrol officers, and prison guards will be termed "marshals." Actually, there were 123 deputy marshals, 316 border patrolmen, and 97 federal prison guards. *IAOM*, 138.

34. The text of Kennedy's radio speech is from *IAOM*, 149.

35. *TYIM*, 213.

36. "Barnett Blames Marshals: Here's Eyewitness Story," *Atlanta Journal*, October 2, 1962.

37. *The University of Mississippi and the Meredith Case* (University, Mississippi: University of Mississippi, 1962).

38. *TYIM*, 250.

39. Ibid., 251, 270.

40. "Mississippi Gives Meredith Degree," *NYT*, August 18, 1963.

41. *TYIM*, 322.

Chapter Twenty-five: Not Another Oxford

1. *RKIOW*, 331.

2. *KJ*, 163.

3. *RKIOW*, 159.

4. "Civil Rights Memorial: Dedication," leaflet announcing the dedication of the Civil Rights Memorial in Montgomery, Alabama, November 5, 1989.

5. Alabama State Archives, Governor's papers, vol. 2, 10/1/45–9/30/62, "Governor's Conference — Southern," drawer 383; Mississippi State Archives, archive MP 86.01, Citizens Council Forum Files, Reel 129, 1961; Ernest Hollings, *The Case Against Hunger* (New York: Cowles Book Company, 1970), 165.

6. Press release: "Address by Governor Ernest F. Hollings to the General Assembly of South Carolina, Wednesday, January 9, 1963."

7. Opinion by U.S. Court of Appeals in *Harvey B. Gantt v. The Clemson Agricultural College of South Carolina*, January 16, 1963, in *RRLR* (1962), 1116.

8. "Atlanta Mayor Tells NAACP City Will Not Shun Duties" ("from Wire Reports"), *AH*, July 3, 1962.

9. The *Birmingham Post-Herald* referred to Folsom, who was from the town of Cullman, as "the big Cullmanite." The paper quoted Folsom as telling a group in Talladega during the campaign: "Believe nothing smear artists say about me and only half of what I tell you myself. After all, it's an election year, and I've got to do a heap of promising." *Birmingham Post-Herald*, September 5, 1961.

10. *CHN*, 579.

11. "Dr. King Asks End to Rights Discord," *NYT*, July 16, 1962.

12. *CHN*, 576.

13. *Plans for Progress: Atlanta Survey* (Atlanta: Southern Regional Council, 1963).

14. *KJ*, 172; *CHN*, 577.

15. *RRLR* (1962), 1.

Chapter Twenty-six: Mississippi: Caught Up in the Tradition

1. Watters and Cleghorn, in *Climbing Jacob's Ladder*, note that VEP financed voter registration campaigns everywhere in the South — in urban centers, small towns, and the rural areas. "A main purpose of VEP was research to determine the causes and remedies of the abnormally low voter registration in the South," write the authors. "But the method of research was the very direct one of encouraging persons not registered to attempt to register." *CJL*, 46.

2. *CJL*, 59; *IS*, 79.

3. *IS*, 80, 81.

4. *CJL*, 60.

5. Ibid., 62.

6. Ibid.

7. *CJL*, 60.

Chapter Twenty-seven: Peace in the Valley

1. Charles Morgan, *A Time to Speak* (New York: Harper & Row, 1964), 49.

2. Harrison Salisbury, *NYT*, April 12, 1960, reprinted in *POAD*, 153; "Birmingham Gets Racial Unity Plea," *NYT*, January 5, 1961.

3. "Ruling Is 7 Years Old," United Press International dispatch in *NYT*, May 18, 1961.

4. Barbara Patterson, "Defiance and Dynamite," *New South* (May, 1963), 7.

5. "Eighteen Affidavits for Alabama," *New South* (June, 1964), 3.

6. ". . . Must Earn Acceptance," part two of series on Birmingham, *Atlanta Journal*, December 30, 1961.

7. "Meeting the Challenge," part three of series on Birmingham, *Atlanta Journal*, December 31, 1961. Morgan, who went on to become a noted civil rights lawyer and the head of the American Civil Liberties Union's Atlanta office, was a student at the University of Alabama in 1956 when Autherine Lucy tried unsuccessfully to enter. When white violence forced Lucy to leave the campus, she told the press that her one moment of hope had come when a student leader had called and told her he would do his best to facilitate her entry. Morgan was the caller.

Chapter Twenty-eight: So Nice to Have You in Birmingham

1. Martin Luther King, Jr., "Letter from Birmingham Jail" (see following note).

2. "Letter from Birmingham Jail": Letter from Martin Luther King, Jr., to Bishop C.C.J. Carpenter, Bishop Joseph A. Durick, Rabbi Milton L.

Grafman, Bishop Nolan B. Harmon, Rev. George H. Murray, Rev. Edward V. Ramage, and Rev. Earl Stallings, from Birmingham City Jail, April 16, 1963. Quotations are from a typescript provided to the press at the time by the Southern Christian Leadership Conference. A slightly different version, which is addressed also to Bishop Paul Hardin, appears in Martin Luther King, Jr., *Why We Can't Wait* (New York: New American Library, 1963), 76.

3. *FITS*, 218.

4. Ibid., 219.

5. Ibid.

6. *MOBR*, 312, 315.

7. Statement by Henry Lee Shambry concerning events of May 3, 1963, from files of Birmingham Inter-Citizens Committee.

8. *POAD*, 162.

9. *FITS*, 220.

10. *POAD*, 165.

11. Charles and Barbara Whalen, *The Longest Debate: A Legislative History of the 1964 Civil Rights Act* (New York: New American Library, 1985), xxi; "Birmingham and Beyond," *New South* (October–November, 1963), 21.

Chapter Twenty-nine: The March

1. "Birmingham and Beyond," *New South* (October–November, 1963), 19; "Civil Rights: Year-End Summary," Southern Regional Council (December 31, 1963), quoted in *IS*, 90.

2. *LBH*, 240.

3. *IS*, 90, 76.

4. "Danville, Virginia," Student Nonviolent Coordinating Committee (August, 1963).

5. Mary King, *Freedom Song: A Personal Story of the 1960s Civil Rights Movement* (New York: William Morrow, 1987), 118.

6. *CJL*, 153, 343.

7. *TYIM*, 320.

8. *CJL*, 135.

9. Ibid., 212, 213.

10. For a discussion of the Baldwin meeting, see *KJ*, 113.

11. Whalen and Whalen, *The Longest Debate*, xxi.

12. Carson writes (*IS*, 91) that President Kennedy met with thirty civil rights leaders and tried to talk them out of marching. James Farmer writes (*LBH*, 243) that the Kennedys feared violence and tried to get the march called off; "failing in that, they sought to ensure that the march's nature would not be inimical to the political interests of the administra-

tion," and they made "every effort to shape the character" of the demonstration.

13. *LBH*, 244.

14. "Proposed Program — Lincoln Memorial," undated, in March on Washington files, A. Philip Randolph Institute.

15. *Jet* (September 12, 1963); *Time* (September 6, 1963); March on Washington files, A. Philip Randolph Institute.

16. Grant, ed., *Black Protest*, 375.

17. *LBH*, 331, 333.

18. *MOBR*, 219.

19. Quoted in *KJ*, 226.

20. *LBH*, 245.

Chapter Thirty: You Always Have to Worry

1. Theodore H. White, "Power Structure, Integration, Militancy, Freedom Now!" *Life* (November 29, 1963), 78.

2. John Fischer, "What the Negro Needs Most: A First Class Citizens' Council," *Harper's* (July, 1962), 12.

3. Undated, untitled memorandum in March on Washington files, A. Philip Randolph Institute.

4. Bayard Rustin, "From Protest to Politics: The Future of the Civil Rights Movement," *Commentary* (February, 1965). Rustin defined "revolution" not as a process involving violent overthrow, but as "the qualitative transformation of fundamental institutions, more or less rapidly, to the point where the social and economic structure which they comprised can no longer be said to be the same."

5. *CJL*, 64.

6. Morgan, *A Time to Speak*, 13.

7. "Birmingham and Beyond," *New South* (October–November, 1963), 22.

8. Historian David Garrow finds that Levison was an "inactive party member" during the period. *BTC*, 117.

9. White, "Power Structure," 78.

Chapter Thirty-one: The Education of Sharon Burger

1. "Prospectus for the Summer," undated, mimeographed copy of a SNCC working paper in author's collection.

2. Both Lowenstein and Frank went on to become U.S. congressmen. SNCC veterans remained skeptical about Lowenstein's motives for involving himself in the Movement; many felt that he wanted to counteract SNCC's growing antisystem attitude on behalf of what they called the

"liberal-labor establishment." Dorothy Miller Zellner thought of him, she said, as "a right-wing liberal."

3. *IS*, 113.

4. Ibid., 115.

5. Civil Rights Education Project, *Free at Last: A History of the Civil Rights Movement and Those Who Died in the Struggle* (Montgomery: Southern Poverty Law Center, 1989), 66.

6. *PP*, 242.

7. Act of the 1965 session of the Louisiana legislature, effective July 9, 1965, in *RRLR* (1965), 1370.

8. Sharon Burger, "Canvassing in Louisiana," *Mishawaka Enterprise*, July 30, 1964, reprinted in Jim Peck, ed., *Louisiana — Summer, 1964: The Students Report to Their Home Towns* (New York: Congress of Racial Equality, 1964).

9. *IS*, 117, 121.

10. *PP*, 244.

11. *CJL*, 139.

Chapter Thirty-two: No Plan, No Program

1. *World Almanac and Book of Facts* (New York: World-Telegram and The Sun, 1965), 172.

2. An excellent source of information on the Civil Rights Act of 1964 is Whalen and Whalen, *The Longest Debate*.

3. Rustin, "From Protest to Politics"; *BTC*, 343; *MOBR*, 368.

4. Paul Cowan, *The Making of an Un-American* (New York: Viking, 1970), 46.

5. *IS*, 124.

6. Ibid., 127.

7. Alcohol was the drug of choice among the activists when they were able to get away from the battle's front lines. James Farmer of CORE recalls that his group's let-your-hair-down sessions were called "COREgies" and involved much drinking. "CORE parties were something to behold," said Farmer. "CORE people drank gallons. It was a way of letting off steam. SNCC was into sex a lot, much more than CORE was. CORE people generally were about ten years older than SNCC people." Interestingly, some SNCC veterans remember that *they* were into drinking and that it was CORE that concentrated on sex. After the middle sixties, marijuana became a problem for SNCC, according to James Forman.

Chapter Thirty-three: Segregation Is Broken

1. *MOBR*, 366.

2. Daniel P. Moynihan, *Maximum Feasible Misunderstanding:*

Community Action in the War on Poverty (New York: Free Press, 1969), 67. Emphasis in original.

3. The details of Hoover's COINTELPRO operation are found in *Supplementary Detailed Staff Reports on Intelligence Activities and the Rights of Americans, Book III, Final Report of the Select Committee to Study Governmental Operations with Respect to Intelligence Activities, United States Senate, 94th Congress, 2d session, April 23, 1976, Report No. 94-755* (Washington, D.C.: Government Printing Office, 1976).

4. Moyers has since gone on to become a well-known television journalist who has examined weighty subjects.

5. *KJ*, 18.

6. Student Nonviolent Coordinating Committee, "SNCC Programs for 1965," February 23, 1965, in author's collection.

7. Henry G. Alsberg, ed., *The American Guide* (New York: Hastings House, 1949), 872.

8. U.S. Commission on Civil Rights data, cited in Student Nonviolent Coordinating Committee, "Selma, Alabama; Marion, Alabama; The Black Belt — Special Report" (February 4, 1965), in author's collection.

9. Howard Zinn, *SNCC: The New Abolitionists* (Boston: Beacon, 1964), 157.

10. *CJL*, 251.

11. Student Nonviolent Coordinating Committee, "Special Report" on "Justice Department Activity in Dallas County, Alabama" (February 25, 1965), in author's collection.

12. James Forman's version of the events is that the Justice Department wanted King to call the march off but King at first said he could not do that. Then the Justice Department got Judge Johnson to issue his injunction. Then King and the government made a deal: King would lead the marchers a few feet beyond the Pettus Bridge, pray, then march the crowd back to Selma to await a ruling on the injunction. "A favorable ruling had been promised by the U.S. Government," wrote Forman. *MOBR*, 441.

13. *RRLR* (1965), 1364.

14. *World Almanac and Book of Facts* (New York: World-Telegram and The Sun, 1966), 57, 58.

Chapter Thirty-four: The End of Terror

1. *CJL*, 34.

2. Ibid., 244.

3. Ibid., 300.

4. Ibid., 299.

5. Ibid., 342.

6. L. C. Dorsey, *Freedom Came to Mississippi* (New York: Field Foundation, 1977), 25.

7. Student Nonviolent Coordinating Committee, "Statement by the Student Nonviolent Coordinating Committee on the War in Vietnam" (January 6, 1965), in author's collection.

8. *RRLR* (1966), 1349.

9. "Klan Members of the '90s See Themselves as Victims," *Washington Post*, August 31, 1990.

10. "Helms Aide in Furor over Racial Accusation," *NYT* (national edition), July 21, 1990.

SELECTED READINGS

■ ─────────────────────────

The serious student of the civil rights movement has available a great amount of material, almost all of it written but some on videotape and phonograph record. What is not in large supply, and sadly so, is contemporaneous accounts, thoughts, and assorted papers of the most active participants in the struggle. Most of those participants never stopped to think of what a valuable resource these would come to be; none of them had the luxury of an hour or so at the end of the day during which they could collect and put down their thoughts.

Still, the flavor of the Movement comes through in dozens of books and articles, many of them written by the key activists themselves. What follows is a highly selective, somewhat eccentric bibliography for readers who want to explore further.

For thorough histories of the Movement, or of significant portions of it, there is a growing selection. *Climbing Jacob's Ladder: The Arrival of Negroes in Southern Politics*, by Pat Watters and Reese Cleghorn (New York: Harcourt, Brace and World, 1967), is concerned primarily with the vote, but it remains one of the best half-dozen books on the struggle, written by trained reporters who witnessed most of it. *Black Protest: History, Documents, and Analysis: 1619 to the Present*, second edition, Joanne Grant, editor (New York: Fawcett, 1968), tells the story of the Movement through original speeches, proclamations, and other readings. Other important and valuable publications include:

David J. Garrow, *Bearing the Cross: Martin Luther King, Jr., and the Southern Christian Leadership Conference* (New York: William Morrow, 1986). The Movement as seen through the contributions of its best-known participant.

Taylor Branch, *Parting the Waters: America in the King Years, 1954–63* (New York: Simon and Schuster, 1988). Another look from the King perspective.

Aldon D. Morris, *Origins of the Civil Rights Movement: Black Communities Organizing for Change* (New York: Free Press, 1984). One of the few valuable academic contributions to an understanding of the Movement. The author fails to recognize the contributions made by younger activists, but his account is nevertheless useful.

Harvard Sitkoff, *The Struggle for Black Equality, 1954–1980* (New York: Hill and Wang, 1981). A thorough survey of the era.

Clayborne Carson, *In Struggle: SNCC and the Black Awakening of the 1960s* (Cambridge, Massachusetts: Harvard University Press, 1981). This is the best coverage of SNCC's stormy history.

Pat Watters, *Down to Now: Reflections on the Southern Civil Rights Movement* (New York: Pantheon, 1971). An examination, late in the Movement years, by a white Southerner who sympathized with the struggle every step of the way.

A considerable number of books illuminate specific issues that concerned the Movement. Among the best of these are *Simple Justice* by Richard Kluger (New York: Vintage, 1975), the be-all book of the *Brown* decision; Victor Navasky's *Kennedy Justice* (New York: Atheneum, 1971), about Robert Kennedy, his Justice Department, and (among other things) civil rights; and three publications by Howard Zinn: *The Southern Mystique* (New York: Knopf, 1964), *SNCC: The New Abolitionists* (Boston: Beacon, 1964), and *Albany: A Study in National Responsibility* (Atlanta: Southern Regional Council, 1962). *Robert Kennedy: In His Own Words. The Unpublished Recollections of the Kennedy Years*, edited by Edwin O. Guthman and Jeffrey Shulman (New York: Bantam, 1988), provides helpful insight into the thinking of the attorney general and of the Kennedy administration.

Bayard Rustin's article, "From Protest to Politics: The Future of the Civil Rights Movement" (*Commentary*, February, 1965), is an important explanation of the feelings of many of the Movement's Northern sympathizers. Anthony Lewis's collection of material from the *New York Times* and its magazine, *Portrait of a Decade: The Second American Revolution* (New York: Bantam, 1965), provides interesting material from the period 1954–65.

Other works include Russell H. Barrett, *Integration at Ole Miss* (Chicago: Quadrangle, 1965); Will D. Campbell, *Race and the Renewal of the Church* (Philadelphia: Westminster Press, 1962); Stokely Carmichael and Charles V. Hamilton, *Black Power: The Politics of Liberation in America* (New York: Vintage, 1967); L. C. Dorsey, *Freedom Came to Mississippi* (New York: Field Foundation, 1977); David Garrow, *The FBI and Martin Luther King, Jr.* (New York: Penguin, 1983); William Bradford Huie, *Three Lives for Mississippi* (New York: WCC Books, 1965); and Louis E. Lomax, *The Negro Revolt* (New York: Harper, 1962).

Walter Lord examined Mississippi after Meredith in *The Past That Would Not Die* (New York: Harper & Row, 1965). Burke Marshall explained (though somewhat condescendingly) the Kennedy administration's reluctance to get involved in civil rights in his *Federalism and Civil Rights* (New York: Columbia University Press, 1964). And there are Henry Lee Moon's *Balance of Power: The Negro Vote* (Westport, Connecticut: Greenwood Press, 1977 — original edition issued in 1948 by Doubleday); James W. Silver's *Mississippi: The Closed Society* (New York: Harcourt Brace Jovanovich, 1964); Calvin Trillin's *An Education in Georgia: The Integration of Charlayne Hunter and Hamilton Holmes* (New York: Viking, 1963); the U.S. Commission on Civil Rights publication, *Political Participation* (Washington, D.C.: Government Printing Office, 1968); Charles and Barbara Whalen's *The Longest Debate: A Legislative History of the 1964 Civil Rights Act* (New York: New American Library, 1985); Robert F. Williams's *Negroes with Guns* (New York: Marzani & Munsell, 1962); and Miles Wolff's *Lunch at the Five and Ten: The Greensboro Sit-ins* (New York: Stein and Day, 1970).

The personal experiences and recollections of those who participated in the Movement are especially valuable. One of these is James Farmer's *Lay Bare the Heart* (New York: New American Library, 1985), the story of his experiences at CORE as the head of one of the most feisty civil rights organizations. James Meredith's account of his battle to enroll at, and stay in, the University of Mississippi is beautifully and nobly told in his *Three Years in Mississippi* (Bloomington: Indiana University Press, 1966). Mary King's *Freedom Song: A Personal Story of the 1960s Civil Rights Movement* (New York: William Morrow, 1987) is a moving memoir of the author's time on the staff of SNCC. *A Time to Speak*, by Charles Morgan, Jr. (New York: Harper & Row, 1964), tells the story of Birmingham through the eyes of one of the few whites there who publicly opposed racism and segregation.

Martin Luther King, Jr., produced several memorable documents. Among them are *Why We Can't Wait* (New York: New American Library, 1963), which contains the text of King's "Letter from Birmingham Jail," and *Where Do We Go from Here: Chaos or Community?* (Boston: Beacon, 1967).

For an understanding of the region in which both segregation and the Movement against it flourished, there is *Who Speaks for the South?*

by James McBride Dabbs (New York: Funk & Wagnalls, 1964). *Southern Politics in State and Nation*, by V. O. Key, Jr. (New York: Vintage, 1949), is helpful, as is Ralph McGill's *The South and the Southerner* (Boston: Little, Brown, 1963).

Two books in particular help to explain the nature of white political resistance. They are Numan V. Bartley's *The Rise of Massive Resistance: Race and Politics in the South During the 1950s* (Baton Rouge: Louisiana State University Press, 1969) and Benjamin Muse's *Virginia's Massive Resistance* (Bloomington: Indiana University Press, 1961).

The Movement years produced a number of publications that are especially helpful to anyone seeking to understand what happened — and even what is yet to happen — in American race relations. The Southern Regional Council (604 Walton Street, Atlanta, Georgia, 30303) consistently turned out reports and assessments during the sixties, and still does. Leslie Dunbar, who served as the council's director, wrote many of those documents himself. Two of his many thought-provoking essays are "The Annealing of the South" (*Virginia Quarterly Review*, vol. 37, no. 4, autumn, 1961) and *The South of the Near Future* (Atlanta: Southern Center for Studies in Public Policy, Clark College, 1980). The *Race Relations Law Reporter*, now extinct, was published by the Vanderbilt University School of Law; it provided a comprehensive and reliable source of information on the ongoing legal and legislative battles.

The U.S. Commission on Civil Rights published a number of helpful documents during the years when it was a real force for improved race relations. Among them are *Freedom to the Free, 1863-1963: Century of Emancipation* (Washington, D.C.: Government Printing Office, 1963) and its *1961 Commission on Civil Rights Report* (Washington, D.C.: Government Printing Office, 1961). The latter is a five-volume report (with an additional volume of excerpts) on the state of voting, education, employment, housing, and justice.

An extremely important reference book for students of the Movement is *The Chronological History of the Negro in America*, by Peter M. Bergman and a staff of compilers (New York: Harper & Row, 1969). The book has a seventy-page index and more than twenty thousand entries, as well as a bibliography of bibliographies, and it covers events in race relations going back to 1441.

The Movement was a moral struggle, but it was also rich in visual and aural excitement. The high-technology equipment of today's broadcast communications did not exist then, but many feet of film and audio tape were used to record the events and people who made up the Movement. It is sad and a little surprising, then, that we have so little in the way of a visual record or explanation of those years. A prominent and wonderful exception to this is the public television series, *Eyes on the Prize*, created by Henry Hampton and Blackside, Inc., of Boston. The series ran in 1988 and was followed in 1990 by a second part that examined the struggle's later years. It was (and remains, for it is reshown from time to time) an example of what public television should be (and nonpublic television, too, for that matter). The original series was accompanied by a book of the same title by Juan Williams (New York: Viking, 1987) and by a collection of readings, *Eyes on the Prize: A Reader and Guide*, edited by Clayborne Carson et al. (New York: Viking, 1987). The second series was accompanied by *Voices of Freedom*, by Henry Hampton and Steve Fayer (New York: Bantam, 1990).

For anyone who was there, a part of the Movement that will last forever is the music. For those who were in Albany, that was the *best* music. One of those who belted out the songs in Albany's Shiloh and Mount Zion churches, Bernice Johnson Reagon, went on to become the director of the Smithsonian Institution's Program in Black American Culture, and was the guiding spirit behind a fine three-disk collection of phonograph recordings, *Voices of the Civil Rights Movement: Black American Freedom Songs, 1960–1966* (Washington, D.C.: Smithsonian Collection of Recordings, 1980).

INDEX

Page references in italics refer to the photographic insert following page 328.

323.1196
P888

85013

LINCOLN CHRISTIAN COLLEGE AND SEMINARY

323.1196Powledge, Fred.
P888   Free at last?

                    85013

DEMCO